Overleaf:
Birth and baptismal certificate written out by Francis Portzline 1838

This example of Pennsylvania Dutch writing shows how the same type of decoration could be applied equally to other artefacts, and indeed appears in samplers, ceramics, painted woods and similar items.

Reproduced by permission of the Philadelphia Museum of Art, gift of J. Stogdell Stokes, 28.10.89

Geburt und Taufschein.
Diesen beiden Ehegatten. als . Wilhelm Portzeline und seine
Eheliche hauffrau Gertraut eine Geborne Zelerin ist ein Sohn zur
welt geboren den 7 ten Junius nachts um 11 uhr im jahr unseres herrn
1838 in Greenwood Taunschip junietta Caunty im Staat Pennsylvania
und erhielt durch die heilige Taufe den namen Benjamin durch den
Ehrwürdigen Prediger Frederich Seiberd. die Taufzeugen sind
Abraham Zeller und seine Ehefrau Nänzi.
Francis Portzline

Introduction

CALLIGRAPHY is the art of fine writing, and is derived from two Greek words, *graphein* meaning 'to write' and *kallos* meaning 'beauty'. It should not be confused with 'palaeography', which also comes from the Greek and means the study of ancient writing. In this book the emphasis is for the most part on the aesthetic aspect of penmanship, so that although some legal and business hands are included, most of the examples are taken from handwritten books and ceremonial documents, or, at a later period from the works of professional writing masters and scribes. For the most part only examples of good handwriting are illustrated, and they by no means tell the whole story, since not everyone wrote on the same high level all the time, and, as we know from our own day, the highest standards are reached only by comparatively few practitioners.

To attempt a full history of western calligraphy would be presumptuous on the part of one who cannot claim to be an authority on all aspects of so wide a subject. Both calligraphy and palaeography have been studied in depth in recent years by specialists who have divided their interests into individual areas of the subjects. This book simply aims to provide a wide range of pictorial coverage, amplified by a general linking text. For those who wish to delve more deeply into specific topics, such as, for example, the uncial or italic scripts, a bibliography of the main specialist works is provided. Since it is intended that this book may also be used as work of reference, a certain amount of information has been repeated in the various sections for the benefit of those who wish to study particular periods rather than to read the work straight through. For those seeking more detailed information on the manuscripts and books illustrated here, much of this will be found, for material in the Victoria and Albert Museum, in the catalogue of the exhibition *The Universal Penman*, by J. I. Whalley and V. C. Kaden, HMSO, 1980. This exhibition enabled the Library of the Victoria and Albert Museum to display many of the calligraphic items from its own collections. The present book, while including some of the more important books and manuscripts described in the catalogue, has been able to make a far wider selection of material from the Museum's holdings than the scale of the exhibition permitted. Of the international importance of these holdings, both catalogue and book make abundantly clear. Details of items from other institutions will be found in the relevant catalogues of those institutions.

Calligraphy is only one of the many manifestations of the arts and crafts of any period, reflecting current styles in the same way that silver, ceramics or furniture do. It is also the product of the political, social and economic conditions of its time. To assist the link with other art forms and with the history of the various periods, the selection is arranged more or less in chronological order, though with the various national hands grouped together within each period. It is hoped that in addition to providing an historical survey of calligraphy, the illustrations will also prove a source of inspiration to all who may wish to practise the ancient art of the scribe, whether as amateurs or as professionals.

The first part of the survey is concerned exclusively with manuscripts produced before the invention of printing in the middle of the 15th century, when there was no alternative to the handwritten book. It is a period that has been studied in great detail, though for the most part it has been the beauty of the decorations rather than that of the scripts which has occupied scholars. This survey draws much of its material from the less well-known collections of the Library of the Victoria and Albert Museum (the National Art Library) so that for the most part the calligraphy is not overshadowed by the familiarity of the illuminated pages; many of the manuscripts do, of course, contain very fine decorations of this kind, but for the purposes of this book illustrations of the illuminated pages have purposely been kept to a minimum.

1 Two thousand years of literacy

THE STANDARD and extent of literacy in any of the periods covered by this survey varied considerably and it had an effect on the actual writing, as well as on the availability of reading matter. If we consider as 'Romans' those who were free-born citizens, it would appear that there was a high standard of reading and writing among them, often in Greek as well as Latin. Letters of Roman schoolboys have been preserved as well as those of men of standing such as the younger Pliny, and business documents have survived as well as ceremonial inscriptions. Since it was customary to place inscriptions in public places, on buildings, altars and gravestones for example, it can be presumed that people were expected to read them. That Rome produced a great deal of literary work is a matter of common knowledge. Roman writing, as we shall see, took account of the differing requirements of business and ceremony by the use of both informal and formal hands, and this practice was continued by the Christian Church after its official establishment by Constantine in 311 AD.

The 5th century saw the break-up of the Roman Empire and the irruption of pagan tribes throughout much of western Europe. The Romans withdrew to guard their own land and Rome itself was sacked by the Goths in 410. Communications deteriorated and each small community tended to look to its own affairs and try to defend itself against outside attacks. The organised and civilised life known throughout the Empire disintegrated and with it went much of the common literacy. Only the Church kept alive the lamp of learning in what have been with reason called the Dark Ages. In isolated centres monks continued to copy out the much needed Bibles and Psalters, and other writings so vital to the survival of Christianity. As the great missionary movements of the 7th and 8th century began to bring many a pagan land back to the Christian fold, there was an even greater demand for the written word. Books had become precious if essential objects, but the only way to acquire them was to copy them. Desirable works were lent from one monastery to another, so that they could be copied. Benedict Biscop, Abbot of Wearmouth, made several visits to Rome in the late 7th century, each time returning with valuable books which could be transcribed and spread throughout a wide area. Not only did texts move in this way from place to place, but so of course did the scripts. The uncial script thus was brought into Britain by missionaries and later, Irish monks took the Anglo-Celtic minuscule with them on their travels, as far as St Gall in Switzerland and other European communities where they settled.

Diepenveen Bible
Netherlandish c1450-53

One of the many illustrations to be found in medieval manuscripts which show the scribe at work in his cell. In this instance it depicts St Jerome, and is taken from a Bible written out by an anonymous nun in the House of the Canonesses of the Congregation of Windesheim, near Deventer in the Netherlands. St Jerome, who was responsible for the Vulgate version of the Bible used during the Middle Ages, was frequently portrayed in medieval manuscripts as well as the four Evangelists, where they can be taken as representative of the many monkish copyists who preserved the written word in the centuries before the invention of printing.

V&AM Reid 23 f.1r 35 × 21.5

Libellus valde doctus
by Urban Wyss 1549

With the spread of printing and the decline of the scribe, the writing master came to the fore. Here we see one at work, surrounded by the various instruments of his craft. With the increase in literacy among the laity following the impetus given to learning by religious and secular events in the 16th century, this type of scene must have become much more common.

V&AM L.840-1880 14 × 21

As conditions in Europe gradually changed and states settled down after the upheaval of the barbarian invasions, the business of government once again began to call for clerkly skills, and these, inevitably, were provided by the church, in the shape of the *clericus* or clerk. In the early Middle Ages even the highest in the land might be illiterate. There is the well-known story of King Alfred's mother promising a book to whichever of her sons should first be able to read it – a prize which the young Alfred was determined to win. Charlemagne, whose name will always be associated with the finest of medieval scripts, the Carolingian minuscule, tried very hard to learn his letters, taking his writing tablets to bed with him. But as his biographer Einhard says, he had started too late and never learnt to write. There were of course always some rulers who could read and write with fluency – Henry I of England was known as 'Beauclerc' for just so unusual a proficiency. But for the most part the population was divided into those who fought, those who prayed – and the rest who worked – and only one group of the three needed to read and write.

As the Middle Ages progressed and life became more complex, the need for people who could read and write increased. 'Clerks' ceased to be clerics, and manorial business and commerce alike made use of the literate layman. This in turn led to a division in writing styles. In his cloister the monk continued to copy out the grand volumes for ceremonial occasions in the church, using the traditional book hands. When he wanted a text for his own use he probably copied it out in an abbreviated form and in a much less formal script. The many lay clerks were doing the same sort of thing. The lawyers and the doctors, the merchants and the estate managers, alike wrote a much less formal hand, and often, since the reader would know what to expect, the text of the writing was abbreviated by conventional contractions. In England in the 15th century we find the *bastarda* script (a mixture of cursive and book hands) being used for informal and business matters, while Bibles and Books of Hours were still being written in gothic letters. But as people became more familiar with bastarda, we find that on occasions it too is elevated into a fine book hand, and achieves a certain dignity as such. In the 16th century the

The universal penman
by George Bickham London 1743

The spread of trade in the 18th century gave rise to an increased demand for clerks, especially in England, and not all copybooks were aimed at the schoolboy learner. It is obvious that many a would-be clerk in a commercial firm needed to be able to produce a good business round hand, and this is no doubt what the young people in this illustration would be practising.

V&A M L.3085-1960 41 × 26.5

secretary hand was developed for most business affairs, but the writer's signature, an important passage of text, or document designed to impress, would be written in italic script – the symbol of the educated man or woman.

The invention of printing in the 15th century brought about many changes. It was no longer necessary to go through the slow labour of hand-copying every book that was needed; multiple copies allowed many people to possess a work and of course reduced its cost to them. Reading and writing became more important, and the medieval copyist scribe, bereft of one job turned in some instances to the new trade of writing master. The writing master would teach his craft in schools or he would take private pupils, but also, if he could, he would publish his copies in order to spread abroad his ideas and his systems, and of course widen his fame. The methods used by the writing masters to propound their various styles and theories are well illustrated in the present book. But all their styles and fine ideas gradually fell before the increasing demands of commerce, where a plain businesslike hand was all that was required. In the 18th century the spread of international trade gave employment to an ever-increasing band of clerks, as did the growth of national bureaucracies.

During the 19th century there was an increase in primary education in all west European countries and North America. It was accepted that everyone should have the opportunity to learn to read and write, even if not everyone wished to, or did in fact become literate. Today the ability to read and write is taken for granted – sometimes unwisely perhaps. Writing styles still display national characteristics but the universality of literacy has led to a certain uniformity and dullness in the scripts. An acknowledgement of this state of affairs is manifest by the number of books on calligraphy which are published every year and by the officially sponsored manuals and schemes on how to improve standards of writing. But before we congratulate ourselves on at least having got back to the literacy standards of the Romans, we should pause to consider whether or not the advent of the telephone, the typewriter, and the computer, is making the ability to read and write redundant in the modern world. Perhaps after all we are heading for another Dark Age, when only a few specialists will continue to wield the pen in cloistered solitude.

A manual of writing founded on Mulhauser's method of teaching writing, published under the auspices of the Committee of the Council on Education. 3rd ed. London 1849

Literacy increased with the spread of general education. From this illustration we can see one of the reasons for the uniformity and lack of character in much of 19th century writing.

V & A M L.11175-1974 19 × 12

2 Writing materials

ONLY a brief account of writing materials is given here since a full account of their history is available elsewhere.* But the effect of writing implements and materials on the shape of writing has always been so significant that a brief survey of the subject is essential to a proper appreciation of calligraphy in all its aspects.

The alphabet with which this survey begins is the Roman square capital, familiar to most people in the form of incised inscriptions on stone or marble. But transferred to another medium, such lettering inevitably underwent a transformation. The main material used by the Romans as a writing surface was papyrus. This was made from the pith of a reed growing most profusely in Egypt. When adequately treated it provided a fairly smooth surface for writing, which was done with a reed pen. Writing with a reed pen on papyrus produced very different letter-forms from those produced by a chisel on stone, and the resulting brushlike quality is especially obvious in the shapes of the so called 'rustic capitals' in which much Roman non-inscriptional writing was done. There was also a less formal running hand, which was written in the same way, namely with a reed pen on papyrus. But for quick notes and similar memoranda the Roman would sometimes use waxed writing tablets, and a metal stylus was used to write on this kind of surface. The advantage of the wax tablet was that it could be re-used once the original writing had been smoothed away, so that it had something in common with the old fashioned school slate. Written papyrus was usually kept rolled up, and 'books' were supplied with a tag or *titulus* at one end to aid identification. Although papyrus was fairly tough it was not really suitable for writing on both sides of the sheet, a matter of little importance as long as supplies were adequate.

An alternative source of writing material was parchment or vellum. This material was possibly developed at Pergamon in Asia Minor, and the German word for vellum (*pergament*) recalls this fact. For some time the two materials, papyrus and vellum, co-existed. But the designation of Christianity as the official religion of the Roman Empire in the early years of the 4th century brought about a change in the relative importance of them both. Supplies of papyrus declined along with the power of Rome, and the deterioration of the Mediterranean trade routes. The impact of Christianity made itself manifest in two ways: in the actual form of books and in the importance attached to the

***Writing implements and accessories*, by J. I. Whalley, 1975. (reprinted 1980)

Illustrations of the Evangelists or of St Jerome are frequently to be found in illuminated manuscripts, and these provide useful examples of writing implements.

In this picture of St John the Evangelist we see his symbol, the eagle, holding the saint's penner and ink-horn for him, while St John himself carefully surveys his quill.

V & A M MS L.2385-1910

Opposite:
This enlarged miniature from a Book of Hours shows the monkish scribe mending his quill, which he holds in his left hand, while with his right hand he prepares to use his pen knife on it.

V & A M Reid MS 23

A medieval inkpot of cuir bouilli *with a stamped pattern of figures of saints.*

Reproduced by permission of the Museum of London A.28570

writing of them. To the Christian the importance of the written word was underlined by the significance of the Bible as the revealed Word of God, and by the duty of the Church to further the knowledge of this revelation. Christian teachers found that they needed to make frequent reference to the Scriptural texts, and this was not easy when the 'book' consisted of a scroll. Gradually sheets took the place of the roll, and were joined together much as several waxed tablets had been joined together with a thong. It was in this way that the book as we know it today developed, in which references to individual pages are relatively easy. Vellum is made from the prepared skins of an animal: sheep, goat or cow; it can be tough and long lasting. Moreover, it proved possible to write on both sides of a vellum sheet, so that it was comparatively economical. This economy of use was further enhanced by the medieval practice of the autumn slaughter of animals for whom there were inadequate feedstuffs for overwintering. Nevertheless, the amount of vellum to be obtained from any one animal was limited, so that it was always a precious commodity for the medieval scribe.

It was of course possible to use a reed pen on vellum, but the quill pen, with its much harder point, was gradually found to be more satisfactory. The quill pen was made from the primary wing feathers of a bird, usually a goose, crow or swan. Like vellum and papyrus, it needed a considerable amount of preparation before it was ready for use as a writing implement. Even then, the point or 'neb' needed constant renewal. Nevertheless the use of vellum and the quill pen (*penna* is the Latin for feather) continued for centuries, and nearly all the manuscripts illustrated here were written in this way. The quill itself played an important part in the form taken by the writing, and this form changed over the centuries. The type of point or edge given to the quill and the angle at which it was held, affected the resulting letters. It could be sharpened to a fine point, or given a chisel edge; it could be held parallel to the top of the page, or held at an angle to it – all these possibilities were fully realised when writing manuals began to be published, and 'correct positions' for holding the pen were illustrated in many copy books, which also often included instructions on how to make a pen.

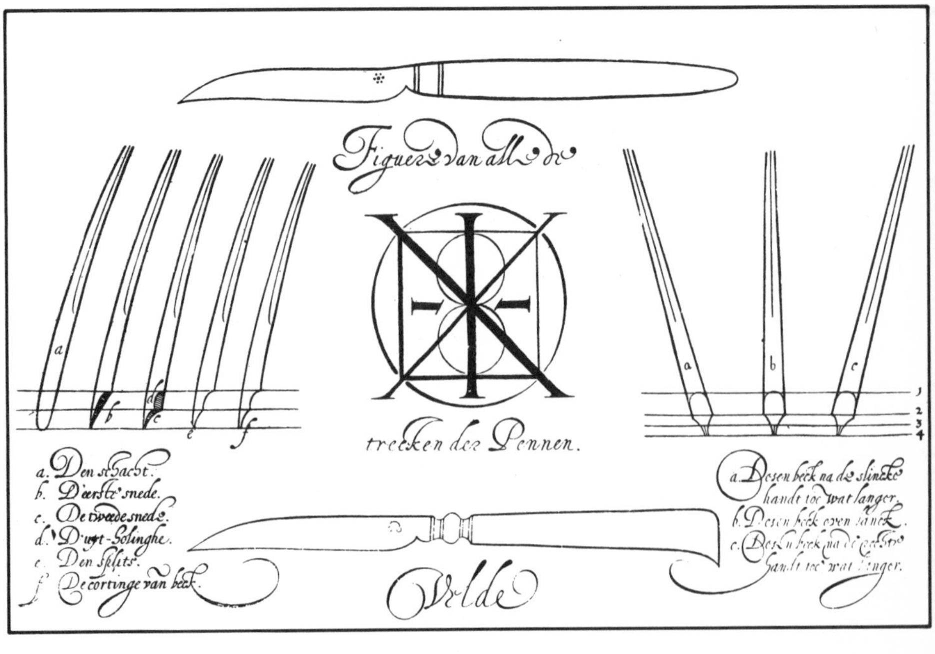

This type of illustration, in one form or another, was common in writing books for centuries. It not only shows how to cut the quill to form the right sort of point, but it also illustrates the type of pen knife most suitable for the operation.

From Spieghel der Schrijfkonste by Jan van den Velde 1605
V & A M 3.xii.1873 23.5 × 35

A selection of writing implements, including quill cutter or pen knife, a pounce pot, an inkstand which has a bell for summoning the servant, and an elaborate inkwell.

From L'art d'écrire by C. Paillasson, 1783 (V & A M L.1908-1911)

In view of the disadvantages of the quill pen it is not surprising that efforts were repeatedly made to find a better writing implement. Indeed some sort of metal pens were available from Roman times on, but they proved to have even more disadvantages than the quill. The medieval desire for fresh meat ensured a plentiful supply of geese and swans (and therefore of feathers), whereas a supply of suitable metal could not always be depended upon. The metal pen also lacked the flexibility of the hand-cut quill, at least until the 19th century, when methods of mass production made well-produced steel pens easily and cheaply available. Contemporary inks also tended to corrode the metal pen. These inks came in two kinds. One was made from a combination of oak galls and iron salts, and this kind, known as *encaustum*, literally burnt into the writing surface; it became dark brown with age. The other type of ink gave a blacker result, but was inclined to flake off, being composed of a suspension of carbon (lamp black for example) in a mixture of gum and water. Both kinds were used for centuries and their varied effects can be seen in the manuscripts illustrated in this book. The first ink factory producing, so it claimed, non-corrosive ink, was set up by Henry Stephens in 1834, but it was only with the discovery of aniline dyes in 1856 that a really satisfactory ink could be produced. This, having proved itself suitable for both steel dip pen and fountain pen, finally ended the long reign of the quill. However the modern scribe still finds that on occasions the hand-made quill is more suitable for his work than any machine-made pen, and a number of the 20th century examples of calligraphy in this book have been written with the

Quills being plucked from the living goose, as illustrated in Scenes of British wealth in produce, manufactures, and commerce for the amusement and instruction of little Tarry-at-home travellers *by Isaac Taylor, 1823.*

V&AM

traditional quill. Indeed the whole revival of calligraphy by Edward Johnston in the 20th century was influenced by his discovery of the secret of medieval scribal practice. Early attempts to reproduce the writing of the medieval scribe had either been done with the steel pen, or by using the quill as if it were itself a steel pen. Johnston realised that the correct way to use the pen as the medieval scribe had used it depended on the chisel-shaped edge to the quill and the angle at which it was held.

Paper was first introduced into Europe by the Moors in Spain and from there it spread out to France and Italy and eventually to the north. Early paper was made from rags and was unsized, or at least imperfectly sized (so that it was more like blotting paper). But once perfected it could be used in the same way as vellum, in that it could be folded to form a book and could be written on on both sides of the page. With the advent of printing in the middle of the 15th century, paper really came into its own, since vellum was unsuitable for use in the printing press. Paper, lacking the 'life' of a skin, could be kept flat to take the type, or the impression from engraved plates. But when it comes to fine writing, the modern scribe frequently prefers the effect of the pen on vellum, rather than the essentially dead effect on paper, so that some of the 20th century calligraphy shown in this book is not only written with the quill, but may well have been written on vellum.

Some of the illustrations which accompany this section show the scribes or the writing masters at work. They are seen surrounded by the various implements of their craft: the pen knife, for erasing mistakes, smoothing the writing surface, or 'mending' the quill; the sander or pounce pot, for drying up the ink – all the various aids to writing are shown. But the basic need has always been the same: a good pen, a smooth surface, a flowing ink – and an eye for the beauty of the written word.

The correct posture at the desk, shown together with the necessary writing implements.

From L'art d'écrire by C. Paillasson, 1783 (V&AM L.1908-1911)

Most of the manuscripts illustrated in this book, including many of the 20th century ones, were written on vellum. This illustration is taken from Denis Diderot's Encyclopédie; ou, dictionnaire des sciences, des arts et des métiers *published between 1751 and 1780. Although it shows the contemporary method of preparing the vellum for writing, the processes had not changed greatly over the centuries. Even when these men had finished, the individual scribe still needed to prepare the final writing surface to his own satisfaction.*

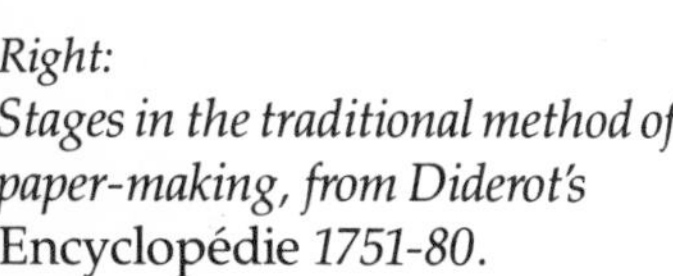
Right:
Stages in the traditional method of paper-making, from Diderot's Encyclopédie *1751-80.*

By contrast with the manuscripts, the copy books were printed or engraved on paper, and the informal writings illustrated in this book, together with many of the later manuscripts, were also on paper rather than vellum. This illustration from *Galerie industrielle; ou, applications des produits de la nature aux arts et métiers* 1822, shows the preparation of paper at a time when it was beginning to be mechanised. Earlier the paper had been hand-made, as shown in the illustration from Diderot's *Encyclopédie* (p. 19), and even today many scribes prefer to work on handmade paper if they are not using vellum, since the mechanical woodpulp product offers a less suitable surface for the calligrapher.

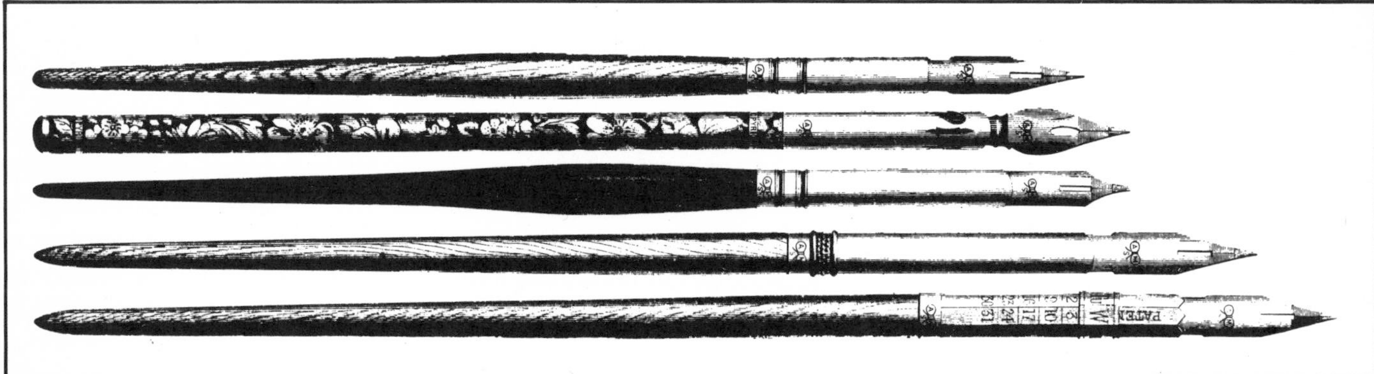

A selection of steel pens, which from about 1830 onwards gradually supplanted the quill. Such pens could be mass-produced quite cheaply and were reasonably long-lasting. This illustration is taken from an advertisement of about 1880.

3 Roman, early Christian and early medieval scripts

THIS survey begins with a study of the basic Roman alphabet, the type of letters which most people think of as 'capital letters'. Since the Romans made great use of inscriptions on their buildings and other monuments such inscribed letters are probably better known today than many later scripts. They are the letter-forms to which calligraphers and typographers have constantly returned over the centuries, and from which they have drawn fresh inspiration and devised new shapes. The Roman Empire was widely spread throughout parts of Europe, Africa and Asia, and wherever they went, the Romans left traces of their passing: temples, triumphal arches or simple gravestones. Marble and stone are long-lasting, hence the familiarity of the monumental inscribed letter-forms even to this day. The Romans were a literate people, with poets, historians and other writers whose names are still well-known and whose works have always been widely read. Moreover the administration of an Empire required considerable ability to read and write. Not surprisingly however the form taken by the written documents of the Romans differed considerably from the monumental inscriptions. As we have already seen, the medium affected the style of writing, and the documents produced by the Romans in the course of public or private business exemplified this. The 'square capitals' of the inscriptions were certainly used for special books and important literary works, but only fragmentary examples remain of such works. Writing these formal letters on papyrus or vellum was laborious and wasteful of material. The pen-written letters tended to take less angular forms, encouraged by the ease with which the pen moved over the unresisting writing surface. The resulting form of capital letter has been named 'rustic', a somewhat derogatory title which is unjust in view of the gracefulness of such writing. The charm of this pen-written majuscule or capital letter form was acknowledged by its longevity, for we find it still in use for headings and other forms of emphasis long after it had ceased to be used for the main text.

Although marble and stone provide the main source of Roman letters for us today, we are fortunate in that there has survived another equally important one. In 79 AD the volcano Vesuvius erupted, burying the cities of Pompeii and Heculaneum which were situated on the slopes of the mountain. With the cities were buried all the evidences of daily life, to be rediscovered in later centuries. Excavations have revealed writings of all kinds throughout the two cities. In the Villa of the Papyri at Herculaneum were discovered many closely written scrolls – a whole library of books, which even now can only be deciphered with difficulty in view of their carbonised state. More important for this study are the humbler evidences of writing that have survived: the accounts chalked up on the walls of the inn; the graffiti, political, libellous or bawdy, just like their modern counterparts; election notices – all the scribbles and passing thoughts of a population going about its daily life without a thought of the tomorrow it was not to see. The writing on the walls in the buried cities shows the two main scripts in use: the rustic capitals and the informal cursive hand. The cursive hand arises naturally as scripts are written quickly on an easy surface; it also tends to deteriorate into illegibility. Nevertheless, the Roman cursive hand was the hand of Roman government and business, and of informal letters. As such its use was widely diffused and its influence great. Looking at such examples as have survived, it is difficult to make out the individual letters, and the appearance of the writing is unfamiliar. Partly this is because the material most used was papyrus or wax tablets, neither of which survive easily, except in dryer parts of the Roman world such as Egypt. Nevertheless the future lay with this somewhat unprepossessing hand, rather than with the monumental scripts and the majuscule letters, since speed and economy were always much in demand.

In the year 311 AD an event occurred which was to have an important effect on the art of the book and on writing itself. In this year the Emperor Constantine proclaimed Christianity as the official religion of the Empire. Up to this time, Christianity had been only one of a number of faiths which had flourished in the late Roman world, but now, with official blessing upon it, it was to spread and overcome most other religions. Roman religion had possessed no sacred books and relied almost entirely on outward ceremonial. Christianity was different. The Christian possessed in his holy book, the Bible, the revealed Word of God, and it was his duty to diffuse this Scripture and the commentaries upon it, as widely as possible. The desire to propagate the Word of God and the works of His martyrs and prophets, and the immense amount of copying that this entailed, inevitably affected the form taken by the actual handwriting. Christianity spread out along the lines of communication of the late Roman Empire, taking with it the vellum codex, the quill pen, and the current forms of script – and, of course, the Bible, a word derived from the Greek *biblos* meaning 'book', since for the Christian there was only one Book.

Understandably the common form of script was not thought to be good enough for sacred writings and church ceremonial. Important literary works had been written in square capitals, which were time consuming and wasteful. Rustic capitals were perhaps easier to write and were certainly used for important writings. But another majuscule script had developed during the Roman period, possibly as early as the 3rd century AD, and was certainly in use by the 4th century. This was the script known as uncial, and from the 5th to the 8th century it was to be the dominant book hand of the west. Some of the oldest and finest Biblical texts were written in this script, which many consider to be the most beautiful of all book hands. There were various reasons for its continued use over so many centuries. It was essentially a pen-formed hand, whose characteristic letters were rounded and whose main vertical strokes generally rose a little above, or fell below, the line. It was a very beautiful script and one that scribes have always found pleasing to write. It was, moreover, the script in which many of the most important early Christian texts had been written – St Jerome's revision of the Bible, the works of St Augustine, and the early Christian Fathers. As such it had an importance for all copyists as a hand worthy for the service of God, and thus maintained its long supremacy in ecclesiastical texts. When, towards the end of the 8th century, the uncial script began to break down and a certain carelessness in execution became manifest, it still retained its importance as a ceremonial hand. It also continued to be used for display purposes, in headings and important passages, long after it had been superseded by the minuscule hands of later centuries, and it gave majesty to those passages where it was used. The uncial was spacious and massive in appearance, with its fine curved letters, but it was slow to write and wasteful of vellum. Such a formal and extravagant hand could never be used for business or indeed for anything except very special works. There was obviously a need for a script which could be written speedily and with economy of material, and the answer to this requirement was the development of the minuscule or small letter script, the great medieval contribution to handwriting.

It has already been noted that there existed a cursive informal hand for use in business and day-to-day affairs. It was not surprising therefore that on occasion some writings, especially those for private or semi-formal use, would show a mixture of scripts, with letters taken from both formal and informal hands. In time this mixed hand could itself be elevated to a book hand. As the 'half-uncial' or pre-Carolingian minuscule its importance lay mainly in its influence on the later development of the various national hands.

As long as communication within the Roman Empire remained intact, the language and script of Rome prevailed throughout the Empire. But with the breakdown of Roman power, the various parts of the Empire became increasingly isolated. Thus cut off one from another, the various areas began to follow their own development, in language and in script. The effect was gradual, and it was some time before the scripts, starting from the same models, had so diverged as to become truly national. Among the main areas of the old Roman Empire which developed national scripts of importance were Spain, Italy, France and the British Isles. In Spain the Visigothic script remained uninfluenced by later developments, although it eventually succumbed to the undoubted superiority of the Carolingian minuscule; nevertheless examples of the national script can be found as late as the 12th century. In Italy, development varied between the north and the south of the country. Beneventan script, evolved around Monte Cassino and areas further south, remained in use until the 13th century. But in the north, French influence was experienced, especially with the extension of the Frankish empire under Charlemagne, and this led to what has been called the Franco-Lombardic style. All the national scripts, including the Merovingian hand in France, were characterised by a certain involved quality leading to a lack of legibility, and by a mixture of letters taken from cursive, uncial and half-uncial forms.

In Ireland and England, the national scripts followed a rather different pattern. Ireland was never conquered by the Roman army, and Roman cursive hands had little or no influence on Irish handwriting. The manuscripts brought to Ireland by the missionaries from Rome were probably written in half-uncials. This fact can only be deduced from the subsequent development of Irish scripts, which owing to the isolation of the country evolved along quite different lines from the continental hands. The finest of the Irish manuscripts are outstanding and many are well-known – perhaps the Book of Kells is the most famous of these. Irish monks were great missionaries, and, taking their scripts with them, settled in places as widely separated as Luxeuil in France, Würzburg in Germany and Bobbio in Italy. On occasions it can be difficult to tell whether a manuscript is in the hand of a native-born scribe or of a writer following the same tradition in one of the continental Irish-founded monasteries.

Perhaps more important for the English speaking world was the fact that the Irish missionaries also went, first to Iona, and then, in 634, to Lindisfarne, so taking their brand of Celtic Christianity and their script to Northumbria. Some of the best productions of the Anglo-Celtic school have also long been well-known, perhaps the most famous of these manuscripts being the Lindisfarne Gospels, written in about the year 700. But in the south of England other influences were at work. Here the scribes were affected by the manuscripts brought over by the Roman missionaries who followed St Augustine's arrival at Canterbury in 597. Rustic capitals, uncials and half-uncials were thus introduced into Britain. But it was the influence from the north which was to predominate and produce the characteristic insular hand. This spread back to the continent during the missionary ventures of Anglo-Saxon monks in the 8th century. In England the Anglo-Saxon or insular minuscule only began to be supplanted by the continental minuscule during the 10th century, and even then it still tended to be employed for works written in the vernacular.

Inscription on a Roman grave slab, Rome 2nd century AD

This is the kind of Roman lettering which is most familiar today. It shows Roman square capitals incised on marble. The most famous example and the one considered to provide the best models for the forms of the letters, is the inscription on the base of Trajan's Column in Rome, of which a cast exists in the Victoria and Albert Museum. Most western scripts derive, in one form or another, from this type of lettering, and throughout the centuries calligraphers and typographers alike have returned to the Roman capitals as a source of inspiration.

Reproduced by permission of the University of London Institute of Archaeology.
29 × 36

ABCDEFGHILMN

special positions

Normal pen position

OPQRSTVXY AJKUWZ

Suggested modern A & JKUWZ forms

"SQUARE CAPITALS" freely copied with a pen from a photograph of a 4th. or 5th. Century MS. (Vergil) – abt. 2ce. the height of originals

ACCEDENS AVTEM TRIBVNVS, DIXIT
ILLI: DIC MIHI SI TV ROMANVS ES?
AT ILLE DIXIT: ETIAM· ET RESPONDIT
TRIBVNVS: EGO MVLTA SVMMA CI-
VILITATEM HANC CONSECVTVS SVM·

Example of (modern) Writing. Note: the words are 'packed' and separate now: in the early MSS. there was no such division. (Actus Apostolorum XXII.27)

ABCDEFGHILMNOPQ

RSTVXY ✣ AHJKUWZ

for thin stems (varies)

Normal pen position for thicks

Suggested modern A, H, & J, K, U, W, Z forms to match.

"RUSTIC CAPITALS" freely copied with a pen from a photograph of a 3rd. or 4th. Century MS. (Vergil) — abt. 2ce. the height of originals.

Edward Johnston: Manuscript & inscription letters for schools and classes & for the use of craftsmen London 1928

This illustration from a teaching portfolio by Edward Johnston, shows the two main Roman majuscule scripts: the square capitals and the rustic capitals. They have been written out here by Johnston, but are based on actual originals; for the use of modern scribes he has added the letters which were not found in the original Roman alphabet.

Author's collection

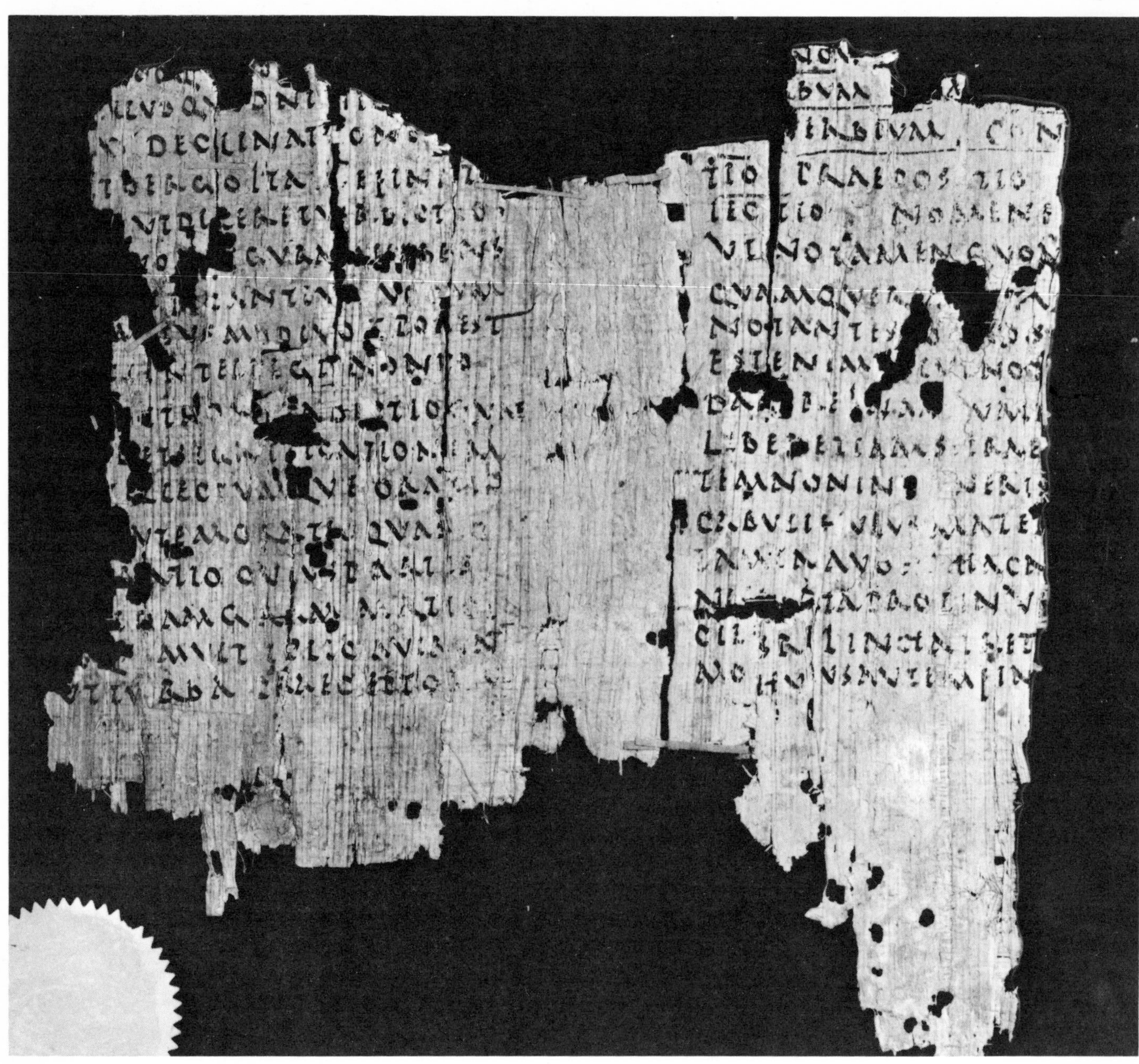

Part of a Roman school grammar,
found at Karanis,
Egypt, after 172 AD

This fragment is written in two columns in rustic capitals, and it will be noticed that as in the earlier fragments, and indeed as in Roman inscriptions, there is no punctuation and no separation between the words. These only began to appear in about the 7th century.

Reproduced by permission of the British Library. Papyrus 2723 (verso)

Two examples of Roman writing from Pompeii. At the top is an election notice, using rustic capitals and painted on a wall. Below, graffiti written in Roman cursive, the hand commonly used for informal communications and business. Pompeii was destroyed in AD 79.

From L'écriture latine de la capitale romaine à la minuscule *réunis par J. Mallon, R. Marichal & C. Perrat. Paris 1939*

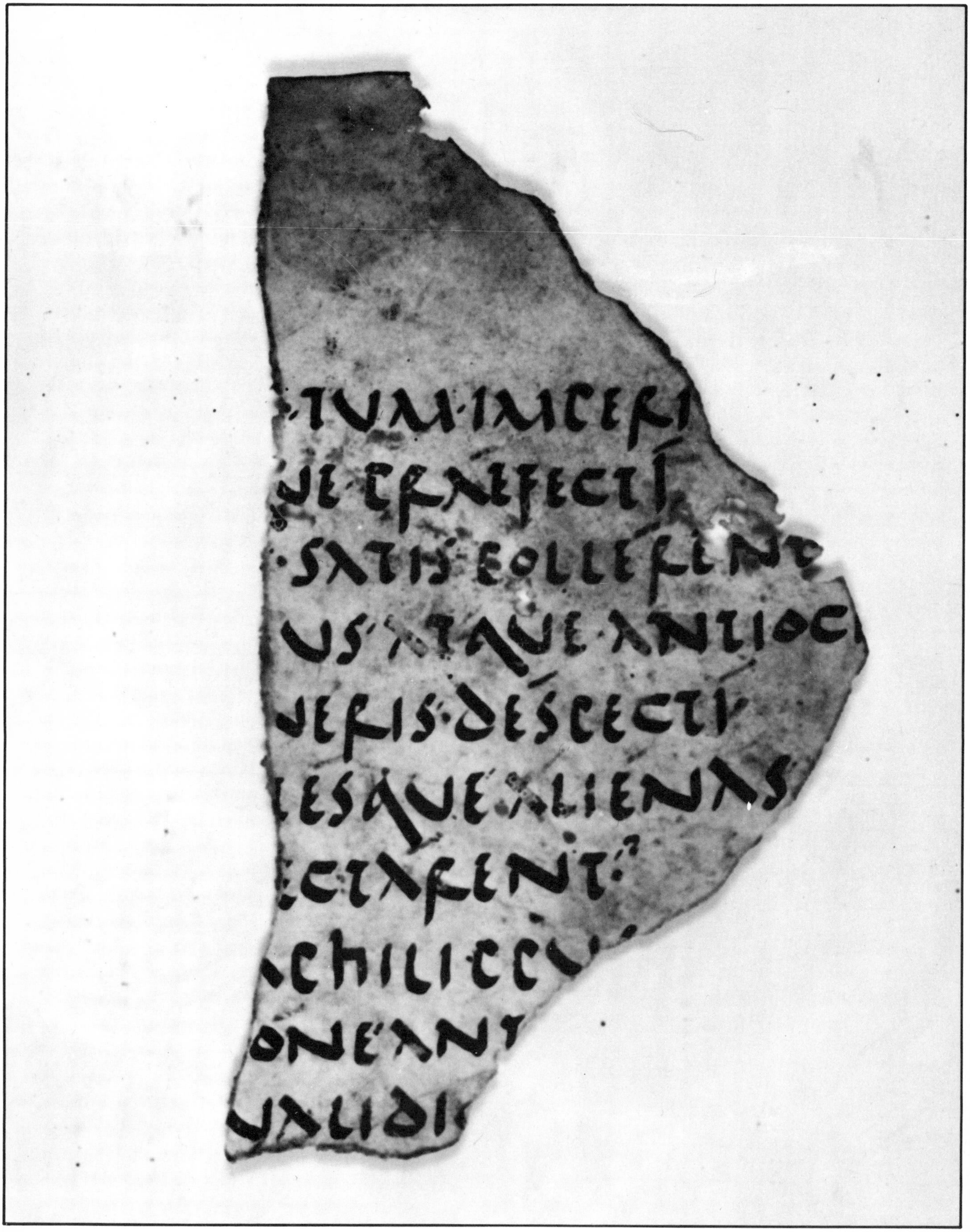

Opposite:

Fragment of a Roman book, found at Oxyrhynchus, Egypt 2nd/3rd century.

This fragment, which is written on vellum (although numbered as papyrus) is especially interesting because of the admixture of scripts which it displays. It is a blend of rustic capitals (A and M), uncials (D, F and R), and rustic capitals influenced by cursive script (R). This sort of mixture must have been frequent during the early centuries of the Christian era, when no one script had found more or less universal acceptance, such as was to take place in later centuries.

Reproduced by permission of the British Library. Papyrus 745

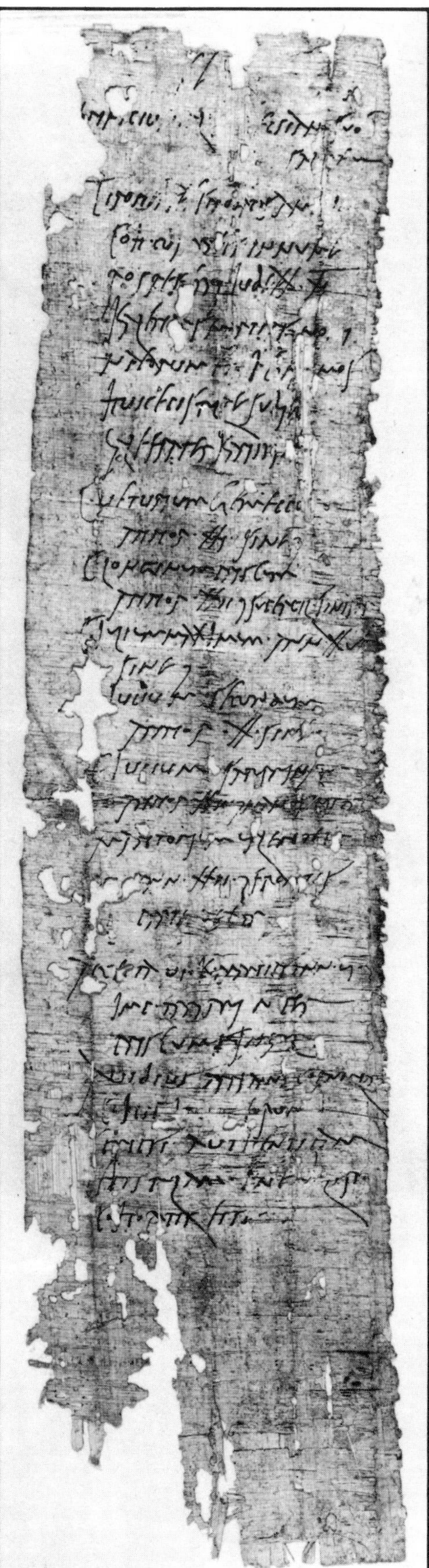

Letter from a Roman officer, found at Oxyrhynchus in Egypt. AD 103

This letter is written in Roman cursive handwriting which was the informal and business hand of the Roman Empire. It had a long life, from at least the second century BC until the 7th century AD. It was this cursive informal hand rather than ceremonial script which eventually influenced the medieval writing. Although it cannot have been so difficult for the recipient to read as it is for us today, nevertheless, like all cursive scripts it very easily deteriorated into illegibility. It has been suggested that the forms of the letters were originally determined by the fact that they were written on wax tablets *(see p. 13)**. This particular letter concerns the enrolment of six new recruits.*

Reproduced by permission of the British Library. Papyrus 2049

audita morte eius reuersus est
de aegypto
miseruntq; et uocauerunt eum
uenit ergo hieroboam et omnis
multitudo israhel
et locuti sunt ad roboam dicentes
pater tuus durissimum iugum
inposuit nobis
tu itaq; nunc inminue paululu(m)
de imperio patris tui durissimo
et de iugo grauissimo quod in
posuit nobis et seruiemus tibi
qui ait eis
ite usq; ad tertium diem
et reuertimini ad me
cumq; abisset populus init
consilium rex roboam
cum senibus
qui adsistebant coram salomone
patre eius dum adhuc uiueret
et ait quod mihi datis consilium
ut respondeam populo
qui dixerunt ei
si hodie oboedieris populo huic
et seruieris
et petitioni eorum cesseris
locutusq; fueris ad eos uerba lenia
erunt tibi serui cunctis diebus
qui dereliquit consilium senum
quod dederant ei
et adhibuit adulescentes qui
nutriti fuerant cum eo
et adsistebant illi
dixitq; ad eos quod mihi datis
consilium ut respondeam
populo huic
qui dixerunt mihi leuius fac
iugum quod inposuit pater
tuus super nos
et dixerunt ei iuuenes qui
nutriti fuerant cum eo
sic loqueris populo huic qui
locuti sunt ad te dicentes
pater tuus adgrauauit iugum
nostrum tu releua nos
sic loqueris ad eos
minimus digitus meus grossior
est dorso patris mei
et nunc pater meus posuit
super uos iugum graue
ego autem addam super iugum
uestrum
pater meus caecidit uos flagellis
ego autem caedam uos
scorpionibus
Uenit ergo hieroboam et omnis
populus ad roboam die tertia
sicut locutus fuerat rex dicens
reuertimini ad me die tertia
responditq; rex populo dura
derelicto consilio seniorum
quod ei dederant
et locutus est eis secundum
consilium iuuenum dicens
pater meus adgrauauit
iugum uestrum
ego autem addam iugo uestro
pater meus caecidit uos flagellis
et ego caedam scorpionibus
et non adquieuit rex populo
quoniam auersatus eum
fuerat dns
ut suscitaret uerbum suum
quod locutus fuerat in manu
ahiae silonitae ad hieroboam
filium nabat
Uidens itaq; populus quod nolu
isset eos audire rex
respondit ei dicens
quae nobis pars in dauid
uel quae hereditas in filio isai
in tabernacula tua israhel
nunc uide domum tuam dauid
et abiit israhel in tabernacula sua
super filios autem israhel
quicumq; habitabant in ciui
tatibus iuda regnauit roboam
Misit igitur rex roboam

Opposite:

Leaf of a Bible (known as the Greenwell Leaf).
(Wearmouth/Jarrow)
English 689-716 AD

This is a leaf from one of the large Bibles written in uncial script in the scriptorium at Jarrow, showing the influence of the continental models brought back by travellers, such as Abbot Benedict Biscop, from their visits to Rome and other important continental centres. It shows clearly the curved pen strokes of this most majestic of majuscule scripts, here seen to advantage on the large spacious page. This surviving leaf from the Bible was used after the Reformation as part of a book cover — by such chances are these early manuscripts preserved!

Reproduced by permission of the British Library. Addl. MS. 37777 (verso)
47 × 33

Ecclesiastical Canons
Italian? 6th/7th Century

This handsome uncial shows clearly the characteristics of the script. According to E A Lowe it 'is an expert graceful uncial, but not of the oldest type'. As usual at this date the words are not separated, but the text is pleasantly set on the page.

Reproduced by permission of the Bodleian Library, Oxford Ms e Mus 100
f.7v. 26 × 18.5

Ecclesiastical Canons
Italian? 6th/7th Century

Another page of the handsome uncial text from the manuscript in the Bodleian Library, Oxford. It contains no punctuation and few abbreviations; the only decoration comes from the occasional use of red — in the headings, titles, or sometimes in the first lines of text.

Reproduced by permission of the Bodleian Library, Oxford. *Ms e Mus 100*
f.10r *26 × 18.5*

Opposite:
Primasius in Apocalypsim
English? 7th/8th century

This version of the half-uncial hand was based on French models, though written in England, possibly by a scribe who was more used to insular methods of writing. It will be noted that the script is well on the way to being a true minuscule. The form of the r *and the* s *in this hand (eg line 3) can be confusing. The initials in the manuscripts are filled with red and yellow.*

Reproduced by permission of the Bodleian Library, Oxford. *Ms Douce 140*
f.1v *24 × 18.5*

Tuis uiri inlustris et religiose cas
tori persuasionibus, adquiescens sic
librum apocalypsis beati iohannis mul
tis misteriis opacatum in adiutorio dni nri ihu
xpi licet exiguus susceperim uiribus expo
nendum. ut non meis tantum solis fuerim con
tentus inuentis, sed quamquam numero pau
ca aliqua tamen a sco quoque augustino tes
timonia exinde exposita fore repperi in
dubitanter adiunxi; sed etiam et ticonio
quondam donatista certa quae sano con
gruunt sensui deflorabi, et ex eis quae eli
genda fuerant, exundantia ne praemerent
inportuna resecans et inpolita compo
nens catholico moderamine temperaui,
multa quippe in ipso eius opere repperi
et super uacua et inepta et sane doctri
ne contraria; ita ut et de causa quae
inter nos et illos uertitur. secundum
prauitatem condicionis sui loca prouendi, cap
taret, nostrae quae ecclesiae noxia expo
sitione putaret mordacitate. inludendum.
nec enim minimum quod hereticus rem sibi congruam
faceret sed uel quod inuenire potuit deplo
randum quod tamen ille facere inuistigate
tauit, nobis curae fuit locorum opportuni
tatibus nactis uenaciter exsequi, eorum
que sermonem conuincendo castigare; sicut
autem praetiosa in stercore gemma pru

Regula S. Benedicti
English (probably Canterbury)
7/8th century

This uncial manuscript is written in two columns, in a very dark ink — 'an expert bold uncial' is how E. A. Lowe characterises the script. The large initials are outlined in black, filled with red, and surrounded by red dots, as we can see here. In this hand the bow of the a *has been given an extra ornamentation and the stem of the* g *ends in a thick triangle, eg line 3.*

Reproduced by permission of the Bodleian Library, Oxford. MS Hatton 48 f.4r 30 × 21.5

Opposite:
Evangelia (parts of St Luke and St John) Irish 8th century

This manuscript shows a fine example of insular majuscule script; it was probably written in Ireland, and displays 'bold Irish majuscules' according to Lowe. It is interesting to note the three dots which are often used at the end of the sections, and decorated initials which follow them. These are in black, filled with yellow, red or mauve, and surrounded by red dots; sometimes the whole of the first word may be decorated with dots in this way — several examples of this occur here. The Irish hand was based on the half-uncial rather than the pure continental uncial.

Reproduced by permission of the Bodleian Library, Oxford. Ms Rawl. S 167 f.25r 32.5 × 24.

a quibus dam quia iohannis surrexit a morTu
is. A quibus dam uero quia helias apparuit
ab aliis autem quia propheta unus deantiquis
surrexit. Et ait herodis iohannem ego decola
ui. quis est iste de quo audio ego talia. Et que
rebat uidere eum. Et reuersi apostoli narra
uerunt illi quae cumque fecerunt. Et adsum
tus illis secessit seorsum in locum desertum
qui est bethsaida quod cum cognouissent
turbae secutae sunt illum et excepit illos et loque
batur illis de regno dī et eos qui cura indigebant (sanabat)
Dies autem ceperat declinare et accedentes xii
dixerunt illi dimitte turbas ut euntes in castella
uillas que quae circa sunt deuertant et inuenia
nt escas quia hic in loco deserto sumus. Ait
autem ad illos uos date illis manducare. At
illi dixerunt non sunt nobis plus quam .u. pan
es et duos pisces. nisi forte nos eamus et emamus
in omnem hanc turbam escas. Erant autem fere
uiri quinque milia. Ait autem ad discipulos
suos facite illos discumbere per conuiuia.

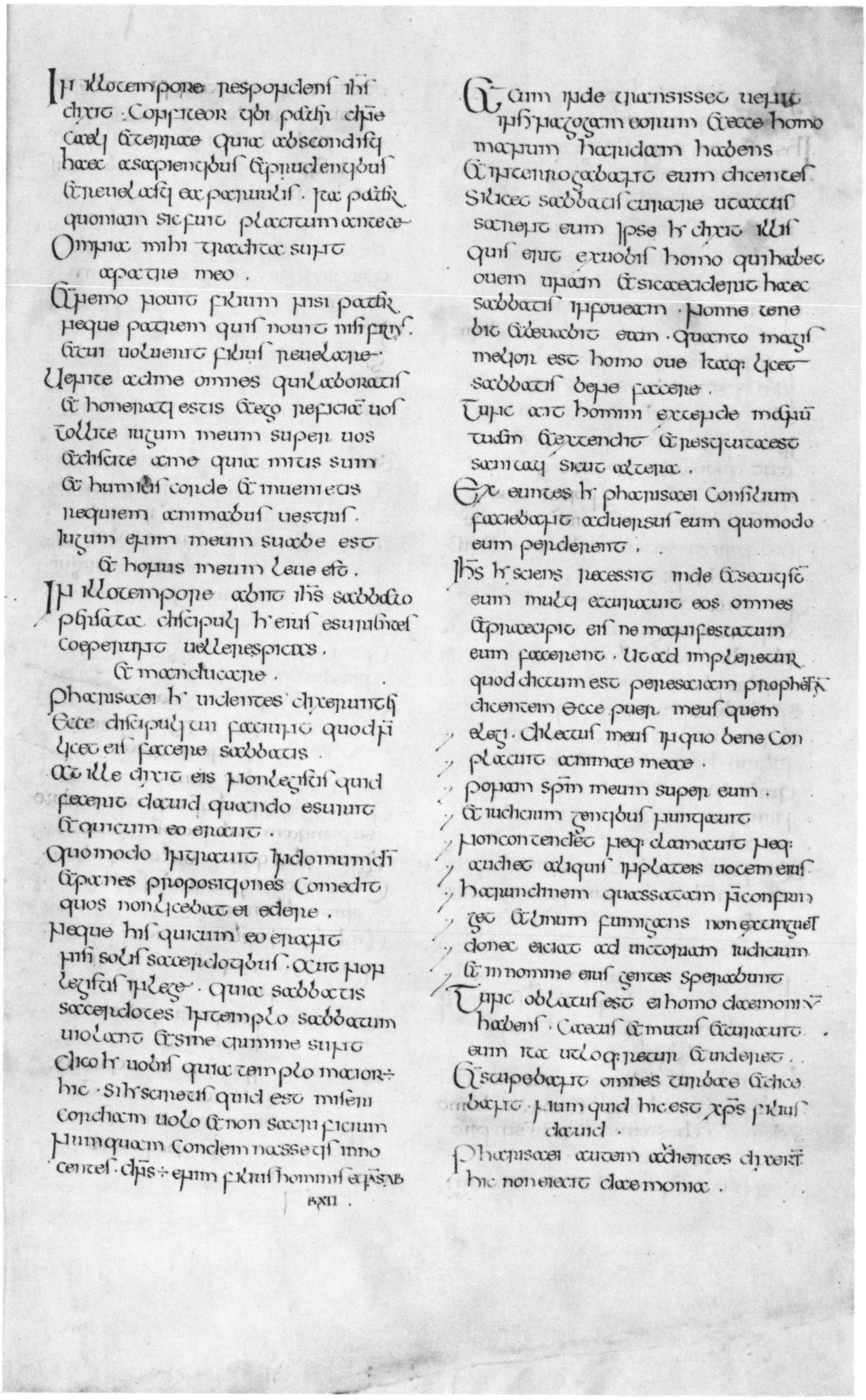

The Canterbury Gospels
English 8th century

This very elegant example of Anglo-Saxon majuscules was written in the south of England and certainly was at Canterbury by the 14th century. The manuscript contains some very fine illuminated pages, but the script can also make its own impact. Closer inspection reveals certain idiosyncrasies in the individual letters, some of the ascenders having an apparent quiver in them (eg In illo tempore) and the a *looks like an* o *joined to a* c.

Reproduced by permission of the British Library. Royal MS 1EVI, f.14r
47 × 34

Opposite:

Psalterium Romanus cum canticis [etc.] English 8th century

This splendid volume was probably written at Canterbury, where it seems to have remained until the time of the Dissolution in the 16th century. It is a good example of the uncial hand written in the south of England, and the layout and decoration should also be noted. The interlinear gloss is written in Anglo-Saxon minuscules of the 9th century and the two hands, appearing together here, form an interesting comparison — certainly the amount of space required by the uncial hand is made very evident.

Reproduced by permission of the British Library, Cotton Vespasian A1, f.55v 23.5 × 18

IN ME SUNT DS UOTA QUAE REDDAM LAUDATIO
NIS TIBI QUM ERIPUISTI ANIMAM MEAM DE MOR
OCULOS MEOS A LACRIMIS. PEDES MEOS A LAPSU
UT PLACEAM CORAM DNO IN LUMINE UIUENTIU
IN FIN. NE DISPERDAS DD IN TIT. INSCRIPT. CUM FU
LVI MISERERE MEI DS MISERERE MEI QUM IN TE
CONFIDIT ANIMA MEA. ET IN UMBRA ALARUM
TUARUM SPERO. DONEC TRANSEAT INIQUITAS.
CLAMABO AD DM ALTISSIMUM. ET AD DNM QUI BE
NE FECIT MIHI... GERET A FACIE SAUL. CONCULCANTES ME
DP MISIT DE CAELO ET LIBERAUIT ME DEDIT IN OPPROBRI
MISIT DS MISERICORDIAM SUAM ET UERITATEM SUA
ERIPUIT ANIMAM MEAM DE MEDIO CATULORU
LEONUM DORMIUI CONTURBATUS... IN SPELUNC
FILII HOMINUM DENTES EORUM ARMA ET SAGIT
TAE ET LINGUA EORUM MACHERA ACUTA..
EXALTARE SUPER CAELOS DS ET SUPER OMNEM
TERRAM GLORIA TUA...
LAQUEOS PARAUERUNT PEDIB' MEIS ET INCUR
UAUERUNT ANIMAM MEAM...
FODERUNT ANTE FACIEM MEAM FOUEAM.
ET IPSI INCIDERUNT IN EAM... DIAPSAL MA

quae in nobis completae
sunt rerum
sicut tradiderunt nobis
qui ab initio ipsi uiderunt
et ministri fuerunt
sermonis
uisum est et mihi
adsecuto a principio omnia
diligenter ex ordine tibi
scribere optime theophile
ut cognoscas eorum
uerborum de quib:
eruditus es ueritatem

·II· Fuit in diebus
herodis regis
iudaeae sacerdos
quidam nomine
zacharias de uice abia
et uxor illi de filiab: aaron
et nomen eius elisabeth
erant autem iusti ambo
ante dm

incedentes in omnibus
mandatis et iustificatio
nib: dni sine quaerella
et non erat illis filius eo
quod esset elisabeth
sterilis
et ambo processissent
in dieb: suis
factum est autem cum
sacerdotio fungeretur
in ordine uicis suae
ante dm
secundum consuetudinem
sacerdoti
sorte exiit ut incensum
poneret ingressus
in templum dni
et omnis multitudo erat
populi orans foris
hora incensi
apparuit autem illi
angelus dni stans
a dextris altaris
incensi

Opposite:

The Lindisfarne Gospels
English 8th century

This manuscript, written in Anglo-Saxon majuscules with a later gloss, is probably one of the best known of early English works. According to the colophon it was written by Eadfrith, Bishop of Lindisfarne (698-721), but the inter-linear gloss is of the 10th century and is written in Anglo-Saxon minuscules. During the 9th and 10th centuries the manuscript accompanied the relics of St Cuthbert during their many wanderings and was always considered as an outstanding object. For the most part it is the decoration which holds the eye, especially the four full-page miniatures of the Evangelists, but this illustration shows the majesty of the script in which the whole work is written.

Reproduced by permission of the British Library, Cotton Nero D. IV f.139v 34 × 24.5

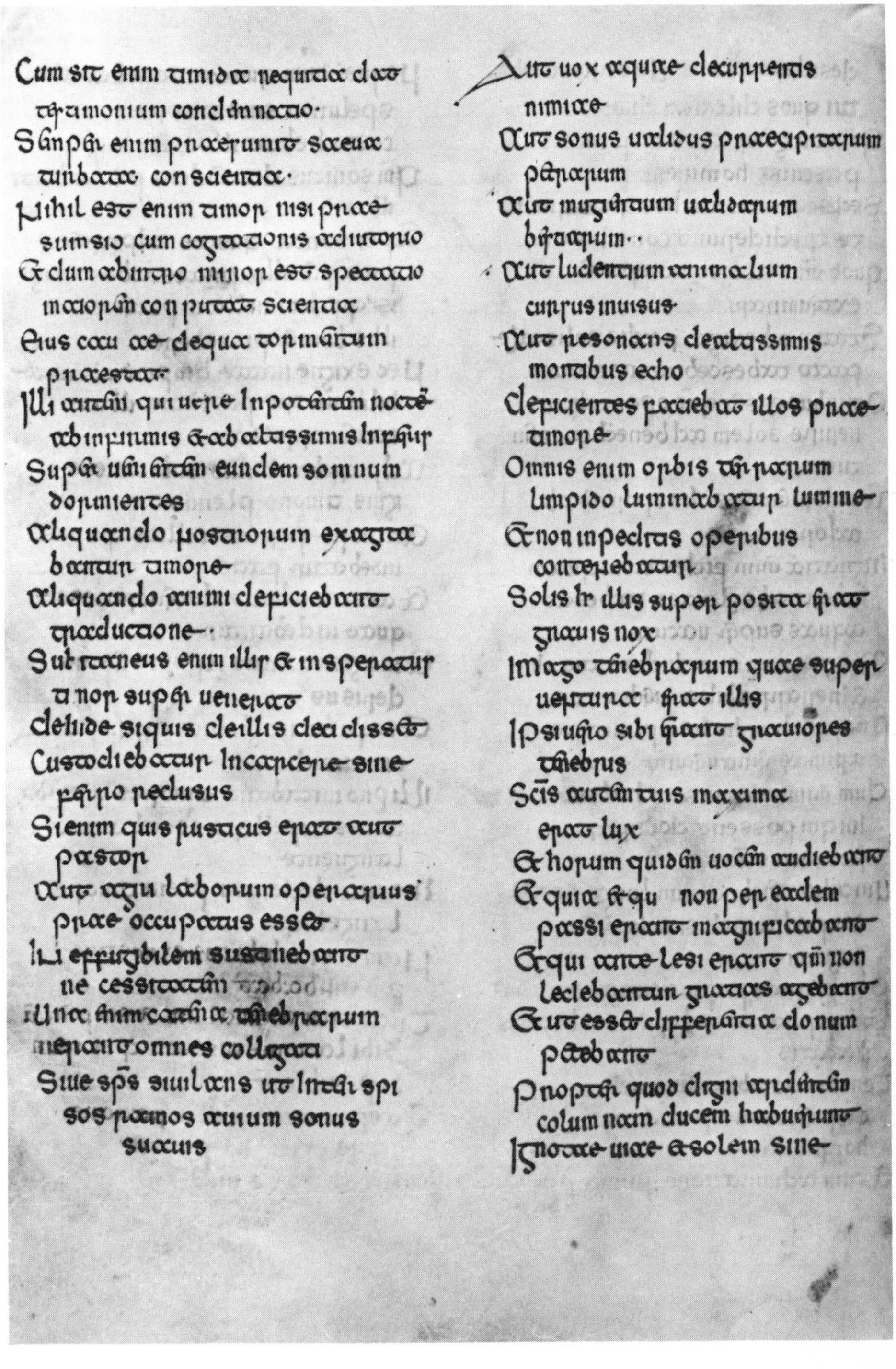
Cum sit enim timida nequitia dat
testimonium condemnatio·
Semper enim praesumit saeva
turbata conscientia·
Nihil est enim timor nisi prae-
sumsio cum cogitationis adiutorio
Et dum ab intro minor est spectatio
maiorem conputat scientia
Eius causae de qua tormentum
praestat
Illi autem qui vere inpotentem noctem
ab infimis et ab altissimis inferis
Super unum eundem somnum
dormientes
Aliquando monstrorum exagita-
bantur timore
Aliquando animi deficiebant
traductione·
Subitaneus enim illis et insperatus
timor supervenerat
dehinc siquis de illis decidisset
Custodiebatur in carcere sine
ferro reclusus
Si enim quis rusticus erat aut
pastor
Aut agri laborum operarius
prae occupatus esset
Ineffugibilem sustinebat
ne cessitatem
Una enim catena tenebrarum
ligati omnes colligati
Sive spiritus sibilans aut inter spi
sos ramos avium sonus
suavis
Aut vox aquae decurrentis
nimiae
Aut sonus validus praecipitatarum
petrarum
Aut mugitum validarum
bestiarum··
Aut ludentium animalium
cursus invisus
Aut resonans de altissimis
montibus echo
deficientes faciebat illos prae
timore
Omnis enim orbis terrarum
limpido illuminabatur lumine
Et non inpeditis operibus
continebatur
Solis autem illis superposita erat
gravis nox
Imago tenebrarum quae super
ventura erat illis
Ipsi ergo sibi erant graviores
tenebris
Sanctis autem tuis maxima
erat lux
Et horum quidem vocem audiebant
Et quia et qui non per eadem
passi erant magnificabant
Et qui ante lesi erant quod non
ledebantur gratias agebant
Et ut esset differentia donum
petebant
Propter quod ignis ardentem
columnam ducem habuerunt
Ignotae viae et solem sine

Sapiential Books of the Old Testament English (Northumbria) 8th century

This manuscript illustrates two Anglo-Saxon scripts, the majuscule and the minuscule, and both were apparently always part of the same work. The long-stemmed r*, looking rather like an* n*, and the curiously curled* g *are characteristic of this script. The manuscript is written in a black ink, and by this date the words are clearly separated one from another.*

Reproduced by permission of the British Library. Egerton MS 1046 f.30v 31 × 23

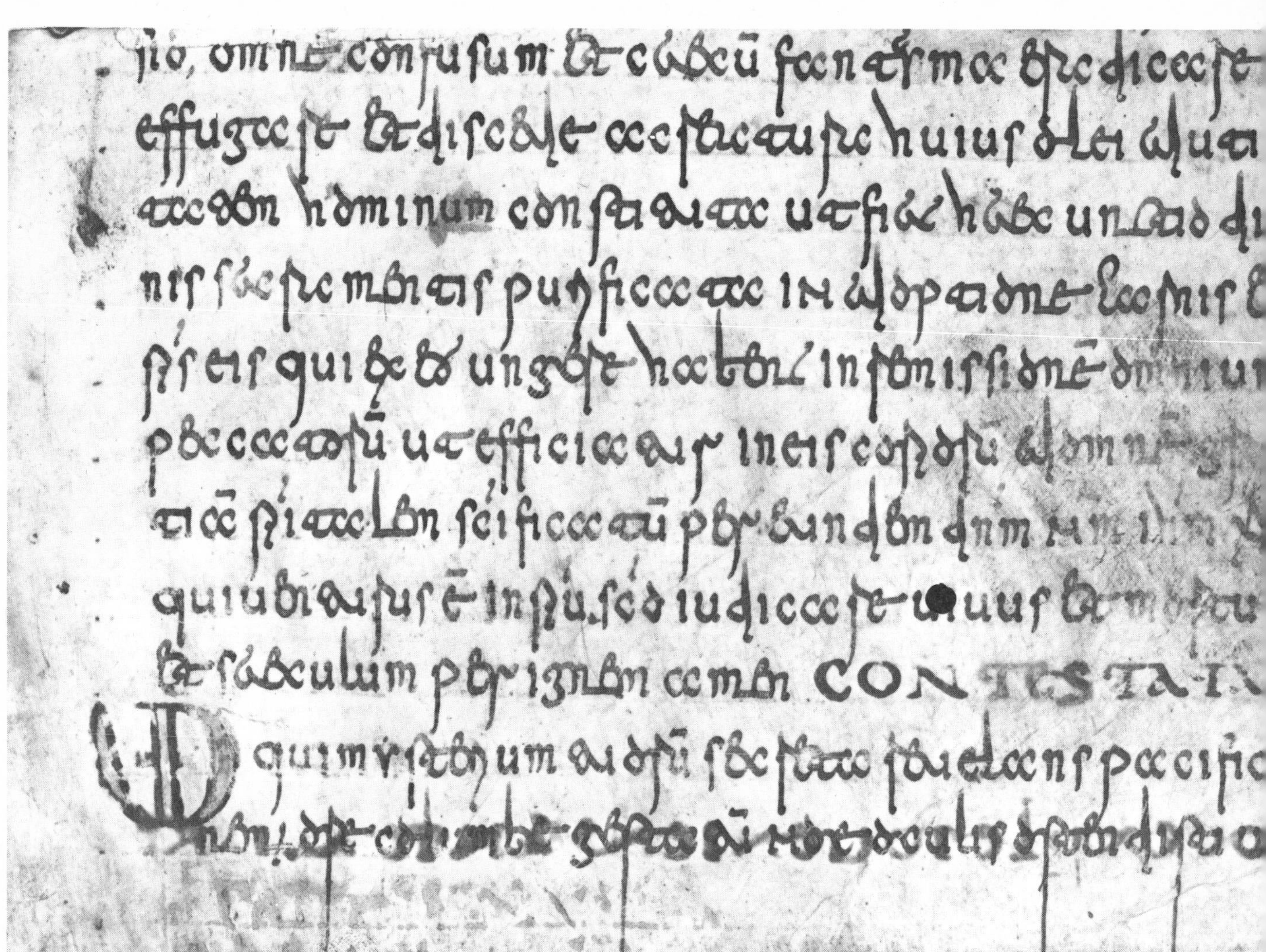

Sacramentum Gelasianum
French 8th century (second half)

This fragment, one of several removed from a binding, shows the Merovingian hand of the pre-Carolingian period in all its complexities. It is extremely difficult to read, a number of the individual letters assuming unfamiliar forms — the a *for example, often appears as two c's. The hand is considered as a precursor of the 'Corbeil a-b' script (p. 44). It was this type of writing which Charlemagne sought to reform by the development of the script which bears his name — the Carolingian minuscule.*

Reproduced by permission of the Bodleian Library, Oxford. Ms Douce f.1 f.1v 15.5 × 21

Opposite:
Evangelia 'Gospels of Mac Regol'
Irish 8th/9th century

This late form of the Irish majuscule script was written in part at least by Mac Regol (identified as 'scribe and bishop'), the abbot of Birr who died in 822. It has coloured capitals in brick red, purple, green or yellow, and decorated with red dots. It is interesting to compare this late and somewhat slacker version of the hand with the other Bodleian manuscript, p. 35 (Ms Rawl. S 167). The Anglo-Saxon interlinear gloss is of the 10th century, and forms a complete contrast to the script of the main text.

Reproduced by permission of the Bodleian Library, Oxford. Ms Auct D II 19 f.93v 35 × 27

Qui fuit arphaxat Qui fuit iareth
Qui fuit sem Qui fuit malelel
Qui fuit noe Qui fuit cainan
Qui fuit lamech Qui fuit enos
Qui fuit mathusale Qui fuit seth
Qui fuit enoc qui fuit adam

se hælend soðlice full gaste rede wæs godes

Cap: 4. Ihs autem plenus spu Qui fuit di

halge eftcerde wæs from iordane 7 wæs gelæded in gaste

2 sco regresus est aiordiane et agebatur inspu

on westenne dagas feowertig 7 wæs gecostad from dioble

in desertum diebus xl. et temptabatur adiabu

7 nowiht ne geæt on dagum ðæm 7 miððy gefylled

lo et nihil manducauit in diebus illis et consum

3 wærun ða gehyngerede cwæð soðlice him se dioful

matis illis essurit dixit autem illis zabulus

gif ðu arð godes sunu cweð ðisum stane ðætte hlaf se

si filius di es dic lapidi huic ut panis fiat

4 7 geondsworade to him se hælend awritten is forðon

et respondit adillum ihs scriptum est enim

ðætte ne on hlafe anum lifeð mon ah in eghwelcu

quia non in pane solo uiuit homo sed in om

5 worde godes 7 lædde hine eum se dioful 7 ætëowde him alle

ni uerbo di et duxit zabulus et ostendit illi omnia

6 rice ymbhwyrftes eorðe in huile tide 7 cwæð

regna orbis terrae in momento temporis et ait

him ðe ic selo mæhte ðas alle 7 wuldor

ei tibi dabo potestatem hanc uniuersam et glori

hiora forðon me gesald arun 7 ðæm ðe ic wyllo

am illorum quia mihi tradita sunt et cui uolu

de ilca ðu forðon gif ðu worðas biforan me

7 ero do illa tu ero si adoraueris coram me

biodun ðine alle 7 geondworde se hælend cwæð

8 erunt tua omnia et respondens ihs dixit

him awritten is drihten god ðinne weorðas 7 him

illi scriptum est dnm dm tuum adorabis et illi

anum gehersumas 7 lædde hine in 7 sette

9 soli seruies et duxit eum in hierusalem et statuit

[i. daemones]
ET IGNORAVIT QUOD GIGANTES IBI SINT ET IN
[i. daemones]
PROFUNDIS INFERNI CONVIVAE EIUS;
Nescit adultera. nescit haereticus quia inmundi spiritus
suas domos habitant. et qui in profundis inferni
portas luunt aeternas. ipsi actibus luxuriosorum.
ipsi haereticorum dogmatibus quasi conviviis delectan
tur omnis; at cum intra ecclesiam Christi sacramenta
celebrantur. Christi verbum auditur et conservatur
quae sapientia dei constat quod angelicae virtutes ibi
sint. et in ecclesiis caelorum convivae fidelium.
panem caeli dedit eis. panem angelorum mandu
cavit homo. Incipit liber II
PARABOLAE SALOMONIS. Novum ponit
titulum. quia novum genus locutionis incipit.
Ut non sicut prius de singulis bonorum malorum
ve partibus diutius disputet. sed alternis versibus
[dictus] actus utrorumque describat; — vero stultus
[i. populus christianus]
FILIUS SAPIENS LAETIFICAT PATREM. FILIUS
[i. aecclesia]
MAESTITIA EST MATRI SUAE; qui accepta fidei
mysteria bene servat. laetificat deum patrem. qui
vero habitu in mala actione vel haeresi commaculat.
matrem contristat ecclesiam;—

Bede: Expositio in Lucam
French (Tours) c820, with late 10th century additions

This fine Carolingian minuscule emanates from the scriptorium of Tours, which produced a number of outstanding manuscripts, especially during the rule of Alcuin of York (Abbot of St Martin's from 796 to 804). This illustration offers a good example of what came to be known as 'the hierarchy of scripts'. The idea of the relative importance of the various scripts (square capitals, rustic capitals, uncials etc.) indicates an awareness also of their antiquity. In this passage we can see that the major headings (the explicit *and* incipit *lines) have been written in rustic capitals, while the first line of the* Liber tertius *is in uncials.*

Opposite:
Beda In Proverbia Salomonis
English (Northumbria: Jarrow or Wearmouth) 8th/9th century

This manuscript is written in Anglo-Saxon minuscules, which continued to be used long after the Carolingian minuscules had become accepted in Europe. It is basically a pointed form, though the scribe uses a round uncial for his headings. After his main statements it will be noted that he uses a charming ivy-leaf device. Among the idiosyncracies of the letter forms the tall c *stands out, together with the fact that the* p *resembles an* r.

Opposite:

Theodore of Mopsuestia: Commentary on St Paul's Epistle to the Colossians
French 8th/9th century

This manuscript was written in north-eastern France in the minuscule script known as 'Corbeil a-b', after the monastery with which it was associated. The reason for its name can be seen in the very first word on the page shown here, where the opening word 'Paulus' includes the typically curious form of the a, *which looks more like* ic, *and the* b *which appears several times in the second line has a disconcertingly open bow. The script looks attractive but its idiosyncracies of letter-form and the amount of contraction make it difficult to read. It was such difficulties that the Carolingian script sought to eliminate from existing hands such as this.*

Reproduced by permission of the British Library. Harleian MS 3063 f.112 26 × 20

'Isidorus Pacensis' Chronicon
Spanish 8th/9th century

An example of the Visigothic script of Spain, described by Lowe in this example as a 'broad easy flowing minuscule of the older type'. The Visigothic hand in Spain remained in use until the 12th century, when, as in other countries, it was displaced by the Carolingian minuscule. Although this example of the script is not as contorted as some, it does show the difficulties encountered in deciphering these manuscripts.

Reproduced by permission of the British Library, Egerton MS 1934. f.1v 49.5 × 37

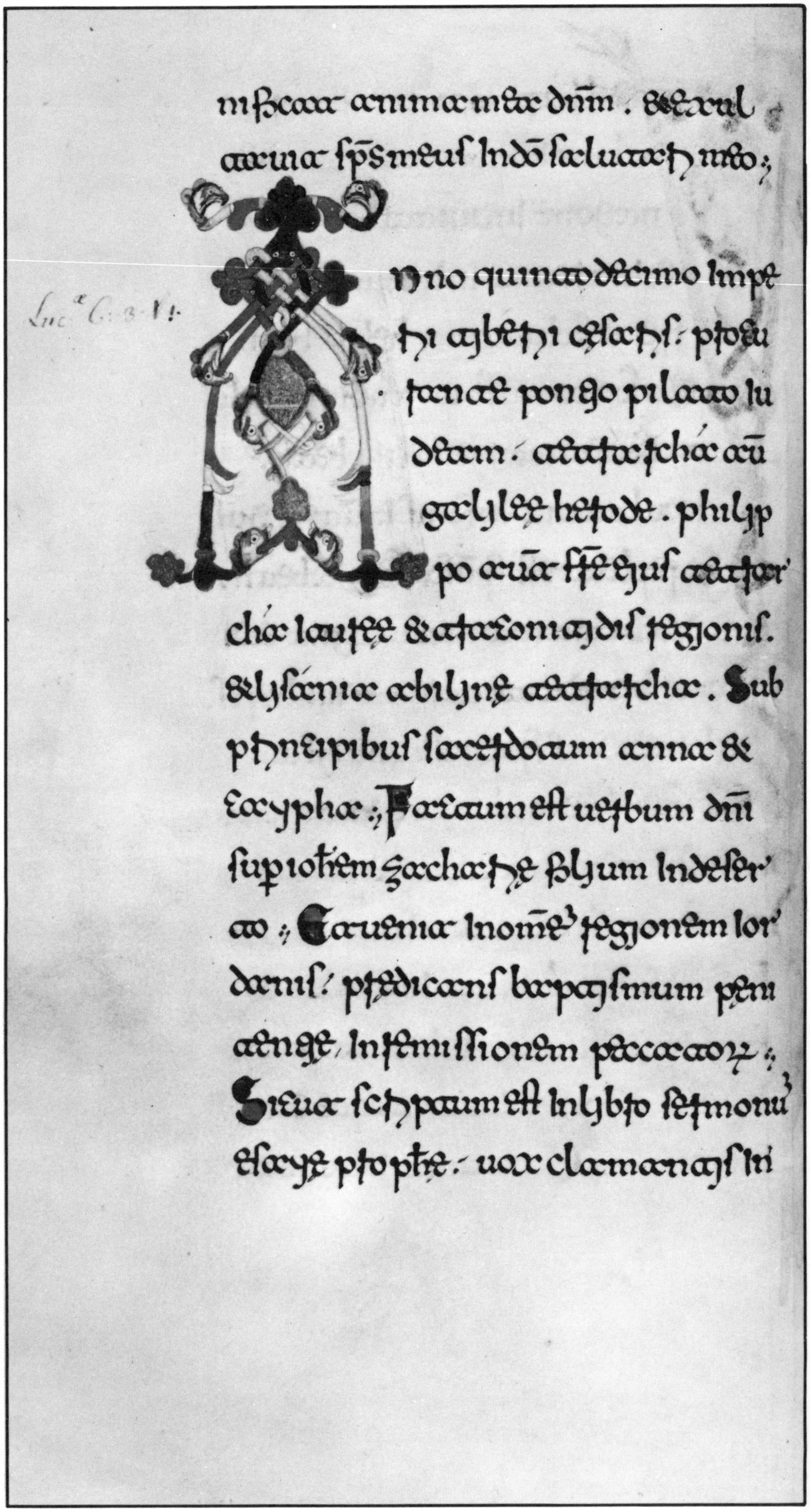

Gospel Lectionary
Dalmatia (Zadar)
late 11th century (1081-86?)

This is an example of the Beneventan script, which remained in use in southern Italy for nearly five hundred years. Although it has an attractive appearance on the page, especially with its simple coloured decoration as here, it is not easy to read — the a *and the* e *are by no means easily picked out in this text.*

Reproduced by permission of the Bodleian Library, Oxford. *Ms Canon Bibl Lat 61 f.7v* 28.5 × 18.5

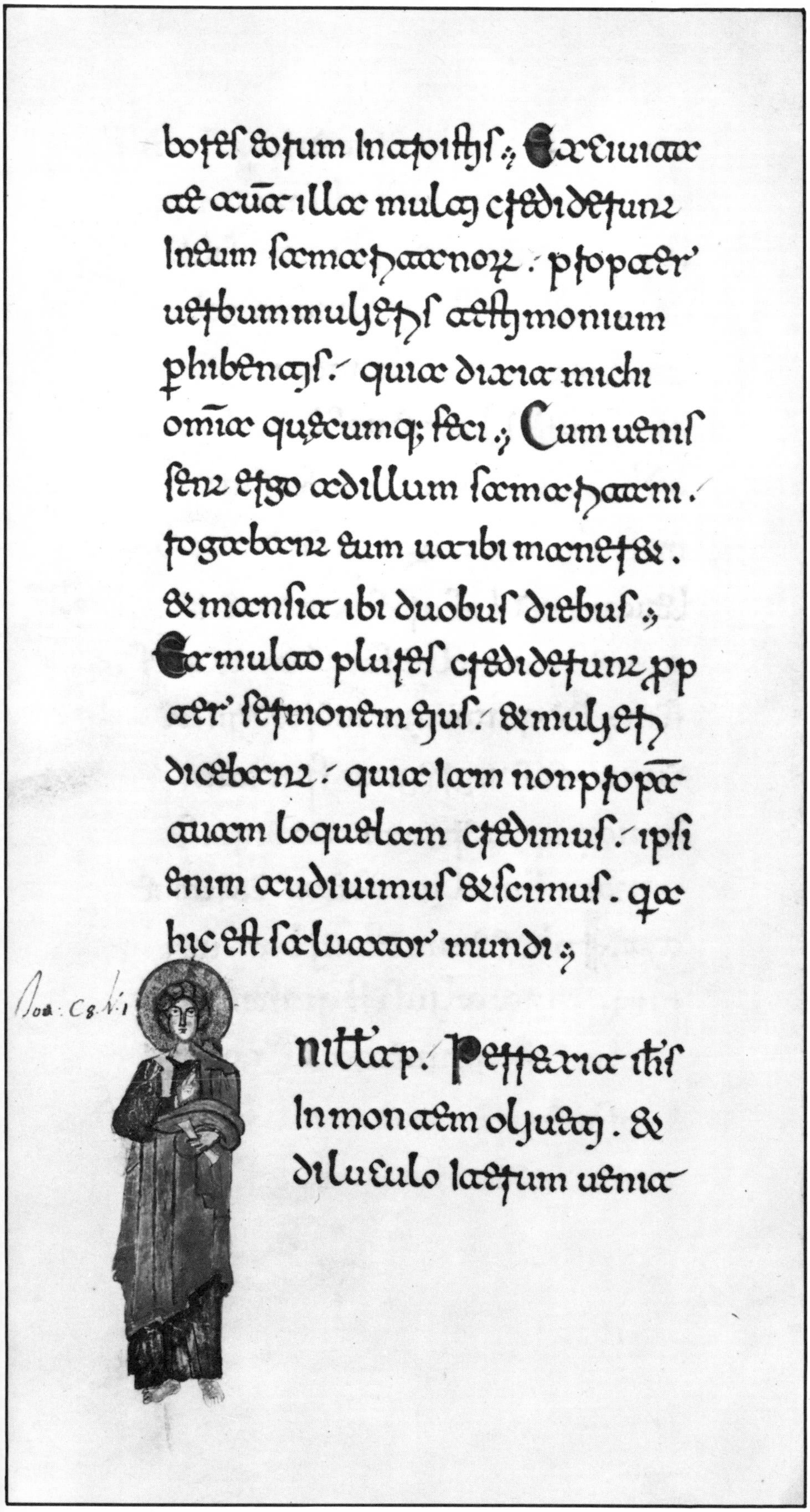

Gospel Lectionary
Dalmatia (Zadar)
late 11th century (1081-86?)

A further example of the Beneventan script, where again the a, *written more as a double* c, *is so compressed as to look more like* oc. *Nevertheless, as the two illustrations from this manuscript show, the general appearance of the script on the page is not unpleasing — but it is difficult to read without a knowledge of the letter-forms.*

Reproduced by permission of the Bodleian Library, Oxford. Ms Canon Bibl Lat.61 f.50v 28.5 × 18.5

4 Later medieval scripts: Carolingian, romanesque, gothic and bastarda

THE IMPORTANCE of the Carolingian minuscule and the fact that it continued in use for some centuries, makes the reign of Charlemagne a convenient dividing point in the history of scripts. Charlemagne succeeded his father Pepin the Short in 768 as joint heir with his brother Carloman. When Carloman died in 771, Charlemagne assumed control of the whole Merovingian empire. From then until his death in 814 Charlemagne continued to be occupied with wars within and around the borders of his empire. But he was more than a warlike king and a good administrator. Although illiterate himself, he had a genuine love of learning, and he gradually assembled at his court in Aachen many of the most learned men of the time. In 782 he summoned Alcuin of York, who in 796 became Abbot of Tours, a monastery whose scriptorium played a major part in the development of the script forever associated with the reign of Charlemagne. During Charlemagne's reign many reforms were undertaken; among them the revision of the church service books, in order to bring the Gallican church more into line with Rome. This entailed the production of large numbers of manuscripts, and at the same time there was a renewed interest in the copying of secular texts, especially those of the classics. Under the personal patronage of the king, the Carolingian renaissance flourished, and with all the literary and artistic activity going on, the need for a more suitable script than the existing ones was even more obvious. Thus the re-modelling of current penmanship became yet another of the cultural activities of the peripatetic court school which accompanied Charlemagne on his many travels.

The Carolingian minuscule evolved from the Merovingian national hand in use at the time, but refined, regularised, and raised to the status of a fine book hand – one that was to dominate the writing of western Europe for some centuries. It certainly arose out of the activity at the court of Charlemagne, but the Carolingian empire itself, by the year 800, included much of what is now France, Germany, Austria, the Low Countries, part of northern Spain and much of Italy. As a result it was not surprising that the calligraphic reforms of the Carolingian empire spread far and wide, even if not so far and wide as those of the Roman empire. Moreover the time was ripe for such a reform, as was manifest by the rapidity with which this new style of handwriting was taken up and maintained in so many countries. The Carolingian minuscule hand was characterised by the roundness of its letter-forms, minimal use of ligatures and contractions, a sense of spaciousness on the page, and a general elimination of cursive features. The script tended to slope slightly on occasions, and the ascenders developed clubbed ends. Although not a fast script, it was nevertheless speedier to write than the older majuscule scripts and more economical, while at the same time preserving both beauty and legibility. But the older, grander scripts were not forgotten, and an order of importance became apparent. This, known as the 'hierarchy of scripts', was first made evident in works from the influential scriptorium at Tours. Square capitals, the most ancient of hands, were placed in the most important position, usually at the heading of the page, to be followed progressively by rustic capitals, uncials and half-uncials, with the main text in minuscules. Not all the scripts were used in all manuscripts, but the way they were used indicates an awareness by the scribes of their relative importance in the history of western writing.

Having spread outwards from France, the Carolingian minuscule was inevitably affected by the existing vernacular scripts in the countries where it was adopted. In England its acceptance was late, and the insular minuscule continued in use well into the 10th century, and even later when the native language was being written. After reaching the peak of perfection in the 9th century the form of the Carolingian minuscule could only become slacker in the next century, and its bold strokes become gradually thinner, though as always styles varied from country to country. By the 11th century the establishment of national variations of the minuscule script was evident. It was perhaps the 12th century however which saw the final flourish of all that was best in the older tradition, especially in the production of the large volumes so characteristic of the romanesque manuscript style. Of these later manuscripts Maunde Thompson has written 'perfect symmetry of letters, marvellous uniformity in their structure, sustained contrast of light and heavy strokes, and unerring accuracy of the practised hand'.

But 12th century Europe also saw the beginning of the evolution of the new gothic style, which among other things was to transform the rounded romanesque arch into the pointed form so typical of the gothic style. In calligraphy too a similar change was to take place, and the grand style and large scale volumes of the 12th century began to decline. The popularity of the university lectures in Paris and other seats of medieval learning led to an increased demand for religious books, and for Bibles in particular. The enormous length of the Bible texts has always caused problems for those who would write or print the complete text. Many of the 13th century scribes solved the problem (as others later were to do) by writing in a very small hand. This also enabled them to produce a smaller book, more portable and more personal than the earlier large volumes, and many small finely written Bibles have survived from this period. But the desire to place as much on the page as possible also affected the style of the writing, which began to show a considerable amount of lateral compression. Gradually the round strokes of the letters became more angular until in the 14th century they frequently appeared to be a series of straight lines; the oblique strokes were fined down to hairlines, and slowly the characteristic gothic or 'textura' script evolved, to hold sway north of the Alps for some centuries. Here again there were regional differences, as can be seen from the examples illustrated in this book. When printing from movable types was invented in Germany in the middle of the 15th century, it was the local form of the gothic script which was used as the model for the first printed works, thus further perpetuating its use in books at least. Even when the gothic or 'black letter' script had been superseded for almost every other purpose, the law, that most traditional of professions, kept it alive, so that even today it can be found in the heading or opening words of wills and other legal documents. Its persistence in England was so long-lived (books were still being printed in black letter in the 17th century) that it has regularly been chosen to represent the essence of antiquity, hence the prevalence of the almost unreadable pseudo-gothic lettering to be found over buildings labelled 'Olde Tea Shoppe' or 'Antiques'.

It has been noted earlier that there was a considerable increase in literacy in the later Middle Ages, as settled town life became more feasible and trade and commerce increased. In their business and private affairs people wrote a cursive informal hand, which differed considerably from the formal book hands. It was speedy and small, with many letters joined together, and with a much rounder quality than the prevailing gothic script. It frequently made use of contractions (or word abbreviations), especially in legal and similar documents. Inevitably those accustomed to write both hands would on occasions mix the two styles, and by the 15th century this mixed hand or 'bastarda' was common. It became so familiar that it was not infrequently employed for literary works, and eventually for liturgical works and books of private devotions such as Books of Hours.

Characteristics of the bastarda script were the curved letter-forms, and a tendency to eliminate serifs and to taper individual strokes – especially prominent was the long *s*. When well written the script achieved a considerable grace and majesty, as a number of late medieval works illustrated in this book indicate. Like all cursive hands it could easily deteriorate, and this fact, together with the complication of the joined letters, meant that it was never seriously considered as a typographic model when printing took over from the hand-written book.

The general increase in literacy and the growing demand for books of all kinds, had not only led to the production of a wider range of secular manuscripts (often written in bastarda script), but had also encouraged changes in the methods of book making. The much needed theological, legal and medical treatises had already been largely mass-produced, and the increased production of reading matter required during the 15th century led in turn to something almost akin to modern publishing. It was no longer a question of a monk in his cell, laboriously copying out a whole work for the glory of God. The texts and the scribes might now be controlled from a central source, each scribe probably only copying one part of a volume, which was then assembled from the work of many different hands. The time was ripe for a more efficient way of producing books, and this took place when in 1455 the first large book, a Bible, issued from the printing press at Mainz. The invention of printing from movable types was to transform not only the whole method of book production as it then existed, but also the scribal art and the lives of those who practised it. Gutenberg had introduced printing into a medieval Germany, but already, south of the Alps in Italy, the Middle Ages had given place to the movement known as the Renaissance, and this too was to have a dramatic effect on the written word.

Pontifical from Exeter
English before 1072

This fine manuscript was written in the English version of the Carolingian script, which reached England about 950, although the Anglo-Saxon minuscule still continued in use as well for some time after this date. The manuscript contains ceremonies normally performed by a Bishop and the formulae for blessings. It is one of a group produced for, or under the direction of, Leofric, Bishop of Crediton and later Bishop of Exeter from 1046 until his death in 1072. It was probably one of the books he bequeathed to the Cathedral.

Reproduced by permission of the British Library. Addl MS 28188 f.73v/74r 18 × 12.5

Opposite:
Missal of Lesnes Abbey
English c1200

This manuscript was written at the transitional period of English art, between romanesque and gothic. However here it would appear that the script already shows gothic tendencies, with the roundness of the letters becoming more angular. Nevertheless the romanesque tradition is still strong enough to give the text a spacious and pleasant appearance.

V & A M L404-1916 f.113v 33 × 22.5

Gloria.

Maiestatem tuam Sci Andree apli.
dne suppliciter exoramus.
ut sicut eccle tue beatus
andreas apls extitit predi
cator & rector. ita aput te sit p nobis
ppetuus intercessor. p dnm. Secretu.
Sacrificiu nrm tibi dne qs beati andree
apli tui precatio sca conciliet. ut cuius
honore solempnit exhibetur. eius meritis
efficiatur acceptu. p. pf. Te dne supplicit.
Sumpsimus dne diuina misteria pco.
beati andree apli tui festiuitate le
tantes. que sicut tuis scis ad glam. ita
nobis qs ad ueniam pdesse pficias. p.
Sci Nicholai epi & conf. Colla.
Ds qui beatum nicholaum
pontificem tuum innume
ris decorasti miraculis. tri
bue nobis qs. ut eius meritis & pcib a ge
henne ignis incendiis liberemur. p. Secr.
Scifica qs dne munera que in uene
ratione sci antistitis tui nicholai

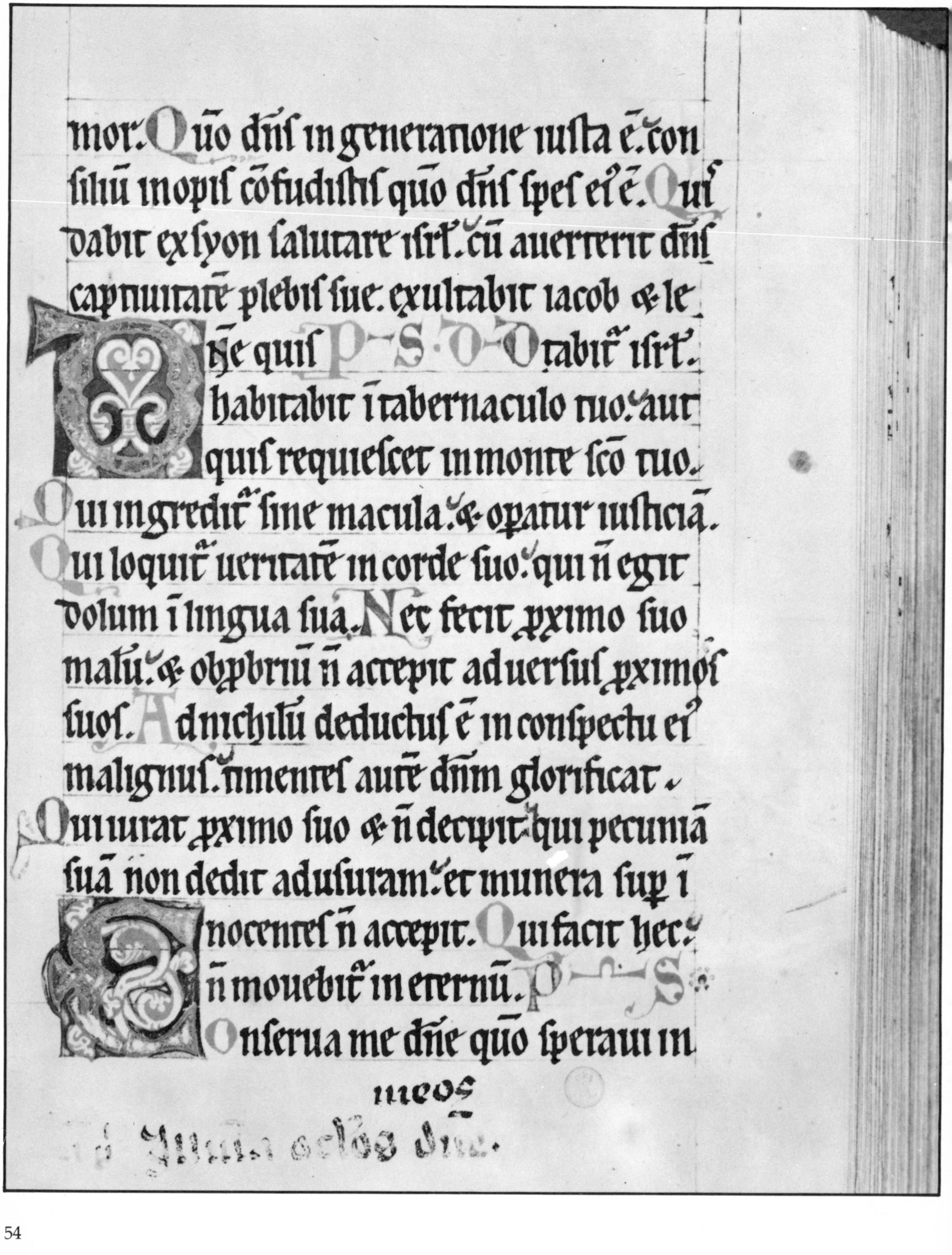

mor. Quō dn̄s in generatione iusta ē. con
siliū inopis cōfudistis quō dn̄s spes ei' ē. Qui
dabit ex syon salutare isrl̄. cū auerterit dn̄s
captiuitatē plebis sue. exultabit iacob & le
Dn̄e quis P. S. D. tabit' isrl̄.
habitabit ī tabernaculo tuo. aut
quis requiescet in monte scō tuo.
Qui ingredit' sine macula. & opatur iusticiā.
Qui loquit' ueritatē in corde suo. qui n̄ egit
dolum ī lingua sua. Nec fecit pximo suo
malū. & obpbriū n̄ accepit aduersus pximos
suos. Ad nichilū deductus ē in conspectu ei'
malignus. timentes autē dn̄m glorificat.
Qui iurat pximo suo & n̄ decipit. qui pecuniā
suā non dedit ad usuram. et munera sup i
nocentes n̄ accepit. Qui facit hec.
n̄ mouebit' in eternū. P. S.
Conserua me dn̄e quō speraui in

meos

Opposite:

Psalter (with canticles), bound with a calendar and part of a breviary; from an unidentified Cistercian house.
German (Worms?) c1260

Written in gothic minuscules on a thick vellum, the script is bold and clear. The words are well separated, although it will be noted that there is a certain amount of abbreviation in the text. It is a vertical script, with the letters t *and* d *being very upright.*

V & A M MS 23. iii. 1870

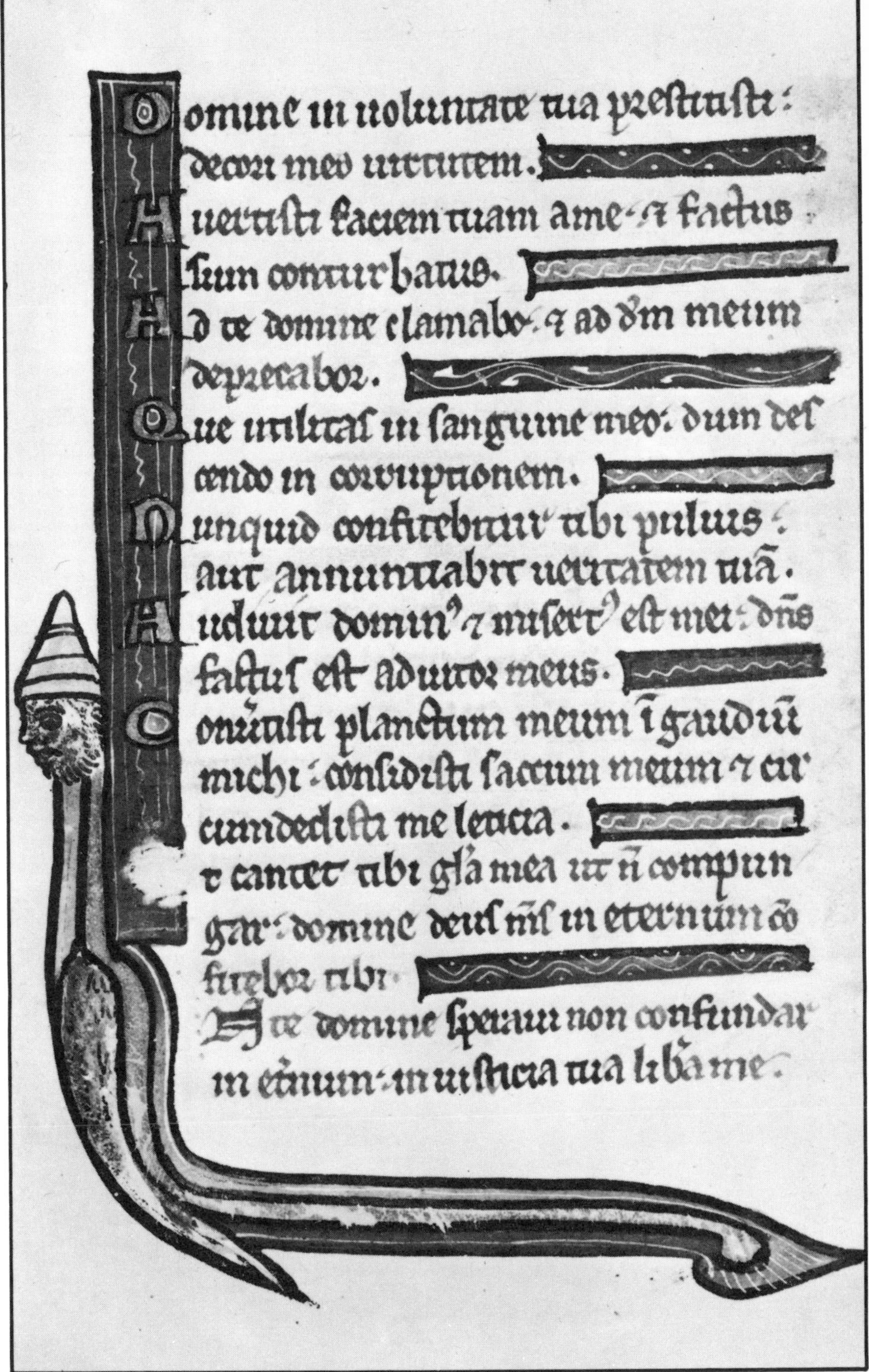
Domine in uoluntate tua prestitisti :
decori meo uirtutem.
Auertisti faciem tuam a me · et factus
sum conturbatus.
Ad te domine clamabo · et ad dm̄ meum
deprecabor.
Que utilitas in sanguine meo : dum des
cendo in corruptionem.
Numquid confitebitur tibi puluis :
aut annuntiabit ueritatem tuã.
Audiuit dominus et misertus est mei : dñs
factus est adiutor meus.
Conuertisti planctum meum in gaudiũ
michi : conscidisti saccum meum et cir
cumdedisti me letitia.
Ut cantet tibi gloria mea et non compun
gar : domine deus meus in eternum con
fitebor tibi.
In te domine speraui non confundar
in eternum : in iustitia tua libera me.

Psalter (with calendar and canticles); South Netherlandish c1280

This script, in gothic minuscules, is small with a certain lack of firmness about its formation; it is much less vertical than p. 54 as can be seen in the letters t *and* d. *The breaks between the minims in letters like* i, u, m *and* n, *can lead to confusion, as in the last line of the text.*

V & A M Reid MS 24

Biblia Sacra English?
13th/14th centuries

This small Bible is typical of its period, when the increased interest in university lectures led to a greater demand for Bibles. There was a trend away from the grander volumes of the previous century to smaller, more portable and more personal books. The vellum of this Bible is very thin and smooth, the writing is small, and considerable use is made of contractions. As a result, the whole of the Biblical text has been contained in a comparatively small volume, without undue sacrifice of legibility. Exactly the same effect can be seen in the printed Bibles of our own day, where the small double-columned text is set on specially thin 'india' paper.

V & A M Reid MS 21 16 × 11

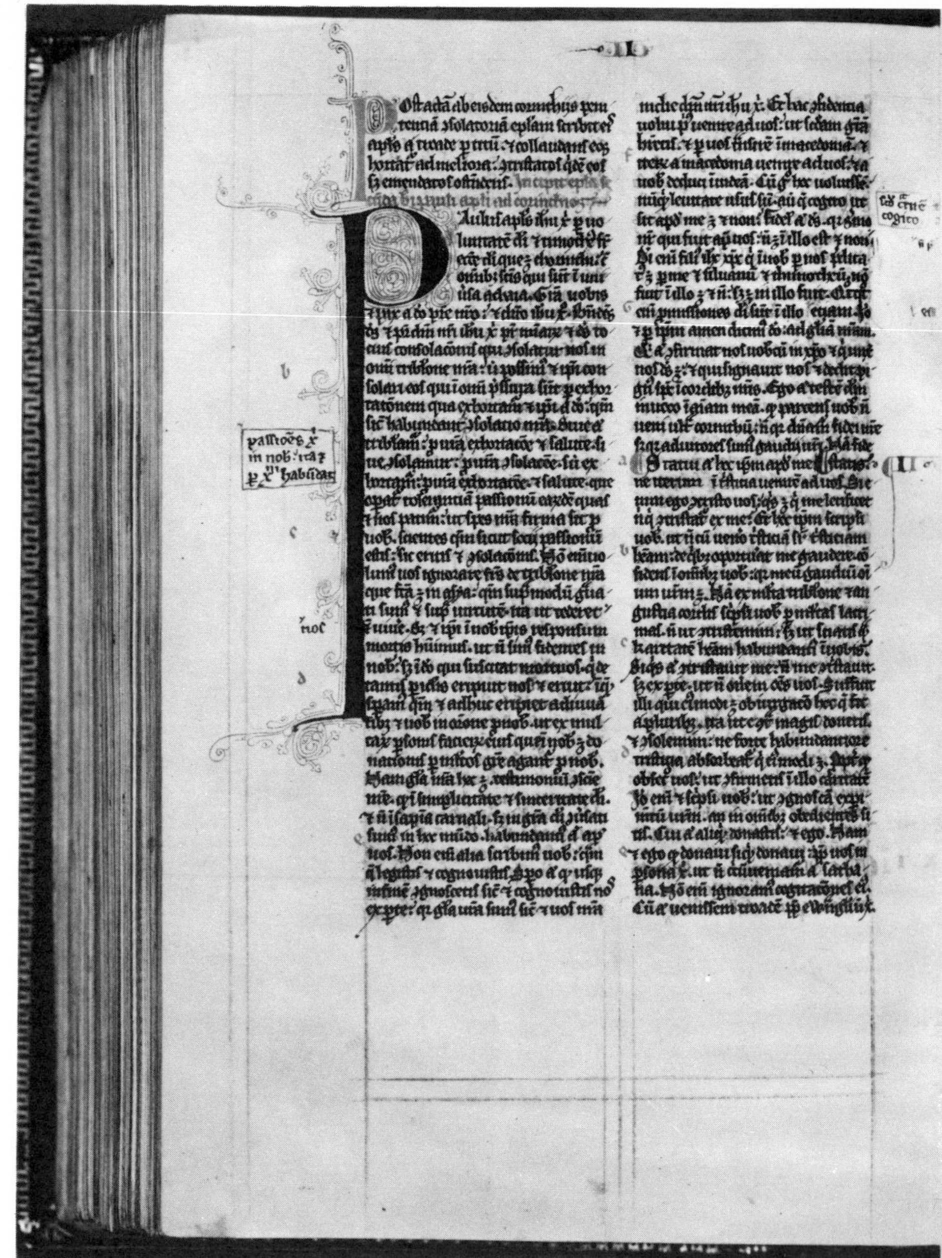

Leaf from an Antiphoner
Flemish c1300

This leaf from an Antiphoner, containing the choral parts of the service, has an elaborate initial D *(Dum) showing the Descent of the Holy Spirit; outside the initial kneels the Abbess, and her name,* Domina Abbatissa Soror Heylwigis *is written in an abbreviated and much less formal hand at the foot of the leaf. The main text, written below the lines of music, is in a very angular script with ascenders and descenders going very little above or below the line.*

V&AM MS 8997.1

Opposite:
Missal of St Denis Abbey, Paris
Paris c1350

Most Missals contain one or two illustrations only, but the St Denis Missal is remarkable in that it has many miniatures, mostly in grisaille, relating to the legendary founding of the Abbey and the life of St Denis. Here is an example of text, including a choral part of the service, showing how the compression and cramped appearance of the writing compares with the spaciousness of the margins and their decoration — the scribe and the decorator were, of course, different people, while the miniatures were probably painted by yet another artist.

V & A M MS L 1346-1891
f.242r 23.5 × 17

Collectarius for a Cistercian house;
German c1380

This manuscript is written in a very black ink, and the effect is further emphasised by the thickness of the pen strokes. The lateral compression and use of abbreviations make reading difficult, although the general appearance is not unpleasing. It is this type of Gothic or 'textura' script which has continued in use today as a supposedly typical medieval style of writing.

V & A M Reid MS 51 15 × 12

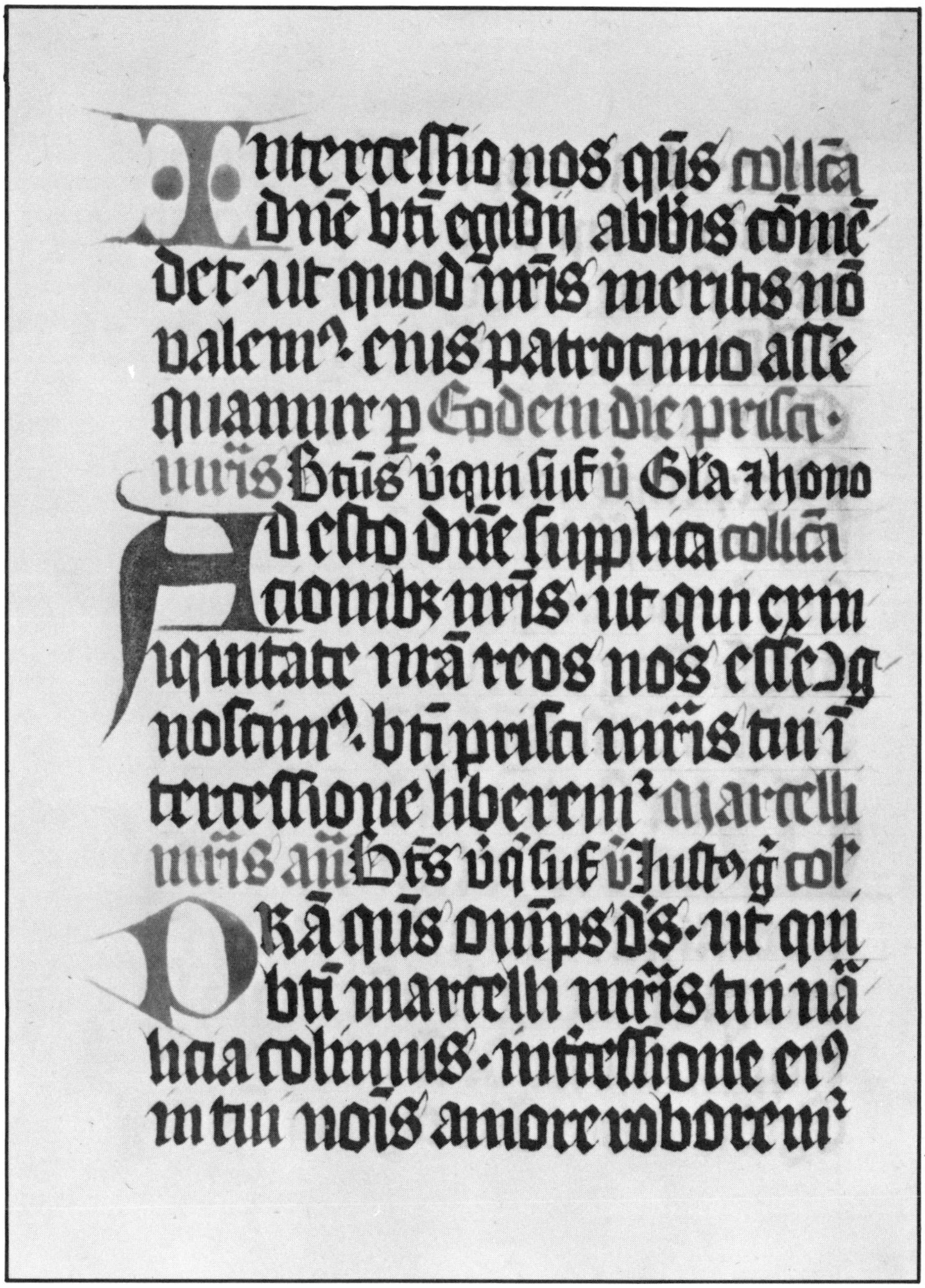

A.a.a.b.c.d.
e.f.g.h.i.k.
l.m.n.o.p.q.r.r.s.
s.t.v.u.x.y.z.&.9.

Pater noster qui es in celis sanctificetur no

Opposite:

Calendar, alphabet, prayer and hymns for private devotions
French   last quarter of the 14th century

*This interesting manuscript contains a clearly written out gothic alphabet. For some letters (*a, r *and* s *for example) more than one form is given. Not only can the letters be examined individually, but they can then be seen in context in the lower half of the page, in the passage beginning* Pater Noster. *The arms in the bowl of the initial* P *are those of Guillaume d'Orgemont.*

Reproduced by permission of the Bodleian Library, Oxford.   MS Rawl Liturg e 40 f.40

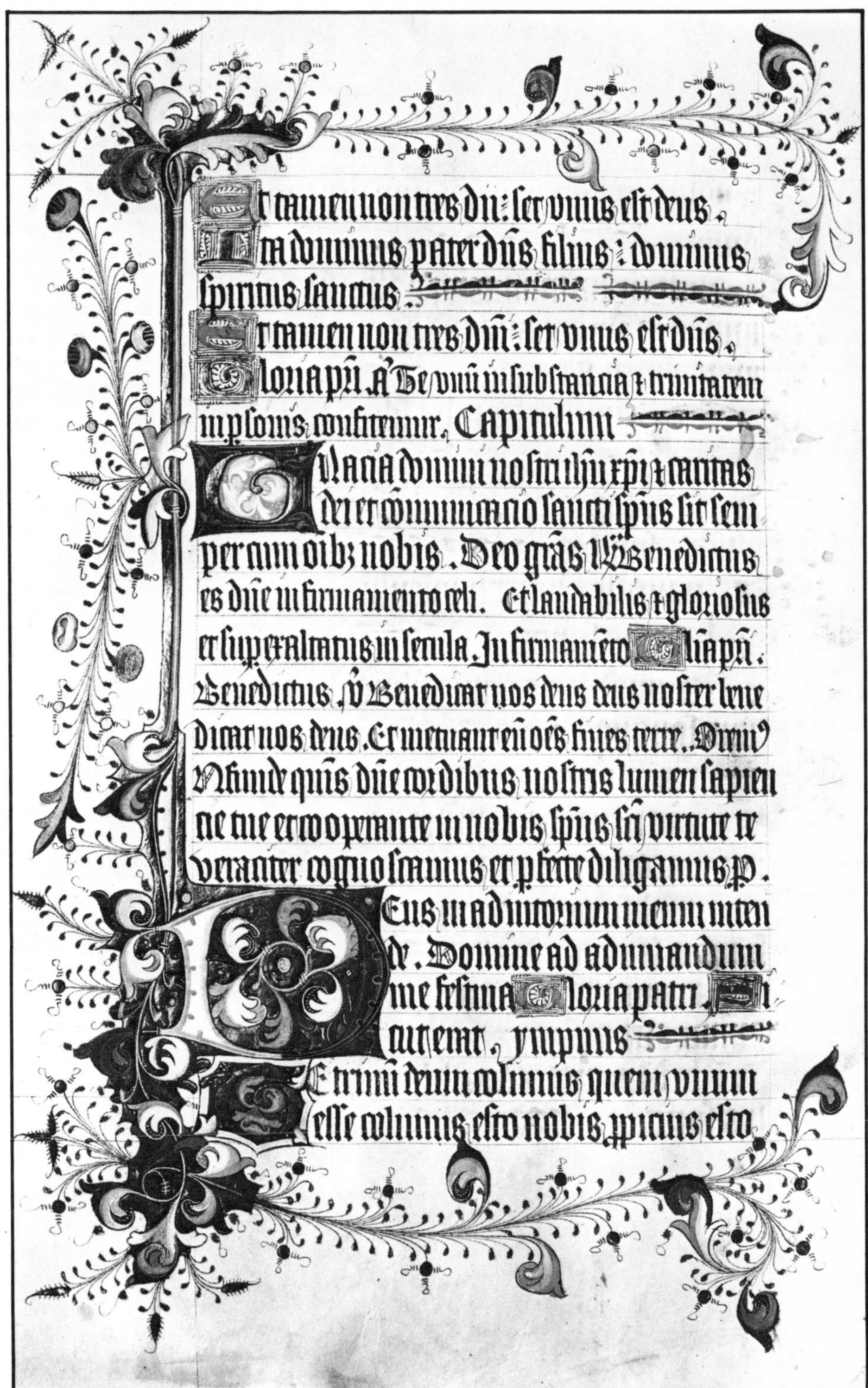

Psalter   English, possibly from the Diocese of Winchester   c1420

This manuscript is of special interest, for in the 19th century it belonged to the artist Owen Jones. He was among those who promoted the production of 'illuminated books' in England, once colour printing had become commercially viable. Undoubtedly it was manuscripts such as this one which influenced his own work, an example of which is illustrated in the present book (p. 316), namely the Victoria Psalter. *This printed Psalter which Owen Jones designed in 1861 took its name from the Queen, to whom it was dedicated.*

V&AM   Reid MS 41   38 × 27

Psalter English, possibly from the Diocese of Winchester c1420

This further page from the Owen Jones Psalter, showing the list of saints in the Litany, clearly displays the difficulty experienced by the modern reader when confronted by this style of writing. Most of the lines begin with the word 'Sancte', but the n *in some cases looks much more like a* u. *This style of gothic script is probably most familiar today from its use on the monumental brasses which have survived from the Middle Ages.*

V & A M   Reid MS 41   38 × 27

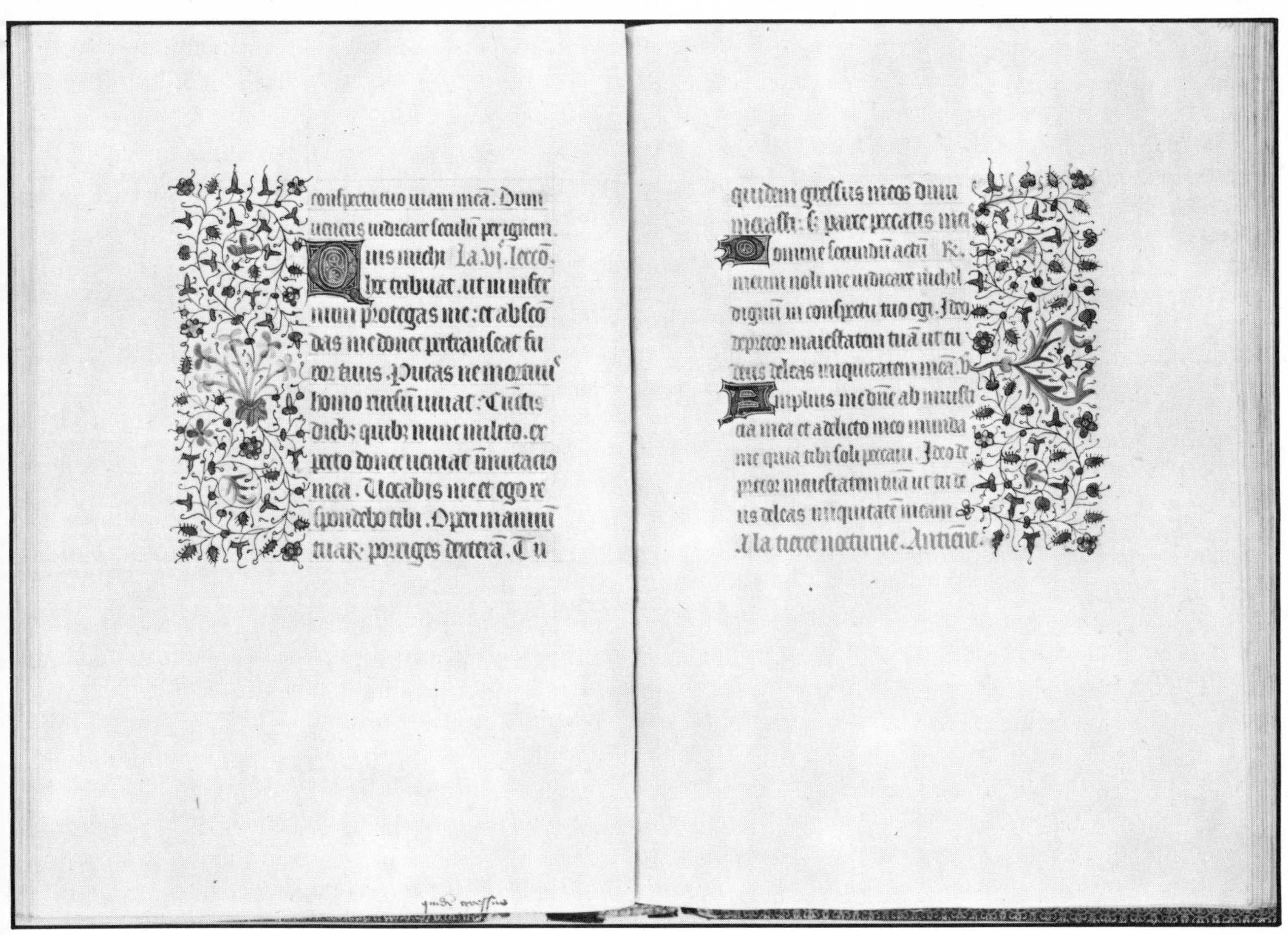

Book of Hours (Use of Paris)
French (Paris?) c1430-40

The main interest of this manuscript lies in its splendid illuminations, which have affinities with the Bedford Book of Hours. However, the written pages are also finely decorated and show a typical gothic hand. At the bottom of the left-hand page there are written, in an abbreviated cursive hand, the words quidem gressus; *the same words are repeated at the top of the right-hand page in the gothic script common to the rest of the manuscript. This was to ensure that the binder would place the gatherings of pages in the correct order, for it will be noted that the pages are not numbered and the binder probably could not read the Latin text.*

From the Caird Collection, on loan to the Victoria and Albert Museum

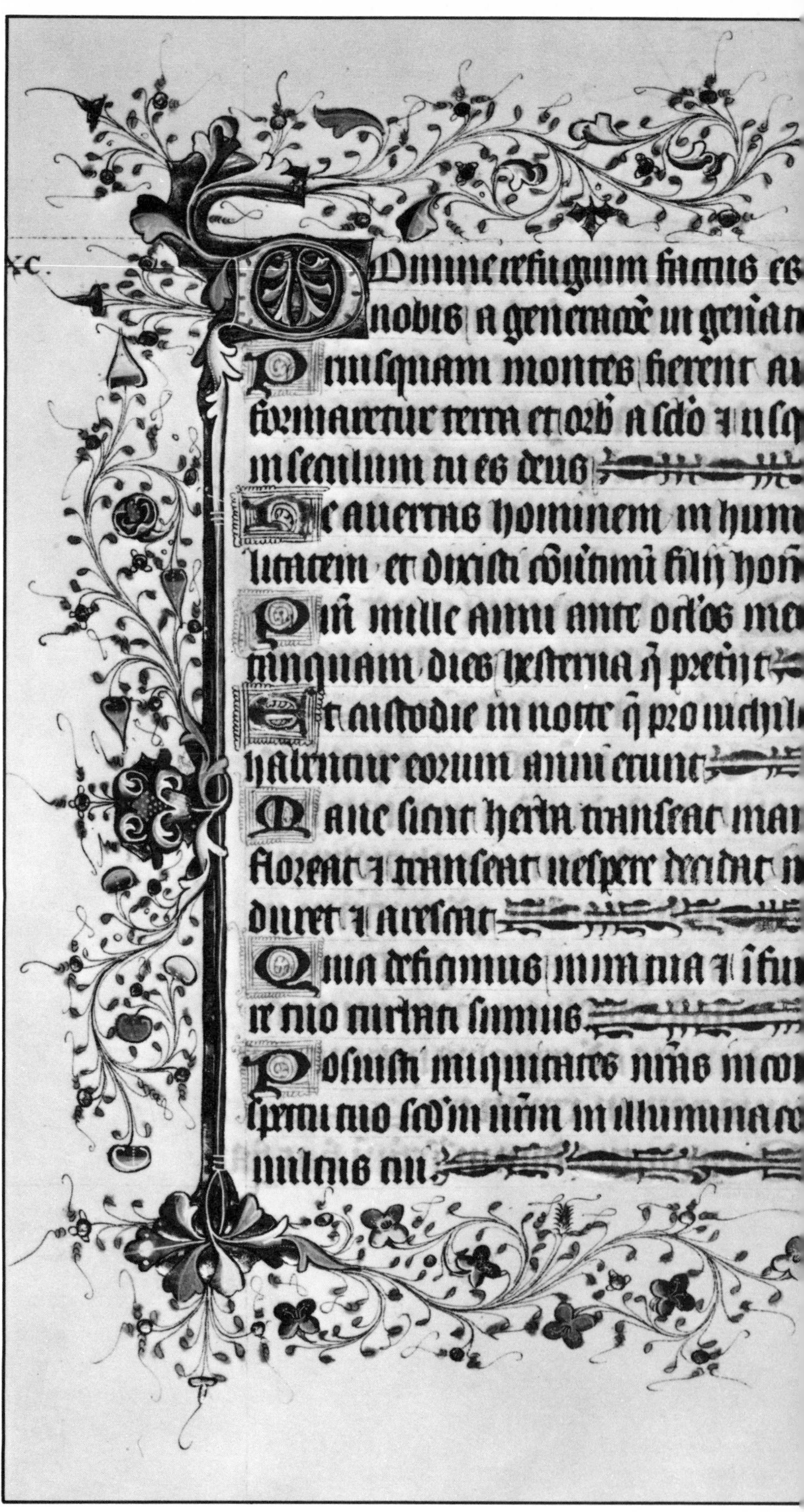

Psalter (with Sarum calendar), known as the Plantagenet Psalter
English c1435-45

Anyone trying to read the first line of text in this illustration (Domine refugium factus es) *will be immediately confronted with the problem of the textura script. All the letters appear at first sight to be composed of single strokes, although some of the bowed letters become apparent on closer inspection. The problem is emphasised by the tendency of the scribe to break the lower part of the bow in his* a *and* u, *thus accentuating the lateral compression of the text as a whole. The scribe has also added decorative hairline strokes to the end of some of his words.*

V & A M Reid MS 42 f.106v
28.5 × 19.5

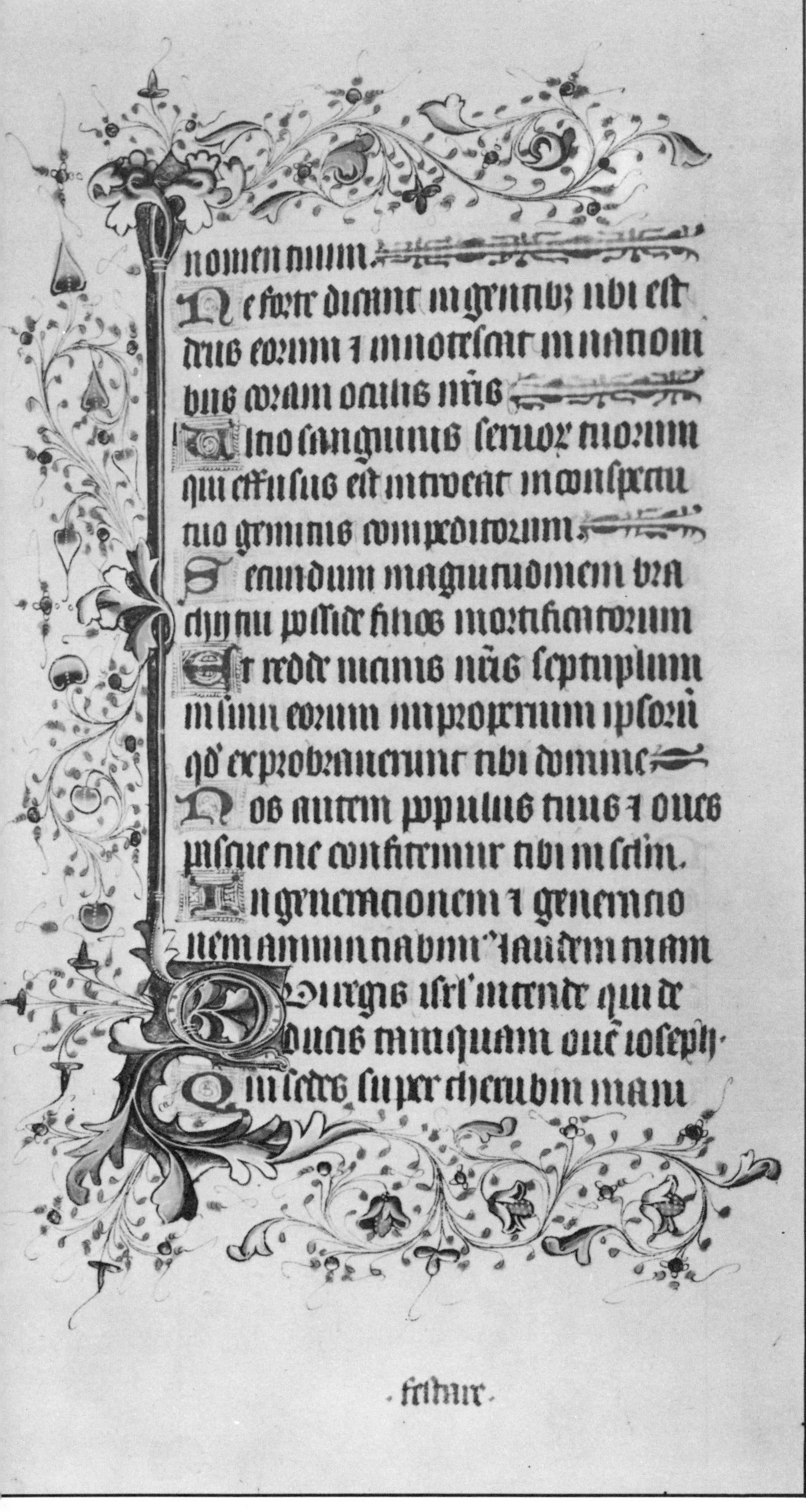

nomen tuum.
Ne forte dicant in gentibus ubi est
deus eorum & innotescat in nationi
bus coram oculis nostris
Ultio sanguinis servorum tuorum
qui effusus est introeat in conspectu
tuo gemitus compeditorum.
Secundum magnitudinem bra
chii tui posside filios mortificatorum
Et redde vicinis nostris septuplum
in sinu eorum improperium ipsorum
quod exprobraverunt tibi domine.
Nos autem populus tuus & oves
pascue tue confitebimur tibi in seculum.
In generationem & generatio
nem annuntiabimus laudem tuam
Qui regis israel intende qui de
ducis tamquam ovem ioseph.
Qui sedes super cherubim mani

·festare·

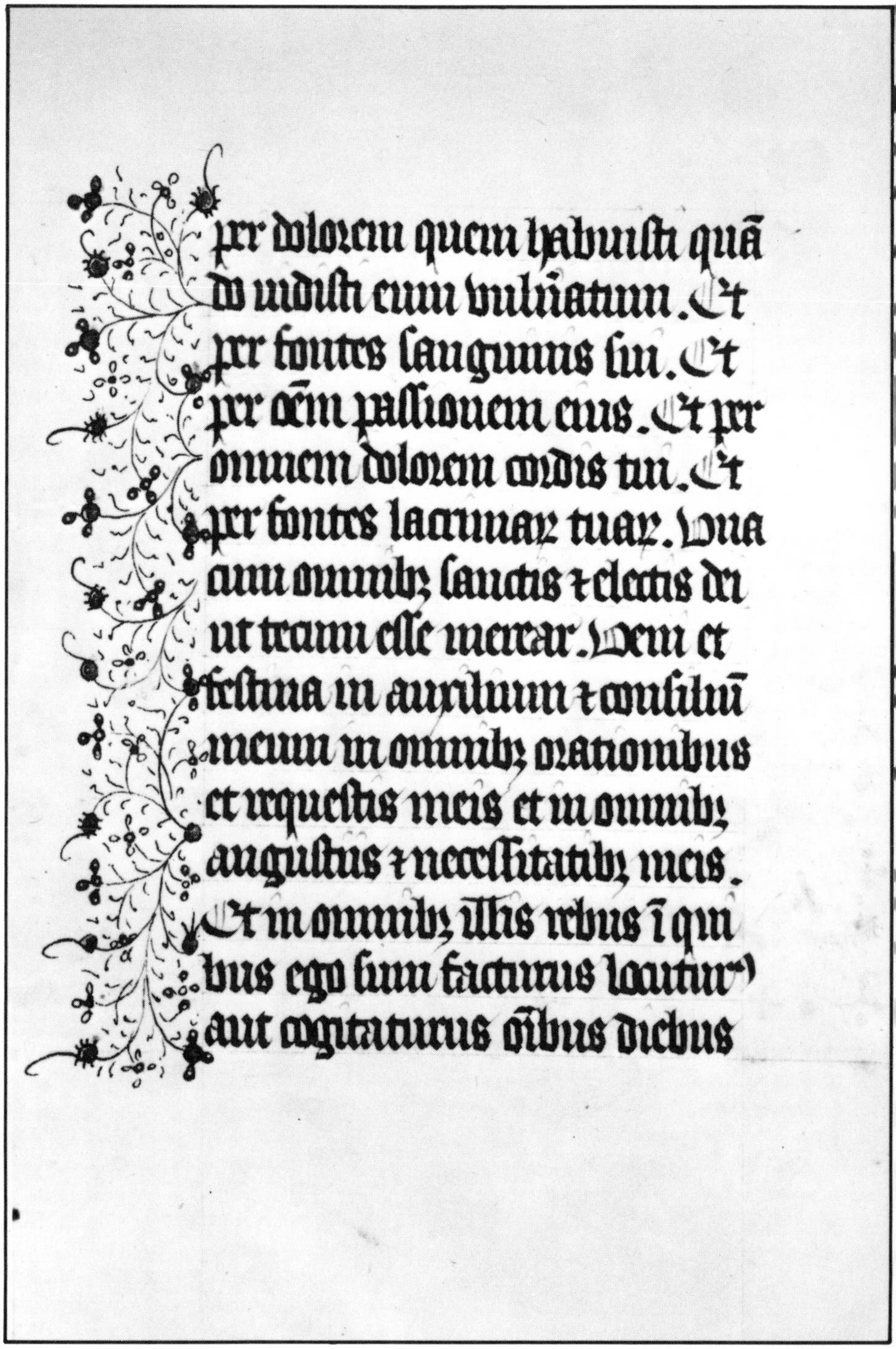
per dolorem quem habuisti quā
do vidisti eum vulneratum. Et
per fontes sanguinis sui. Et
per oēm passionem eius. Et per
omnem dolorem cordis tui. Et
per fontes lacrimaꝝ tuaꝝ. Una
cum omnibꝫ sanctis & electis dei
ut tecum esse merear. Veni et
festina in auxilium & consiliū
meum in omnibꝫ orationibus
et requestis meis et in omnibꝫ
angustiis & necessitatibꝫ meis.
Et in omnibꝫ illis rebus ī qui
bus ego sum facturus locuturꝰ
aut cogitaturus oībus diebus

Book of Hours (Use of Bayeux)
French c1450

The guide-lines (on or between which the scribe wrote) of this manuscript are drawn in red in the original, and so to some extent form part of the decoration of the page. It is noticeable how few of the letters go more than a fraction below this line, which helps to emphasise the fish-tail effect at the end of the stems of the p *and* q. *The scribe also tends to extend the hairline stroke at the beginning and end of some of his words, so that they are almost joined together. Nevertheless, the script offers a good clear example of textura script in the middle of the 15th century.*

V&AM Reid MS 8 f.71r
19 × 13.5

Book of Hours (Use of Bayeux)
French c1450

A further example from the same Book of Hours shows how the scribe has combined some of the catchwords with little decorative drawings. The catchwords were to ensure that the binder assembled the volume correctly.

V & A M Reid MS 8 f.21v
19 × 13.5

Glōa eterno p̄ri et agno mitissīo
qui frequēter ymolat᷑ p manet q3
integer vnus deus in natura cū
spūamē amen Panem celestē
accipiā et nomē dn̄i inuocabo
Laudans ī uocabo dn̄m et ab
inimicis meis saluus ero Cor
✠ pus dn̄i nr̄i iesu xp̄i prosit m̄i
in vitā eternā Perceptio corporis
tui dn̄e iesu xp̄e quā ego indig
nus peccātor hodie sumere p̄sumpsi
nō veniat michi in iudiciū et cō
dempnacōn̄ aīe mee sed psit m̄i
ad tutamentū corporis et aīe Ps
vi. Quid retribuā dn̄o p oībus
q̄ retribuit michi Calicē salu
taris accipiā et nomē dn̄i in

Opposite:

Missal (Use of Salzburg) Austria (Salzburg) c1450?

The script in this manuscript varies considerably throughout the work; some pages are written in a hybrid of textura and rotunda, but the section beginning at the Canon of the Mass is written in a large black gothic, as here. The letters are written with a thick pen and end with a heavy wedge-shaped serif in many cases, so that, together with the lateral compression and use of contractions, the text can be difficult to decipher. The date of the work is important, since it is the period when Gutenberg was experimenting with printing from movable types, and it was this style of script which was to be taken up by the early printers.

V & A M Reid MS 39 22.5 × 16.5

Book of Hours (Use of Châlons-sur-Marne) French c1470

This manuscript is unusually large for a Book of Hours, since these prayer books were for the layman's private devotions. The ink is very black and the text is set spaciously on the page. The letters are all written between the guide-lines, but the scribe has a tendency to elongate his hairline strokes and also to add them to some letters, so that they form a conspicuous part of the writing. The effect can be clearly seen in the words Amen *and* genitrix *at the bottom of the page.*

V & A M Reid MS. 12 23 × 16.5

qui pro nobis ex te natus reg
nat super ethera ut sua carita
te nostra deleantur peccamina
Tu autem domine miserere no
stri. Deo gratias. Responsorium
Beata es virgo maria que dominum
portasti creatorem mundi Genu
isti qui te fecit et in eternum perma
nes virgo. Vsus. Ave maria gratia
plena dominus tecum. Genuisti
qui te fecit et in eternum permanes
virgo. Iube domine benedicere
Sancta dei genitrix sit nobis au
xiliatrix Amen.
Sancta dei genitrix que

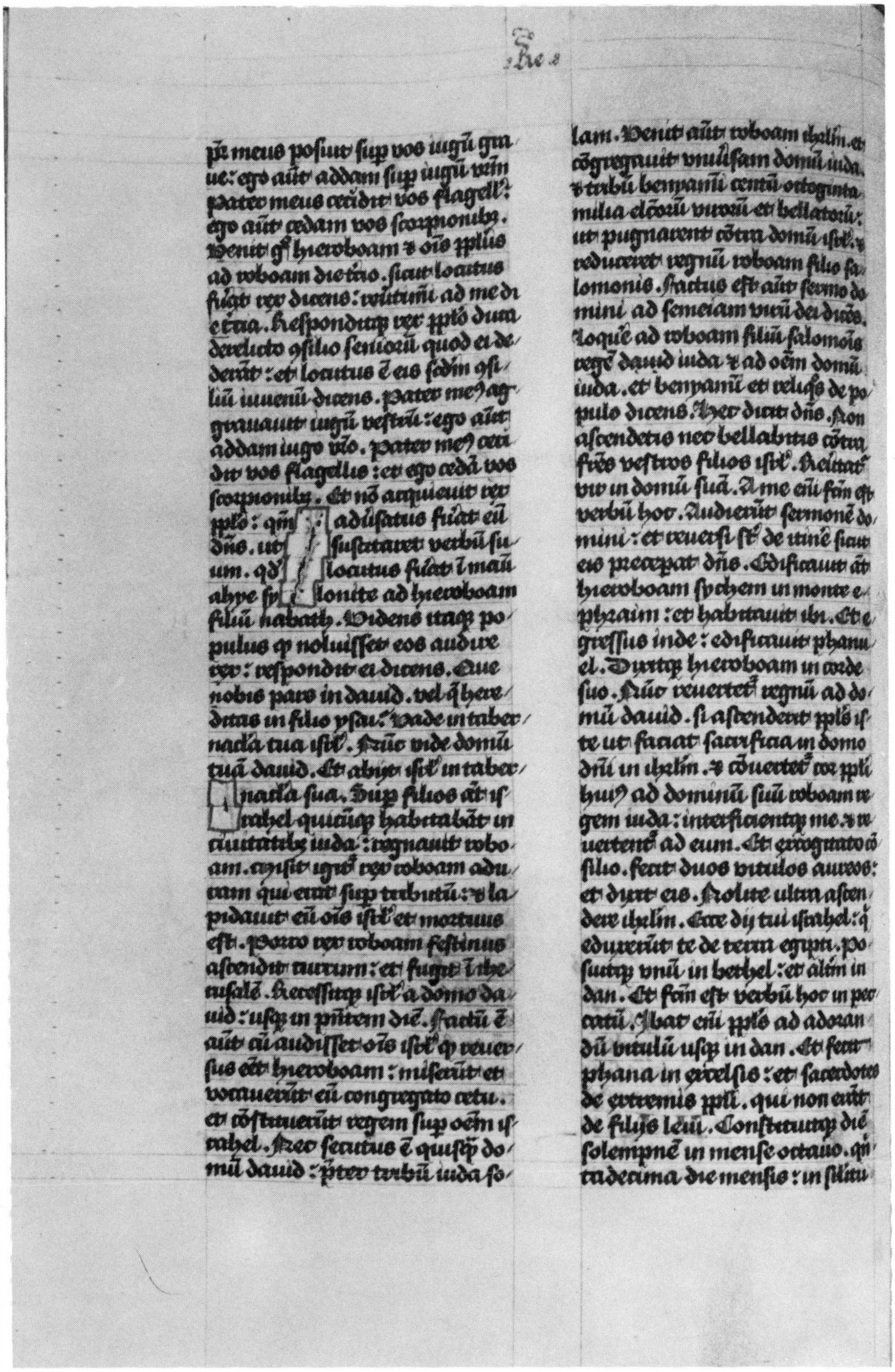

Opposite:

Diepenveen Bible
Netherlands c1450-53

This Bible was written out in a gothic script by an anonymous nun in a house of the Canonesses of the Congregation of Windesheim, near Deventer. She has dated her work as she progressed. This is the opening page of the manuscript, showing St Jerome at work; the script is neat and even, and, since the Bible was probably intended for use by the nun herself or her fellows, considerable use is made of contractions. The manuscript is quite large, and it will be noted that as frequently happens with Biblical texts, it is written in double columns.

V & A M Reid MS 23 f.1r
35 × 21.5

Diepenveen Bible
Netherlandish c1450-53

In this further page from the Diepenveen Bible *the preciousness of the writing material is clearly emphasised. There were faults in this sheet of vellum, but the scribe could not afford to waste it, so she has neatly written round the holes, and then incorporated them into the page by putting a line round them! The pricking for the guidelines is visible on the outer edge of this page.*

V & A M Reid MS 23 f.112v
35 × 21.5

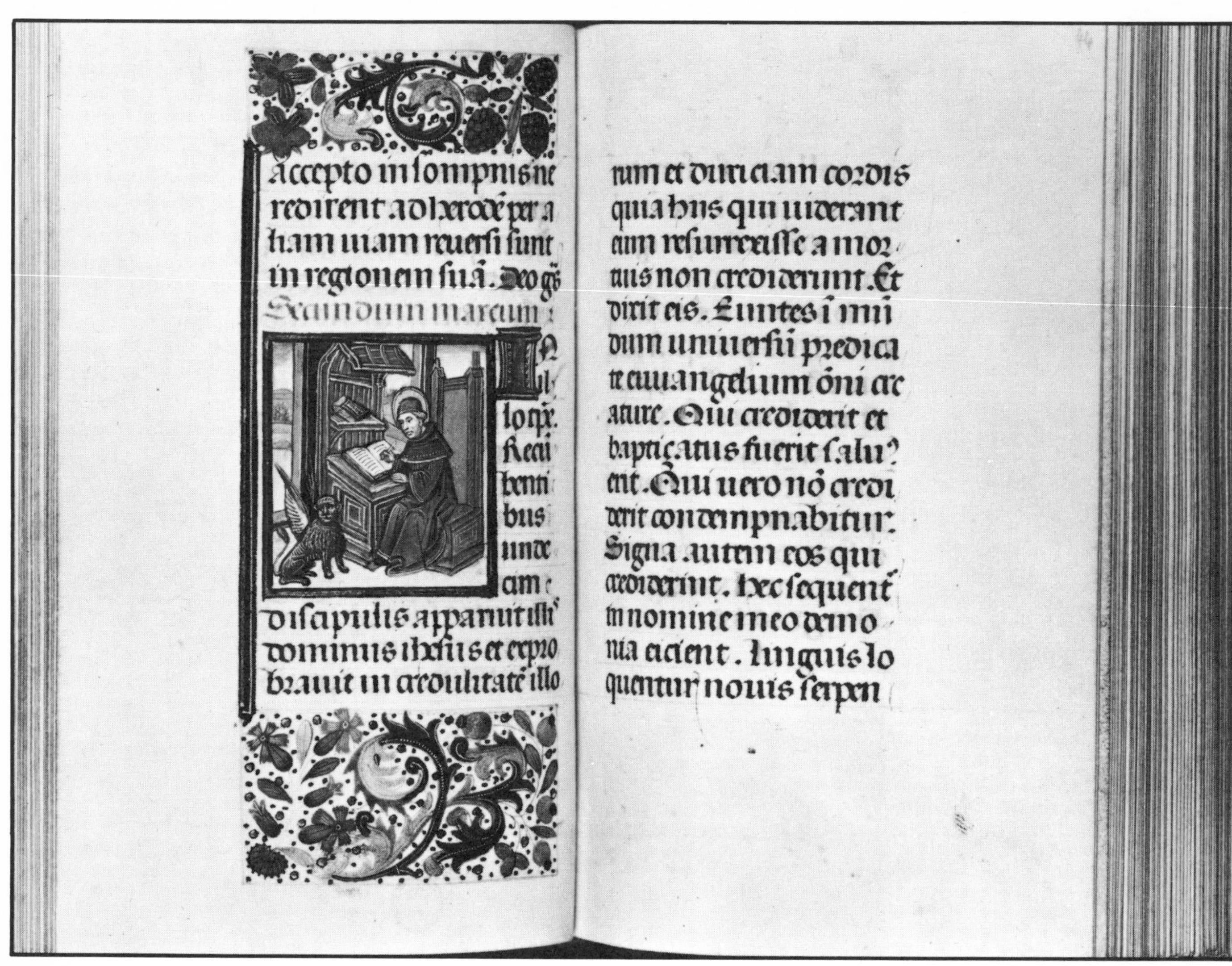

Book of Hours (Use of Rome), known as the Hours of Cardinal Hohenembs Netherlands (Bruges) c1475

This is an elegant little manuscript, fit for a prince of the church. It is written in a fine even rotunda script, in a very black ink which often suggests Spanish influence. It will be noted how rarely the letters go above or below the line of text. Manuscripts were very portable objects and as such were a common means of transmitting artistic styles from one country to another. The miniature shown here depicts St Mark at work on his Gospel, with his symbol, the lion, beside him.

V & A M *Salting MS 4478*
f.43v/44r *11 × 7.5*

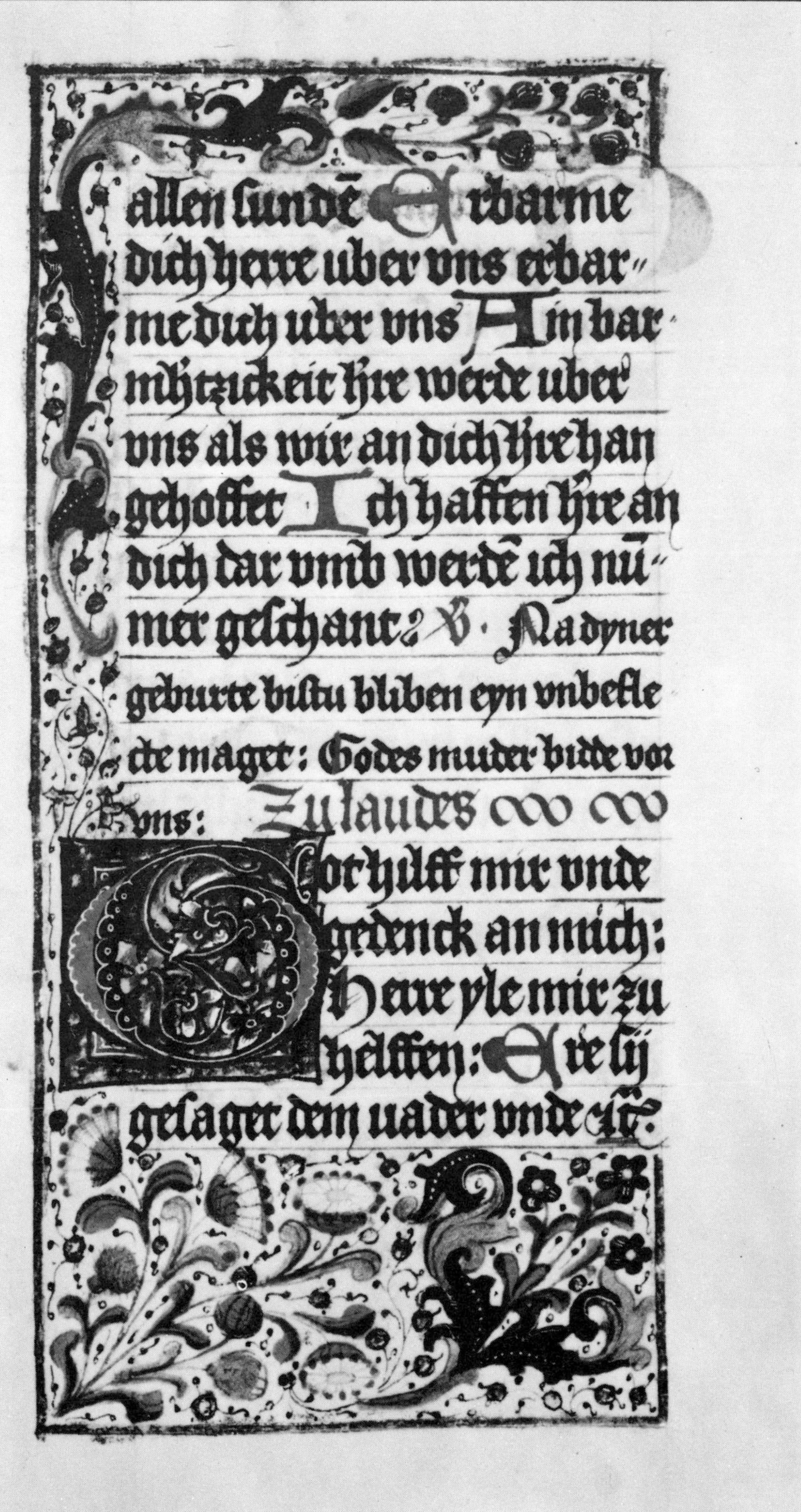

allen sundē Erbarme
dich herre uber vns erbarme dich uber vns Ain bar
mhtzickeit hre werde uber
vns als wir an dich hre han
gehoffet Ich haffen hre an
dich dar vmb werdē ich nū-
mer geschant. V. Na dyner
geburte bistu bliben eyn vnbefle
cte maget: Godes muder bidde vor
vns: Zu laudes
Gor hulff mir vnde
gedenck an mich:
herre yle mir zu
helffen: Ere sij
gesaget dem uader vnde

Book of Hours (for use in the Diocese of Trier)
German c1475-1500

Unlike most of the manuscripts illustrated in the early part of this book, this one is written not in Latin but in the vernacular — German in this instance. The textura script is in very black ink on a fine smooth vellum, and the guide-lines are clearly inked in. The writing is kept in the middle of these lines, so that only the letters h *and* y *go below them, while the ascenders such as* k, h, b *etc. are given a fish-tail decoration.*

V & A M MS L 1253-1949
f.29r 13.5 × 9

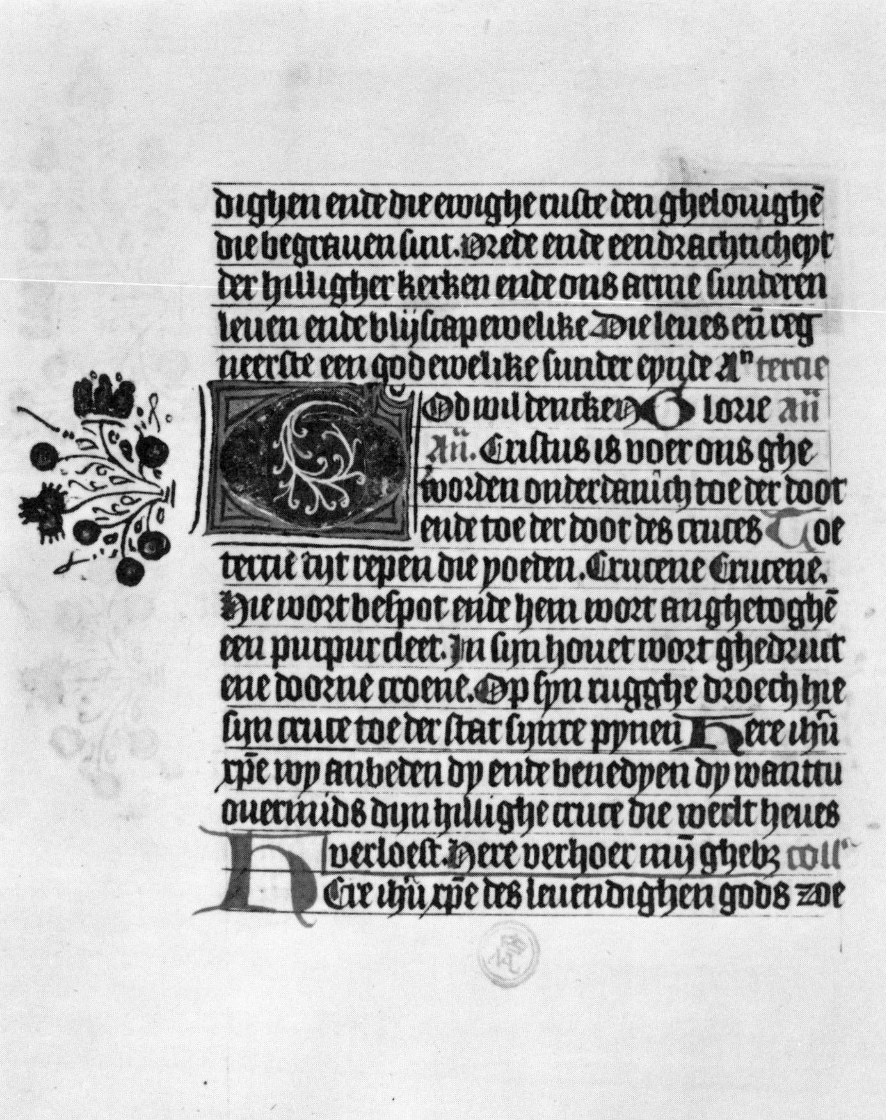
dighen ende die ewighe ruste den ghelouighē
die begrauen sijn. Vrede ende eendrachticheyt
der hilligher kerken ende ons arme sunderen
leuen ende blijscap ewelike. Die leuet eñ reg
neerste een god ewelike sunder eynde. An tercie
God wil dencken. Glorie aū
Añ. Cristus is voer ons ghe
worden onderdanich toe der doot
ende toe der doot des cruces. Toe
tercie tijt repen die ioeden. Crucene Crucene.
Hie wort bespot ende hem wort aengetoghē
een purpur cleet. In sijn houet wort ghedruct
ene doorne croene. Op sijn rugghe droech hie
sijn cruce toe der stat sijnre pynen. Here ihū
xpē wy anbeden dy ende benedyen dy want tu
ouermids dyn hillighe cruce die werlt heues
verloest. Here verhoer my gheb3 coll'
Here ihū xpē des leuendighen gods zoe

Office of the Dead, and other fragments and prayers.
Netherlandish (Utrecht?) c1490

The appearance of this manuscript, written in textura script in Dutch, is pleasing, with its text set firmly amid spacious borders. But closer inspection shows that the amount of lateral compression makes reading surprisingly difficult. The words are all written between the lines, so that the ascenders and descenders have little prominence.

V & A M *Reid MS 33* *14.5 × 10*

Opposite:
Office of the Dead, and other fragments and prayers.
Netherlandish (Utrecht?) c1490

Another example (enlarged) from this manuscript showing the textura script in Dutch, together with the more elaborate decorations and initials which appear on some pages.

V & A M *Reid MS 33* *f.35*
14.5 × 10

God wil dencken Glorie Ant.
Cristus is voer ons gheworden o-
derdanich toe der doot ende toe der
doot des cruces. Toe prime tijt
wort ihesus gheleyt toe pylatum ende mit valschen
tughen wort zeer ouer hem gheclaghet. Syn
hals wort gheslaghen syn handen ghebonden
syn aensicht bespoghen alsoe als die prophete
toe voren hadden ghesproken. Here ihesu
xpe wy aenbeden dy ende benedyen dy want
du ouermids dynen hilighen cruce die werlt
heuelste verloest. Here verhoer my. Collecte
Here ihesu xpe des leuendighen godes
zone sette dyne pyne dyn cruce en
dyn doot tusschen dyn gherichte en
myne zele nu op dese tijt ende in der tijt dat myn
zele van den lichame scheyden sal ende ghif le-
ue here ghenade ende barmherticheit den leuen

Videbunt iusti et timebunt et sup eum ri-
debunt et dicent: ecce homo qui non posuit deum adiutorem suum. sctm sct
Sed speravit in multitudine divitiarum
suarum: et prevaluit in vanitate sua.
Ego autem sicut oliva fructifera in domo
dei: speravi in misericordia dei in eternum et in
Confitebor tibi in seculum quia fecisti: et expec-
tabo nomen tuum quoniam bonum in
conspectu sanctorum tuorum. Deus
Dixit insipiens in
corde suo: non est
Corrupti sunt et
abominabiles
facti sunt in iniquitatibus
non est qui faciat bonum
Deus de celo prospexit sup filios hominum:
ut videat si est intelligens aut requirens deum.

Psalter (Cistercian), known as the Kinloss or Boswell Psalter
Scottish c1500

This Scottish manuscript was probably written for the Cistercian Abbey of Kinloss, Morayshire. It is in a bold textura script, and is an especially fine example of Scottish writing and illumination. An enlarged detail of the decorated initial D and its surrounding text is also shown here (opposite), so that the form of the letters can be studied more closely.

V & A M Reid MS 52 f.48v
38 × 30

tabo nomen tuum quon
conspectu sanctorum tuo

Deus de celo pspexit sup fil
ut videat si est intelligēs

Nota in aduentu dn̄i ad matutinas et ad vs. dicat col
lecta sequens loco. Concede nos famulos. etc. Coll.
Deus qui de beate marie virginis vtero
verbū tuū angelo annūciante carnē
suscipere voluisti. presta supplicibz tuis. ut q
vere eam dei genitricē credimus. eius apud te
intercessionibz adiuuemur. P eundē dnm.
Nota A natiuitate dn̄i vsqz ad festū purificacionis
ad matutinas et ad vs dicat collcā sequēs loco. Con
Deus qui salutis eterne btē Coll. cede.
marie virginitate fecunda. humano
generi premia prestitisti. tribue quesum9. ut
ipsam pro nobis intercedere sentiam9. p quā
meruim9 auctorem vite suscipere. Ad compl.
Aue maria grā plē. dn̄s tecū bn̄dcā tu i mulier.
Conuerte nos deus salutaris nr̄.
Et auerte iram tuā a nobis.
Deus in adiutoriū meū in
tende. Dn̄e ad adiuuandū me
festina. Glā pri et filio et s.s. Sicut erāt. Ps.

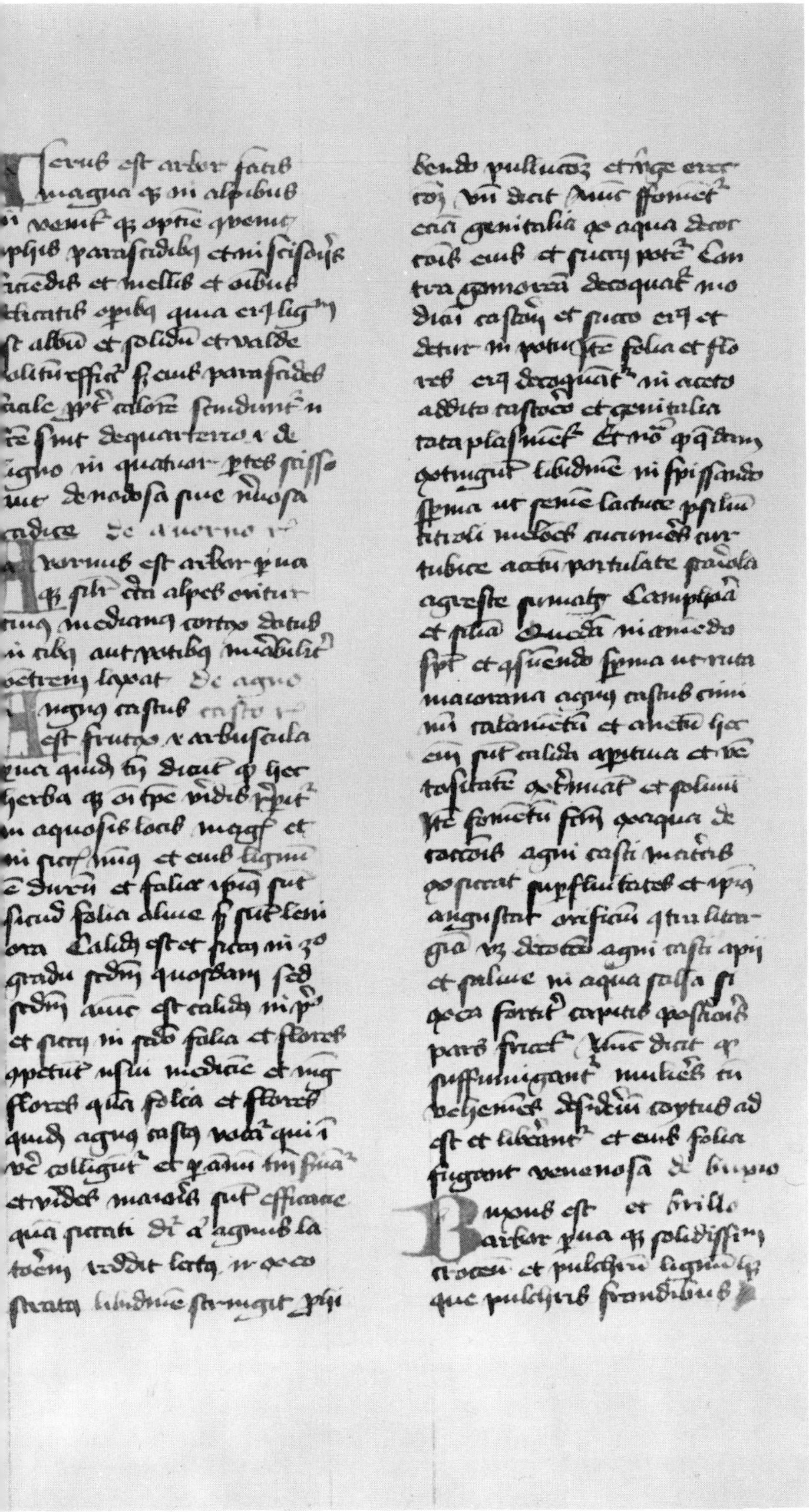

Opposite:

Books of Hours (Use of Utrecht) Netherlandish (or possibly Westphalian) 1510.

This is another quite large manuscript for a work of private devotions, and the text is written in a correspondingly large script. The guide-lines are very evident and form part of the pattern of the page. This type of textura script was reproduced in early printed books, and so the manuscript comes at the end of the long tradition of hand-written prayer books, which the invention of printing in the middle of the 15th century had already made redundant.

V & A M Reid MS 37 25 × 18

P. de Crescentiis: Ruralium commodorum, libri XII German c1460

This manuscript is written out in bastarda script, with only a few decorations in the form of coloured initials — those on this page are written in red. The emphasis on the cursive nature of bastarda and the use of contractions all suggest that this volume was written out for strictly practical use — perhaps for the copyist himself. In the Victoria and Albert Museum Library there is a printed version of the same text, dated 1471. A comparison of the two emphasises the labour involved in the copying of such texts, compared with the comparative ease with which multiple copies could be produced for scholars after the invention of printing from movable types.

V & A M MS L 98-1945 28 × 20

Opposite:

Egidio Colonna, Romano, Archbishop of Bourges: Libro . . . que trata del regimiento de los principes Spanish c1470-80 (with later additions).

This interesting manuscript is unlike any others illustrated here. The script would seem to fall between gothic and bastarda, partaking of both styles. The main text, in the centre of the page, is written out in a formal hand. The commentary, by Alphonso Tostado de Madrigal, which surrounds it, is in a more cursive style, and contains more contractions. With the simple penwork initials, the pages form attractive patterns. It is a very large folio.

V & A M MS L 2463-1950 41 × 21

Book of House (Use of Rome) Flemish (Hainault) c1480

This manuscript is written in bastarda script, a mixture of the cursive informal hand and the gothic. The angularity of the individual letters is maintained, but the cursive tendency is also obvious. The descenders, especially the long s, *taper away and reveal a slight slant. The effect is pleasing to the eye and shows how an informal script could be elevated to a book hand with considerable grace.*

V & A M Reid MS 31 16.5 × 11

Breviary (incomplete) of Utrecht
Netherlandish (Delft?) c1490

This manuscript is written in a clear bold bastarda script in Dutch. There are few decorations in the work apart from the historiated initials — this one shows Mary Magdalene, who is wearing contemporary dress. By writing in double columns the scribe has managed to get a lot of text on the page and yet retain legibility.

V & A M Reid MS 36 f.211r
20 × 13

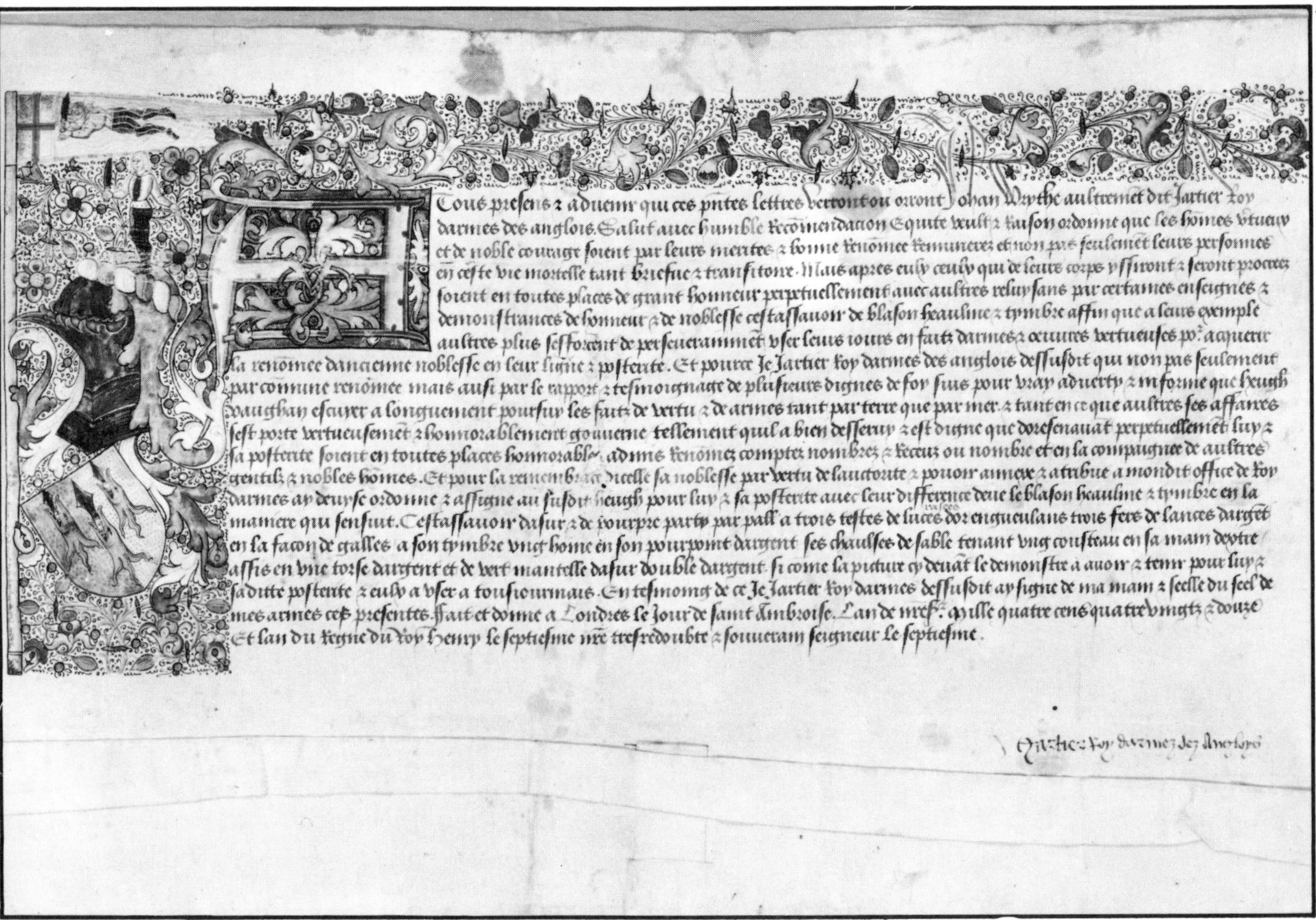

Above:

Grant of arms by John Wrythe, Garter King of Arms, to Hugh Vaughan, 1492

Not many legal documents are illustrated in this book, but this is interesting for the fine bastarda script in which it is written, and it should also be noted that it is written in French, even at so late a date. The characteristics of the bastarda script are clearly shown here, with the tapering descenders and the long s being especially distinctive.

V & A M   MS L 4362-1948

Die hemelen vertellen die glorie gods: ende dat firmamẽt
openbaert die wercken sijnre han
den Die dach wtcondicht den
dach dat woort: eñ die nacht wiset
den nachte wetentheyt. Alsoe
moet sijn die sprake eñ redene: die
men haer stemme niet en hoort.
Der hemelen gheluyt is wt ghe
gaen in alle aertrijcke: ende haer
woorden inden eynde van aertrij
ke. Sijn tabernakel sette hi in die
sonne: ende hi is voortghegaẽ als
een brudegom wt sinder slaepca
mer. Hy verhuechde hem seer te
loopen den wech als een reuse: sijn
wtganc was vanden opperstẽ des

Book of Hours (Use of Utrecht), and collection of prayers.
North Netherlandish? c1500

A very clearly written example of bastarda script, showing both its gothic and cursive affinities, but chiefly the former. The words are well separated and the letters show no extremes or idiosyncracies.

V & A M   Reid MS 35   12.5 × 9

Account of the trials, condemnation (1431) and rehabilitation (1450) of Joan of Arc · c1530-40

This fine manuscript was written for Diane de Poitiers, mistress of Henri II of France and a keen bibliophile. It is of course written long after the events it records, and in this illustration the court of Henry VI of England is portrayed. By the time this manuscript was written out, printing was in common use for most books, but there was still a certain cachet *about the specially produced hand-written book, especially among court circles. The bastarda script, here used for a secular book, still carries gothic overtones in the formation of some of the letters, although people like Diane de Poitiers must have been very familiar, with the humanistic scripts.*

From the Caird collection, on loan to the V&AM

Domine
sancte
pater omni
potens eter
ne deus: qui
coequalem
et consub
stancialem et
coeternum
tibi ante omnia secula filium
ineffabiliter genuisti: cum quo
atque cum sancto spiritu existente
eodemque filio procedente. celum
terram atque omnia quecunque
existunt visibilia et invisibi
lia mirabiliter creasti. Tibi gra
cias ago. te adoro. te laudo. te be
nedico. te magnifico. Esto queso
propicius mihi miserrimo peccatori

Book of Hours (Use of Sarum) known as the Playfair Hours French (Rouen?) late 15th century.

This is a fine example of the bastarda script elevated to a book hand. Though the letters are closely joined the text remains quite legible; the forms of the letters perhaps show more of a gothic than a cursive tendency but the typical long s *of the bastarda script is prominent.*

V&AM MS L 475-1918
f.149r 22.5 × 12

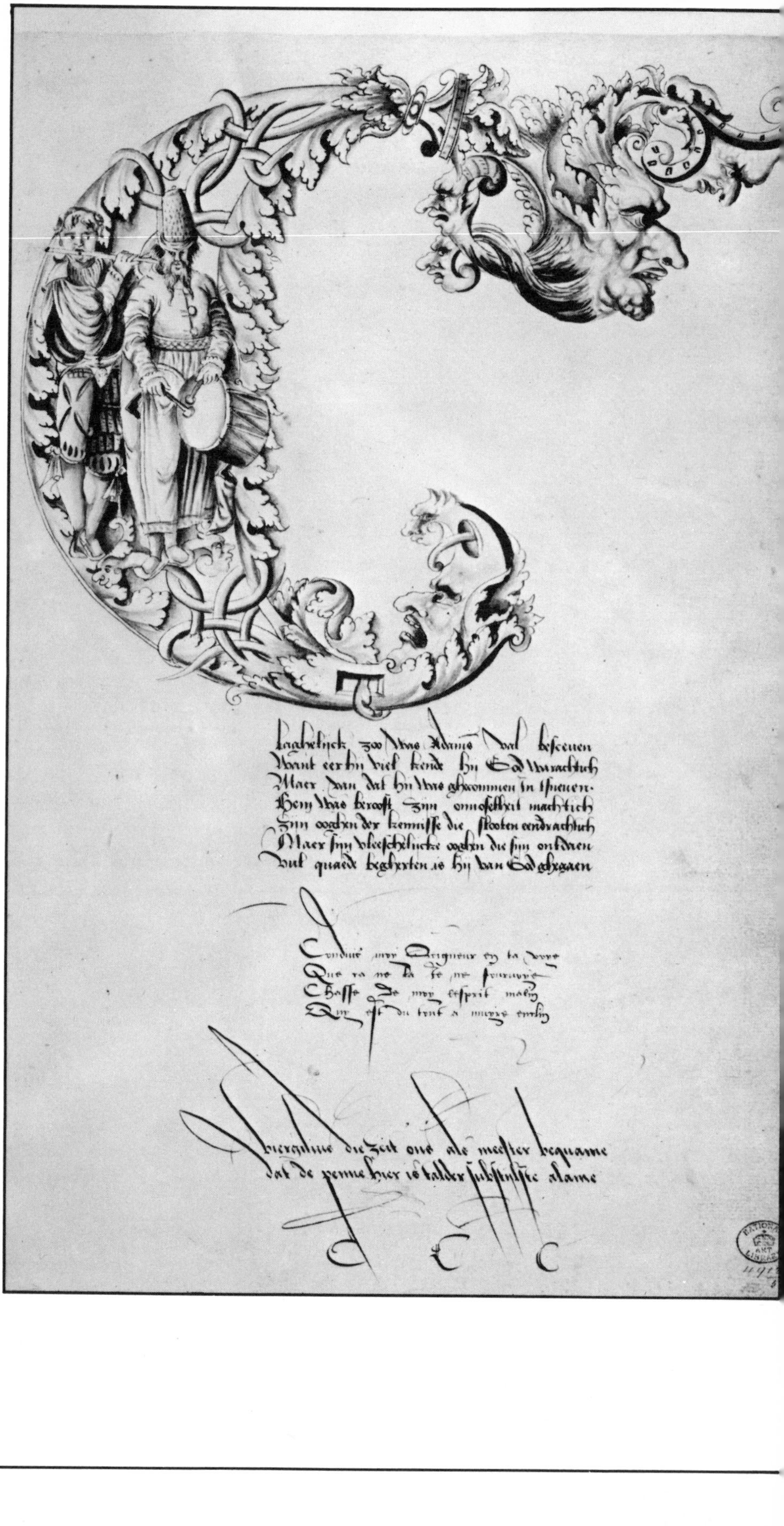

Grotesque alphabet c1520

This and the succeding illustrations are taken from a grotesque alphabet now in the Victoria and Albert Museum. The date of the work is uncertain, but the artist has signed himself 'Marcus van Ypres' — though it is not known whether he was the originator of this alphabet or whether he copied it from an earlier example. Such grotesque alphabets were a feature of the late Middle Ages, and other examples (both of 16th century date) can be seen in pp. 90-93. In addition to the finely drawn initial letter, each of the plates in this manuscript has examples of calligraphy, usually in both Flemish and French, as in the four examples illustrated here.

V&AM MS 4912/5 41 × 27

Grotesque alphabet c1520

Plate 16 from the Grotesque alphabet of c1520

V & A M MS 4912/16

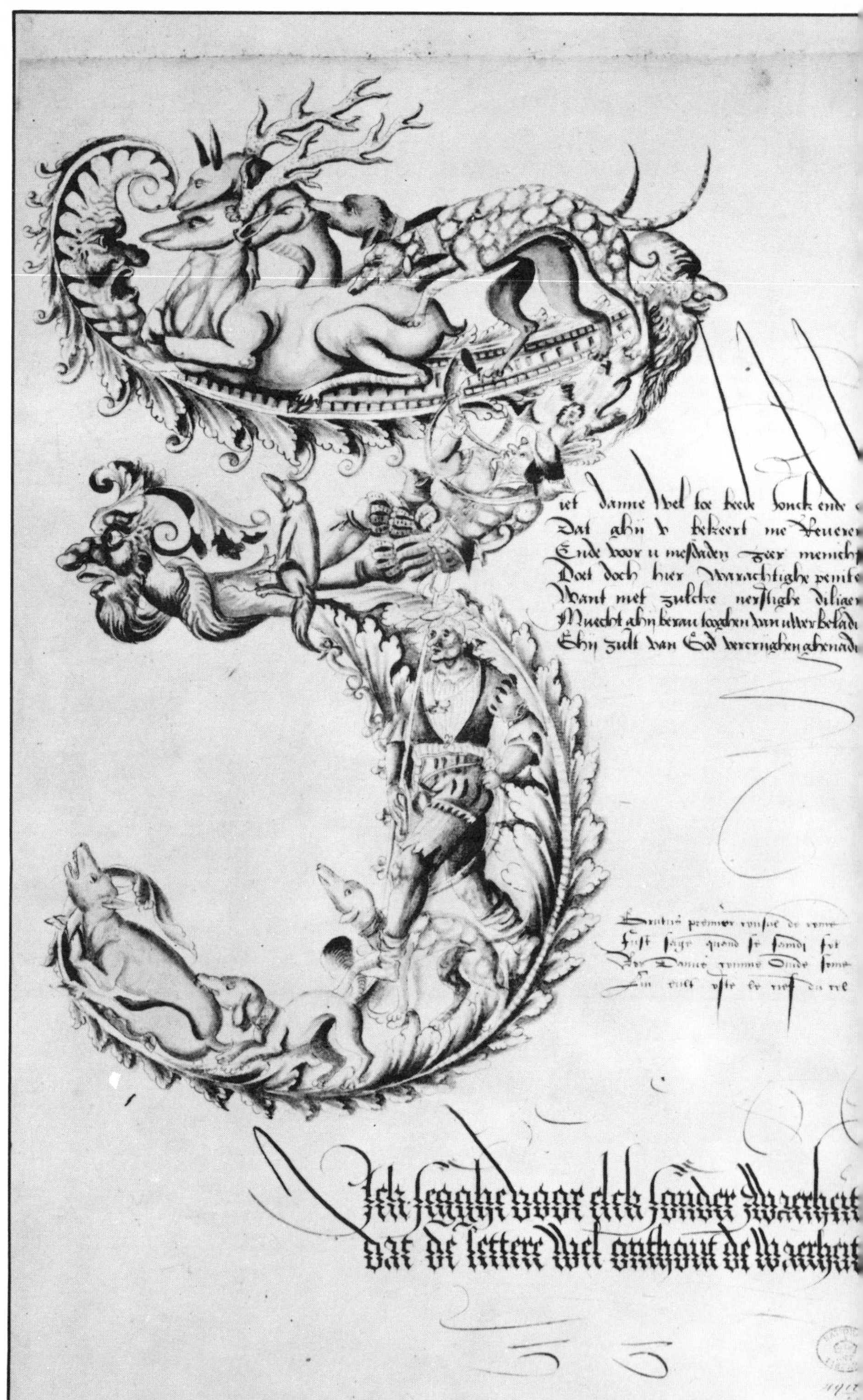

Grotesque alphabet c1520

Plate 25 from the Grotesque alphabet of c1520

V&AM MS 4912/25

Grotesque alphabet c1520

Plate 21 from the Grotesque alphabet of c1520

V&AM MS 4912/21

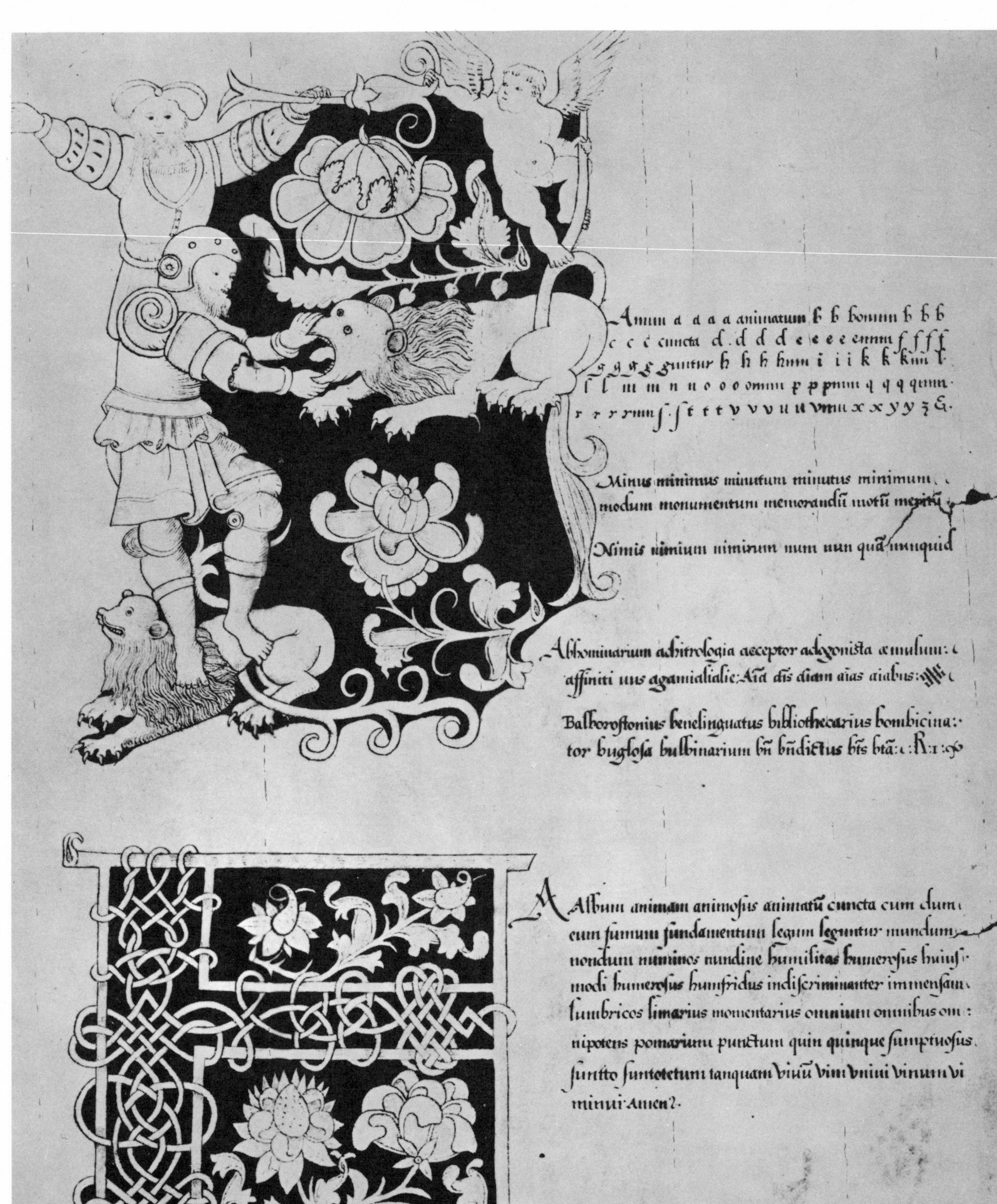

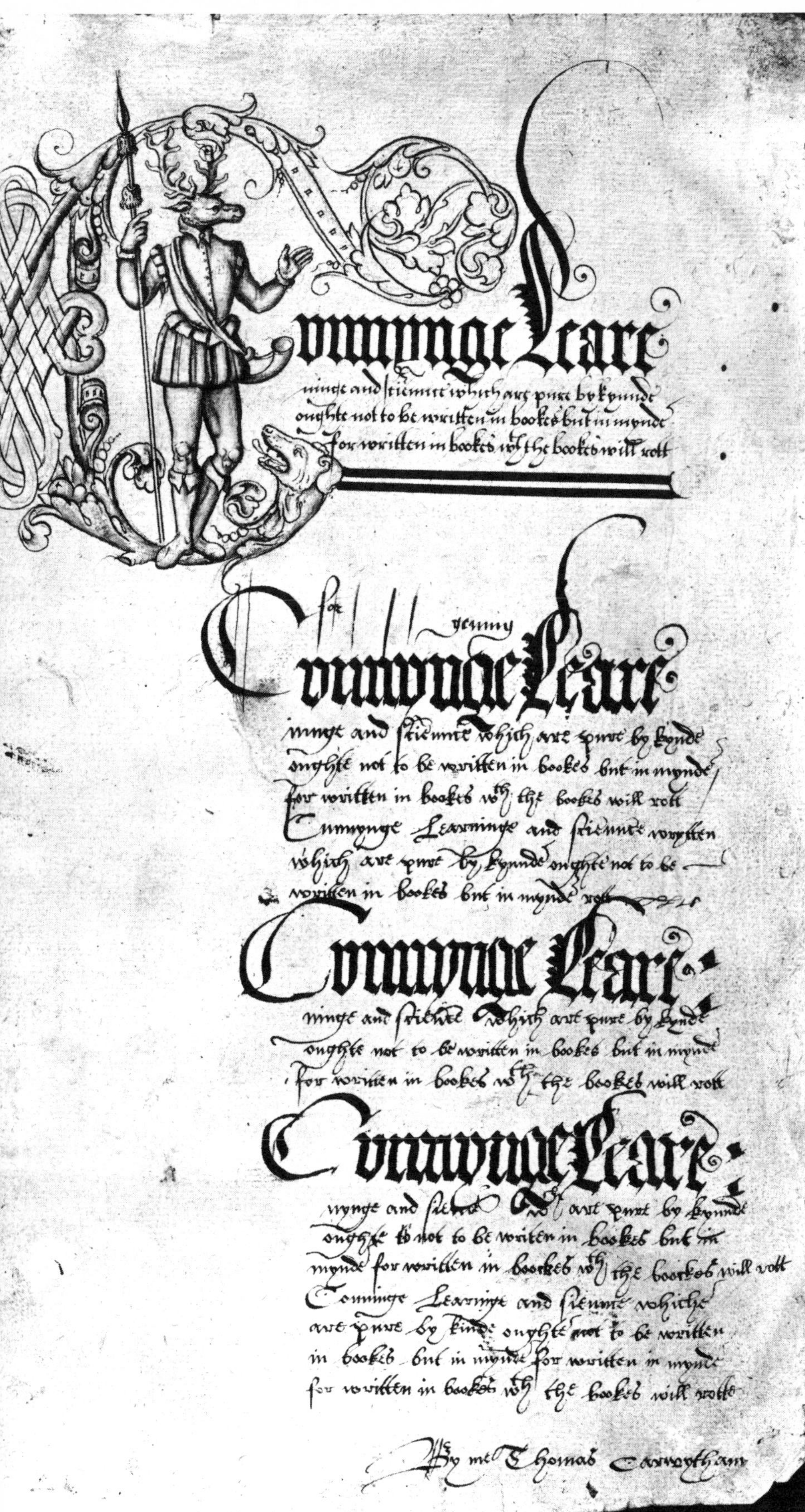

Cunnynge Leare
ninge and sciennce which are pure by kynde
oughte not to be written in bookes but in mynde
for written in bookes wth the bookes will rott

Cunnynge Leare
ninge and sciennce which are pure by kynde
oughte not to be written in bookes but in mynde
for written in bookes wth the bookes will rott
Cunnynge Learninge and sciennce written
which are pure by kynde oughte not to be
written in bookes but in mynde rott

Cunnynge Leare
ninge and sciennce which are pure by kynde
oughte not to be written in bookes but in mynde
for writen in bookes wth the bookes will rott

Cunnynge Leare
nynge and sience wch are pure by kynde
oughte not to be writen in bookes but in
mynde for written in bookes wth the bookes will rott
Cunninge Learninge and sciennce whiche
are pure by kinde oughte not to be written
in bookes but in mynde for written in mynde
for written in bookes wth the bookes will rott

By me Thomas Carwytham

A writing master's copy sheet. c1600

The writing master has written out the first copy at the top of the page and the pupil has followed, not very expertly, becoming progressively worse as he got to his third copy! He has wisely not attempted the very elegant grotesque initial C at the beginning of the text (which is written in a neat secretary hand) but he was still proud enough to sign his name at the bottom of the sheet 'By me Thomas Carwytham'.

V&AM MS L 1482-1945 31 × 11.5

Opposite:

A book of alphabets, with examples of calligraphy. c1540-c1567

Little is known about this manuscript, which may have been a scribe's sample book, or perhaps a record of scripts and alphabets which especially interested him. The two major grotesque alphabets are taken from the Master of the Banderolles (second half of the 15th century) and Noël Garnier (1470/75-c1544), so both were quite old-fashioned when the English scribe copied them. He has added a variety of examples of current scripts; those shown here display the italic hand.

V&AM MS L 2090-1937 29.5 × 21

A book of alphabets, with examples of calligraphy c1540-c1567

Two further examples from this English manuscript, showing additional scripts as well as two more of the elaborate initials taken from the engraved set by Noël Garnier

V & A M MS L 2090-1937 29.5 × 21

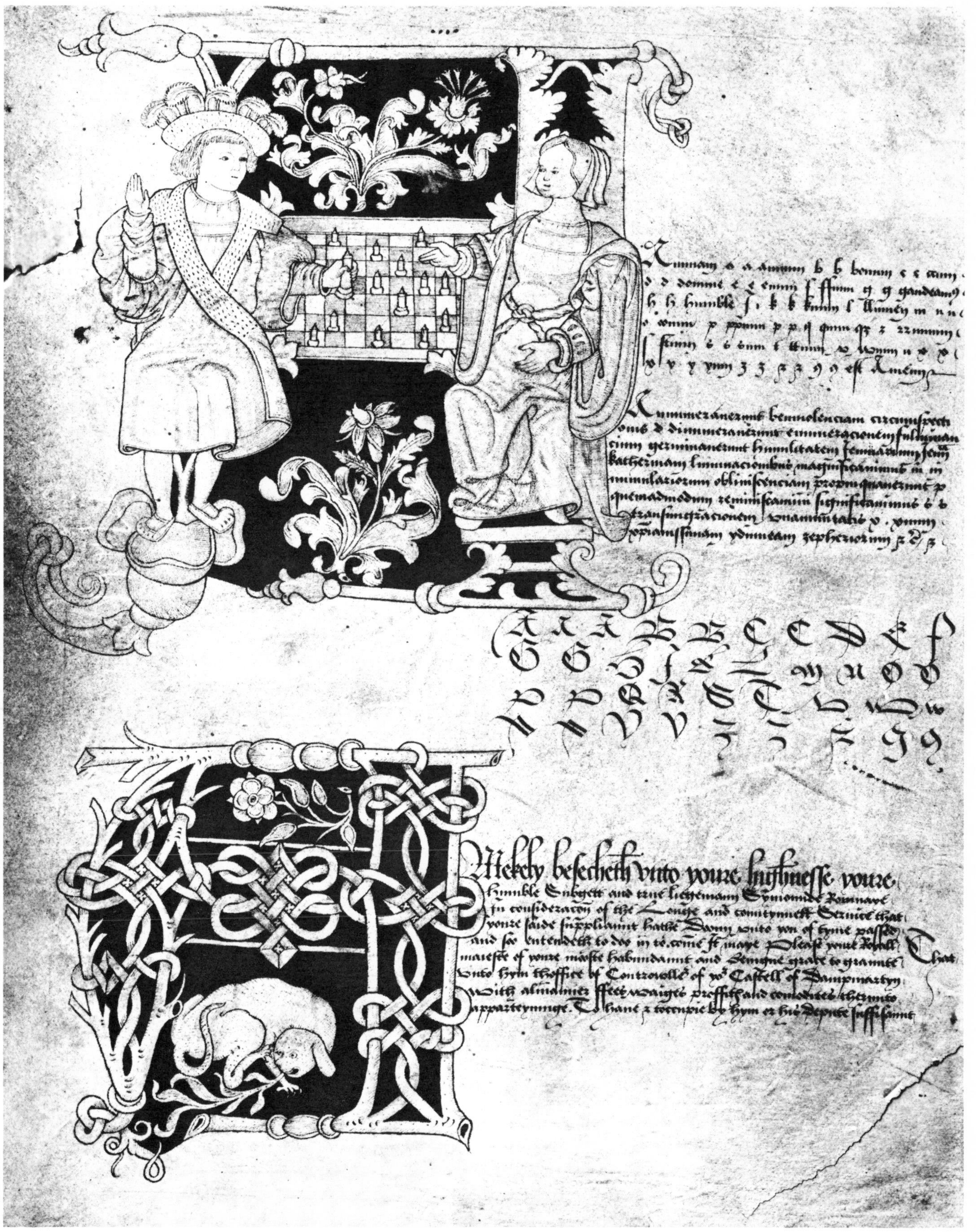

5 Italian and post-medieval scripts

JUST AS medieval forms of writing originated in Italy and spread, via the Roman Empire, to the rest of western Europe, so the new script that was to conquer the west also arose in Italy. In post-Imperial and medieval Italy both formal and informal hands were widespread. With the break-up of the Empire, communications became as difficult in the peninsular as they were elsewhere in Europe. In the south of Italy the Beneventan script remained the dominant hand for some centuries, but in the north of Italy handwriting was much more vulnerable to foreign influences. Here invasions both military and economic had a profoundly modifying effect on the scripts in common use. Although somewhat isolated by physical conditions, Italy was not uninfluenced by the gothic style of the north. Rome remained one of the most important of Christian shrines and the pilgrimage route south was only one of the ways in which ideas and styles were interchanged. Buildings and paintings alike, from Milan cathedral to the art of Siena, testify to the gothic influence in Italy. But it was by no means so prevalent as in the north nor was it carried to the same extremes. At the back of much Italian medieval art was the conscious memory of Roman art, traces of which lay all around, often profoundly influencing artists, as can be seen for example in the work of a sculptor like Giovanni Pisano in the 13th century.

The peculiarly Italian aspect of the gothic style in the fine arts had its counterpart in contemporary scripts. Medieval Italian manuscripts were written for the most part in a script known as 'rotunda', a name which indicates the much more rounded form taken by gothic hands in Italy. At first sight manuscripts in rotunda script give the impression of having nothing gothic about them; the general appearance is one of roundness and spaciousness. But a closer inspection reveals that there is still a certain angularity about the individual letters, with a considerable differentiation between the thick and thin strokes in the shading, which was so characteristic of gothic hands, together with the fusion of certain letters. Certainly the words were more widely and clearly spaced than was usual in northern manuscripts, and this gives a recognisable difference to the rotunda script of Italy. Its use was widely propagated by the activities of the northern universities such as Padua and Bologna, which were well-known throughout the European scholastic world. Nevertheless the rotunda script was directly affected by the Renaissance interest in classical learning, which had considerable influence on Italian handwriting. Even so, the rotunda script continued to be employed for liturgical and similar works long after it had been abandoned for secular texts, and it certainly gave a majestic appearance to the pages where it was so used, as illustrations in this book demonstrate.

The scripts of the Italian Renaissance have been studied more than any others in recent years, and although much information about them has been revealed, it has also been made apparent that there is still much more to be learnt. The Renaissance was many sided in its appeal and in its effects, but for the study of handwriting perhaps its most important aspect was the impetus it gave to the study of classical texts – the re-birth of classical learning and art manifest in the written word. The commencement of this interest in the past of Greece and Rome may be in dispute, as scholars trace its origins ever further back. But the years around 1400 form a useful if somewhat arbitrary date, when the new style could be seen expressed in architecture, painting and sculpture, in the work of Brunelleschi (1377-1446), Masaccio (1401-28) and Donatello (1386?-1466) among many others. Conscious that Rome and Italy had once been the centre of the civilised world, the 15th century Italian humanists desired to revive something of the grandeur of the ancients. Remains of this earlier world lay all around in the form of brick and stone, often bearing finely carved inscriptions. But the scholars desired much more than this material evidence, and the actual writings of the classical world were now eagerly sought after. Collectors and scholars alike went in search of classical texts throughout Italy and Europe, the richer among them sending agents far afield. When the much desired classical texts were found, the manuscripts were frequently those which had been copied during a previous renaissance, namely that of the court of Charlemagne. They were thus written out in the fine Carolingian hand of that period, with all its clarity and beauty. This writing greatly impressed 15th century scholars, who felt that the new learning needed a complete break from the prevailing scripts in order to express the new spirit of the age.

The script that was evolved was called 'lettera antiqua', because it was based on the Carolingian scripts of the 9th and 10th centuries. It was widely practised by the humanist scholars of the 15th century and was also taken up by the professional scribes. It was, like its progenitor, a fine, clear, rounded hand, suitable for the presentation of the light of learning that was being let in upon the scholasticism of the Middle Ages. The Renaissance was very much a period of individualism, and hence the personal variations of the humanistic minuscule were considerable; a selection of them is represented in this book. But, as has been repeatedly noted, the natural tendency for all scripts is to change, usually because of an innate desire in most writers for speed, all too often at the expense of legibility. The fine humanist minuscule was also eventually affected in this way. The tremendous desire for more and yet more texts involved considerable work for the professional copyist, but many a scholar was his own scribe, and was more concerned with acquiring a copy of the text he wanted than the method of its production or writing.

Other events were also affecting the output of written material. The rise of nation states in Europe led to the formation of national bureaucracies. Among the most important of these was the Papal Chancery, whose correspondence extended to almost every west European country. Trade and travel were alike on the increase, all giving rise to more and more documentation and thus an increased demand for scribes, and for those scribes to work speedily. When written quickly, the rounded form of the letter *o* tends to become oval, and so do other characters based on the circle; letters become joined, a slope develops, and a cursive hand arises. This was what happened to the humanist hand in Italy. The resulting cursive script was adopted by the influential chanceries of Rome and Venice in the middle of the 15th century, whence it became known as the chancery hand, or *cancellaresca corsiva*. In England, where it arrived a few decades after its appearance in Italy, it was, not surprisingly, known as 'italic', and was also referred to as the Roman hand. Shakespeare mentions it in a well-known passage in 'Twelfth Night', when Malvolio, referring to Olivia's supposed note to him, says 'I think we do know the sweet Roman hand'.

The chancery or italic hand could perhaps be considered as the Renaissance hand *par excellence*, and its influence and importance was considerable. It was a very individualistic script, as can be seen by the varied examples illustrated in this book, and it could also be a very beautiful hand. Although the scribes of the great chanceries and offices might use it, and it appeared as one of the hall-marks of the educated person, it was by no means the common hand of Europe in the 15th or 16th century. Italic was certainly much less prevalent in Germany and central Europe, although it was taken up with enthusiasm by certain sections of the population in England, France and the Low Countries. For more ordinary writing, the gothic influence was still felt north of the Alps, where the bastarda script became more cursive, eventually developing into a form which in England was known as the 'secretary hand' – a very suggestive nomenclature. This hand, which was one of considerable illegibility, continued in use almost to the end of the 17th century, and was regularly taught by writing masters in addition to the italic hand, itself so clear and legible. One of the noticeable features of much 16th century writing in England, was that the main body of a letter or document was written in the common secretary hand, while the signature of the writer appeared in a clear italic. This is the reverse of its modern counterpart, which is usually clearly written or typed, while the writer's signature is often so illegible as to require it to be clearly spelt out underneath. So prevalent is this now that not so long ago a lengthy and complaining correspondence appeared in *The Times* under the heading 'Yours sincerely Squiggle'.

The importance of the Italian scripts of the Renaissance to the rest of Europe is obvious, but their significance went even further. When the first Italian printing press was set up at Subiaco in 1464, the printers, as in Germany, turned to the local scripts for their type. The early Italian printed books therefore appeared, not in the textura of the north, but in the Roman letters of the south. Eventually the Roman form of letter was to conquer the gothic type in all but a few countries, and this book is printed in a type that derives directly from the humanist script of the Renaissance. When Aldus Manutius of Venice desired to print editions of the classics cheaply and in small portable volumes, it was to the italic script he turned to provide suitable models. Both Roman and italic types are still in use today, and both go back to these handwritten forms.

Missal (Roman)
North Italian c1300

This manuscript provides a good example of the form taken by the gothic script in Italy. Here the 'rotunda' script placed greater emphasis on roundness and spaciousness. Nevertheless its gothic affinities are recognisable in the angular quality of many of the bowed letters, such as o *or* d*. The manuscript, which is incomplete, is interesting in that it shows how the work of the scribe and decorator was carried out. On this page we can see that one of the larger initials remains in outline only, the intended gold and colour never having been added.*

V&AM Reid MS 65 18.5 × 13

Opposite:
Epistle Book Italian, possibly for Franciscan use and connected with Assisi. 1368

This manuscript shows the form taken by the gothic minuscule in the northern half of Italy. The letters have the angularity expected of the textura script, and the joining strokes of the minims tend to disappear, but the general appearance remains one of roundness, with the words clearly separated from each other.

V&AM MS 25.i.1861 33.5 × 25

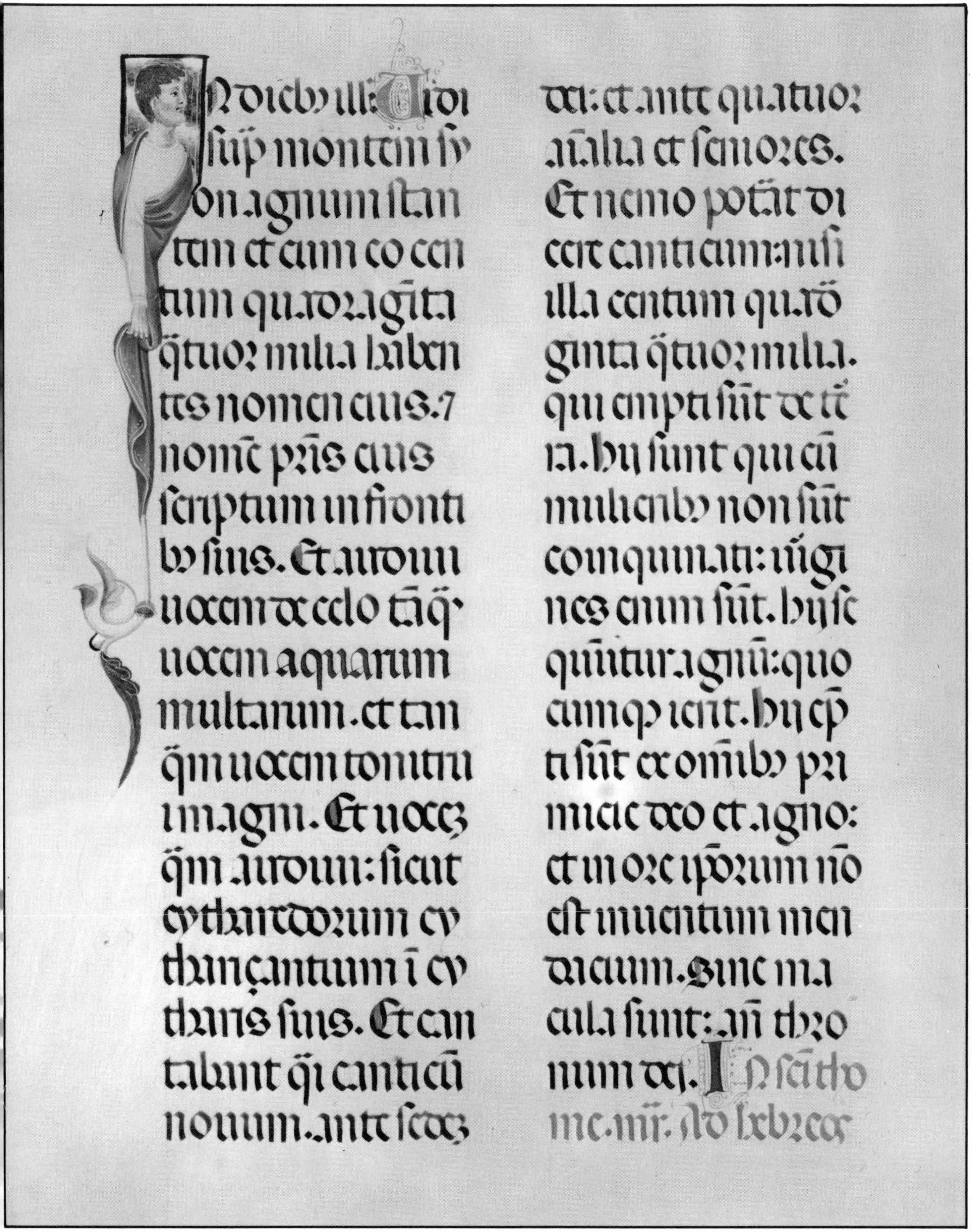

IN diebȝ illis: Vidi
sup montem sy
on agnum stan
tem et cum eo cen
tum quadragīta
q̄tuor milia haben
tes nomen eius. 7
nomē pris eius
scriptum in fronti
bȝ suis. Et audiui
uocem de celo tāq̄
uocem aquarum
multarum. et tan
q̄m uocem tonitrui
magni. Et uocē
q̄m audiui: sicut
cytharedorum cy
tharizantium i cy
tharis suis. Et can
tabant q̄si canticū
nouum. ante sedē
dei: et ante quatuor
aīalia et seniores.
Et nemo poterat di
cere canticum: nisi
illa centum quadrā
ginta q̄tuor milia.
qui empti sūt de ter
ra. Hii sunt qui cū
mulieribȝ non sūt
coinquinati: uirgi
nes enim sūt. Hii se
quūtur agnū: quo
cumq; ierit. Hii em
ti sūt ex omnibȝ pri
micie deo et agno:
et in ore ipsorum nō
est inuentum men
dacium. Sine ma
cula sunt: ante thro
num dei. In sci tho
me. mr. ad [illegible]

habetis. credite in lucem. ut filij lucis sitis.
Hec locutus est yhs ⁊ abijt ⁊ abscõdit se
A Cunctis nos dñe qs reati Sec. eis.
bus ⁊ periculis propitiatus absolue.
quos tanti mistery tribuis esse ꝯsortes.
Per dñm. Pt com.
D Iuini muneris saciati largitate qs dñe
deus nr̃. ut hui' semper ꝑticipatiõe ui
uamus. Per do. Oro sr po.
T Ueatur qs dñe dextera tua ppl'm depre
cantem. ⁊ purificatũ dignant' erudiat
ut ꝯsolatione presenti ad futura bona ꝓ
ficiat. Per. Dñica in ramis palmar. j.
D Eus quem diligere ⁊ amare iu Oro.
stitia est ineffabilis grẽ dona in nobis
multiplica. ⁊ qui fecisti nos morte filij
tui sperare q credimus. fac nos eodẽ resur
gente puenire quo tendim'. Qui tecũ.

Opposite:

Missal (Roman), for the use of a religious house in Milan, possibly the Trinitarians   Italian (Milan) c1390-1400

This manuscript shows a further example of the rotunda script of Italy. In spite of the angularity of some of the letters (the a *for example) the general appearance is one of spaciousness. The last few lines of the text show clearly the breaks occurring in strokes forming the tops of the* m *and* n.

V & A M   Reid MS 66   19 × 13.5

Book of Hours (Use of Rome)
Italian (Milan?)   1446

This small manuscript written in rotunda script was probably produced in the north of Italy, and the border on this page indicates a possible French or Netherlandish influence. It may even have been added at a later period. The interesting fact about the manuscript is that it is signed and dated, on f.266, where we read Frater Paulus de Mediolano ordis sci B'tholomei de hermineis scipsit MCCCC 46. *The gothic aspect of this example of rotunda script is pronounced, making for difficulties in reading; this is not helped by the 'see-through' from the next page.*

V & A M   Reid MS 60   f.71r
13 × 9.5

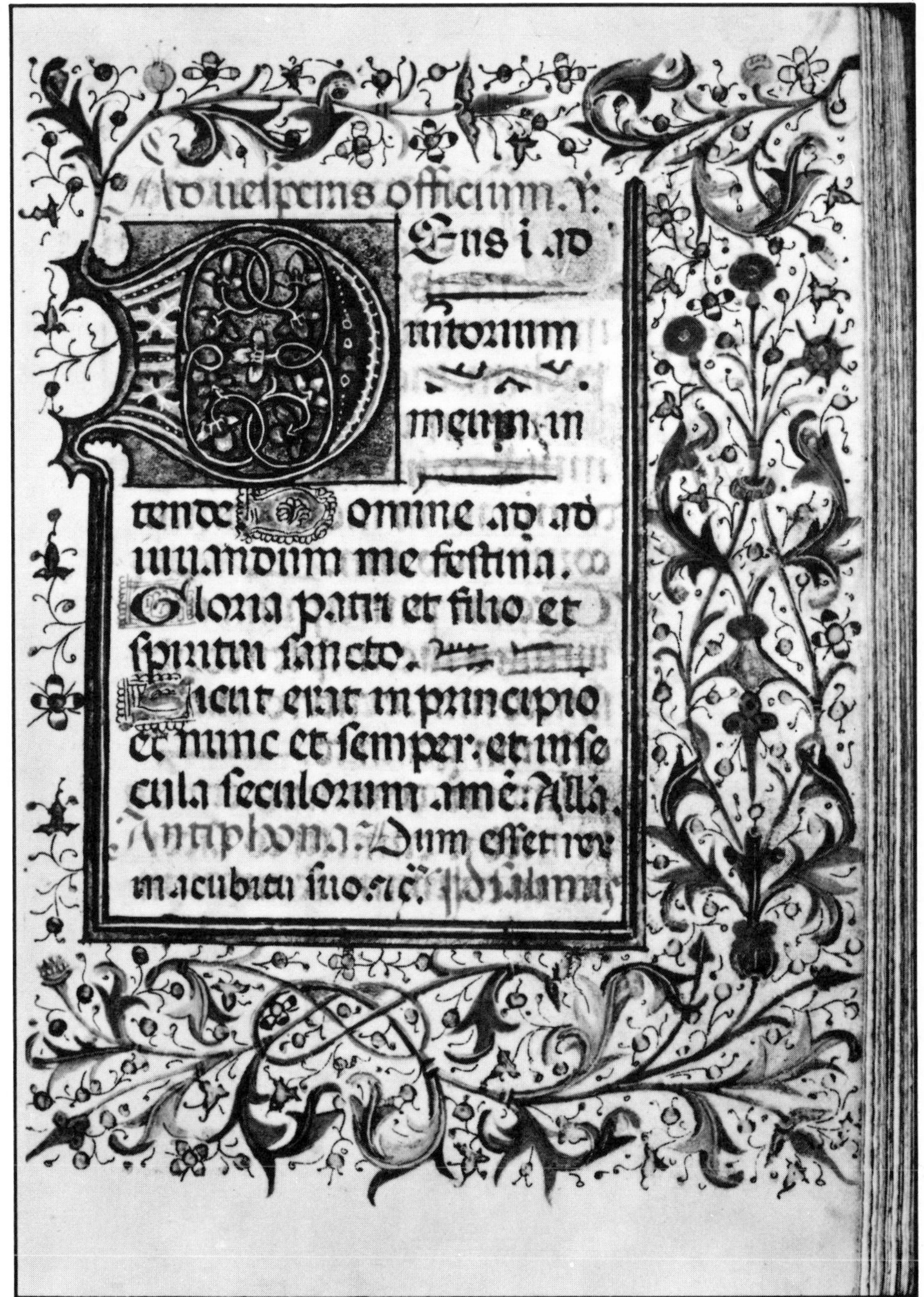
Ad vesperas officium. V.
Deus i ad
iutorium
meum in
tende. domine ad ad
iuvandum me festina.
Gloria patri et filio et
spiritui sancto.
Sicut erat in principio
et nunc et semper. et in se
cula seculorum amē. Alla.
Antiphona. Dum esset rex
in accubitu suo.

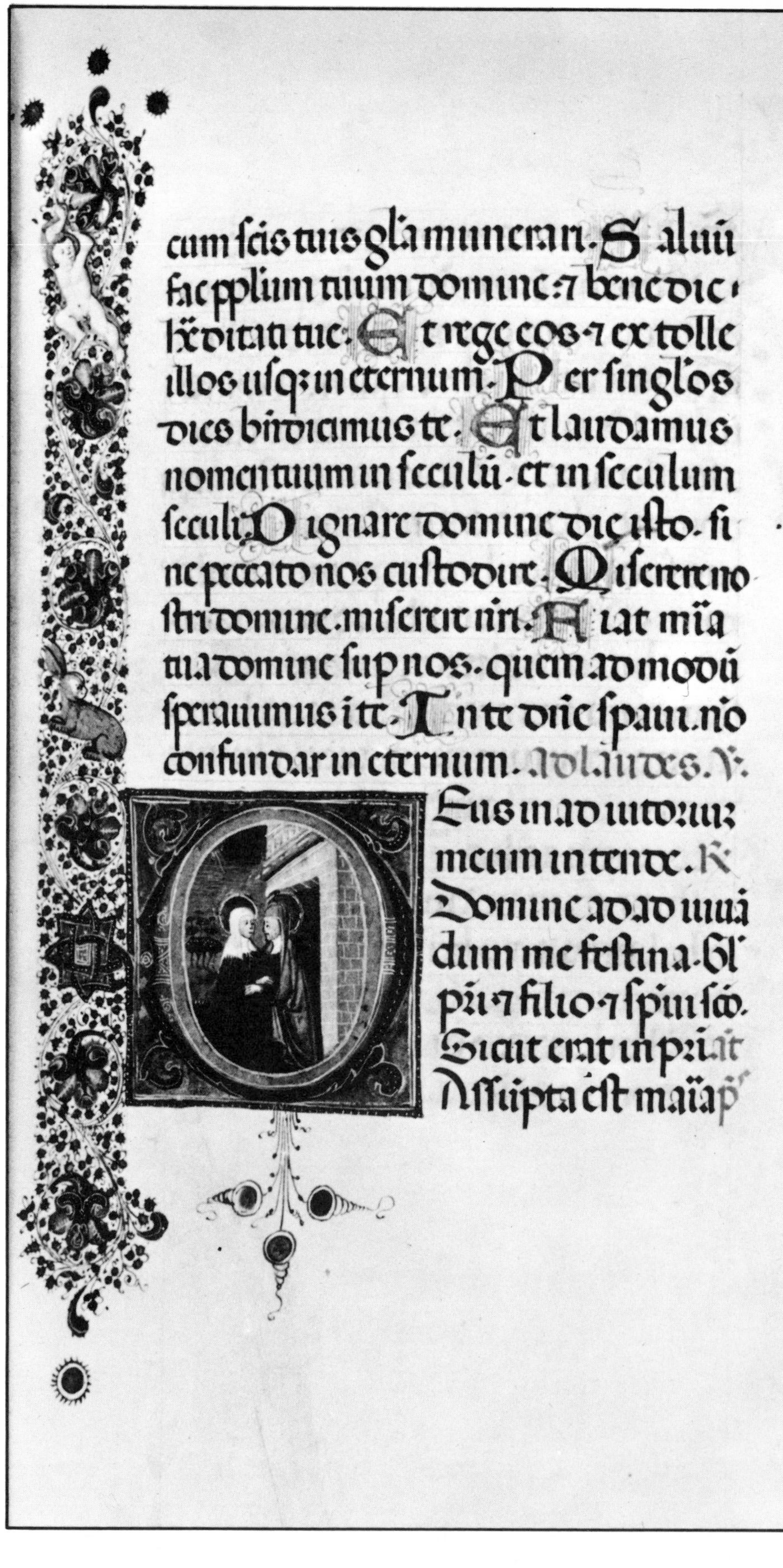

Book of Hours (Use of Rome), known as the Hours of Alfonso of Aragon   Neapolitan   c1480

This magnificent manuscript, written in rotunda script, is chiefly remarkable for its illuminations. This page shows one of the historiated initials, the letter D containing an illustration of the Visitation. The enlarged detail which follows shows the same initial and the text surrounding it, thus enabling the form of the script to be more closely studied.

V & A M   Salting MS 1224
f.20r   25 × 27

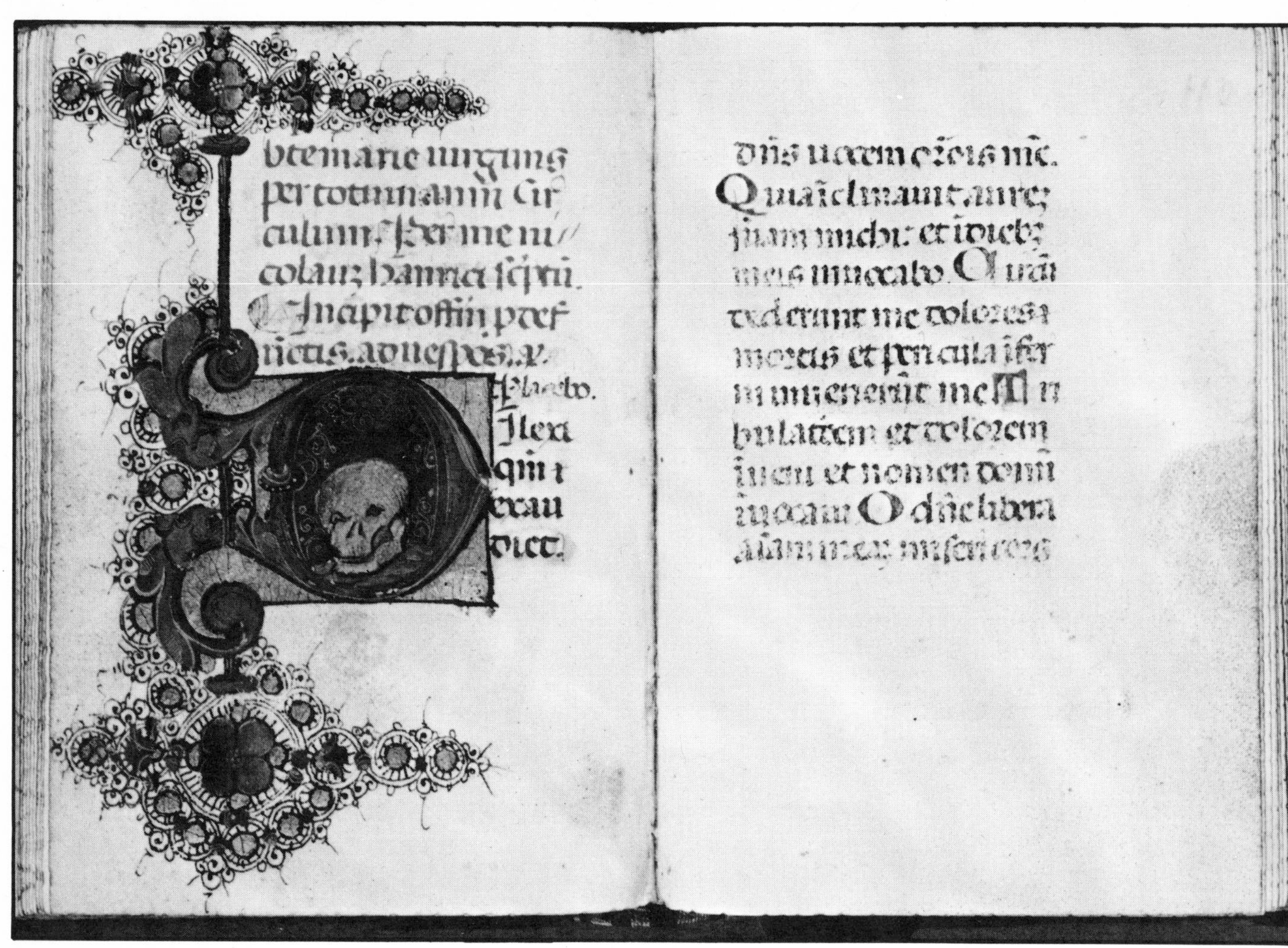

Book of Hours (Use of Rome)
North Italian c1470

This small manuscript, written in rotunda script, would be considered a fairly insignificant production, typical of the period, but for one interesting fact, namely that it has been signed by the scribe. On the left-hand page in this illustration, beginning in the third line, can be seen the words Per me ni/colaus hanrici sc'ptu. *Nothing further is known about Nicolaus Henricus, and few such manuscripts are signed in this way.*

V & A M Reid MS 62
f.109v/110r 9 × 6.5

Opposite:
Dominican Gradual
North Italian late 15th century

The Gradual was a large choir book containing the choral parts of the Mass. It would have been placed on a lectern around which the monks could gather. The letters which appear in this illustration are therefore much larger than any others that appear in the earlier sections of the present book. The spaciousness of the rotunda script and the size of the individual letters would ensure that the words would be clearly visible at a distance.

V & A M MS L 3691-1963
f.79v 56.5 × 40.5

ce
oculi do mini super
timentes e ii spe
rantes in misericordi

Book of Hours (Use of Rome)
Spanish? c1500

This manuscript can be compared with p. 108 of about the same date. In both cases the attribution is debatable because of the close connection between Spain and Naples at this period. It is thought that this manuscript, written in very black ink in rotunda script, may be Spanish in origin. But it could equally well be Neapolitan, or possibly written by a Spaniard working in Naples or south Italy. A former owner, George Reid, obtained it in Sicily 'from an ancient monastic library in Sicily (Messina)', which contained many volumes of early Spanish printing.

V & A M Reid MS 71 f.43r
14 × 10.5

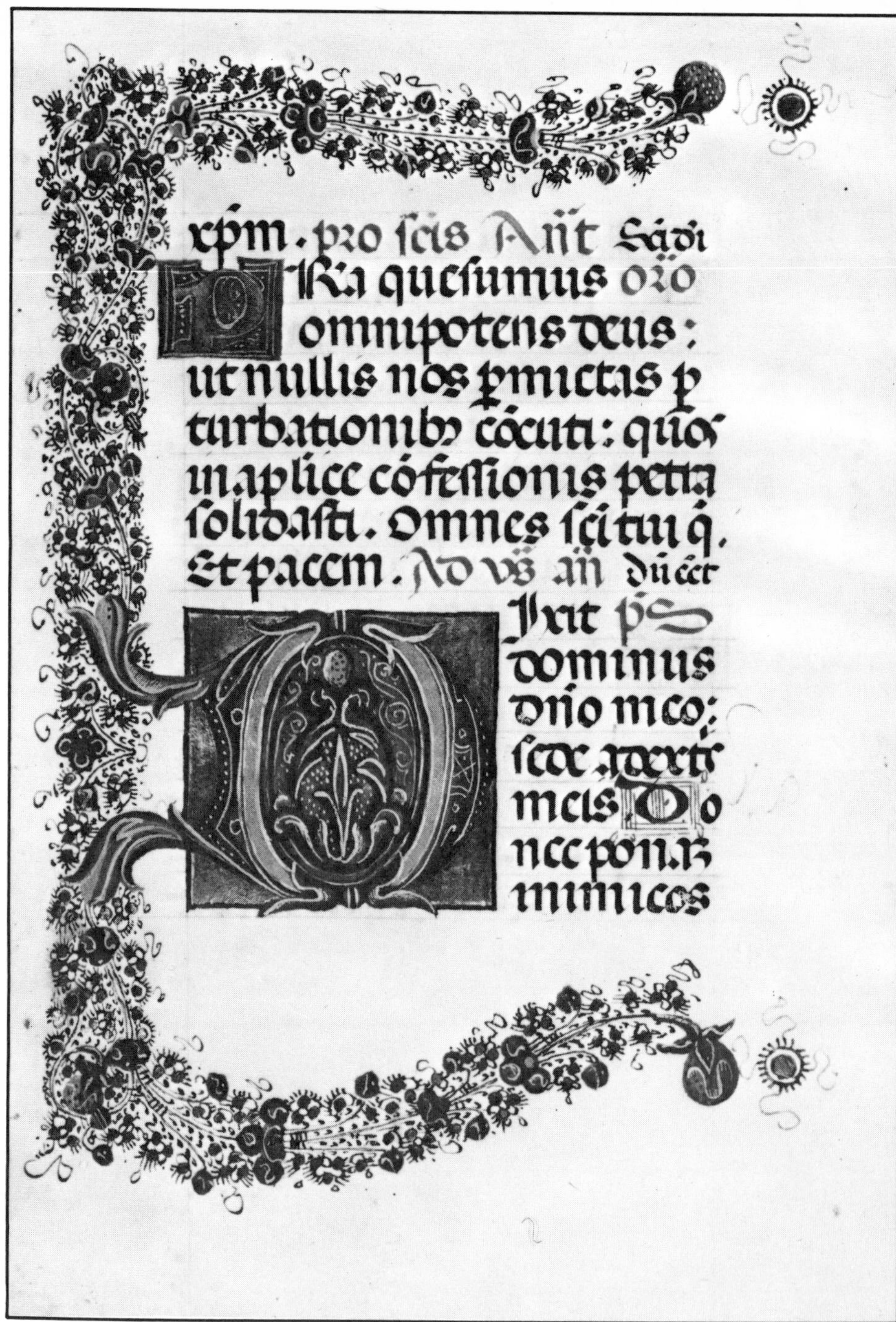

xpm. pro scis Ant Sacdi
Nra quesumus dño
omnipotens deus:
ut nullis nos pmictas p
turbationib9 cocuti: quos
in aplice cofessionis petra
solidasti. Omnes sci tui q.
Et pacem. Ad vs an Duect
Dixit ps
dominus
dño meo:
sede adextris
meis. Do
nec ponam
inimicos

Opposite:
Book of Hours (Use of Rome)
Spanish? c1500

One of the later pages (enlarged) in this manuscript, showing the elaborate decoration which surrounds the script at the beginning of the different sections. This page shows the commencement of the Hours of the Holy Cross.

V & A M Reid MS 71 f.60r
14 × 10.5

bone uoluntatis tue coronasti nos Re
quiem eternam. An Dirige domine ⁊
deus meus in conspectu tuo uiam me
am. An Conuertere. Ps.
D Omine ne in furore tuo arguas me ne
q; in ira tua corripias me Miserere mei
domine quoniam infirmus sum sana ⁊
me domine: quoniam conturbata sunt
omnia ossa mea Et anima mea tur
bata est ualde: sed tu domine usq; q
quo Conuertere domine et eripe aĩ
mam meam: saluum me fac propter ⁊
misericordiam tuam Quoniam non
est in morte qui memor sit tui in ĩfer
no autem quis confitebitur tibi La
boraui in gemitu meo lauabo per sin
gulas noctes lectum meum lachry

Opposite:
Book of Hours (Use of Rome), known as the Bentivoglio Hours
Bologna c1500

This manuscript provides a sumptous example of a work made for a noble owner, in this instance, Giovanni II Bentivoglio. It is written in humanist antiqua script, and is lavishly decorated in bright colours. The variety of ligatures and flourishes suggested to Wardrop and others that it might be the work of Pierantonio Sallando, but the hand has not yet been positively identified.

V & A M Reid MS 64 21 × 15

Book of Hours (Use of Rome) known as the Bentivoglio Hours
Bologna c1500

A detail from this manuscript which shows an initial letter D, containing a depiction of St Bernardino of Siena, and the text surrounding it, thus permitting a closer study of the script.

V & A M Reid MS 64 f.103r 21 × 15

negligentia plectimur tum maxie in amicis & dili-
gendis & colendis pposteris .n. utimur consilys
& acta agimus qui uetamur ueteri puerbio. Nam
implicari ultro & citro uel usu diurno uel etiam offi
cijs repente inmedio cursu amicitias exorta aliqua
offensio dirumpimus Quo etiam mag' uituperanda e
reimaxie necessarie tanta incuria Vna n. e amicitia inrebus humanis de cuius utilitate oms uno
ore consentiunt q̃q̃ amultis uirtus ipsa contemni
et uenditatio quedam atq; ostentatio ee dicitur.
Multi etiam diuitias despiciunt quos paruo contentos
tenuis uictus cultus q; delectat. Honores uo q'z
cupiditates quida inflamantur q̃ multi ita contep-
nut ut nihil inanius nihil ee leuius existiment
Item q; ceteri que quibusdam admirabilia ee uide-
tur permulti sunt qui pnihilo putet. De amicitia oms adunum ide sentiunt. & hy qui ad res
publicas se contulerunt & hij qui rerum cognitie
doctrina q; delectantur & hy qui suu negotiu
gerunt ostiosi. Postremo hij qui se totos tradiderunt uoluptatibus sine amicitia uitam ee sentia-
unt nullam. sinmodo uelint aliqua ex parte li-
beraliter uiue. Serpit .n. nescio quom p omnium
uitam amicitia nec ullam etatis degende rōnez
patitur ee expertem sui. Quin etiā si quis asperita-
tem eam ē & inmanitatem nāe congress ut satie-
tatem hominum fugiam atq; oderit qualē fuisse
athenis Thymonem nescio quē accepimus tum

Marcus Tullius Cicero: De Amicitia and De Senectute
Florentine? c1460

This is a businesslike humanist hand, which by its use of contractions suggests that the text, rather than the writing of it, was most important. But it is neatly and evenly written, with large margins, although the scribe has certain idiosyncracies, writing his Q well above the line and his S with the larger bowl at the top.

V & A M MS L 937-1951 20.5 × 12

uō suasionis illecebras renuere in nobis est cur tu materiam abscidis corona
rum industrieq: et probitatis occasionem tollis. Ad hec si illum sciens fore
insuperabilem cunctosq: deuicturum ita illum dimisisset deus: nec sic qui
dem ista hesitatio locum habuisset. Nam tum quoq: quod ille obtineret
quod uinceret non reluctantes: sed sponte sibi cedentes atq: succumbentes
a nobis profecto manasset. Quod si plurimi quidem illius potentiam ac
uires frangunt. complures item posthac illum superaturi sunt. quid tu
futuros probatissimos clarissimaq: uictoria insignes tanto priuas honore.
Idcirco enim eum dimisit ut illum deuicant qui fuerant ab eo superati qd
illi omni supplicio grauius ac dirius est. At non omnes inquies illum supe
raturi sunt. Quid hoc ad rem. Profecto enim multo melius multoq: con
uenientius est uistis occasiones suppeditari. quibus ad uirtutem se exer
ceant uoluntatemq: ostendant suam. Eos uō qui non sunt huiusmodi
ex propria puniri negligentia q̄ istorum causa illis etiam coronas suas adi
mi. Nam modo is qui malus ac uecors est: non aduersarii uiribus sed suo
potius torpore superatur. quod indicat uincentium illum multitudo
tunc uō studiosi quiq: atq: alacres malorum causa meritis honoribus
fraudati fuissent non habentes ubi uires exercerent suas: ueluti si ago
nitheta quis athletas duos nactus alterum quidem aduersario congre
di paratum omnemq: tolerantiam ostendere coronamq: ex certamine
referre: alterum uō labori illi et erumpne otium delitiasq: preferentē
cōpare atq: aduersario de medio sublato ambos re infecta dimittat. Sic
enim strenuus ille propter alterius ignauiam graui iniuria affectus [illegible]
retur. Ignauius autem non fortissimi socii causa malus esset uerum ob [illegible]
cordiam suam. Sed enim hec istorum questio cum de diabolo agitari
uideatur si suo ordine procedat: plurimis in rebus dei prouidentiam in
simulat cunctamq: simul creaturam perimit. Accusat enim oris atque
oculorum fictionem quippe cum per istas queq: illicita concupiscant
atq: in adulterium corruant plurimi. Per hoc autem blasfemant et per
nitiosa dogmata proferant alii. Num ergo sine oculis et lingua debue
runt homines fieri: Pedes quoq: abscidere et amputare manus necesse
erit. cum iste plene singuine. illi uō prompti ad malum currant. Ne ipse
quidem aures immanitatem rationis huius effugere poterunt. Nam

Thesaurus adversos hereticos, by St Cyril, Patriarch of Alexandria, and De Providentia Dei ad Stagirium libri tres, by St John Chrysostom, Patriarch of Alexandria (both texts in Latin versions probably by Georgius Trapezuntius)
Florentine 1460-70

This is a good example of the humanist hand of the earlier period of the Renaissance, which clearly shows its affinities with the Carolingian hand of the 9th and 10th centuries. It also continues the rotund characteristics of the Italian script, which had never been entirely superseded by the textura style of the north. The writing is clear and even, and is set spaciously on the page. In the original manuscript the rulings for the margins and the prickings for the guidelines are clearly visible. The scribe remains anonymous, although other manuscripts have also been attributed to the same hand.

V&AM Reid MS 78 30 × 22

Ars completa geomantiae
Italian c1460-70

This treatise on geomancy was possibly written in Rome. The illustration shows one of the astrological diagrams which appear in the book, and it can be seen how suitable the humanist hand was for use in maps and diagrams such as this. Although the writing is quite small (and in coloured inks in the original manuscript), yet the inscriptions are entirely legible. It will be noted that the Latin text of the work includes many abbreviations and contractions, suggesting that it was meant for scholarly use.
In the front of the volume of Ars completa geomantiae, *a note on the work by the late James Wardrop has been attached to the fly-leaf. This is reproduced here, to show the essentially humanist character of his own script, which can be compared with the manuscript on which it was based (below).*

V&AM MS L 2464-1950
f.64v 33.5 × 23.5

figura & IV & hec dupliciter qa uel ex pte ante & sic est a pma ad IV
aut ex pte post & sic a pma ad X & ultimus eor fortior est pmo A spe
ctus sextilis dicitur aspectus mediae amicitiae qa fit communiter inter si
gna concordantia in una qualitate & dicitur sextilis qa continet VI pte
circuli s II signa integra ita q habet fieri inter pma figura & III & hec pot

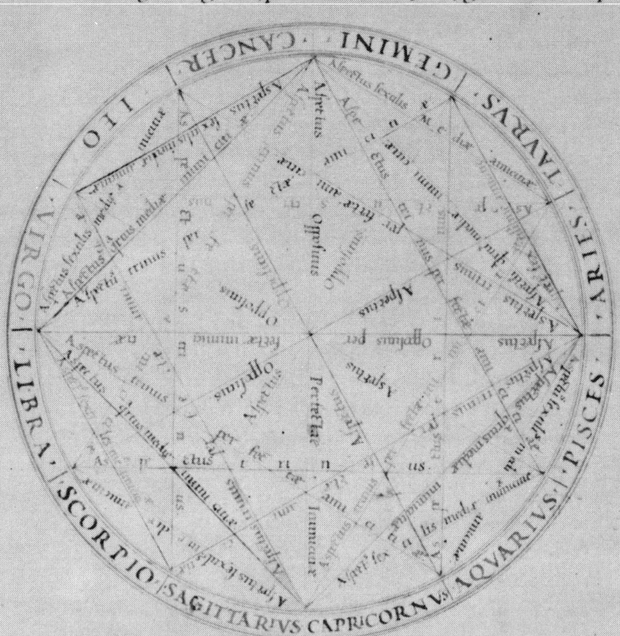

ee dupliciter s ex pte ante & sic est a pma ad III uel ex pte post & sic
est a pma ad XI & iste ultimus s a pma ad XI est fortior alio quae est
a pma ad III & haec oma patent in figura Et nota q fortior & me
lior est aspectus qn figurae sese aspicientes concordant in qualitatibus q
quando discrepant qa qn concordant in qualitatibus tunc est duplex ami
citia una ex pte qualitatu quae dicitur ee ex pte mediae & alia ex pte lo
cor quae est ex pte formae sed siue concordent in qualitatibus siue discor
dent ratione locor tenet aspectus cu forma dignior sit media est tamen
fortior & melior cu concordia q sine ea Et nota q omes domus quae
respiciuntur ab ascendente sunt fortes aliquae tam plus & aliquae minus

For a description of this manuscript see Robinson, W. H., Ltd. Catalogue 81 : A selection of precious manuscripts historic documents and rare books, London, 1950, no. 50. According to this catalogue "Thorndike & Kibre: Catalogue of Incipits, 1937, p. 602, quote an anonymous treatise which is almost certainly identical with this, though there is a slight variation in the initium (i.e. quamplurimos instead of quamplures) This treatise, which they knew only from an entry in an inventory of the Francesco Gonzaga library made in 1407 is there entitled Liber theoretice et practice in Geomancia."

equestrē & pedestrē replicabis opti
me & alia omīa quae supradicta
sunt sine magno labore mō uelis
cū diligentia te exercere aliter fru
stra laboras.

P OSTREMO non inutile mihi
uisum est pro illis maxīe q centū
duntaxat locos hēbunt modū
dare delendi imagines ex locis
ut alias de nouo collocare possīt
qa nisi hac regulā siue modum
haberet non possent aliquo pacto
illis centū locis uti nisi semel tā
tum. nā occupatis locis aliqbus
imaginibus si uelles alias appo
nere nemini dubiū est q illico
sequeretur confusio non pua nā
recitando pores eēnt impedimēto

Jacobus Ragona: De artificiali memoria Italian c1465

This script was originally considered to be the hand of Antonio Tophio but later researches have identified it as that of Bartolomeo Sanvito, to whom more and more important manuscripts of this period are being attributed. The work is written out in a sloped Roman script, and a distinctive feature is the form taken by the contraction mark over the various abbreviations, and the shape of the serifs on the ascenders. The space left between the initial P *and the rest of the text suggests that such capitals were added at a later stage.*

V&AM MS L 1349-1957 16.5 × 10.5

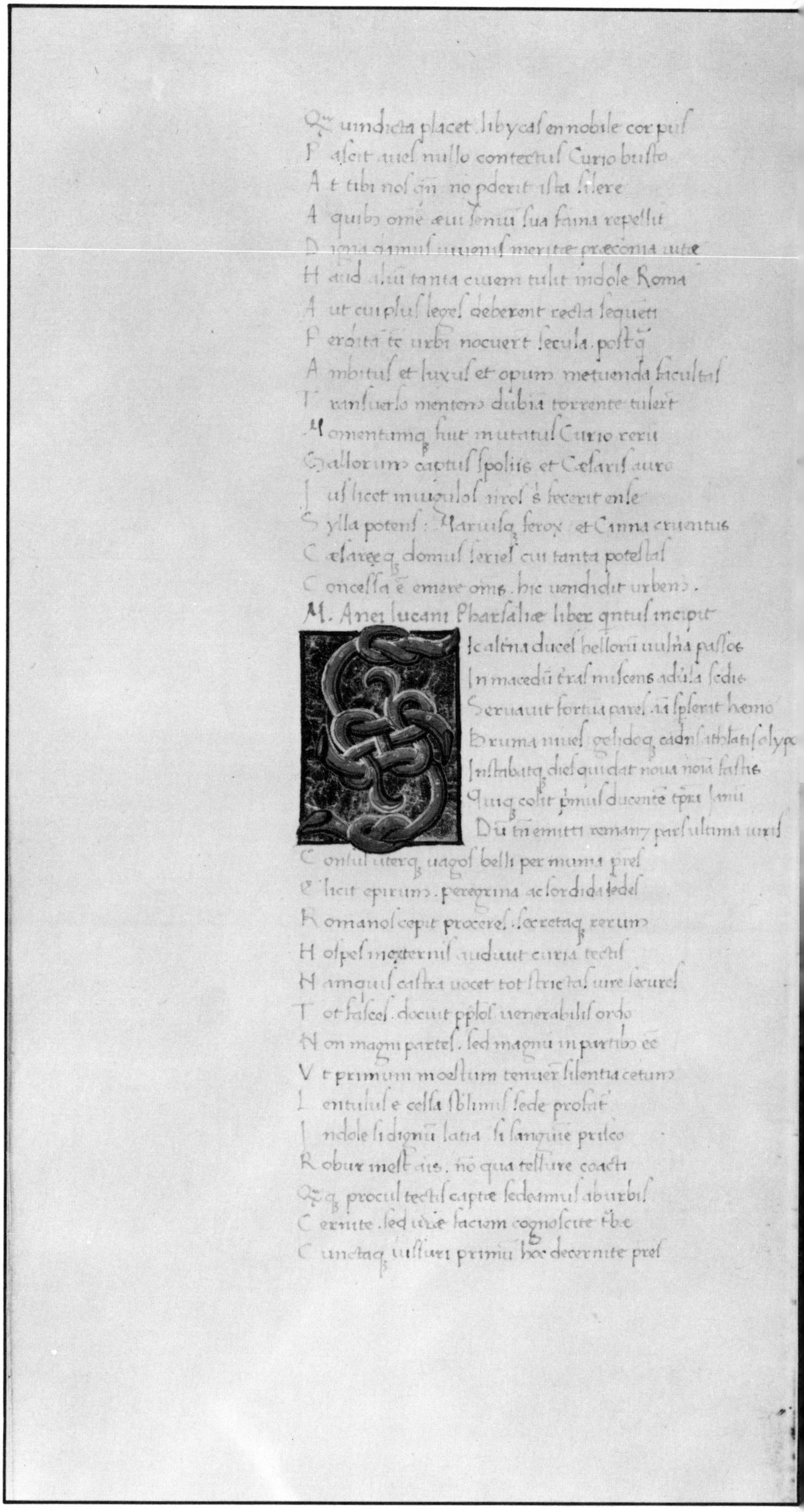

Marcus Annæus Lucanus: Pharsalia
Italian(Mantua)
finished 20th October 1471

This manuscript has been signed and dated at several stages of the work; the earliest states finis per me Iohannem Franciscum Genuesium de Mantua die 19 Iunii 1471. *It is written in a fine humanist hand on smooth vellum, and the page size is unusually long and narrow. The volume contains a number of strapwork initials, similar to the one illustrated here; they are in green, blue or pink, on burnished gold grounds.*

V&AM MS L 366-1956 23 × 12

ET tartari seguendo con gran cura
Trouando egypto forte pe paludi
Non uollon seguir lor disauentura
ET benche fussin delle vista gnudi
Non uolson trapassar sanza riguardo
Sendo admoniti ad bellicosi ludi
ET quando euano fuor collo stendardo
Guardon se posson essere traditi
Et perche modo ognhor cō prōpto sguādo
ET molto bene intendono e partiti
Seglie da prolungare o darui dentro
Et se aduantaggio o no sono assaliti
VAnno col sole a tanto scaltrimento
Accio nō impedisca allor lauista
Et uan uoltando anchor secondo il uento
Nella battaglia sanguinosa et trista
Di canne, vulturno il uento fe gran dāno
Con poluere et con labe insieme mixta
ET per non esser vincti con ingāno
Della natura dello ro aduersario
Sopra ogni cosa intender stima fāno
Seglie bestiale o seglie temerario
Voglion sapere o timido o audace
O cauto o prudente il lor contrario.

Marianus Gualterius: De re militaris. Dedicated to Jacobus IV, Lord of Piombino   Italian (Florentine?) late 15th century

This manuscript book of verses offers an unusual and very personal version of a humanistic hand with cursive tendencies. The bulbous terminals of the ascenders are especially noticeable, and there is a dash and a flourish about some of the minuscules.

V & A M   MS L 1346-1957   21 × 14

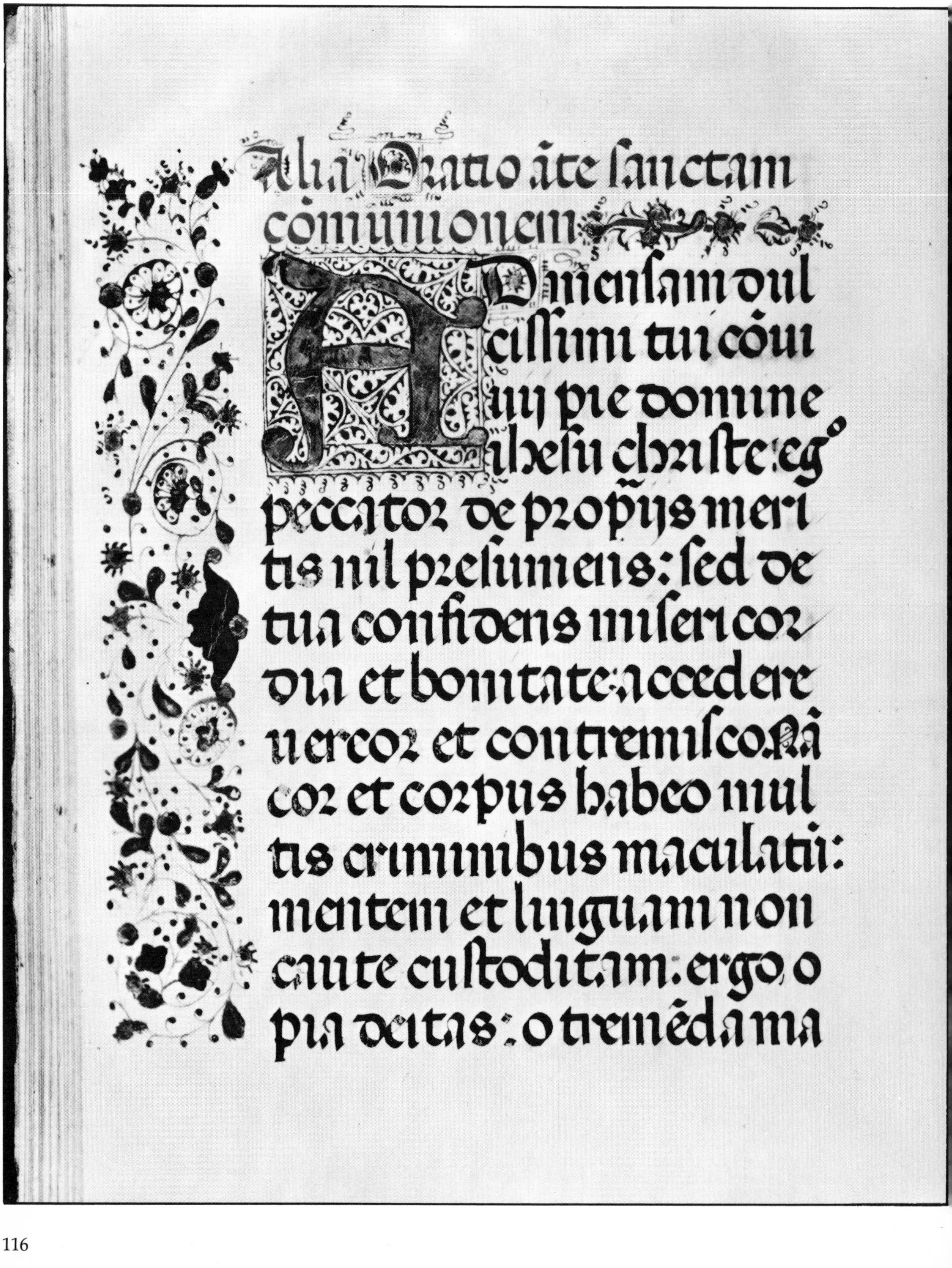

Alia Oratio ãte sanctam
communionem
Ad mensam dul
cissimi tui cõui
uij pie domine
ihesu christe: eg°
peccator de propijs meri
tis nil presumens: sed de
tua confidens miseri cor
dia et bonitate: accedere
uereor et contremisco. Nã
cor et corpus habeo mul
tis criminibus maculati:
mentem et linguam non
caute custoditam: ergo, o
pia deitas: o tremẽda ma

tuam pijſſime domine : ut conce
das mihi diem futurum ſic per
agere in tuo ſancto ſeruitio . cum
omni humilitate et diſcretione :
quatenuſ gratum ſeruitium tibi
exhibere ualeam : Qui uiuis et
regnas in ſecula ſeculorū . Amen.

O Ratio dicenda dum homo
accedit ad ſtratum.

Ratiaſ tibi ago
domine qui me di
gnatuſ eſ in hac die
cuſtodire : depre
cor clementiam tuam pijſsime
domine : ut concedaſ mihi hanc
noctem ſic mundo corde pertran

ſire :

ſire et corpore : ut mane ſurgens
gratum tibi ſeruitium exhibere
poſſit Qui uiuis et regnas in ſe
cula ſeculorum . Amen .

Q Veſti ſono edodici articoli
de la fede .

Redo in deum patrē
omnipotentem creato
rem celi et terre . E t
in ieſum xp̄m filium eiuſ unicū
dominum noſtrum . Q ui cō
ceptuſ eſt de ſpiritu ſancto nat'
ex maria uirgine . P aſſus
ſub pontyo pylato crucifixus
mortuus et ſepultus . D eſcē
dit ad inferos tertia die reſurre

Book of Hours (Use of Rome)
Florentine c1522

This style of humanist script, based on earlier models, continued to be used in Italy for liturgical works until well into the 16th century and it has certain affinities with the printed book of the period. It is clearly and evenly written on fine smooth vellum, and the original manuscript makes considerable use of coloured inks to supplement the few illuminated initials. The catchword, written at right angles to the page at the bottom, was to ensure that the binder assembled the book correctly — the same word appears at the top of the next page, the first of the new gathering.

V & A M Salting MS 1223 f.147v/148r 14 × 9

Opposite:
Collection of prayers (Liber precum) written for Ettore Pignatelli (d.1535) Count of Borello, created Duke of Monteleone, Sicily, in 1526
Spanish or Neapolitan c1500

Boldly written in black ink in rotunda script, the style is considered to indicate Spanish influence, which was strong in the south of Italy at this time. The size of the manuscript is quite large for a book of private devotions, but it permits a more careful study of the formation of the individual letters.

V & A M Reid MS 74 19 × 13.5

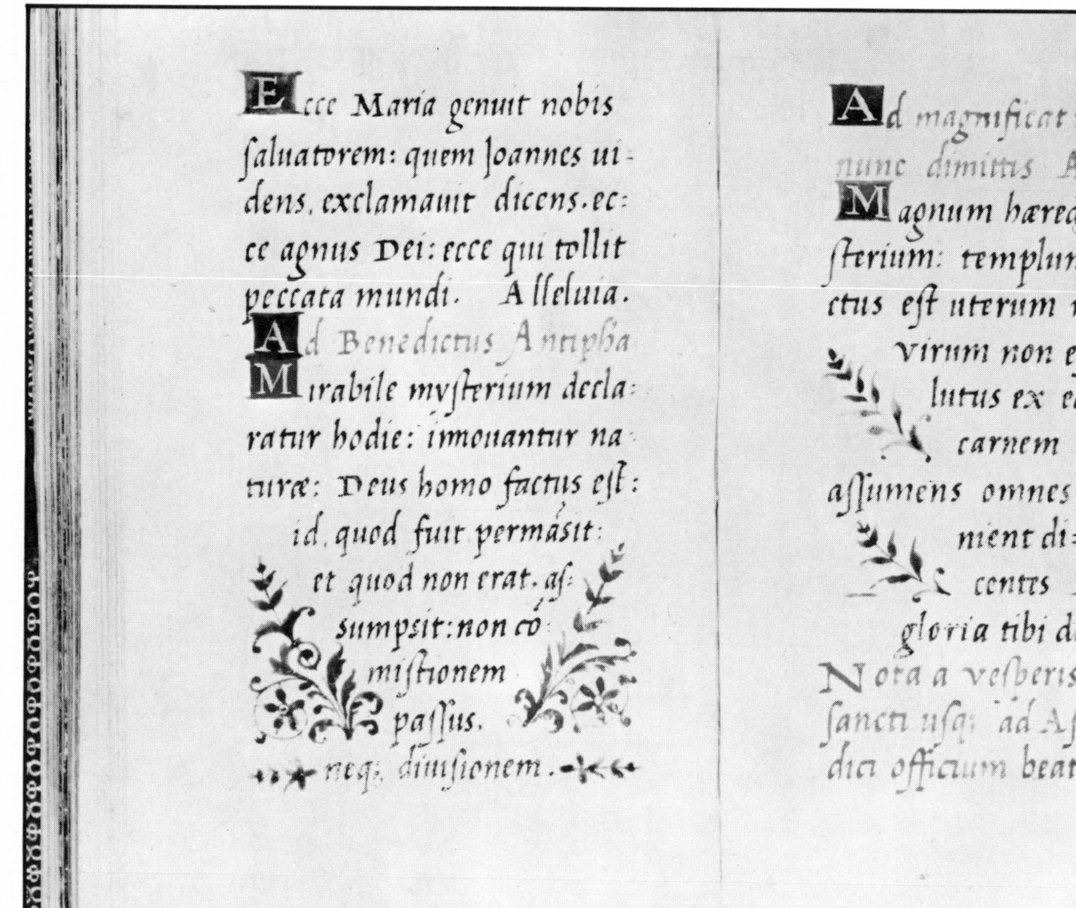
Ecce Maria genuit nobis
saluatorem: quem Joannes uidens. exclamauit dicens. ecce agnus Dei: ecce qui tollit
peccata mundi. Alleluia.
Ad Benedictus Antiphona
Mirabile mysterium decla-
ratur hodie: innouantur naturæ: Deus homo factus est:
id. quod fuit permasit:
et quod non erat. as-
sumpsit: non cō-
mistionem
passus.
neq; diuisionem.

Ad magnificat: & ad
nunc dimittis Antiphona
Magnum hæreditatis my-
sterium: templum Dei fa-
ctus est uterum nesciens
virum non est pol
lutus ex ea.
carnem
assumens omnes gentes ue
nient di-
centes
gloria tibi domine
Nota a vesperis sabbati
sancti usq; ad Ascensionē
dici officium beatæ Mariæ

Book of Hours (Use of Rome),
known as the Hours of Eleanora
of Toledo Florentine
signed and dated 10th February 1540

The hand-written book still made its appearance in court circles in 16th century Italy; this one is signed Aloysius scribebat Floren', *but the scribe's identity remains unknown. Of his work the late James Wardrop wrote 'the script is a good example of* cancellaresca formata, *brought to perfection in Italy in the second quarter of the 16th century'.*

V & A M *MS L 1792-1953*
90v/91r *13 × 8.5*

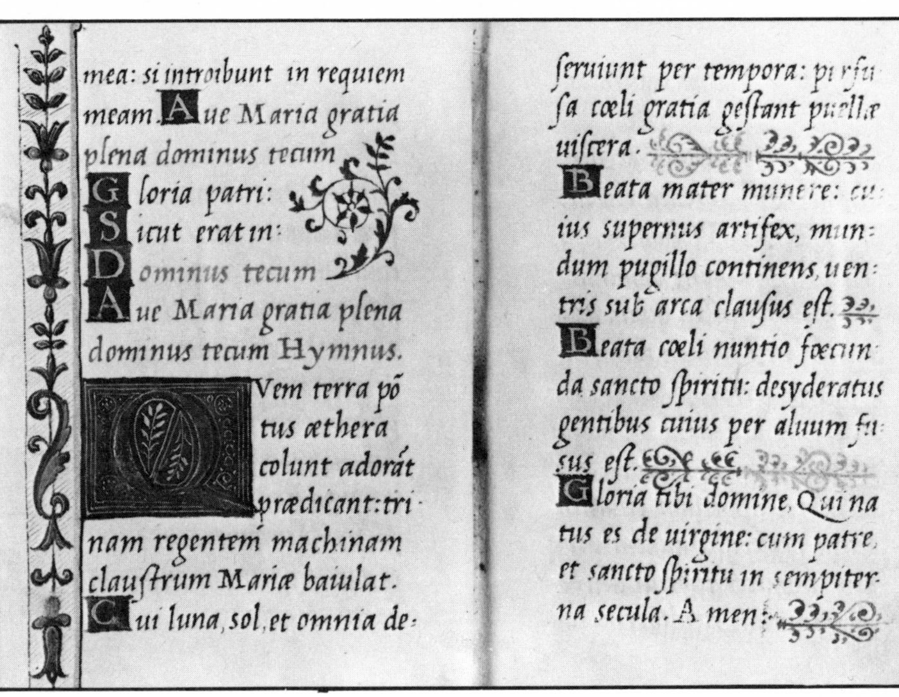

mea: si introibunt in requiem
meam. Aue Maria gratia
plena dominus tecum
Gloria patri:
Sicut erat in:
Dominus tecum
Aue Maria gratia plena
dominus tecum Hymnus.
Quem terra pō
tus æthera
colunt adorát
prædicant: tri
nam regentem machinam
claustrum Mariæ baiulat.
Cui luna, sol, et omnia de:

seruiunt per tempora: perfu
sa cœli gratia gestant puellæ
uiscera.
Beata mater munere: cu
ius supernus artifex, mun:
dum pugillo continens, uen:
tris sub arca clausus est.
Beata cœli nuntio fœcun:
da sancto spiritu: desyderatus
gentibus cuius per aluum fu:
sus est.
Gloria tibi domine, Qui na
tus es de uirgine: cum patre,
et sancto spiritu in sempiter:
na secula. A men:

O EMANVEL
Periit et fuga à me et non
est qui requirat animam
meam: clamaui ad te domīe
dixi tu es spes mea: portio
mea in terra uiuentium.
O CHRISTE
Confiteantur tibi domi
ne omnia opera tua: et san
cti tui benedicant tibi.
Gloria patri, et filio.
et spiritui sancto.
Sicut erat in principio
et nunc et semper: &c:-

ORATIO AD DE
VM PATREM
Pater noster qui
es in cœlis sancti
ficetur nomen
tuum
Adueniat regnum tuum
Fiat uoluntas tua sicut in
cœlo et in terra
Panem nostrum quotidia
num da nobis hodie: et dimit
te nobis debita nostra sicut et
nos dimittimus debitorib[us] nr̄is
et ne nos in ducas i tentationē
sed libera nos a malo. Amen:-

Book of Hours (Use of Rome), known as the Hours of Eleanora of Toledo Florentine
signed and dated 10th February 1540

Another two examples from this charming small Book of Hours, with its elegant cancellaresca script and simple decoration.

V&AM MS L 1792-1953 13 × 8.5

S e de le mie ricchezze care et tante
Et si guardate; ond'io buon tempo uiſsi
Di mia sorte contento, et meco diſsi
Neſsun uiue di me piu lieto amante;
I o ſteſso mi disarmo: et queſte piante
Auezze a gir pur la; dou'io scopriſsi
Quegli occhi uaghi, et lharmonia sentiſsi
De le parole si soaui et sante;
L ungi da lei di mio uoler sen'uanno:
Laſso chi mi dara Bernardo aita?
O chi m'acquetera, quand'io m'affanno?
M orrommi: et tu dirai mia fine udita;
Queſti, per non ueder il suo gran danno,
Laſciata la sua donna uscio di uita.

S ignor, che parti et tempri gli elementi,
E'l sole et laltre ſtelle e'l mondo reggi.
Et hor col freno tuo santo correggi
Il lungo error de le mie uoglie ardenti;
N on lasciar la mia guardia, et non s'allenti
La tua pieta; perch'io tolto a le leggi
M'habbia d'amor, et diſturbato i seggi,
In ch'ei di me regnaua alti et lucenti.
C he come audace lupo suol de gli agni
Stretti nel chiuso lor; cosi coſtui
Ritenta far di me lusata preda.
A ccio pur dunque in danno i miei guadagni
Non torni, e'l lume tuo ſpegner si creda;
Con fermo pie dipartimi da lui.

Pietro Bembo: Rime [etc.]
Italian 1543?

A small beautiful italic script, with the words clearly written although the general appearance is of a flowing cursive hand. There are no decorations in the manuscript, and it is evident that text and script alike were intended to indicate their own importance. The scribe has satisfactorily managed to integrate the capital letters at the beginning of each line with the rest of the text — a problem always accentuated where verse is concerned.

V&A M *MS L 1347-1957* *21.5 × 14*

GVIDVS VBAL-
DVS. II. FELTRIVS
DE RVVERE VRBI-
NI DVX. IIII. Ꝗ. PISA-
VRI ET SENOGAL-
LIAE DOMINVS.
MONTISFERETRI.
AC DVRANTIS
COMES. ALMAEQ.
VRBIS PRÆFECTVS

ILLVSTRI, ET MAGNIF. COMITI
PETRO BONARELLO PATRITIO ANCONITANO, SALVTEM, AC
sinceræ dilectionis affectum. Ex omnibus ornamentis, & præsidijs, in quæ
cum sibi, tum posteris suis in perpetuum comparanda PRINCIPES ciuitatum
toto animo incumbere debent Illud unum firmissimum, ac præclarissimum semper
existimauimus, quod, in eorum hominum qui ab ætatis initio uirtutem amplexati ea
nihil unquam antiquius habuerint, fidelitate, beneuolentiaq; positum esset; Tunc n.
promptius, & alacrius amplissima quæq; negotia bello ac pace gerere possumus cum ta-
lium uirorum in maximis rebus credendis; fidem in prouidendis autem, atq; administra-
dis consilium, et prudentiam præsto nobis esse cognoscimus. Quamobrem ut in reliquum
tempus ad fidelissimam operam suam nauandam uehementius incendantur, alij hoc
exemplo admoniti ea, quæ ad tuendam, atq; augendam dignitatem nostram attinent
diligentius exequantur Hos egregios Viros honorificentissimis præmijs decorandos esse iudicauimus. Cum igitur superioribus annis Illustri Viro. Antonio Landria-
no auunculo tuo Camillam filiam nostram Naturalem in matrimonium collocauerí-
mus, Cumq; & eius filios mares ex legitimo matrimonio procreatos per subinfeuda-
tionem (ut aiunt) Castro VRCEANI cum tota eius Iurisditione donauerimus,
quod ut faceremus complures quidem eius uiri excellentes uirtutes Nos impulerunt,
sed præcipue singularis, & in maximis, ac grauissimis rebus erga Nos, Domumq; nostram spectata fidelitas, Is autem non sine grauissima animi nostri molestia, nulla
uirili prole suscepta, decesserit, Nos maxime cupientes te optime spei Adolescente,
ob egregias animi tui dotes nostra liberalitate complecti, uehementer lætati sumus
quod [illegible] nobis carissimi consanguineum, ea quæ decet beneuolentia prosequeremur,
cumq; nobis pro dignitate augendum et honestandum censeremus. Te enim lectissi-
mæ fœminæ Margharitæ prædicti Antonij Sororis filium auunculi tui optimis, ac
sanctissimis moribus admirabili modestia, incredibili prudentia, & non ab adolescente id ætatis expectanda simillimum præbuisti, ut cum te uideamus tantopere a nobis
dilectum Auunculum tuum præsentem intueri uideamur, nam cum te nobis multos
abhinc annos a poculis esse uoluerimus, & paulo post centum leuis armaturæ equiti-
bus ad nostri corporis custodiam conscriptis, præfecerimus, in utroq; munere, in quo
uitæ nostræ rationes præcipue consistunt, tanta fide, modestia, probitate, ac prudentia te gesisti, et continenter geris ut nihil in te desiderari possit quod a fidelissimo,
& eodem prudentissimo atq; integerrimo uiro sit expectandum. Accedit quod,
cum te de grauissimis negocijs ad Nos, Statumq; nostrum maxime pertinentibus, in
consilium nostrum adhibuerimus, et adhibeamus taciturnitatem tuam cum rarissi-
ma fide coniunctam tuamq; operam quotidie nobis gratiorem, & fideliorem experi-
mur. Cum igitur nihil tam magnum, nihil tam amplum sit, quod de te sperare

An act of investiture by Guidobaldo II, of Montefeltro and Rovere, Duke of Urbino, bestowing on Pietro Bonarelli of Ancona, the castle of Orceano, with the title of count and other privileges.
Urbino 4th September 1559

This document is written out in a fine flowing italic hand, which is pleasant to look at and easy to read; it contains few contractions. It was this ceremonial use of calligraphy, for which the mass production of the printing press was unsuitable, that ensured continuing work for scribes working in the old traditions of illumination and writing.

V&AM MS L 1519-1957
f.1v/2r 27.5 × 19

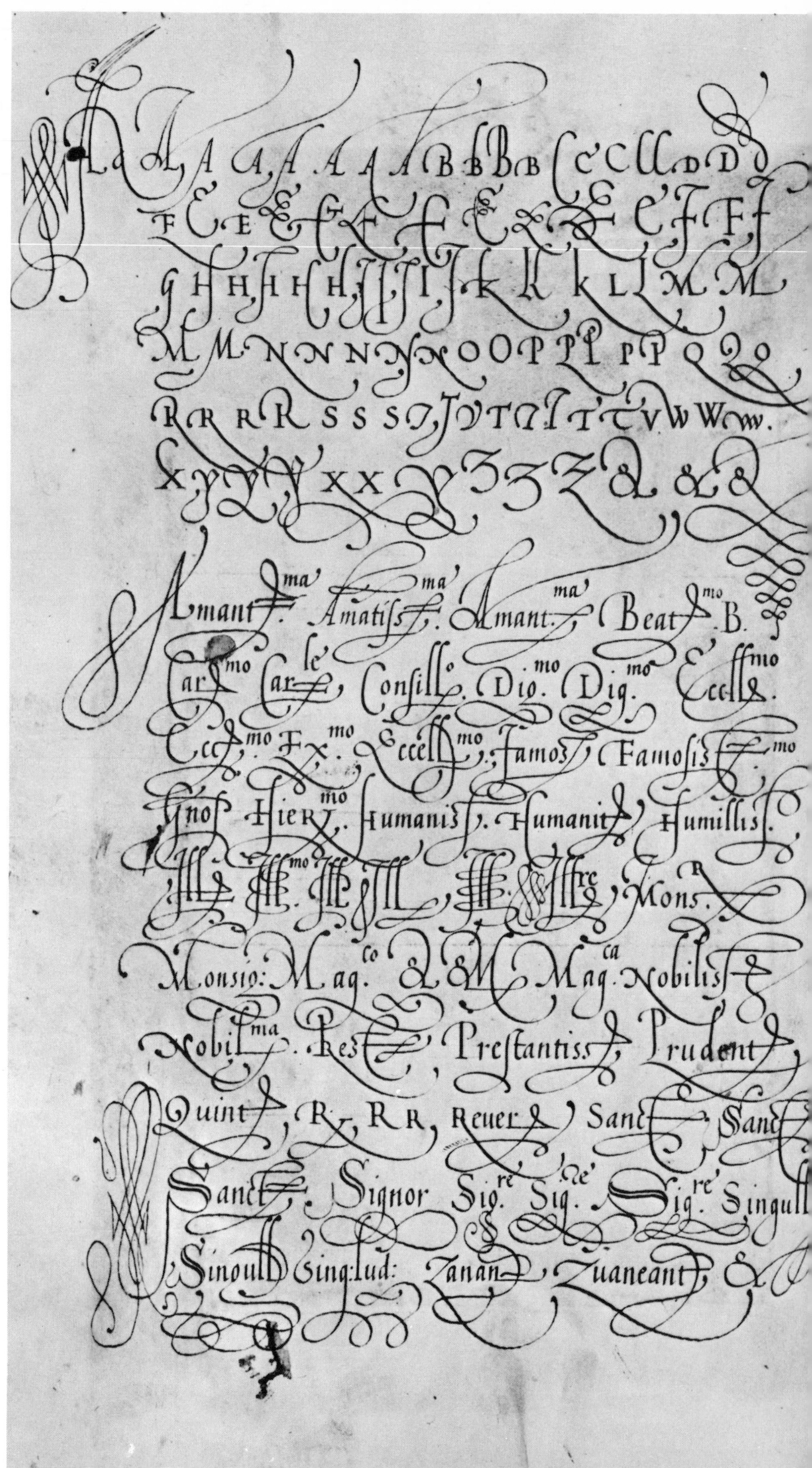

Francesco Moro, of Pozzoveggiano: Arte della strozaria e farsi perfetto stroziero c1560-70

In spite of the title of this work, only the first 15 pages relate to the treatise on hawking. The rest of the book consists of calligraphic specimens, written on vellum and mostly in italic script. As can be seen from the 2 plates here, there is a variety of alphabets and addresses. A few are in colour, or in white-on-black, and are touched with gold or silver. Moro is mentioned by Conretto da Monte Regale in his own book published in 1576.

V & A M   *MS L 1485-1946*   *23 × 15.5*

IGLIA RAVET VIDELICET REOBARBARO mumia uidelicet rubba tintorum et rubet In tutto onze una tanto di luno quanto di laltro et farai pasta et sel sparauiero fusse quasi morto gli darrai di questa una pirola auolta nel bambaso et, a, sacchetto et gorga uodda In questo gela darrai et subito che la hauera gettata la matina guarira perche, e, medicina eccellentissima et e cosa approbata

Rimedio al Mal della testa quando e sgonfia con gliocchi piccoli et mesti

IGLIA PEVERE GRANI TRE GAROFOLI grani tre semencina quanto basta et farai pestar tutte queste cose Insieme In poluere et per tre giorni continui nelle narre et palato del sparauiero à degiuno gli ponerai de detta poluere et quando hauera cessati gli stranuti uno terzo di hora dapoi: di bon et caldo pasto lo passerai et di subito guarira perfettamete.

Al male della testa quando dalle Nare gli uenga mazza puzolente

Hystri tela manu iacientes sollicitabant. Hinc Vergilius eundem locum de incluso Turno, gratia elegantiore composuit.

Ergo nec clypeo iuuenis subsistere tantum
Nec dextra ualet: obiectis sic undique telis
Obruitur: strepit assiduo caua tempora circum
Tinnitu galea: et saxis solida aera fatiscunt.
Discussaeque iubae capiti: nec sufficit umbo
Ictibus: ingeminant hastis et troes: et ipse
Fulmineus Menestheus: Tum toto corpore sudor
Liquitur: et piceum [Nec respirare potestas]
Flumen agit: fessos quatit aeger anhelitus artus. Homerus ait.

FVRIVS IN QVARTO ANNALI.

ressatur pede pes: mucro mucrone: uiro uir. Hinc Vergilius ait: Heret pede pes: densusque uiro uir. Homeri est. Hunc secutus hostius poeta in libro secundo belli hystrici ait. Non nisi mihi linguae centum: atque ora sit etiam totidem uocesque liquatae. Hinc Vergilius ait. Non mihi si linguae centum sint oraque centum. Homerica descriptio est equi fugientis: in haec uerba.

Ennius hinc traxit.

Et cum sicut equus qui de praesepibus actus
Vincla suis magnis animis abrupit: et inde

Opposite:

Ambrosius Theodosius Macrobius: Saturnalia   Italian (Rome) completed 14th August 1465

This is a fine example of cursive italic script. It is legible, and yet gives the appearance of an informal but speedy hand, with a pleasing appearance on the page. The late James Wardrop said of this manuscript that it was an example of 'humanistic cursive at its best, before it had become over-formalised'.

V & A M   MS L 1769-1952
f.113r   30 × 20

Miscellany of tracts on various (mainly classical) subjects by Valerius Probus and others
Italian   Last quarter of the 15th century

This volume contains a number of tracts, probably all written out by the same scribe, though at different times and in different scripts. These pages show a cursive italic, and also demonstrate the care taken over the placing of the texts on the page. In the original manuscript the scribe has made use of coloured inks to make his points clear, using green and purple in addition to the more usual red. In spite of its smallness and compression, the script remains clear and businesslike.

V & A M   MS L 1348-1957
ff.12v/13r   15 × 9

Bartolomeo Sanvito: M. Tullii Ciceronis Officiorum Liber I (II, III)
Italian (Rome)
dated 2nd November 1495

On the last page of this manuscript (f.121) it states M.T.C. Officiorum Lib. finit Romae die Lunae II November. MCCCCLXXXXV B.S. *The scribe, Bartolomeo Sanvito, was first identified by James Wardrop, and further studies have led to many other manuscripts being attributed to him. One of the most skilled and influential scribes of the Renaissance, he practised all the contemporary hands; this example shows his italic, and Wardrop believed that it was this which may have influenced the italic types of Aldus Manutius.*

V & A M *MS L 1609-1954*
f.72r *16.5 × 11*

LIB · II ·

est. Deinde. C. Claudius Appij filius. — C. Claudius: App
Multi post Luculli Hortensius Syllanus.
Omes aut. P. Lentulus me consule uicit — P. Lentulus.
supiores. Hunc & Scaurus imitatus. — Scaurus.
Magnificentissima uo nostri Pompeij mu — Pompei muner
nera secundo Consulatu: in qbus omi
bus qd mihi placeat uides? Vitanda
Tam est suspitio auaritiae. Nam Ma — Mamercus.
merco hoi ditissimo praetermissio aedi
litatis Consulatus repulsam attulit.
Quare &si postulatur a populo bonis
uiris si non desiderantibus: attamen
approbantibus faciendu est: modo pro
facultatibus nos ipsi ut fecimus. Et si
quando aliqua res maior aut utilior
populari largitione acqritur: ut Ore — Orestes.
sti nup prandia in semitis/decumae no
mine magno honori fuerunt. Ne M. — M. Seius.
quid Seio uitio datum est: qd in cari
tate annonae/asse modiu populo de
dit. Magna .N. se & inueterata inui
dia nec turpi iactura quando erat
Aedilis: nec maxima liberauit. Sed
honori sumo nup nostro Miloni — Milo.
fuit: qd gladiatoribus emptis rei.p.

LIB III

aliqd uoluptati/condimenti fortasse nō
nihil: utilitatis certe nihil habebit.

HAbes a patre munus Marce fili: mea
quid sententia magnū: sed perinde erit:
ut acceperis. Quanq̃ hi tres libri inter
Cratippi cōmentarios tanq̃ hospites erūt
recipiendi. Sed ut si ipse uenisse Athe-
nas: qđ quid ēēt factū: nisi me e medio
cursu clara uoce patria reuocasset: aliqn
me quoq. audires. Sic qm his uolumini
bus ad te profecta vox mea est: tribue
his tribus quantū poteris: poteris aūt
quantū uoles. Cum uero intellexero te
hoc scientiae genere gaudere: tum & prae
sens tecū propediem (ut spero) & dum
aberis absens loquar. Vale igr mi Cicero: tibiq. psuade: te mihi quidem ēē
carissimum: sed multo fore cariorem:
si talibus monumentis praeceptisque
laetabere.

M·T·C· OFFICIORVM LIB·FINIT
ROMAE DIE LVNAE II NOVEMBR
MCCCCLXXXXV

B S

Bartolomeo Sanvito: M. Tullii Ciceronis Officiorum Liber I (II, III)
Italian (Rome)
dated 2nd November 1495

The last page of this manuscript, showing the colophon with Sanvito's initials.

V & A M MS L 1609-1954
f.121r 16.5 × 11

Aug · Pius · cos · iij · Trib · pot · ij · P · P · Aquedu
ctum in nouis Athenis coeptum á diuo hadri
ano patre suo consummauit : dedicauitque.

Apud Butrotum i Epyro Troia.

· C · Clodio Zosimo pri : & Juliae Euterpe Matri : et · T ·
Pomponio luperco Suo Potine Monumentum
D · S · sibi et Suis fecit.

Tragurię in Basilica Virginis ex Muros.

· Imp · Caesar Diui · F · Aug · parens Coloniae
Murum · et Turris dedit ·

· Ibidem ·

· T · Julius optatus Turis vetustate consumptas
impensa sua restituit ·

Delphis in Templo Pythij Apollinis i pariete.

ΘΕΟΙΣ ΕΠΙ ΑΡΙΣΤΑΓΟΡΑ ΑΡΧΩΝΤΟΣ
ΕΝΔΕΛΦΟΙΣ ΠΥΛΑΙΑΣ ΗΡΙΝΗΣ ΙΕ
ΡΟΜΝΙΜΟΝΟΥΝΤΩΝ ΑΙΤΩΛΩΝ ΠΟ
ΛΕΜΑΡΧΟΥ ΑΛΕΞΑΜΕΝΟΥ ΔΑΜΩΝΟΣ.

Ibidem

· ΠΥΘΙΝ ΜΑΝΤΙΣ ·

Ν ΑΥΘΕΣΩ ΑΥΚΟΕΡΓΕ ΕΜΟΝ ΠΟΤΙ ΠΙΟΝΑ
ΝΗΟΝ ΓΗΝΙΦΙΛΟΣ ΚΑΙΠΑΣΙΝ ΟΛΥΜ.

Publius Victor: P. Victoris De Notis Antiquis [silloge of classical inscriptions] c1500

This manuscript is interesting on many accounts. It is historically of interest in that it provides a collection of classical inscriptions written out in the period of the Renaissance. It is also a fine piece of calligraphy, not only for the beauty of its script, but also in the way it is set out on the page; showing only two sample pages here fails to do it justice. Early in this century the manuscript was in the possession of Edward Johnston, who particularly admired it. He reproduced passages from it in his important book Writing & Illuminating, & Lettering, *published in 1906, and commented on the work itself. A copy of Johnston's manual came into the hands of the young James Wardrop, who modelled his own writing on the reproductions Johnston had provided. On Johnston's death Wardrop acquired the original manuscript, which is now in the Victoria and Albert Museum.*

V & A M   MS L 5161-1977   28 × 20

Opposite:
James Wardrop: Iter Italicum Anno Salutis MCMXLVIII

This manuscript should be compared with p. 128, for it was on that 15th century script that James Wardrop based his own writing. The present manuscript, sadly incomplete, is a record of manuscripts examined by Wardrop, then Deputy Keeper of the V & A Library, during a tour of Italian libraries. Not only was he a fine calligrapher, as can be seen from this document, but he was one of the first scholars to study the humanist manuscripts and scribes in detail. It is fitting that this manuscript should now have found a permanent home in the V & A Library in view of the Library's connections with both Johnston and Wardrop, and its well-known interest in calligraphy.

V & A M   MS L 4287-1964   25 × 20.5

Vat. Lat. 3595.

Statius. Vellum. (21 × 12) cm. No foliation. Typical decoration – spolia opima; Emperor on horseback. Shield blank. f. 1v (3v if blanks are counted), leaf of rose-stained vellum with coarsely executed design: inset, poem in gold "AD LIBRVM" evidently by B.S. Initials, headings and caps. also in his style. Miniature of Orpheus at 6th leaf from end. (no. 56 in Vatican Exhibition, 1950. "Written in Rome by Partenio Minuzio Paolino, the friend of Pomponio Leto." See Cat. p. 43)

B. S.

Vat. Borg. Lat. 336.

Fra Giocondo. On paper, without decorations (21 × 14) cm. Written in brown and red inks. An early work of il nostro※. In dedication, f. 26 reference to Alessandro Cortesio (see supra, Vat. Lat. 10228).

※ I am now disposed to give most of this MS. to Questenberg, for several reasons; but particularly for the peculiar &t ligature. B.S. perhaps wrote the Calendar

B. S. See Campana's letter 4·IX·'48

A. Cortesius

Vat. Lat. 13679.

A. Cortesius, but not, apparently, autograph. (See Vat. schedario)

A. Cortesius

Ottob. Lat. 2989.

Augustino Mafeo. (Questenberg). Writing resembles that of B.S. marginal notes in red, reminiscent of his style.

Questenberg

Ottob. Lat. 1732.

On paper. (Questenberg) Capitals, but not as accomplished as with B.S. For Questenberg see G. Mercati, "Questenbergiana". (Opere Minori, IV, pp. 437–461)

Questenberg

Vat. Lat. 3366.

Xandra. Vellum (18·5 × 11) cm. Christoforo Landino's autograph copy presented to Bernardo Bembo. The script is interesting, & seems to be related to※ MS. Bodl. Canon. Class. Lat. 85; N. York Public Lib. MS. 28; and Modena Cod. Est. Lat. K. 6. 15. Sepia & blue inks. At f. 3 fine initial of Leda & the swan. [See for this MS. Nolhac p. 240]

C. Landino

B. Bembo

※ but not identical with

Ex Tibur in Templo · S · Marię de horto in
Sepulchro Corroso ab uno Latere ·

C · Sextilius · V V & Tiburtium · vod · L · Alphenatius

Lib · Ephebus
herculanius
Augustalis
Curator ·

IIII · K · Septembres · F ·
Cognita petitione
Et Basim Marmo
Herculis et Augu
Auctoritas per
vm · C · Sextilius · Sa
Phebus Non hod
Exornatus S · ET ·
henes auro herc ·
Jacere grate ext
quoque nominus
subscriptione lo
Acilius ue
Exequtub ·
Ensue
Aulla et
Arpendo
Attius ·

Publius Victor: P. Victoris De Notis Antiquis [silloge of classical inscriptions] c1500

A further page from the Italian manuscript linked with both Edward Johnston and James Wardrop.

LA discordia nel ciel prima fu nacque
Fra gli anzoli che furo a Dio rebelli
Spiriti del Phlegetonte in le ardēte acque.
Gli elementi fra lor sempre in flagelli
Di corrumper lun laltro: & generarsi
Nel conflicto si fanno ogni hor piu belli.
Nel uacuo Regno quante prede farsi
Vedessi da gli ucelli: et quante in terra
Fra gli animanti: el pesce i mar uorarsi?
Per ho stado non fu mai senza guerra
Et da neccessita per causa honesta
Chi e constretto a deffendersi non erra.
Sel mal vicino el gregie tuo molesta
O pacti infringa cum dextreza tenta
Prima remouer quel che piu te infesta.
Ma lultimo remedio quando e spenta
Iustitia in tutto: e uindicar cum larmi
Iniuria: che ragion frena et paueta.
Adonq. in consuar el stado parmi
Che la militia sia ferma tutela
Non lasciando ella poi roder da tarmi.

Antonio Vinciguerra, called Cronaca: De principe Libellus [a poem celebrating the appointment of Leonardo Loredano as Doge of Venice] (2 October 1501)
Italian c1502

A cursive italic with no contractions, since no doubt this manuscript was meant for show. The only regular form of decoration the scribe allows himself is the curious extension of the ascenders on the top line of the text, and occasional swash letters, as in the L of the last line. This fast hand is considered by some to have affinities with that of Arrighi and Tagliente.

V & A M MS L 2320-1947
f.10r 22 × 14

Quod Iudices Procuratorum non se impediant de domibus, Statijs, et affictibus ad Ecclesiam Sancti Marci pertinentibus. Capitulũ. C xviij:–

L. 1490. Die. 5. Martij. Inter Dominos Consiliarios:–
A nostra Ill.ma Signoria cõmanda à uoi Signori Zudesi de Procurator, che non debbiate impedirue in alcuna cosa delle Case, Botteghe, Statij, et affitti pertinenti alla Chiesa nostra di San Marco. Saluo tanto, quanto. i. Signori Procuratori de ditta Chiesa richiederà. Però che à loro comesse sono, et voleno, che comesse siano tutte le cose pertinente alle affittation, et exattion d'affitti delle dette Case, et Statij, si come hanno la liberta i Signori del Sal delli affitti pertinenti ad esso suo officio et si come sempre è stato osseruato per. i. detti Signori Procuratori.

Consiliarij

S Ioannes Mauro. S Dominicus Marino.
S Hieronym⁹ de Ca da Pesaro. S Philippus Trono.

Procuratores Sancti Marci non possunt esse Sapientes Consilij, et de additione, nisi vnus tantum pro Procuratia. Capitulum. C xix:–

C. 1495. Die 7 Februarij. In maiori Consilio.
Aptum opportune fuit in maiori Consilio, quod pro

· 80 ·

oßerua al presente. sua Ser^{tà} non s' habbia à impedir, ma li Procuratori di eßa Chiesa habbino il carico di gouernar et amministrar dette entrade, come li parerà per ballotta: tion, et termination della maggior parte di loro. Et se il Ser^{mo} Principe si resentiße d'alcuna cosa, che faceßero li det- ti Procuratori circa le dette entrate, sua Ser^{tà} poßa dedurre tal materia trà li sopranominati, ouero etiam al Consiglio di pregati, come meglio li parerà. Restando etiam ogn'al: tra giurisdittione, et authorità, ch' ha sua Ser^{tà} nella ditta Chiesa, alla presente parte non repugnante, et sempre sia, et eßer s'intenda riseruata l'authorità, ch' ha il Zudegà nostro di Procurator quanto alle cose al suo officio pertinenti :-

IL FINE.

Presbyter Joannes de Vitalibus Brixiæ scripsit, et literis aureis celestinisq; ornauit hunc librum Anno Domini. M.D.L VIII.

Laws and regulations to be observed by the Procurators of the Basilica of St Mark, Venice.
N. Italian signed and dated 1558

This is a most beautifully written north Italian manuscript, of the kind for which printing offered no substitute in view of its limited appeal. Moreover, as this illustration shows, the scribe 'Presbyter Joannes de Vitalibus Brixiæ' signed and dated his work at the end. At first appearance the manuscript looks as though it is a printed book, but in fact the writing is perhaps far more even than would have resulted from contemporary typography in the same style.

V&AM MS L 2158-1947 25.5 × 19

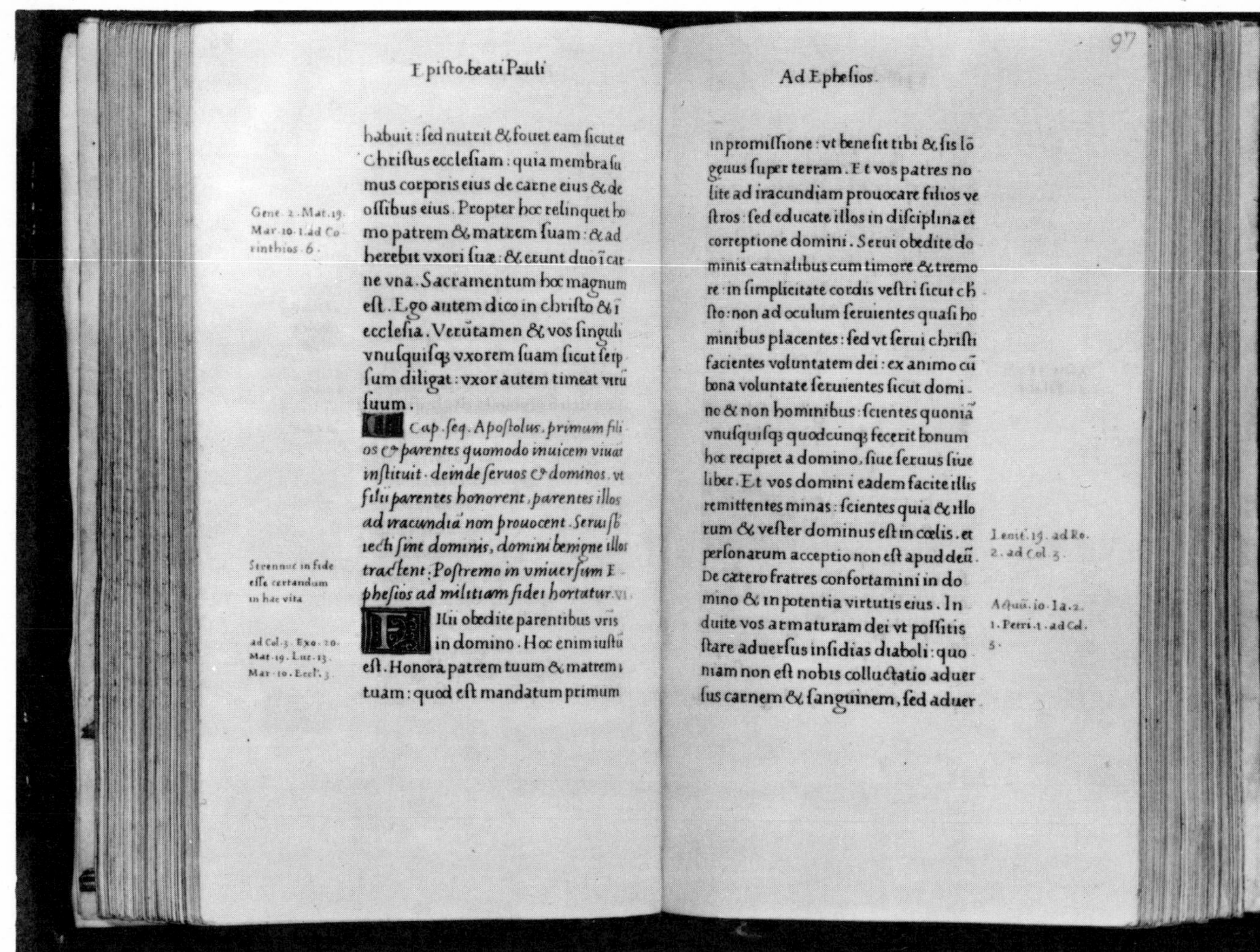

Episto. beati Pauli

habuit: sed nutrit & fouet eam sicut et
Christus ecclesiam: quia membra su
mus corporis eius de carne eius & de
ossibus eius. Propter hoc relinquet ho
mo patrem & matrem suam: & ad
herebit vxori suæ: & erunt duo ī car
ne vna. Sacramentum hoc magnum
est. Ego autem dico in christo & ī
ecclesia. Verūtamen & vos singuli
vnusquisq; vxorem suam sicut seip
sum diligat: vxor autem timeat virū
suum.

Gene. 2. Mat. 19. Mar. 10. 1. ad Corinthios. 6.

*Cap. seq. Apostolus. primum fili
os & parentes quomodo inuicem viuat
instituit. deinde seruos & dominos. vt
filii parentes honorent. parentes illos
ad iracundiā non prouocent. Serui sb
iecti sint dominis, domini benigne illos
tractent. Postremo in vniuersum E
phesios ad militiam fidei hortatur.* VI

Strennue in fide esse certandum in hac vita

Filii obedite parentibus vris
in domino. Hoc enim iustū
est. Honora patrem tuum & matrem
tuam: quod est mandatum primum

ad Col. 3. Exo. 20. Mat. 19. Luc. 13. Mar. 10. Eccl. 3.

97

Ad Ephesios.

in promissione: vt bene sit tibi & sis lō
geuus super terram. Et vos patres no
lite ad iracundiam prouocare filios ve
stros: sed educate illos in disciplina et
correptione domini. Serui obedite do
minis carnalibus cum timore & tremo
re: in simplicitate cordis vestri sicut chri
sto: non ad oculum seruientes quasi ho
minibus placentes: sed vt serui christi
facientes voluntatem dei: ex animo cū
bona voluntate seruientes sicut domino & non hominibus: scientes quoniā
vnusquisq; quodcunq; fecerit bonum
hoc recipiet a domino. siue seruus siue
liber. Et vos domini eadem facite illis
remittentes minas: scientes quia & illo
rum & vester dominus est in cœlis. et
personarum acceptio non est apud deū.
De cætero fratres confortamini in do
mino & in potentia virtutis eius. In
duite vos armaturam dei vt possitis
stare aduersus insidias diaboli: quo
niam non est nobis colluctatio aduer
sus carnem & sanguinem, sed aduer

Leuit. 19. ad Ro. 2. ad Col. 3.

Actuū. 10. Ia. 2. 1. Petri. 1. ad Col. 5.

Epistles French c1500

This beautifully written little manuscript uses the antiqua script for two-thirds of the book, while the remainder is written in italic. However, occasionally both scripts are used together, with great effect, as we can see here. Both scripts are finely written on a smooth white vellum, and although the letters are very small, the words are easily read — even the tiny annotations and references in the margins.

V&AM *MS L 1721-1921*
f.96v-97r *11 × 6.5*

Book of Hours (Use of Rome)
Southern French? c1520

This manuscript probably originated in the south of France and it exhibits a blend of two different styles. It is written in a fine humanist script, and the architectural motifs of the miniature on the left also reflect Renaissance trends. But the right-hand page depicts a border in the Flemish style, so that the work stands as an interesting example from a period of transition. The southern part of France was a natural meeting place of Italian and northern influences.

V&AM Reid MS 73 f.35v/36r
15 × 9.5

Alors ſeront tous nous liubres ouuers,
Et de noz cœurs les ſecretz decouuers,
De noz deſirs, & noſtre fantaſie,
Las ne ſeront aulcuns maſques diuers,
Habitz entiers, ou barres de trauers,
Aultant vauldront les noirs comme les vers,
Pour deguiſer la faulçe hypocriſie.

Soubz beau parler; et doulce contenance,
Soubz frans propoz et modeſte semblãce
Appareſtra mainte orde punaiſie,
Mainte luxure en guyſe d'attemprence;
Pour charite, vne occulte vengence,
Pour humble port, vne eſtreme arrogance,
Et pour amour, ſans amour ialouſie.

Opposite:
Victor Brodeau: Traicté à la louenge de Dieu French
'escrit a Rome l'an Iubile du 1550'

Although written by a Frenchman for a Frenchman ('pour Monsieur Claude d'Urfé'), the manuscript was produced in Rome and shows the influence of contemporary Roman scripts. It will be noticed that while the d *and the* l *are simply made, the* s *tends to be given very special prominence with clubbed terminals — but not in all cases, which suggests that the manuscript was not the work of a professional scribe.*

V&AM MS L 1964-1957 19.5 × 13.5

Victor Brodeau: Traicté à la louenge de Dieu French
'escrit à Rome l'an Iubile du 1550'

The final page of this manuscript, showing the colophon set below a pagan altar on which a lamb is being sacrificed, the whole set in a landscape with a river and ruins — the classical influence on contemporary lettering is thus emphasised.

V&AM MS L 1964-1957
f.30r 19.5 × 13.5

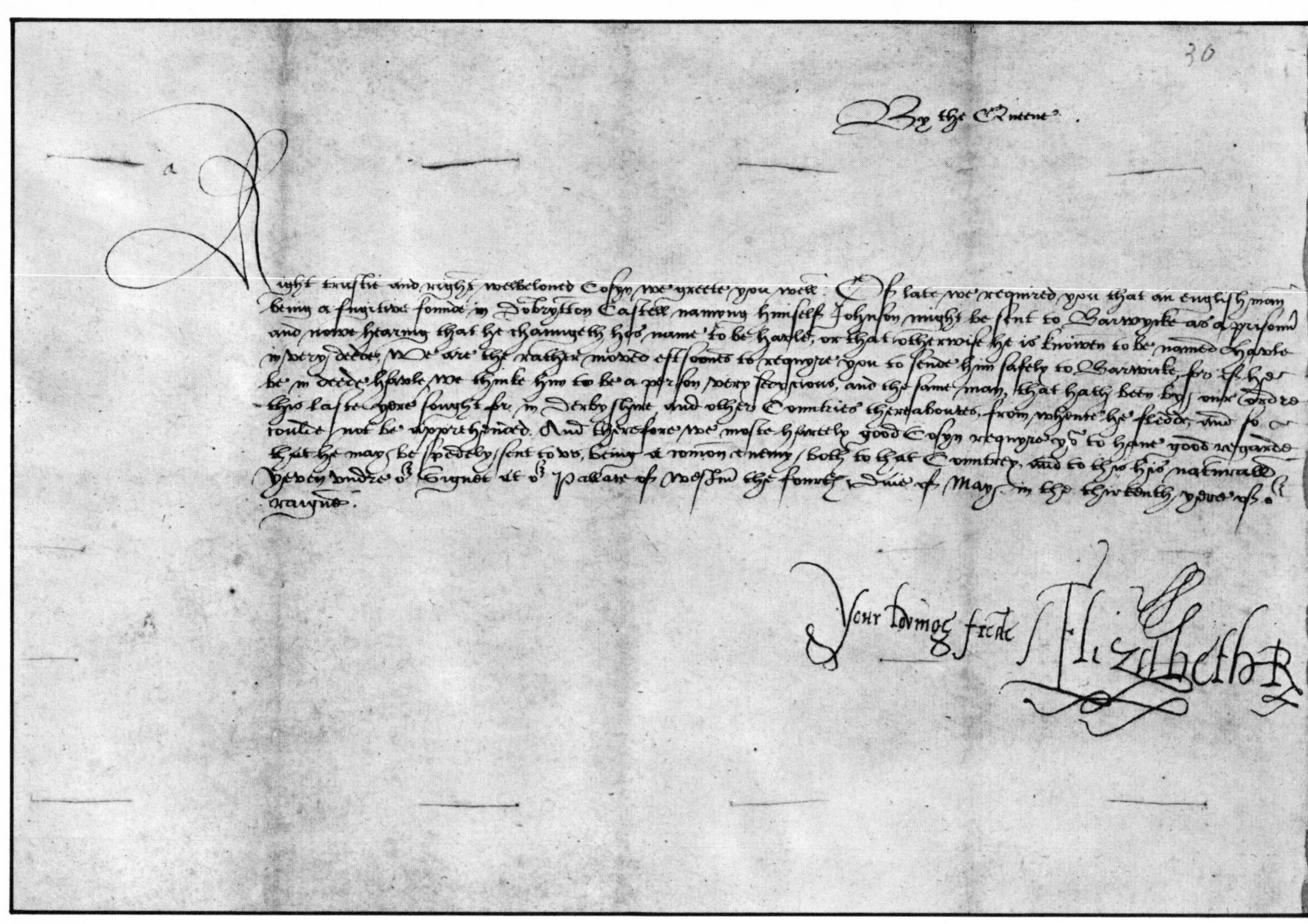

30

By the Quene.

Right trustie and right welbeloved Cosyn we grete you well. Of late we required you that an englishman being a fugitive founde in Dobrytton Castell naming himself Johnson might be sent to Barwyke as a prisoner and nowe hearing that he chaungeth his name to be Harle, or that otherwise he is knowen to be named Harle in very dede, we are the rather moved effsones to require you to sende him safely to Barwike, for if he be in dede Harle we thinke him to be a person very sedicious, and the same man that hath ben by our order this laste yere sought for in Derbyshire and other Countries therabouts, from whence he fledd, and so coulde not be apprehended. And therfore we moste hartely good Cosyn require you to have good regarde that he may be spedely sent to us, being a comon enemy both to that Countrey and to this his naturall. Yeven under our Signet at our Pallace of Westm the fourth daie of May in the thirtenth yere of our raigne.

Your lovinge frede Elizabeth R

Queen Elizabeth I: Letter written to the Earl of Lennox, Regent of Scotland, 1570

The main part of this letter, which would have been written by a secretary or other official, provides a good example of the contemporary English 'secretary hand'. It was the script commonly used for business, either public or private. Even when carefully written, as here, it was quite difficult to read, and it always had a tendency to deteriorate, like most cursive hands. The Queen herself signed the letter, 'Your loving fre(n)de Elizabeth R', and she has done so in an italic script, which she wrote very proficiently.

V & A M   Forster MS 190   22 × 30.5

Amos Lewis: A copy book dedicated to Sir John Petre of West Thorndon, c1580-85

No other writing book is known from the pen of Amos Lewis apart from this manuscript. He states in his 'Epistola' that it is his first work, so it is possible that something further by him may yet be discovered. His examples are charmingly ornamented with strapwork and grotesques in the contemporary style. The 'letter frizée' illustrated here appears in a number of 16th century writing books, presumably as proof of the master's dexterity.

Reproduced by permission of Mr Simon Jervis 9.5 × 14

Esther Inglis: Summarie expositions upon sundrie notable sentences of the Olde Testament made in form of praiers. Last quarter of the 16th century

Esther Inglis is one of the few known women calligraphers. Her family were Huguenot refugees who settled in Edinburgh, where much of her work was done. This manuscript is unsigned, but is very similar to other attributed works. She specialised in small volumes and often decorated them with paintings of flowers. The first part of this manuscript is written out in a fine italic hand, but the second part contains examples of many different scripts then current, including some very exotic (and scarcely legible) ones.

V&AM MS L 3087-1960 8.5 × 6

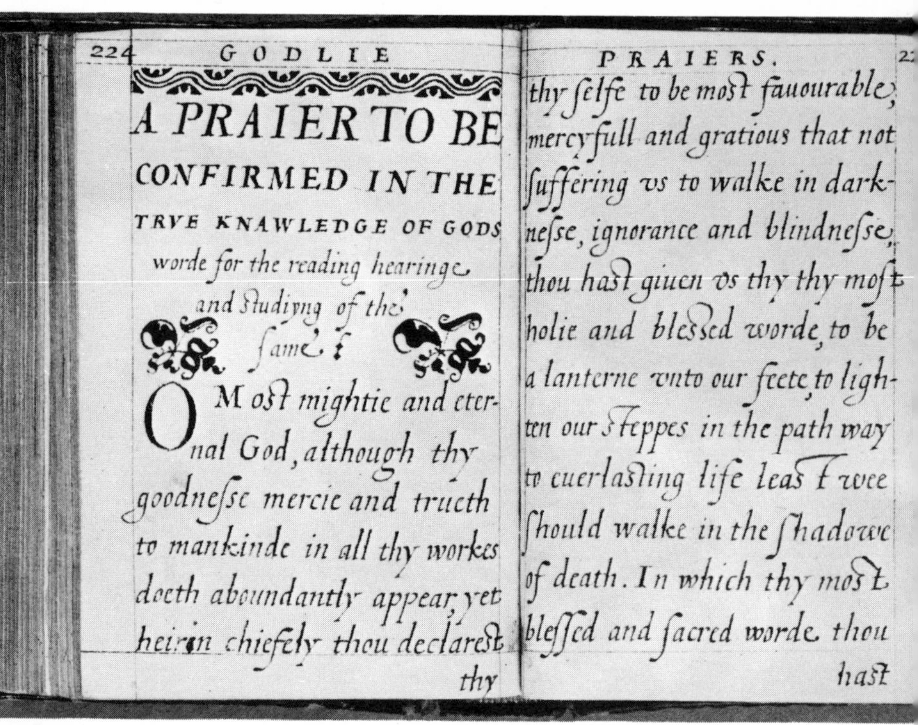

224 GODLIE

A PRAIER TO BE CONFIRMED IN THE TRVE KNAWLEDGE OF GODS worde for the reading hearinge and studiyng of the same.

O Most mightie and eternal God, although thy goodnesse mercie and trueth to mankinde in all thy workes doeth aboundantly appear, yet heirin chiefely thou declarest thy

PRAIERS.

thy selfe to be most fauourable, mercyfull and gratious that not suffering vs to walke in darknesse, ignorance and blindnesse, thou hast giuen vs thy thy most holie and blessed worde, to be a lanterne vnto our feete, to lighten our steppes in the path way to euerlasting life least wee should walke in the shadowe of death. In which thy most blessed and sacred worde thou hast

Esther Inglis: Summarie expositions upon sundrie notable sentences of the Olde Testament made in form of praiers. Last quarter of the 16th century

A further example from the work of one of the few women calligraphers known from the early period. In this illustration it will be noted that Esther Inglis uses the clubbed form of the ascenders.

V&AM MS L 3087-1960 8.5 × 6

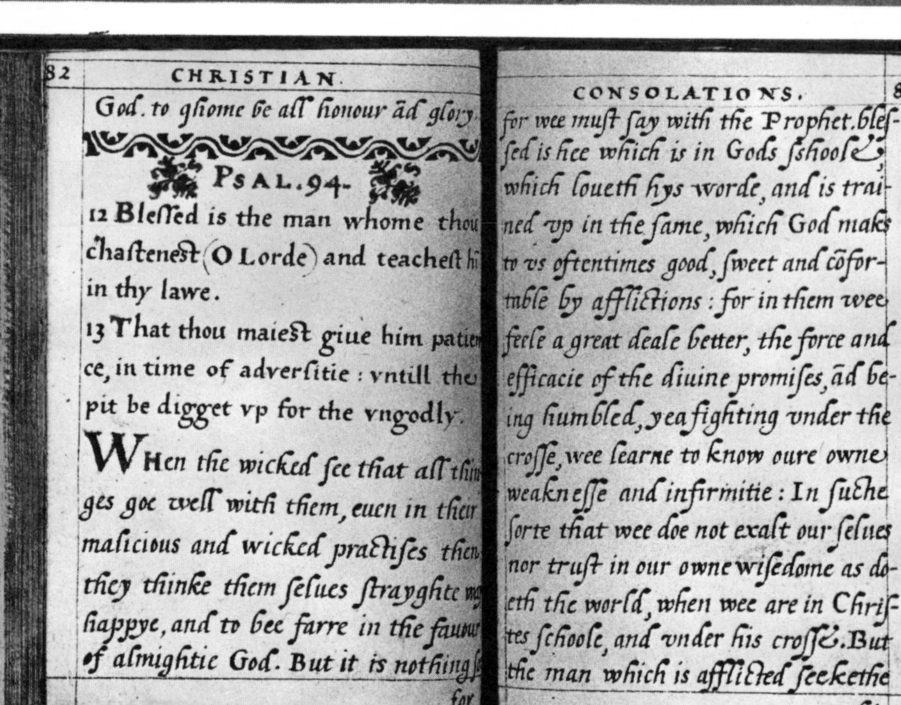

82 CHRISTIAN.

God. to whome be all honour ād glory.

PSAL. 94.

12 Blessed is the man whome thou chastenest (O Lorde) and teachest hi[m] in thy lawe.

13 That thou maiest giue him patience, in time of adversitie: vntill the pit be digget vp for the vngodly.

WHen the wicked see that all thinges goe well with them, euen in their malicious and wicked practises then they thinke them selues straighte way happye, and to bee farre in the fauour of almightie God. But it is nothing so for

CONSOLATIONS. 83

for wee must say with the Prophet. blessed is hee which is in Gods schoole, which loueth hys worde, and is trained vp in the same, which God maks to vs oftentimes good, sweet and cōfortable by afflictions: for in them wee feele a great deale better, the force and efficacie of the diuine promises, ād being humbled, yea fighting vnder the crosse, wee learne to know oure owne weaknesse and infirmitie: In suche sorte that wee doe not exalt our selues nor trust in our owne wisedome as doeth the world, when wee are in Christes schoole, and vnder his crosse. But the man which is afflicted seeketh his

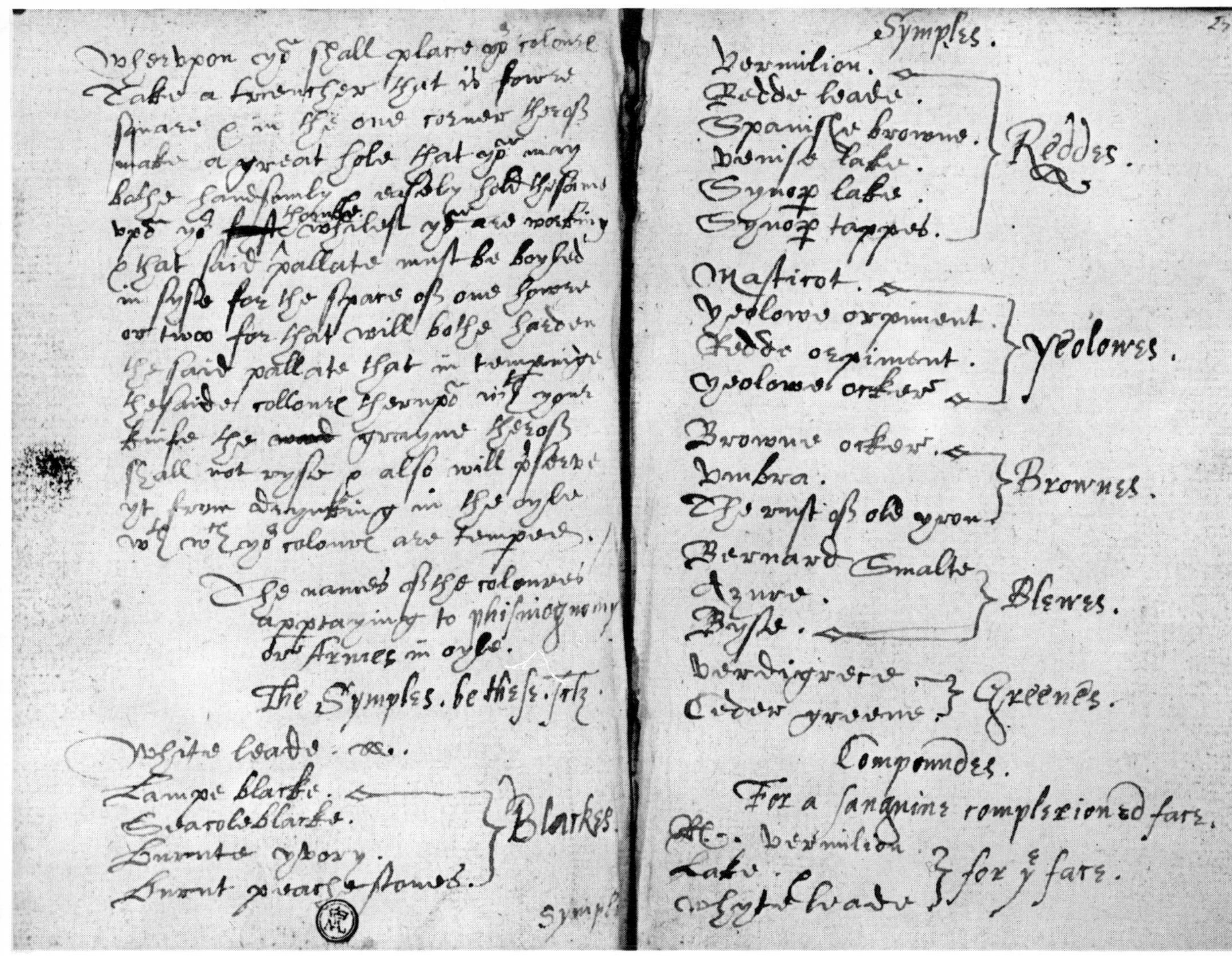

Wherevpon you shall place yor colours
Take a trencher that is fowre
square & in the one corner thereof
make a great hole that yo[u] may
both handsomly & easely hold the same
vpon yor thumbe whilest you are working
that said pallate must be boyled
in syse for the space of one hower
or two for that will both harden
the said pallate that in temperinge
the said colours therupon wt yor
knife the grayne thereof
shall not ryse & also will preserve
yt from drynkinge in the oyle
wherwith yor colours are tempered.

The names of the colours
appertayninge to phisiognomy
and Armes in oyle.

The Symples be these. viz

White leade . &c.

Lampe blacke. } Blackes.
Charole blacke.
Burnte yvory.
Burnt peache stones.

Symples

Symples.

Vermilion. } Reddes.
Redde leade.
Spanishe browne.
Venise lake.
Synop lake.
Synop tappet.

Masticot. } Yeolowes.
Yeolowe orpiment.
Redde orpiment.
Yeolowe orker.

Browne orker. } Brownes.
Vmbra.
The rust of old yron.

Bernard Smalte. } Blewes.
Azure.
Bysse.

Verdigrece. } Greenes.
Cedar greene.

Compoundes.

For a sanguine complexioned face.

Vermilion. } for ye face.
Lake.
Whyte leade

The way how to lyme & howe thow shalt lay thy colours & make syse for lyminge [etc] c1582-1600

This is a practical work for an illuminator or miniature painter, and it is interesting in that the writer uses both secretary and italic script. The main body of the text is written in the typical Elizabethan hand, secretary, but the headings, and the colours listed on the right-hand page, are given prominence by being written in an italic script.

V&AM MS L 1774-1935 15 × 10

SEMPER
EADEM
ER
ER
Qui voudra figurer, d'vn ouurage parfect,
La beauté, la Vertu, l'Ornement, et les graces,
De Nature, des Dieux, de l'vniuers, des Graces,
Accoure contempler la grand' ELIZABETH.

6 The sixteenth century and the rise of the writing masters

Opposite:
Jean de Beauchesne: Hymne à très-haute . . . Princesse Elizabeth Royne d'Angleterre (a poem to Queen Elizabeth I by Georges de la Motthe) 1586

The name of Jean de Beauchesne, the Huguenot scribe of this work, is of considerable importance in the history of handwriting in England. With his collaborator, John Baildon, he published in 1570 the first English copy book, 'A booke containing divers sortes of hands'. He was identified as the scribe of this manuscript by Berthold Wolpe. The work of another Huguenot calligrapher, Esther Inglis, is also illustrated here (p. 140).

Reproduced by permission of the Bodleian Library, Oxford. MS Fr.e.i. f.7 21.5 × 16.5

PRINTING from movable types originated in the mid-15th century in Germany, with the publications of Johann Gutenberg at Mainz. The effect of this revolutionary process on the work of professional scribes was dramatic. The invention of printing did not mean that scribes would no longer be needed, but it did seem that fewer of them would be required. The hard labour of mere copying of books was now removed from the scribe to the printing press, which was able to produce multiple copies of texts, each one exactly the same as the other, and the method was both speedier and cheaper. But where multiple copies were not required, the professional scribe remained in demand, and would do so for centuries. Letters, business records, ceremonial and legal documents – all the items for which it was uneconomic or unpractical to set the printing presses going, would continue to be handwritten, until the invention of the telephone and the typewriter in the 19th century. All this meant that there was still work for the professional scribe, while the fact that more people could now possess books for themselves gave an added stimulus to the skills of reading and writing. To this factor was added the effect of the increase in scholarly and investigative studies brought about by the Renaissance, and all the theological controversies of the Reformation and Counter-Reformation in the 16th century. The voyages of discovery in the same century opened up new trade routes, stimulating commerce and increasing the need for clerks who could write a good clear fluent hand, for printing was of no use in the counting house.

So if the copyist had largely lost his employment, the art of writing had if anything become even more important. Moreover, since printing was essentially something for the masses, there were always some people who despised it accordingly, and continued to require their books to be handwritten specially for their own libraries. By this means work of high quality continued to be carried out for a long time after printing had taken over most work, though in a very limited way and mostly within court circles or at least aristocratic ones. Hence such late works were in the *de luxe* tradition, and some are illustrated in this book. At least this somewhat limited patronage helped to keep the skills of calligraphy and illumination alive, as did such items as ceremonial documents, which were usually individually designed. And of course, in spite of the printing press, scholars continued to borrow and to copy out texts just as they always had, but such writings were usually done in informal scripts, unlike the specially commissioned works. Examples of both kinds can be found illustrated here.

If the 16th century saw the end to a great extent of the copyist scribe, it also saw the rise of a new kind of professional writer, who in many cases actually made use of the printing press to put forward his own work. The new profession was that of the writing master, and the works he produced were in the form of copy books. The number of pupils who could be taught by a master at any one time was obviously limited. If he produced writing copies for his students, then more could obtain instruction. If the master went further, and published these copies, there was no end to the people whose writing skills he could influence. The writing masters of the 16th century quickly realised this, and the number of copy books which issued from the presses proliferated from then on. The first of the writing manuals, and one that has remained of importance, was *La Operina*, by Ludovico degli Arrighi, called Vicentino, which was published in 1522. Arrighi was a writer of briefs in the Papal Chancery, and so ideally placed to teach the new cursive hand. At this period both text and examples were printed from wood blocks, although Arrighi himself had a further significance as a designer of a fine italic type for the printers.

The importance of a type design based on the italic script should not be overlooked. The publication of books in this type will always be associated in particular with the work of Aldus Manutius in Venice, and it has been suggested that Arrighi was associated with him in this. The Aldine italic type enabled complete works of length, such as those of many classical writers and contemporary academics, to be printed in a comparatively small volume. But for the most part the printed book in Italy was based on the Roman script, which was the prevailing hand at the time when the first Italian printing press was set up at Subiaco in 1464. North of the Alps, where the gothic script had continued in fashion, the first books were printed in a gothic black letter or *fraktur* type.

The second important writing book to be produced in Italy was that of Giovanni Antonio Tagliente, who taught handwriting in the Venetian chancery. Tagliente made an important departure when he had part of the text of his book set in italic type, to match some of the alphabets he taught. This work was his *Lo presente libro* . . . published in 1524. The third of the great Italian writing masters was Giovanni Battista Palatino who included a great variety of hands in his manuals, the first of which was *Libro nuovo d'imparare a scrivere* issued in 1540.

By the middle of the 16th century, the writing master and his profession were sufficiently well established to allow for a certain amount of criticism. Francesco Cresci in his book *Essemplari di piu sorti lettere*, 1560, for example, criticised the models of Palatino for being too slow to perform. Indeed one of the enduring features throughout the 16th, 17th and 18th centuries was the continual carping and quarrelling between exponents of different styles of writing. Some of their differences may appear so slight to the modern eye as to cause wonder at all the fuss. But by far the greatest source of controversy was to be opened up with the publication in 1571 of Giulantonio Hercolani's work *Essemplare utile*. . . . The significance of this publication was that it used copperplate engraving in place of the more usual woodcut. Hercolani employed the new medium with restraint, but it was obvious that the burin (or graver) could reproduce the strokes of the pen with considerable facility –

or even improve on them. It was this new development which was to prove the undoing of so many later writing masters, who sacrificed the greater legibility of the new scripts in favour of sheer virtuosity. The first to start what was to prove an extremely popular fashion was Tomaso Ruinetti in his *Idea del buon scrittore*, published in 1619. In this were seen for the first time the involved calligraphic flourishes which were to be such a feature of 17th century copy books.

During the late 15th and early 16th centuries the new styles of writing and the new invention of printing spread out from the lands where they had originated, to be taken up in other west European countries. Caxton issued the first books printed in England in the last quarter of the 15th century, and the humanist scripts arrived at about the same time. As the 16th century progressed, the impact of printing was felt ever more widely among the population, but the humanist learning and scripts remained much more limited in their impact, the court and the universities being the places most affected by the ideas of the Italian Renaissance. Elsewhere the gothic tradition remained strong, further augmented by the acceptance by the first English printers of the textura letters for their type models. Developments in Italy were quite well known to the intelligentsia of the day, but an additional bar to communication was set up following Henry VIII's break with Rome in the 1530's, and all the subsequent turmoil of the Protestant Reformation. The equation of the Pope, as Bishop of Rome and ruler of Italian lands, with all that was inimical to the new Protestant settlement, inevitably had an effect on the importation of Italian and humanist ideas throughout the second half of the 16th century. But the embargo was never complete, as the records of the time make clear, since Italian influence, whether of fashion or learning, was constantly referred to in both the official and the informal writings of the time.

It comes as no surprise therefore to learn that the first English copy book appeared much later than those in Italy or some other European countries. *A book containing divers sortes of hands*, by John de Beauchesne, a Huguenot refugee, and John Baildon, was published in 1570. It contained a variety of the hands then current in England, of which the two most frequently to be met with were the secretary and the Italian hands, although for many years to come legal documents continued to use the more traditional scripts – and the writing masters to teach them.

The contacts between Italy and Spain in the 16th century were close, and no doubt emboldened by the success of the early Italian writing books, in 1548 Juan de Yciar produced *Recopilacion subtilissima intitulada orthographica pratica*, better known from its second enlarged edition of 1550 by the title of *Arte subtilissima. . . .* This first Spanish writing book was a very fine production, produced by woodcuts of which the engraver was Juan de Vingles. The book contained some especially remarkable examples of white-on-black printing. Towards the end of the century there appeared another important Spanish copy book by Francisco Lucas *Arte de escrevir . . .*, 1580. This book was to prove especially significant in the subsequent development of two major Spanish hands, of which Lucas offered his own version. These were forms of the *bastarda* and the *redondilla* which remained in use in Spain for several centuries.

Other countries of western Europe also produced important copy books during the 16th century, most of them based largely on Italian models. Indeed, *Literarum Latinarum . . .* by Gerard Mercator, published in Antwerp

The portrait of Giovanni Battista Palatino from the title-page of his Libro nuovo *. . . 1540. Palatino lost no opportunity to indicate his pride in his Roman citizenship* — 'cittadino romano'.

V&AM L 1532-1952

in 1540, was in fact only the third manual, chronologically, to deal with th italic script, the two preceding ones being those of Arrighi and Tagliente. I Germany however, existing traditions of handwriting produced a rathe different style of copy book. The textura or gothic script, as noted earlie remained in use much longer in Germany and was used as the model for th first printed books, which inevitably prolonged its life. Humanism and it scripts were of course known in German lands, but the gothic letter prove too strong to be supplanted in daily use. It was Johann Neudörffer the Elde who gave a definitive form to German handwriting by the use of *Fraktur* scrip in his *Ein gute Ordnung . . .* published in Nuremberg in 1538. This was th style of writing which continued to be published and used in German land for over four centuries. A version of it was transplanted in the 18th century b German immigrants to the United States, where it re-emerged in its characteristic form as 'Pennsylvania Dutch' (*Deutsch*).

Apart from those published in Italy, there has been little general study o the 16th century copy books, although individual publications or master have been the subject of detailed surveys. The survival of such books ha inevitably been haphazard, since they were not obvious candidates for preservation, but rather objects for practical use. It is possible that more remain t be discovered as the interest in them grows. Certainly by the end of the 16t century Italy, France, Spain, the Netherlands, Switzerland, Germany an Britain had all produced similar copy books. These generally containe examples of the various hands then current in each country, with a sprinklin of foreign scripts. But by the end of the century, the almost universal use o engraving on copperplates to reproduce the line of the pen brought about considerable transformation in the whole style of the copy book, and reverse the relative importance of the pen and the graver.

The portrait of Juan de Yciar from his Arte subtilissima *. . ., 1550.*

V&AM L 412-1895

Graue fatica non ti fia ad imparar fare le
littere Maiuscule, quando nelle pic=
cole harai firmato bene
la mano, et
eo maxime ch'io ti ho
dicto che li dui principij delle
Piccole sonno anchora quelli delle Grandi
come continuando il scriuere, da te
medesimo uenerai
cognoscendo
Non ti diro adunque altro, saluo che te
sforzi imparar fare le tue Maiuscule
Come qui apresso ri=
trouerai per esse=
pio designato

A XI

Ludovico degli Arrighi, surnamed Vicentino: Regola da imparare scrivere varii caratteri de littere con li suoi compassi et misure. Et il modo di temperare le penne secondo la sorte de littere che vorrai scrivere [etc]. 1533

This work is a re-issue of one published the previous year, which itself was printed from the blocks of the original 1522 edition of Arrighi's La Operina, *considered by many to be the finest of all copy books. The first part of this book is written in chancery cursive, or cancellaresca, of which Arrighi, a writer of briefs in the Papal Chancery, was an elegant exponent. The second part uses an italic hand among others. Arrighi was also a type designer, with a special interest in italic types, which are essentially calligraphically based.*

V&AM L. 960-1901 19 × 13

Ludovico degli Arrighi, surnamed Vicentino: Regola da imparare scrivere [etc]. 1533

Another page from Arrighi's manual in which he demonstrates the form of letters used in writing Papal briefs. This illustration is taken from the 1533 reissue of the work published the previous year, itself printed from the blocks of the original 1522 edition of La Operina. *This probably accounts for the form of the date given here.*

V&AM L 960-1901 19 × 13

LITERA DA BREVI:

A a b c d e e f g g h i k l m n o p q r s s t u x y z

:~: Marcus Antonius Casanoua :~

Pierij vates, laudem si opera ista merentur,
Praxiteli nostro carmina pauca date.
Non placet hoc; nostri pietas laudanda Coryti est;
Qui dicat hæc; nisi vos forsan uterq; mouet;
Debetis saltem Dijs carmina, ni quoq;, et istis
Illa datis. iam nos mollia saxa sumus.

A A B B C C D D E E F F G G H H I I
K L L M M N N O P P Q Q R R S
S T T V V V X X Y Z & & & &

Ludouicus Vicentinus scribebat Romæ anno salutis MDXXIII

Dilecto filio Ludouico de Henricis laico
Vicencio familiari nostro.

Opposite:

Giovanni Antonio Tagliente: Lo presente libro insegna la vera arte delo excelle(n)te scrivere de diverse varie sorti de litere [etc]. 1524

Tagliente's work was mostly conducted in the north of Italy, and especially in the area of the Veneto; this book was published in Venice. Some of the pages in Tagliente's manual were printed from types cut to resemble italic script. This illustration shows an example of his cursive hand.

V&AM 5.x.1874 20.5 × 15

Eglie manifesto Egregio lettore, che le lettere Cancellaresche sono de uarie sorti, si come poi ueder nelle scritte tabelle, le quali to scritto con mesura e arte, Et per satisfatione de cui apitisse una sorte, et cui unaltra, Io to scritto questa altra uariatione de lettere la qual uolendo imparare osserua la regula del sottoscritto Alphabeto :

A a. b. c. d. e e. ff. g. h. i. k. l. m. n. o. p p. q. g. r. s. s. t. u. x. y. z. &.

Le lettere cancellaresche sopranominate se fanno tonde longe large tratizzate e non tratizzate & per che io to scritto questa uariacione de lettera la qual imparerai secundo li nostri precetti et opere.

A a a b. c. d. e e. f. g. h. i. k. l. m. n. o. p. q. r. s. s. t. u. x y z &.

Seguita lo eſſempio delle lre che pono
ligarſi con tutte le ſue ſequenti, in tal mo=
do cioe

aa ab ac ad ae af ag ah ai ak al am an
ao ap aq ar as aſ at au ax ay az

Il medeſmo farai con d i k l m n u.
Le ligature poi de c f s ſ t ſonno
le infra=
scritte

ct, fa ff fi fm fn fo fr fu fy,
st st
ſt ſſ ß ſt, ta te ti tm tn to tq tr tt tu
tx ty

Con le reſtanti littere de lo Alphabeto, che
ſono, b e g h o p q r x y z z
non ſi deve ligar mai lra
alcuna ſequente

Ludovico degli Arrighi, surnamed Vicentino: Regola da imparare scrivere varii caratteri de littere con il suoi compassi et misure 1533

A further page from Arrighi's influential manual (taken from another copy) which shows the method of making the ligatures so characteristic of this style, as well as the joining strokes of other letters.

V & A M L 3077-1960

See below an example of the letters
that can be joined with any that follow
to Wit

aa ab ac ad ae af ag ah ai ak al am an
ao ap aq ar as aſ at au ax ay az,

The same can be done with d i k l m n u.
The ligatures for c f s ſ t are
written
below

ct, fa ff fi fm fn fo fr fu fy,
st st
ſf ſſ ß ſt, ta te ti tm tn to tq tr tt tu
tx ty

Concerning the other letters of the Alphabet,
which are b e g h o p q r x y z z
one ought not to tie any to
the letter following.

John Howard Benson: The first writing book: an English translation & facsimile text of Arrighi's *Operina*, the first manual of the Chancery hand, with introduction and notes by J. H. Benson, 1955.

This interesting tour-de-force shows what can be done with the calligraphic models included in this section of the present book. Not only has Benson translated the Arrighi text, but he has planned it as a counterpart to the Italian original, with all the complexities of adaptation that implies.

V&AM L 873-1955 21.5 × 14.5

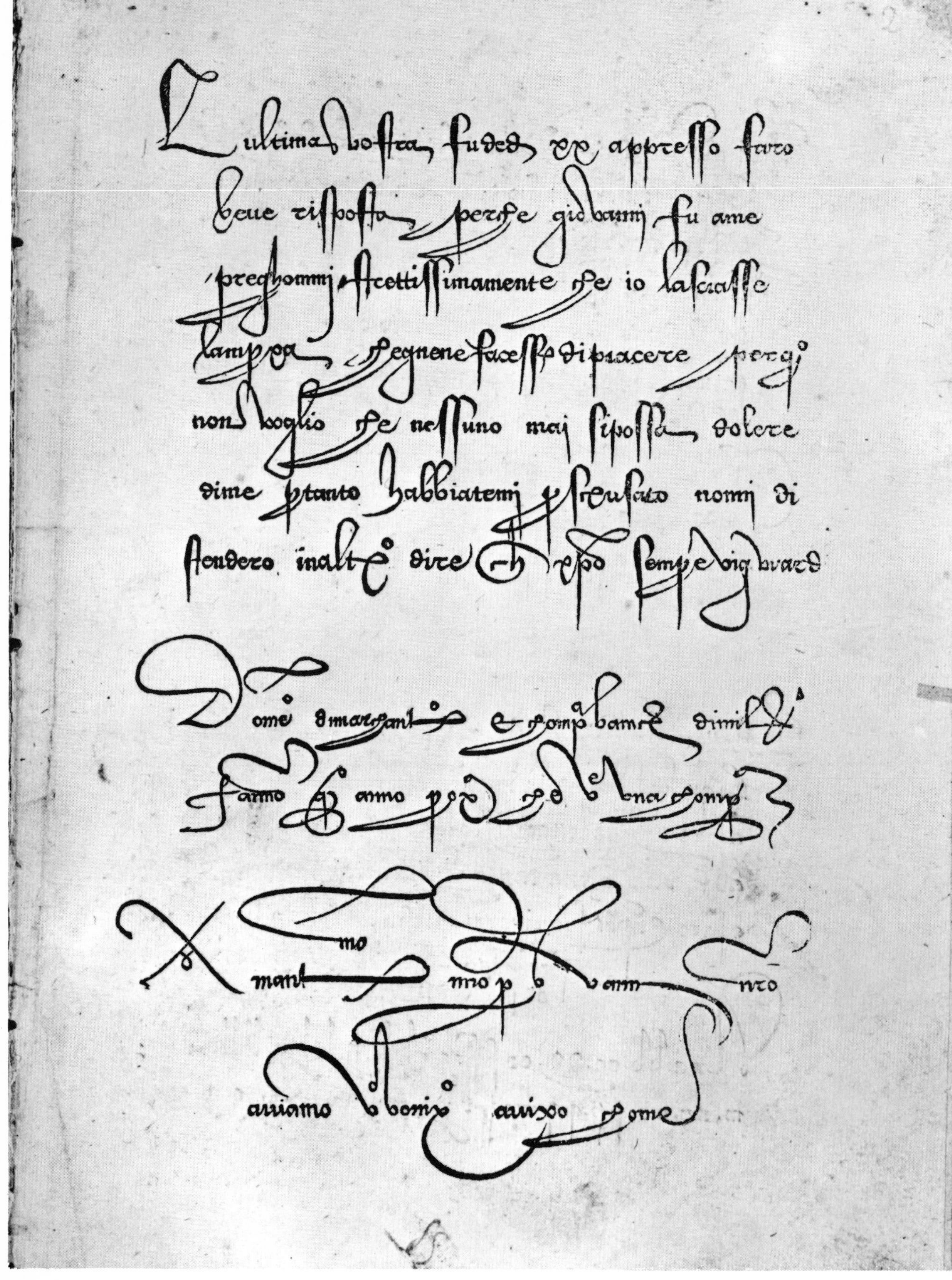

Lultima vostra fu de [illegible] xx appresso faro
breve risposta perche giovanni fu a me
preghommi affettissimamente che io lasciasse
la impresa segnene facesse di piacere perche
non voglio che nessuno mai si possa dolere
di me per tanto habbiatemi per scusato non mi
stendero in altro a dire che Xpo sempre vi guardi

Opposite:
Giovanni Antonio Tagliente:
Lo presente libro insegna la vera arte delo excelle(n)te scrivere de diverse varie sorti de litere [etc]. 1524

Tagliente was, with Arrighi, one of the most important calligraphers and writing masters of the 16th century. At least thirty editions of this work were published in that century alone. The examples show various scripts and alphabets including italic; this page shows the tortured forms which some of the scripts were to assume at the end of the century.

V&AM 5.x.1874 20.5 × 15

Giovanni Battista Palatino: Libro nuovo d'imparare a scrivere tutte sorte lettere antiche et moderne di tutte nationi [etc]. 1540

This work, like all the earliest copy books, was engraved on wood. The first part shows the chancery script (used in the Papal Chancery), which was still considered fashionable. The second part of the book deals with cryptography, and the third demonstrates unusual alphabets.

V&AM L1537-1952 20.5 × 14

Et che' senza esso non si puo
scriuere' pure vna sola
lettera,
Et conseguentemente, la poca
auuertenza di essi che l'han
pretermesso, & imperfettio
ne de' loro precetti.
Et se' auuertirete' trouarete' ques to
Secondo Tratto in tutte' le' lre'
de l'Alphabeto
per
modo diretto, quale' e'l
modo suo naturale,
Et quattro sole' ne' truouo che' lo conten-
gono per modo obliquo, che' son queste.
s x y z

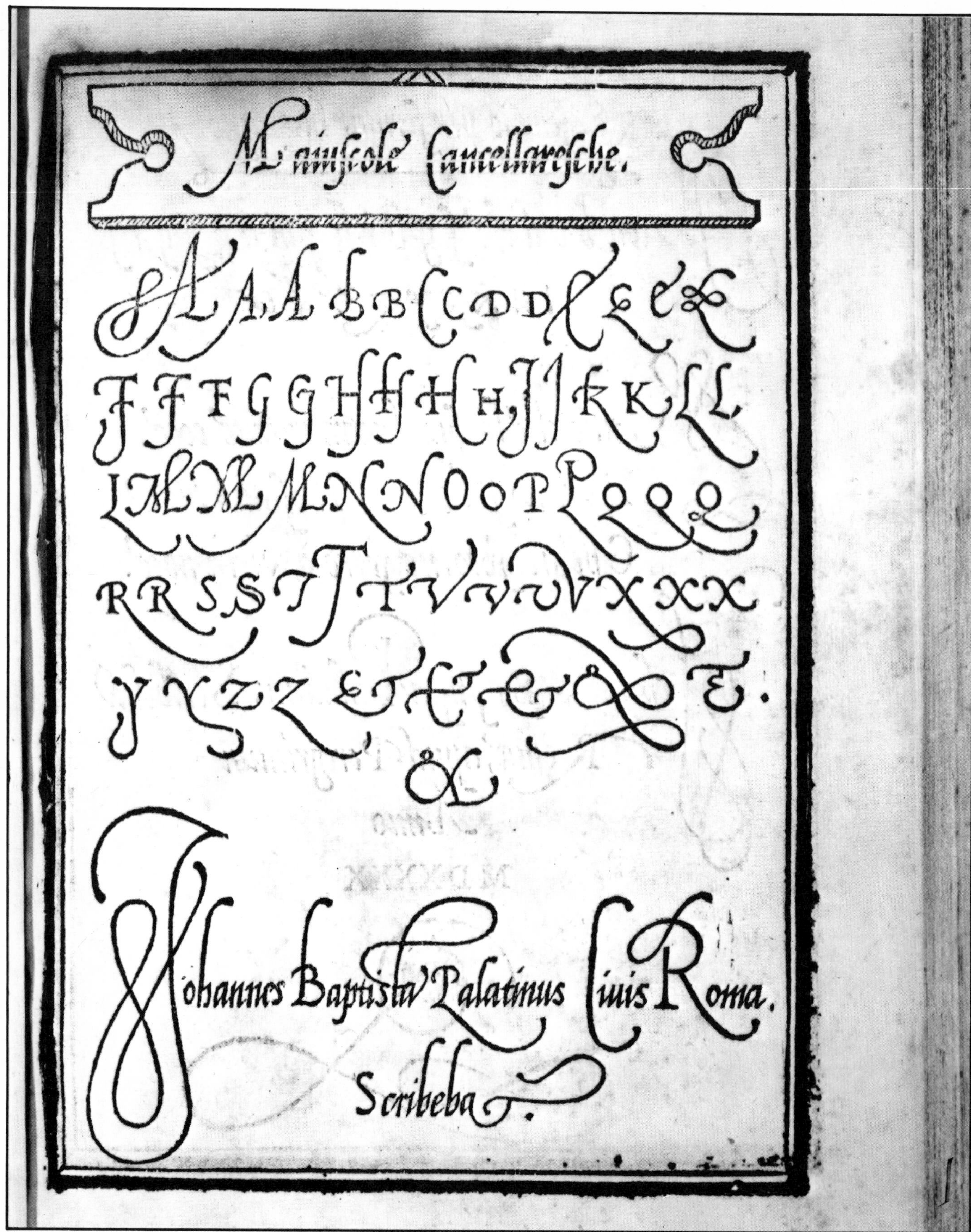
Maiuscole Cancellaresche.
Iohannes Baptista Palatinus Ciuis Roma.
Scribeba.

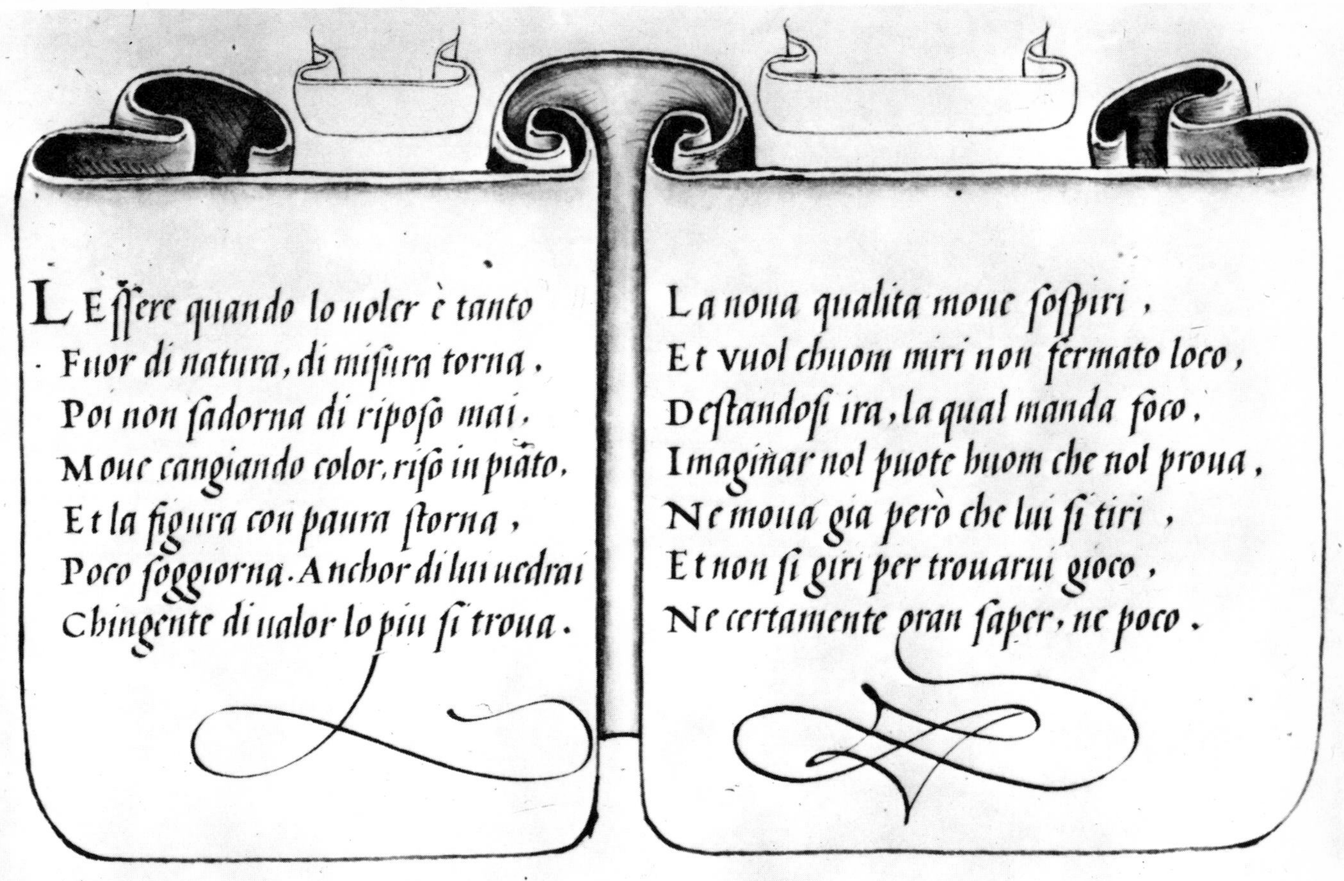
L Essere quando lo uoler è tanto
Fuor di natura, di misura torna .
Poi non s'adorna di riposo mai .
Moue cangiando color, riso in piãto .
Et la figura con paura storna ,
Poco soggiorna . Anchor di lui uedrai
Chi gente di ualor lo piu si troua .

La noua qualita moue sospiri ,
Et vuol ch'huom miri non fermato loco ,
Destandosi ira, la qual manda foco .
Imaginar nol puote huom che nol proua ,
Ne moua gia però che lui si tiri ,
Et non si giri per trouarui gioco ,
Ne certamente gran saper, ne poco .

Giovanni Battista Palatino:
Writing book
Italian (Rome)   1541 or later

This interesting manuscript by Palatino forms a fitting complement to his important published copy books also illustrated here (p153, 154). The manuscript, like the copy books, contains examples of different hands, including the chancery script for which he was much admired.

Reproduced by permission of the Bodleian Library, Oxford.   MS Canon. Ital. 196 f.36r   16.5 × 23.5

Opposite:
Giovanni Battista Palatino: Libro nel quale s'insegna a scrivere ogne sorte lettere   1548

This is a re-issue of the work first published in 1545; Palatino's manuals were very popular, although little is now known of his life. He was, however, very proud of his Roman citizenship, which he acquired in 1538 and frequently alluded to, as in this illustration. It is interesting to note the various forms of capital letters which Palatino offers in his cancellaresca hand.

V & A M   L 2138-1952

Ugo da Carpi: Thesauro de scrittori 1535

The title-page of this work, illustrated here, could not be more explicit. Ugo da Carpi was known primarily as an accomplished wood block cutter, who is believed to have assisted Arrighi in the production of La Operina *in 1522. Sigismondo Fanti, to whom Ugo da Carpi makes reference here, produced a book in 1514 on geometrically constructed letters. The work by Ugo da Carpi is indeed a treasury of scripts and of other information relating to handwriting.*

V&AM L 1990-1884 20 × 14

THESAVRO DE SCRITTORI

Opera artificiosa laquale con grandissima arte si per pratica come per geometria insegna a Scriuere diuerse sorte littere: cioe Cancellarescha: merchantescha: formata: Cursiua: Antiqua: moderna: et bastarda, de piu sorte: cum uarij, e bellissimi exempli. & altre sorte littere de uarie lingue: cioe Grecha: hebraicha: Caldea & Arabicha: Tutte extratte da diuersi et probatissimi Auttori: & massimamente da lo preclarissimo SIGISMVNDO fanto nobile ferrarese: mathematico: et Architettore eruditissimo: dele mesure, e ragione de littere primo inuentore: Intagliata per Ugo da Carpi: Cum gratia: et Priuilegio

A S

Anchora insegna de atemperare le Penne secundo diuerse sorte littere, e cognoscere la bontade de quelle, e carte: e fare inchiostro et Verzino. Cenaprio, e Vernice: cum multi altri secreti pertinenti alo Polito: et Eccellente Scrittore: come per te medesimo legendo imparara. Ne lanno di nostra salute.

M·D·XXXV

A A B C D E F G J K L M N O P Q R S T V.

Se dal mondo sempre non fussero state in somma ueneratione le sacrosante lettre humanissimo lettore non haurebbono gli antichi cosi longamente conteso à cui douesse donar la palma della inuentione di esse Imperoche alcuni attribuiuano q̃ gloria al Magnanimo Hercule, alt. a Nicostrata od'à Carmenta, altrj a Palamede nella guẽ Troiana, moltj a Numa Pompilio à cuj erano diuine cose reuelate dalla Nimp. Egeria, & pure erano quelle dal suo principio roze, et mal formate, Pensa tu adunque di che laude siano degni q̃lli che ornate et terse anoi le dimostrano &

A a a b b c d d e f ff g Giouan Batt. Car.mo b y j k.mo l m n o p q r.mo

Vespasiano Amphiareo: Un novo modo d'insegnar a scrivere et formar lettere di piu sorti [etc]. 1548

Little is known about Amphiareo, a Franciscan friar, though his only printed work is important in the history of the development of the chancery cursive script. His use of the loops and joins more common in mercantile scripts helped to produce a more speedy hand.

V & A M L 2037-1931 15 × 21.5

A A a. b b. c c. d d. e e. f ff. g g. h h. ij. k k. l l. m m

Humanissimo & osseruandissimo S. mio, Tra tutti gli deuoti serui di V. R.ma S.ig.
Vespasiano Amphyareo Ferrarese Minoritano Conuentuale, porta scolpita nel=
li intimi precordij la uostra diuinissima imagine; et con animo tutto pieno di religio=
so affetto, appende alla clementissima sua cortesia, la presente tabula, non altrimete
che sogliano quelli che saluati da maritimi naufragij lieti consagrano uoluntarij
doni alli honorati altari del gran p.dre Nettuno. Et con piatoso core pregano il
terribil Eolo che con piaceuol aura gli riduchi à lor paterni lidij. Et aquella mi R ac.o

N n. o o. p p p. q q. R r. s ss. s s. ß. t t. u. x. y. z. &.

A A c o a b b c d e f ff g h ij k l m n o p q r s s t u x y z &.

Sereniss.o Principe hoggi il R.mo et Illustriss. Cardinal di Lorena mi hà introdutto in cam.a
di sua M.ta Christianissima, & hò esposto à quella quanto haueuo in mandatis da
V. Sublimità laquale mi hà udito con allegra faccia, E dipoi molte parole si hà rissolto
in quanto V. Celsitudine potrà uedere per la l.ra Ziffrata la contra Ziffra della q.le,
è apresso il Segretario nouello, uscito dalla presentia del Rè Christianiss.o ho ren=
gratiato assai sua R.ma et Illus.ma Signoria della introduttione, con parole à ciò ac=
commodate, Ne altro per hora à V. Serenità mi raccomando & offero &c.

D. V. S.ta Fideliss.o Ser. Frate Vespasiano Amphiareo.

Opposite:
Vespasiano Amphiareo: Un nuovo modo d'insegnar a scrivere et formar lettere di piu sorti, che da altri non prima c'hora usate 1548

Two further plates from this work

Ferdinando Ruano: Sette alphabeti di varie lettere, formati con ragion geometrica 1554

Ruano, although a native of Spain, was employed as scrittore latino *in the Vatican Library from 1541 until his death in 1560. This is his only published work, and in it he tried, not very successfully, to give Renaissance hands a geometric basis, for which the cancellaresca is especially unsuited. The printing of this volume in italic type should also be noted, since the influence of the humanist scribes was so significant in its development.*

V&AM L 1387-1896

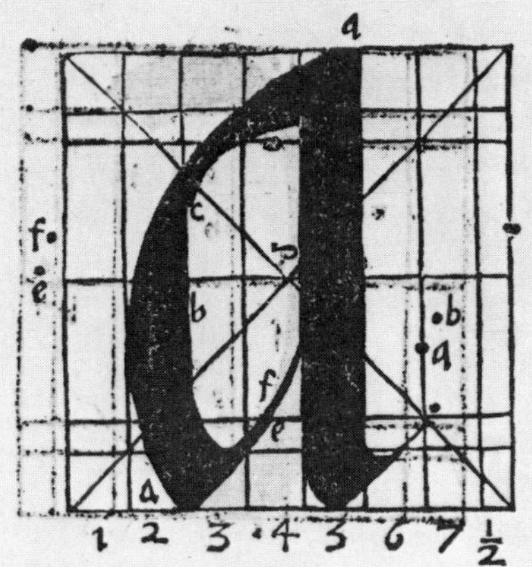

LA lettera .A. ſi forma nel ſuo quadro il qual tu partirai come io t'ho detto: & per far il ſuo caſo metterai il compaſſo nel punto del.a. che ſta nella 7. linea ſotto il diametro, & riſponda ſopra la.6. linea doue ti ſegna un'altra.a. & farai mezo circolo che forniſca alla.3.linea doue trouarai un'altra.a. Il ſuo ouato, ouer cauo ſi forma in tre mezi circoli, cioè mettendo il compaſſo nel punto del.b. che trouarai alla.7. linea ſotto il diametro, & riſponda alla.3.linea, & cominciarai dal detto diametro doue ti ſegna l'altro.b. & uenirà al mezo della terza teſta: il ſecondo ſarà il punto del.c. il qual trouarai nella linea che ſerra il quadro à mano manca ſopra il diametro, & riſponderà il compaſſo alla.3. linea cominciando dal detto diametro, et andarà di ſopra fin alla linea angolare: il terzo ſarà il punto del.d. il qual trouarai nella.5. linea ſopra il diametro, & riſponda di ſopra la medeſima linea, & alla prima linea ſotto quella del quadro, & uenirà fin alla angolare, che ſi lieghe con quella del.c. La ſua tondezza di ſotto ſi forma mettendo il compaſſo nel punto del e, & riſponda ſotto la.3.linea, & farai mezo circolo che arriui alla.5.linea ſotto il diametro, farai unaltro mezo circolo ſopra queſto, & diſcoſto un quinto mettendo il compaſſo nel punto del.f. liquali due punti.e, & .f. trouarai a man dritta di fuora al quadro, & sarà formato il caso. La ſua gamba uuole eſſer dritta, et diſcoſta dal detto caſo due teſte. In loco di baſe farai una teſtina ſguinza conforme a i punti che trouarai. E te biſogna auuertire che come hai fatto queſta.a. farai il b.c.d.e.g.h.o.p.q.x. con quelli medeſimi punti, et circoli. Et queſto ti baſti hauendo l'eſſemplare inanzi.

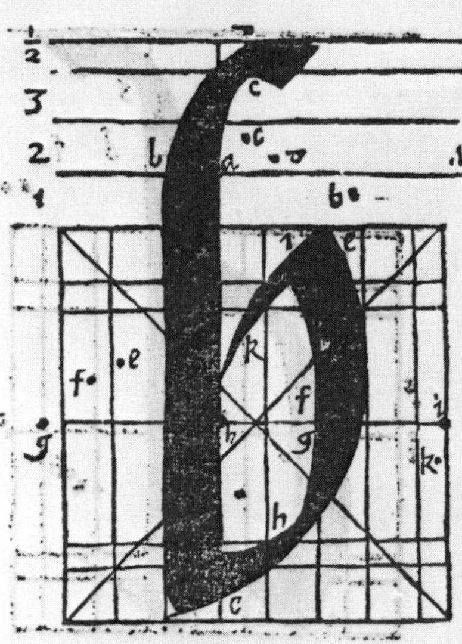

LA lettera .B. ſi forma come l'a, ſaluo chel ſuo aſtillo eſce fuora del quadro tre teſte, & meza, & della prima teſta ſopra il quadro farai la ſua tondezza con un poco di teſtina anchora in tondo: & per farla ſeguirai l'ordine de i punti come nell'a. & queſto aſtillo ti ſeruirà per d.f.h.l.

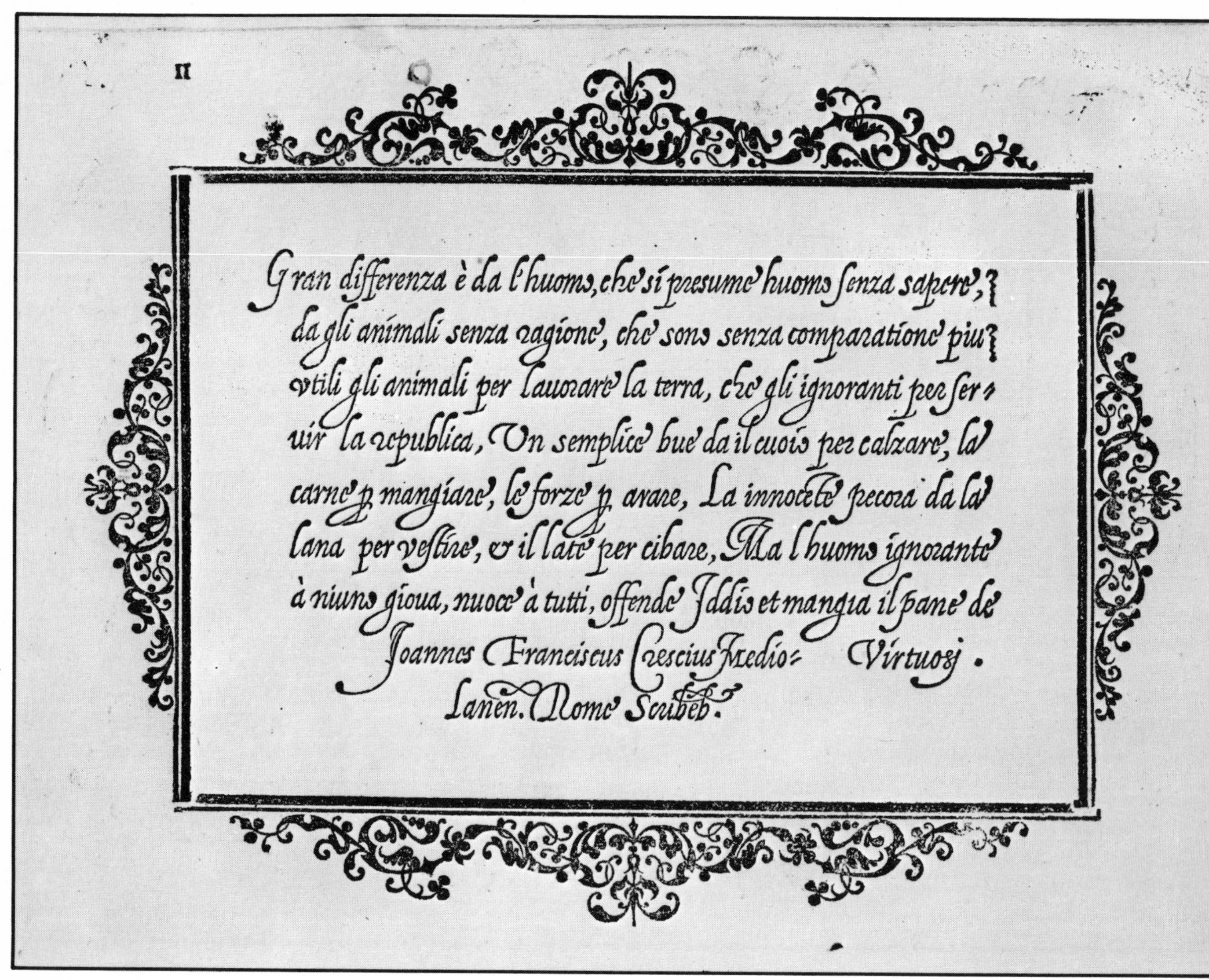

II

Gran differenza è da l'huomo, che si presume huomo senza sapere,
da gli animali senza ragione, che sono senza comparatione piu
vtili gli animali per lauorare la terra, che gli ignoranti per seruir la republica, Vn semplice bue da il cuoio per calzare, la
carne p mangiare, le forze p arare, La innocēte pecora da la
lana per vestire, & il latte per cibare, Ma l'huomo ignorante
à niuno gioua, nuoce à tutti, offende Iddio et mangia il pane de
Ioannes Franciscus Crescius Medio- Virtuosi.
lanen. Rome Scribeb.

Giovanni Francesco Cresci:
Essemplare di piu sorti lettere
1560

Cresci has been called the first calligrapher of the Baroque, and certainly he brought changes into current styles of writing. He considered existing forms too slow and heavy, and endeavoured, by making greater use of joins to the letters, to produce a more flowing hand. The result gave his writing a pronounced slope as well as introducing certain idiosyncracies such as the heavily clubbed ascenders.

V & A M L 133-1954 15 × 21.5

ODISTI Omnes qui operantur iniquitatem,
perdes omnes qui loquuntur mendacium. Virum
sanguinum, & dolosum abominabitur dominus. ego
autem in multitudine misericordiæ tuæ. Introibo
in domum tuam, adorabo ad templum sanctum
Crescius Romæ Scribebat.

Giovanni Francesco Cresci:
Il perfetto scrittore 1570

This is the second of Cresci's published copy books and in it he reiterates the need for a speedier hand. This example shows again his characteristic clubbed ascenders, while the writing itself sits uneasily inside its heavy and unrelated frame.

V&AM L 3068-1948 20 × 26

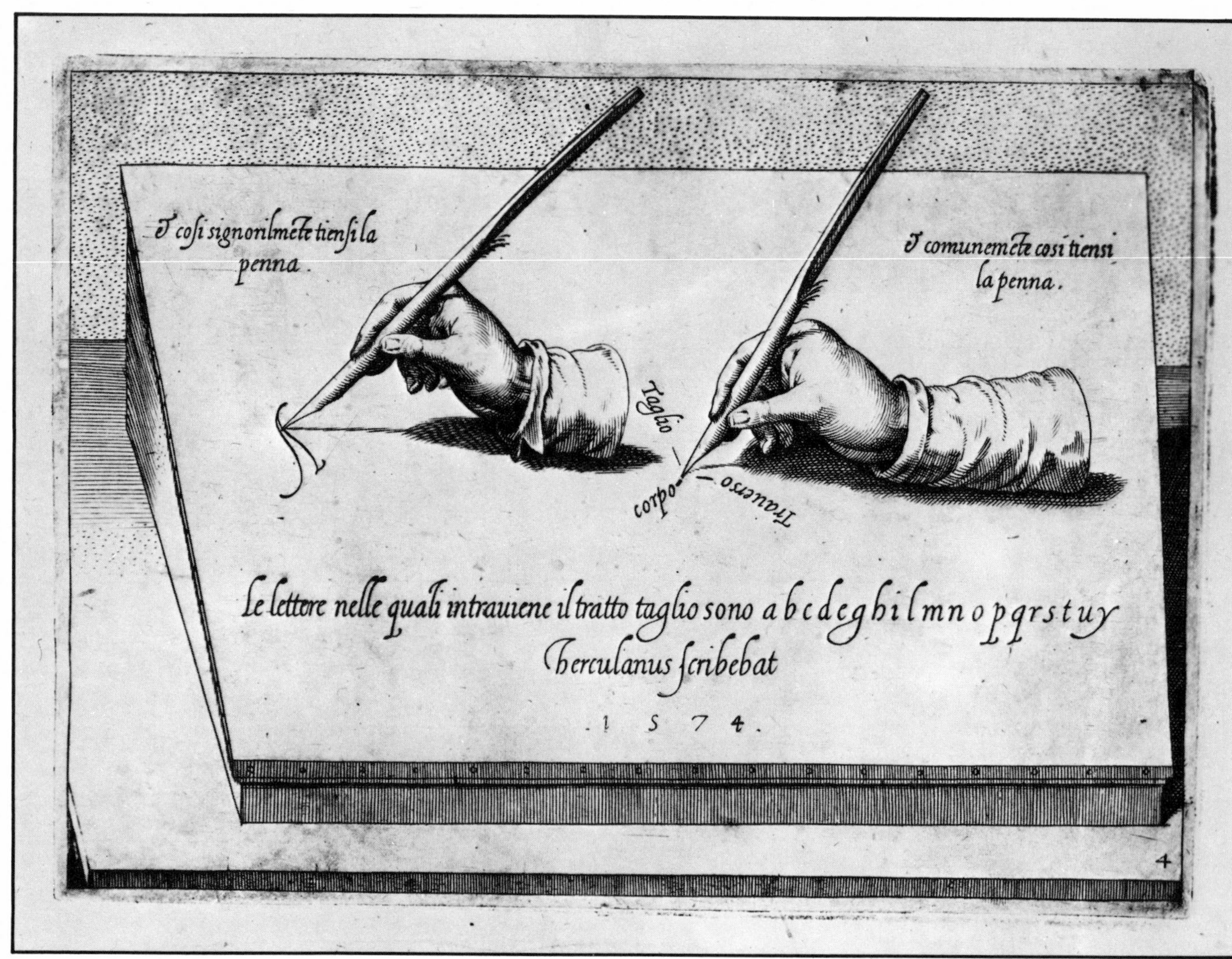

Giulantonio Hercolani:
Essemplare utile di tutte le sorti di l(ette)re cancellaresche correntissime, et altre usate 1574

Hercolani's works were the first to be produced by means of copperplate engraving; the first edition of this book was published in 1571. The introduction of copperplate instead of wood engraving was to have a significant effect on calligraphy at a later date; at first, however, the result was very satisfactory since the burin or graver more easily reproduced the strokes of the pen.

V&AM L 1955-1949 19 × 27

De profundis clamaui ad te dñe: dñe exaudi uocem meam. Fiant aures tuæ intendentes in uocem deprecationis meæ
Herculanus scribebat
1574.

Questa lrã cancellaresca commune, & l'altre lettere tutte uuole pendere uerso mano destra, essere uguale, diritta, netta; il spacio fra le righe sia equale, fra le parole et fra le lrẽ ancora.
A a a b bb cc dd e e d e ff gg hh hh ii l m n o p p petrus pp qq rr
ss t tt u u u v x y z re ee w p p st Vigilantibus acquiritur. &c.
Herculanus scribebat 1574

Si iniquitates obseruaueris dñe domine quis sustinebit? Quia apud te propitiatio est: & propter legem tuam sustinui te domine Deus.
1574

Beneficentia è una uirtù, la quale solamente in se contiene il fare beneficio ad altri senza aspettatione alcuna d'esserne rimunerato; et è propio dell'huomo grande et magnanimo qual debbe seguitar nō il frutto ma il beneficiare. 1574.

cancellaresca circonflessa

Sappia ciascuno che li spacij che sono fra lrã et lrã uogliono essere equali et non più grandi che si sia il bianco che è dentro il spacio dei corpi delle lrẽ, fra le parole li spacij capiscano una i.
Herculanus scribebat. 1574

Maiuscole cancel. che più facili
A A A A B B C C C C D D E E
E F G G H I J L M M N O P P Q
R R R S S T T T V V X Y Z &
1574

Questa cancellaresca formasi sciolta e tondeggiante per tutto doue in essa intrauiene il tratto taglio à differenza della cancellaresca acuta. et il taglio intrauiene in queste lrẽ a b c d e g h i l m n o p q r s u x y &

Giulantonio Hercolani:
Lo scrittor' utile 1574

The previous work by Hercolani (p. 162) and this one, both contain plates bearing the date 1574. This illustration not only provides examples of the various hands contained in Hercolani's manual, but also gives an idea of the freedom conferred on the scribe by the new method of copperplate engraving.

V&AM *L 1061-1901*

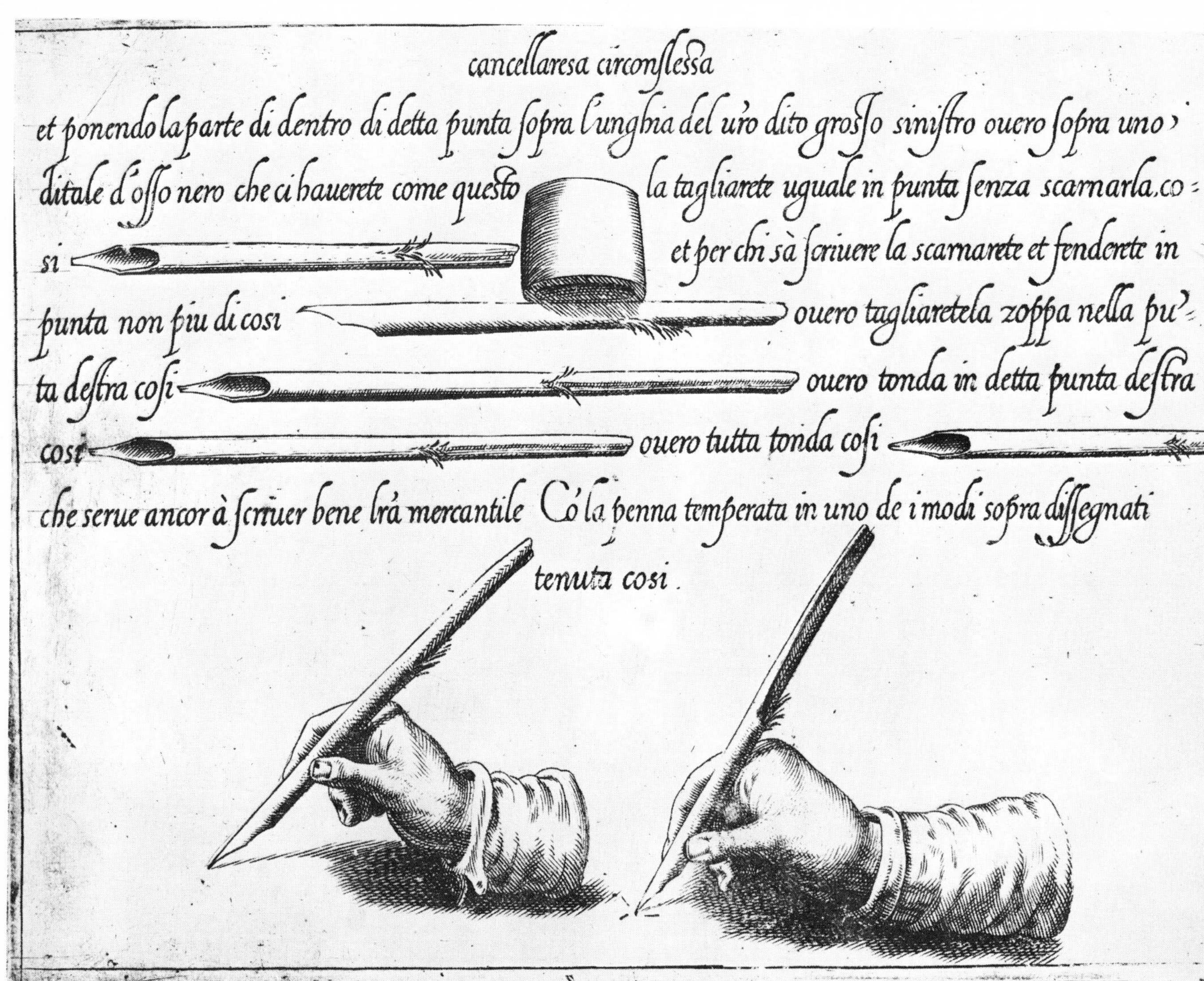

cancellaresa circonslessa

et ponendo la parte di dentro di detta punta sopra l'unghia del uro dito grosso sinistro ouero sopra uno ditale d'osso nero che ci hauerete come questo la tagliarete uguale in punta senza scarnarla co-si et per chi sà scriuere la scarnarete et fenderete in punta non piu di cosi ouero tagliaretela zoppa nella pu-ta destra cosi ouero tonda in detta punta destra cosi ouero tutta tonda cosi

che serue ancor à scriuer bene lrã mercantile Cō la penna temperata in uno de i modi sopra dissegnati tenuta cosi.

Giulantonio Hercolani:
Lo scrittor' utile 1574

A further plate from the copperplate engraved work of Hercolani, showing the restraint practised when this method of reproducing copy books was first employed. This illustration also shows Hercolani's instructions for making a quill suitable for his style of cancellaresca script.

V&AM L 1061-1901

Salvatore Gagliardelli: Per il Signor Girolamo Sommai, il Gagliardelli scriveva 1580

This work consists of pages with an elaborately engraved border; the same one is repeated throughout the book. Within the border, the text has been written out in manuscript — in this instance passages from Dante's Inferno *have been chosen. Gagliardelli's best known published work is his* Soprascritte di lettere in forma cancellaresca corsiva appartenenti ad ogni grado di persona, *1583 (below).*

V&A M MS L 2879-1947 21 × 27.5

Salvatore Gagliardelli: Soprascritte di lettere in forma cancelleresca, corsiva, appartenenti ad ogni grado di persona. 1583

This illustration, taken from Gagliardelli's only known published work, enables the script as shown here to be compared with the manuscript version in his own hand which is also illustrated. The method of writing addresses correctly and elegantly frequently featured in copy books.

V&A M L 2549-1949 18.5 × 25.5

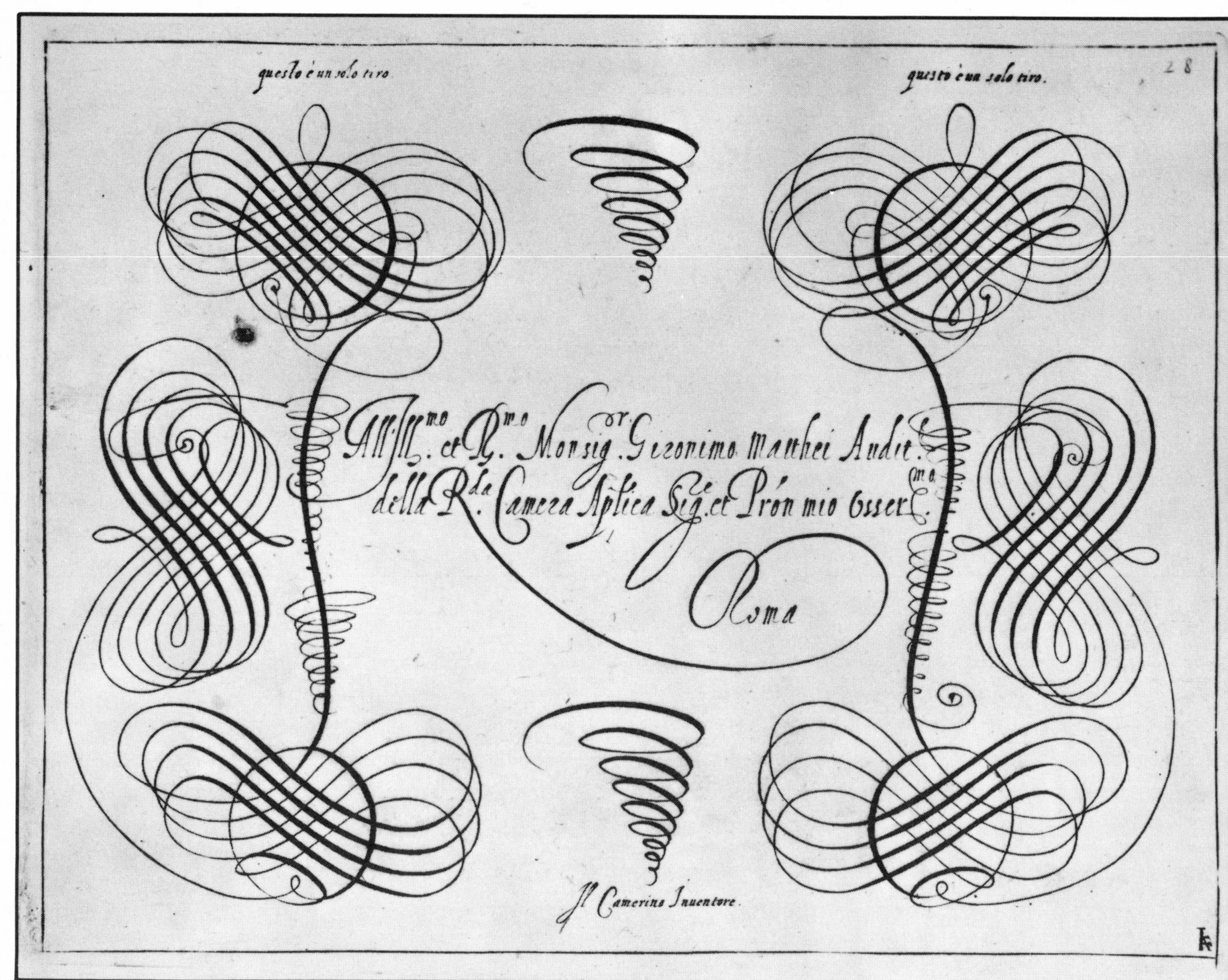

Marcello Scalzini, called Il Camerino: Il secretario di Marcello Scalzini, detto il Camerino 1587

The first edition of this book was published in 1581. In it Il Camerino *as he signs himself, concentrated almost entirely on the* cancellaresca corsiva, *the hand developed in the Papal Chancery, with especial emphasis on the need for speed. This example shows the elaborate form of address considered appropriate for letters, though the flourished decoration, so typical of the period, was not an essential part of it!*

V & A M L 560-1913 17 × 23.5

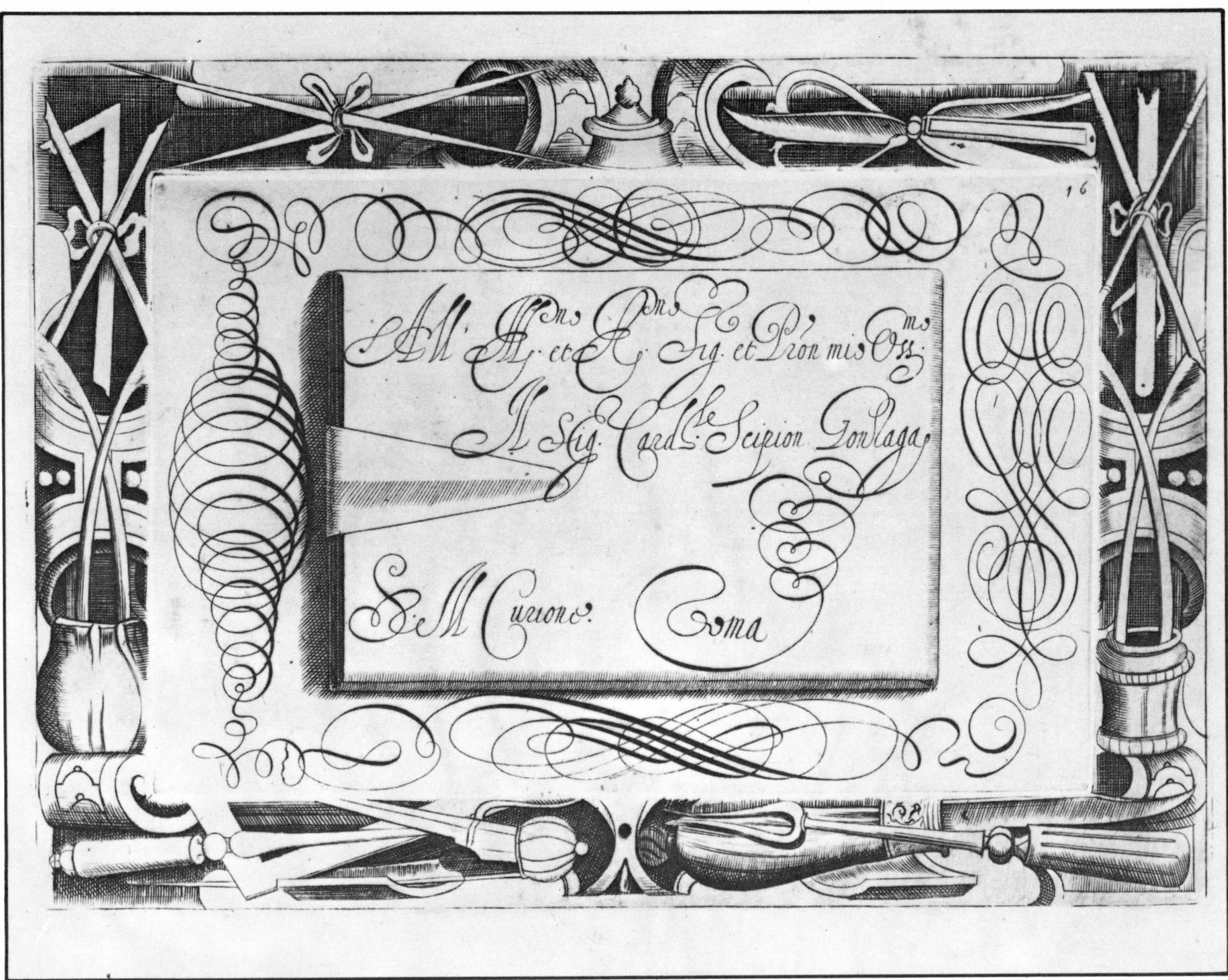

Ludovico Curione: La notomia delle cancellaresche corsive & altre maniere di lettere 1588

Curione's book is mainly devoted to the chancery hand. In the example shown here we can see the beginning of the flourishes known as 'command of hand' or 'strikings' which were to become such a feature of later writing books. The engraved border shows various writing implements, while the example itself is shown in the form of an address on the outer cover of a letter.

V & A M L 1683-1882

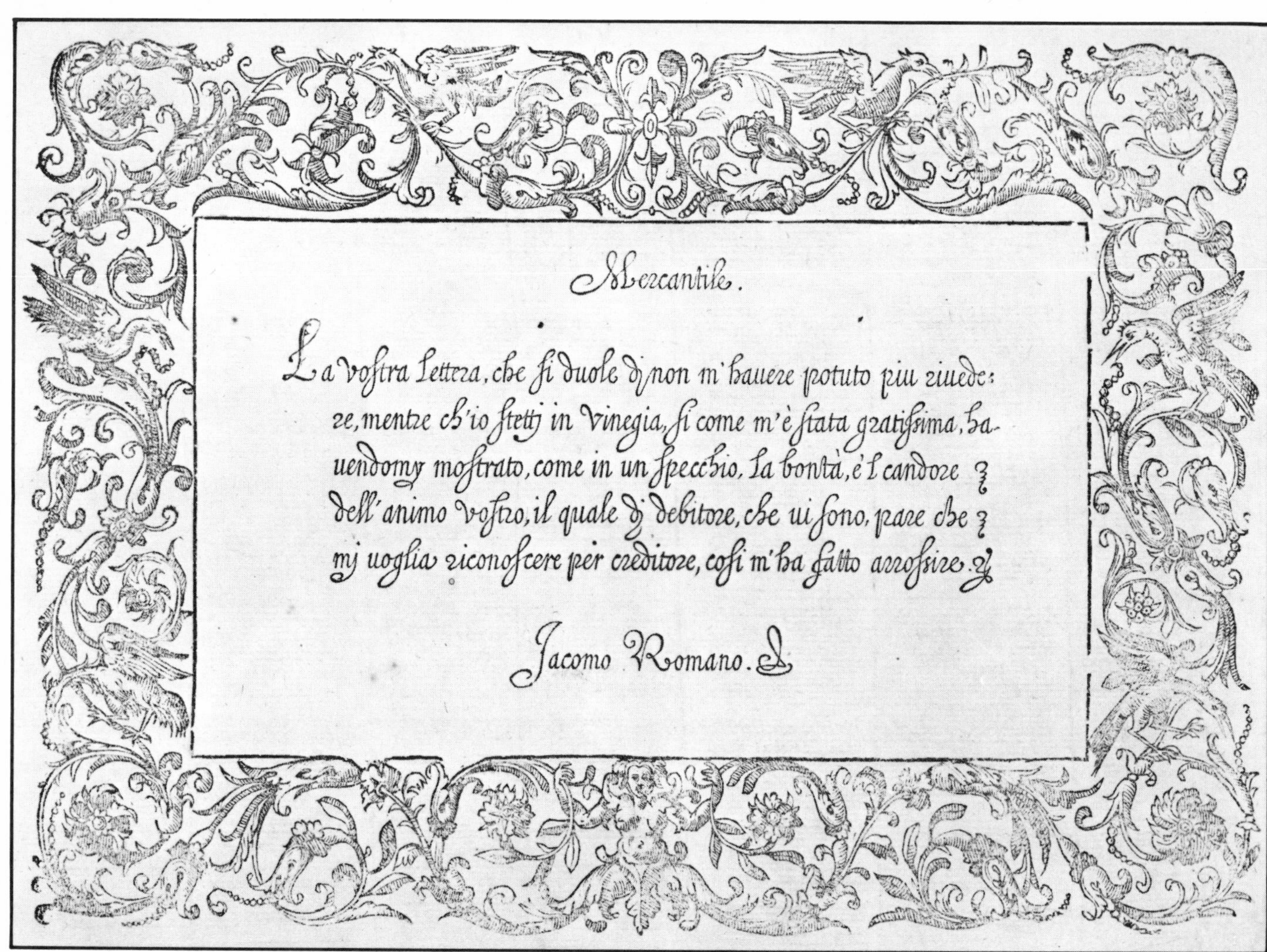

Mercantile.

La vostra lettera, che si duole di non m'hauere potuto piu riuede:
re, mentre ch'io stetti in Vinegia, si come m'è stata gratissima, ha-
uendomy mostrato, come in un specchio, la bontà, e'l candore
dell'animo vostro, il quale di debitore, che ui sono, pare che
mj uoglia riconoscere per creditore, cosi m'ha fatto arrossire.

Iacomo Romano.

Giacomo Romano: Il primo libro di scrivere di Iacomo Romano, dove s'insegna la vera maniera delle cancellaresche corsive [etc]. 1589

Romano's work follows very closely the style set by Cresci in his depiction of cancellaresche corsive *but the illustration shown here is of the mercantile hand; it was this hand which was eventually to assist in the development of the 'round hand' so popular in the 18th century.*

V&AM L 4101-1948 17 × 24

Juan de Yciar: Arte subtilissima, por la qual se ensena a escrevir perfectamente 1555

The first edition of this work, under a different title, was published in 1548. Juan de Yciar has been described as the founder and patriarch of Spanish calligraphy. The examples are engraved on wood, some of them showing the effect of white letters on a black background as here.

V&AM L 412-1895 17.5 × 12.5

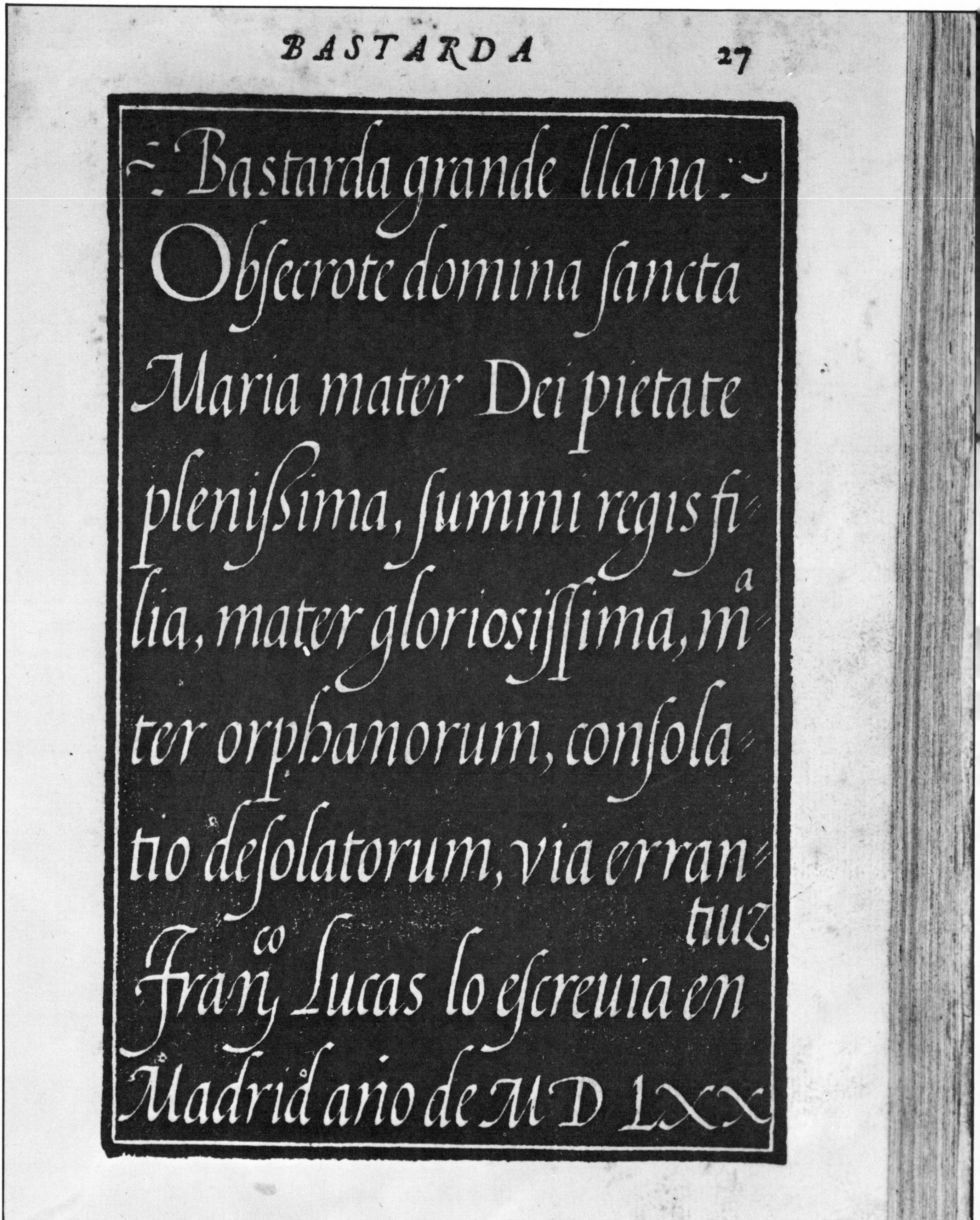

Bastarda grande llana

Obsecrote domina sancta
Maria mater Dei pietate
plenissima, summi regis fi-
lia, mater gloriosissima, m[a]
ter orphanorum, consola
tio desolatorum, via erran
tiuz
Fran[co] Lucas lo escreuia en
Madrid año de M D LXX

Opposite:
Francisco Lucas: Arte de escrevir
1577

Lucas's book was particularly significant for Spanish calligraphy since the forms he introduced retained their importance for nearly two centuries. He developed a script that was a combination of italic chancery and local mercantile hands. In this book the first and longest part is devoted to bastarda script.

V&AM 19 × 14

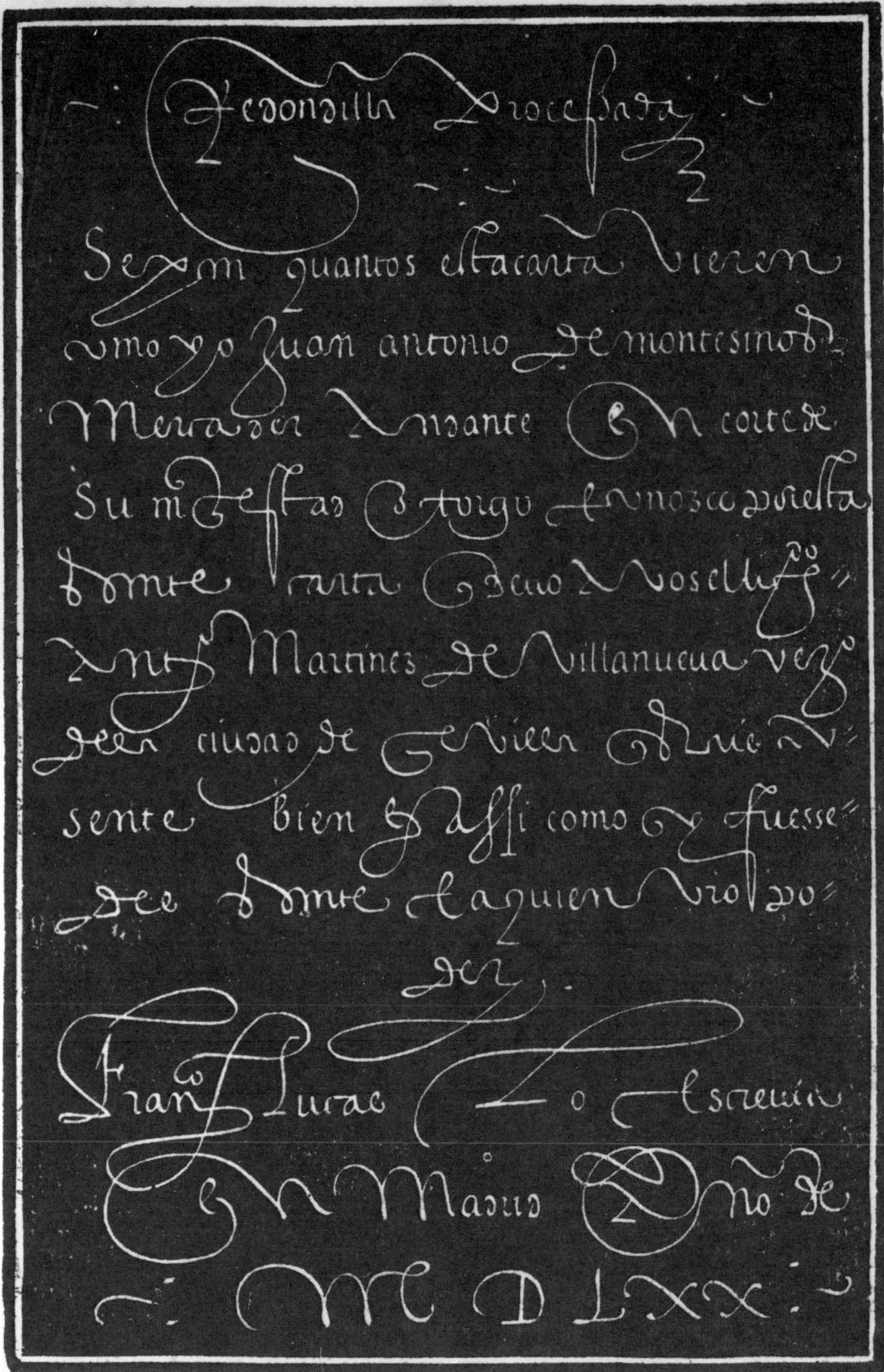

Francisco Lucas: Arte de escrevir
1577

The second illustration from Lucas's important copy book shows one of his examples of the redondilla script, again with white-on-black.

V&AM 19 × 14

Urban Wyss: Libellus valde doctus elegans & utilis, multa & varia scribendarum literarum genera complectens 1549

This was one of the most important manuals on writing published in northern Europe in the 16th century: the name of Wyss, and many of his examples, appear in later copy books in various countries. Wyss, who was Swiss, was also the printer and engraver of his own book, which was done on wood.

V & A M L 840-1880 14 × 21

Opposite top:
Johann Neudörffer, the Elder: Ein gutte Ordnung [etc]. 1561

This manuscript was possibly written out by Neudörffer himself, or at least by one of his pupils. The original work was published in 1538, and was an important landmark in the development of German 'Fraktur' script. Apart from the difficulty experienced by those accustomed to the Roman forms of the letters as used today, this illustration also provides an example of the additional problem of separating out the minims in some of the words — and indeed of separating the words themselves in the heading to this text!

V & A M MS L 2607-1936 17 × 29

Opposite bottom:
Johann Neudörffer, the Elder: Ein gutte Ordnung [etc]. 1561

A further illustration from the manuscript of Neudörffer's important work, in which the forms of the individual letters can be more clearly studied. It is interesting to note how many versions he offered for some of the letters, from the simple to the almost unrecognisable.

V & A M MS L 2067-1936 17 × 29

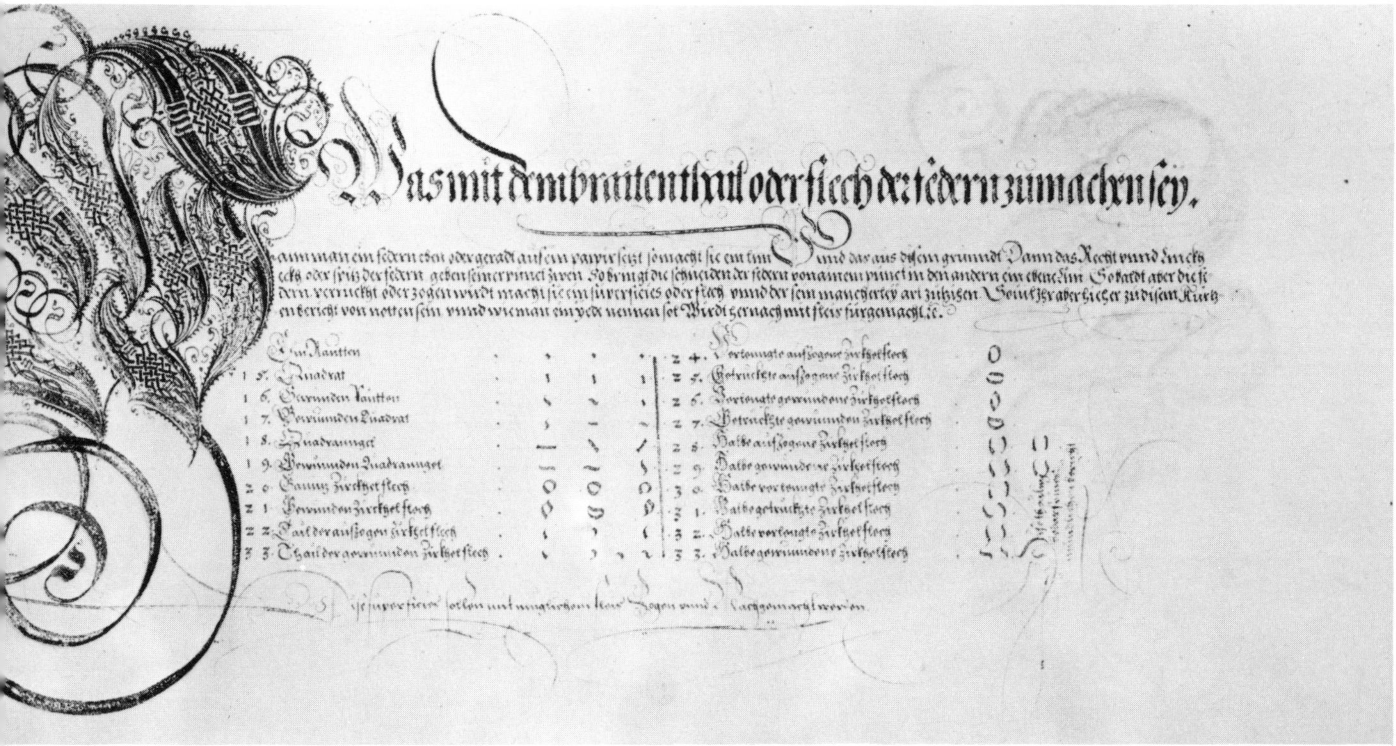

Was mit dem braiten thail oder flech der federn zu machen sey.

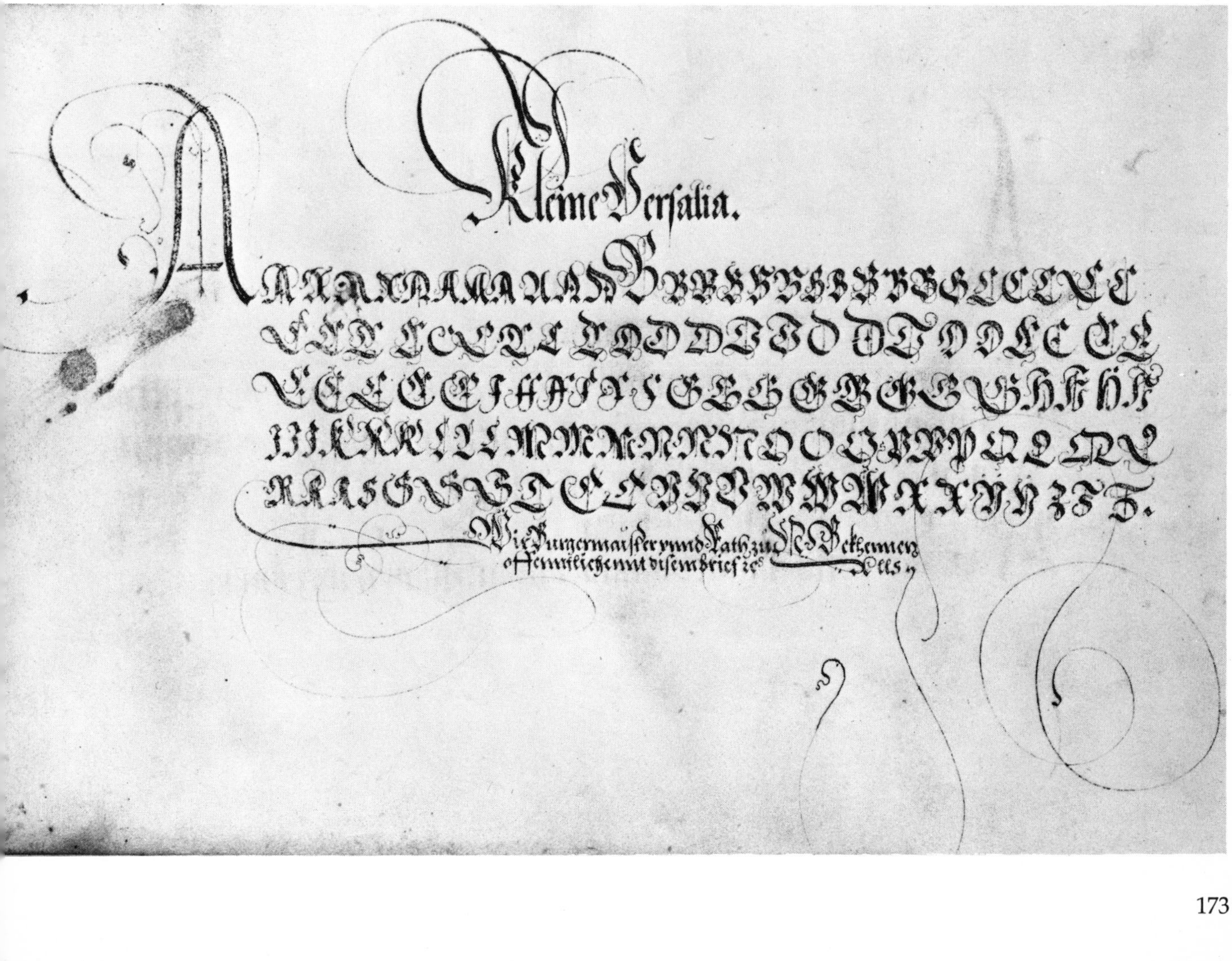

Wann man ein federn eben oder geradt auf ein papir setzt so macht sie ein lini Und das aus disem grundt Dann das Recht vnnd lincks ecks oder spitz der federn geben seiner lini zwen So bringt die schneiden der federn von ainem punct in den andern ein ebene lini So baldt aber die federn verruckht oder zogen wirdt macht sie ein superficies oder flech vnnd der sein mancherley art zu zaigen Seind hierab hieher zu disem kurtzen bericht von notten sein vnnd wie man ein yede nennen sol Wirdt hernach mit fleis fürgemacht ꝛc.

Ein Kantten	24. Verlengte aufzogene zirckhel flech
15. Quadrat	25. Getruckhte aufzogene zirckhel flech
16. Gewunden Kantten	26. Verlengte gewundene zirckhel flech
17. Gewunden Quadrat	27. Getruckhte gewunden zirckhel flech
18. Quadrangel	28. Halbe aufzogene zirckhel flech
19. Gewunden Quadrangel	29. Halbe gewundene zirckhel flech
20. Gantz zirckhel flech	30. Halbe verlengte zirckhel flech
21. Gewunden zirckhel flech	31. Halbe getruckhte zirckhel flech
22. Tail der aufzogen zirckhel flech	32. Halbe verlengte zirckhel flech
23. Thail der gewunden zirckhel flech	33. Halbe gewundene zirckhel flech

Dise superficies sollen mit [illegible] zogen vnnd [illegible] gemacht werden.

Kleine Versalia.

Wir Burgermaister vnnd Rath zu N. Bekhennen offenlich hiemit disem brief ꝛc. Alls

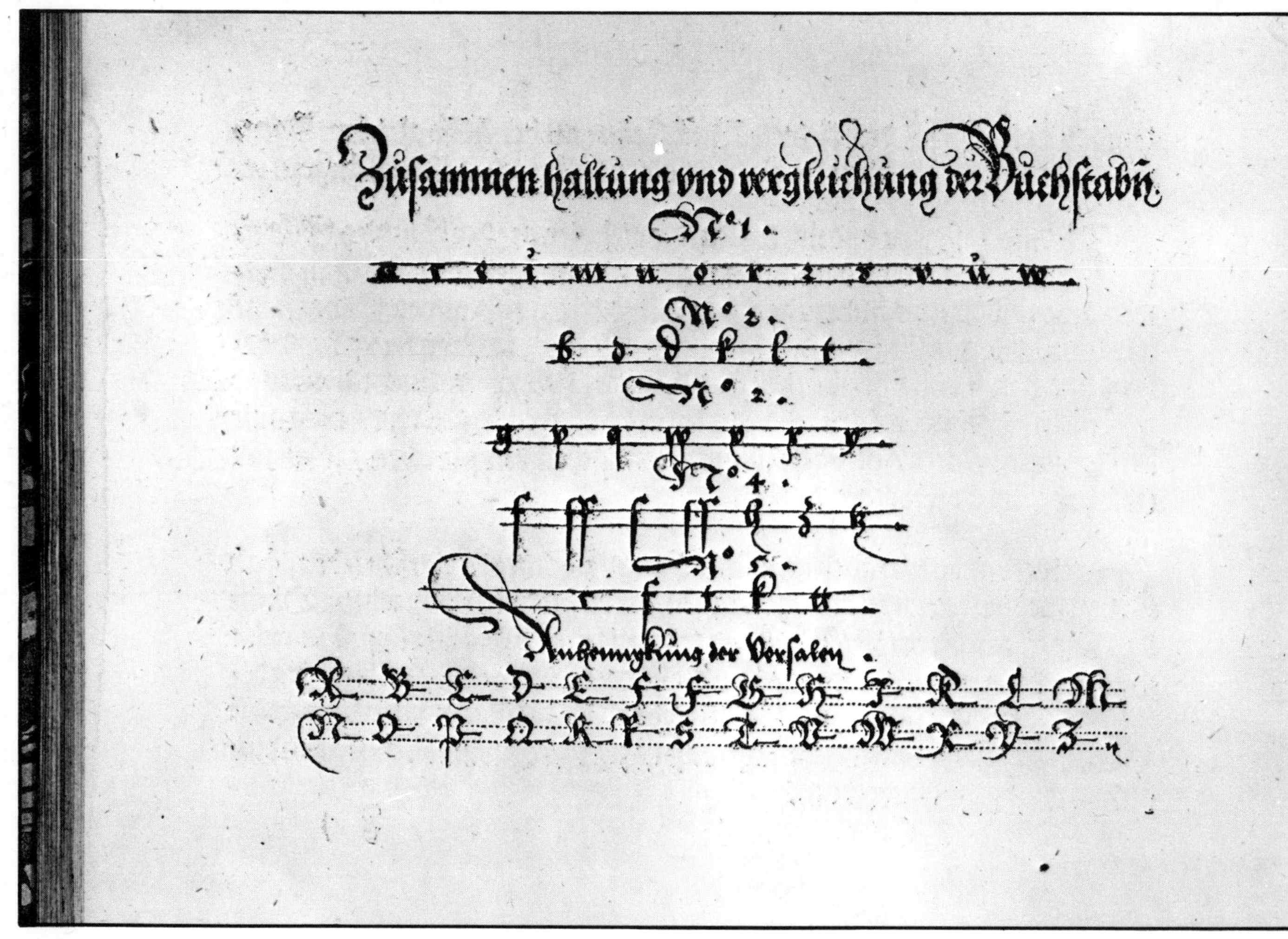

Wolfgang Fugger: Ein nutzlich und wolgegrundt formular manncherley schöner schrifften, als teutscher, lateinischer, griechischer, und hebrayischer Buchstaben [etc]. 1553

Despite the date on the title-page this work is in fact the second edition, published between 1597 and 1605. Fugger himself was a printer and a pupil of Johann Neudörffer. His writing book is one of the most important of the earlier manuals to come from Germany. In this example it is interesting to see how Fugger places the alphabet within lines, either real or invisible, which control the relationship of the individual letters.

V&AM L 2741-1950 15 × 20

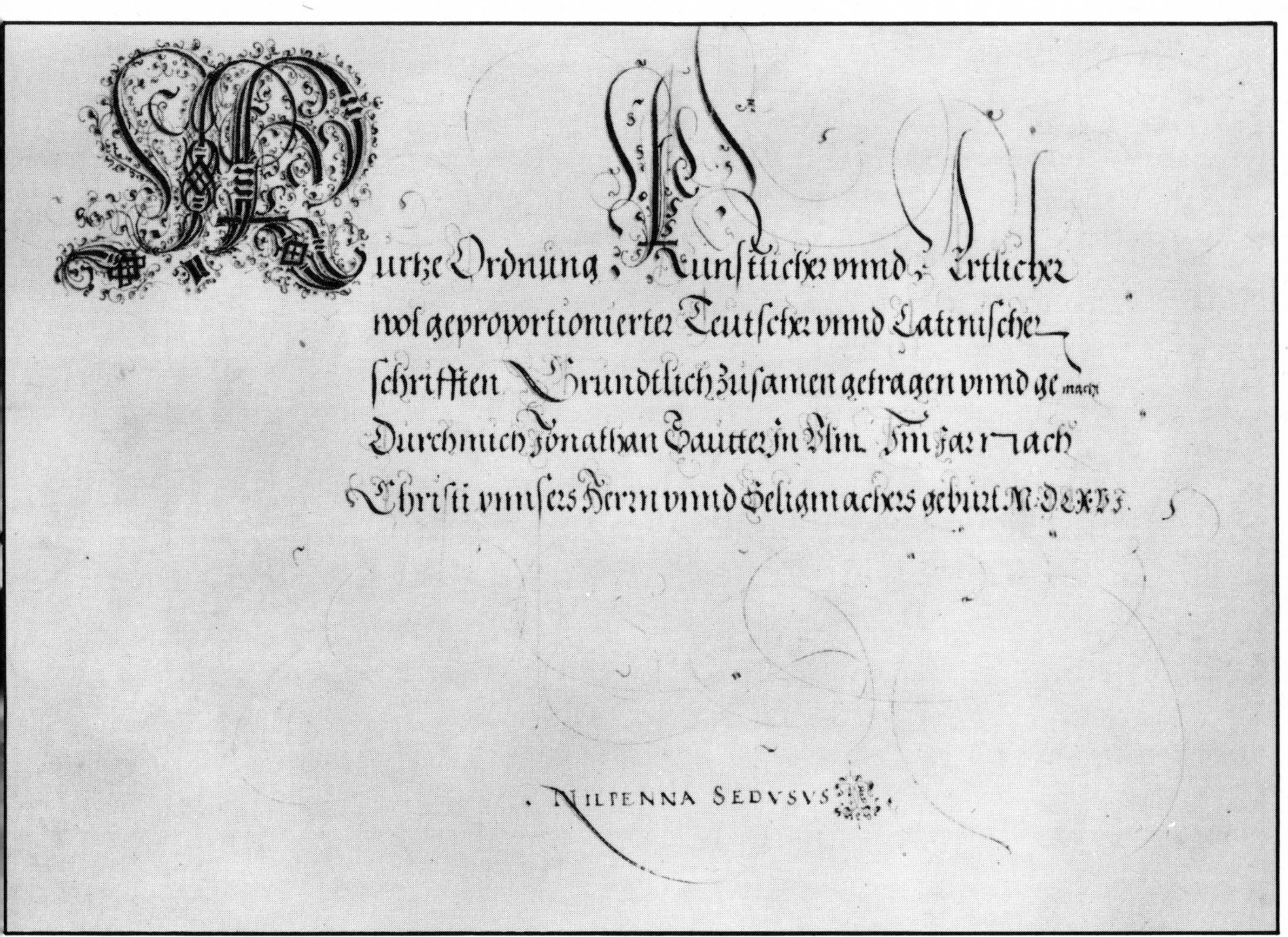
Kurtze Ordnung Kunstlicher vnnd Artlicher wol geproportionierter Teutscher vnnd Latinischer schrifften Grundtlich zusamen getragen vnnd gemacht Durch mich Jonathan Sautter in Ulm. Im Jar nach Christi vnnsers Herrn vnnd Seligmachers geburt M.D.LXVI.

NIL PENNA SED VSVS

Jonathan Sautter: Kurtze Ordnung kunstlicher unnd artlicher . . . schrifften 1566

Little is known about the writer of this manuscript, although Sautter seems to have been an engraver and portrait painter. In this work he appears as a very competent calligrapher, working in the style of his famous contemporary, Johann Neudörffer. Although the title-page shown here is written in German script, Sautter shows his familiarity with the Roman hand in the inscription at the foot of the page.

V & A M MS L 2740-1950 11.5 × 17

Johann Theodor and Johann Israel de Bry: Alphabeten und aller art Characteren 1596

Published in Frankfurt, this work is an anthology of scripts in different languages, of a kind that was to become increasingly popular. The calligraphic plates are followed by alphabets decorated with flowers, animals, insects and birds.

V&AM 10.x.1871 14 × 20

Clément Perret: Excercitatio alphabetica nova et utilissima 1569

The highly ornamental borders almost dwarf the calligraphic example, but certainly place the art of writing in its contemporary stylistic setting: the script echoes the decorative exaggerations of its surroundings. Perret's work was the first copy book to be published in the Netherlands (Brussels).

V & AM 19.v.1857 21 × 28

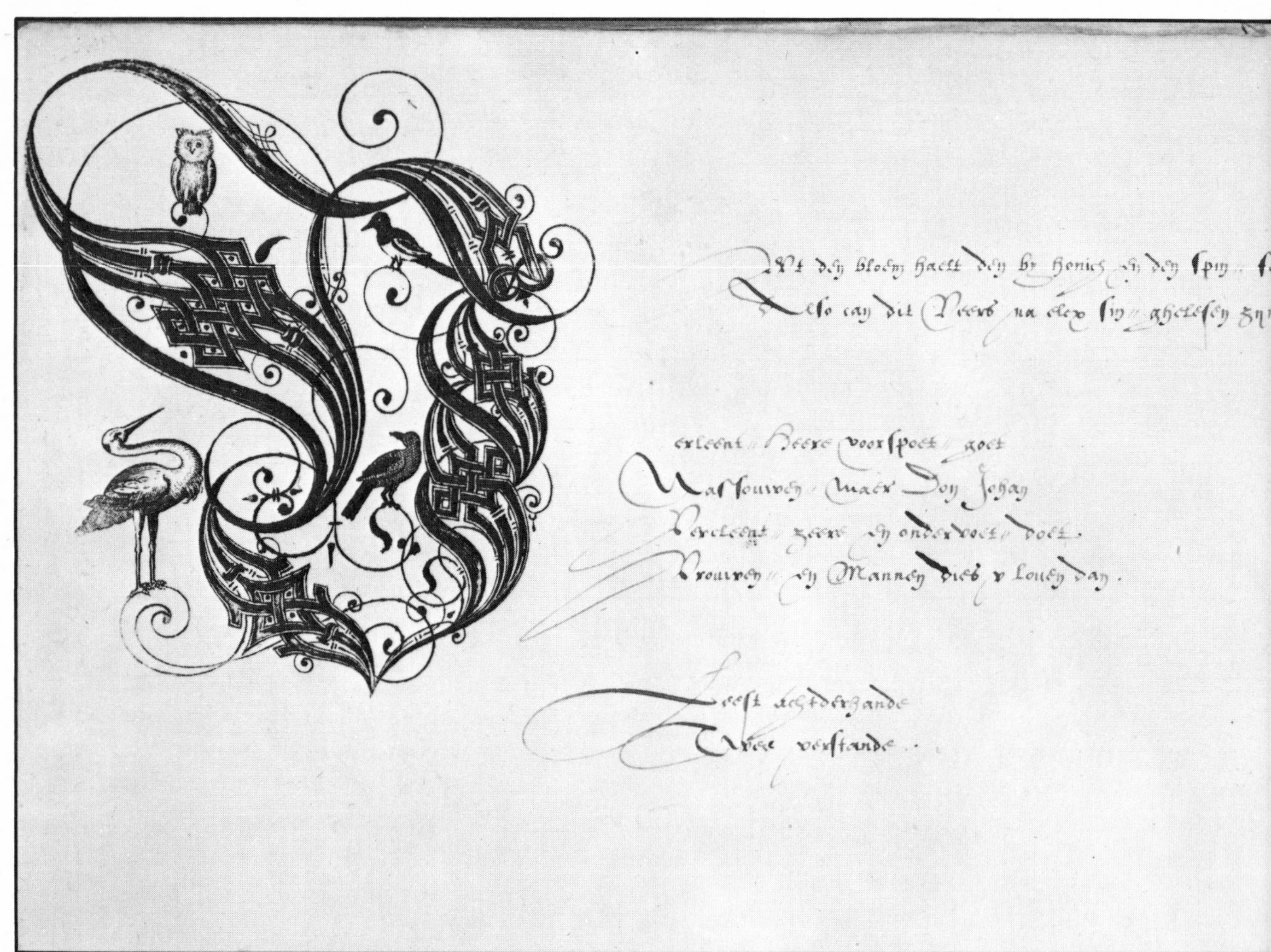

Aert van Meldert: Alphabet; ou, ABC pour la jeunesse 1585

This copy book consists of a series of wood engraved initials of considerable elaboration, such as the one shown here, and the rest of each page contains a variety of contemporary scripts. Meldert is said to have been a French schoolmaster, which the title of his work would support, and the scripts, written in Dutch, may have been added later.

V&AM MS L 785-1884 15 × 20

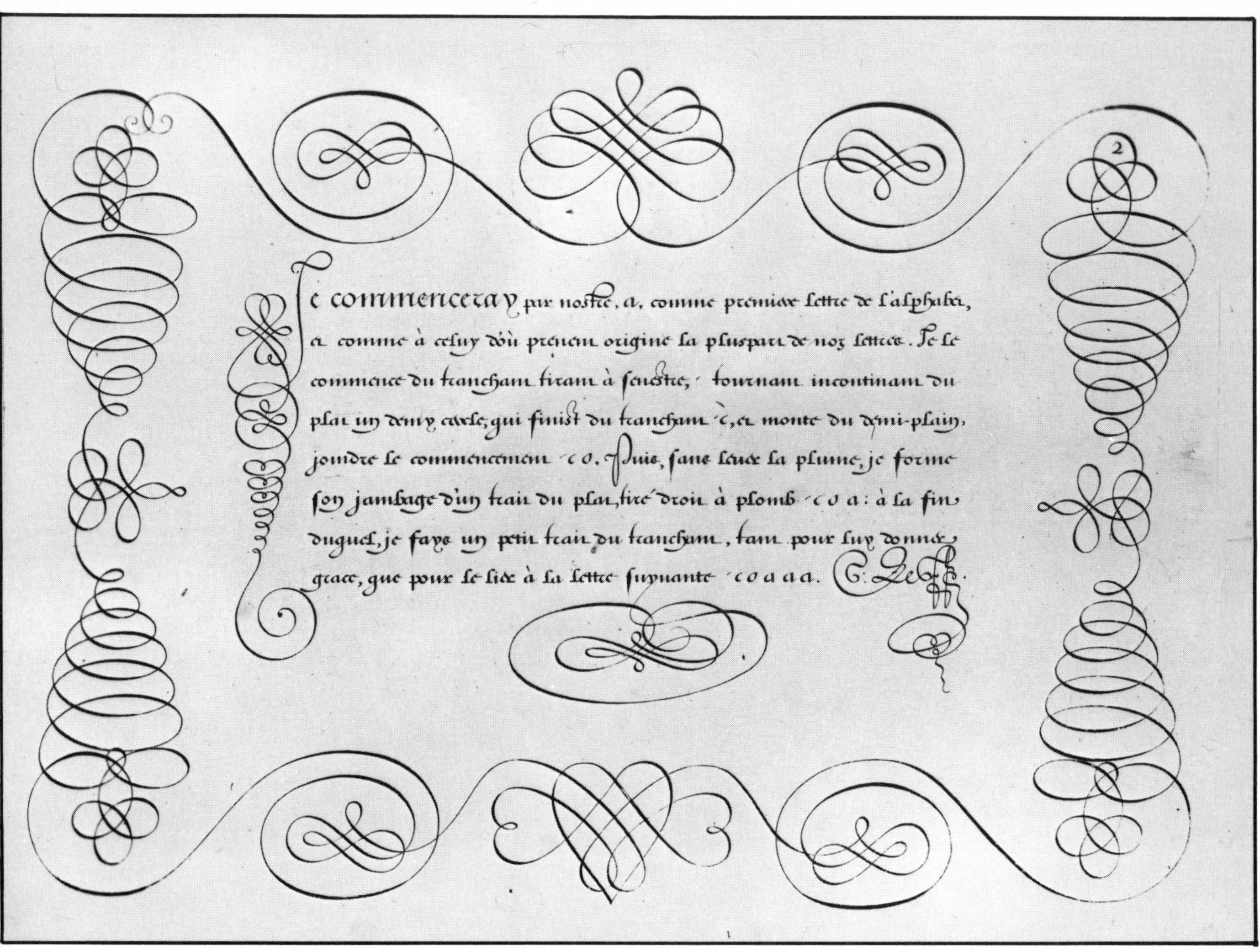

2

Je commenceray par nostre, a, comme premiere lettre de l'alphabet, et comme à celuy d'où prenent origine la pluspart de noz lettres. Je le commence du tranchant tirant à senestre, tournant incontinant du plat un demy cercle, qui finist du tranchant c, et monte du demi-plain, joindre le commencement c o. Puis, sans lever la plume, je forme son jambage d'un trait du plat, tire droit à plomb c o a: à la fin duquel, je faye un petit trait du tranchant, tant pour luy donner grace, que pour le lier à la lettre suyvante c o a a. G. Le G.

Guillaume Le Gangneur: La technographie ou briefve methode pour parvenir à la parfitte connoissance de l'escriture françoise 1599

Le Gangneur was secretary to Henri IV and a highly accomplished writing master. Most of his plates in this book are decorated with 'command of hand' flourishes or other ornaments.

V&AM L 946-1899 19.5 × 27

Jodocus Hondius, the Elder: Theatrum artis scribendi 1594

This work is an anthology of scripts by various calligraphers, and is indicative of the fame of the various writing masters outside their own countries. The example illustrated is by Hondius himself, and shows his impression of the English secretary hand. His signature, as often happened at this period, was written in an italic script. The engraved borders of this work are especially fine.

V&AM L115-1886 16 × 23

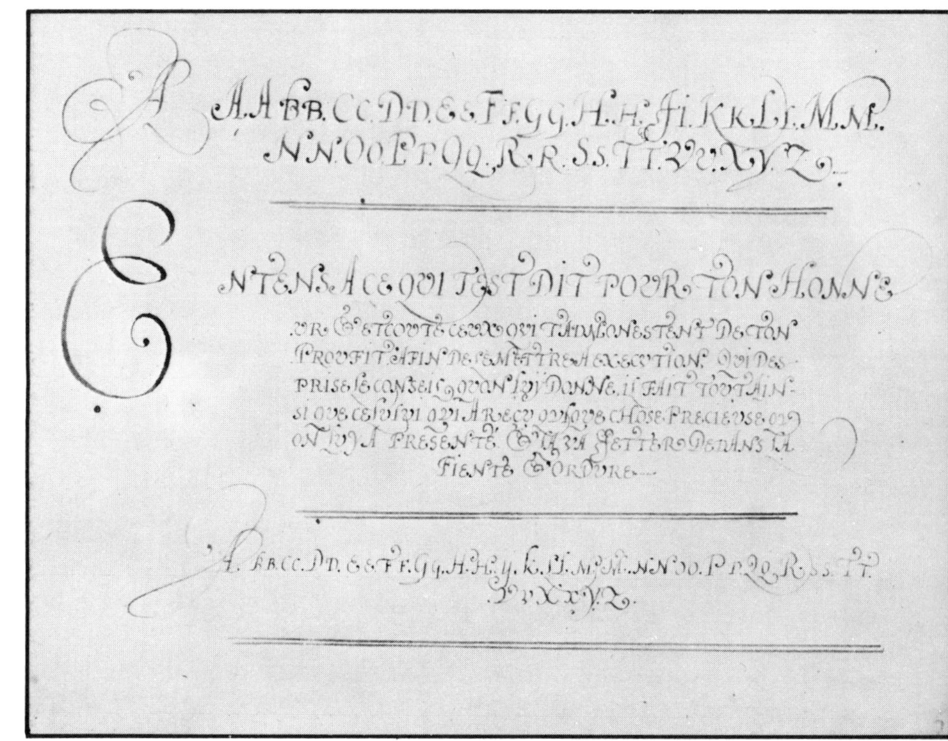

Guillaume Beeck: Copy book 1596

Nothing is known about the calligrapher who wrote this manuscript, though he would appear to have been working in the South Netherlands. This example shows the ornamented form of script which is frequently to be found in French copy books of this period.

V&AM MS L 2328-1904 14 × 19

7 The seventeenth century, and the heyday of the copy books

THE 17th century was undoubtedly one of the greatest centuries for the sheer volume and variety of copy books produced in west European countries. It also saw the influential position of the Italian writing masters decline in favour of northern scribes. The copy books of the 17th century reflected the spirit of the age in many ways, but chiefly in the exuberance of their decoration, which led to the deterioration of the scripts offered. The reason for both these factors, the decoration and deterioration, can be traced back to the use of copperplate engraving to reproduce the pen strokes. This form of engraved writing could accurately copy the master's style, and could follow the pen in its most intricate movements. But it was perhaps too successful in its results, so that the writing masters were tempted to try ever more brilliant strokes, knowing that the engraver could reproduce them as well, if not better, than the master's hand had written them. Competition among the teachers of writing increased as more took upon them the task of instructing pupils of all ages and ranks in the art of the pen. It was difficult to make each new copy book different from its rivals, unless it offered some outstanding feature. So the style of the writing was distorted into strange loops, ever more clubbed ascenders, or convoluted initials. The margins of the pages were alive with florid figures of animals, birds, men, or sheer mazes of line, as each writing master strove to outshine his contemporaries.

The writing masters' position in society was somewhat ambiguous. The earlier teachers, in Italy, had had their posts about the Papal court or elsewhere, and many of them enjoyed a considerable academic standing among their fellows. But the new race of writing masters were primarily teachers rather than scholars. They might instruct their pupils privately, or they might be employed in a school. Their pupils moreover, might not be children at all but adults, who wished to improve or add to their writing skills. The link with the higher forms of learning was maintained as far as possible by the writing masters, who endeavoured in their copy books to show their familiarity with a variety of different languages, which might include Latin, Greek and even Hebrew. The texts they chose to write out were also intended to show the wide range of learning they possessed. In some cases the display was one of genuine knowledge, but far more frequently it was but superficial. Nevertheless, it all made for lively productions, and when the writing masters ceased to concern themselves so much with their status in society, the copy books were the poorer in appearance, as the late 18th century books show.

The most characteristic feature of the 17th century copy book, and one which lasted in to the early years of the 18th century in some countries, was the baroque decoration known as 'striking' or 'command of hand'. In this the penman produced a variety of flourishes by the dexterous use of his pen, often, so it was claimed, without lifting it from the paper. The many examples shown in this book indicate the widespread nature of the fashion for this kind of decoration, which of course was only possible when the skill of the engraver matched that of the penman. Thus the position of the engraver of calligraphic works became increasingly important, and the prefaces to some of the copy books indicate a degree of strain creeping into the relationship between the writing master and his interpreter, the engraver. Some writing masters (Edward Cocker was one) were able to engrave their own works, and this saved them a lot of problems. Others specially learnt the skill in order to produce their own work. Sometimes the engraver was himself a good calligrapher, as George Bickham was to prove in the next century. There is no doubt that many writing masters envied the engraver his skill, and gradually began to produce scripts which followed the style of the burin (or graver) rather than making them truly pen-formed. It can be seen from some of the examples illustrated in this book, that virtuosity had taken over from beauty in all too many cases, and the learner must have had the greatest difficulty in trying to make with his quill pen those shapes so easily produced on the copperplate.

By the 17th century printing was so well established that to many people it must have seemed as common-place as it does today – it had always existed in their life-time and that of their parents. But handwriting continued to be of importance in certain fields where printing was uneconomic, or where the status of a specially hand-produced object was of significance. For the most part however those scribes who continued in the profession made little impression on contemporary styles – their work was essentially traditional, and was written out in traditional scripts. Such professional scribes were almost entirely concerned with legal documents of various kinds, or ceremonial manuscripts. In the case of legal documents, traditional semi-gothic hands certainly continued in use, and with them many of the old contractions – for after all, the majority of such documents were written on behalf of lawyers for lawyers (or their clerks) who would be able to interpret this now almost forgotten type of script. But the ceremonial document was different. Here legibility was important, for the proud owner of a diploma or patent of nobility would want to be able to read it, and to ensure that others could too. So that it is in these areas that we find true calligraphic skills continuing, albeit at a rather low standard, since few patrons wanted anything too much out of the ordinary. This section of the book therefore includes a range of handwritten documents that continued to be produced throughout the century, many of a kind that still continue to be handwritten today.

There is one group of manuscripts illustrated here which is different. This is the selection of those produced for the court of Louis XIV, especially the manuscript books associated with the name of Nicolas Jarry (*c.* 1615-1670). The handmade object has always attracted a certain cachet which the mass-produced item does not possess, and it is obvious that a specially commissioned hand-written book would appeal to an aristocratic clientèle. Most of the French court calligraphy was expressed in religious or devotional works, many of them obviously intended for the ladies of the court – such manuscripts often appear to be more like ornaments or adjuncts to dress than books for actual use, and they are also often very prettily bound. Many of them show by the style of their script that the calligrapher was more influenced by typographical than by pen-formed letters, but nevertheless, each of the manuscripts was unique, even if the general style was fairly consistent among them.

Thus the course of the 17th century provided a great variety of writing styles. The many copy books showed ever more exotic and distorted forms in their efforts to attract, until the inevitable reaction began to take place towards the end of the century. In France and in England the emphasis then turned towards the practical business hand, and writing styles sobered down in the interests of legibility and commerce. Diplomas and grants of nobility however continued the calligraphic tradition, and this was especially true of Spain, where the *carta executoria de hidalguìa* continued to feature in importance. These *cartas* were peculiar to Spain, where the nobility needed to prove the purity of their blood and lineage following the long years of Moorish domination. Although the Moors had been driven out of Spain several centuries ago, the results of a certain amount of inter-marriage with the Moriscos remained. The implications for Spanish calligraphy were most beneficial. As can be seen from the examples illustrated in this book, the high standard continued well into the 19th century, so that the document of 1804 appointing Manuel de Godoy as governor of Teruel was worthy to stand beside the best work of any age. Elsewhere standards fell to a generally low level of competence, and remained there throughout the next century.

1

Al Molto Ill.re e R.mo Mons. Cimbardo Cimb. Vesc. di Colle.

Quantunque io mi troui tenuto à tutta Casa Cimbarda, per molti benefizi che ne ho riceuuti, singularmente, nondimeno mi sento di strettissimi nodi d'obligazione legato à V.S. R.ma, che prima comincio a rileuarmi, ed à mettermi in grazia a' generosissimi suoi fratelli. Facciami dunque degno de' suoi comandamenti, poi che io con desiderio gli attendo. Il Pericciòli scrisse.

Francesco Pericciòli: Il secondo libro delle cancellaresca corsive 1610

In this plate the border tends to dominate the script! Pericciòli uses the heavy clubbed ascenders, but makes use of loops for most of his descenders. The h, *which has almost entirely lost its bow, should also be noted.*

V&AM L 1060-1901 21 × 28.5

Gio. Batta Marino Poeta Eccell.mo

Poiche con altro piu espresso argomento d'affettuosa diuotione non m'è conceduto palesare al mondo come infinitamente io stimo il sommo ualore di V.S. godero almeno che n q.sti miei carattori appaia uiuamente espresso alcun segno, come anch'io con gli altri alzai gli occhi al marauiglioso splendore delle sue rare uirtu, et hebbi ricca la mente nelle sue lodi, se ben pouera la lingua in darle tributo di riuerenza et d'honore Et me le raccomando. Di Genoua il primo di Marzo 1604.

Segaro

Giuseppe Segaro:. Dell'idea dello scrivere 1607

This work has a very elaborate architectural title-page, on which it gives the date and states that the work was engraved by a priest, Don Epifanio del Fiano Vallombrosano. But A. S. Osley discloses that the work was in fact published by Segaro's son in 1624, who may have had the architectural borders added. However, the work offers a very fine example of contemporary styles.

V&AM L 1681-1951 27 × 36.

Tomaso Ruinetti: Idea del buon scrittore 1619

Ruinetti was the first of the writing masters to use copper-plate engraving to reproduce not only a variety of scripts (as Hercolani had been the first to do in 1574) but also the very elaborate borders showing 'strikings' or 'command of hand'. These calligraphic flourishes already threaten to dominate the page, and later writing masters were to take up this aspect of the copy books with great enthusiasm and virtuosity.

V&A M *L 2323-1952* *23 × 32*

All' Emin.mo e R.mo Sig.re e Pron mio Colen.mo Il Sig. Cardinal Pallotto

Porta V.ra Emin.za splendore alla nostra Prouincia della Marca più col valore, che con la porpora, anzi questa arrossisce di uedersi fatta inequale à premiar degnamente i singolari suoi meriti, a i quali han seruito di Teatro le Corti più riguardeuoli d'Europa e di spettatori i più sourani Principi dell'Vniuer so. Io, che miro sepolto il mio nome nell'oscurità de miei inchiostri, e ristretta la mia diuotione uer so V. Emin.za nell'angustie dell'animo, hò uoluto nel publicar queste mie fatiche testificarle l'humi lissima seruitù mia, e fregiar delle sue glorie i miei caratteri, perche quelle potranno communicar lo ro perpetua chiarezza, et à me principale ornamento

Di V.ra Em.za R.ma Deuot.mo Ser.re

Leopardo Antonozzi Osimano

Leopardo Antonozzi:
De caratteri, Libro primo 1638

Antonozzi was scriptor to the Pope, like cresci, whom he greatly admired. His chancery script, shown here, although pleasant to look at, also contains the curious h *whose bowl is raised above the line. The elaborately engraved surround can be matched by similar ones in the copy books of many masters in the 17th century.*

V & A M L 123-1903 20 × 29

18

Al molto Ill.re S.r mio e Prone osser.mo Il Sig.a Horatio Felici Scr.e eccellent.mo

S'io publicassi la presente mia opera di scriuere senza fregiarla del nome di V.S.
mostrerei di non conoscere il pregio ch'ella può dar ad essa, ch'à quell'eccellenza di
questa nobil professione si è auuanzata, alla quale l'altrui penne in vano di giun
ger's'affaticano. Piacciale, ch'io mi prenda da lei quest'honore, e che faccia palese ad
vn'hora a gli altri, quanto io riuerisca in V.S. quella virtù, che non posso aggua:
gliare, che sarà pur vn'accrescere à se stessa lode, et à me nuouo obligo di seruir:
la, benche ne tenga già mille cagioni della singolar humanità sua.

Oblig.mo Ser.re
Leopardo Antonozzi
Osimano

Leopardo Antonozzi: De caratteri,
Libro primo 1638

A further plate from Antonozzi's copy book, showing the decorative element which was to become such a feature of English copy books in the second half of the 17th century, where birds and fish were especially selected for such treatment.

V&AM L123-1903 20 × 29

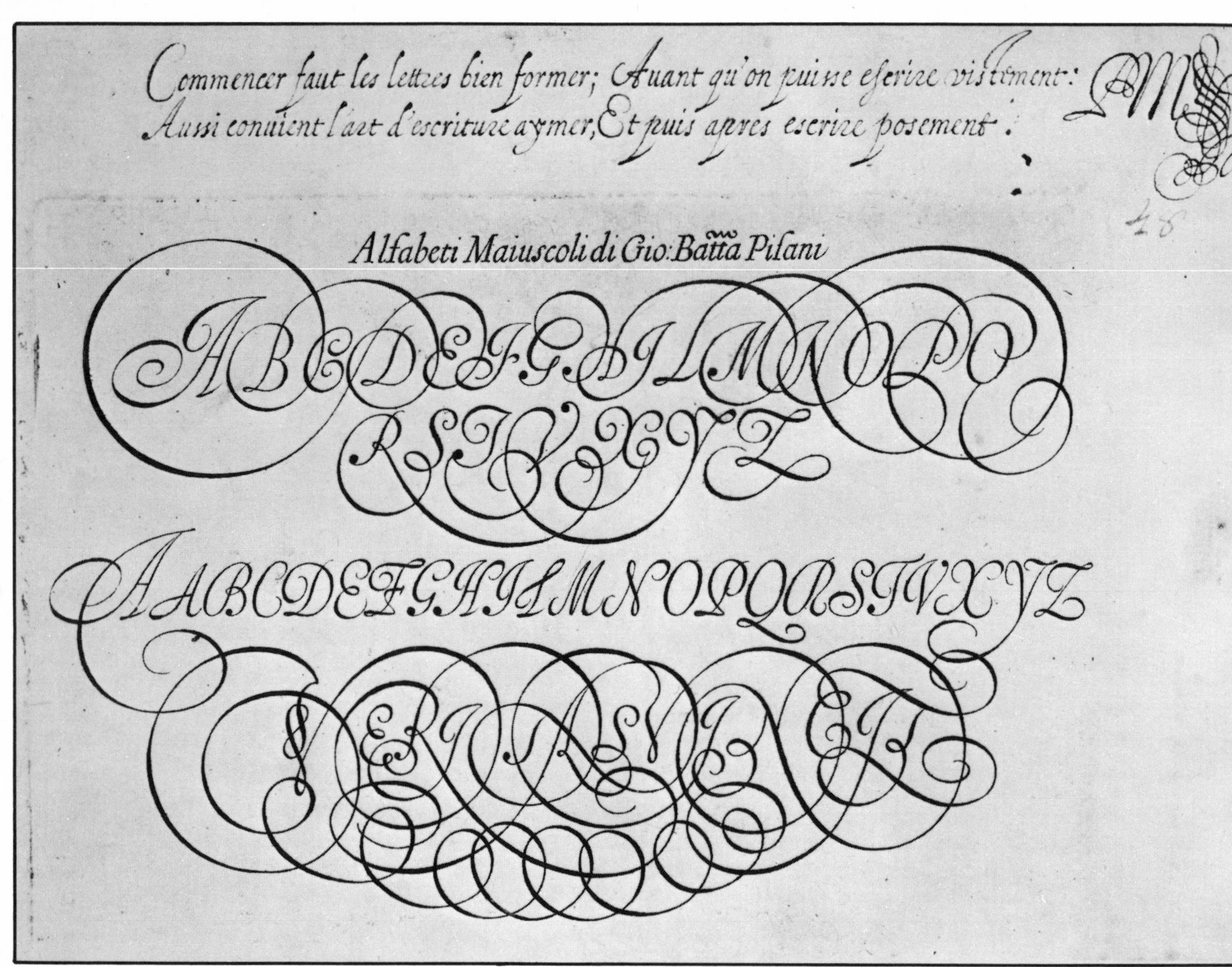

Giovanni Battista Pisani: Il primo libro di lettere corsive moderne
1641

The plate-line surrounding the engraved calligraphy is clearly visible in this illustration. Above it are written two lines of script in French, and these are in manuscript — a fact which the illustration unfortunately does not reveal. The writer has signed his work with his unidentified initials; the script is very professional as are his remarks on calligraphy!

V & A M L 1233-1970 16 × 22.5

Severo Binotti: Rime nel Dottorato dell'Illmo sig. Conte Francesco Gambara 1603

This laudatory poem is written out in a competent italic hand, but obviously not by a professional calligrapher; it gives the impression of a piece carefully produced to catch the eye of a potential patron. It is such examples of contemporary writing that bring life to the exact but cold models of the writing masters.

V&AM MS L778-1863 24 × 17

NEL DOTTORATO DELL'ILL.^{MO} SIG.

Che piu ? merta ogn'honor, merta ogni gloria
Ornamento del Cielo, e della Terra
Vedra' l'eta futura in ogni Historia
Il nome suo, che tutti i nomi atterra
Col Mondo eterna fia la sua memoria
E in uan s'armerà il tempo a'fargli guerra,
Che troppo e' grande di Francesco il pregio
E troppo e pien di merto il nome egregio.

Nocchiero esperto con sicuro legno
Solca nel uasto golfo de le leggi
E con miracoloso, & alto ingegno
I più dotti in saper uien che pareggi
E di Philosophia potente il Regno
Sa' pur ogn'huom com'ei lo signoreggi
Sia poi tall'hor tra' Dame, e tra Guerieri
Ben sa' l'Arti d'Amor d'Armi il mestieri.

Lectorum dicti celeberrimi Studij Patauini Magcum et admodū Reuerendū Dñum FRANCISCVM Magci Domini, ALEXANDRI RIATI Patauini, Filium {qui post multa, et longa studia, ac meditationes, variaq. eius probitatis, et eruditionis documenta, fidem Catholicam verbis iuxta Bullæ bonæ memoriæ Pij Papæ IV. tenorem conceptus palam et solemniter coram nobis professus est} a Promotoribus suis adductum, et nobis oblatū ad subeundum suum rigorosum examen, punctisq; ei {vt moris est} in sacra Theologia præassignatis, fecimus coram Nobis, et admodum Rdo Decano, ac alijs prædicti sacri Collegij Doctoribus, et Magistris ibidem existentibus diligenter, & rigorose examinari, qui autem in huiusmodi examine, sua Puncta assignata magistraliter recitando, argumenta quæcunq;, et dubia omnia, et

quasli=

Opposite:
Pages 190, 191 and 192 show three diplomas issued between 1614 and 1686 by the University of Padua. They not only span most of the 17th century, but by their variety of scripts they show how calligraphy continued to be kept alive by the need to produce such ceremonial 'single occasion' documents, for which printing was uneconomic. P. 190 confers a Doctorate in Theology on Franciscus Riatus in 1614; it is written in a clear rounded hand, which owes more to the printed page than to calligraphy. The important parts of the document are in gold.

V&AM L 2494-1886 23.5 × 16.5

re ſoluendis, in omni deniq; periclitatione sui tam
egregie, prudenter, docte, honorifice, laudabiliter,
excellenter, magiſtraliter, & Doctoreo more ſe
geſsit, talemque, ac tantam ingenij, memorię, do=
ctrinę, cæterarumque rerum, quę in conſūma=
tiſsimo Iuris Vtriuſque Doctore deſiderari
solent vim oſtendit, vt magnam sui expectatio=
nem, quam apud omnes concitauerat, non ſo=
lum ſuſtinuerit, ſed etiam longe superauerit: &
ob eam rem ab omnibus Excellentiſsimis dicti
Sacri Collegij Doctoribus ibidem continuo
exiſtentibus, VNANIMITER, ET CON=
CORDITER, CVNCTISQVE SVF=
FRAGIIS, AC EORVM NEMINE
PENITVS, ATQVE PENITVS DIS=
CREPANTE, AVT DISSENTIEN=
TE, NEC HÆSITANTE QVIDEM,
idoneus, & sufficientiſsimus in Vtroque Iure
fuerit iudicatus, & merito quidem approbatus;
sicut ex eorum votis ſecreto in scrutinio No=
bis

P. 191 conferred a Doctorate in Law on Quintilio Carbò in 1627. It is written in italic on vellum and is signed by the scribe, Bartholomæus Bredda, on the last leaf; this diploma also has important passages in gold.

V&AM L 2493-1886 23.5 × 16.5

omnes concitaverat non sòlum sustinuerit sed etiam longissime superaverit.
Quamobrem ab Exc: Inclyti Ordinis prefati Doctorib: ac publ: Profess: omnib: ibi=
dem continuò existentib. Unanimiter, et Concorditer Cunctisq. Suffragijs
ac Eorum NEMINE PENITUS ATQ. PENITUS Discrepante aut Dissentien=
te, Nec Hæsitante Quidem, Idoneus, aptissimus ac sufficientissimus Philosoph.
ac Medicus fuerit iudicatus, ac merito quidem approbatus, sicut ex eorum Votis
et singulorū suffragijs secreto in Scrutinio Nobis porrectis evidenter, et perspicuè
constitit. Nos itaque antiquam sequentes consuetudinem, et Sententiā Privi=
legiorum Patavinę Academiæ habita ratione scientiæ, eloquentiæ, peritiæ, facul=
tatis interpretandi, methodi curandi, et aliarum Virtutum, ac morū eiusdē
quorum omnium certissimū specimen exploratus, atq. pertentatus dedit, de
consilio, et sententia omniū Excellentissimor, predicti Venerandi Consessus
Doctorum ac Patrum præsentium, et hoc ipsum postulantium pro Tribunali se
dentes eundem Præclarissimum D. IO. BERNARDUM WINTERBA
CHIUM, Virum quidem doctissimum atque ita universis naturæ Artisq: do=
tibus ornatum, ut nihil amplius ei deesse videatur Doctorem Philosophiæ, et
Medicinæ in Dei Nomine approbavimus et approbatum esse volumus; pro=
nuntiantes, et declarantes eum esse optimè habilem, idoneum, ac dignum offi=
cio munere dignitate, et honore Doctoratus in Philosophia et Medicina ipsumque
continuò Philosoph: et Medicinæ Doctorem publicè, et solemniter fecimus, et cre=
avimus, ac per presentes literas facimus et creamus, tribuentes ei tanquā verè
idoneo, ac optime merito, et hac promotione, honorisque apicè dignissimo libe=
ram, et plenam potestatem, Cathedram Magistralem ascendendi atque Insignia
Doctoratus à Promotoribus suis petendi, et recipiendi, ipsisque Promotorib: illa
sibi impertiendi, liberam facultatem ut in posterum liberè et plenariè publi=
cè, et privatim in quibuscumque Philosophicis, et Medicinalibus disciplinis le=
gere, repetere, consulere, disputare, quæstiones terminare, controversias deci=
dere, et practicare possit, atque earum singulas partes aut universas profite=
ri docere, glossare, interpretari, et commentari hic, et ubique in rarum omneq:
Medicinam facere, Scholas regere, Baccalaureos constituere omnibusque, et
singulis uti frui, ac gaudere privilegijs, prerogativis, exemptionibus, imunitatib.
libertatibus, concessionibus, honoribus, favoribus, gratijs, ac indultis alijs quibus=
cumque quocumq. nomine censeantur, quibus alij Doctores atq. Magistri almæ
Parisiensis, Salamaticensis, Papiensis, et Bononiensis Academiæ ex quibuscumq.
Ecclesiasticis vel temporalib. concessionib. aut indultis gaudent et utuntur vel
uti et gaudere possunt, ac poterunt quomodolibet in futurū iuxta formā Privile=
gior, Almę Universit: nræ Patavinæ antiquitus, et absolutè concessor: Quibus ita
gestis, ac declaratis ut supra Præclarissimus et Excell: D. Alexander Bor=
romeus Patavinus Phil: et Medic: Doct. Comes Cast. Arquati et Burgi Val=
lis de Tarro, in prefato Lyceo ad Theor: extraord: Med: in p.° loco, et I. N. G. Protector

P. 192 is similar to p. 191, being neatly written out in black and gold italic script. The diploma confers the degree of Doctor of Philosphy and Medicine on Johannes Bernard Winterbach, and is dated 1686. The pages are modestly decorated with foliage patterns in blue and gold on the natural vellum ground.

V&AM L 596-1872

Opposite:

Anton Neudörffer: Schreibkunst [etc]. 1601 (1631)

Anton Neudörffer was a grandson of Neudörffer the Elder, the father of German calligraphy. This splendidly baroque title-page shows the state of German writing at the turn of the century. The work is in three parts, two of which are on wood and the third has been engraved on copper. A great variety of scripts is included.

V&AM 19.5 × 12.5

Schreibkunst
Das erste Theil
Inn
Welchem die Künstliche Außtheil-
ung des gantzen Kils Temperierung vñ
Proportionierung derselben, auch wie-
man die feder recht fassen sol. Nachmals
der Grund des zierlichen Teutschen Schreiben
vffs klerlichst angezeigt vnd angewisen,
das ein anfangender gar leichtlich dar-
aus schreiben lernen kan
Mit angehengten 2 newen schönen ver-
sal Alphabeten dergleichen niemals gesehen worden
Durch
Antonium Neudörffer Rechenmaister vnd
Modist der Statt Nürnberg
NVLLA DIES ABEAT, QVIN LINEA DVCTA SVPERSIT.

A
B

M I

Lettre fort propre pour Dames.

DEMETRIUS Phalerius admonnestoit souuent le Roy Ptolo
se pouruoir de toute sorte de liures traictans de l'administration des Royaumes,
et du gouuernement du faict de la guerre. Car il disoit que les choses desquelles
les familiers n'osoyent admonnester les Roys, estoient escrites es dicts liures,
ausquelz on congnoist la verite & n'espargnent aucunement personne.

Maurice Jausserandy: Le miroir d'escriture ou sont representées plusieurs sortes de lettres & charactères 1600

Jausserandy describes himself on the title-page of this work as escrivain et aritmeticien en Avignon. *Materot (p. 196) also came from Avignon, which indicates the continuing importance of this former Papal capital as a meeting place for Italian and French influences. It will be noted that in common with other writing masters Jausserandy offers a special hand for ladies!*

V&AM L 2899-1950 26 × 18.5

Opposite:

Anton Neudörffer: Schreibkunst [etc]. 1601 (1631)

Anton Neudörffer's manual contains a number of gothic alphabets of considerable elaboration. Many similar ones appear in later copy books, especially in England. It is fortunate that Neudörffer also includes a key to the letters he has so elaborately decorated as on occasions it would be difficult to decipher them!

V&AM 19.5 × 12.5

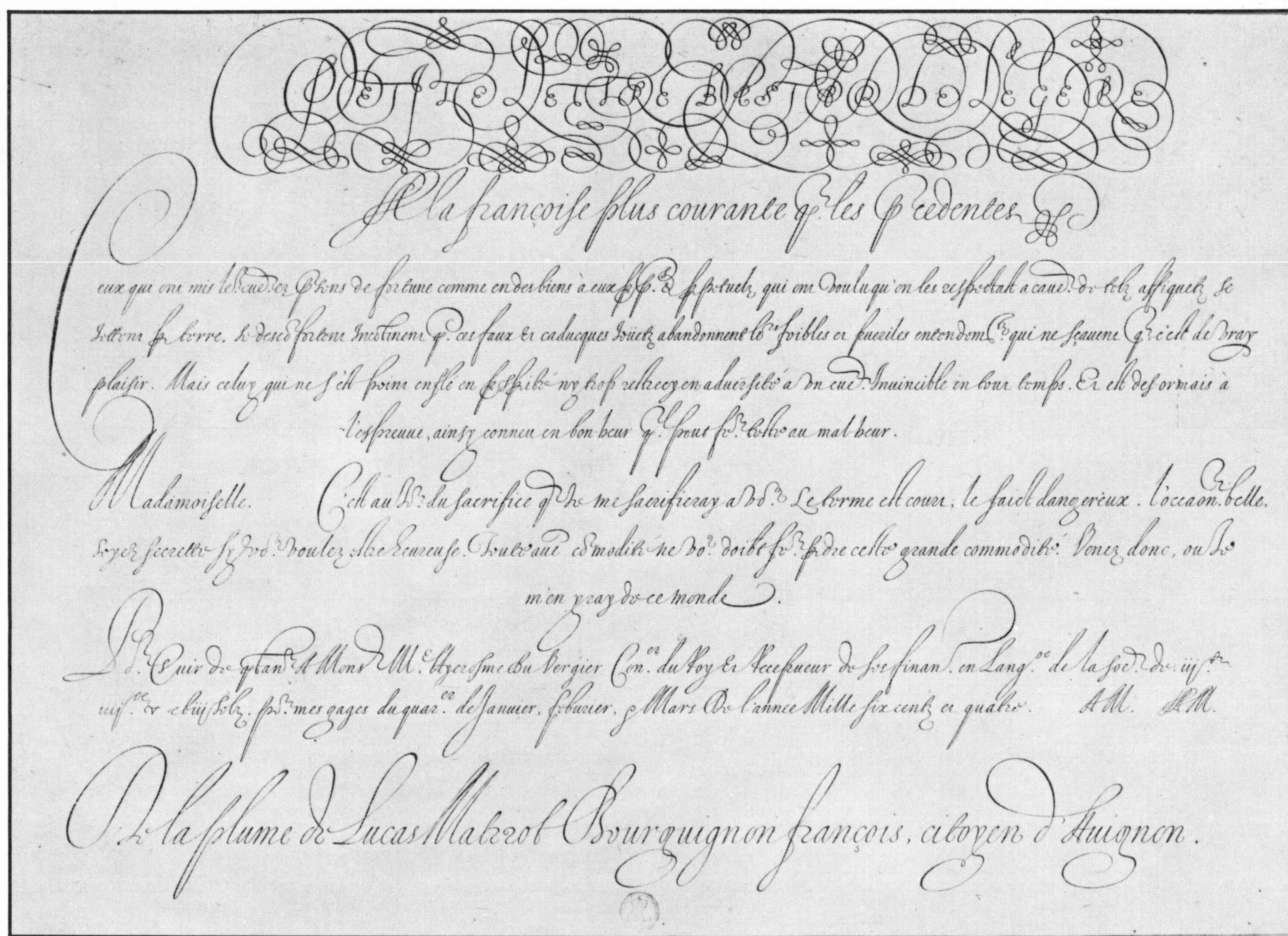

A la françoise plus courante q. les precedentes

De la plume de Lucas Materot Bourguignon françois, citoyen d'Avignon.

Lucas Materot: Les Œuvres
1608

Materot here gives an example of cursive writing in the 'lettre bastarde plus courante que les precedentes'. *But, as so often happened, the greater speed did not make for legibility, and the flourishes Materot employed make this an extremely difficult piece to decipher — especially the entwined heading! Nevertheless, the name of Materot was greatly revered by later writing masters.*

V & A M *2.viii.1874* *14 × 21.5*

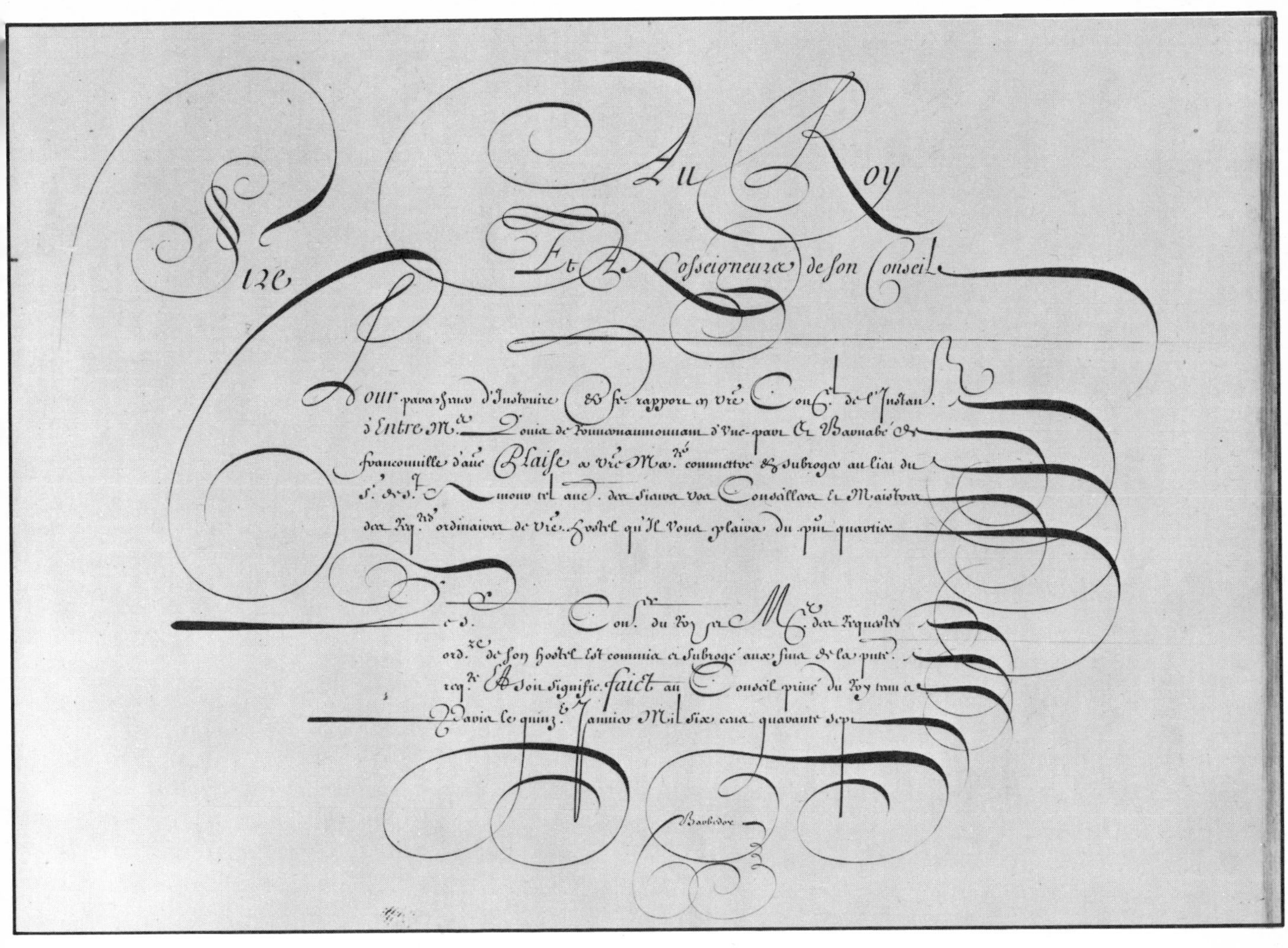

Louis Barbedor: Les ecritures financieres et italienne-bastarde dans leur naturel. 1650?

Barbedor was one of the most important 17th century French writing masters. He was given the task of revising the scripts used in official documents in France, and so helped to develop the round hand in that country. Even for official writings a certain amount of flourish was still encouraged!

V & A M L 3413-1938 33 × 41

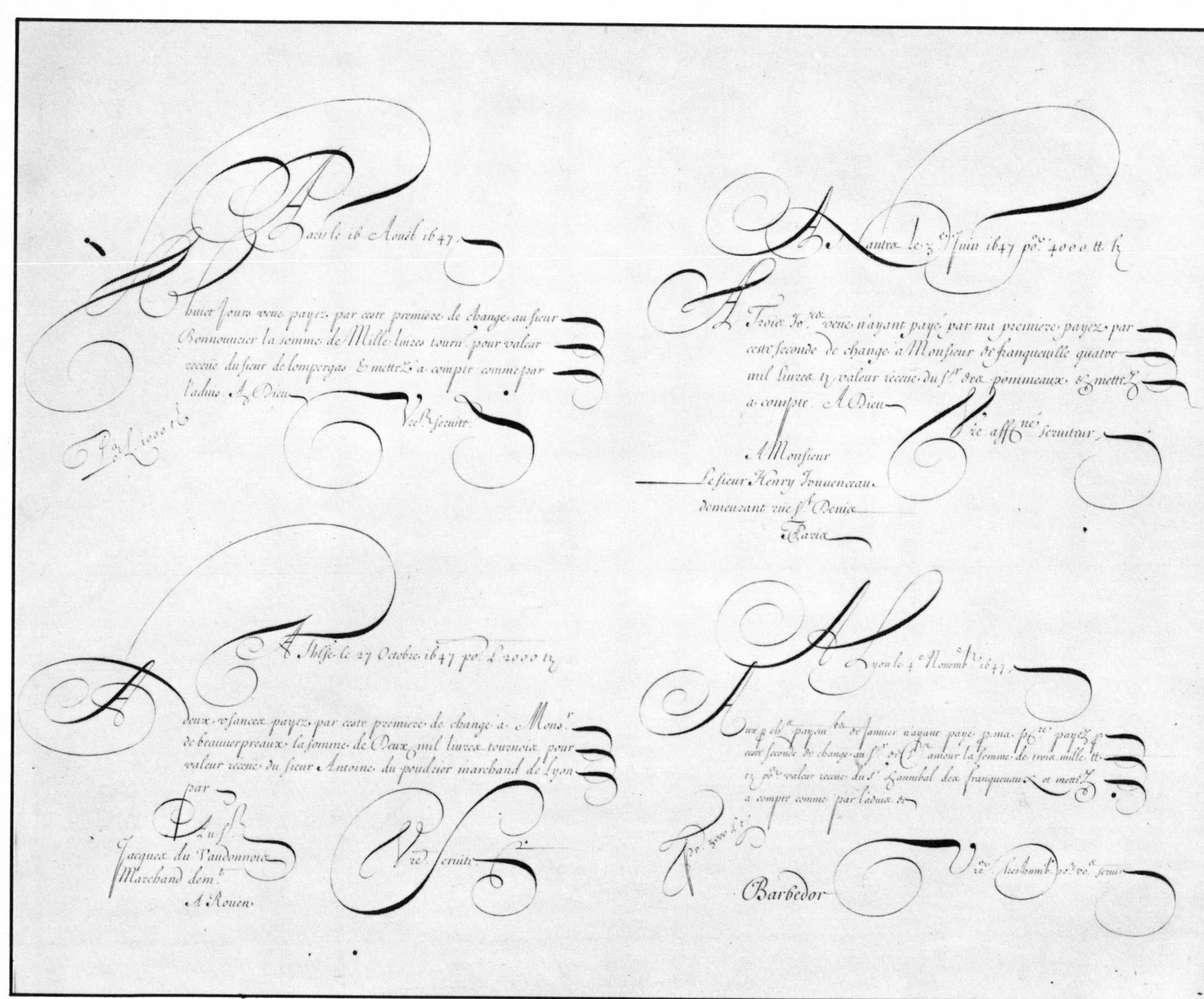

Louis Barbedor: Les ecritures financiere et italienne-bastarde dans leur naturel. 1650?

This further illustration from Barbedor's influential (and large!) manual, shows the script he advocated being put to practical commercial use.

V & A M L 3413-1939 31 × 41

Opposite:

Louis Senault: Les rares escritures financieres et italiennes-bastardes 1670?

Senault's work was characterised by the use of a neat sloping Roman hand, and he was his own engraver. The script shown here is relatively undecorated, but elaborate 'strikings' still have a place on the page.

V & A M L 1690-1888 37.5 × 25.5

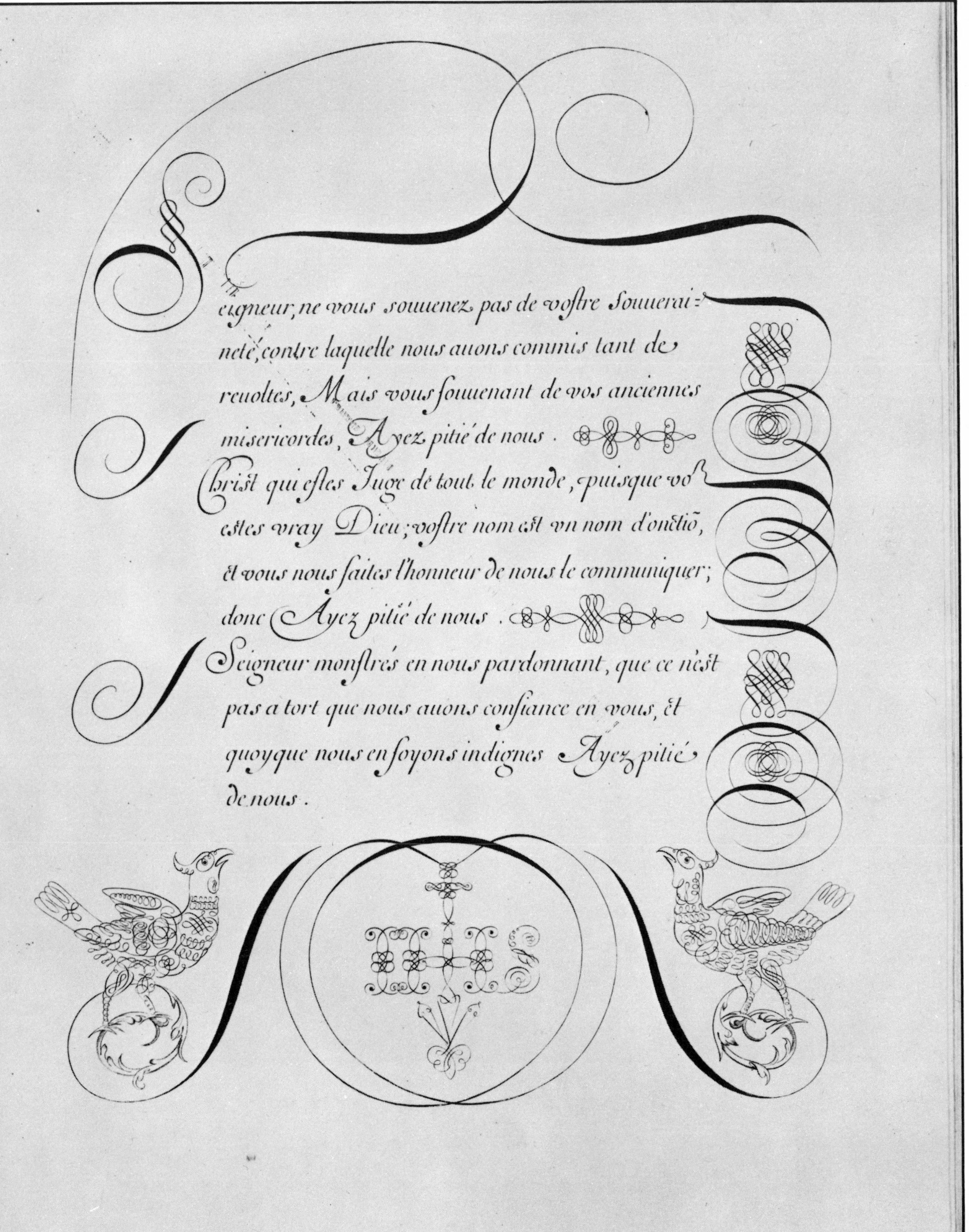
Seigneur, ne vous souuenez pas de vostre Souuerai-
neté, contre laquelle nous auons commis tant de
reuoltes, Mais vous souuenant de vos anciennes
misericordes, Ayez pitié de nous.
Christ qui estes Juge de tout le monde, puisque vo
estes vray Dieu; vostre nom est vn nom d'onctiõ,
et vous nous faites l'honneur de nous le communiquer;
donc Ayez pitié de nous.
Seigneur monstrés en nous pardonnant, que ce n'est
pas a tort que nous auons confiance en vous, et
quoyque nous en soyons indignes Ayez pitié
de nous.

A PRIME

E vous saluë Marie pleine de grace &c. O Dieu venez a mō secours. Gloire soit au Pere &c.

HYMNE

Chriſte Redemptor omniū.

Christ Redempteur de tout le mōde,
Du Principe éternel diuin écoulement
Dieu qui né sans commencement
Viens naître dans le temps d'vne
Vierge ſeconde.
Toy qui du Pere des lumieres

Heures Nouvelles dediées à Madame la Dauphine. Ecrites et gravées par L. Senault.

This work by Senault is undated but is presumably from the last quarter of the 17th century. It forms an interesting contrast to his copy book (p. 199), and is far more in the tradition of the handwritten devotional works of the school of Jarry. If you could not afford to commission such a work, then this engraved prayer book, which looked so like some of the manuscript ones, made a good substitute.

V&AM 14.vii.1870 19 × 12

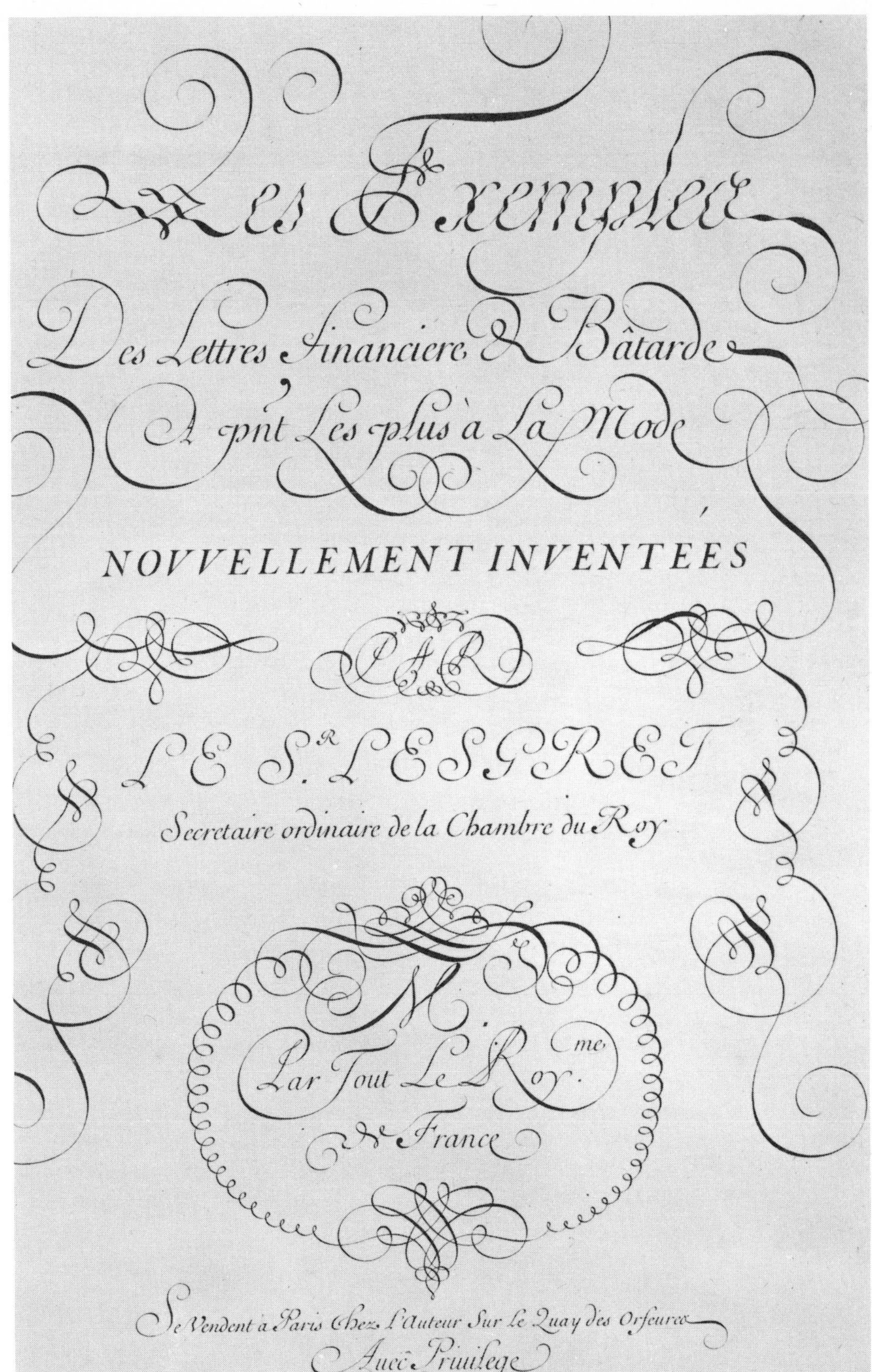
Les Exemples
Des Lettres Financiere & Bâtarde
A qnt Les plus a La Mode
NOUVELLEMENT INVENTEES
PAR
LE S.R LESGRET
Secretaire ordinaire de la Chambre du Roy
M.
Par Tout Le Roy. me
France
Se Vendent a Paris Chez l'Auteur Sur le Quay des Orfeures
Auec Priuilege

Nicolas Lesgret: Le livre d'exemplaires composé de toutes sortes de letres de finance & italienne bastarde, avec des instructions familieres touchant les preceptes generaux qu'il faut observer, pour bien imiter les examples qui y sont compris 1694.

Like Barbedor before him, Lesgret was in the employ of Louis XIV, and his copy book has many similarities with that of the earlier writing master. The terminal flourishes which Lesgret gave to so many of his letters were typical of the contemporary French style of writing.

V&AM L1672-1888 37 × 24.5

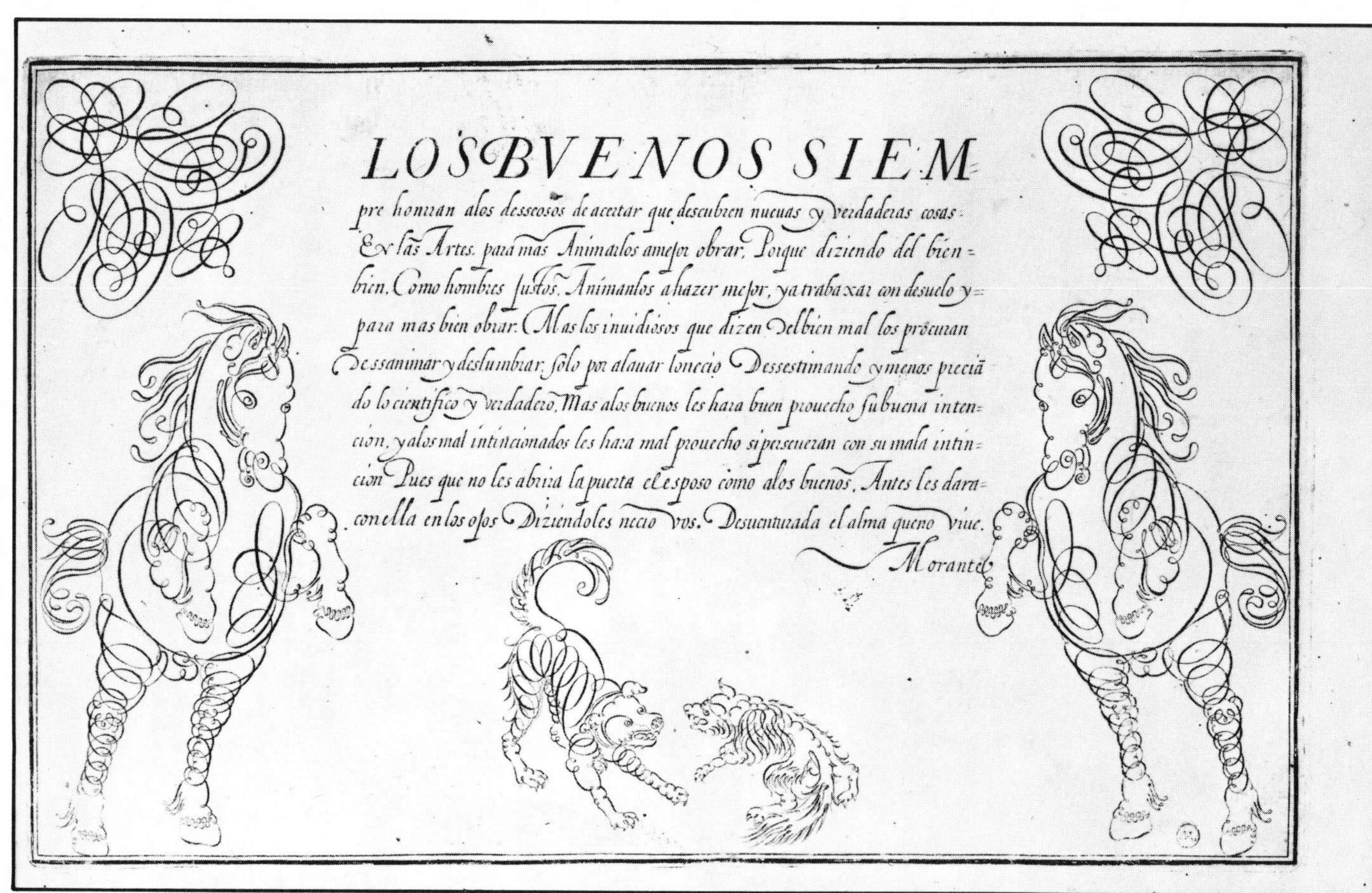

Pedro Diaz Morante: Nueva arte de escrevir 1615

Diaz Morante was one of the important 17th century Spanish calligraphers, but, as can be seen from this example, he was much influenced by the Italian writing masters in his cursive chancery script. His style was typical of its period in the clubbed effect of his ascenders and descenders, and in his fondness for elaborate decorative flourishes.

V & A M L 2051-1965 20 × 29.5

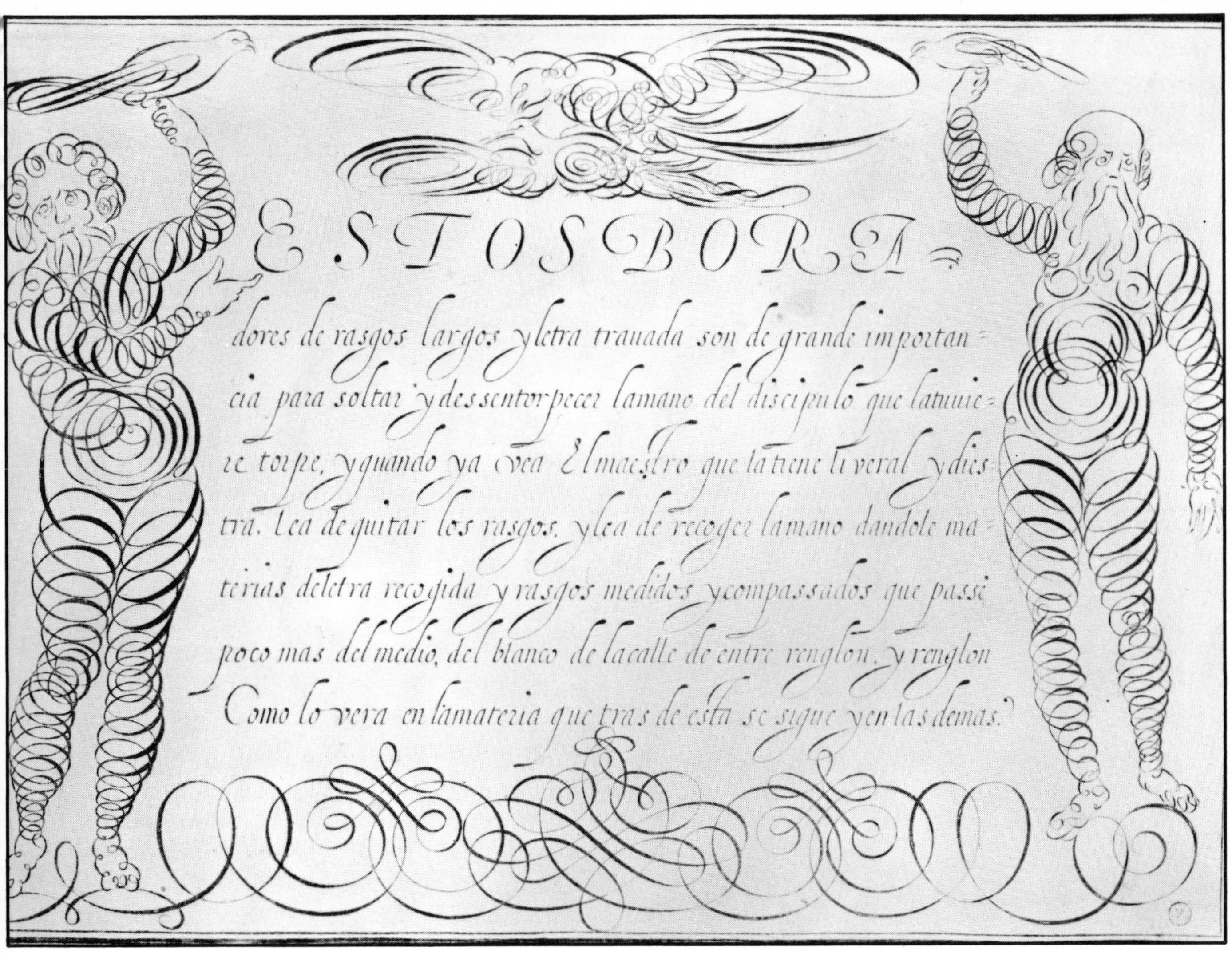

Pedro Diaz Morante: Nueva arte de escrevir 1615

This particular example from the important copy book of Diaz Morante has been selected for a special reason. When the Liber Collectarum [etc] 1620 *(p. 204), was purchased by the Library of the Victoria and Albert Museum, an attempt was made to trace the possible source of the calligraphic decorations in the manuscript. A careful comparison of the two figures which ornament this plate should be made with those illustrated in the* Liber Collectarum. *It seems almost certain that the scribe of the Italian manuscript must have had a copy of the Spanish writing book before him when he drew the two later figures — only the objects which the figures hold differ from the originals.*

V&AM L 2051-1965 20 × 29.5

Liber Collectarum iuxta ritum Sac. Ordinis Cartusiensis . . . 1620

This manuscript was purchased by the Library of the Victoria and Albert Museum as an example of contemporary Italian calligraphy. The source of the style of at least part of the manuscript is indicated by the very great similarity between the two figures illustrated here and those which appear on one of the plates of the copy book by Diaz Morante (p. 203). The widespread influence of the published copy books is proved by this interesting link.

V&AM   MS L 6630-1978   32 × 22

Giovanni Battista and Francesco Pisani: Engraved copy book.

Both the Pisani published copy books in the 1640s and this volume contains samples signed by Giovanni and Francesco, but lacks a title-page — it may be merely a gathering together of their work from various sources. The interest lies in the two engraved figures here, which exactly match the manuscript volume illustrated adjacent to this, although being so much later they can hardly have formed the original models.

V&AM L 3076-1960 18 × 25.

José de Casanova: Primera parte del arte de escrevir todas formas de letras 1650

Casanova displays a great variety of hands in his book, but the most important was the lettera bastarda *which he did much to introduce into Spain. It was included in many contemporary copy books in different countries and was of considerable significance in the evolution of the later round hand. Casanova, in common with many writing masters, was not satisfied with the available engravers, and so learnt the art that he might engrave his own work. The plate shown here is typical of the script and decoration of Spanish official documents, a style which lasted until the 19th century.*

V&AM 16.x.1871 30 × 21

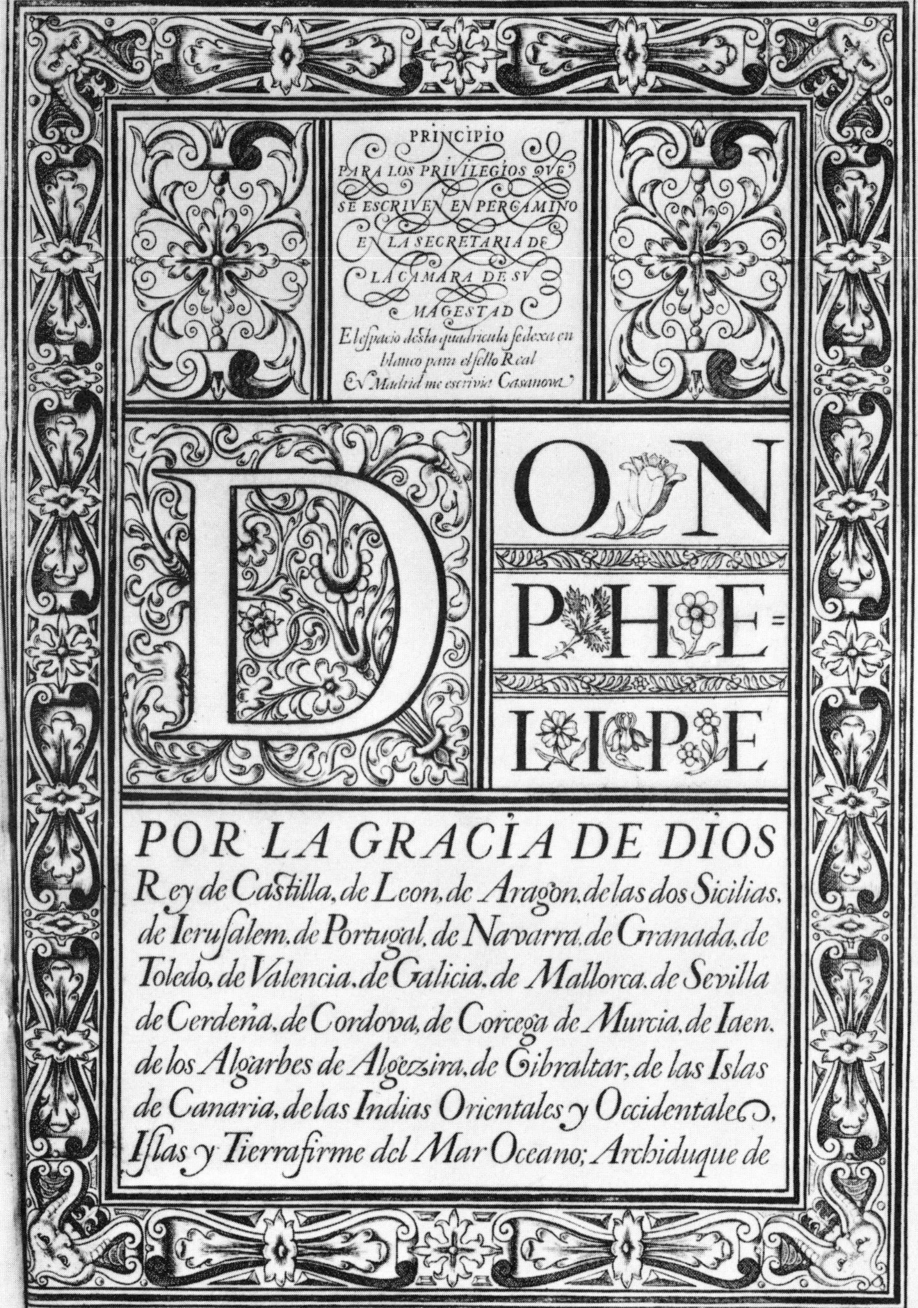

PRINCIPIO PARA LOS PRIVILEGIOS QVE SE ESCRIVEN EN PERGAMINO EN LA SECRETARIA DE LA CAMARA DE SV MAGESTAD

El eſpacio desta quadricula ſe dexa en blanco para el ſello Real

En Madrid me escrivia Casanova

DON PHELIPE

POR LA GRACIA DE DIOS

Rey de Caſtilla. de Leon. de Aragon. de las dos Sicilias. de Ieruſalem. de Portugal. de Navarra. de Granada. de Toledo. de Valencia. de Galicia. de Mallorca. de Sevilla de Cerdeña. de Cordova. de Corcega de Murcia. de Iaen. de los Algarbes de Algezira. de Gibraltar. de las Islas de Canaria. de las Indias Orientales y Occidentales. Iſlas y Tierrafirme del Mar Oceano; Archiduque de

Carta executoria de hidalguìa
1625

Cartas executoria *were documents issued in Spain to prove purity of blood and nobility of descent. Introduced during the reign of Ferdinand and Isabella, they continued to be issued until about 1800, although the majority date from c1550-1700. They were not often of very high artistic quality, but since few copies were required, it was not a profitable field for printers, and they remained in the hands of scribes and illuminators. This example relates to the family of Berbinçañas y Licarazos, and is written in a very distinctive script, with its swash letters and clubbed ascenders.*

V & A M MS L 101-1864 f.102r 29 × 20

Hijo legitimo y natural de Pedro de Berbinçana Liçaraçu escrivano
real, y del Juzgado dela Villa de Peralta, y Lo fue por raçon que
estando Cassado el dicho Pedro de Berbinçana Liçaraçu Con Mª
Lopez de Dicastillo en segundas nupcias, ansi enla dicha Villa de
Peralta Como en esta Villa de Viana le conocio, y vio tenia en su cassa
y Compañia tres hijos, que el Vno dellos era el dicho Joan de Berbinçana
a quien este testigo Conuerso, y comunico mucho siendo muchachos y
al dicho Pedro de Berbinçana su Padre este testigo le oyo decir y Confesar
que el dicho Joan de Berbinçana Padre delos Supplicantes hera su hijo legitimo procreado en el primer Matrimonio, que celebro enla Villa de Cor-
lla Con Vna tal Fernandez, y en este Credito, opinion y fama
este testigo se lo Vio tener, Criar, tratar, y alimentar, llamandolo
hijo, y el a el Padre, y por tal fue hauido, tenido y reputado, sin que
se sepa aya oydo, ni entienda Cossa en contrario, y que esto que a dicho
y depuesto en este su dicho es Verdad, y como en tal siendole leydo
lo ratifico y firmo. Pedro Ruyz. Ante mi Bartholome de s.t
Martin es.º

tes.º En la Villa de Viana, los dias, mes, e año dhs
por ante mi el dicho escrivano, el dicho D. Joan de Liçaraçu por si
y en el dicho nombre, en su prueva de su articulado presento por tes.º
a Martin Serrano Vezino dela dicha Villa, de quien tome

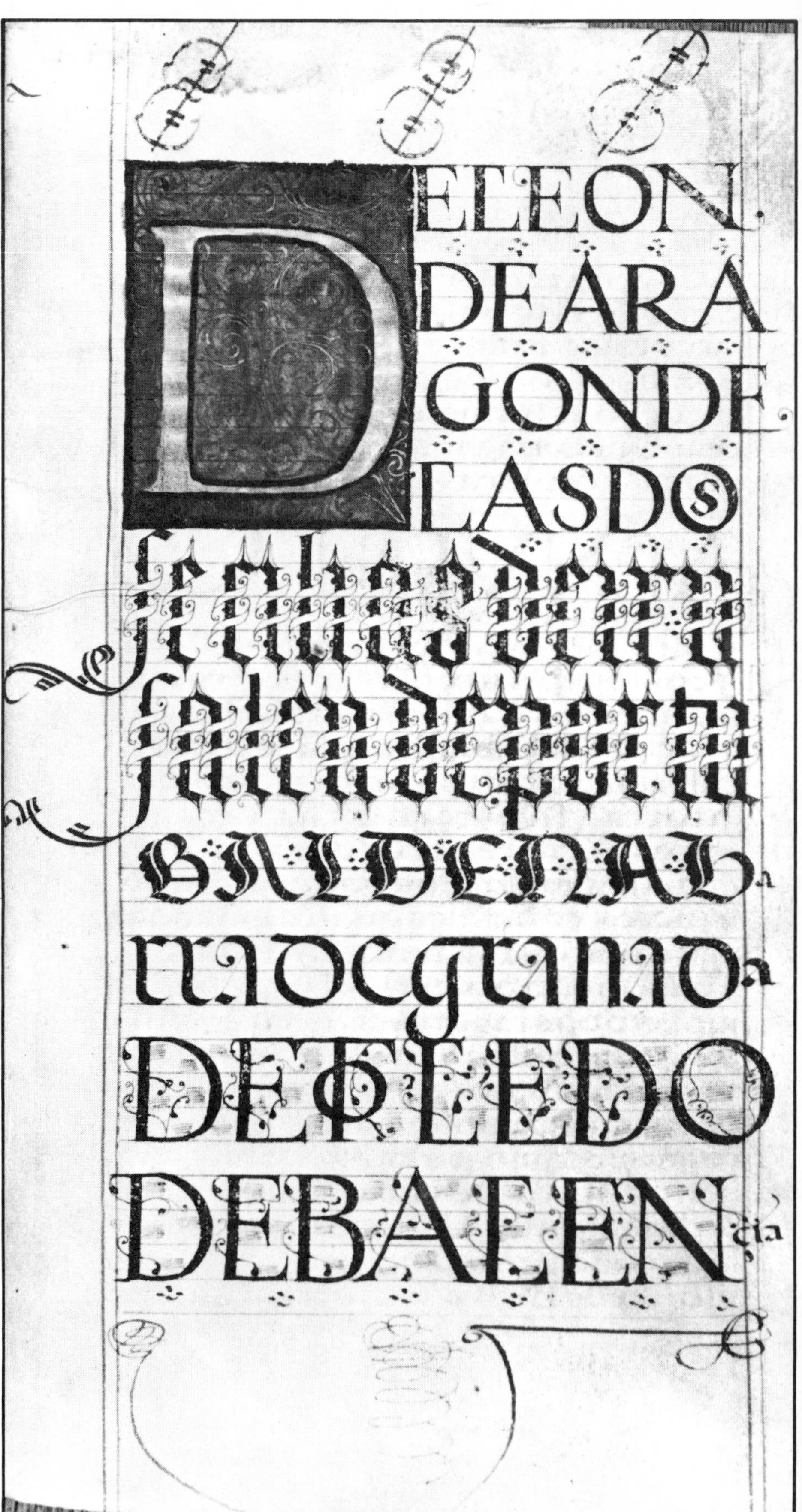

Carta executoria de hidalguìa
29 May 1595

The main part of this attestation of nobility is written out in a rotunda script, but this page has been chosen to show the elaboration which might be given to certain important passages in such documents. The text here contains part of the Spanish King's titles. The beginning on the previous page is illuminated and reads Don Phelipe por la gracia de Dios Rey de Castilla *and continues here with* De Leon, de Aragon [etc].

V&AM L116-1938 f.4r 31 × 21

Plate 1
Breviary (incomplete) of Utrecht
Netherlandish (Delft?) c1490

This manuscript is written in Dutch on a fine white vellum, and the whole aspect of the work suggests that it may have been written and decorated in a convent in Delft. The bastarda script is written in a neat hand in very black ink.

V & A M   Reid MS 36   f 42r
20 × 13

Overleaf: Plate 2
Book of Hours (Use of Rome), known as the Hours of Alfonso of Aragon   Neapolitan   c1480

This kind of large and lavishly decorated prayer book continued to be in demand among the aristocracy and court circles long after printing had taken over for the more humble productions. It is written in rotunda script in a very black ink; this page shows the beginning of the Office of the Dead.

V & A M   Salting MS 1224   f 91r
25 × 17

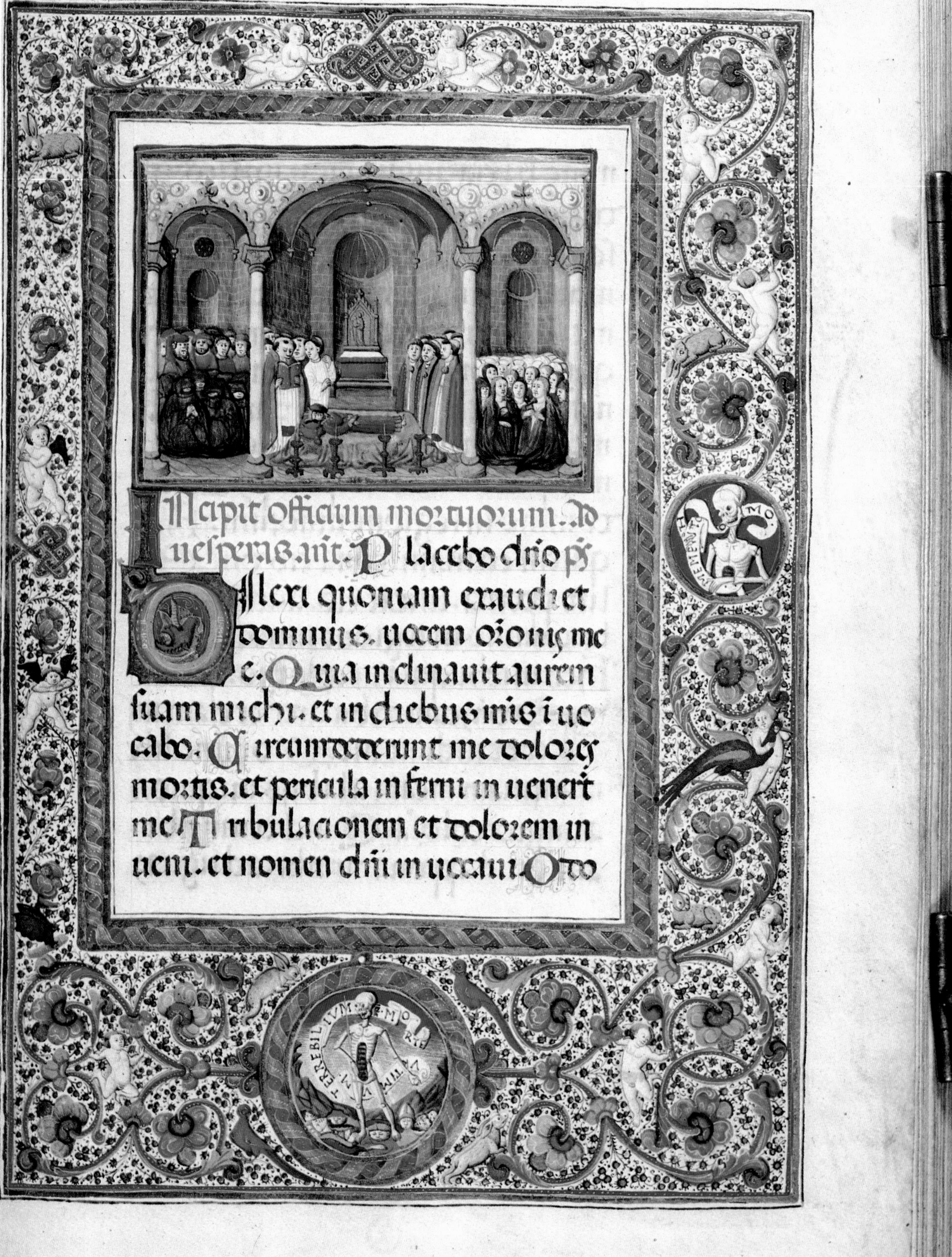

Incipit officium mortuorum. Ad
vesperas. ant. Placebo dno ps.
Dilexi quoniam exaudiet
dominus. vocem orõnis me
e. Quia inclinauit aurem
suam michi. et in diebus meis inuo
cabo. Circumdederunt me dolores
mortis. et pericula inferni inuenerut
me. Tribulacionem et dolorem in
ueni. et nomen dñi inuocaui. O do

Plate 3
Adrien Baltyn: Traicté de l'antiquité & preeminence des maisons d'Habsbourg [etc] 1616

This is a large and well illustrated volume, probably intended as a presentation copy. Throughout the scribe has used various scripts in order to emphasise different aspects of his text. This illustration comes from the end of the book, and shows the writer busy at work, while below the illustration begins the list of related books. A delightful depiction of scripts and scribe!

V & A M MS L 3542-1979 f 227r
25 × 21

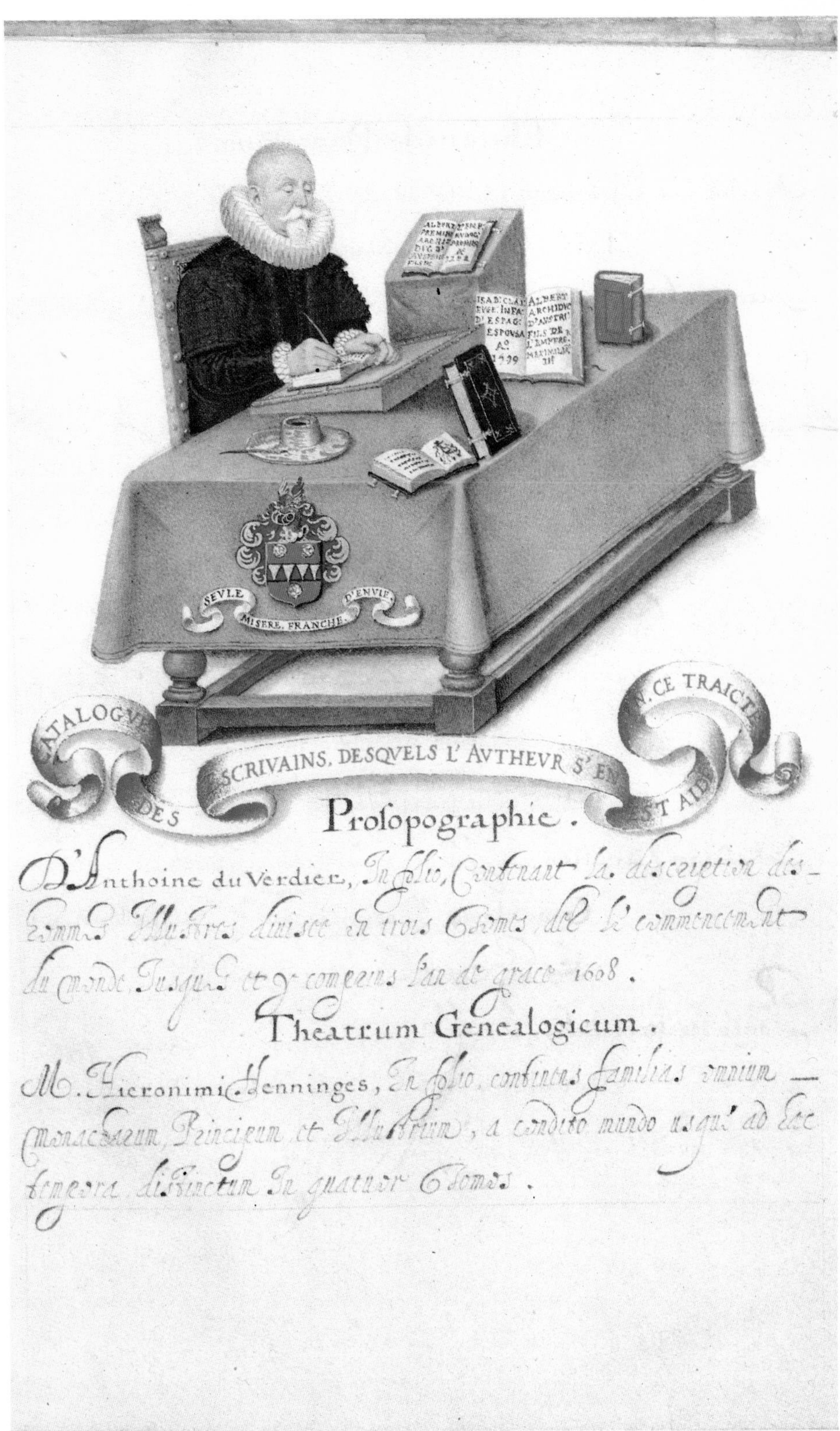

Overleaf: Plate 4
Book of Hours (Use of Rome) known as the Bentivoglio Hours
Bologna c1500

The manuscript is written in antiqua tonda *script, with a great variety of ligatures and flourishes, which to James Wardrop and others has suggested the work of Pierantonio Sallando. Although the decorations are perhaps the most outstanding feature of this manuscript, the text is entirely worthy of so fine a manuscript.*

V & A M Reid MS 64
21 × 15

AD SEXTAM. V.

DEus in ad
iutorium
meum inte
de. R. Do
mine ad
adiuuan
dum me
festina. V.
Gloria
patri et filio et spiritui sancto. Si
cut erat in principio et nunc et sem
per et in secula seculorum. amen Al
leluya uel Laus tibi domine rex
eterne glorie. HYMNUS.
MEmento salutis auctor q no
stri quondam corporis ex illi

Plate 5

Document appointing Manuel de Godoy, Prince de la Paz, Duke of Alcudia, as governor of Teruel 1804

This elegant document indicates the continuing high standard which prevailed in Spanish calligraphy, especially within the court circle. The decoration of the borders and the initials is of an equally high quality, and includes a series of tiny genre scenes in grisaille set within minute gilded frames.

V & A M MS L 4763-1978
30.5 × 20

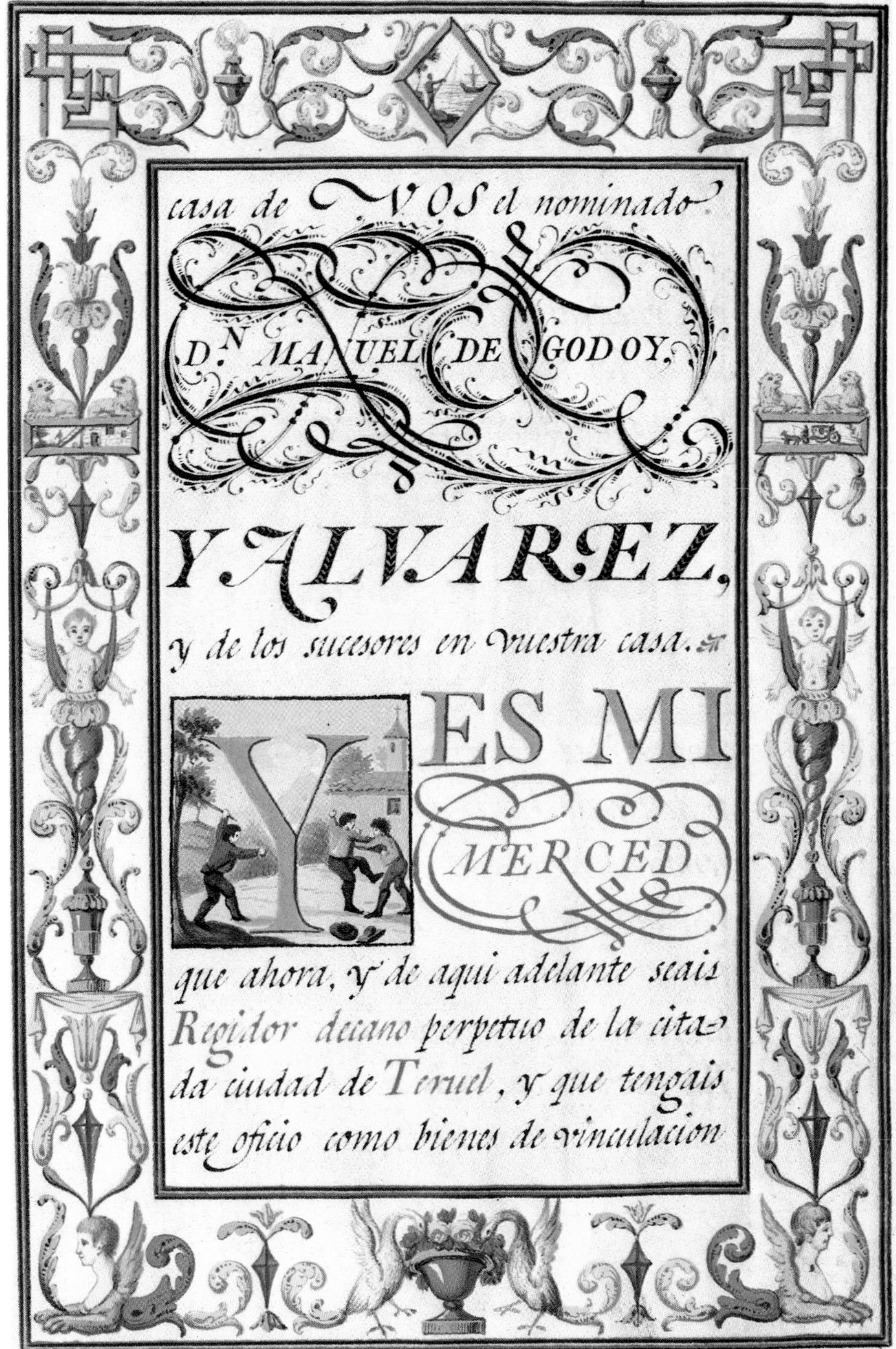

casa de VOS el nominado
D.N MANUEL DE GODOY,
Y ALVAREZ,
y de los sucesores en vuestra casa.
YES MI
MERCED
que ahora, y de aqui adelante seais
Regidor decano perpetuo de la cita-
da ciudad de Teruel, y que tengais
este oficio como bienes de vinculacion

Overleaf: Plate 6

Idylls of the king, by Alfred Lord Tennyson 1862

This lithographed text and the outlines for illuminating were published by Winsor & Newton, colour merchants, who also sold the necessary artists' materials. This type of work, which was published in large numbers in the 1860s, was no doubt intended for those amateurs who did not feel capable of producing their own designs. Such publications were symptomatic of the interest in all things medieval at that time, among them the manuscript book. The script is a 19th-century gothic and the illustrations are coloured by hand.

V & A M L 5838-1970

SIR BE DIVERE
Queen Guenevere
had fled the Court & sat
There in the holy house at Amesbury
Weeping none with her save a little maid
A novice one low light betwixt them burn'd
Blurr'd by the creeping mist for all abroad
Beneath a moon unseen albeit at full
The white mist like a face cloth to the face
Clung to the dead earth & the land was still.

Plate 7
Edith B. Crapper: The Bell of Atri by H.W. Longfellow 1927

The 20th century has seen a revival of interest in the handwritten book, based on medieval practice but still essentially contemporary. This charming work was specially commissioned from the scribe, who was also her own decorator and illuminator.

V & A M *MS L 5444-1975* *17 × 13*

Plate 8
Hella Basu: 'Non nobis . . .' by Henry Cust 1969

An interesting piece of modern calligraphy in which the scribe has combined a formal script with a collage of illustrations disposed to form letters.

V & A M *MS L 5315-1971*

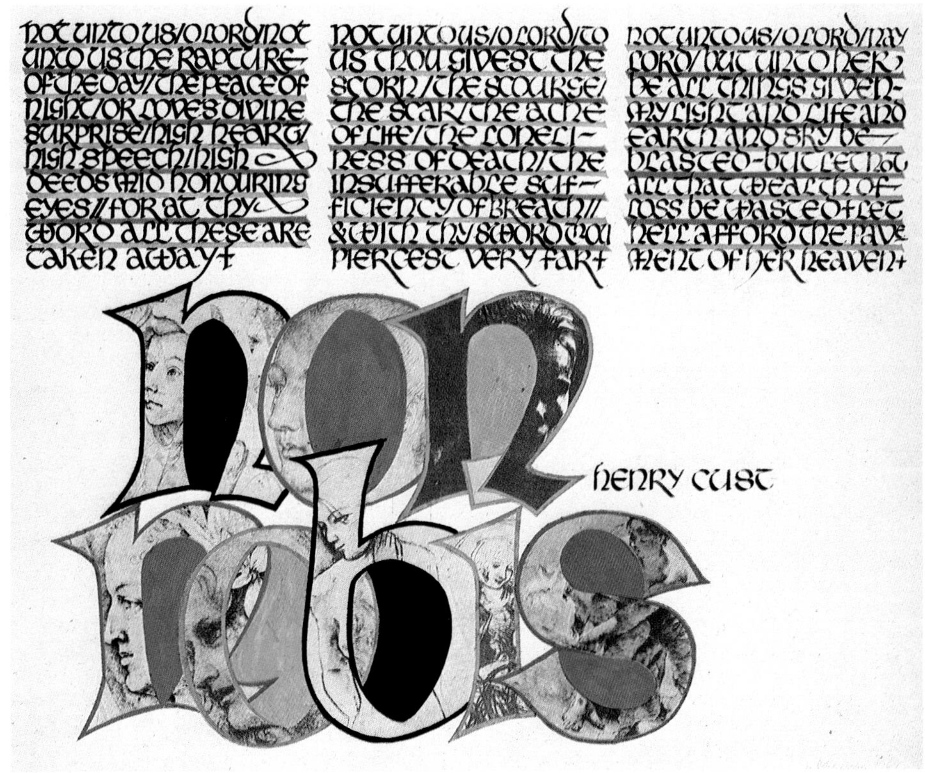

Overleaf: *Plate 9*
Marie Angel: You never enjoy the world aright . . . From words by Thomas Traherne 1979

Marie Angel is probably best known for her drawings of plants and flowers. Her delicate work is particularly suited to the miniature style of most of her manuscripts, many of which are in private collections. In this illustration her calligraphy blends especially well with the subject.

Reproduced by permission of the artist.

YOU NEVER ENJOY THE WORLD ARIGHT,
till the Sea itself floweth in your veins,
till you are clothed with the HEAVENS,
and crowned with the STARS:
AND PERCEIVE YOURSELF
TO BE THE SOLE HEIR OF THE WHOLE WORLD,
and more than so, because men are in it who
are every one SOLE HEIRS as well as You.

Las Armas, y Blason gentilico que pertenecen àssi al expresado Don Andres como del Capitan Don Andres dela Gādara por este esclarecido Linage se òrganizan en Campo de Blao, Castillo de Plata, y àla puerta del vna muger Armada con espada, vn escudo embraçado que defiende la entrada, y el Castillo ha de estar sobre hondas, de àgua delas quales han de salir, dos Cisnes Volantes hacia el Castillo, vno por vn lado, y òtro, por el òtro, como se manifiesta en el primer quartel de las Armas, de Costados que va al principio de este geneolosico, àcto, y se obstenta en el presente Escudò.

CHRO, ROLARIO.

El Campo Nobilissimo de este Escudo que en àraldico estilo llamamos! Blaò, denota, y representa, el notorio justificado Celo, delos Varones Illustres de este Linage

Carta executoria de hidalguìa
1724

In this document the scribe has used a Roman script for quotations and special passages, while the main text is written in a neat italic. Cartas executoria *were an important factor in helping to keep alive the scribal art in Spain, where the general level of calligraphy remained high until a late date. This document relates to the Gandara family.*

V & A M MS L 7121-1978 30.5 × 20.5

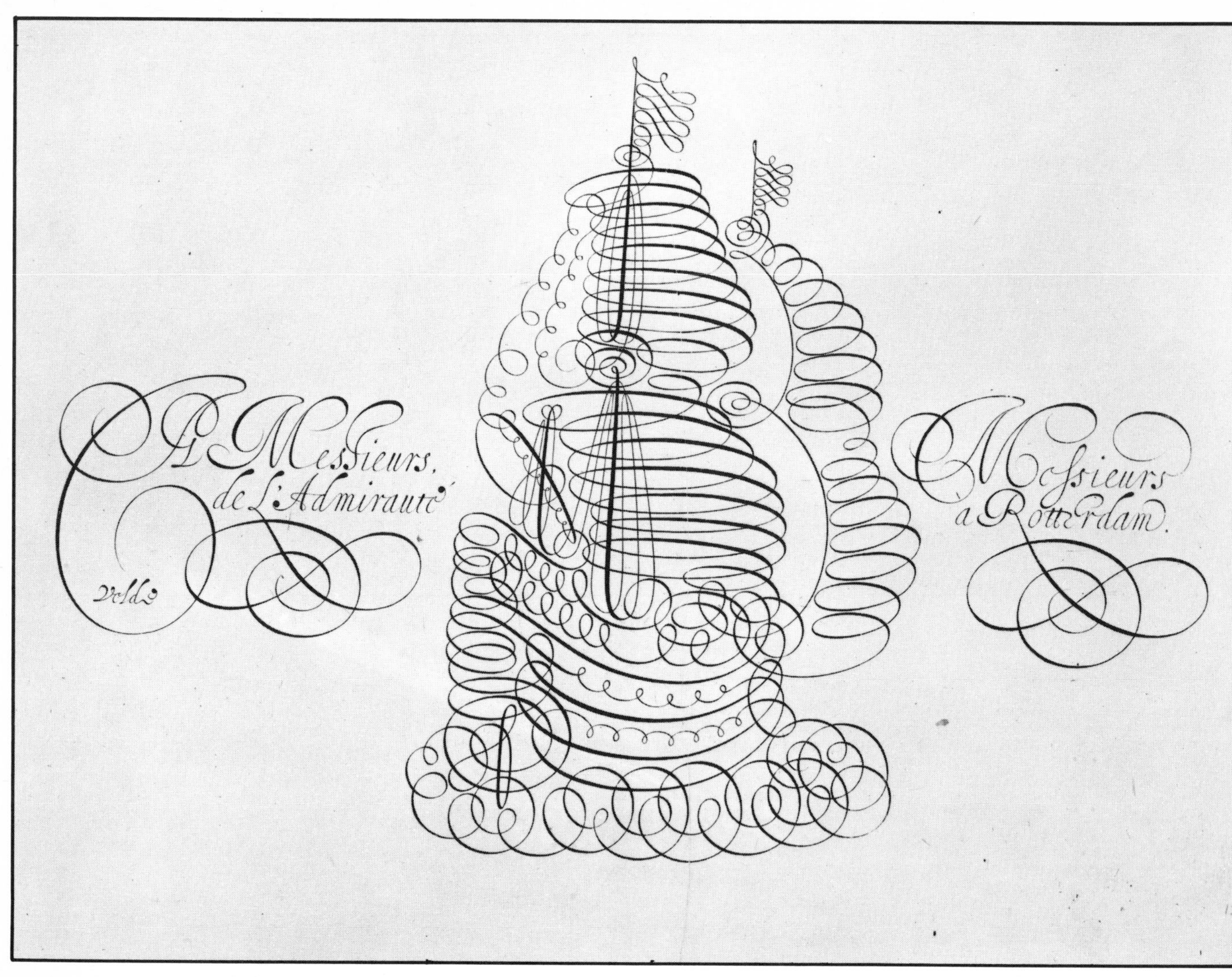

Jan van den Velde: Spieghel der Schrijfkonste, in den welcken ghesien worden veelderhande Gheschriften met hare Fondementen ende onderrichtinghe wtghegeven door Jan van den Velde. 1605

Van den Velde was one of the most important of Dutch writing masters, and was mentioned with respect by colleagues in various parts of western Europe. His copy book was of much larger format than most contemporary works. Many of his versions of the gothic letters were very ornate, as were his flourished decorations, but in the latter he was very much a man of his time.

V&AM 3.xii.1873 23.5 × 35

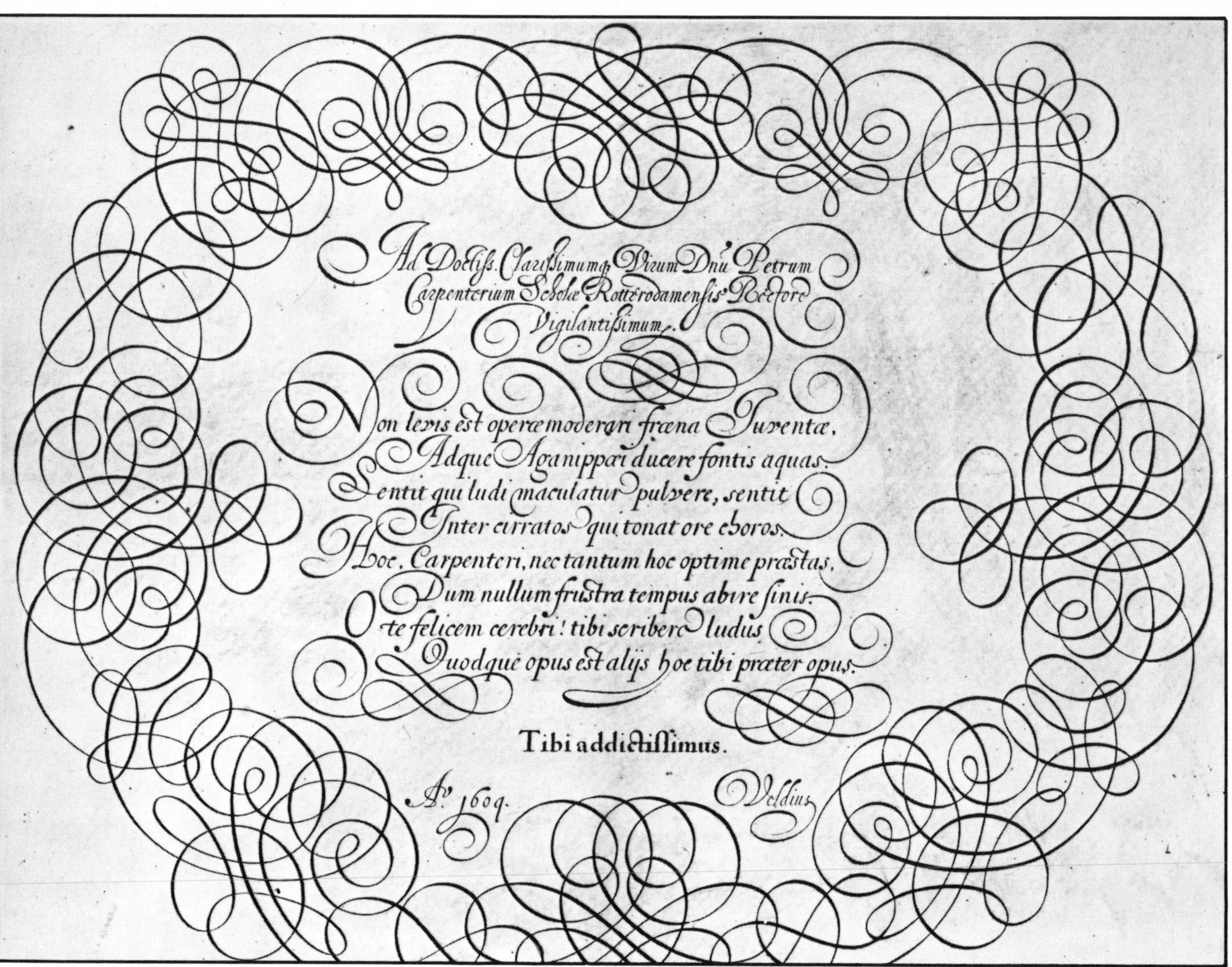

an van den Velde: Spieghel der
ichrijfkonste [etc]. 1605 (1609)

'his further plate from a later part of 'an den Velde's important work shows is script as a link between the French orms of Materot and the later levelopments of the English round and. The use of Latin examples by the riting masters was all part of their ttempt to link their work with that of rofessional academics, and so improve heir own status.

' & A M 3.xii.1873

David Roelands: T'magazin oft-pac-huys der loeffelijcker penn-const 1616

Roelands was a writing master in Antwerp and Vlissingen, but little else is known about his life. The two plates illustrated here show him to have been an extremely competent calligrapher, in the tradition of his near contemporary Jan van den Velde, who has remained so much better known. But there is no doubt that the over-elaboration common to so many copy books of the period detracts from the usefulness of the examples.

V & A M Circ. 171-72-1972

Alle dinck heeft synen Tyd. Eccle. 3.

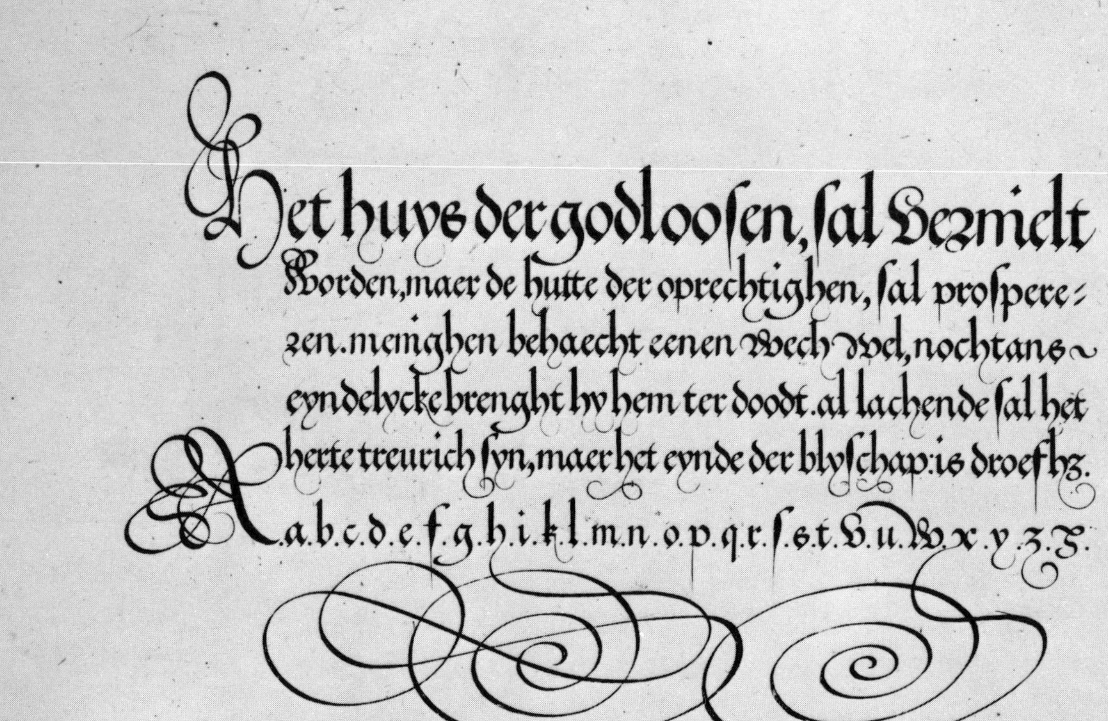

Simon de Vries: Lust-hof der schriif-konste 1610

Simon de Vries is best known as engraver, chiefly of landscapes, but in this book he shows himself a competent calligrapher. Many engraved illustrations often carried beautifully written captions (also engraved) so it is no surprise to find calligraphers as engravers and engravers as expert calligraphers.

V&AM 28.vii.1870 20 × 31

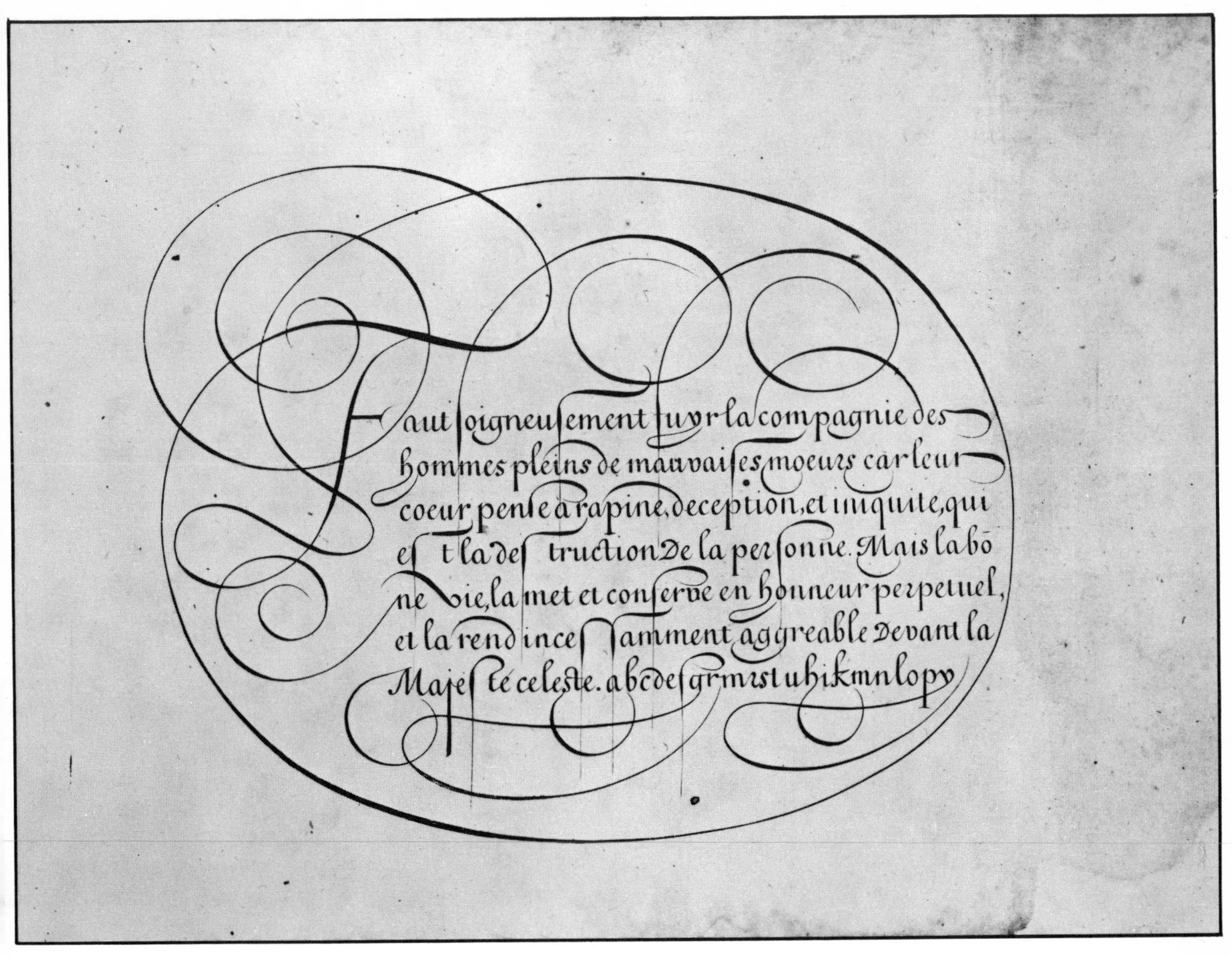

Faut ſoigneuſement fuyr la compagnie des
hommes pleins de mauvaiſes moeurs car leur
coeur penſe a rapine, deception, et iniquite, qui
eſt la deſtruction de la perſonne. Mais la bō
ne vie, la met et conſerve en honneur perpetuel,
et la rend inceſſamment aggreable devant la
Majeſte celeste. abcdeſgrmrstuhikmnlopy

Jean de la Chambre:
Verscheyden geschriften 1638

The title of this copy book is to be found below a portrait of the author painted by Frans Hals and engraved by J. S. Hoef; this gives some idea of his contemporary importance, though little is now known about him. His calligraphy here is decorative rather than practical, as he carries some of his ascenders and descenders over or below other parts of the words.

V&AM L 3639-1960 20 × 28

When an humour is strong and predominant, it not onlie converteth his proper nutriment, but even that which is apt for contrarie humours, into it owne nature and qualitie. Of like force is a strong and wilfull Desire, in the minde of man: For it nott only feeds upon agreeable motions, but makes even those reasons, which are strongest against it, to be most for it.

Æger animus, falsa pro veris videt.

Martin Billingsley: The pens excellencie; or, the secretaries delighte 1618

Billingsley was chiefly noted for his Italian hand, of which this is an example, but his copy book contained a variety of different hands in the styles then current. Sir Ambrose Heal considered this work to be 'the first English copy book of any pretensions'.

V&AM L 3061-1960 13 × 18

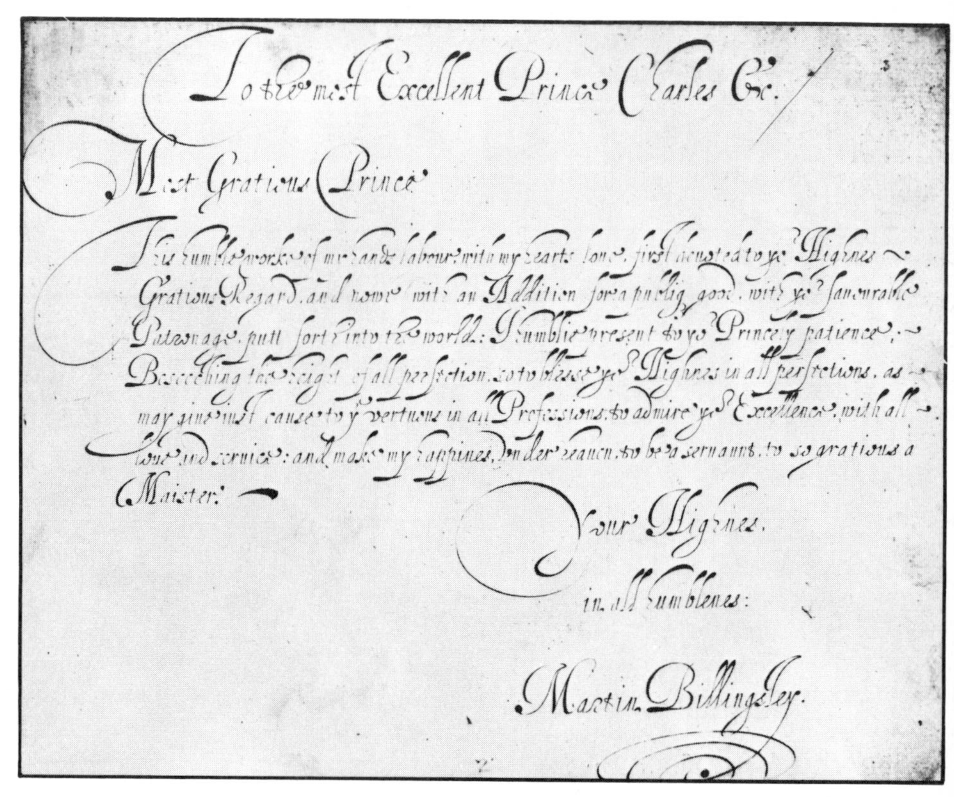

To the most Excellent Prince Charles &c.

Most Gratious Prince.

This humble worke of my hande & labour with my hearts love, first devoted to yor Highnes Gratious Regard, and nowe with an Addition for a publiq good, with yor favourable Patronage, putt forth into the world: I humblie present to yor Princely patience: Beseeching the height of all perfection, so to blesse yor Highnes in all perfections, as may give most cause to ye vertuous in all Professions, to admire yor Excellence, with all love and service: and make my happines, under heaven, to be a servaunt, to so gratious a Maister.

Your Highnes.

in all humblenes:

Martin Billingsley.

Martin Billingsley: The pens excellencie; or, the secretaries delighte 1618

Billingsley taught writing to Charles I when he was Prince of Wales, and this work is dedicated to him; an example of the King's own writing later in life can be *seen on p. 218.*

V&AM L 3061-1960 13 × 18

32

May it please your Lo: &c.

I was vppon my way to haue waited vppon yor Lo: too Mr Hackary
but when I was about stocke I had certen word yor L. came
not before night, and went a longe iorny to morrowe
so as to haue visited yor L. theare to night had been to
haue iniured Mr Hackar (though he very courteously waited
me) and to haue importuned yor Lo: Therfore I humblie pray yor
L. to take the affect for the effect, and to vouchsafe to accept
the humble remembrance of my seruice. I humblie thanke yor
L. for yor noble fauour in sending me these inclosed the
collections of one I haue seene heere like to proue very
seruisable. this Chappell is cum to this perfection since I
was at florence yet then in doinge. Yor L. knows those
parts better then I though I haue been there twise this not
withstanding is my opinion yt the Ruins of the Ancient
Romans both at Roome and at Prouinces ar fairer
then the greatest buildings in all Europe yt ar not
ancient; If yor L. desier to increase yor magnificence
then my Lo: let me haue the honnor to persuade you to
imploy Mr Cooke to prouide you of the works of Benedick
Palma at Venise, who exceeds in doinge large pictures
as mutche as the hole side of a greate chamber vppon
cloth [illegible] history. for Pictors of Counterfet let him send you
of the workes of Sipion Gaetano in Roome who is longe
in finishing but [illegible] most excellent. for Statua most
esteemed amongst the Italians there is a litle ould
man called John Bollognia the Ducks seruant and at florence who is not inferiour mutch
to Michell Angello. 2 of these I sawe and for John Bollognia
I count him the rarest man yt I sawe of any profession
for his profession. pardon my L. this my presumption
vanitie and make full accompt if yor L. thinke me
worthy of so mutch honnor yt I am yor Lo:

Most humble seruant

W. Burghley

Wth your L. permission I
humblie desier likewise to be
remembered as a most humble
seruant to my most honorable Lady
to whome I wishe a prosperous iorny
and all other happines whatsoeuer.

Letter from Lord Burghley to the Earl of Shrewsbury 23 July 1609

This letter was the equivalent of the modern telephone call; it was not the writing of a professional scribe, though certainly that of a man who had frequent occasion to write. The script was based on the italic pattern, but it also shows some characteristics of the secretary hand. The letter remains as an example of the hasty note between acquaintances, in which the content was of greater importance than the way it was written.

V & A M *Forster MS 66* 31 × 20

Oxford 10. Aprill 1646.

Nepueu/ this is to your satisfaction to acknowledg to you, that my going to the Scots Army is of such eminet danger [to my person], in respect of the numbers & placing of the Rebells Forces betweene this & where I am to goe, that your opinion is, I should not undertake it, so far you ar from giuing me any aduyce for it; but you must lykewais acknowledge to me, that [the reason of] my resolution in this, is not because I [am] ignorant of the Danger, (in that, differing litle or nothing from you) but to eschew a certaine mis= cheefe, wch otherwais I must [(according to my sence)] undergoe: you must also remember, that you must conceale this, untill the Action be ouer; & in the meane tyme, assist me, as hartely, in it, as if you fully concurred with me in opinion: Charles R.

King Charles I: Letter to his nephew Prince Rupert 1646

This letter, although from a royal hand, is not a formal piece of writing but rather a hastily penned note. It is interesting because Charles I was taught writing by Martin Billingsley, whose copy book is also illustrated (p. 216).

V & A M Forster MS 101

For that the Italian hands practized in this Kingdom haue bin, and still are corruptlie taught, especiallie by Mountebancke and circulatorie professors of impossibillities, to the dishonour of our Nation and abuse of learners in generall, being hands soe much desired, and growing more and more in vse amongst vs. For rectifieing whereof I haue in some of these my ensuing endeauours and varied examples selected, exactlie traced and followed, certaine peeces; (both in character and language) of the ablest Calligraphotecknists and Italian Mr. that euer wrot, hoping a good satisfaction to the iudicious and those, that are indulgent that waie, and for the rest, I leaue them (as they are) willfullie ignorant.

Non omnibus omnes

Gething

Richard Gething: Chiro-graphia; or, a book of copies containing sundrie examples.
1645

Gething was a somewhat austere practitioner in an age of baroque endeavour. He conforms to a certain extent in the decoration of his pages, but always with restraint. In his published work he offered the best of the contemporary hands as he saw them, and in this passage, written out in 'bastarde italique' he makes a scathing attack on less able 'calligraphotecknists' as he calls them.

V&AM L1898 19 × 29

to write and name please is much, to please and not to write is paine then rather write and serue thy god then spende thie tyme in vaine. october 16. Anno Domini 1620.
precepts coucht in this globes rou
worlde well to obserue

OF IOHN DAVIES OF HEREFO THE LIVELY PORTRAITVRE
The Writing Schoolemaster
or The Anatomy of Faire Writing. Wherein is exactlie expressed each severall Character, Together with other Rules and Documents coincident to the Art of faire & speedy writing 1631

John Davies: The writing schoolemaster or the anatomie of faire writing 1648

This work was probably published posthumously, and was reprinted many times — it will be noted that the date on the engraved title-page shown here is 1631, whereas the printed title-page of the same copy bears the date 1648. This constant reprinting of copy books meant that older styles of writing could persist over a long period, especially away from the main cities.

V & A M L 3070-1960 13 × 18

Opposite:
Richard Jackman From a book of copies, mostly in legal hands 1620

Nothing is known about the manuscript from which this unusual illustration is taken, except that it was found in one of the beams of Tangley Manor in Surrey. But apart from being an attractive jeu d'esprit, *it does provide a good example of an elegant English italic hand written by someone who was probably a tutor or writing master in a private family.*

V & A M L 3051-1960 15 × 27

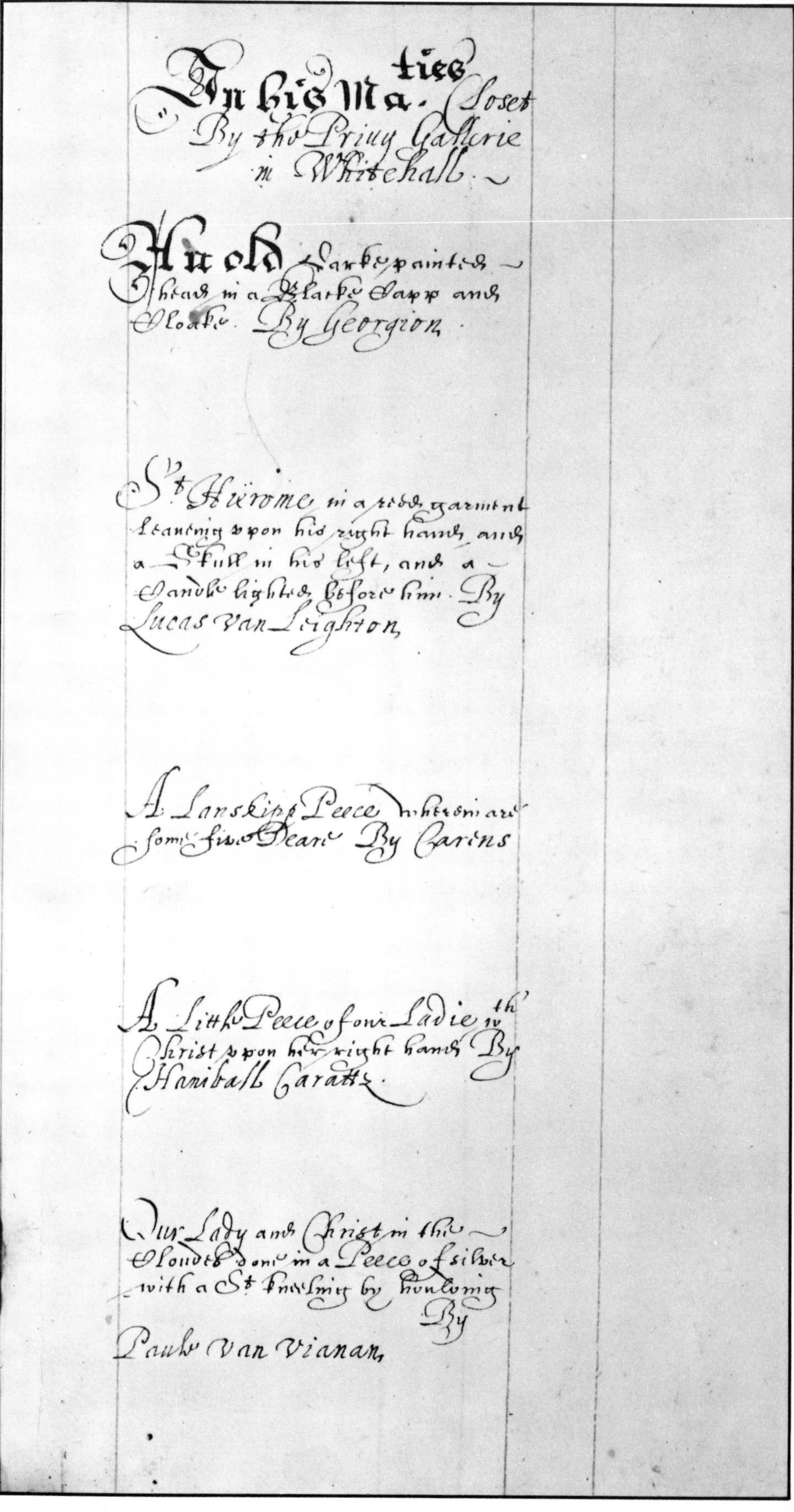
In his Ma.ties Closet
By the Privy Gallerie
in Whitehall.

An old darke painted head in a Blacke Capp and Cloake. By Georgion.

St Hierome in a redd garment leaning upon his right hand, and a Skull in his left, and a Candle lighted before him. By Lucas van Leighton

A Lanskipp Peece wherein are some five Deare By Carins

A Little Peece of our Ladie with Christ upon her right hand By Haniball Caratz.

Our Lady and Christ in the Cloudes done in a Peece of silver with a St kneeling by kneeling By Paule van Vianan.

Page from a catalogue of the art collections of King Charles I at Whitehall and St James's Palace. 1640-41

This catalogue shows the use of the various scripts to be found in the copy books of the time. It will be noted that there is a mixture of the italic and the gothic hand, which sit uncomfortably together on the same page; nevertheless the scribe obviously felt that these were suitable for such an important document.

V & A M   MS L 1753-1907   35 × 25.5

Opposite:
A page from an instruction book for making purse-strings, including patterns for working every letter of the alphabet.   c1640

This is a working account of how to make braided silk, examples of which can be seen in the illustration. The writing is very clear and firm and essentially businesslike, and shows the application in practice of the copy book instructions.

V & A M   MS L 1012-1938   18.5 × 14

To make the Diamond poynte./

2

Take 7 boes of red one partie. and 7 boes of whyte the other. placinge 4 boes on the out hands and 3 on the inward then worke the spanish bredth takinge the priuate stich:—

To make the waine poynte./

2

Take ech partie 4 boes of red on the out hands. and 3 boes of whyte on the inward hands alike. then worke the spanish bredth takinge the priuate stich:— — —

To make the brode Arrowe heade and staffe.

3

Take 5 boes of whyte the midle worker. and the: Rh: 5 boes of red. and the out worker 5 boes of greene. then worke the spanish bredth takinge the priuate stich. but the Rh: Changeth wth the midle worker allwayes once and the midle worker Changeth wth the other out worker allwayes twice:— — — — — — — — — —

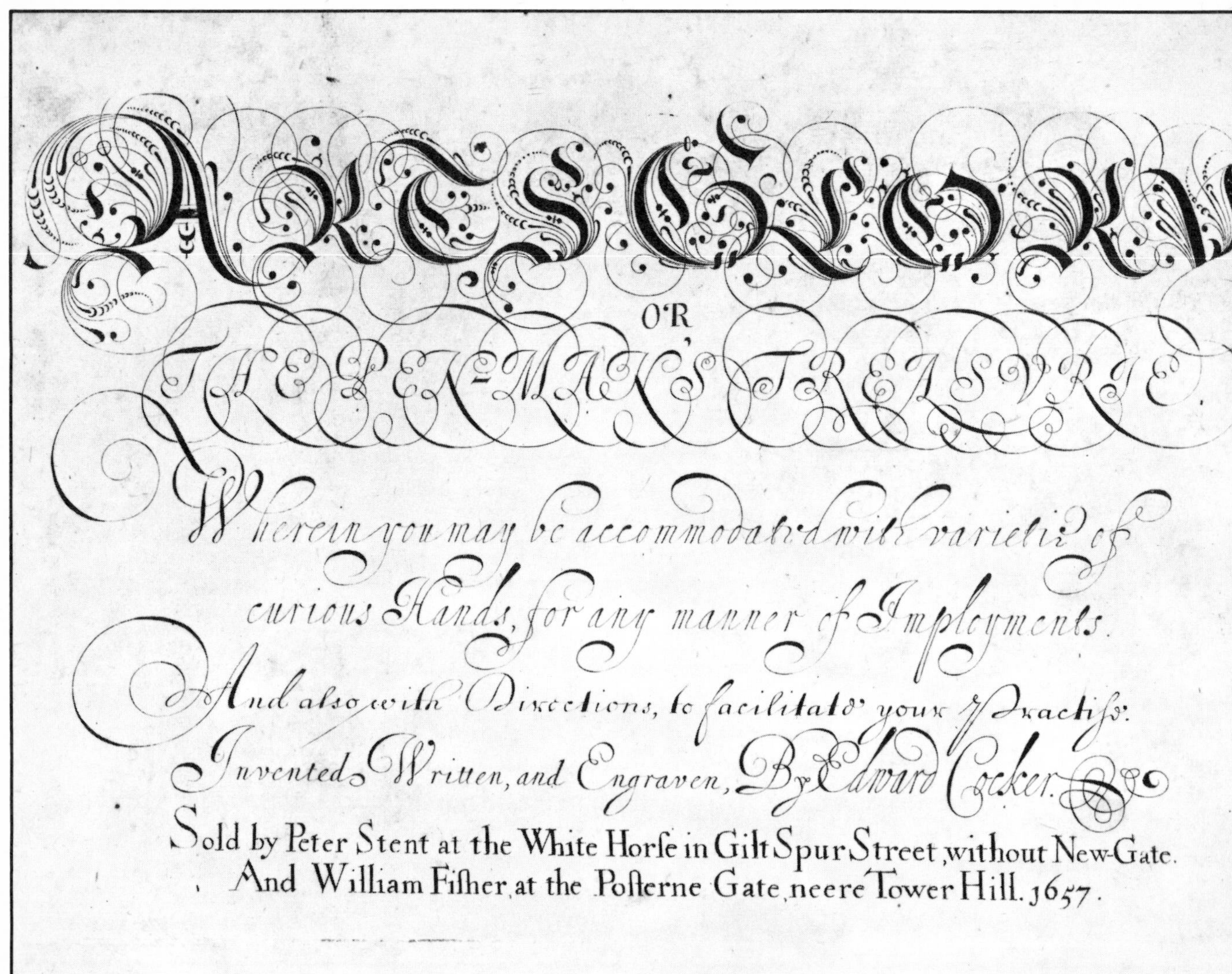

ARTS GLORY

OR

THE PEN-MAN'S TREASVRIE.

Wherein you may be accommodated with varietie of curious Hands, for any manner of Imployments.

And also with Directions, to facilitate your Practiſe:

Invented, Written, and Engraven, By Edward Cocker.

Sold by Peter Stent at the White Horſe in Gilt Spur Street, without New-Gate.
And William Fiſher, at the Poſterne Gate, neere Tower Hill. 1657.

Edward Cocker: Arts glory; or, the pen-man's treasurie.
1657

This is the earliest surviving book by Cocker, who was one of the most prolific of 17th century English writing masters. He frequently engraved his own work, which he decorated with exuberant 'strikings' or flourishes 'done by command of hand'. The title-page shown here indicated some of the variety of styles to be found within.

V & A M　　L 3055-1960　　15.5 × 20

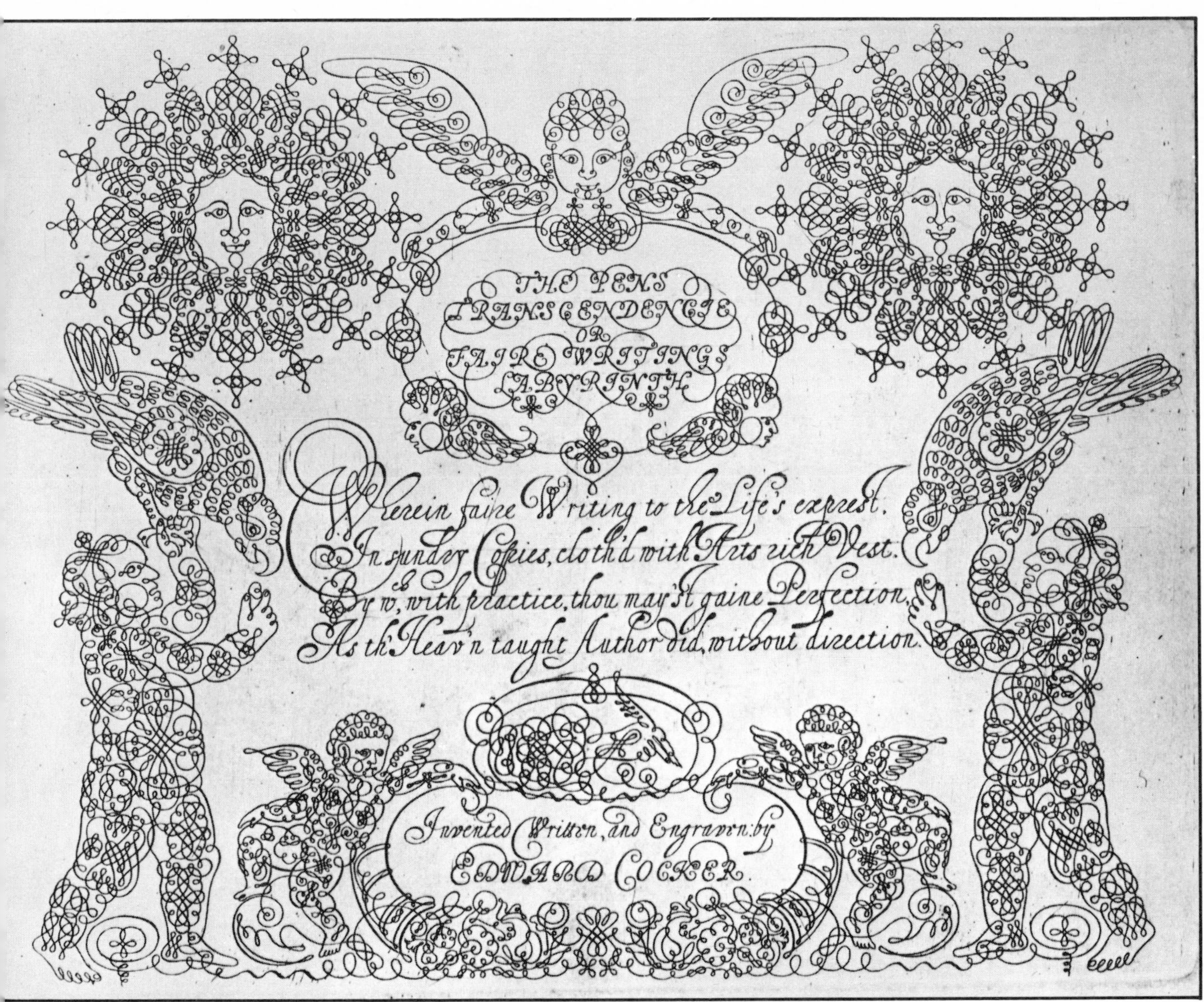
THE PENS
TRANSCENDENCIE
OR
FAIRE WRITINGS
LABYRINTH

Wherein faire Writing to the Life's exprest,
In sundry Copies, cloth'd with Arts rich Vest.
By w, with practice, thou may'st gaine Perfection,
As th' Heav'n taught Author did, without direction.

Invented Written, and Engraven: by
EDWARD COCKER.

Edward Cocker: The pens transcendencie, or faire writings labyrinth 1657

This page from one of Cocker's writing books shows how easily he could be overwhelmed by the sheer exuberance of his own virtuosity. It will be noted that he was his own engraver, which was no doubt just as well! The intricacies of his line would also appear to have affected his letter forms, to their detriment.

V&AM L 3064-1960 18.5 × 26

Edward Cocker: Penna volans; or the young man's accomplishment 1661

Cocker, that most exuberant of penmen, could on occasion produce a simpler hand. But the thickness of the pen strokes and inclusion of irrelevant decoration shows how contrary to his spirit and that of the age, he felt this commercial simplicity to be.

V&AM L 3071-1960 18 × 25.5

Edward Cocker: The pens transcendency or fair writings store-house 1668

This little rhyme contains Cocker's reply to those who criticised his over-decoration and 'strikings'. He suggests 'Some may be drawne, as I was, by delight/In apish ffancies and so learn to write' — but did he and other practitioners of this style of decoration really believe that? The interesting point about Cocker and others who enjoyed 'strikings' and 'command of hand' decoration, was that they could also produce simple scripts when required.

V&AM L 3058-1960 18 × 25.5

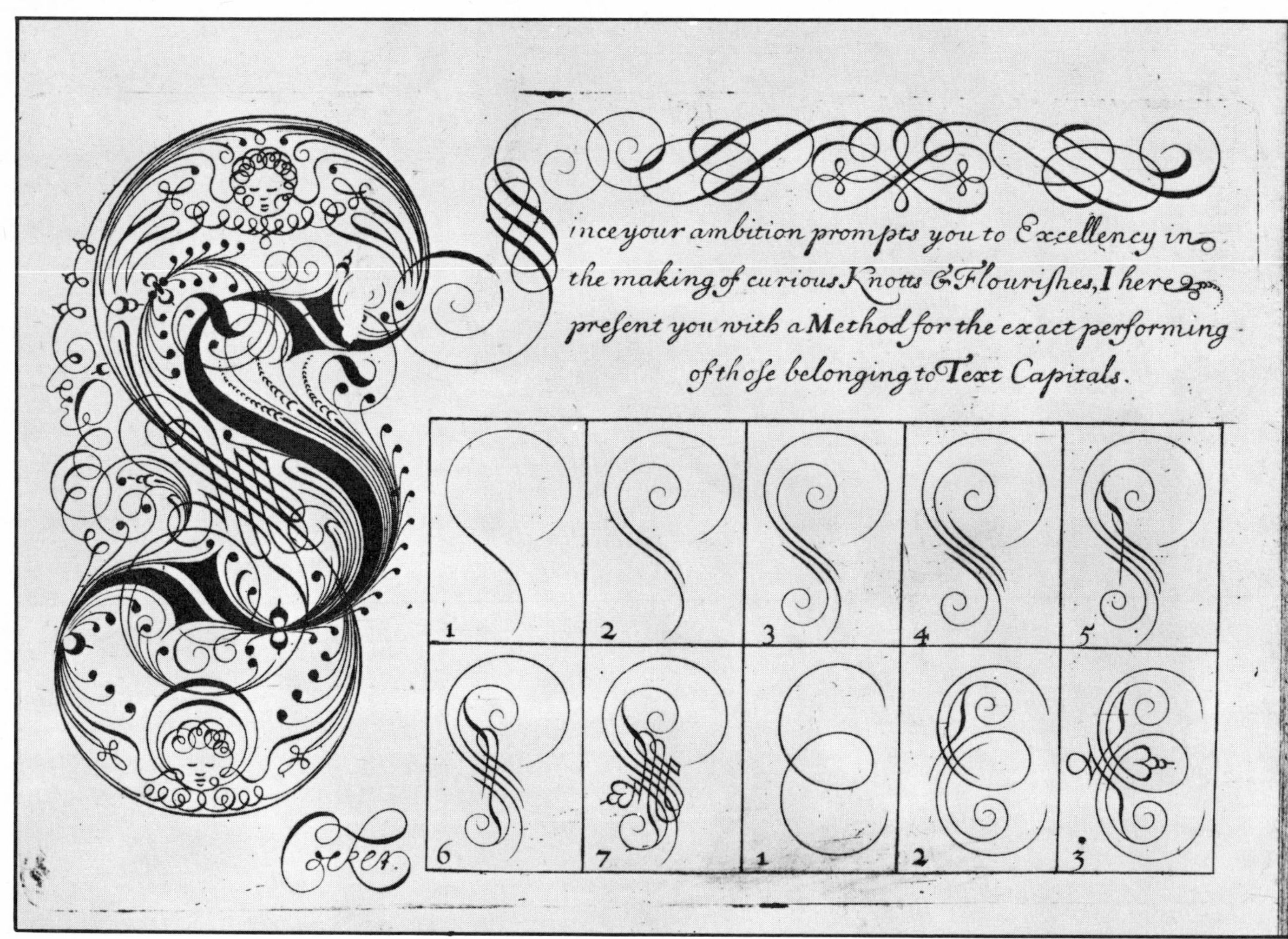

Edward Cocker: Magnum in parvo; or, the pen's perfection. 1672

This plate, from one of Edward Cocker's many writing books, shows the stages by which the 'curious knotts and flourishes' of the text capitals could be performed — or so Cocker says!

V&AM L114-1889 15 × 20

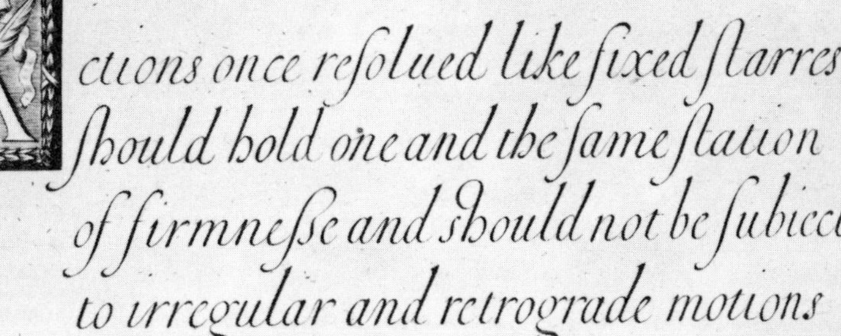

35

Actions once reſolued like fixed ſtarres
ſhould hold one and the ſame ſtation
of firmneſſe and ſhould not be ſubiect
to irregular and retrograde motions

Peter Gery: Gerii viri in arte scriptoria quondam celeberrimi opera c1667

Gery's work has a certain austere quality about it, in contrast to that of many of his contemporaries. It is likely that this, his only known copy book, was published after his death, since apparently he was not satisfied with the engraved results of his work. His attempt here at a decorative initial owes more to typography than calligraphy, and sits uncomfortably on the written page.

V & A M L 3082-1960 21 × 32.5

9

Mixed Secretarie

Keepe not company with wine bibers and with riotus eaters of flesh for such shall com to poverty and he that is given to much sleep shall goe with a ragged coate; Andrew

The world:s much like a fair deceitfull nut: whereto when once the knife of truth is put: and it is opend a right Judicious eye; find:s nothinge in it but meer vanitye;

Andrew Andrewes: A coppie booke of some severall hands used 1667

This manuscript would appear to be the work of a pupil rather than a master, and some of the pages reveal a rather uncertain hand. But the work contains a variety of scripts, some of considerable elaboration, as here. The difficult 'mixed secretarie' script illustrated here was soon to be completely ousted by the simpler 'running hand'.

V & A M MS L 3067-1960 14.5 × 18

Opposite:

John Stonestreet: Copy book, probably written out by John Stonestreet 1688.

The persistence of older styles of writing is clearly indicated by the two illustrations from this manuscript. The 'letter frisée' appears in the example by Amos Lewis (p. 139) of one hundred years earlier, and the jester musician also appears in the Baildon-Beauchesne copy book of 1570.

V & A M MS L 3052-1960 13 × 19.5

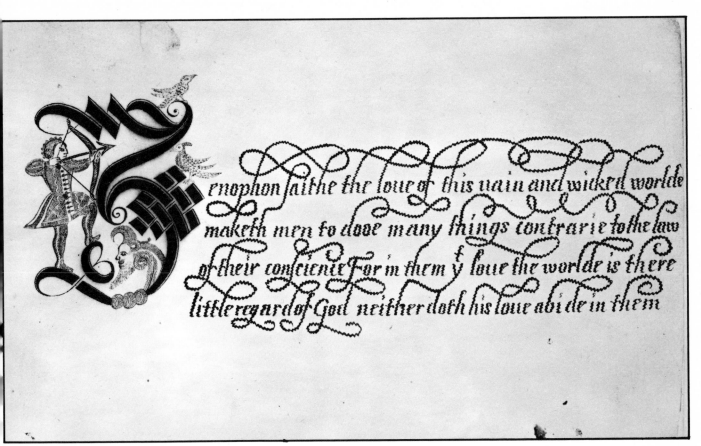

Xenophon saithe the loue of this vain and wicked worlde
maketh men to dooe many things contrarie to the law
of their conscience For in them yt loue the worlde is there
little regard of God neither doth his loue abide in them

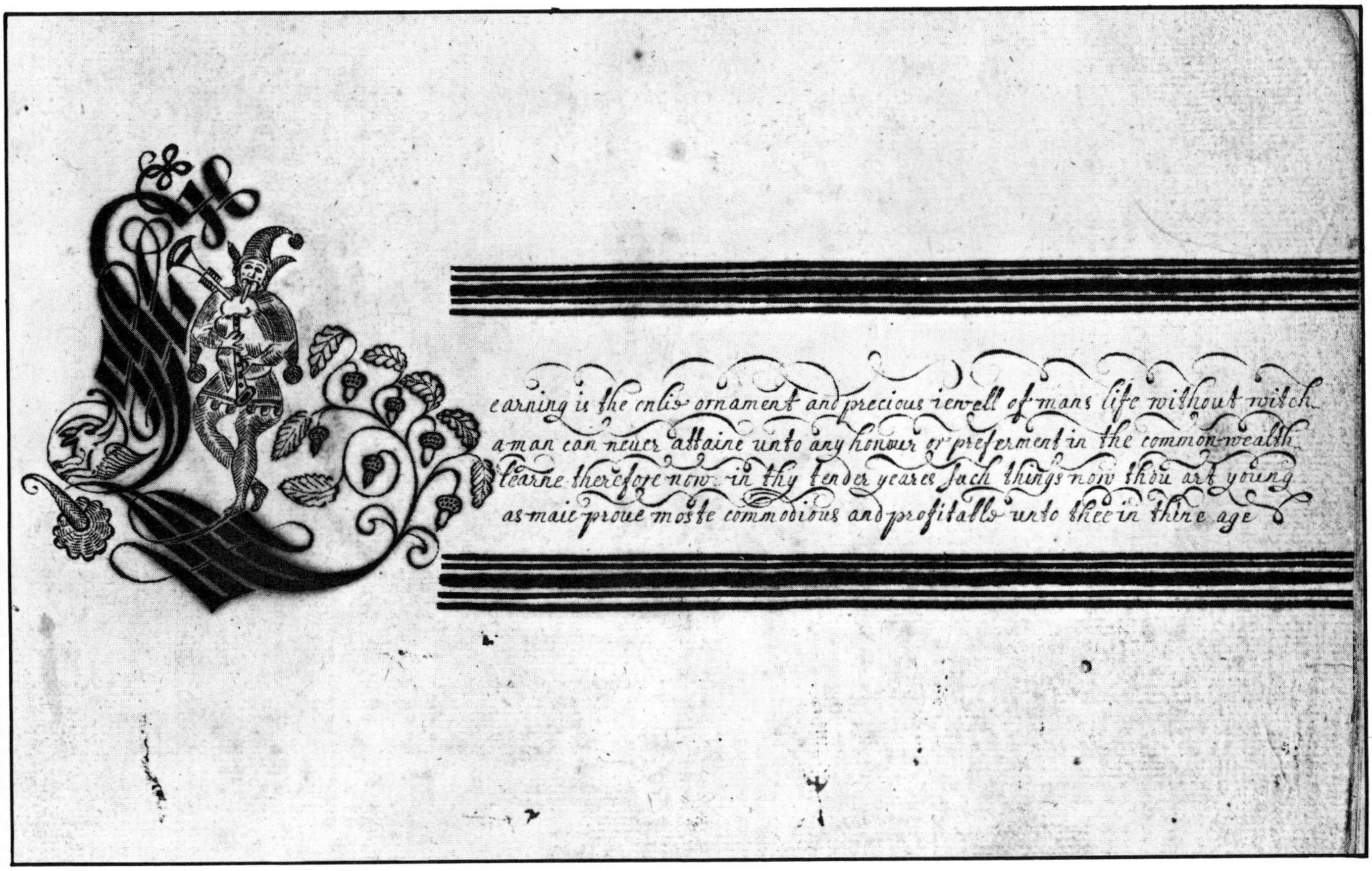

Learning is the onlie ornament and precious iewell of mans life without witch
a man can neuer attaine unto any honour or preferment in the common-wealth
learne therefore now in thy tender yeares such things now thou art young
as maie proue moste commodious and profitable unto thee in thine age

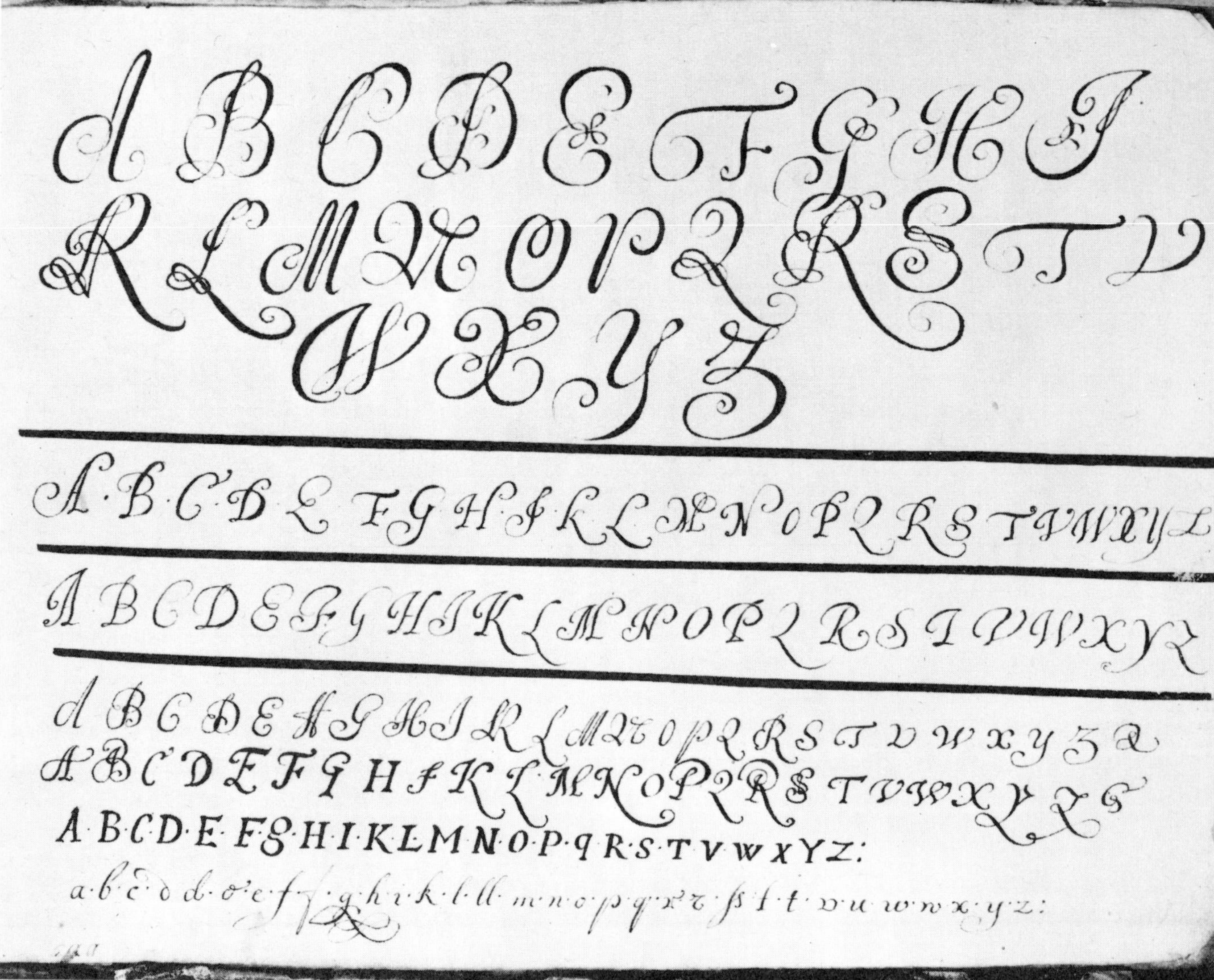

John Stonestreet: From one of two copy books written out and signed by John Stonestreet. 1688

It is sometimes more helpful to see the less-than-perfect efforts of a pupil rather than the exact performance of the master. Here we see John Stonestreet's attempt to reproduce the florid alphabets so common in the copy books of the period.

V&AM *MS L 3080-1960* *15 × 19.5*

Opposite top:
Thomas Watson: A copy-book enriched with great variety of the most useful & modish hands. c1690

This copy book stands out because of its unusual capital letters, although a rather similar style is to be found later in an American copy book. Compared with the text, the ornamental capital is very large, while the writing itself has certain affinities with French scripts.

V&AM *L 1019-1920* *27.5 × 37*

Opposite bottom:
William Elder: The modish pen-man, or, a new copy book, containing variety of all the usual hands now practised in England. c1691

Elder was a Scot working in London, and was known as an engraver of portraits. In 1687 he published Enchiridion Calligraphiae, *and many of the plates were re-used in the present work. In this copy the first lines of some songs and their tunes have been written in a contemporary hand on the blank pages.*

V&AM *L 7115-1888* *16 × 25*

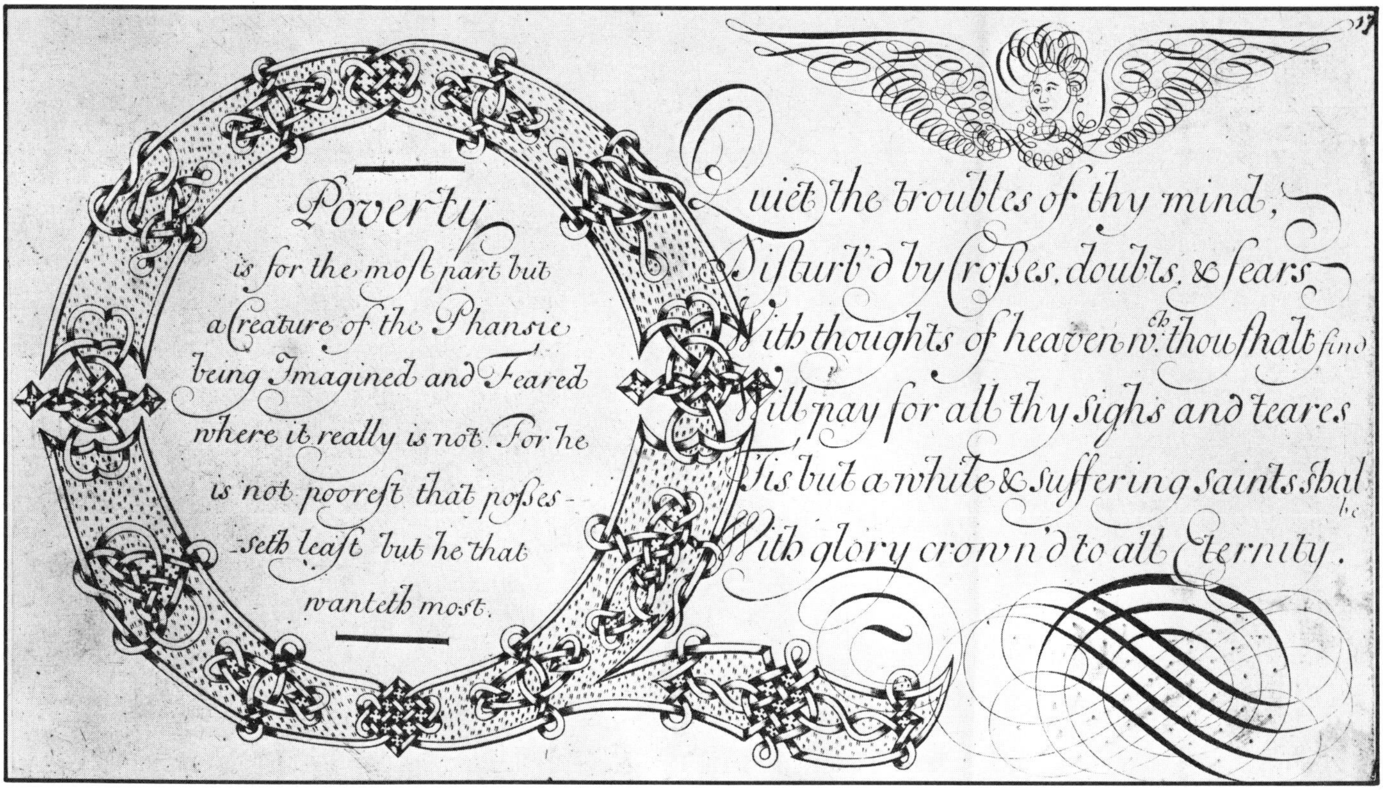

Poverty
is for the most part but
a Creature of the Phansie
being Imagined and Feared
where it really is not. For he
is not poorest that posses-
-seth least but he that
wanteth most.

Quiet the troubles of thy mind,
Disturb'd by Crosses, doubts, & fears
With thoughts of heaven wch thou shalt find
Will pay for all thy sighs and teares
Tis but a while & suffering saints shal be
With glory crown'd to all Eternity.

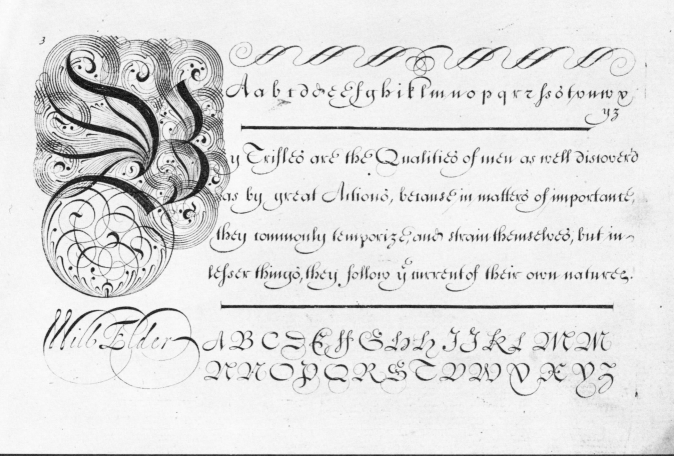

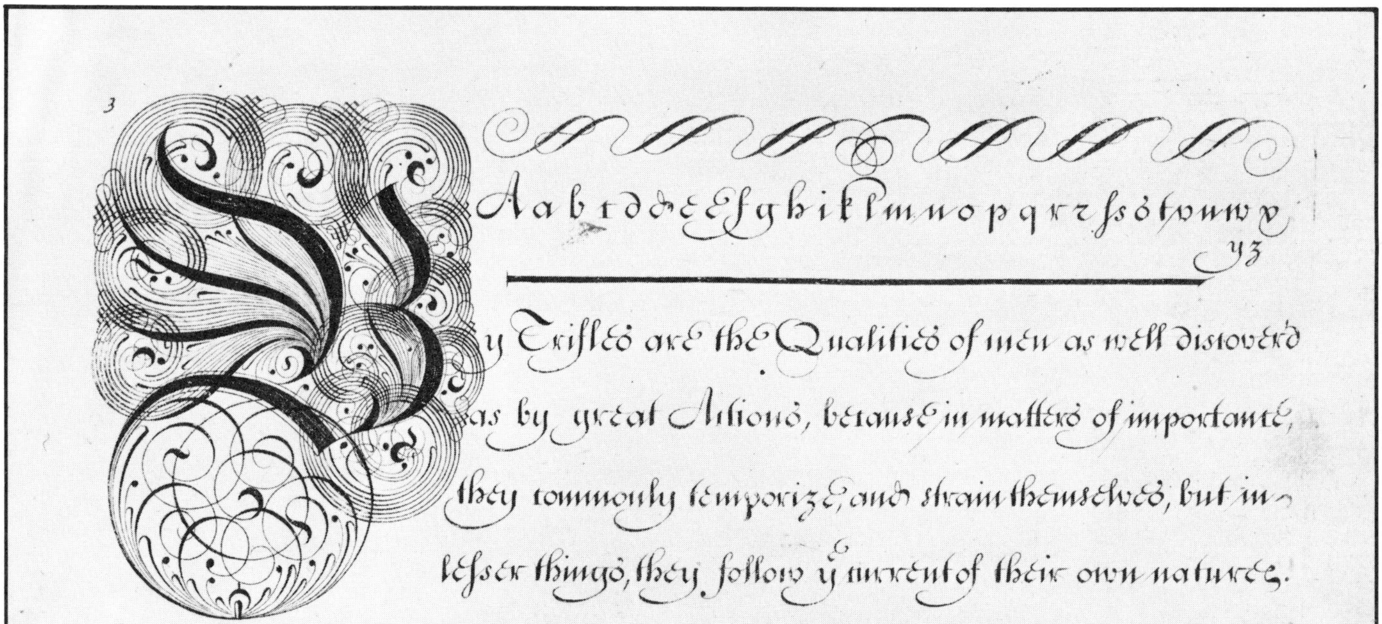

A a b c d e f g h i k l m n o p q r s t u v w x y z

By Trifles are the Qualities of men as well discovered as by great Actions, because in matters of importance, they commonly temporize, and strain themselves, but in lesser things, they follow ye current of their own natures.

Will Elder

A B C D E F G H I J K L M N O P Q R S T U W V X Y Z

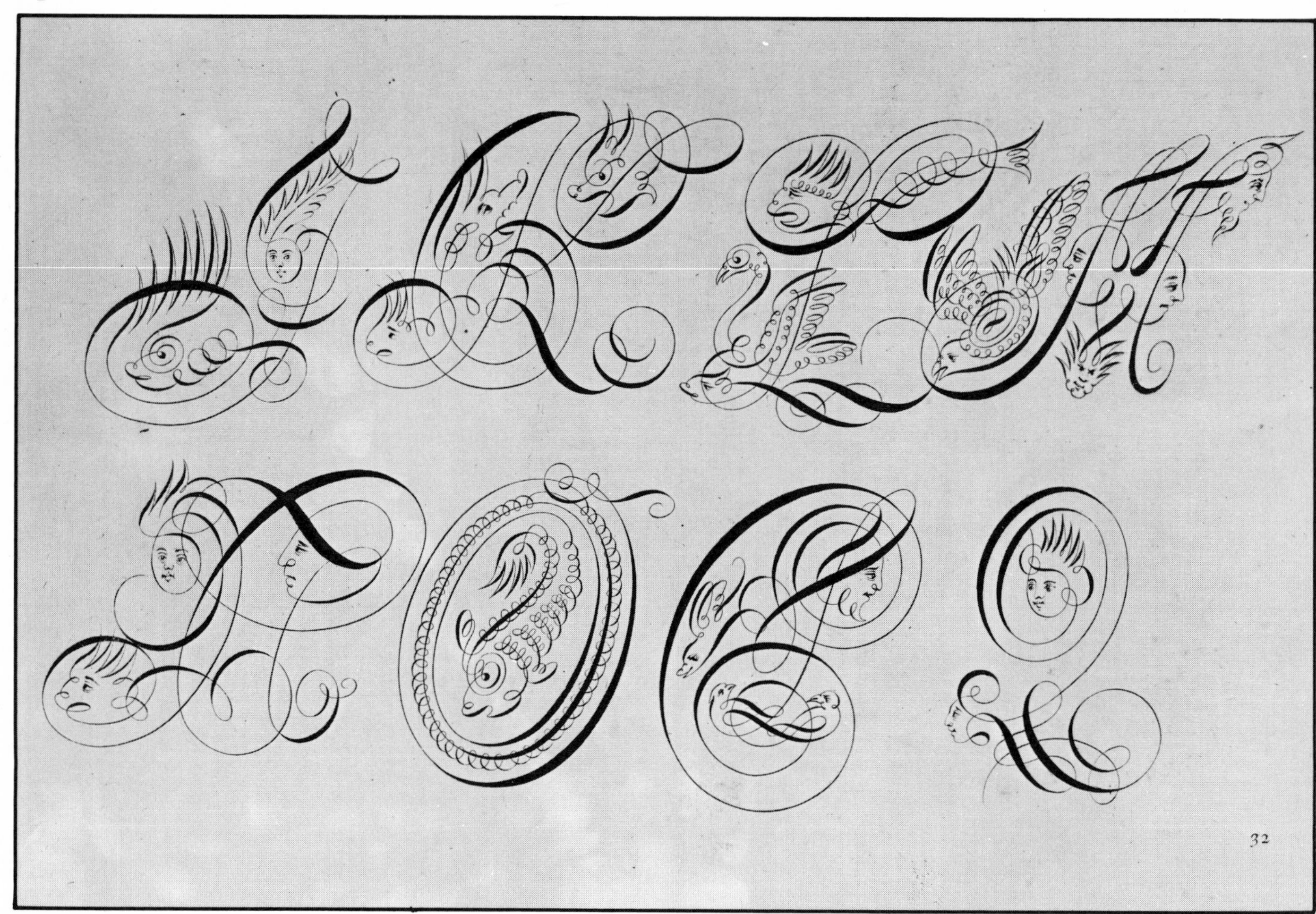

John Seddon: The pen-man's paradis, both pleasant & profitable. 1695

John Seddon was highly regarded by his contemporaries, although he was one of the writing masters who continued the earlier tradition of ornamenting his writing with decoration 'done with one continued and entire tract of the pen'. The alphabet shown here displays considerable virtuosity but can have had little practical application!

V&AM 11.iv.1872 34 × 22

Opposite:
Richard Carter: Arithmetic book. 1695

This is a pupil's arithmetic book, but one very much of its period. Not only does the calligraphy provide a practical example of the style taught by contemporary writing masters, but the student has embellished his work with 'strikings' which were such a feature of the copy books of the time, as we can see from the many examples illustrated in the present book.

V&AM MS L 842-1969 20.5 × 16.5

If 10 Brick-layers make a Wall of 100 foot long and 20 foot high in 12 days how many Brick-layers will make a wall of 236 foot long & 20 foot high in 16 days

If Feet 100	———	Brick-l 10	———	236
If 12	———	$23\frac{60}{100}$	———	16

236 × 10 = 2360; 1/00) 23|60

$23\frac{60}{100}$
100
2360
12
16) 28320 (1|00 (17|7 $\frac{0}{100}$

16
123
112
112
112
0

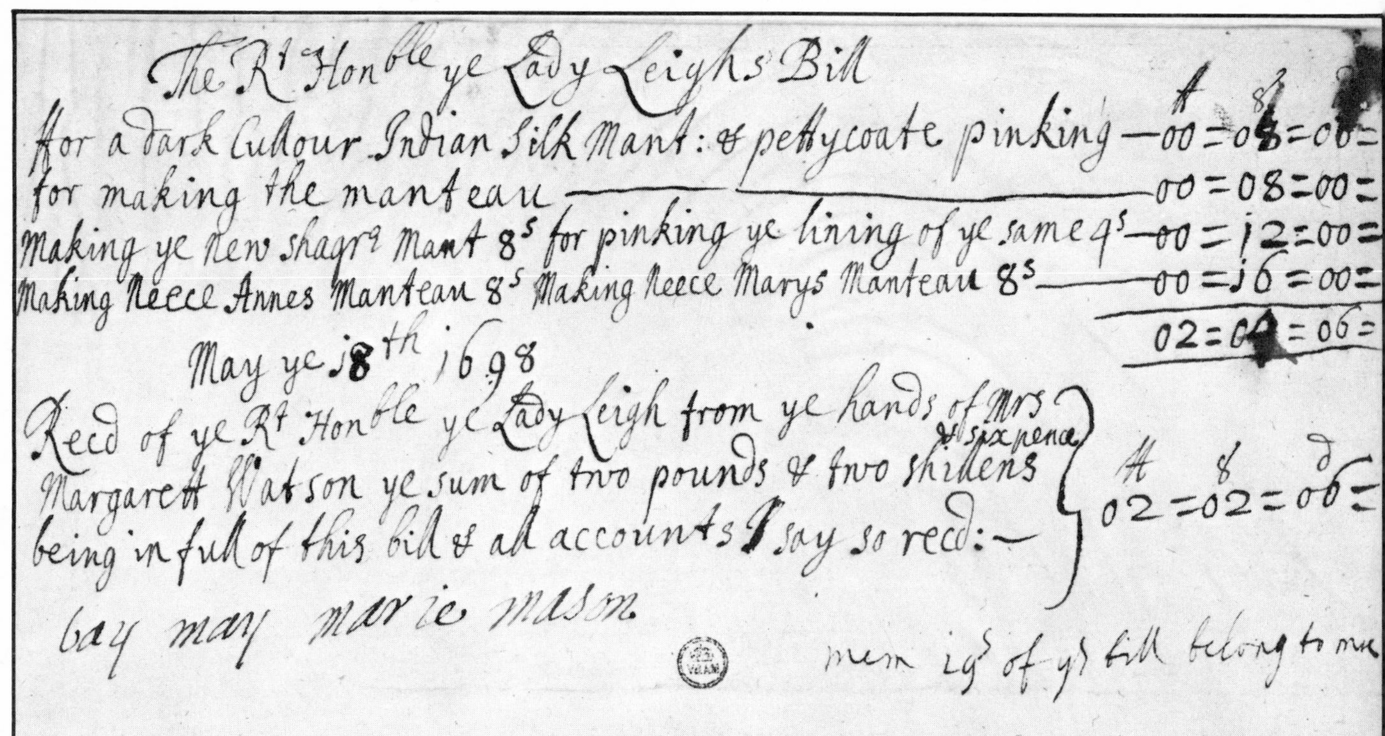

The Rt Honble ye Lady Leighs Bill

	£	s	d
For a dark Cullour Indian Silk Mant: & pettycoate pinking	00	08	00
for making the manteau	00	08	00
Making ye New shagrd Mant 8s for pinking ye lining of ye same 4s	00	12	00
Making Neece Annes Manteau 8s Making Neece Marys Manteau 8s	00	16	00
	02	04	06

May ye 18th 1698

Recd of ye Rt Honble ye Lady Leigh from ye hands of Mrs Margarett Watson ye sum of two pounds & two shillens & sixpence being in full of this bill & all accounts I say so recd:— } £ 02 = s 02 = d 06 =

bay may marie mason

mem 19s of ys bill belong to me

He that loveth pleasure shall be a poor man. He that loveth wine and oyl shall not be rich. Look not thou upon the wine when it is red when it giveth his colour in the cup when it moveth it self aright. At the last it biteth like a serpent & stingeth like an adder

Aa abbcdef ffg ghikkl mnnopqr r s ss ttuvwxyz

Proverbs

CH.XX.17. CH.XXIII.31.

Ayres

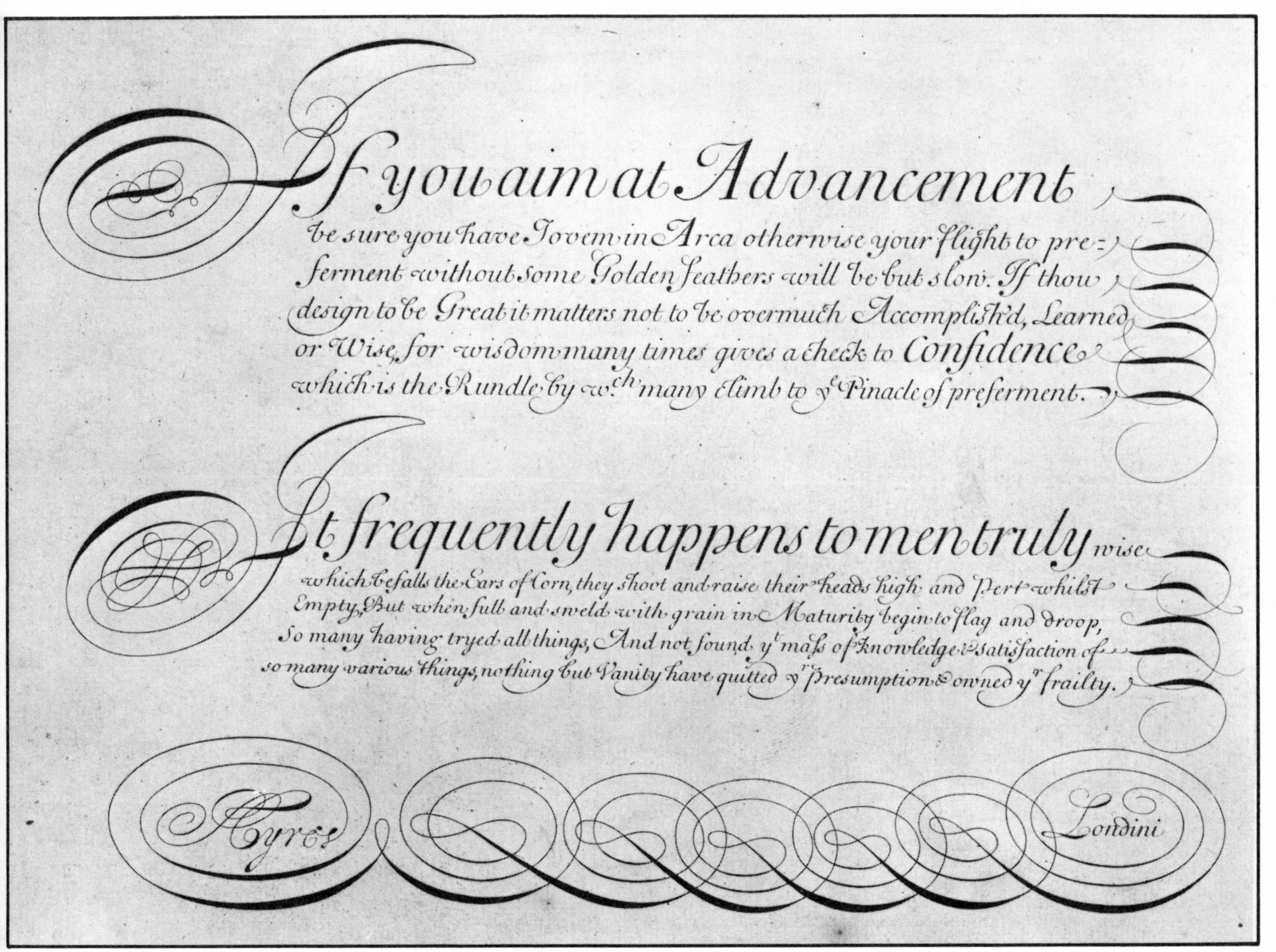

If you aim at Advancement be sure you have Jovem in Arca otherwise your flight to pre= ferment without some Golden Feathers will be but slow. If thou design to be Great it matters not to be overmuch Accomplish'd, Learned or Wise, for wisdom many times gives a check to Confidence which is the Rundle by wch many climb to ye Pinacle of preferment.

It frequently happens to men truly wise which befalls the Ears of Corn, they shoot and raise their heads high and Pert whilst Empty, But when full and sweld with grain in Maturity begin to flag and droop, So many having tryed all things, And not found yt mass of knowledge & satisfaction of so many various things, nothing but Vanity have quitted yr Presumption & owned yr frailty.

Ayres

Londini

Opposite top:
A dressmaker's bill in the name of Lady Leigh, dated May 18th 1698

This bill is clearly written out, obviously by someone familiar with such matters, and it shows the instruction of the copy books put to practical use. The recipient of the money has signed the bill in a less educated hand 'bay may (by me) Marie Mason', while another hand — or was it the informal hand of the original writer of the account? — has hastily scribbled 'mem. 19s of ye bill belongs to mee'.

V & A M from L 427-1943 10.5 × 19

Opposite bottom:
John Ayres: A tutor to penmanship; or, the writing master. 1698?

John Ayres was one of the best-known English writing masters of his time, and was mentioned with respect by later calligraphers. He was a great protagonist of the round hand, which was to become the dominant script in England in the next century. His copy books however include examples of 'all the variety of penmanship and clerkship as now practised in England'. This plate shows the continuing gothic tradition for use in special circumstances, such as the quotation of religious texts.

V & A M L 581-1880 25 × 41

John Ayres: A tutor to penmanship; or, the writing master. 1698

Ayres was greatly admired by that connoisseur of penmanship, Samuel Pepys. This work contained a great variety of alphabets and scripts, and the unnecessary curlicues so typical of the art of the period still find a place in this otherwise straightforward piece of writing.

V & A M L 1581-1880 25.5 × 41

Prières choisies French (Paris?) c1625-50

This tiny manuscript by an unidentified scribe is a very good example of the court art of Louis XIV, when the handwritten book was back in favour. Most of the productions of the court school of calligraphy were no doubt specially commissioned, often with the noble ladies in mind. This manuscript has covers made from lapis lazuli, which, together with its very fine writing and miniature size, all suggest something more in the nature of a toy than a book for practical use, in spite of the devotional nature of the text.

V & A M *MS L 487-1873*
f.49v/50r *6 × 4*

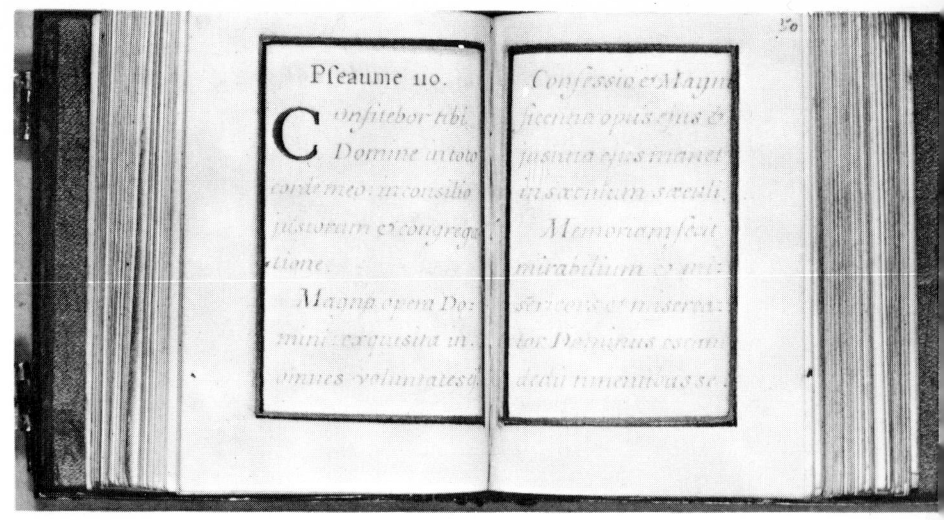

Henriette de Coligny, Countess de la Suze: Le Triomphe de Amarillis [and other poems]
French c1650

The binding of this manuscript has the words écrit par Jarry *on the spine, but the writing is more likely to be by a pupil or someone else within the Jarry circle. The script has a very elegant and feminine appearance, which makes it particularly suitable for the poems of a noble lady.*

V & A M *MS L 1056-1950* *28 × 20.5*

LE PORTRAIT DE
MADEMOISELLE.
STANCES.

Fille du Souuerain des Dieux,
Qui des Arts les plus glorieux,
Merites l'eternel hommage,
Minerue, viens a mon secours,
Ie veux peindre dans cet Ouurage
Le plus rare Objet de nos jours.

Pensant a ce diuin Objet,
Cent fois on si hardy projet
A sçû me flater & me plaire,
Et foible pour ce grand Tableau,
Cent fois de ma main temeraire,
I'ay laissé tomber le pinceau.

QVOY QV'IL SÇACHE plusieurs choses, il ſe croit ignorant, ne pouvant ſçauoir ſi Panthée eſt capable d'aymer.

SONNET.

IE ſçay que par vos ſoins la vertu regne en terre,
Q'vn homme, en vous ſervant, ſe rend égal aux Dieux,
Et que vous pouvez plus, par vn clin de vos yeux,
Que ne peut tout le Ciel, avecque ſon tonnerre.

Ie ſçay que votre eſprit peut animer la pierre,
Qu'il eſt ce que Nature a jamais fait de mieux,
Qu'il change comme il veut la face de ces lieux,
Et met en nos deſirs ou la paix, ou la guerre.

Ie ſçay que les deſtins, par vn ſage conſeil,
Ont reſolu qu'vn jour vous ſerez le Soleil
Qui doit, ſans Occident, luire en nôtre hemiſphere

Ie ſçay qu'il faut frémir quand on vous doit nômer:
Mais tout ce grand ſçavoir ne me peut ſatisfaire,
I'ignore entierement ſi vous pouvez aymer.

Sonnets françois French c1650

This manuscript is very much in the style of Nicolas Jarry, and certain associations of the poems suggest that he was the scribe. Certainly it was written by someone working close to the court school of calligraphy, from which the patronage of such works emanated. The balance of the various letter-forms and the general layout of the manuscript produce a very sophisticated effect, but the script has undoubtedly been influenced by the printed page.

V&AM MS L 316-1948 f.20 30 × 21

L'Office de la Vièrge (Prières de St Augustin) Paris 1661

This manuscript is signed and dated at the bottom of p. 68 'N. Iarry Parisinus scribebat 1661'. *Nicolas Jarry (c1615-1670) was one of the most famous exponents of the court school of calligraphy, which flourished during the reign of Louis XIV, and which kept alive in France the art of fine writing, when standards elsewhere were low. The small size of the manuscript was typical of the works produced by Jarry and his associates.*

V & A M MS L 1171-1949 pp 12, 13
9 × 6

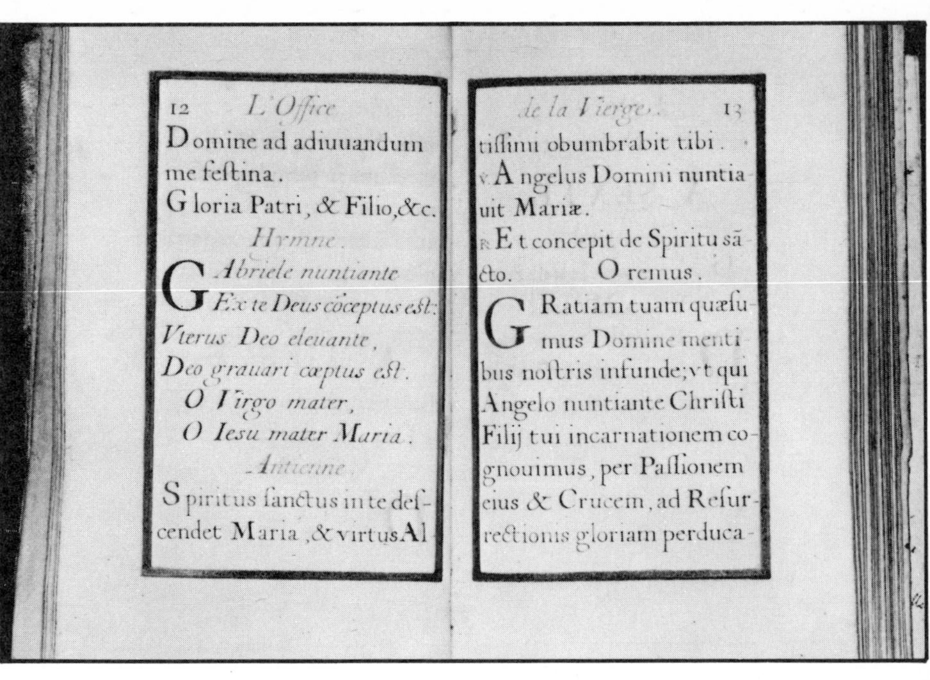

12 L'Office
Domine ad adiuuandum
me feſtina.
Gloria Patri, & Filio, &c.
Hymne.
Gabriele nuntiante
Ex te Deus cõceptus eſt:
Vterus Deo eleuante,
Deo grauari cœptus eſt.
O Virgo mater,
O Iesu mater Maria.
Antienne.
Spiritus ſanctus in te deſ-
cendet Maria, & virtus Al

de la Vierge. 13
tiſſimi obumbrabit tibi.
℣ Angelus Domini nuntia-
uit Mariæ.
℟ Et concepit de Spiritu sã-
cto. Oremus.
Gratiam tuam quæſu-
mus Domine menti-
bus noſtris infunde; vt qui
Angelo nuntiante Chriſti
Filij tui incarnationem co-
gnouimus, per Paſſionem
eius & Crucem, ad Reſur-
rectionis gloriam perduca-

Prières de la Messe, écrites par J. P. Rousselet Paris c1710?

Although Rousselet was a noted calligrapher, this manuscript owes more to the printed page than to calligraphic models. The script is elegant and clear, but the effect it produces could have been made equally well by letter-press; nevertheless like most manuscripts it no doubt had the charm of uniqueness.

V & A M MS L 1340-1950 f.7
16.5 × 10

de la Meſſe
au Kyrie
Quand je vous di-
rois à tous les mo-
mens de ma vie: Sei-
gneur, ayez pitié de
moy; ce ne ſeroit poīt
encore aſſez pour le
nombre & pour la qua-
lité de mes fautes.
Quand vous ne m'é-
couteriez point - Sei-
gneur, je crieray ſans
ceſſe & à châque mo-
ment, d'une voix plus

50

Pratique

III.

Pour temoigner a Dieu que votre penitence est ſincere, recherchez les causes de vos pechez dans vos passions & dans vos mauvaises habitudes, & voyez comment vous pourrez les retrancher: Prevoyez-en aussi les occasions, & prenez resolution de les eviter; mais reconnoissez toujours qu'étant foible comme vous êtes, vous ne pouvez rien vous promettre de vous-même, si vous n'êtes aßisté de la grace divine. Demandez-la par cette Priere de l'Eglise :

51

pour la Confession.

DAignez, Seigneur, nous accorder le ſecours de votre grace, afin que nous accompliſſions ce que vous nous avez inſpiré. Ainſi ſoit-il.

DEVANT LA COMMUNION.

PRIERE DE S.T THOMAS D'AQUIN.

E vous adore avec reſpect, Divinité cachée ſous les figures de ce Sacrement.

Prières durant la Messe, avec pratique pour la Confession et des prières pour Communion
French (Paris?) c1730?

This manuscript is signed on p. 58 'Ecrit par S. Le Couteux'. *As can be seen from the illustration, Le Couteux makes use of both Roman and italic scripts, a style which helps to give emphasis to different parts of the text. The work has elaborate rococo title-page and head-pieces, as well as some charming initials in the rococo style, one example of which appears here.*

V & A M MS L 2324-1952 pp 50, 51
15 × 10

verdadero de la passion de
mi Señor Iesu Christo para
sentir y reformar el desor=
den de mi vida Amen.

63

MYSTERIOS
GLORIOSOS
Se han de rezar Miercoles
y Domingo.

Mysterio I.
Consideracion de la Re
surection.
Marci 16. Luce. 14. Ioan. 20.

Oracion y ofrecimiento
O Muy dulce amorosa y
siempre virgen Maria, yo te
ofrezco humilmente estas
diez Aue Marias, y un Pa=
ternoster, al inefable gozo
que tuviste en la gloriosa
Resurrection de tu Hijo muy
amado (que segun la mu=

Memoria espiritual de devotas y contemplatives oraciones y otras Christianas devociones. En Brusselas escrito por G. H. Wilmart año 1673

Georgius Herman Wilmart has been identified as the scribe of several other manuscripts and the illustration here shows him to have been a very competant calligrapher. He makes use of a variety of different scripts, though the italic hand predominates. The penwork decorations in black and gold are especially charming.

V&AM MS L 1760-1894 pp 62, 63
10.5 × 7

8 The eighteenth century

GENERALLY it may be considered that in the 18th century calligraphy ceased to exist, although of course handwriting continued to flourish. The paradox can be explained by the fact that while more and more people were encouraged to write well, there was little concern for writing as an art, let alone a fine art. Writing was a practical subject and as such it was to remain for a great many years. A work such as George Bickham's *The Universal Penman*, produced almost in the middle of the century, proved that while there were many good writing masters, and a number of individual styles, they were nearly all intended to one end – the making of a good clerkly hand. Important developments in handwriting had gradually been taking place further north since the great flowering of the humanist hands in Italy in the 15th and 16th centuries, and now it was the English round-hand that was to become dominant. For this the English merchant was responsible. English traders sailed the world in pursuit of markets, and where they placed their goods they placed also their bills, their ledgers, and their clerks. The English round-hand was essentially a good business hand, plain and clear, and it was taken up by merchants in other countries, where its origin was sometimes acknowledged (e.g. *lettres anglaises*), and at others the script was re-christened to suit the country concerned. Germany however continued its own tradition based on the older gothic scripts. That the German writing masters knew other scripts, and indeed taught them, is obvious from the copy books. But for their main business, the Germans used their own script and typography. As a result of this, states absorbed into the Austro-Hungarian Empire were forced to learn this script too, if they wished their nationals to take up official posts. An example of this can be seen in the illustration from the work by Ponzilacqua (p. 322) in the next century, produced when the Congress of Vienna handed a part of Italy over to Austria.

But German letter forms and script had an influence far removed from the neighbouring European countries. Writing in the United States was inevitably largely influenced by hands common in England. The Pilgrim Fathers had taken with them to the New World the contemporary English scripts, and trade between the two continents had brought French and Dutch scripts in its wake. But the later German immigrants, settling for the most part in Pennsylvania, brought with them the very different styles of Central Europe – and not just in handwriting but in all the arts and crafts. As a result there developed the very individualistic style known as 'Pennsylvania Dutch' (*Deutsch*), with its colourful folk art traditions. Pennsylvania Dutch *fraktur* script had its basis

A restrained piece of self-advertisement by William Brooks, two illustrations of whose work are included in this book (pp. 255, 256). Nevertheless a subtle indication of his academic abilities is attempted by the inclusion of the French and Latin phrases!

V & A M

This splendid mezzotint by Faber after the painting by M. Dahl was published in 1723. Thomas Weston has scattered on the table before him such objects as he feels will emphasise his claim to fame; his neat inkstand should be especially noticed.

V & A M.

in contemporary German scripts, but developed along its own lines once it became firmly established. A great variety of documents and manuscripts were produced in this style in the late 18th and early 19th century in the Pennsylvania area, and they have great charm and vigour. The quality varies considerably, since it was very much a folk art. There were teachers certainly, but there were also many who took pleasure in producing for their own or their friends' enjoyment those personal items reminiscent of the land of their forefathers. Such productions stand outside the mainstream of American calligraphy, but their existence has nevertheless influenced certain later work.

In western Europe calligraphy was confined to legal documents (still written in traditional scripts) and ceremonial pieces, as in the previous century. But of course there were at all times personal writings in the form of letters and diaries, memoranda, bills, and records of all sorts, and on the whole the script used for these items was at least legible if nothing more. This section of the book includes a number of personal writings of various kinds, to show the general standard of handwriting of the period. But the late 18th century also saw an interesting development, in a form of antiquarianism which in one manifestation has been given the name of 'Strawberry Hill Gothic'.

Antiquarianism was not a new phenomenon. If we consider it in England, we shall find that there had for long been amateurs and scholars who had looked back with interest to the past, and inspected with equal interest the surviving remains of that past. The Reformation in England and the dissolu-

This mezzotint by Faber after T. Stokes differs from many of the portraits of Willis's fellow writing masters in that he is set plainly against a dark background, with nothing but his quill to indicate his profession. But the satisfied look on his face suggests that John Willis was quite assured of his standing without any additional symbols!

V&AM

Joseph Champion, portrayed here in a very grandiose way, contributed no less than 47 plates to Bickham's Universal Penman, *some examples of which are illustrated here (pp. 267-70). Everything in this portrait is intended to emphasise the writing master's status and his abilities.*

V&AM

tion of the monasteries had led to the dispersal of the monastic libraries, while the spread of printing had made many manuscript texts redundant. But there were always some people who regarded this dispersal with sadness, and there is a famous passage in John Aubrey's autobiographical writing in which he says 'in my grandfather's days manuscripts flew about like butterflies'. He goes on to say how in his own schooldays (in the 1630's) he found schoolbooks covered with old manuscript pages, and deplored the various less attractive uses to which such relics were sometimes put. Others after him looked back and wondered, but few gave their interest such a practical expression as Horace Walpole. It was he who built the 'gothick' fantasy which he called Strawberry Hill, and filled it with all the medieval spoils he could lay hands on, including of course medieval manuscripts. Many of the copy books had always included a version of some medieval scripts, and the origin of the alphabet had for long fascinated antiquarian-minded writers. For a study of calligraphy this 'gothick' movement is of considerable interest, since it aroused a desire among some people to try their own hand at a manuscript book, or at least a medieval-style type of script. One such attempted imitation can be seen in p. 314. The interest in medievalism, strengthened by the growth of the romantic approach to the arts, developed even further in the next century. Thus a new attitude to writing was brought about. No longer was it something which had to be done out of necessity, and was usually associated with commerce. It now partook of the romantic aura which surrounded the Middle Ages as seen by the 18th century, and which was to be further exploited later in the writings of Sir Walter Scott.

So as the 18th century drew to a close a number of different trends had become apparent. The plain business script exemplified by the English round hand was generally in the ascendant. Literacy was on the increase and the Sunday School Movement was to bring reading and writing to an even greater number of poorer people – but the writing was to be simple and

A portrait of the exuberant Edward Cocker, which appeared in his Guide to Penmanship, *1664*

V&AM E 849-1965 20 × 30

unadorned of course. One of the effects of the French Revolution at the end of the century was to make people look critically at existing ideas and to cast aside much that was old-established and aristocratic. At the same time the interest in a more remote past was increasing, and the products of that past were looked at with greater awareness. Nevertheless, it must be realised that it was still very difficult for most people to actually see a medieval manuscript, even in reproduction. There were few collections open to general inspection and colour printing was not yet a viable commercial proposition, hence the uninformed nature of much of the study on writing and manuscripts. It was this aspect that the great improvements in the next century were to affect so dramatically.

A portrait of George Shelly, engraved by George Bickham. The writing-master is given a typical baroque background of classical column and billowing drapery, no doubt to emphasise his status (in his own eyes at least!). The implements of his art which surround him should also be noted.

V&AM E 866-1965 29.5 × 19.5

This portrait of Thomas Tomkins is a mezzotint by Charles Turner after the painting by Sir Joshua Reynolds, and was issued in 1805. Tomkins looks out as if assured of his position in society, which his friendship with Reynolds no doubt encouraged, but he was cruelly slated by Isaac D'Israeli who said 'this vainest of writing-masters dreamed through life that penmanship was one of the fine arts, and that a writing-master should be seated with his peers in the Academy!'

V&AM E 874-1965 36 × 25.5

This manuscript contains directions for a tournament held in Bologna in 1710, and was written by an unknown author who used the pseudonym 'Flamarindo'. It would appear that the manuscript was written out either for personal use or as a memento, and the writer was not a professional scribe. Nevertheless he has produced a fine italic script which relates directly to copy book models, though possibly those of an earlier date than that of the manuscript.

V&AM MS L 1937-1880 28.5 × 20

48

Avvertenze al Sarto

IL Cavaliere deve avere una Camiciola di Tela di lino imbuttita di Bombace battuto attilata alla vita con colare che facci il collo alto due dita con i quarti sotto pure imbuttiti, che coprano tutto lo stomaco, avvertendo però, che a dirittura del filo della schiena non deve essere imbuttita, ne avere orli grossi. Le maniche si fanno di roverscio attilate al braccio, e lunghe sino alla snodatura della mano. Si serra sul polso con tre cordelle attaccate da una parte della Manica, e passando per buchi fatti dall'altra parte, s'uniscono in un punto d'una cordella, la quale fasciando il braccio tengono assicurata la Manica, che non s'apre d'avanti; da un fianco all'altro nella centura si fanno diversi buchi, mettendovi sotto una fortezza di tela, dovendo sostenere il peso de' Gambieri.

Attorno a i spalazzi si fanno i medesimi buchi con le stesse fortezze, dovendo sostenere i bracciali. Vi vogliono quattro stringhe lunghe un braccio, et altre quattro lunghe un braccio e mezzo, da mettere abbasso, e queste devono essere di cordella bianca ben forte ferrata da tutte due le parti.

Ve ne vuole un'altra lunga ferrata da un capo solo, la quale deve servire, per serrare la Camiciuola d'avanti principiando dal collarino sino allo stomaco; Sotto li quarti si fanno due borse con il suo cordoncino da serrare, per tenervi dentro qualche cosa sagra, o danari.

In caso bisognasse alzare la Celata, o altro, come si dirà ab=

Opposite:
This calligraphic tour-de-force was produced by John Dundas, junior, and engraved by Joseph Nutting in 1705. It carries everything to extremes, including the two roundels containing minuscule writing — that on the left begins 'Our Father . . .'

V&AM

Non bene faciam sed Iuvat hoc facere
The happy Quills wth wch our Laureats write Hinder ye Birds but raise ye Poets flight
To all kind Judges my Endeavors bow,
I'm not conceited but must faults allow:
Pray ben't too nice my Art is very young,
Then blast it not by a too rigid tongue.
JOHN DUNDAS Iur Scripsit 1703
Joseph Nutting Sculpt. 1705
London Printed for Robt. Sayer at No. 53 in Fleet Street
price 6d.

Sr

Octobr: 6th: 1708.

'ΗΈΛΙΟΣ: hath 4 Times, and MHNH 52 Times Transited MAZZAROTH Since my Immuremt: in Castles Inchanted: About Three years Past you was pleased to make a Descent, visiting me in Limbo &c: for wch: kindness I sent a Letter of thanks, till Acknowledgmt: could be made in Propria Persona, but was Obstructed: for this Arke of my Body hath ever Since been So Agitated, by the Adverse Billows of Fortune and Gradated from Schooles to Colledges, and now at the University of Januæ Novæ am Commencing Doctour; in the great Quadrangle there called Debtors Hall. And if you are yet in the Land of the Living, as for certain I that write am in the dens) and you can Descend also in Tartaro, where no One but a Hercules in Good Will dare Attempt; Cerberus will Admitt you, without ye Fatigue of Carrying him away at yr Return: Excuse this Freedom knowing the Man, at Present in Nubibus, Sed post Nubila PHŒBUS: I hope the Time may be short, and to Contemplate on the ARCANA's of this Infernall Region are not So Terrifying, as yr Presence will be Exhilerating to him Sr: who was, is, and shall Remain:

This Gent: a Quondam Sufferer wth: my Self, can Satisfie how I came here, & the Reason of Imploring Auxilium Deorum ——
Ο'ΜΗ'ΡΟΥ Ι'ΛΙΑ'ΔΟΣ —

yr Humb: Servt: to Command:

John: Watts.

Letter from John Watts to James Sotheby dated 6th October 1708. Watts was in Newgate Prison, London, and he wrote a facetiously learned letter asking Sotheby, possibly his patron, to bail him out. The letter is carefully written and set out on the page, and makes an interesting comment on the formal teaching of handwriting as portrayed in the writing masters' manuals.

V & A M   MS L 1768-1966   20 × 15

Opposite top:
George Shelley: Natural writing in all the hands, with variety of ornament 1709

Shelley's Natural writing *appeared in two parts and this plate is taken from the first part. If we remove the intrusive decoration on this plate, we are left with a plain round hand, of which Shelley was a master. It was this simple and unadorned writing, so suitable for business, that was eventually to supplant all other hands in the course of the 18th century.*

V & A M   L 2035-1884   23 × 36

Opposite bottom:
George Shelley: Natural writing in all the hands, with variety of ornament 1709

This further plate from Natural writing *shows clearly why Shelley's round hand was so much admired. It was his 'sprigg'd fancies' which his opponents derided, and it must be admitted that in this text, for example, they have little relevance, however elegantly performed.*

V & A M   L 2035-1884   23 × 36

There is nothing
so Excellent but
Detraction will
find some fault

Shelley scr.

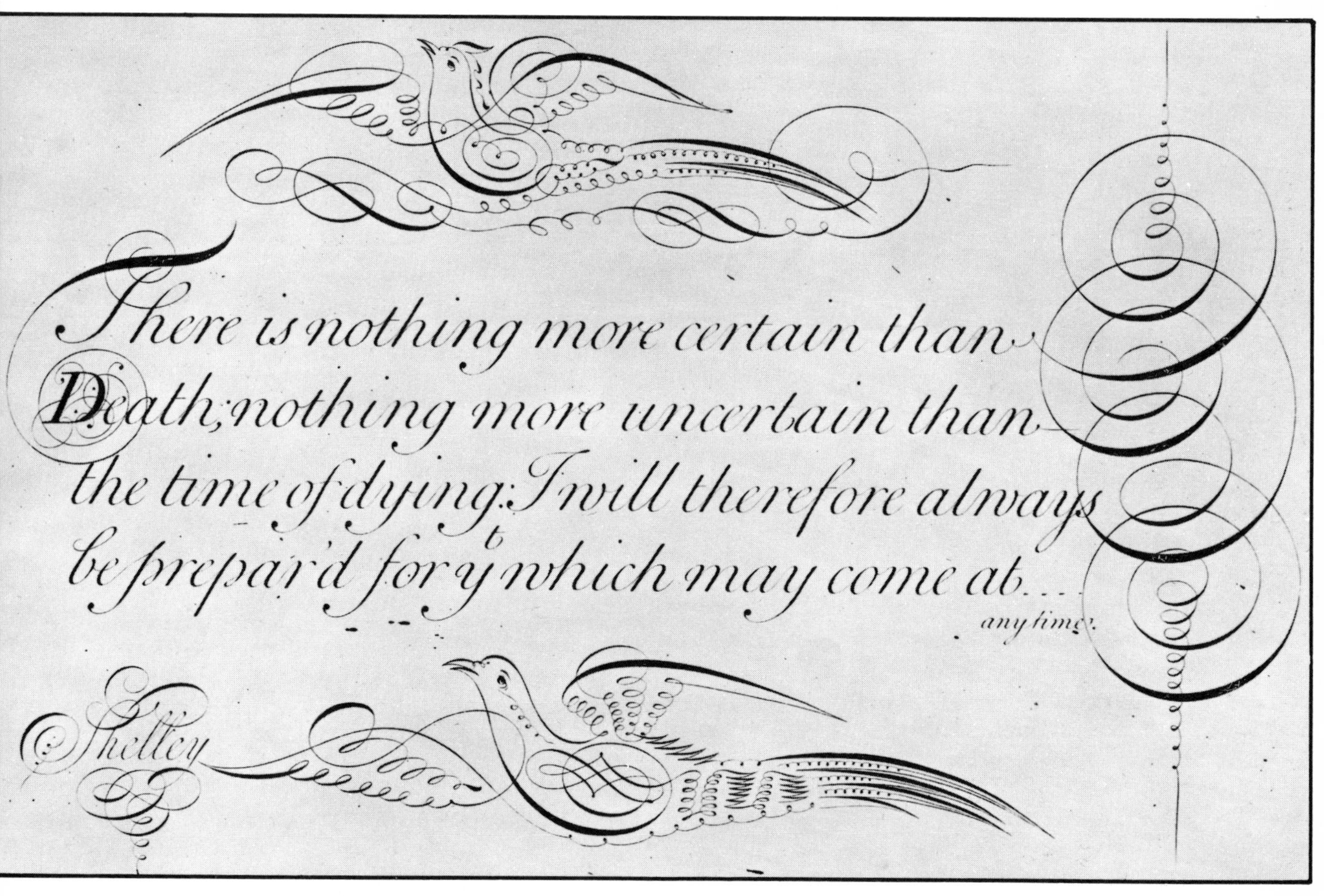

There is nothing more certain than
Death; nothing more uncertain than
the time of dying: I will therefore always
be prepar'd for y^t which may come at...
any time.
Shelley

TO

Mr Peter Monger

and

Mr John Cartlitch Senr

Gentlemen,

Tho I hazard the Loss of Yor Favour by making Your Names Public, yet I cannot Omit ye Opportunity of letting You know, that I shall ever Retain a Grateful Remembrance of the Extraordinary Generosity, and Genteel Treatment, I met wth in my Teaching Yor Sons. They're such Gentlemen as yorSelves yt Invigorate a Master's Endeavors & to whome ye World's oblig'd for all ye Advances made in Penmanship

Yr most Obliged & Obedient Servt.

G Shelley

George Shelley: Penna volans, after ye English, French & Dutch way c1710

In this example Shelley not only provides the student with a model of a formal letter, but he also manages to include a little self-advertisement too — something to which most writing masters were especially prone! It is interesting to see from the title of this work those countries whose hands were considered to be especially important at this period.

V & A M L 537-1939 19.5 × 27.5

An Acco.t of Plate with the Respective Quantity ... Weight and Value, that hath been delivered out of the Jewell Office upon any Occasion from the 13.o of December 1701. To the 29.o of Septemb.r 1711 (Except the Plate deli.d for Her Majesties Own proper Use) Also what Quantity of y.e said Plate hath been discharged by Privy Seal within the said Time and how much stands charged in y.e Books of the said Office within the said Time

On what Acco.t	To whom delivered	Gold Works (oz dwt gr)	Gilt Plate (oz dwt gr)	White Plate (oz dwt gr)	Value (£ s d)	Total Value (£ s d)
Claims at the Coronation	To the Duke of Bedford High Constable One Staff of Silver Gilt at each End		12 3		8 5	
	To the Earle Marshall one Truncheon of Gold	15			90	
	To Ditto One Gold Cup	32 2			176 11	
	To the Earle of Bindon Deputy Earle Marshall to the Duke of Norfolk One Truncheon or Staff of Gold	15 2			90 12	
	To the Champion One Cup of Gold	21			115 10	
	To the Mayor of London Chief Butler One Gold Cup	21			115 10	
	To the Mayor of Oxford Under Butler One Gilt Cup and Cover		112		67 7	
	To the Earle of Bradford One Wedge of Gold for an Offering	12 .. 12			} 100 3 6	
	To Ditto One other Wedge of Gold	8				
	To the Chief Cup Bearer One Gilt Cup and Cover		41 16		25 1 6	
	Twelve Canopy Staves			474 15	213 12 9	
	Eight Gilt Bells		54 13		46 14	
	To the Earle of Lindsey L.d Great Chamberlain Two large Chased Basons Gilt and One Chased Ewer		355		213	
	To the Prebends of Westminster One Silver Standish			69 9	26 .. 10½	
	To the Earle of Exeter as Lord Almoner a Large gilt Bason		151		90 12	
	To the Master of the Ceremonies One Chain of Gold	8 9			46 10 6	
	To D.o One Badge of Gold	1 17			17 8	
	To Garter Principal King at Armes one Scepter of Gold	1 17			31 7 5 [?]	
	To Ditto a Badge of Gold	1 – 20			14 3 4 [?]	
	Carried Forward				1488 13 10½	

This is a piece of business writing albeit a somewhat ceremonial one. It is a formal statement of the account of plate (silver and gold, chains, ewers, cups, truncheons etc) which were delivered out of the Royal Jewell House between 1701 and 1711, mainly to noblemen and court functionaries. Even in this plain businesslike statement, the scribe cannot refrain from a certain elaboration in the capital letters, especially in the headings.

V&AM MS L 1217-1947 22 × 14.5

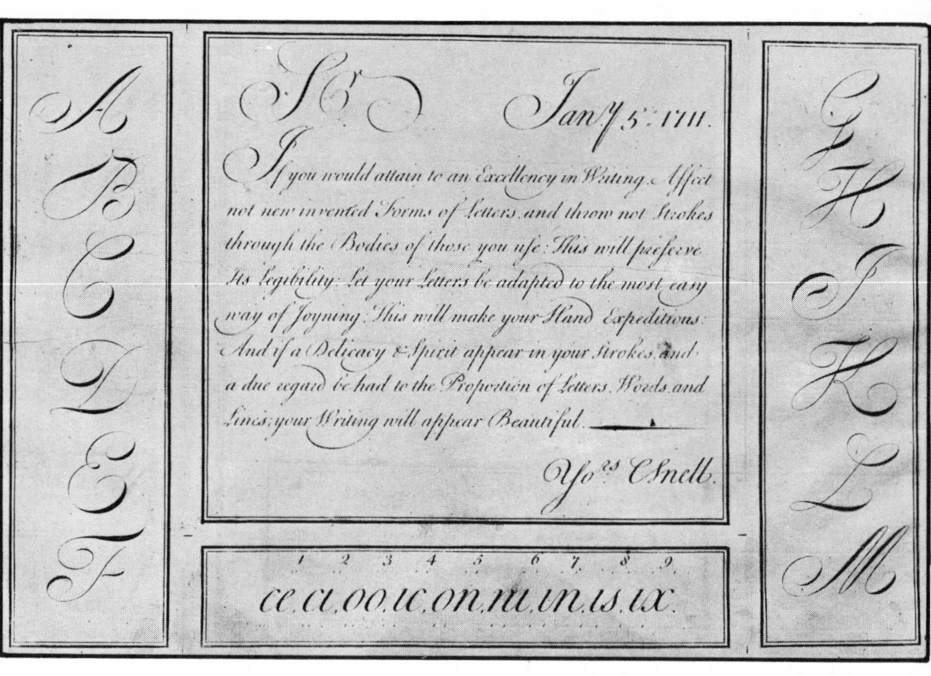

A B C D E F

Sr. Jany 5: 1711.

If you would attain to an Excellency in Writing, Affect not new invented Forms of Letters, and throw not Strokes through the Bodies of those you use: This will preserve Its legibility: Let your Letters be adapted to the most easy way of Joyning: This will make your Hand Expeditious: And if a Delicacy & Spirit appear in your Strokes, and a due regard be had to the Proportion of Letters, Words and Lines; your Writing will appear Beautiful.

Yors. C Snell.

1 2 3 4 5 6 7 8 9

ce. ci. oo. ic. on. ni. in. is. ix.

G H I K L M

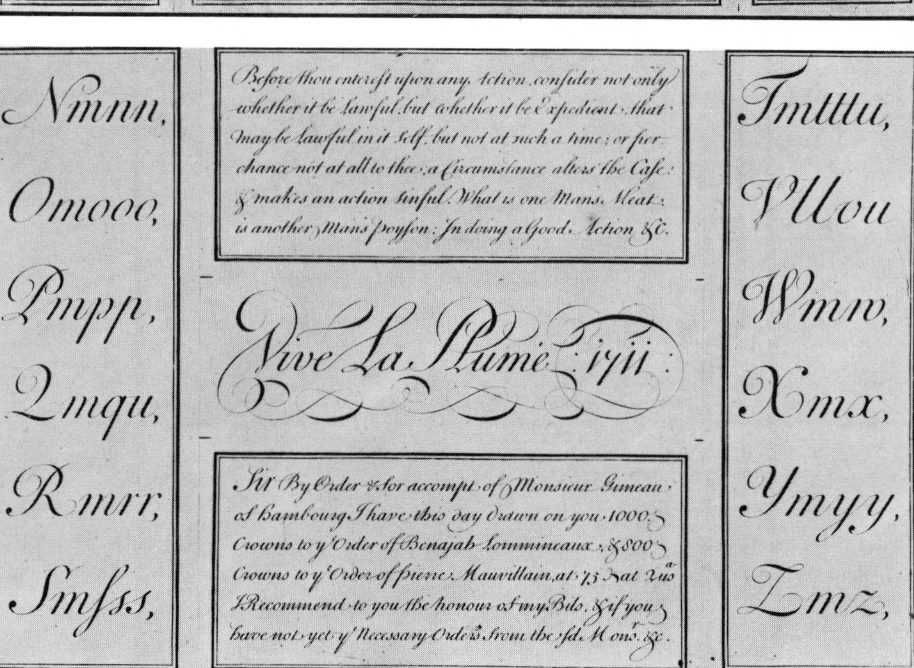

Nmnn, Omooo, Pmpp, Qmqu, Rmrr, Smſss,

Before thou enter'st upon any Action, consider not only whether it be Lawful, but whether it be Expedient: that May be Lawful in it Self, but not at such a time; or perchance not at all to thee; a Circumstance alters the Case: & makes an action Sinful. What is one Mans Meat: is another Mans Poyson: In doing a Good Action &c.

Vive La Plume 1711.

Sir By Order & for accompt of Monsieur Gimeau of Hambourg I have this day drawn on you 1000 Crowns to ye Order of Benajah Lomminecaux; & 800 Crowns to ye Order of Pierre Mauvillain, at 75 at 2 Us. I Recommend to you the honour of my Bils, & if you have not yet ye Necessary Orders from the sd. Mons. &c.

Tmttu, VUou, Wmw, Xmx, Ymyy, Zmz,

Charles Snell: The art of writing in its theory and practice 1712

Charles Snell advocated an unadorned style of writing, and endeavoured to formulate 'standard rules' based on a mathematical approach to letter forms. As can be seen from what he says here, he was concerned with legibility above all. But even he cannot entirely avoid some flourish to his letters, possibly because it was suggested that those who opposed them did so because they were not competent to make them!

V&AM *L 599-1879* *23.5 × 34*

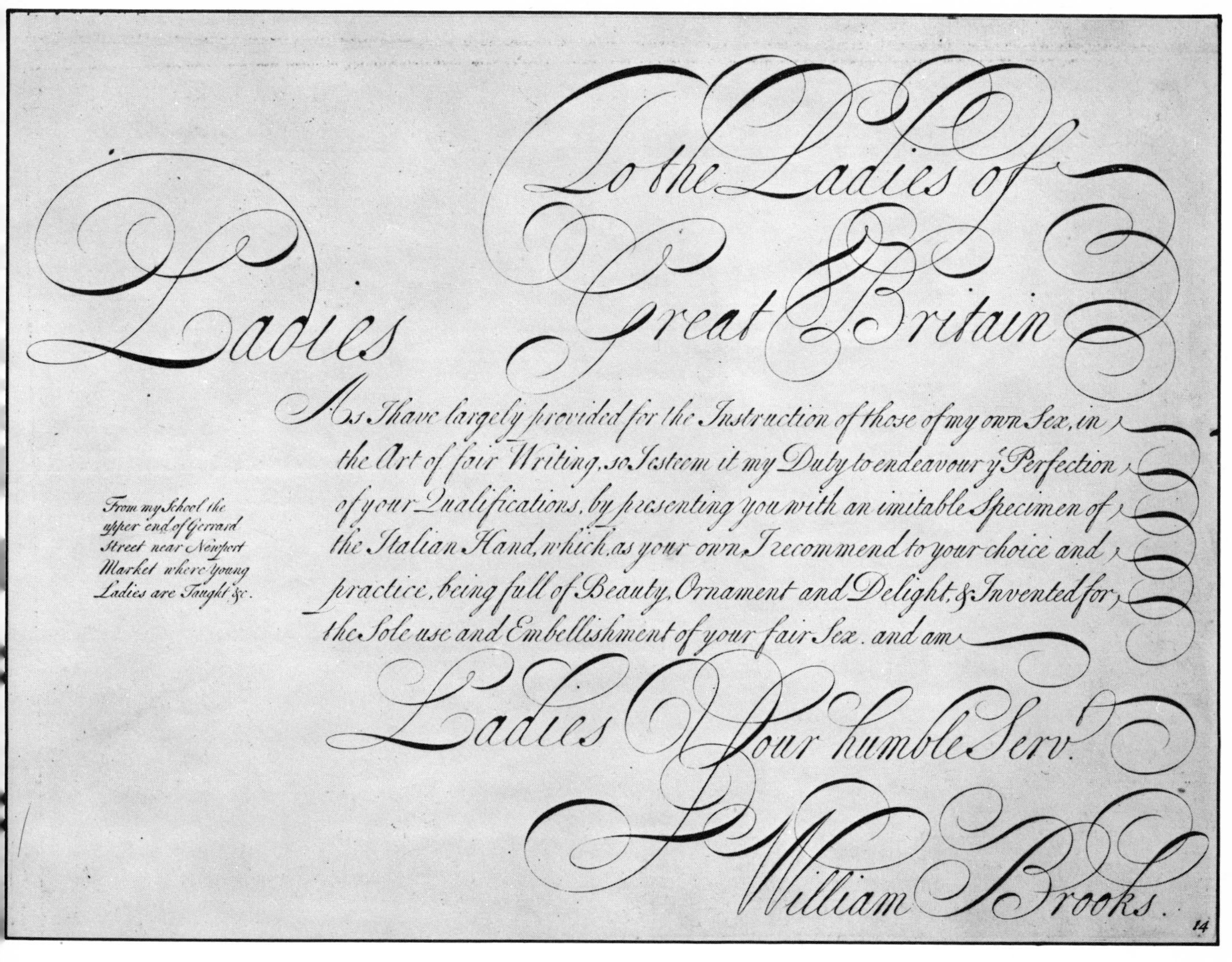

To the Ladies of Great Britain

Ladies

As I have largely provided for the Instruction of those of my own Sex, in the Art of fair Writing, so I esteem it my Duty to endeavour ye Perfection of your Qualifications, by presenting you with an imitable Specimen of the Italian Hand, which, as your own, I recommend to your choice and practice, being full of Beauty, Ornament and Delight, & Invented for the Sole use and Embellishment of your fair Sex. and am

Ladies Your humble Servt.

William Brooks.

From my School the upper end of Gerrard Street near Newport Market where Young Ladies are Taught &c.

14

William Brooks: A delightful recreation for the industrious
1717

This example of the early 18th century Italian hand was expressly aimed at 'the ladies of Great Britain'. Throughout the 17th and 18th centuries writing masters explained that the Italian hand being the easiest to write, was therefore the most suitable for women. For, as Martin Billingsley wrote 'they (having not the patience to take any great paines, besides fantastical and humorsome), must be taught that which they may easily learne . . . because their minds are (upon light occasion) easily drawn from the first resolution'.

V&AM L1744-1922 23 × 36.5

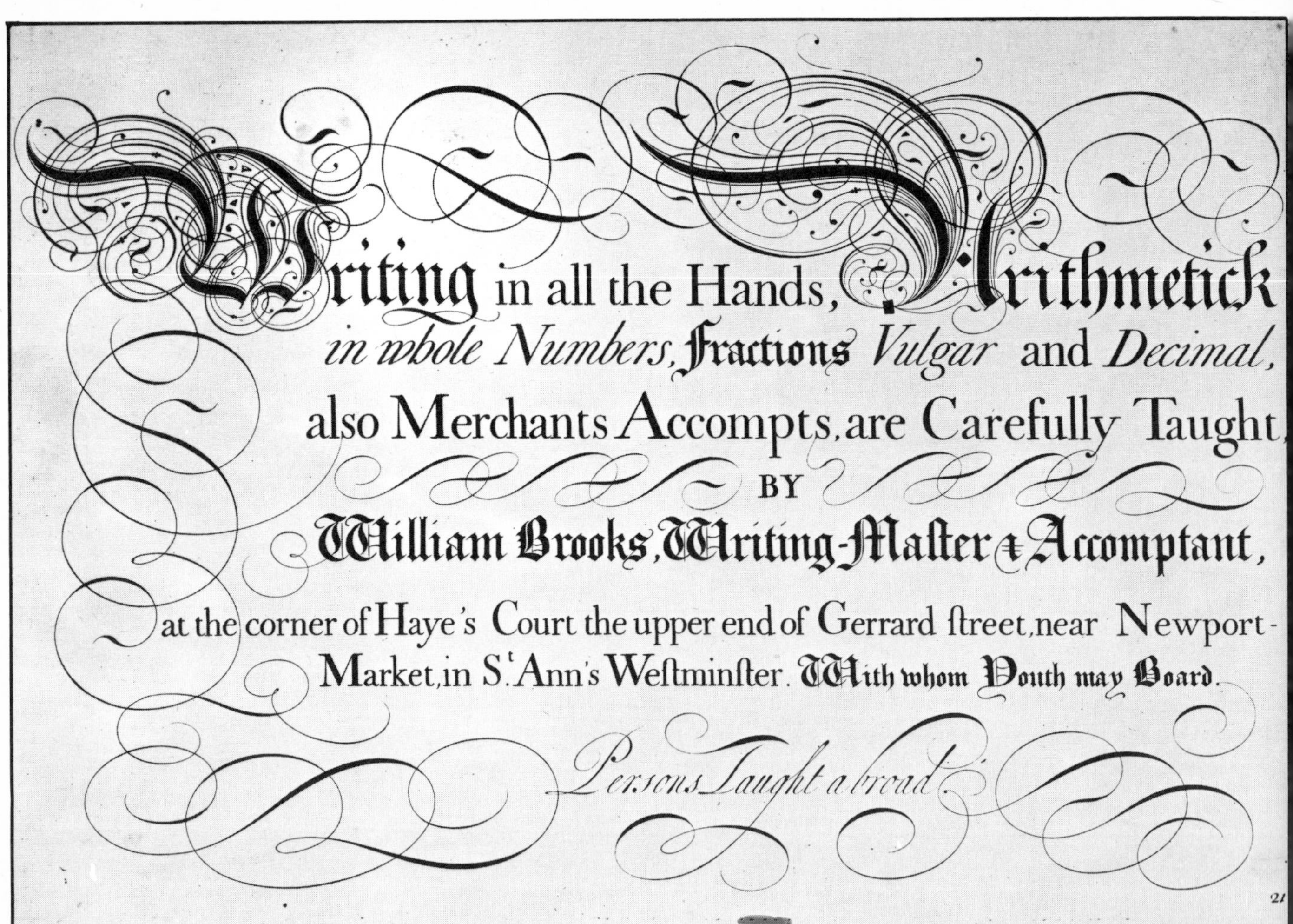

William Brooks: A delightful recreation for the industrious 1717

This illustration shows an advertisement which William Brooks included in his copy book. He has obviously included in it a specimen of all the hands which he was prepared to teach, so that it offers a practical example of the master's abilities. This form of self-advertisement was often used in the title-pages of copy books too.

V&AM L1744-1922 25 × 37

A New Copy Book
Of the Small Italian Hand
Published for the Use
Of Publick and Private Schools
As well as for the Use of Families
By John Langton Writing Master
In Stamford in the County of Lincoln
Where Youth may be Taught Arithmetick
And the Hands in general
John Langton Inv: et Scr.
George Bickham Sculp.

John Langton: A new copy book of the small Italian hand. 1727

This title-page is in the form of an advertisement, since it makes use of all the hands which Langton might be supposed to be able to teach. Although some of the letters show a certain amount of flourish, Langton obviously did not feel the need to attract his pupils by any further decorations. It will be noted that this plate has been engraved by George Bickham, himself no mean calligrapher, and examples of whose work are also illustrated in this book.

V&AM L 1397-1922 19 × 31

Elias Ashmole: The institution, laws & ceremonies of the Most Noble Order of the Garter c1727

This work contains the title-page and index of the printed book, but the rest is mainly an abridgement of Ashmole's work, apparently made for one of the officials or knights concerned. It is a good example of an educated cursive hand, here used for business rather than display.

V & A M Clements MS. 00.10
29.5 × 18

Of the Collar and George.

As it now is it was introduced by K. H. 8. & is an Ornament not of Law, but Ancient invention, & ye wonderfull Consent of most nations plead for it, Sacred Writ sets down ye Collar of Gold for one of ye Ornaments Pharaoh conferred upon Joseph, ye Images of Isis & Osiris, were represented with such like Collars, in a manner extending to their Shoulders as Kircher, informs us, Their workmanship seems wonderfull Curious,

The Collar was of illustrious Original among ye Romans, & gave denomination to ye Family of Torquati, descended from L. Manlius, whom ye Soldiers surnamed Torquatus, because he fought with ye Champion of ye Gauls, anno V.C. 392, & having foiled him in fight cut of his head & yn pulled off his Collar bloody as it was, & put it about his own neck In further memory of wch Action were found several Roman Coins refering to L. Torquatus, consul with L. Catta Anno V. C. 688. & it is remarkable yt one of an other Tribe was adopted into this family, he did also assume this Badge of hon, as in ye Coin of D. Junius Silanus, tho ye fashon of ye Work differed somewhat from ye former,

In pristine Times none but Kings & Princes, wore Collars, & therefore their use seems of Dignity & Power, as is evident from Daniel, where ye Assyrian Kings used this Ornament, afterward men famous for Wisdome & Council, had ym as a distinguishing Badge, as in ye Example

George Bickham: The universal penman 1743

This large folio work was originally issued in parts between 1733 and 1741, and contained examples of writing from twenty-five contemporary writing masters in 212 plates. Bickham was responsible for the engraving of many of the plates and was himself a very competent calligrapher, including some of his own work in this compendium (see right). The volume includes a great variety of scripts, but business hands undoubtedly dominate the work. Nevertheless, the plates are also enlivened with genre scenes and a wealth of rococo decoration, which all combine to make this work one of the most important writing books issued in the 18th century, as well as being one of the most magnificent and attractive. For this reason, a number of examples from the work, by various writing masters, are illustrated here (pp. 259-270).

V&AM 39 × 26.

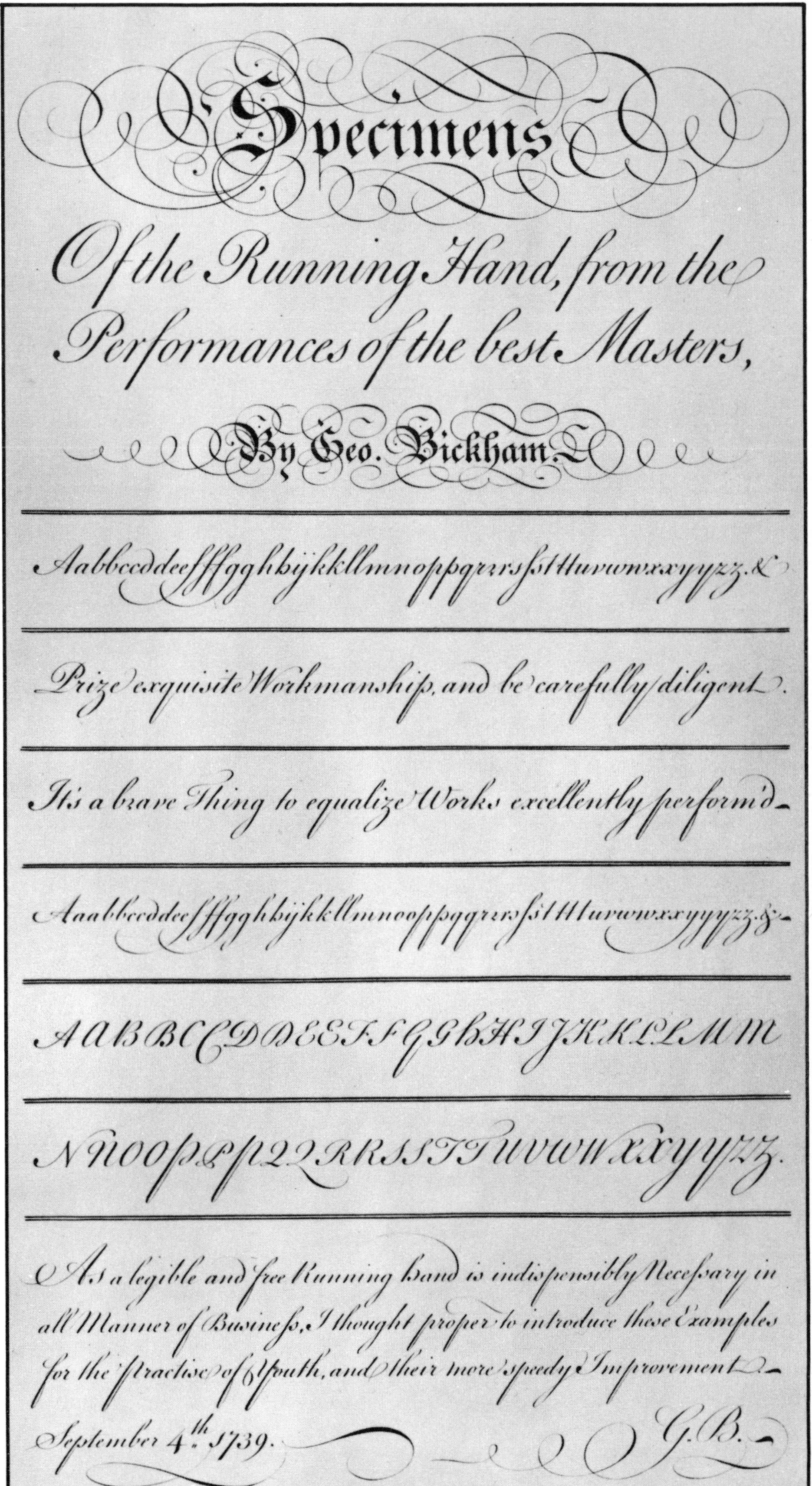

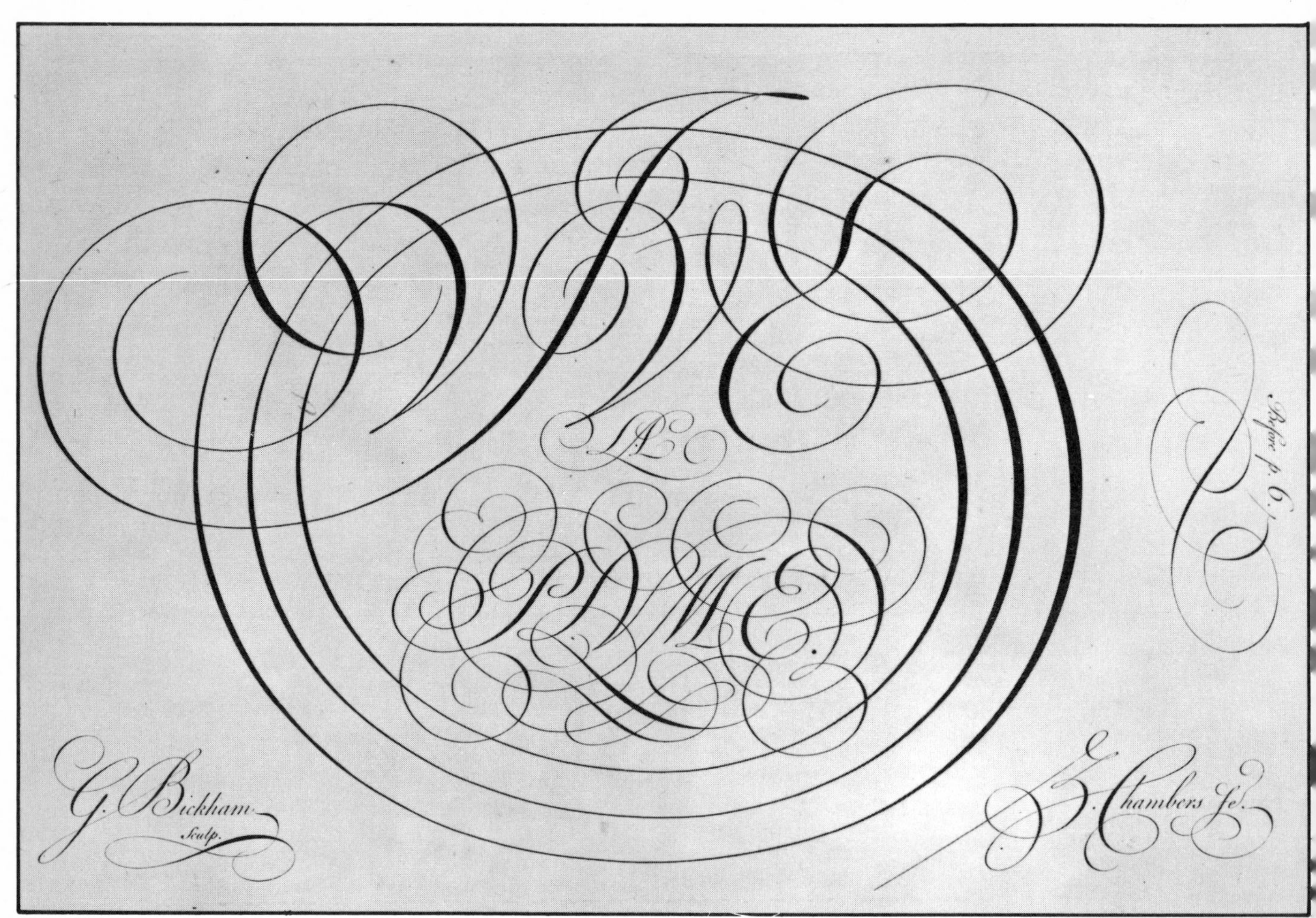

George Bickham: The universal penman 1743

Little is known about Zachary Chambers apart from some plates in various publications. But his work was obviously admired by Bickham who chose to have this example of 'Vive la plume' at the beginning of his great work.

THE

Writing Masters

INVITATION, *AND* INSTRUCTION.

Come Youths this Charming Sight behold!
With Lawrel Plum'd, a Pen of Gold!
If You would win this Glorious Prize,
Do as Your Master shall Advise;
Till You, from Learners, Masters grown,
Make both the Bays & Gold your Own.

Come Listen Youths, and I'll Display
To this Rare Art a Certain Way.
He that in Writing would Improve,
Must first with Writing fall in Love;
For True Love for True Pains will call,
And that's the Charm that Conquers All.

Three things bear mighty Sway with Men,
The Sword, the Scepter, and the PEN;
Who can the leaſt of theſe Command,
In the First Rank of Fame will Stand.

Labor Omnia Vincit.
J. Champion
delin. et scrip.
No IX.
G. B. sculp

George Bickham: The universal penman 1743

Joseph Champion was one of the foremost writing masters of his day and contributed largely to this work; varied examples from his pen are illustrated here.

The Good Samaritan.

Good-Nature.

Good-Nature is the Foundation of all Virtues, either Religious or Civil; Good-Nature, which is Friendship between Man and Man, good Breeding in Courts, Charity in Religion and the true Spring of all Beneficence in General.

Good-Nature and good Sense must ever join;
To err is Human; to Forgive, Divine.

Good Sense and Good-Nature are never separated, tho' the ignorant World has thought otherwise; Good-Nature, by which I mean Beneficence and Candor, is the Product of right Reason, which of necessity will give allowance to the Failings of others, by considering that there is nothing perfect in Mankind.

W: Kippax Scrip!

George Bickham: The universal penman 1743

William Kippax contributed 7 plates to Bickham's work. The scenes and decorations which appear at the top of some of the plates are taken from a variety of sources.

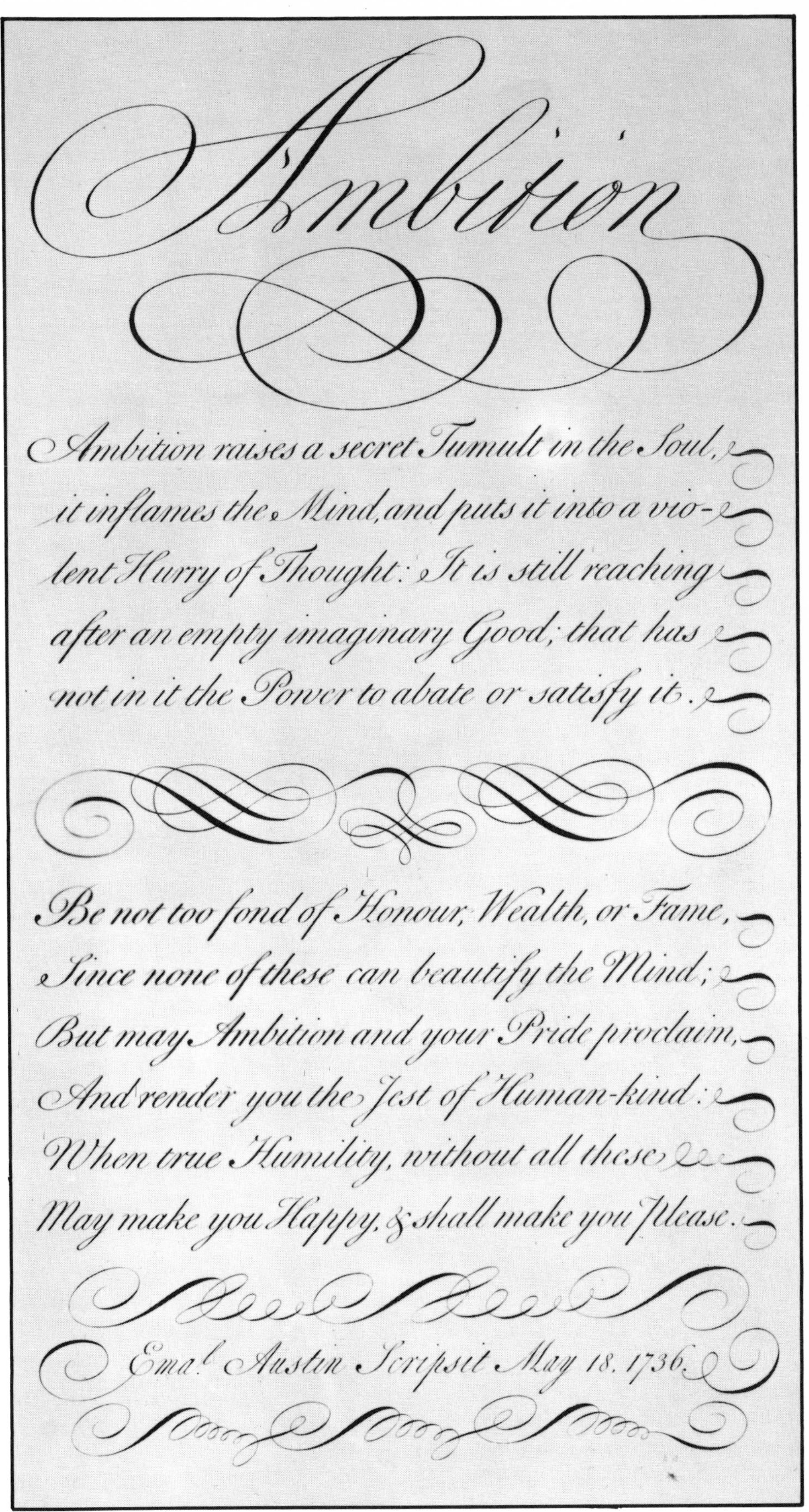

Ambition

Ambition raises a secret Tumult in the Soul, it inflames the Mind, and puts it into a violent Hurry of Thought: It is still reaching after an empty imaginary Good; that has not in it the Power to abate or satisfy it.

Be not too fond of Honour, Wealth, or Fame,
Since none of these can beautify the Mind;
But may Ambition and your Pride proclaim,
And render you the Jest of Human-kind:
When true Humility, without all these
May make you Happy, & shall make you Please.

Ema.l Austin Scripsit May 18. 1736.

George Bickham: The universal penman 1743

Emanuel Austin was an important writing master of the period and 22 examples of his work were included by Bickham.

A ſcanty Fortune clips the Wings of Fame,
And checks the Progreſs of a riſing Name.

Fame is at best but an inconstant Good;
Vain are the boasted Titles of our Blood.
We soonest Loſe what we most highly Prize,
And with our Youth our short-Liv'd Beauty dies.

Fame, due to vaſt Deſerts is kept in Store
Unpaid, till the Deſerver is no more.

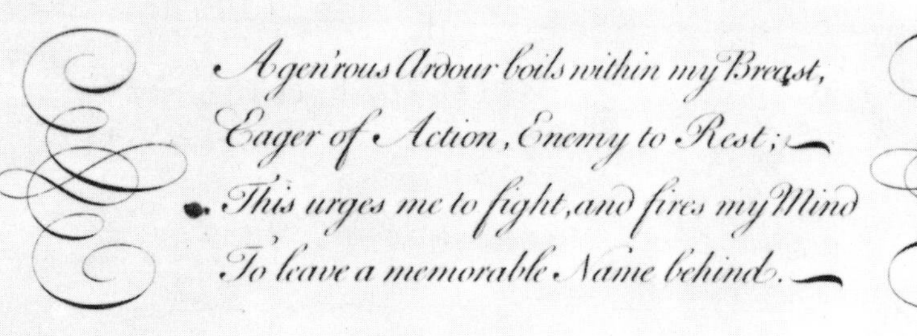

A gen'rous Ardour boils within my Breast,
Eager of Action, Enemy to Rest;
This urges me to fight, and fires my Mind
To leave a memorable Name behind.

The Thing call'd Life, with eaſe I can diſclaim,
And think it over-Sold to purchaſe Fame.

George Bickham: The universal penman 1743

The relationship of John Bickham to the compiler of The universal penman *is not known, and it has proved impossible to decide whether he was brother or father — the two most likely kinships. 3 plates by him were included in this work.*

Too frequent Use does the Delight exclude:—
Pleasure's a Toil when constantly pursu'd.

It is a frivilous Pleasure to be the Admiration of a gaping Croud, but to have the Approbation of a good Man in the Cool Reflections of his Closet, is a Gratification worthy an Heroic Spirit: The Applause of the One makes the Head Giddy; but the Attestation of the other makes ye heart glad.

Fond airy Pleasure dances in our Eyes,—
And spreads false Images in fair disguise.

W. Clark scrip.

George Bickham: The universal penman 1743

Willington Clark was one of the most important contributors to Bickham's work, only two other writing masters had more of their scripts included. In this example and the following one he produces evidence of his versatility.

Liberty.

The Love of Liberty with Life is giv'n,
And Life it self's th'inferior gift of Heav'n.

Lucius seems fond of Life; but what is Life?
'Tis not to stalk about, and draw fresh Air
From time to time, or gaze upon the Sun;
'Tis to be Free. When Liberty is gone,
Life grows insipid, and has lost its Relish.

'Tis Liberty of Choice that sweetens Life,
Makes ye glad Husband & ye happy Wife.

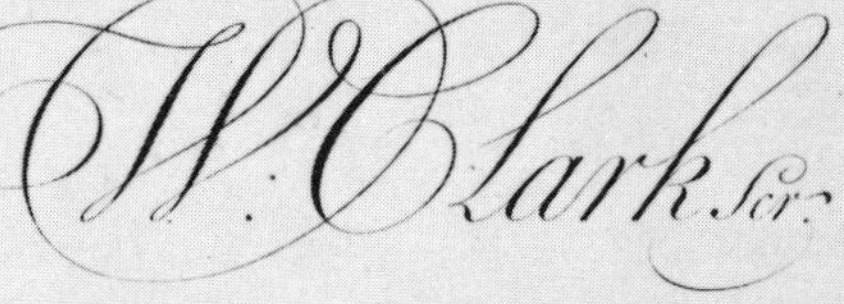

No. XXVII. W. Clark Scr. G. B. sculp.

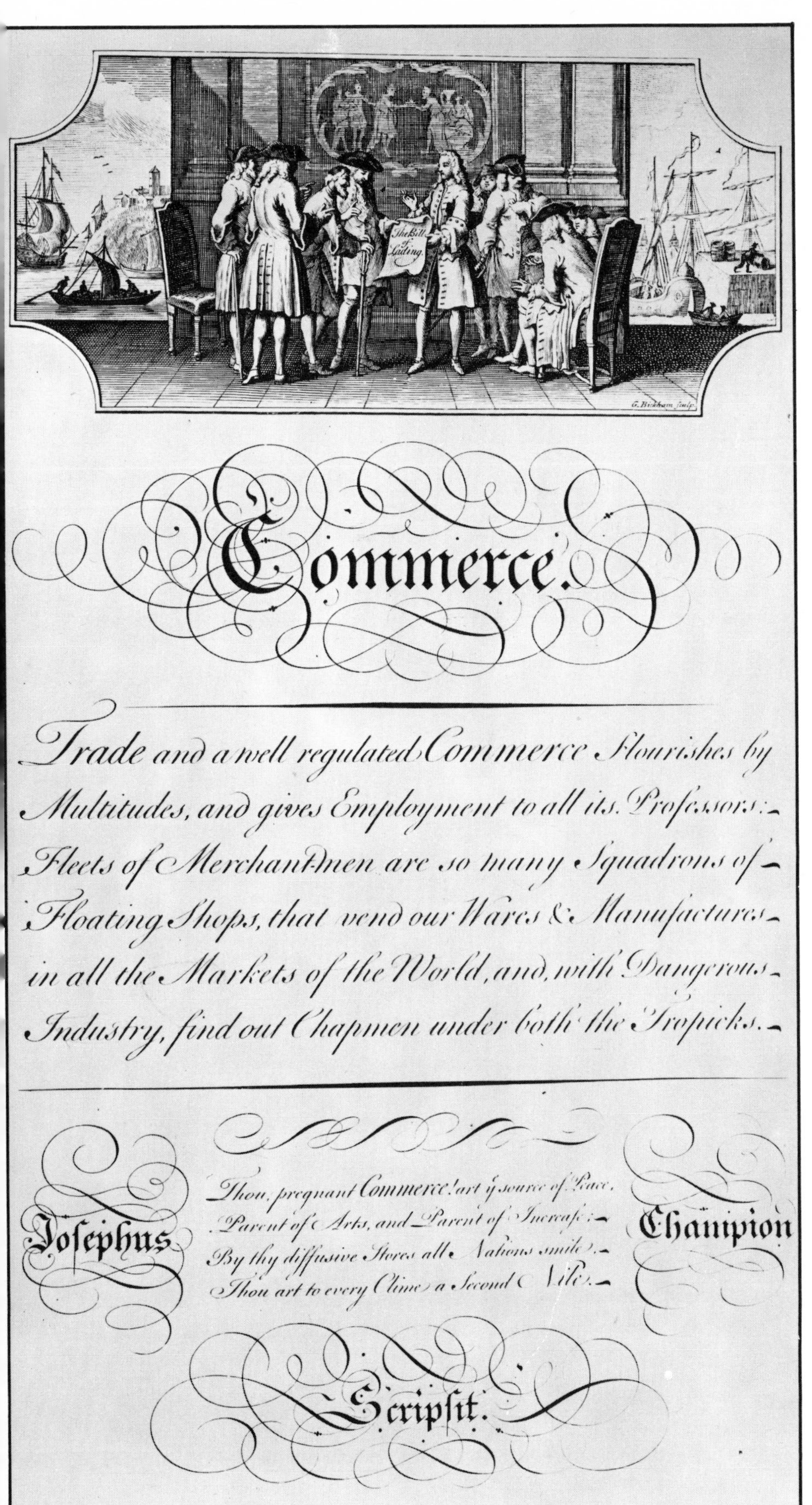
The Bill of Lading

G. Bickham sculp.

Commerce.

Trade and a well regulated Commerce Flourishes by Multitudes, and gives Employment to all its Professors: Fleets of Merchant-men are so many Squadrons of Floating Shops, that vend our Wares & Manufactures in all the Markets of the World, and, with Dangerous Industry, find out Chapmen under both the Tropicks.

Thou, pregnant Commerce! art ye source of Peace,
Parent of Arts, and Parent of Increase:
By thy diffusive Stores all Nations smile,
Thou art to every Clime a Second Nile.

Josephus Champion Scripsit.

George Bickham: The universal penman 1743

The last 4 plates from Bickham's compendium illustrated here are all by Joseph Champion, who was probably the most important contributor. They show a wide range of his scripts, and it will also be noticed that they are quite unadorned except for the headings, which continued to retain an ornamental quality long after it had been rejected elsewhere in writing.

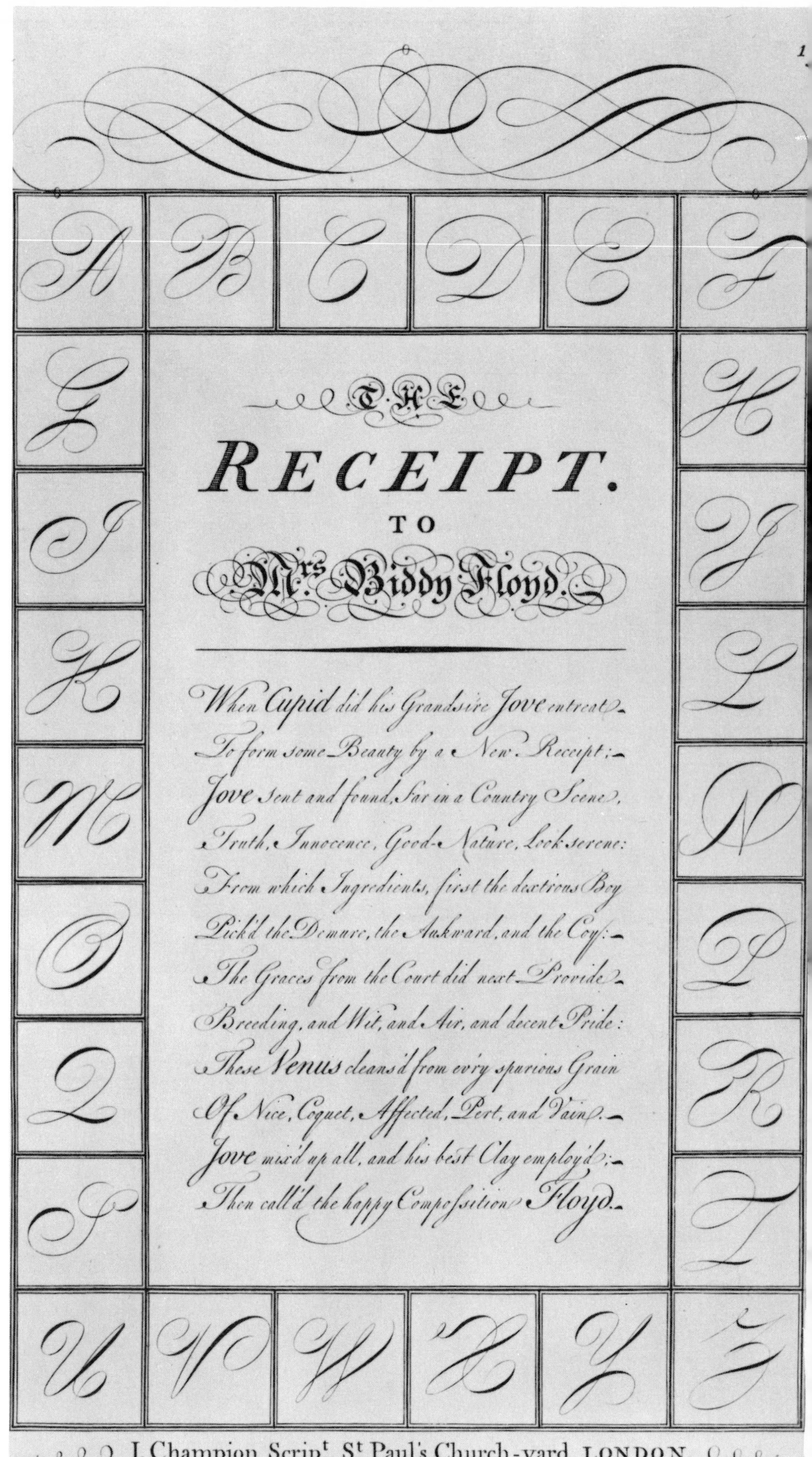
1
THE
RECEIPT.
TO
Mrs Biddy Floyd.
When Cupid did his Grandsire Jove entreat
To form some Beauty by a New Receipt;
Jove sent and found, far in a Country Scene,
Truth, Innocence, Good-Nature, Look serene:
From which Ingredients, first the dextrous Boy
Pick'd the Demure, the Aukward, and the Coy:
The Graces from the Court did next Provide
Breeding, and Wit, and Air, and decent Pride:
These Venus cleans'd from ev'ry spurious Grain
Of Nice, Coquet, Affected, Pert, and Vain.
Jove mix'd up all, and his best Clay employ'd;
Then call'd the happy Composition Floyd.
J. Champion Script. St Paul's Church-yard, LONDON.

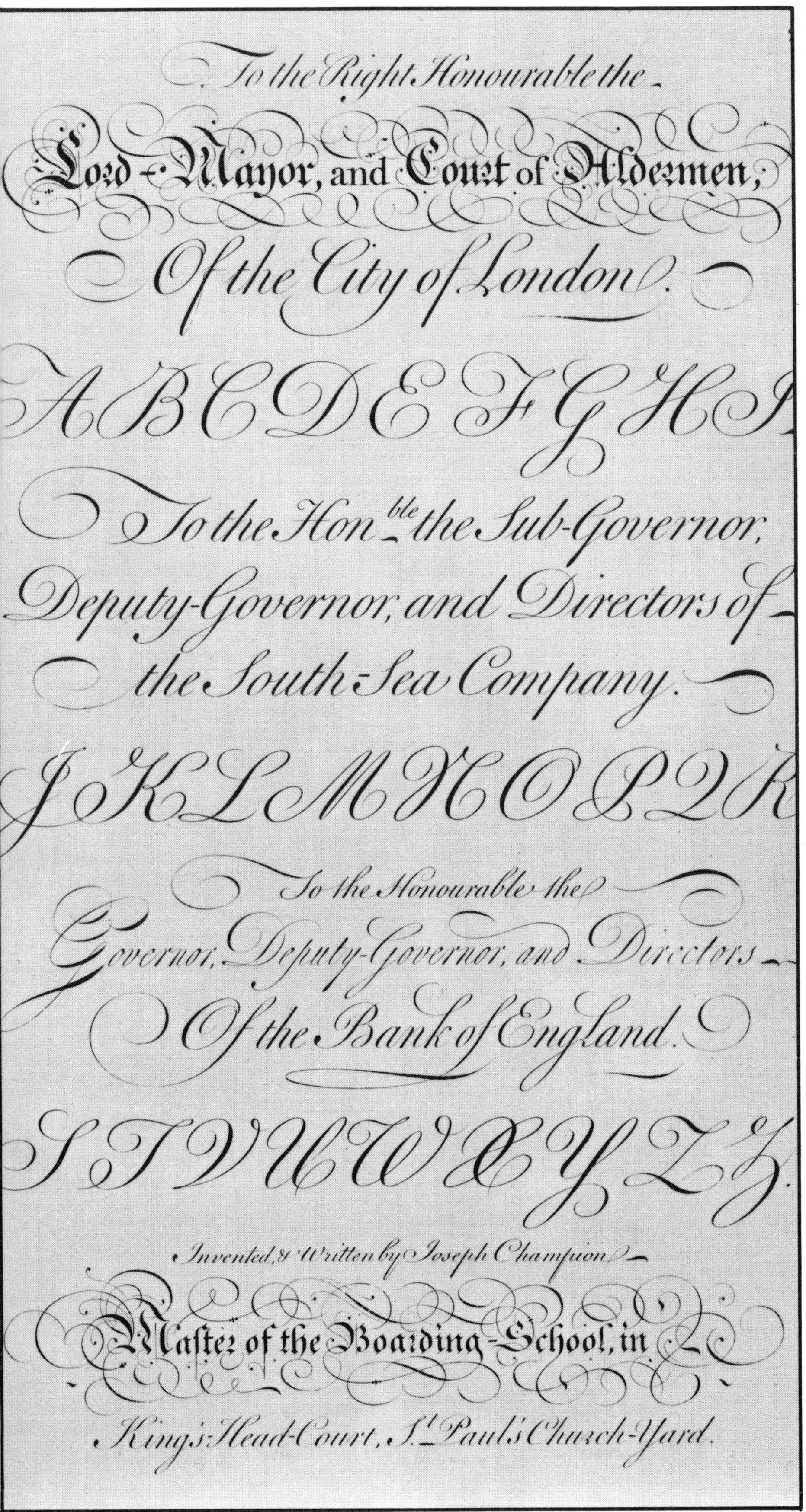
To the Right Honourable the
Lord-Mayor, and Court of Aldermen,
Of the City of London.
A B C D E F G H I
To the Hon.ble the Sub-Governor,
Deputy-Governor, and Directors of
the South-Sea Company.
J K L M N O P Q R
To the Honourable the
Governor, Deputy-Governor, and Directors
Of the Bank of England.
S T V U W X Y Z
Invented, & Written by Joseph Champion
Master of the Boarding-School, in
King's Head-Court, St. Paul's Church-Yard.

Old English Print.

Aabcdefghijklmnopqrſsſſtuvwxyz.&c.

A B C D E F G H J K L M N O P

Q R S T U W X Y Z Z. J. C.

Italick Print.

Aabcdefghijklmnopqrſstuvwwxyz.æœ.

A B C D E F G H I J K L M N O P Q R

R S T U V W X Y Y Z Æ.

Roman Print.

Aabcdefghijklmnopqrſstuvwxyz.

A B C D E F G H I J K L M N O P Q

R S T U V W X Y Z.

Italian Hand.

aabbccddeeffffgghhijkkllmmnoppqrsſsttuvwxyzz.

A B C D E F G H I J K L L M M N

N O P Q R S T U V W W X X Y Z Z.

Court Hand.

[Court Hand alphabet, lower case]

The Chancery

Aa Bb Cc Dd Ee Ffff Gg Hh Iiij Kk Llll Mm Nn

Oo Pp Qq Rr Sſs Tt Uuv Ww Xx Yy Zz &c. Champion Scrip.

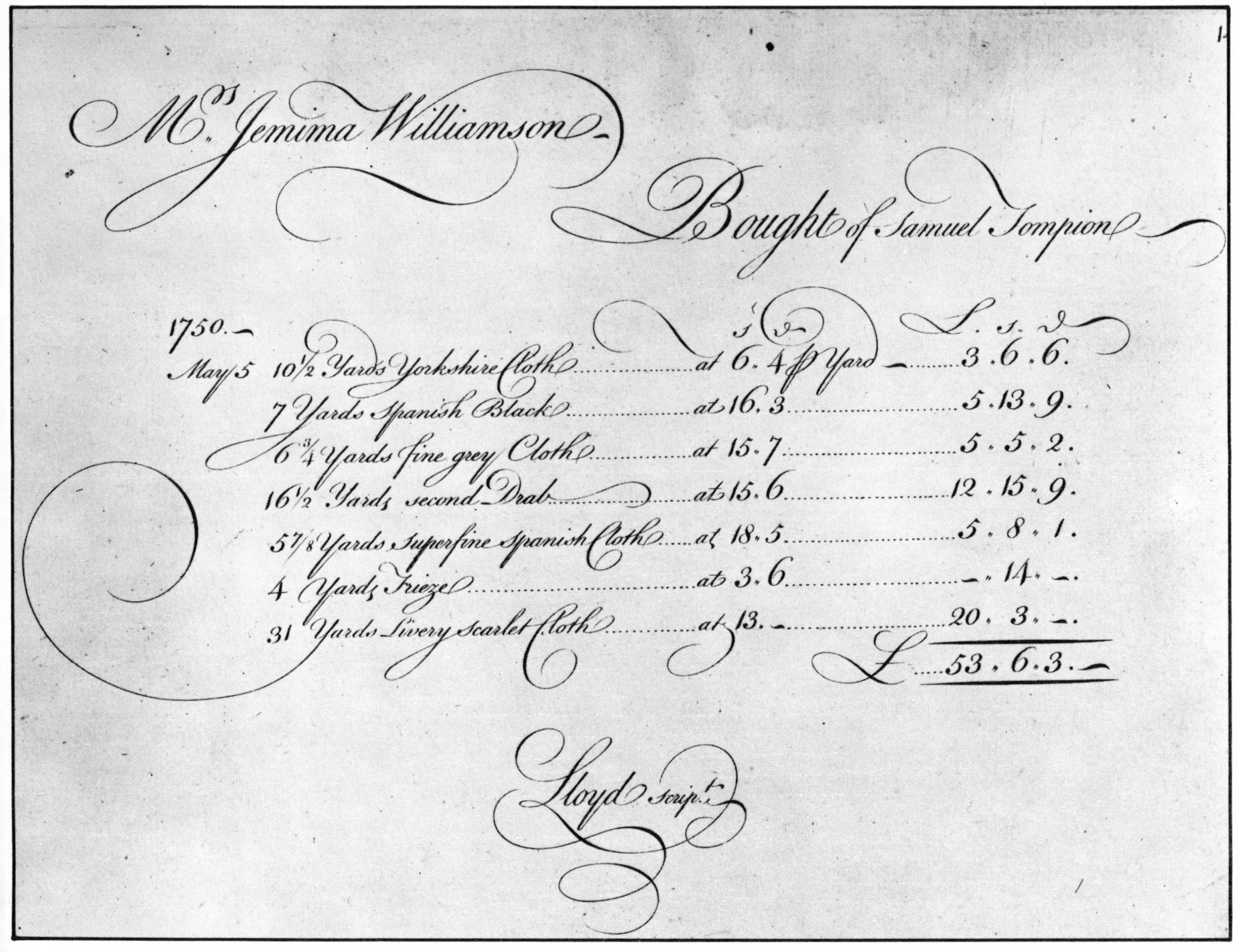

Mrs Jemima Williamson

Bought of Samuel Tompion

1750.			£. s. d
May 5	10½ Yards Yorkshire Cloth	at 6. 4 ⅌ Yard	3 .6 .6.
	7 Yards Spanish Black	at 16. 3	5 .13 .9.
	6¾ Yards fine grey Cloth	at 15. 7	5 . 5 . 2.
	16½ Yards second Drab	at 15. 6	12 . 15 . 9.
	5⅞ Yards Superfine Spanish Cloth	at 18. 5	5 . 8 . 1.
	4 Yards Frieze	at 3. 6	– . 14 . –.
	31 Yards Livery Scarlet Cloth	at 13. –	20 . 3 . –.
			£ 53 . 6 . 3. –

Lloyd Scrip.t

Edward Lloyd: The young merchant's assistant 1751

The title tells us what to expect from this work, and the example shows the English round hand put to use for business affairs. It was the ubiquitousness of the English trader that carried such bills throughout the world, and so familiarised the form of handwriting in which they were made out.

V&AM L 534-1939 23.5 × 37

William Chinnery: Writing and drawing made easy, amusing and instructive (The Compendious emblematist) 1750

Many writing masters added another subject to their abilities, usually either arithmetic or drawing. Chinnery offers the latter. Judging by the number of surviving editions, this work must have been very popular, though possibly more among 'the female practitioners of the art'. The moral text and its application on the right-hand page, is illustrated on the left, together with the relevant letter in a variety of different hands.

V&AM L3066-1960 16.5 × 18

THE MERMAID,

Sweet is the Mermaid's Voice and fair her Face,
But certain Death attends her Soft Embrace.

Application

Beauty without Virtue is a painted Sepulchre.

W. Chinnery Scrip.t — T. Hutchinson Sculp.

Mr Wilson

Feb. 16. Mrs Wilson's Portrait (3/4) — — — 21 " "

March 9th Mrs Wilsons Portrait (3/4) — — 21 " "

may 5 Receved of Mr Wilson for one Picture 21 .. ..

Receved of Mr Skerrow for Mrs Wellson Portrait — 21 " "

na froum —

Mr Brown

Feb. 17 Mr and Mrs Brown's Portraits (3/4) each — 42 " "

Receve'd ——— for Pictures

Viscount Falmouth

Feb. 18. His Lordship's Portrait (3/4) — — 21 " "

May 8 Believes half was received —

June 1st Received of Lord Falmouth 21

1784 for his Portraits —

To Frame Saunders received 3 10

George Romney: Account book of payments for portraits, frames etc 1777-1785

This account book was written in more than one hand: headings follow the correct copy book form for such writings, but the receipts, underneath the accounts for each portrait, are written out in a very hasty and uneducated scrawl.

V&AM MS L3149-1961 32 × 20.5

Opposite top:

Samuel McArthur: A new copy-book for round text, half text and small hand. c1755

A choice of three hands is given in this book, but all alike are plain and unadorned, with the exception of a few flourishes to the capital letters. This was the hand of commerce, which because of the widespread nature of British trade, was to be universally considered as the most suitable of all hands for the conduct of business.

V&AM L 533-1939 23 × 42

Opposite bottom:

Thomas Tomkins: The beauties of writing 1777

Thomas Tomkins was one of the many writing masters who endeavoured to raise the status of the profession. He was a friend of Sir Joshua Reynolds and his portrait was painted by the artist. Tomkins was certainly one who would call writing an art rather than a craft. His pretensions were severely criticised by Isaac D'Israeli in his brief essay on writing masters, in which he referred scornfully to 'the late Tomkins'. Tomkins's even, plain writing was very much in keeping with the needs of his time, and so little did styles change that an edition of The beauties of writing *appeared as late as 1844.*

V&AM L 1787-1952 28 × 44.5

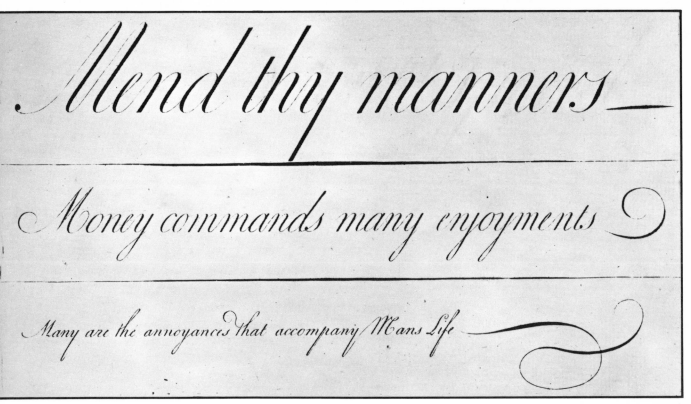

Mend thy manners—

Money commands many enjoyments

Many are the annoyances that accompany Mans Life

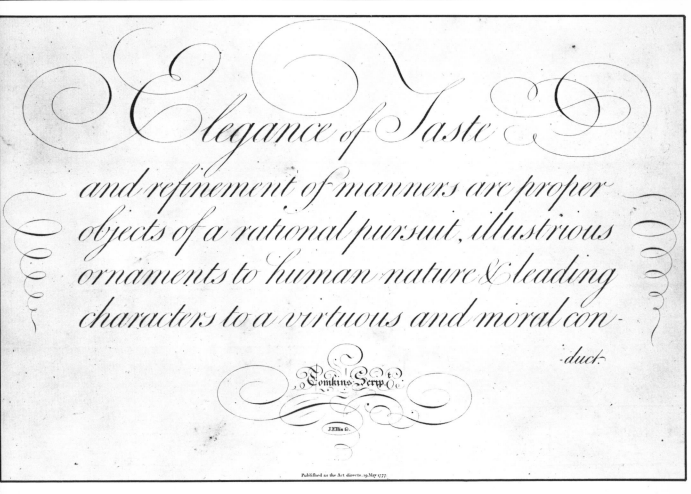

Elegance of Taste

and refinement of manners are proper objects of a rational pursuit, illustrious ornaments to human nature & leading characters to a virtuous and moral con-duct.

Tomkins Scrip.t

J.Ellis fc.

Published as the Act directs, 19 May 1777.

Avoid bad companions. d.

Beware of ostentation. w

Confine your paſsions. ma

Deride no infirmities. ak.

Endeavour to improve. m,

Fear attends the guilty. m,

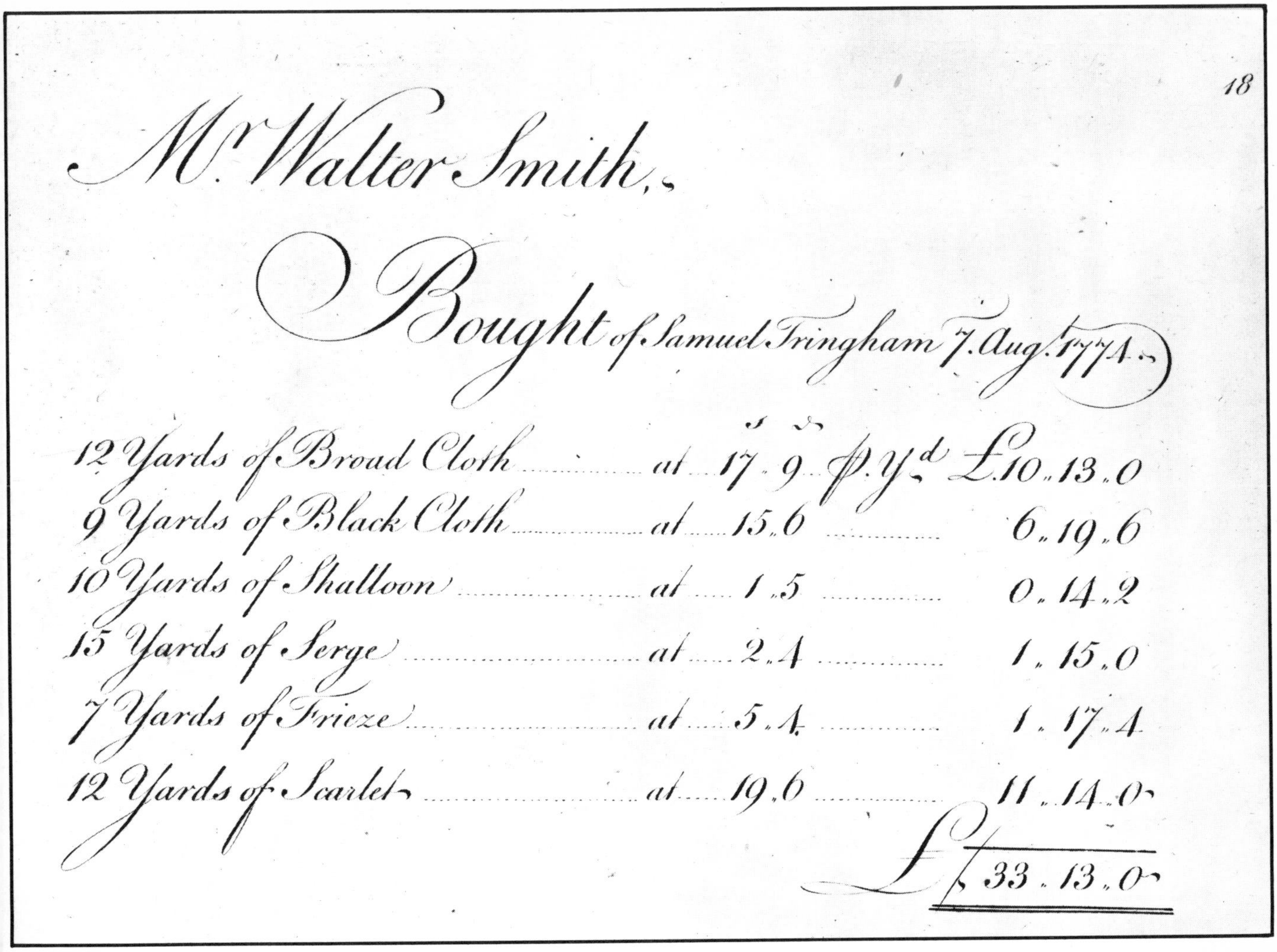

18

Mr. Walter Smith,

Bought of Samuel Tringham 7. Aug. 1774.

12 Yards of Broad Cloth	at 17.9 ℘ Yd	£10.13.0
9 Yards of Black Cloth	at 15.6	6.19.6
10 Yards of Shalloon	at 1.5	0.14.2
15 Yards of Serge	at 2.4	1.15.0
7 Yards of Frieze	at 5.4	1.17.4
12 Yards of Scarlet	at 19.6	11.14.0
	£	33.13.0

Joseph Webb: Useful penmanship 1796

The title alone of this work is indicative of the changes in emphasis that have taken place in handwriting in the course of the century. The example illustrated here is typical of the plain simple hand required by the business needs of the day, here used to show how the commercial clerk should set out his invoice.

V&AM L 542-1939 20 × 29

Opposite:

Duncan Smith: The Academical Instructor 1794

The illustration shows the weakness inherent in this style of writing, with its tendency to undue emphasis on the contrast between the thick and thin strokes. Carried to excess, it could make the writing almost illegible. The Library of the Victoria and Albert Museum possesses another copy book apparently based on a work by Duncan Smith, but published in Russia. This is a further indication of the importance of the English business hand, and the need for countries trading with Britain to be familiar with it.

V&AM L 539-1939 23 × 29

Manuel de Andrade de Figueyredo: Nova escola para aprender a ler, escrever, & contar. . . . Primeyra parte. 1722

Andrade's work, as can be seen in this example, was highly ornamented. He was known as 'the Portuguese Morante' after the Spanish calligrapher Diaz Morante. The figures made 'by command of hand' are to be found in some copy books of nearly every west European country over a period of several hundred years.

V & A M *L 708-1888* *38 × 25*

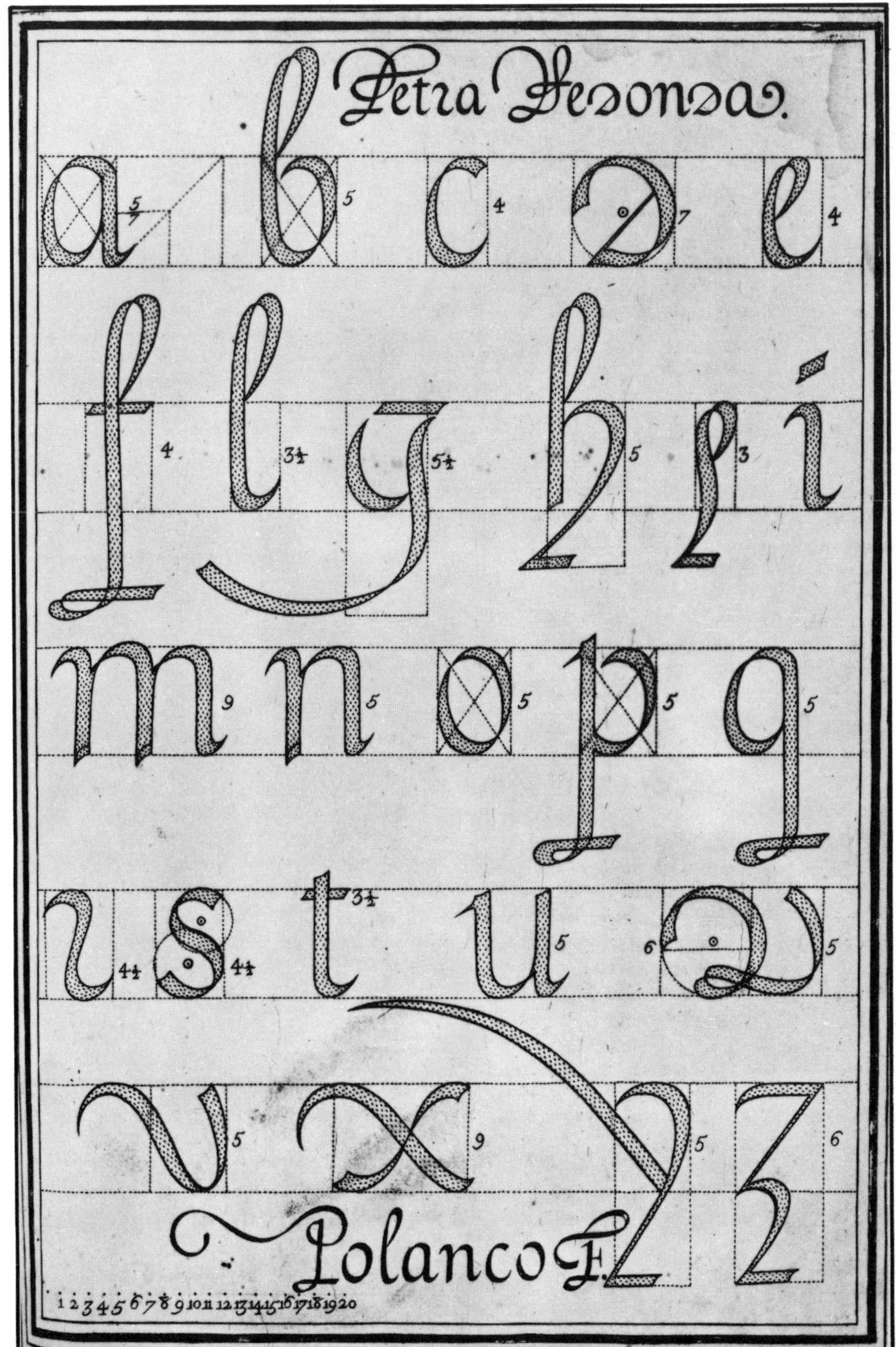

Juan Claudio Aznar de Polanco:
Arte nuevo de escribir por preceptos geometricos y reglas mathematicas
1719

Aznar de Polanco was a mathematician, an architect and a fencing master as well as a calligrapher! Arte nuevo de escribir *was his most important work. Like a number of writing masters at all times since the Renaissance, Aznar de Polanco believed that good writing could be based on geometrical principles, and an example of his method can be seen here.*

V&AM 18.iii.1864 30 × 20

Mucho importa à todos los que desean, que sus Hijos con-
sigan saber escribir con primor, y Ciencia, diestra, y gallardamente
una forma de Letra Bastarda, liberal, y Cortesana, segun se prac-
tica oy en todas las Oficinas, y Secretarias de su Magestad
Que sepan, antes que determinen poner sus Hijos à las Escue-
las, quien son los Mros de mas fama, y credito, que enseñan bu-
en rumbo, forma, y casta de Letra; y lo que adelantan sus Discipulos por medio de su enseñanza, y cuidado Porque el escribir bi-
en es una habilidad tan estimada en todas partes, y necessaria, que
no puede ninguno llamarse Hombre perfecto, sin saber el dho Arte,
por ser el principio de todas las Ciencias, y la llave Mra, que
abre, descubre, y trahe à la memoria las cosas, que supieron los passados.

En la Imperial, y Coronada Villa de Madrid
me escribia Juan Claudio Aznar de Polanco Escritor
General de Formas, y Rasgos, y Maestro del
Arte Cientifico de Escribir, y Contar, en esta Corte.

Juan Claudio Aznar de Polanco: Arte nuevo de escribir por preceptos geometricos y reglas mathematicas 1719

A further example from Aznar de Polanco's work, which shows how his carefully constructed letters appeared when written with speed. The curious form of the r *and the tail of the* p *and the* q *should be especially noted. It will be seen that Polanco describes himself on this plate as* maestro del arte cientifico de escribir.

V&AM 18.iii.1864 30 × 20

Fr. Luis de Olod: Tratado del origen y arte de escribir bien 1768

Father Luis de Olod was a Capuchin monk, and a writing master in Barcelona. His book contains a great variety of examples, from the very simple to the ornate, and includes alphabets and foreign scripts. This plate is especially interesting, since we can see exactly how Olod wished his pupils to practise the particular alphabet shown here — both large and small letters (majuscule and minuscule) are given.

V&AM L 3050-1960 30.5 × 20.5

Francisco Xavier de Santiago y Palomares: Arte nueva de escribir inventada por el insigne maestro Pedro Diaz Morante, e ilustrada con muestras neuvas y varios discursos [etc]. 1776

Palomares was greatly influenced by the 17th century writing master Diaz Morante. He was much concerned by the decline in Spanish calligraphy since then, and, by his own work instituted a revival in the art of fine writing. He offered examples of his own calligraphy together with that of other writing masters whom he admired, as in the example illustrated here.

V&AM L 1915-1913 35.5 × 27

Lam. 28

Es la pluma tan acertado y eminente
instrumento del entendimiento humano, que si tan presto como al primer hombre le fué dado entendimiento, se aprove-
chàra de la pluma, todos fueramos muy
sabios, porque tubieramos ciencia clara
de todas las cosas naturales sin sofiste-
rîa, ni error alguno: — Madariaga.

El doctisimo Lùis Vives Valenciano es-
cribió un dialogo en que enseña los prin-
cipios del Arte de escribir. Quintiliano,
Alexo Vanegas, Erasmo, y otros hom-
bres sabios trataron dignamente de el
mismo argumento. Madariaga.

Fr. Luis de Olod: Tratado del origen y arte de escribir bien 1768

This plate, which acts as frontispiece to Olod's work, was irresistible! It was typical of the extravagances which the writing masters allowed themselves in the portrayal of figures of this kind. The Victoria and Albert Museum Library has a similar series of pictures produced as late as the 19th century, in which actual royal portraits are placed on top of calligraphically executed figures, as in this example.

V & A M L 3050-1960 30.5 × 20.5

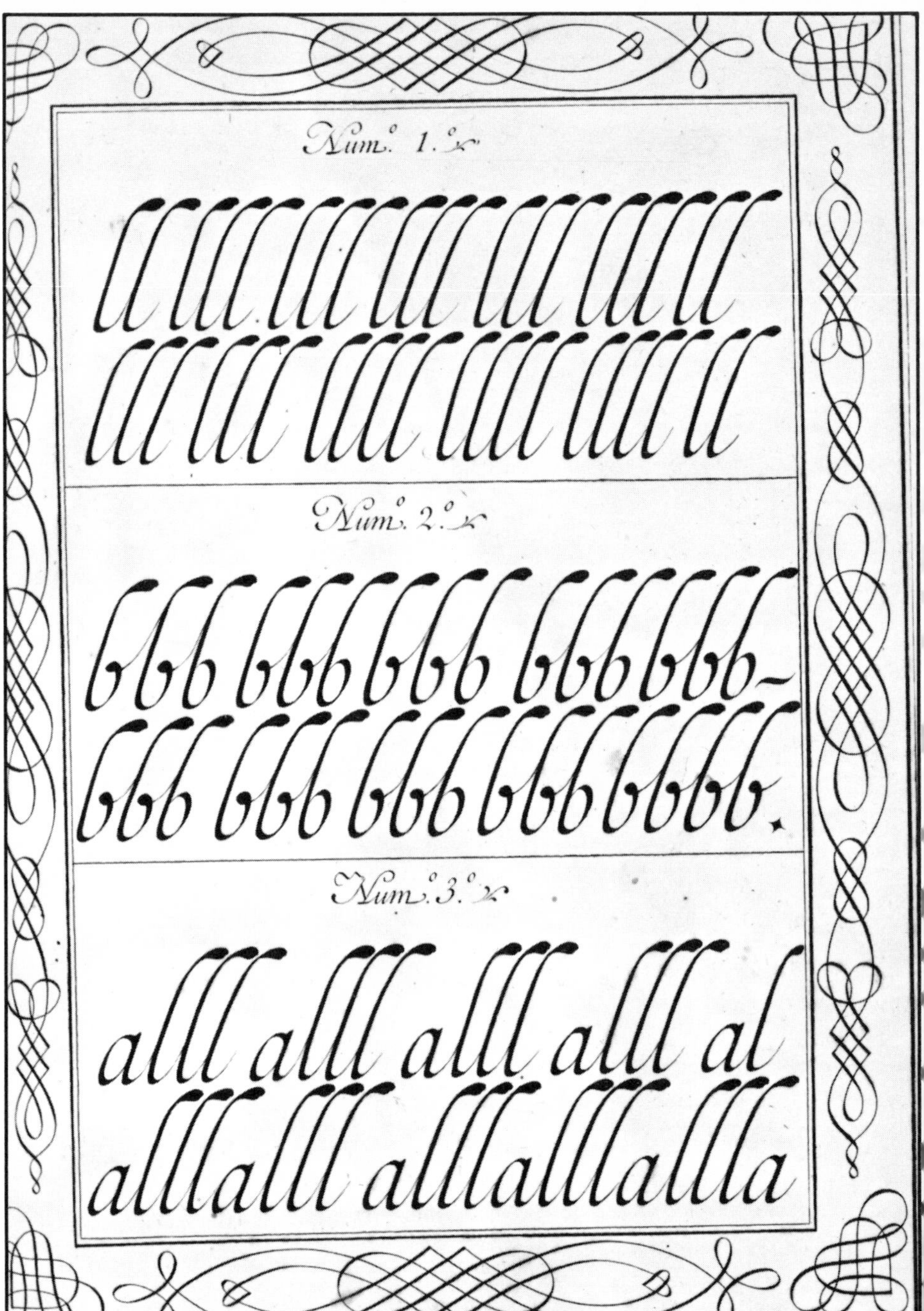

Francisco Xavier de Santiago y Palomares: Arte neuva de escribir [etc]. 1776

A further illustration from Palomares' influential book. This example, showing his own writing, explains the type of practice required to perform this script. The restrained decoration of the borders in this work blends well with the firm directness of the writing.

V&AM L 1915-1913 30.5 × 21

Juan Rubel y Vidal: Breves lecciones de calografía por las quales se puede aprender con facilidad a escribir la letra bastarda española 1796

Rubel y Vidal was a follower of Santiago y Palomares, and an influential calligrapher in Barcelona at the end of the 18th century. In this plate he continues the tradition of showing the correct position for writing and for holding the quill, while the writing table displays a very utilitarian assortment of writing implements.

V&AM L 1721-1950 20 × 14

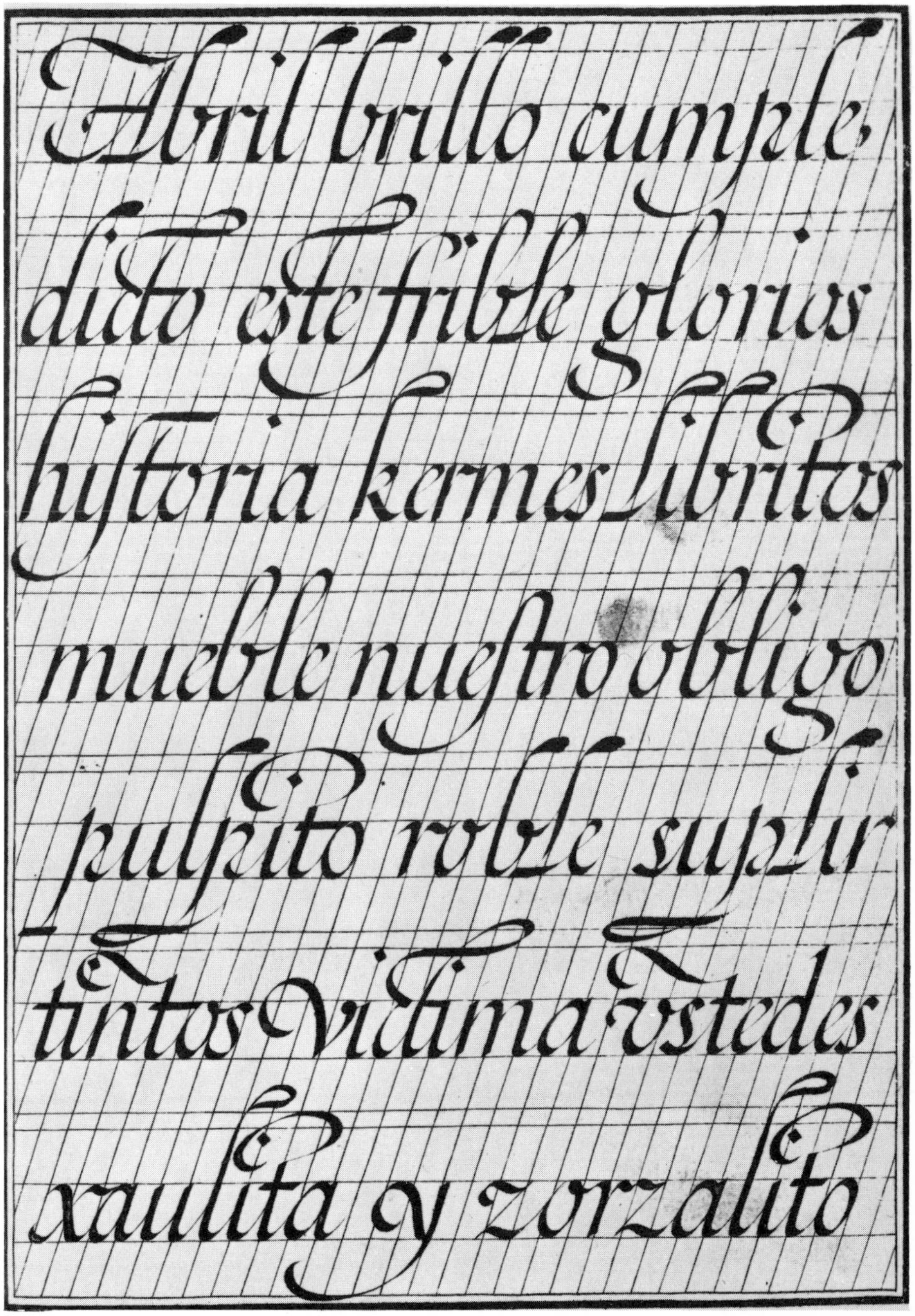

Juan Rubel y Vidal: Breves lecciones de calografía por las quales se puede aprender con facilidad a escribir la letra bastarda española 1796

A further plate from the work published in Barcelona by Rubel y Vidal at the end of the 18th century, which shows how the desire to regulate the method of writing continued to exercise the minds of the writing masters. It will be noticed that each of the words written out here begins with a different letter of the alphabet — a system which originated a century or more earlier.

V&AM L 1721-1950 20 × 14

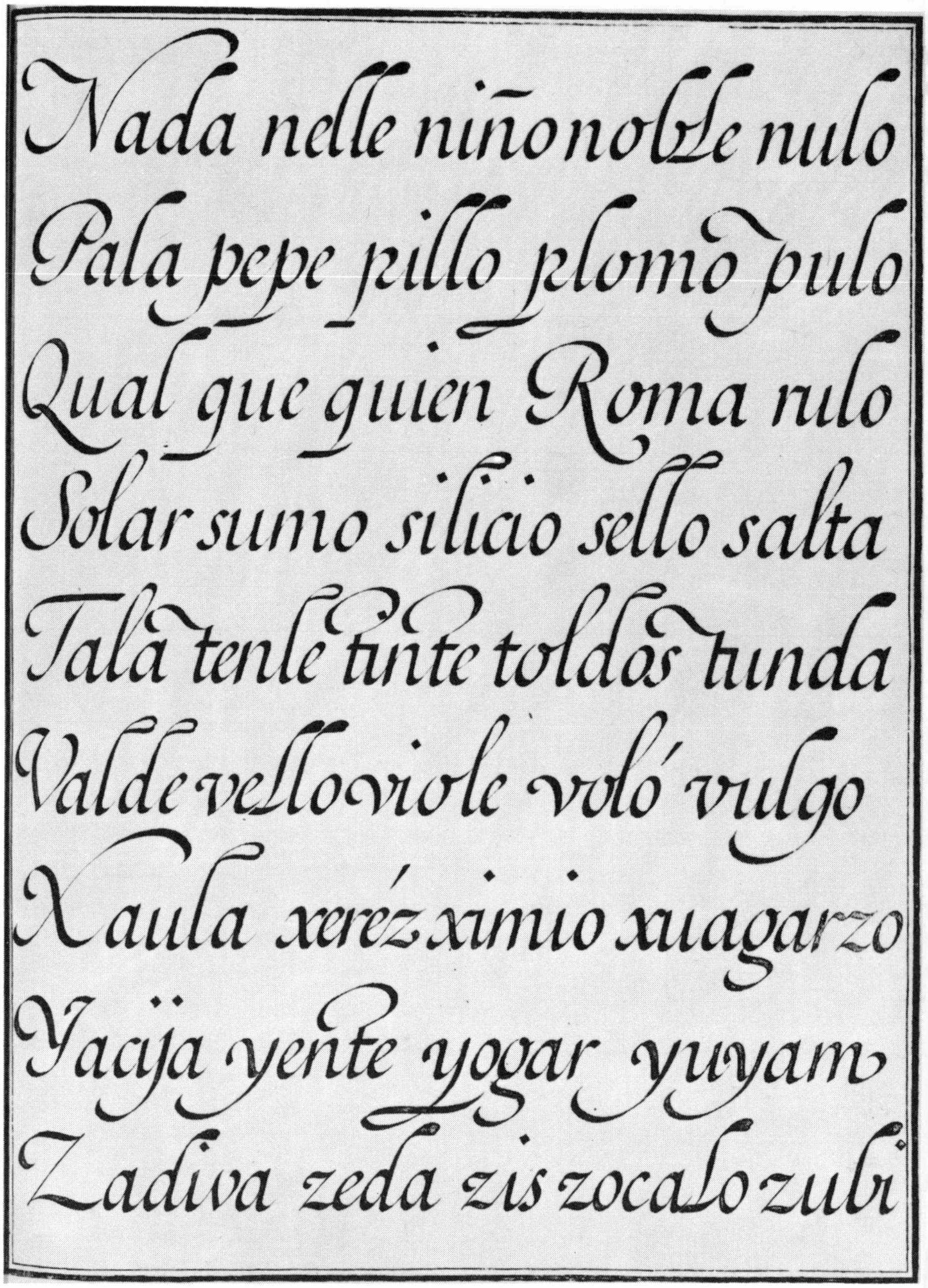

Juan Rubel y Vidal: Breves lecciones de calografía por las quales se puede aprender con facilidad a escribir la letra bastarda española
1796

Another plate from Rubel y Vidal's influential copy book, showing the elegance of his script, and also how traditional the Spanish styles remained — this, which appeared within a few years of the 19th century, would not have been out of place at least a century earlier.

V & A M L 1721-1950 20 × 14

Opposite:
Jean-Baptiste Alais de Beaulieu: L'art d'ecrire, par Alais.
1720

The engraved title-page of this work is rather more explicit: L'art d'ecrire ou le moyen d'exceler en cet art sans maistre. *It would seem that in his profession Alais de Beaulieu followed both his father and his uncle, and his manual may include examples of their work as well as his own. This illustration shows the sort of instruction given to those who wished to 'excel without a master'.*

V & A M L 353-1890 39 × 25

Nada nelle niño noble nulo
Pala pepe pillo plomo pulo
Qual que quien Roma rulo
Solar sumo silicio sello salta
Tala tenle tinte toldos tunda
Valde vello viole voló vulgo
Xaula xeréz ximio xuagarzo
Yacija yente yogar yuyam
Zadiva zeda zis zocalo zubi

Table de L'Ordre quon doit garder dans L'Ecrit.[e]

L'ordre est l'ame et la perfection du Sujet ecrit, Elle regarde L'Ortografe, La distance et rectitude des lignes; proportion et distance des lettres et mots, Caractere, et forme de papier conuenables aux Sujets.

Ortografe — Est d'écrire corectement et par raison chaque mot, et placer a propos les majeures les virgules et les points.

Rectitude des lignes — On peut se seruir de regles, transparants et poncifs Jusqu'a ce que l'exercice ait donné l'hab[de]. d'aligner et distancier également; on les éloignera selon la difference des caracteres et de l'ordre qui suit.

Distance des lignes

compte de 4 corps compte	finance de 4 finance	minute grosse de 4 minute hâtée de 7 Bâtarde minute { de 3. grossé / de 5. hâtée	batarde .... Coulée de 4 ord.[re] de 3 batarde ...... Romaine de 2 et demy

Proportion des lettres et mots et leur distances — La hauteur, largeur, et grosseur des lettres s'aprendront par la table des lettres radicales.
La distance des mots sera d'une (m) du caractere quon sera (m)
La distance des lettres sera de deux becs et demy presque pour la finance, pour la bâtarde de trois et plus.

Caractere et forme de papier conuenables aux sujets, dont les Exemples sont au second Liure.

Placet, Bâtarde.	Lettre Patente. finance	Estat. finance	Compte. compte	Missiues bâtarde
Au Roy Sire marge pareille aux points	Louis par la grace .... 3 doits de marge au haut 4 aux deux extremitez des lignes plus ou moins au bas	Estat Prem.[t] Les 2 marges a costé des lig.[s] seront egalles et celles du haut plus ouuertes q' celles du bas	Compte Ecrire a Marges egallement a vn costé mais de differente largeur a grosseur.	Monseigneur Pour vue puissance Je ....
Bâtarde Placet pour vn Conseiller Plaise a M[r] ... Pour .... Contre .... M[r]. ad.[t] Pion	Commission Le parchemin moins grand q' pour la patente et moins de marge.			C'est pour v[o]. donner auis point ou peu de marge po.[r] vn billet ordinaire.

Pour Le Palais, il regarde plus l'vtile que l'agreable; c'est pourquoy il n'obserue pas tant de regles en sa maniere d'écrire expediant plustost matiere, qu'écriuant d'ordre et d'vn caractere formé.

Les affaires domestiques, châcun les écrit a sa guise, et le marchand donne l'ordre a ses Liures selon son caprice, outre que cela depend plustost de la pratique particuliere que de la demonstration d'une regle generale.

– Marchand: Nouveaux principes d'ecriture italienne avec des exemples suivant l'ordre de Madame de Maintenon pour les demoiselles de la Maison Royale de St Louis établie à St Cyr. Par le maitre à écrire de Madame la Duchesse de Bourgogne.
Paris 1721

This copy book comes with the highest credentials, and it is interesting to note that, as so often when female writing is concerned, it is the Italian hand which is being offered (as the easiest to learn!). This charming illustration, showing the correct posture for writing, probably portrays the young Duchess of Burgundy herself.

V&AM L 2036-1978 19 × 25

Etienne de Blegny: Les elemens ou premieres instructions de la jeunesse. 1732

Blegny's book was first published in 1691, and teaches arithmetic, spelling and manners, as well as writing: obviously it was a popular compendium since it was still in print in 1732. On the title-page Blegny describes himself as expert juré ecrivain pour les verifications des écritures contestées.

V&AM L2833-1972 19.5 × 12.5

Charles Paillasson: L'art d'écrire réduit à des demonstrations vraies et faciles avec des explications claires pour l'Encyclopédie Méthodique 1783-90

This illustration is taken from a collection of sixteen plates of calligraphy used in the section on 'ecriture' in Diderot's great Encyclopédie. *Paillasson, as may be deduced from this fact, was one of the leading calligraphers of 18th century France. In this plate he is demonstrating the correct position for writing, as well as (below) the method of mending and holding the pen.*

V&AM L 1908-1911 42 × 30

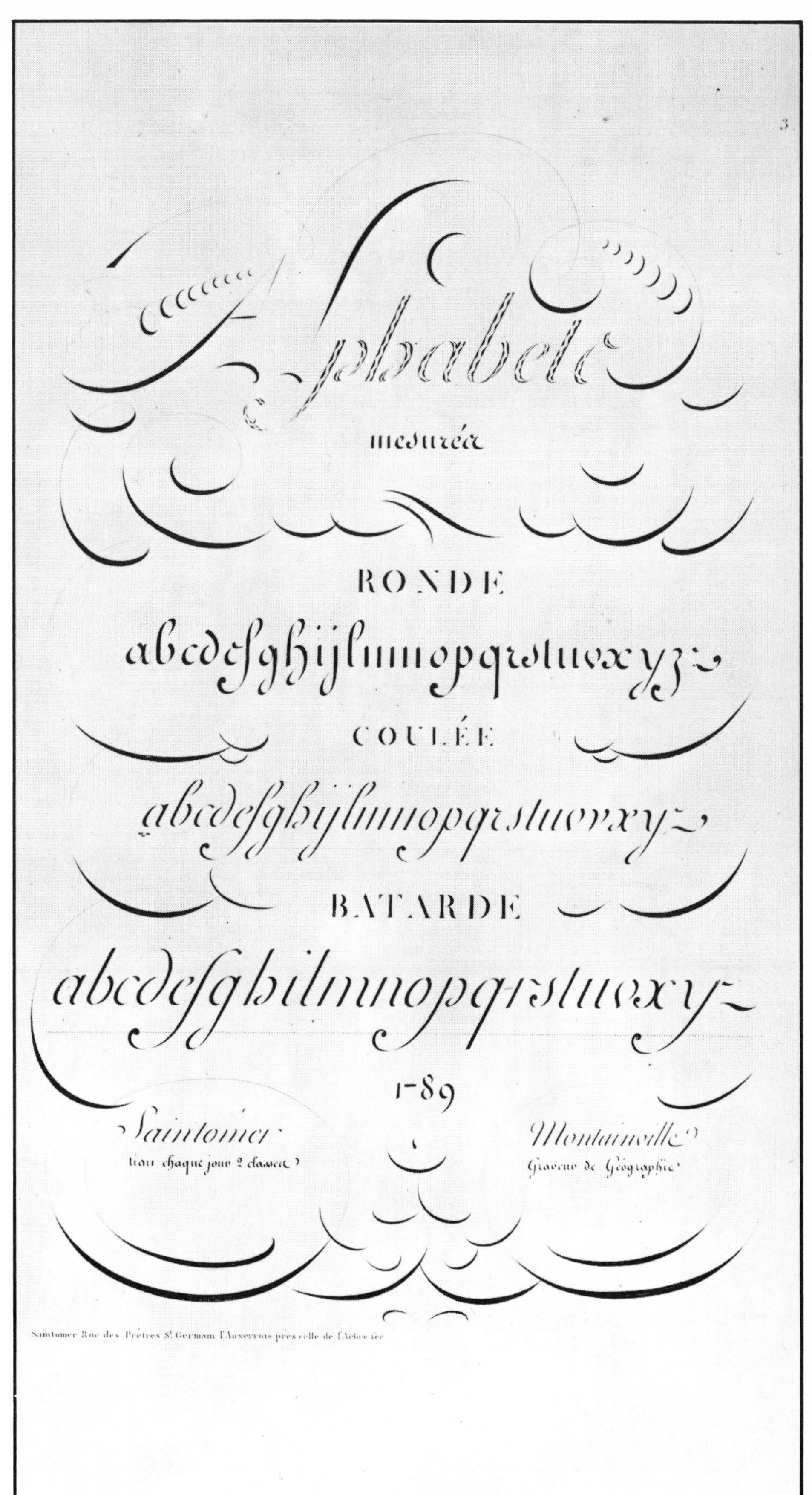

– Saintomer, the Elder: L'écriture démontrée par Saintomer l'ainé, professeur. 1789

Very little is known about Saintomer, even his first name is uncertain. On plate 3 of this work however we are told that he tien chaque jour 2 classes, *and the copy book is obviously intended for his pupils, with Saintomer's address being given on the bottom of the plate, as can be seen in this example. The scripts he taught were relatively unadorned.*

V&AM L1671-1888 43 × 28.5

Più d'un Ingegno Peregrino, e raro
Passa la Vita tenebrosa, e oscura:
E vede sol con suo cordoglio amaro
Trionfar l'apparenza, e l'impostura
La Scienza oppressa
NOTA È A SE STESSA
CORRE LA DEA VOLUBILE
DALLA VIRTÙ VERACE
E SI DIMOSTRA PRODIGA
CON CHI ADULANDO PIACE

Opposite:

Gaetano Giarrè: Alfabeto di lettere iniziali adorno di animali e proseguito da vaga serie di caratteri 1797

Giarrè was a teacher of arithmetic as well as calligraphy, and also a well-known Florentine engraver. His engraved decoration undoubtedly takes precedence over his calligraphy in the plates of this work!

V & A M L 1685-1910 34.5 × 25.5

reichen Fürstenthümen und Länder=
recht gebohrnen Lehens=Turniers=genoß=
und rittermässigen Edlleüthen; Ver=
leihen, geben, gönnen, und erlauben ih=
nen auch obberührtes adeliches Wap=
pen also zu führen, und zu gebrauchen
von Römisch=Kayserlicher Macht=Voll=
kommenheit in Kraft dieses Brieffs;
Meinen, sezen, und wollen, daß nun für=
baßhin mehrermelter **Johann Mel=**
chior Killinger seine künfftige eheli=
che Leibs=Erben, und derenselben Erbens=
Erben Mann=und Weibs=Persohnen,
in alle zeit rechtgebohrne Lehens=Tur=
niers=genoß=und rittermässige Edlleüthe
seyn, und von männiglichen an allen
Orten, und Enden, in allen und jede geist=
und weltlichen Sachen, und Geschäfften
dafür erkennet, geehret, genennet, und
geschrieben werden, auch alle und jede.

Grants of nobility, like diplomas, were among the documents that gave employment to scribes and illuminators at a time when there was little other need for their services. Pp. 293 and 294 both relate to the Austrian Empire in the 18th century. P. 293 dated 1737 is a grant of arms and nobility to Johann Melchior Killinger. The standardisation of such documents had already caused parts of them to be engraved, and only the more individual sections were filled in by the scribe.

V & A M L 167-1923 32 × 23

minder die rothe Wax-Sieglung von nun an zu allen künftigen Zeiten in allen und jeden ritterlichen Sachen, und Geschäften zu Schimpf, u: Ernst, in Stürmen, Schlachten, Streitten, Kämpfen, Turnieren, Gestechen, Gefechten, Ritterspielen, Feldzügen, Pannieren, Gezelten Aufschlagen, Pettschaften, Kleinodien, Begräbnissen, Gemählden, auch sonsten an allen Orten, und Enden nach ihren Ehren, Notdürften, Willen und Wohlgefallen sich gebrauchen, u: geniessen, und dessen sich erfreuen können u: mögen.

Und ergehet solchemnach an alle, und jede Chur-Fürsten, und Fürsten, geistlich und weltliche Prälaten, Grafen, Freye, Herren, Rittere, und Knechte Unser Gesinnen, und Begehren, an Unsere

This grant of nobility and arms to Franz Anton Bihn is dated 1764 and is signed by the Empress Maria Theresa. Part of the text and the decoration is engraved, and the other part is done in pen-and-ink. But only a careful scrutiny with a magnifying glass can reveal which is which, so closely has the work of the scribe approached that of the engraver — at first sight the complete document appears to have been engraved.

V & A M   L 166-1923   36.5 × 31.5

Derer Französischen Buchstaben G

I. Grund-Striche:

II. Theile.

Derselben Anfangs-Buchstaben

I. Grund Striche:

II. Theile.

Bey derley Buchstaben Herleitung, Höhe und Breite, Lage, Setzung auf die Linie, Veränderung, Zusammensetzung, und der Zwischen-Raum ist, wie bey denen Lateinischen, die Stärcke aber etwas schwächer.

Grundliche Unterweisung in der so nothig als nutzlichen Schreibe-Kunst [etc]. 1744

This work is aimed at merchants among others, so in addition to the contemporary German 'Fraktur' script, it also offers various west European styles of writing. The French script shown here (above) must have needed a great deal of practise for the student used to the gothic letters. The frontispiece to this book (right), show the merchants busy at their ledgers, with the merchandise and attributes of commerce also included in the picture.

V&AM 21.ii.1883 17 × 21.5

Johann Muscat: Kurtze doch gründliche Anweisung zur zierlichen Schreib-Kunst c1750?

The date of this work is uncertain — one edition was published in 1743, and this copy is bound with other works by Muscat, one of which is dated 1773. The gothic trend of the script is evident in this title-page, while the rather ponderous composition of the angel leaves the calligraphic decoration supporting a face, two arms and two feet!

V & A M 31.viii.1872 21 × 33

J. G. Schwandner: Dissertatio epistolaris De calligraphiae 1756

This German copy book contains a series of elaborate initial letters, from which the plate containing P and Q is illustrated here. It will be seen that the idea of using letter forms as the basis of abstract patterns is by no means a modern trend.

V&AM Circ.170-1972

A Son Altesse Serenissime
Monseigneur le Prince Charles
Landgrave de Hesse p. Stadhoudre
des Duchés de Slesvic et de Holstein p.
à Gottorff.

Dem Durchlauchtigsten Fürsten und Herrn
Herrn Friedrich, Landgrafen zu Hessen, Fürsten zu Hersfeld, Grafen zu Catzenelnbogen, Dietz,
Ziegenhain, Nidda, Schaumburg und Hanau pp.
Meinem gnädigsten Fürsten und Herrn.
Cassel.

Pater noster qui es in coelis: sanctificetur nomen tuum; adveniat regnum tuum; fiat voluntas tua, sicut in coelo, et in terra. Panem nostrum quotidianum da nobis hodie, et dimitte nobis debita nostra, sicut et nos dimittimus debitoribus nostris; et ne nos inducas in tentationem, sed libera nos a malo. Amen.

Durchlauchtigster Land...

Calender
auf das Jahr
Jesu Christi
1772
Mit Römisch Kayserlicher Maiestat
allergnäd: Privileg.
zu finden in Frankf.

Durchlauchtigster Fürst,
Gnädigster Fürst u: Herr,

Daß Ew: Hochfürstl: Durchlaucht durch ein gnädigstes Rescript sub: dato 13. currentis mir den Character eines Secretarii in Gnaden geschenket haben, dafür statte ich hiedurch den unterthänigst schuldigsten Dank ab, und verharre damit bis in mein Grab

Ewr: Hochfürstl: Durchlt.
unterthänigster Knecht.

Die sieben Wunderwerke der Welt sind:
1, die Mauer zu Babylon; 2, der Colossus in der Insel Rhodus; 3, die Pyramiden in Aegypten; 4, das Mausoleum, oder das von der Königinn Artemisia in Carien erbauete Grabmaal; 5, der Tempel der Göttinn Diana zu Epheso; 6, das Bildniß des Jupiters in der Stadt Olympia; 7, der Thurm Pharus in Aegypten.

Vater unser der du bist im Himel, geheiliget werde dein Name. Zu uns kome dein Reich: Dein Wille geschehe auf Erden, als wie im Himel. Unser tägliches Brod gieb uns heute, und vergieb uns unsere Schuld, wie wir vergeben unsern Schuldigern. und führe uns nicht in Versuchung, sondern erlöse uns von dem Ubel. Den dein ist das Reich und die Krafft und die Herrlichkeit in Ewigkeit, Amen.

Jan: Febr: Mart: April: May, Jun: Jul:
Aug: Sept: Octobr: Novembr: Decembr:

H. Coutgen Sc. Mog.

Das Blut Jesu Christi deß Sohns Gottes macht uns rein von allen Sünden.
1. Joh: am 1. Cap:

a b c d e f ff g h i k l m
n o p q r ꝛ ſ ſſ ſt ß s t tt
v u w x y z tz.

Diesen beyden Ehgatten, als conrad breneise und seine eheliche Haus-
Frau Maria gebohrne ist ein tochter zur Welt gebohren, als:

Maria Breneisin ist zur Welt gebohren, im Jahr
unsers Herrn Jesu 1770 den ten Tag august um 4 Uhr morgens
im Zeichen des
Ist, weil alle Menschen in Sünden empfangen und gebohren, laut Christi Lehre alle Kindlein zu JEsu sollen gebracht werden, wie der Evangelist Marcus 10, v. 15. rc. beschreibet, daß, wer das Reich GOttes nicht empfähet als ein Kindlein, der wird nicht hinein kommen; mithin diese, durch die heilige Taufe in den Gnaden-Bund GOttes einverleibet, und von
Pfarrer den ten Tag september getauft und genen-
net worden, wie oben gemeldt. Tauf-Zeugen sind valentin breneisen und seine
oben gemeldete maria breneisin ist gebohren und getauft
worden, in America in der Provintz Pennsylvania, in
Caunty in Taunschip

Wann wir kaum gebohren werden: Ist vom ersten Lebenstritt, bis ins kühle Grab der Erden, Nur ein kurtz gemessener Schritt. Ach mit jedem Augenblick! Gehet unser Kraft zurück, Und wir sind mit jedem Jahre, allzu reiff, zur Todtenbahre. Und wer weiß in welcher Stunde, uns die letzte Stimme weckt; Dann GOtt hat's mit seinem Munde, keinem Menschen noch entdeckt. Wer sein Haus nun wohl bestelt, geht mit Freuden aus der Welt. Da die Sicherheit hingegen; ewigs Sterben kan erregen.
Geschrieben 1784.

Opposite top:

Johann Gottfried Weber: Calligraphia oder nach der zierlichens Schreib-arth und dem heutigen Cantzley Schreib Stylo eingerichtete Vorschrifften [etc]. 1775

Weber published a number of copy books, and the first edition of this one was issued in 1771. The illustration gives a good idea of the number of scripts current in Germany at this time, showing that in addition to the native 'fraktur' or gothic writing, there was a demand for the styles practised outside central Europe.

V & A M *L 1775-1888* *19.5 × 33*

Opposite bottom:

Johann Jacob Losenawer: Vorschrifft deutsch- lateinisch-, und französischer Schrifften
1719

This work contains examples of various scripts, including the chancery hand and the especially German 'fraktur'. The plates include flourished decorations of great complexity, such as we have seen in other copy books, but there are also additional engravings, such as the charming bird and the flower we see here.

V & A M *1.vi.1872* *18 × 26*

Birth and baptismal certificate by Heinrich and Jacob Otto 1784

The German immigrants to the United States took with them the 'Fraktur' or gothic script of their homeland. In the area of Pennsylvania where they settled they developed a native tradition, based on the arts of their original homeland, which is known as 'Pennsylvania Dutch' (Deutsch). In this example, part of the text has been printed, using a typography based on the traditional gothic letters, and the rest has been written in by the calligrapher, Jacob Otto.

Reproduced by permission of the Philadelphia Museum of Art, gift of J. Stogdell Stokes, 28.10.91. Photograph by A. J. Wyatt, staff photographer.

Hausseegen oder die Engel des Morgens.

Auf

die Schatten

sind vergangen, der Morgenröthe Glanz bricht an! Auf eh der Sonnenstralen Prangen, noch Sodoms Flur erleuchten kan, ermuntre dich aus deinem Schlafe, auf! höre hier des Höchsten Wort: den Augenblick verdirbt die Strafe, des höchsten diesen Sünden Ort. Du zauderst! hier gilt kein verweilen! Gott komt, der nach Verdienste lohnt, das Land bebt schon von Donnerkeulen, dich einig hat der Herr verschont, reich mir die Hand, ich will dich leiten, steig diesen hohen Berg hinan! sieh nicht zurück auf keiner Seite, weil dich sonst niemand retten kan. Der Allmächtig Gott sey mit dir, der segne, erhalte, und beschütze dich im Zeitlichen und im Ewigen, durch unsern Herrn Jesum Christum. Amen.

Elisabeth Bordner

im Jahr unsers Herrn 1830.

Prayer, written out by Elisabeth Bordner 'im Jahr unsers Herrn 1830'

A further example of the Pennsylvania Dutch fraktur-script, in which the extreme gothic nature of the original German writing has become somewhat modified.

Reproduced by permission of the Philadelphia Museum of Art, gift of J. Stogdell Stokes, 28.10.88

9 The nineteenth century

THE 19th century saw many great changes and inventions, which were to make it a watershed between an older way of life and the modern. In calligraphy, too, change and invention played an important part. Copy books continued to be published, or to be re-issued, as they had been for several centuries, but for the most part they appear severe and practical when compared to their predecessors. The 18th century had already seen the type of copy book which contained lines of writing for the pupil to copy again and again (no doubt hoping for ever greater perfection), and this was to be very much the style of the 19th century book, especially for schools. Several of these are illustrated here (pp. 312, 313). In England and America self-help was very much to the fore, and journals and other publications were on hand to give advice to the would-be self-improver, on handwriting as on other subjects. But it was certainly writing rather than calligraphy that was taught – a plain dull hand, which could (and did) deteriorate when written with speed. The increase in formal education in most western countries led naturally to official pronouncements on the subjects to be taught and the methods to be used. This inevitably led to even greater uniformity in one of the basic skills taught to all children, namely writing. In England the Committee on Education recommended the Mulhaüser method, which its originator had used with success in Switzerland. Another important event in England was the institution of examinations for candidates for all government appointments, however lowly, and this in turn led to a recommended 'Civil Service' style of writing, which was based on that commonly taught in schools. In America much the same was happening, with the increasing need for more and yet more clerks. Business schools were set up to teach the best type of writing at the greatest speed, and there too writing manuals also proliferated. Indeed publications of the later part of the 19th century have continued to have a dominating effect on American handwriting to this day, especially that associated with the name of Spencer and the Spencerian system of writing.

The antiquarianism noticed in the previous century was now taken up in a much more scholarly and informed way. It led to a serious study of Medieval art in all its aspects, and among the many results of such studies was the crop of gothic town halls, railway stations and *cottages ornés* throughout various western countries. For all its pedantic scholarship, its style remained very much that of the 19th century, and this revealed itself in manuscripts as much as in architecture and the decorative arts. Many of those who produced works on medieval manuscripts also wrote on other aspects of the Middle Ages, such as costume or goldsmiths' work. It is hard to realise the difficulties then experienced by those who wished to study earlier manuscripts, since today there is almost a superabundance of coloured reproductions available. But Henry Shaw, for example, spent long hours copying the manuscripts in the British Museum (British Library), and produced copies of the greatest beauty. Until a commercially viable form of colour printing was available, such copies could only be published in black-and-white, with hand-colouring for the more expensive editions. But by the 1860's colour printing was reasonably inexpensive, and one result was an immense out-put of works relating to manuscripts, both the illuminating and the writing of them. For the first time it was possible for the interested member of the public to see these works in all their glory, and with this familiarity came the desire to imitate them. A number of 'how to do it' manuals on illuminating date from the 1860's, together with 'outline' copies for the less competent. It became the fashion, especially for ladies, to make manuscript books (or to complete outline copies!) for presentation to their friends, in the same way that they might embroider a text for use as a bookmark or to hang on the wall. And of course the letter-form used in either case was a version of the gothic or textura script.

But there was one great problem in imitating earlier scripts, of which most people were unaware. One of the great inventions of the 19th century had been the steel dip pen. Up to about 1830 the quill continued to be used by the majority of people, although the methods of mass production were making the steel pens cheap, and improved inks were making them convenient and long-lasting. But it was difficult to achieve the same result in writing with a steel pen as had been achieved with the medieval quill, a fact which 19th century calligraphers soon discovered. Either a thin and scratchy result was produced or else in order to achieve the desired medieval effect the letters had to be outlined and then inked in, to give them more body. Either way, the letters were certainly not the same as those the medieval scribe had produced, though no doubt highly satisfying to the many people who thus found themselves trying to write in a style other than 'copperplate' for the first time.

As can be seen from the illustrations in this book, there were a number of people with a scholarly interest in the medieval book in the second half of the 19th century, although the name of William Morris is undoubtedly the best known. In view of Morris's active interest in the Middle Ages and his burning desire to imitate the artefacts of that period, it is not surprising to find him trying his hand at the manuscript book. Several complete works and a number of fragments survive from his hand, and one of the finest is illustrated in this book (p. 320). A facsimile edition of *A Book of Verse* is now in preparation. But Morris's script too is thin, and without obvious models, even as the decoration of his manuscripts was essentially in a very personal style. Nevertheless, Morris's work will always be important in the context of the revival of calligraphy which occurred in the next century, and his concern for the book as a whole, whether manuscript or printed, has continued to influence today's calligraphers. The 20th century scribe has shown a conscious awareness of every aspect of book production, even as Morris did, and modern examples shown that great care has been taken in the choice of paper or vellum, binding, illumination, layout – and of course style of script. All these things Morris himself was concerned about, and he tried to realise his ideal of 'the book beautiful' in the products of his Kelmscott Press, leaving the calligraphic aspect to a later generation.

But the last part of the 19th century had seen another development in calligraphy, and one that was to increase in importance in the next century. This was the use of calligraphic forms in advertisement art. It was not a new departure: bill heads and other kinds of self-advertisement had for long employed pen-made forms. But they had tended to reproduce the style found in so many copybook title-pages, where the writing master showed his versatility by the number of different scripts he could cram on to one page. From the late 19th century onwards we become aware of the application of contemporary art styles in the field of calligraphy, an example of which can be seen in the *Art Nouveau* lettering of Walter Crane illustrated here (p. 313) Immediately the lettering used in the Paris Metro, or on the covers of contemporary journals can be recalled, together with that of various advertisements of the period. During the century a number of books had been published containing alphabets for use in a variety of circumstances. Now however calligraphic styles were being created and used for specific advertising purposes, and this was to be yet another pointer to the future of the hand-written letter.

Joseph Crosfield: Copysheet 1812

Copysheets were very popular in the late 18th and early 19th centuries on both sides of the Atlantic. They were written out by pupils as proof of their writing ability and were no doubt taken home in triumph to their parents. This one has been dated '11th of 12th month 1812', so perhaps it was an end-of-term exercise. The border of the sheet is engraved with highly improving illustrations of the Ten Commandments, but not all copysheets were so elaborate.

V & A M MS L 2534-1979

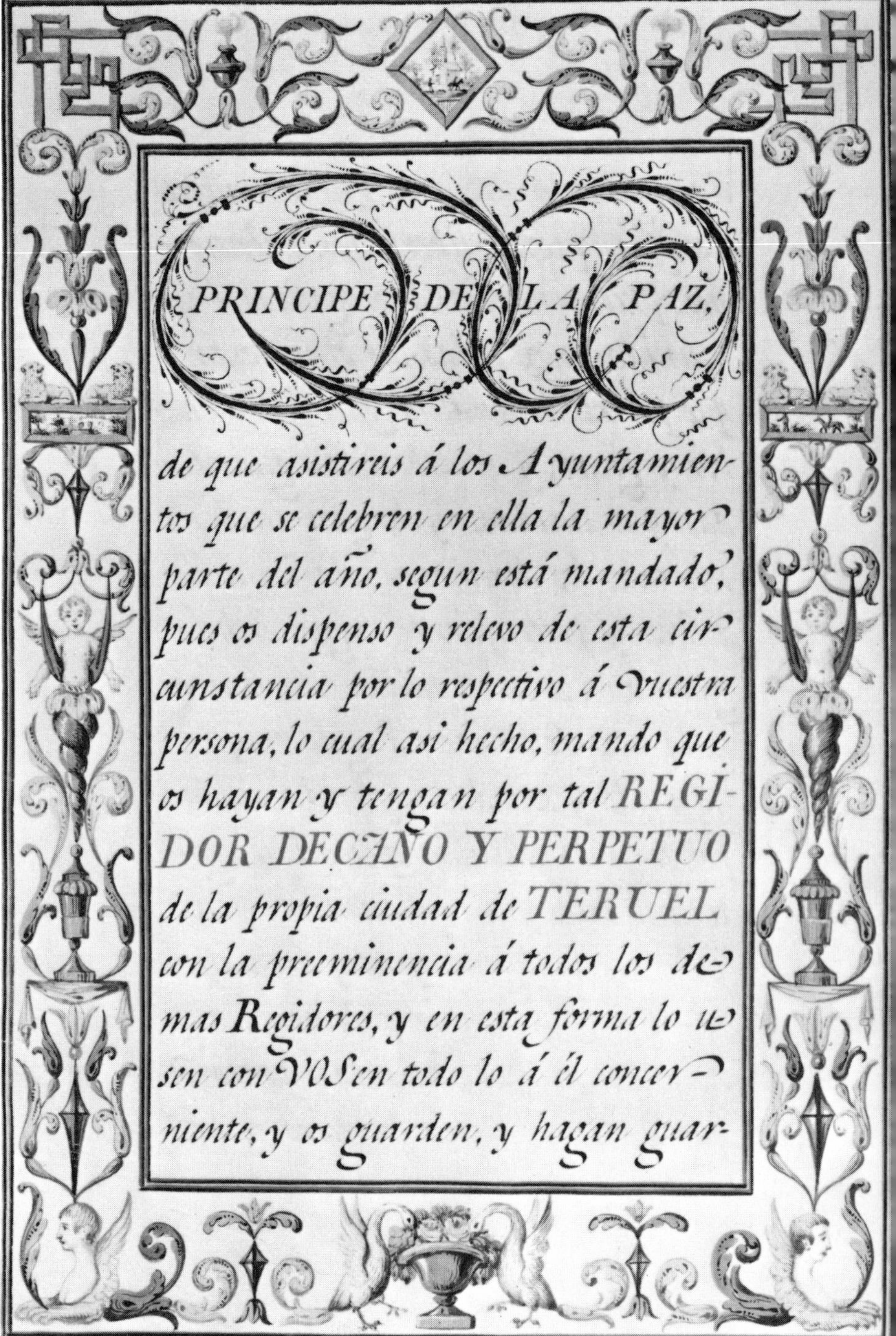

PRINCIPE DE LA PAZ,

de que asistireis á los Ayuntamien-
tos que se celebren en ella la mayor
parte del año, segun está mandado,
pues os dispenso y relevo de esta cir-
cunstancia por lo respectivo á Vuestra
persona, lo cual asi hecho, mando que
os hayan y tengan por tal REGI-
DOR DECANO Y PERPETUO
de la propia ciudad de TERUEL
con la preeminencia á todos los de-
mas Regidores, y en esta forma lo u-
sen con VOS en todo lo á él concer-
niente, y os guarden, y hagan guar-

Document appointing Manuel de Godoy, Prince de la Paz, Duke de la Alcudia, as governor of Teruel. Spanish 1804

This is a most elegant manuscript, although in style it looks back to the 18th century rather than forward to the 19th century. It indicates the high standard maintained by Spanish calligraphy, especially within the court circles, for Manuel de Godoy was virtual ruler of Spain at this period. The decoration that accompanies the calligraphy can be matched in the published works of Spanish writing masters, but the decorative borders and initials are on quite a different plane. Charming river scenes form backgrounds to the initial letters, while genre scenes in grisaille are set in small frames within the borders.

V&AM MS L 4763-1978 30.5 × 20

William Mate: Copysheet 1856

This piece of penmanship was perhaps ntended as a gift since it is signed and lated at the foot of the sheet 'Christmas AD 1856'. Certainly William Mate had eason to be proud of his virtuosity, but he result is so like the engraved xamples of the period that only careful nspection reveals that it is in fact all lone by hand. While its birds and angels o back to similar decorations to be found n 17th century manuscripts, the eneral appearance of the sheet is nmistakably 19th century.

V & A M MS E 847-1951

Newcastle 17 March 1810

Gentlemen

I have this day Shipped on board the Peggy Capt. Bainbridge 5 Boxes or chests containing as follows viz — Box No 3 – 69 Books @ 15s each . 51 .. 15
No 4 68 Do — Do Do . 51 .. —
No 5 65 Do — Do Do — 48 .. 15 —
No 6 – 68 Do — Do Do — 51 —
No 7 – 69 Do — Do Do — 51 .. 15
Books 339 @ 15s each L254 . 5

marked Numbered as p inclosed bill of Lading

Then I hope you will recieve in safety & I shall as soon as possible send you the remainder — The few Books which the Booksellers snatched away from me as soon as they were put in boards. I shall, in any way you please account to you for — as also for 3 or 4 others were got, much in the same way, by my intimate friends here by some others, of the same description I am still teased for more — but this I shall not do without your permission & if you agree to this, be so good as to say how many you may be pleased to allow me to dispose of in this way

I am
Gentlemen
your obliged & obedt
Thomas Bewick

Thomas Bewick: One of a collection of letters written by Bewick to various correspondents concerning business, transactions relating to his publications A history of British birds and A general history of quadrupeds. 17 March 1810

In this letter the artist is his own accountant, and although the copy book models are obviously at the back of his mind, the letter itself is a good example of a late 18th century — early 19th century informal hand.

V&AM MS L 3252-1955 21 × 17

Opposite:

William Thomson: The writing master's assistant 1820

This early 19th century title-page shows that the writing masters still felt a need to prove their ability to teach a variety of different scripts. But the text hands were by now little more than tedious exercises for the pupils, who can rarely have needed them in practice.

V&AM L 536-1939 26.5 × 21.5

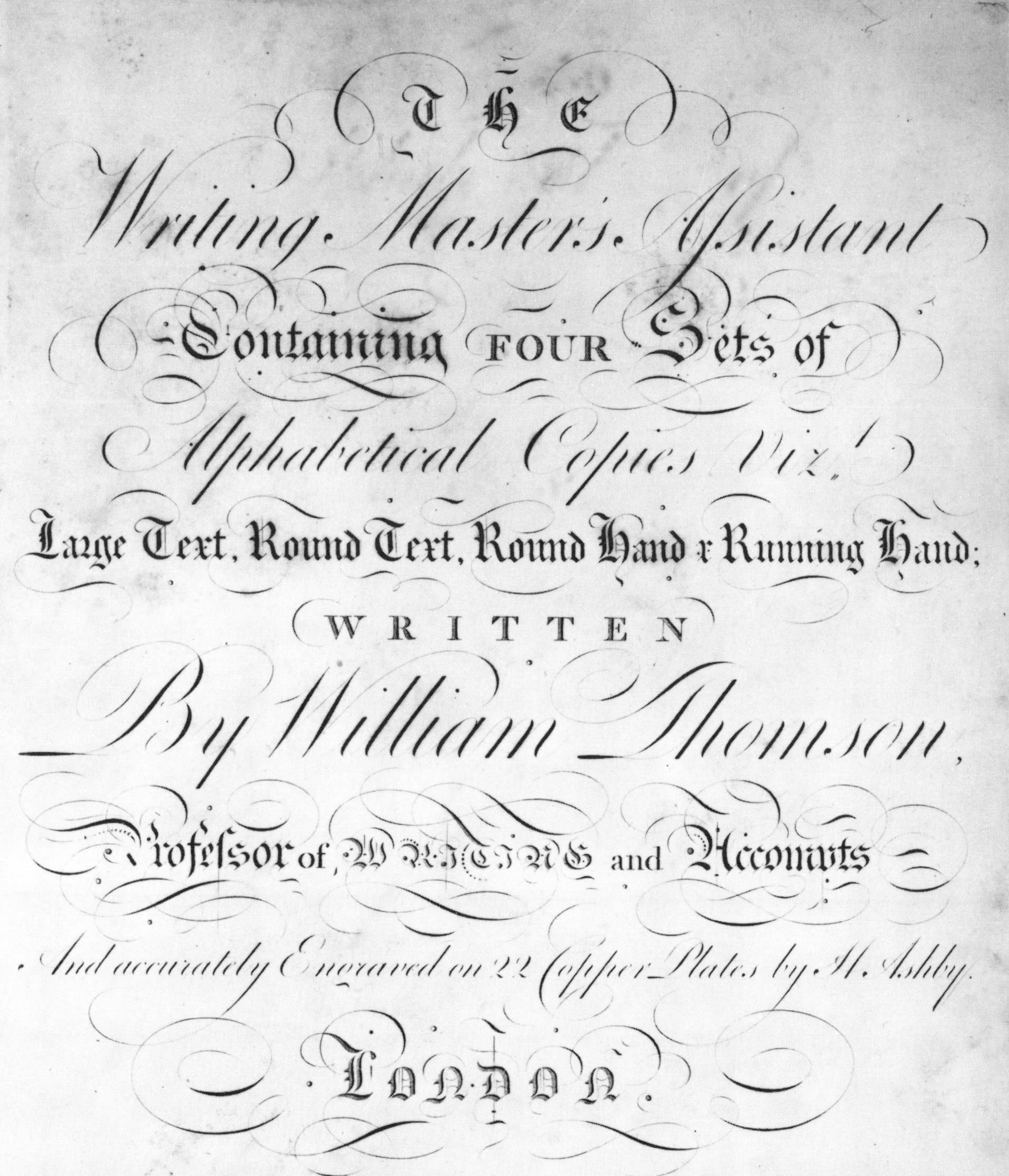

THE

Writing Master's Assistant

Containing FOUR Sets of

Alphabetical Copies Viz.t

Large Text, Round Text, Round Hand & Running Hand;

WRITTEN

By William Thomson,

Professor of WRITING and Accounts

And accurately Engraved on 22 Copper Plates by H. Ashby.

LONDON.

Published Sept.r 16: 1820, by RICHARD HOLMES LAURIE, N.o 53, Fleet Street, London.

Sir Henry Cole: 'The Parch', a book of arithmetical exercises, drawings, and examples of penmanship, written out by Henry Cole in 1821

This exercise book was written out when Cole was a thirteen year old schoolboy at Christ's Hospital, a school long famous for its standard of writing. Even at this late date the decorative aspect of the work was not neglected, and the figure of the bird could have been equally at home in Richard Carter's arithmetic book of the late 17th century (p. 235). Henry Cole was to become one of the principal organisers of the Great Exhibition of 1851, and subsequently the first Director of the South Kensington Museum (later the Victoria and Albert Museum) which houses many of the books and manuscripts illustrated in the present work.

V&AM MS L 1241-1932 23 × 19

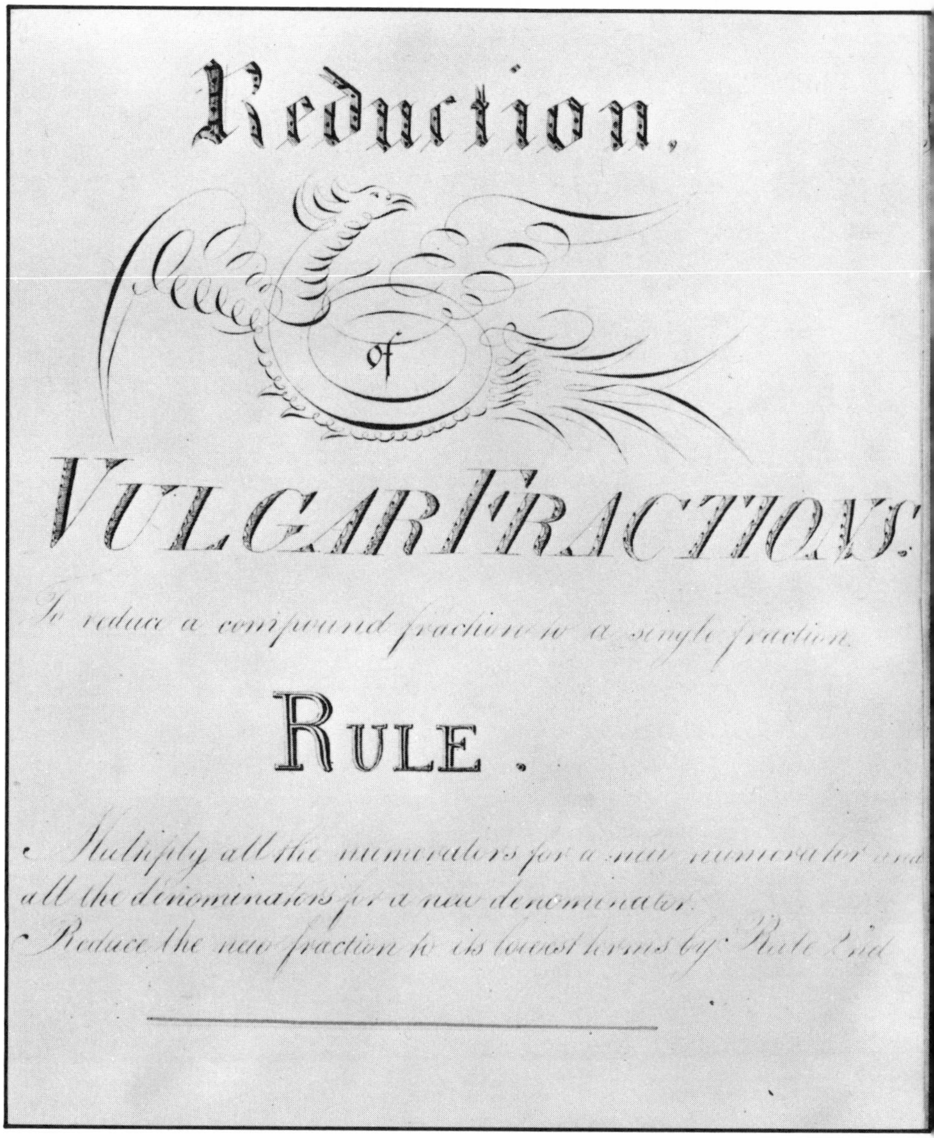

Reduction,

of

VULGAR FRACTIONS.

To reduce a compound fraction to a single fraction.

RULE.

Multiply all the numerators for a new numerator and all the denominators for a new denominator.

Reduce the new fraction to its lowest terms by Rule 2nd

Below:

B. P. Wilme: A manual of writing and printing characters, both ancient and modern, for the use of architects, engineers and surveyors, engravers, printers, decorators, and draughtsmen; also for use in schools and private families. 1845

The list of occupations in the title of this book gives some idea of the widespread uses of calligraphy. These were by no means confined to the period of the 19th century, for the calligrapher and the engraver of calligraphy had been in demand for centuries, producing captions for illustrations, lettering on maps, headings on bills and other similar items. As the 19th century progressed, the engraved effect might be produced by a mechanical means, but behind the resulting bill or advertisement was still the original calligraphic design.

V&AM 30.vii.1877 27 × 22.5

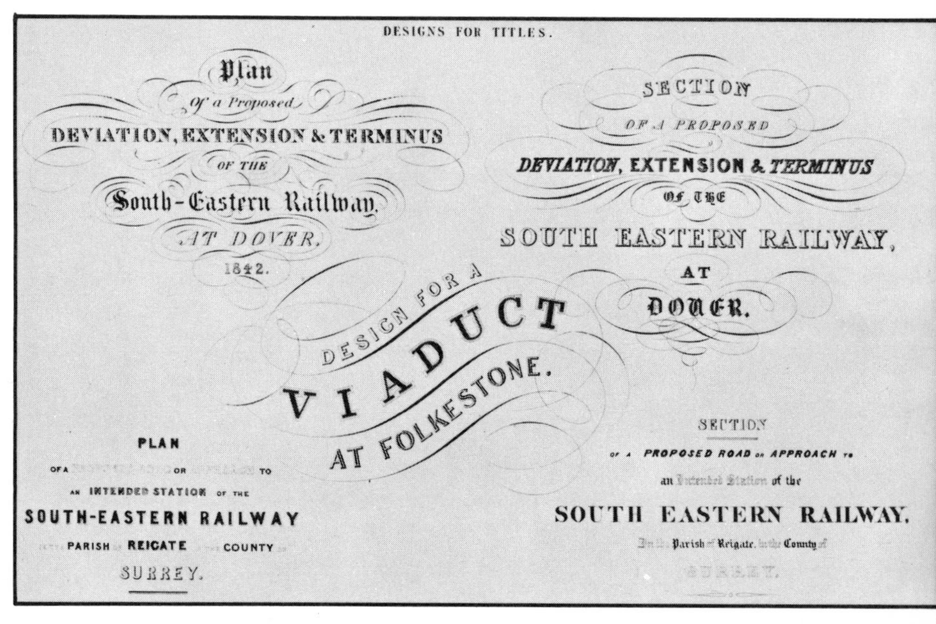

DESIGNS FOR TITLES.

Plan
Of a Proposed
DEVIATION, EXTENSION & TERMINUS
OF THE
South-Eastern Railway.
AT DOVER.
1842.

SECTION
OF A PROPOSED
DEVIATION, EXTENSION & TERMINUS
OF THE
SOUTH EASTERN RAILWAY,
AT
DOVER.

DESIGN FOR A
VIADUCT
AT FOLKESTONE.

PLAN
OF A OR TO
AN INTENDED STATION OF THE
SOUTH-EASTERN RAILWAY
PARISH REIGATE COUNTY
SURREY.

SECTION
OF A PROPOSED ROAD OR APPROACH TO
an Intended Station of the
SOUTH EASTERN RAILWAY.
Parish Reigate, County

A

MANUAL

OF

WRITING;

FOUNDED ON

MULHAÜSER'S METHOD OF TEACHING WRITING.

AND ADAPTED TO ENGLISH USE.

UNDER THE SANCTION

OF THE

Committee of Council on Education.

THIRD EDITION.

Published by Authority,

BY

JOHN W. PARKER, WEST STRAND.

LONDON.

M.DCCC.XLIX.

M. A. Mulhauser: A manual of writing founded on Mulhauser's method of teaching writing. And adapted to English use.
London 1849

The illustration here is taken from the third edition of Mulhauser's manual, which was first published in 1842. As can be seen, it was published 'by authority' under the sanction of the Committee of the Council on Education. It offers a formalised method of teaching large groups of children, so that they may produce a legible if unexciting clerical hand.

V&AM L 11175-1974 19 × 12

21

On, on, with fearful violence, it came, –
The raging tempest, with its voice of thunder:
Its whirlwind breath and eye of lurid flame,
Rending the up-piled granite rocks asunder,
Crushing the forest trees, and making tame
The fiercest animals with awe and wonder;
On, on it came, and at the midnight hour
Had reached its height – the zenith of its power.

22

Then, while the lightning leapt from jag to jag
Of Blocksberg's heights, and all was dire commotion,
Was Henrick seen upon a lofty crag,
Rocked like a ship upon a stormy ocean;
Around him grinned full many a ghastly hag,
And all the demon brood, who pay devotion
To Belzebub, their prince, and mischief work
And blighting ill, where'er they chance to lurk.

23

Oh! 'twas a sight to agonize the brain,
And make the heart with fear grow chill and cold,
To see that dauntless youth, who from the plain
Had ventured up amid them, overbold,
And too presumptuous, yearning after vain
Delusions, things which are not – to behold
Him in that scene of desolation stand,
With fierce and fiendish forms on every hand.

Walpurgis Night: a lay of the Hartz Mountains c1840

This poem was illustrated and written out by the artist Richard Dadd, and the script and the pen-and-ink sketches blend harmoniously throughout. The writing is based on one of the three main scripts which were generally recommended in contemporary copy books, and which has less emphasis on the looped ascenders and descenders than the script usually employed at this period.

V & A M MS L 393-1925 20.5 × 15

Opposite:
Cassell's Popular Educator, vol. II 1853

Symptomatic of the general desire for self-improvement to be found in the Victorian period was the appearance of a number of magazines offering instruction for those whose education had been inadequate. Here is an example of the three styles of handwriting considered most likely to be of use to those seeking to improve themselves. The scripts were of course similar to those commonly taught in schools.

V & A M 27.5 × 19

Easingwold

Encourage all honest and virtuous actions.

Encouragement most commonly animates the mind.

Formentera

Fame most commonly accompanies merit.

Fear is commonly the companion of guilty actions.

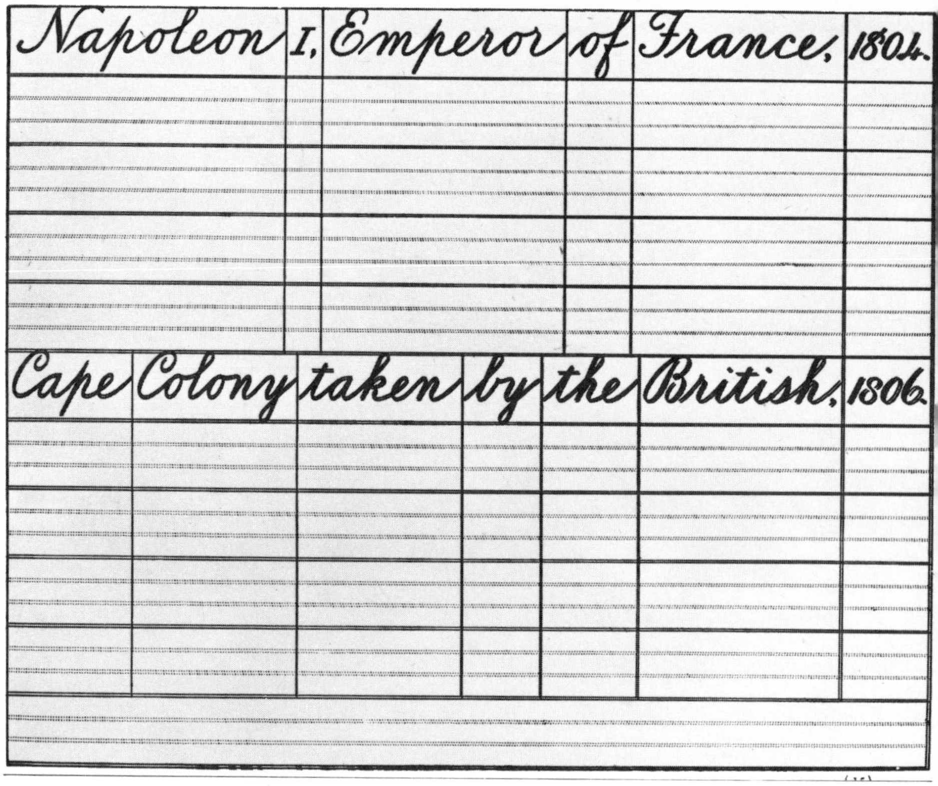

Napoleon I, Emperor of France, 1804.

Cape Colony taken by the British, 1806.

Vere Henry Lewis Foster: Bold writing, or Civil Service series 1870

The pupil would write his copy between the middle lines of each of the four sections shown under the two texts, no doubt in hope that he would improve with each repetition. This style of writing was considered especially suitable for candidates seeking government appointments. The present writer purchased similar copy books, still issued in the same form and with the name of Vere Foster, as recently as a few years ago.

V&AM L 6417-1977 17 × 21

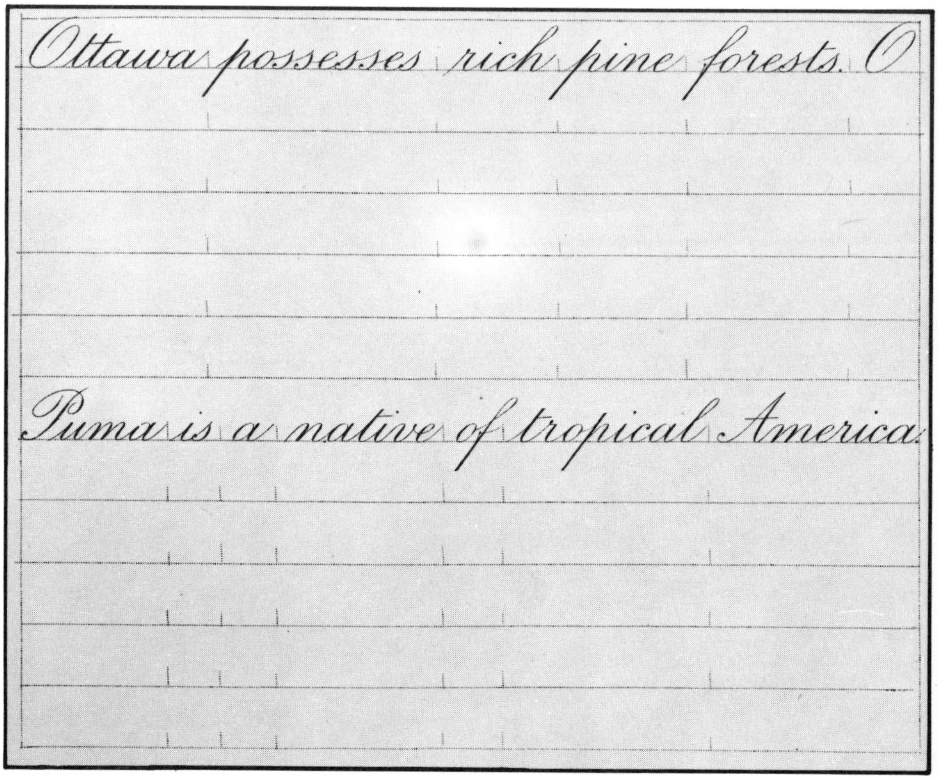

Ottawa possesses rich pine forests. O

Puma is a native of tropical America.

Moffatt & Paige: Moffatt's copy book 1890

This type of somewhat soulless repetition of examples was typical of the copy book in England and America throughout the 19th and much of the 20th century.

V&AM 17 × 21

OLD ENGLISH

London, Dublin, Edinburgh, Glasgow

Liverpool, Manchester, Newcastle

Moffatt & Paige: Moffatt's copy book 1890

Even as late as 1890, children were still expected to produce the type of copies that had been current for centuries, and for which they were unlikely ever to have need in their future careers.

V&AM 17 × 21

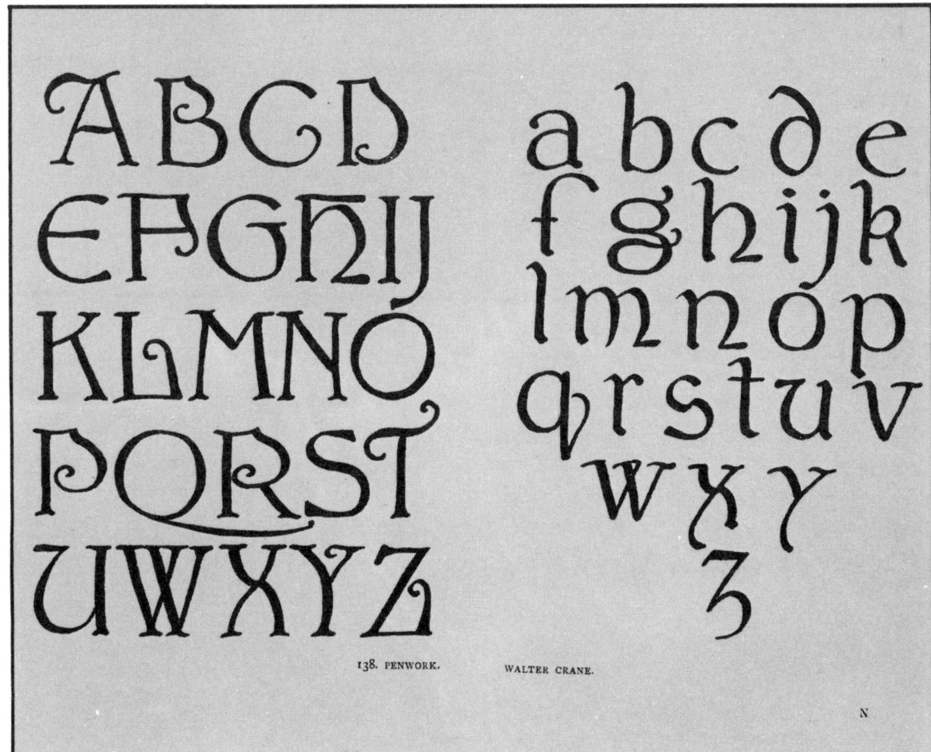
ABCD
EFGHIJ
KLMNO
PQRST
UWXYZ
abcde
fghijk
lmnop
qrstuv
wxy
z
138. PENWORK.
WALTER CRANE.
N

Lewis F. Day: Alphabets old & new [etc]. 1898

This collection of alphabets was published just at the time when Edward Johnston was turning his thoughts to calligraphy, with all that that was to mean for the revival of the art in the 20th century. It was this Art Nouveau *style of alphabet by Walter Crane, however, that was to be much more characteristic of contemporary letter-forms for some time to come.*

V&AM L1185-1898 18.5 × 12.5

Auncient seles affixed to charters, grauntes to abbies, priories, conventes, churches &c. collected by G. C. L[everland]. c1795?

This is a typical page from this curious manuscript, in which the author/compiler has painted a charter and seal, and then written out the description, neither done very expertly. But it is a good example of the late 18th century interest in such antiquities of the Middle Ages, and it will be noted that Leverland has attempted to imitate the gothic script in which such charters were written, as well as using a Chattertonian form of pseudo-medieval spelling!

V&AM MS L 6629-1978 27 × 20.5

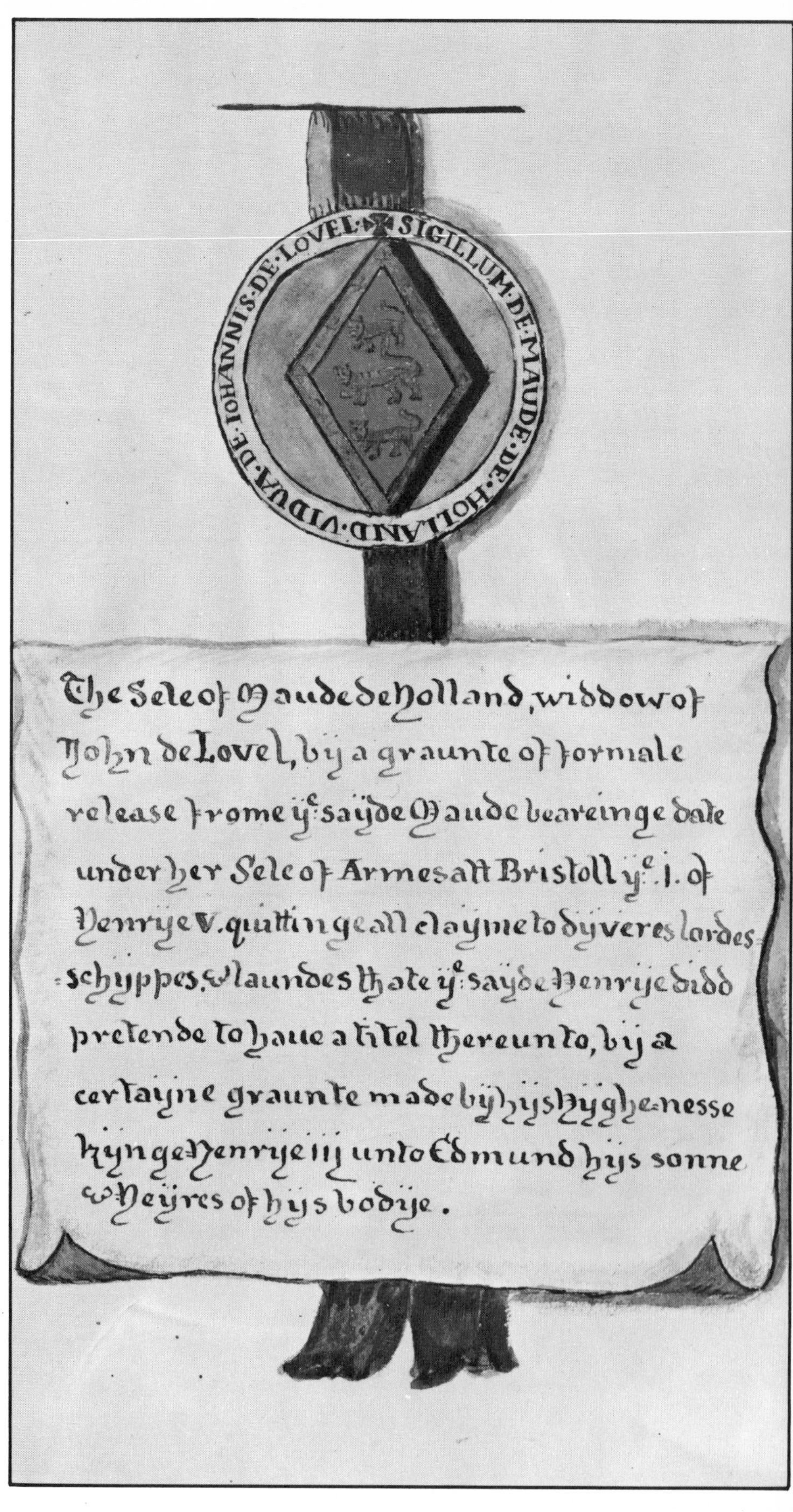

The Sele of Maude de Holland, widdow of
John de Lovel, by a graunte of formale
release frome ye sayde Maude beareinge date
under her Sele of Armes att Bristoll ye 1. of
Henrye V. quittinge all clayme to dyveres lordes-
-schyppes & laundes thate ye sayde Henrye didd
pretende to haue a titel thereunto, by a
certayne graunte made byy hys hyghe-nesse
kynge Henrye iij unto Edmund hys sonne
& Heyres of hys bodye.

Opposite:
Henry Shaw: One of several copies from a manuscript of Aristotle's 'Ethics' in the British Museum c1860

This manuscript which glows with brilliant colour, is a reminder of the problem of producing good copies of manuscripts in the days before photography. Henry Shaw made many such scrupulous copies of early manuscripts, and when published, these were frequently hand-coloured.

V&AM P&D 4844

PROLOGO DEL MVY ILLVSTRE
DON KARLOS PRINCIPE DE VIA
NA PRIMOGENITO DE NAVARRA
DVQVE DE NEMOS E DE GANDIA D
RECADO AL MVY ALTO E EXCELLĒ
TE PRINCIPE E MVY PODEROSO
REY E SENNOR DON ALFONSO T
ERCIO REY DE ARAGON E DE LAS
DOS SEQILIAS ETC SU MVY RED
VPTABLE SENNOR E THIO DE LA
TRANSLACION DE LAS ETHICAS
DE ARISTOTILES DE LATIN EN ROM
ANCE FECHA
PVBLICO. PO
DER. EN. LA
TIERRA. E
YMAGEN
DE LA. DIVI
NA. MAGESTAD
Yo el Principe vro muy humil

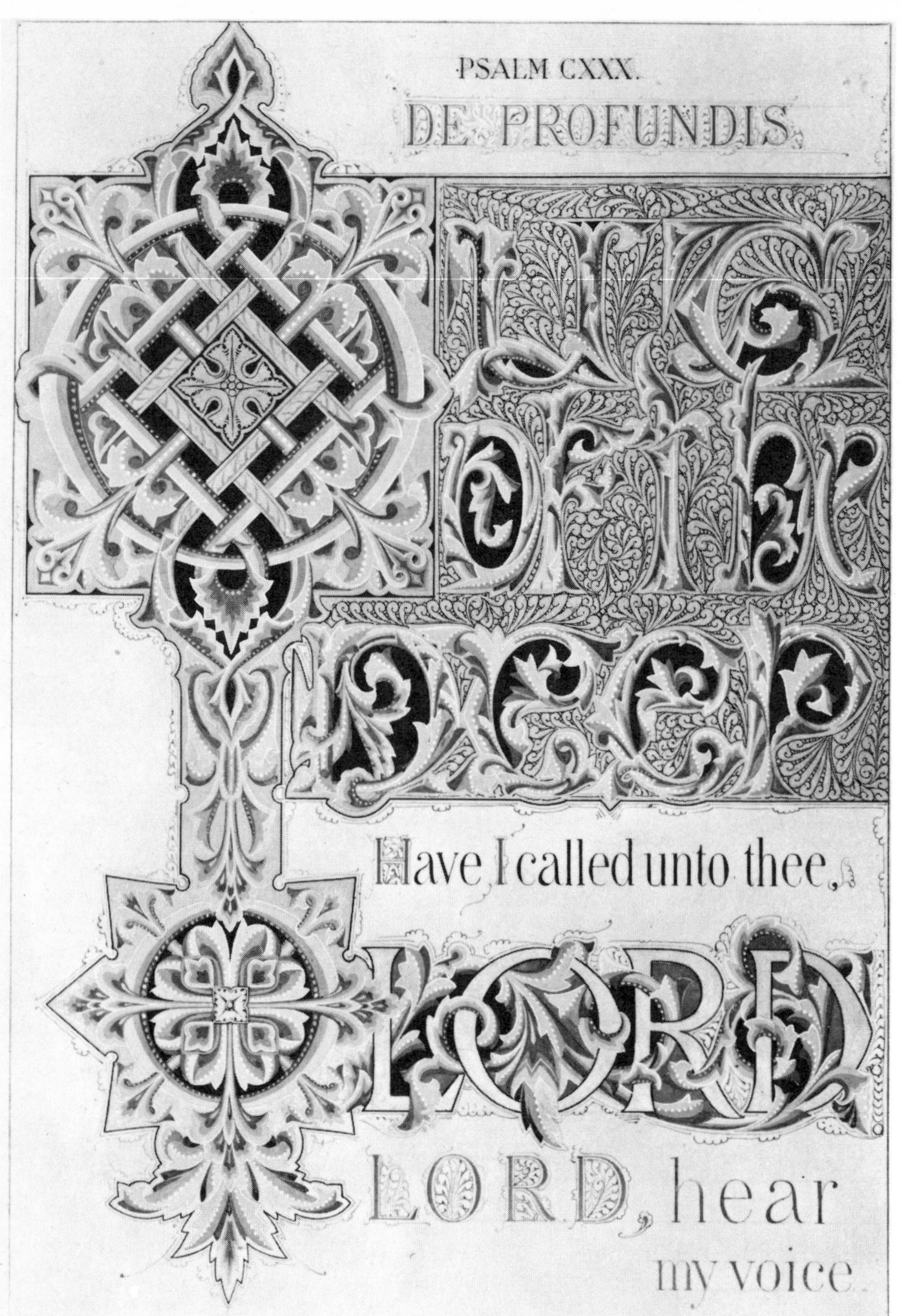
PSALM CXXX.
DE PROFUNDIS
Have I called unto thee,
LORD
LORD, hear
my voice

Owen Jones: The Victoria Psalter
1861

This is one of the original designs for the large work known as The Victoria Psalter *from its dedication to the Queen; the artwork is contained in 5 volumes, and on many pages the printed text is mounted to indicate the final form of the work. This particular page, however, contained no printed text, and was written and illuminated entirely by Owen Jones. A medieval Psalter, formerly in Jones's possession, is also illustrated in this book (p. 61), and it is interesting to see how the artist has here transformed the medieval style into an essentially neo-gothic mid-19th century one.*

V & A M MS L 462-1952

Opposite:
The May Queen,
by Alfred, Lord Tennyson.
Illuminated by Mrs W. H. Hartley
and chromolithographed
by W. R. Tymms.
London: Day & Son, 1861

By the 1860s manuals on illuminating began to proliferate, and copies for the less adept practitioner were also published, where guide lines for text and illuminations were provided. Many of the illuminated gift books were also used as models. As can be seen from this example, the artistic style of most of the illuminated books was very definitely mid-Victorian.

V & AM L 1543-1887 p 13

If you're waking call me early, call
me early mother dear,
For I would see the sun rise
upon the glad New year.
The New year's coming up mother
but I shall never see,
The flower upon the blackthorn,
the leaf upon the tree.

The book

13

art come unto a people which thou knewest not heretofore.

THE Lord recompense thy work, and a full reward be given thee of the Lord God of Israel, under whose wings thou art come to trust.

THEN she said, Let me find favour in thy sight, my lord; for that thou hast comforted me, and for that thou hast spoken friendly unto thine handmaid, though I be not like unto one of thine handmaidens.

AND Boaz said unto her, at mealtime come thou hither, and eat of the bread, and dip thy morsel in the vinegar. And she sat

The Book of Ruth. The illuminations arranged and executed under the direction of Henry Noel Humphreys.
London: Longman, Brown, Green & Longmans, 1850

Owen Jones's dictum 'form without colour is like a body without a soul' received vivid expression in a series of chromolithographed 'illuminated' gift books, designed by himself and Noel Humphreys. The influence of the medieval manuscript is obvious in works such as this, although the script is based more on the 'black letter' of print than on the pen-made forms. However, the copying of this kind of sacred text was considered an especially suitable occupation for the Victorian Sabbath, and was particularly popular with ladies.

V & A M Forster 672

The cheefest harts in Chevy Chase
To kill and beare away.
These tydings to Erle Douglas came,
In Scotland where he lay:
Who sent Erle Percy present word,
He wold prevent his sport.
The English Erle, not fearing that
Did to the woods resort,

Chevy Chase: A ballad.
Illustrated and illuminated
by James Douglas. 1865

In an illustration it can sometimes be quite difficult to know whether one is looking at an original or at a printed piece of work, and this is especially true of the 'illuminated books' of the mid-19th century. This example, however, is in fact a manuscript, and was probably written out with a steel pen, not a quill; as a result the script is almost more 'gothic' than medieval writing ever was. The illuminated book was symptomatic of the great interest in all things medieval during the mid- and late Victorian period, and which affected everything from railway stations and town halls to books.

V & A M LS L 4150-1971 25 × 20

William Morris: A book of verse 1870

This manuscript was made for presentation to Lady Burne-Jones; at the end of it, Morris has written out the names of all who had a share in producing the work. Most of the paintings were by Charles Fairfax-Murray, and much of the ornament was done by George Wardle. But it was William Morris himself who completed the work and who wrote out all his own poems. As can be seen from other illustrations in the present book, Morris was not alone in his desire to produce a medieval-style manuscript book, especially in the second half of the 19th century. But, as this book of poems shows, he was no slavish imitator of earlier work, evolving instead a characteristic style of his own. By his concern for all aspects of book production, including typography, and by his close involvement in the Arts & Crafts Movement, Morris's influence on the book arts and calligraphy was to be of considerable importance in the 20th century.

V&A MS L 131-1953 27.5 × 21 p 11

LOVE FULFILLED.

HAST thou longed through weary days
For the sight of one loved face,
Hast thou cried aloud for rest,
Mid the pain of sundering hours,
Cried aloud for sleep and death
Since the sweet unhoped for best
Was a shadow and a breath —
O, long now, for no fear lowers
O'er these faint feet-kissing flowers
O, rest now; and yet in sleep
All thy longing shalt thou keep.

Thou shalt rest, and have no fear
Of a dull awaking near,
Of a life for ever blind
Uncontent and waste and wide.
Thou shalt wake, and think it sweet
That thy love is near and kind.
Sweeter still for lips to meet;
Sweetest, that thine heart doth hide
Longing all unsatisfied
With all longing's answering
Howsoever close ye cling

historically; but I fear it would not be easy to get a horse into the existing design. You see, it isn't built for it. Possibly one of the Sangreal subjects which Burne Jones is doing for us might suit you. But the Magi as it stands is a very fine tapestry design; and for one thing since it has already been done, would cost less to execute. We shall be in town about 6 p m on Thursday. Won't you, if you are still in England, come over in the evening: dinner at 7 about I suppose, & then we could talk it over.

Yours very truly
William Morris

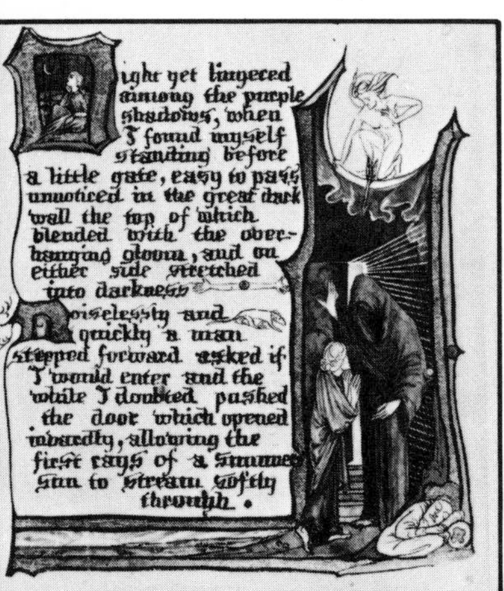
Night yet lingered among the purple shadows, when I found myself standing before a little gate, easy to pass unnoticed in the great dark wall the top of which blended with the overhanging gloom, and on either side stretched into darkness. Noiselessly and quickly a man stepped forward asked if I would enter and the while I doubted pushed the door which opened inwardly, allowing the first rays of a summer sun to stream softly through.

Phoebe Traquair: One wrote the dream . . . 1886

Phoebe Traquair was responsible for every aspect of this little manuscript: the text, the writing, the illumination, and the binding. Her work is typical of the Arts & Crafts Movement, in that it has embraced the book as a whole. The curious script, no doubt meant to suggest medieval writing, was probably done with a steel pen.

V & A M MS L 1765-1936 f.3
9.5 × 9.5

Above:
William Morris: A letter to W. Scawen Blunt.

William Morris's ordinary handwriting forms an interesting contrast to the type of script he thought suitable for his manuscript books (p. 320).

V & A M MS L 2385-1954

Gaetano Giarrè: Gaet.° Giarrè scrittor fiorentino invento, e incise questo Nuovo metodo per bene scrivere. 2ed 1807

We can presume this illustration shows Giarrè himself at work, since the inscription on the paper in front of the scribe gives his address, while the paper by his left hand contains the date. On a number of the plates in the book, he emphasises that he was both calligrapher and engraver, and this was always the best method of ensuring that the published work correctly portrayed the master's hand.

V&AM L 1398-1922 22.5 × 33

Bartolommeo Ponzilacqua: Calligrafia tedesca dimostrante in tavole ragionate, le scritture 'corrente', 'kansley' e la 'gotica' o 'Fractur'. 1819

This is an interesting example of the influence of politics on handwriting. In 1815 the Congress of Vienna, meeting after the defeat of Napoleon, abolished the old Venetian state, and handed it over as a province to Austria. The Austro-Hungarian Empire used the German scripts, so that Italians wishing to work for the new régime had of necessity to learn the different forms of writing current in central Europe at that time.

V&AM L 6037-1978 22 × 30.5

Scrittura Corrente Tedesca.

Elementi, e Lettere minori che respettivamente ne derivano.

Elementi	Lettere che ne derivano.	Elementi	Lettere che ne derivano.
1:		2:	
3:		4:	
5:		6:	

Ponzilacqua scrisse

Pasquali intagliò

Josef de Anduaga y Garimberti:
Compendio del arte de escriber
por reglas y sin muestras
1805

This work was first published 1791, and went through various editions. It was one of a number of similar manuals which attempted to provide strict rules, often based on geometrical examples, for the execution of fine writing.

V&AM L 4465-1977 14 × 9.5

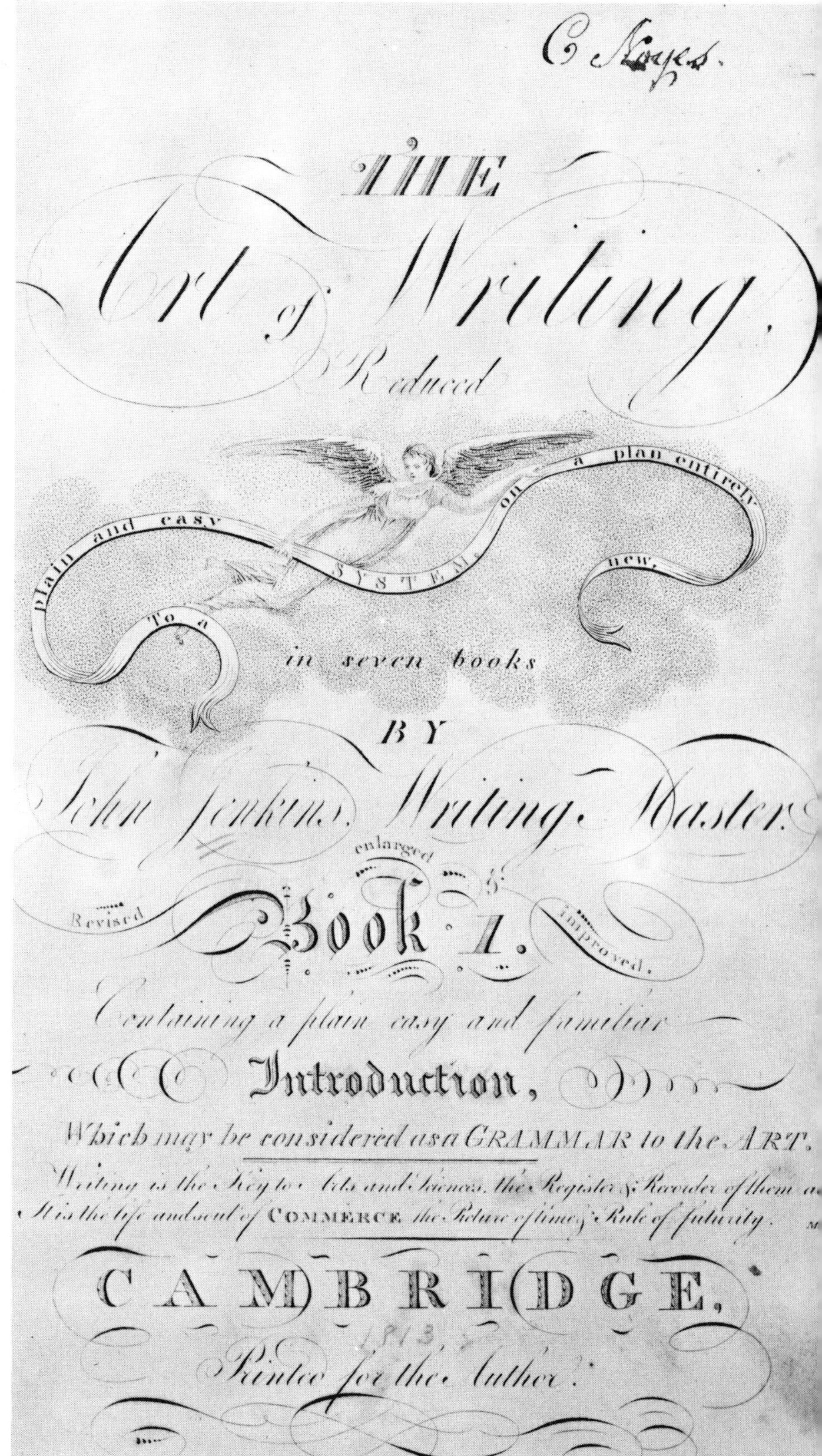

C Noyes.

THE
Art of Writing,
Reduced
To a plain and easy SYSTEM, on a plan entirely new,
in seven books
BY
John Jenkins, Writing Master.
Revised enlarged & improved.
Book I.
Containing a plain easy and familiar
Introduction,
Which may be considered as a GRAMMAR to the ART.
Writing is the Key to Arts and Sciences, the Register & Recorder of them a
It is the life and soul of COMMERCE the Picture of time, & Rule of futurity.
CAMBRIDGE,
1813
Printed for the Author.

John Jenkins: The art of writing reduced to a plain and easy system. 1813

Although Jenkins promised a work in seven books, as we can see from this title-page, only three appeared. He based his system on the theory that the round hand could be divided into six basic strokes of the pen and that having mastered these, anyone could write a good hand. He himself was self-taught, and used his own experience in his teaching. Unfortunately he found that certain letters such as k *and* s *did not fit into his scheme, while* z *was omitted as unnecessary! His work was the first of its kind to be published in America.*

V&AM L 619-1916 21 × 13

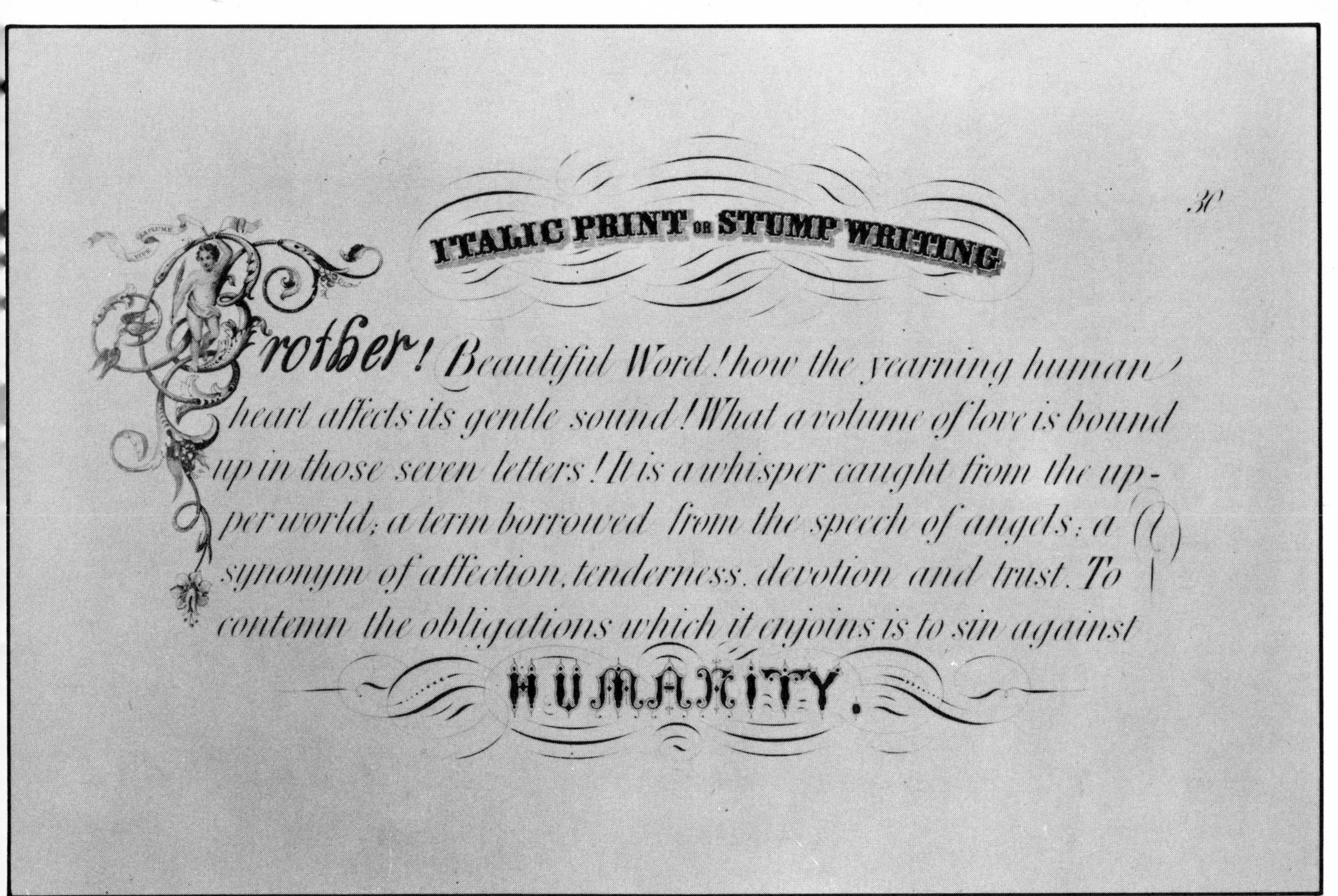

George J. Becker: Becker's ornamental penmanship c1855?

This work, published in Philadelphia, includes a variety of hands and alphabets in the style of earlier copy books. Although German and 'Old English' hands predominate, Becker also includes such items as 'velvet letter' and 'pearl letter'.

V&AM L 616-1916 19.5 × 30

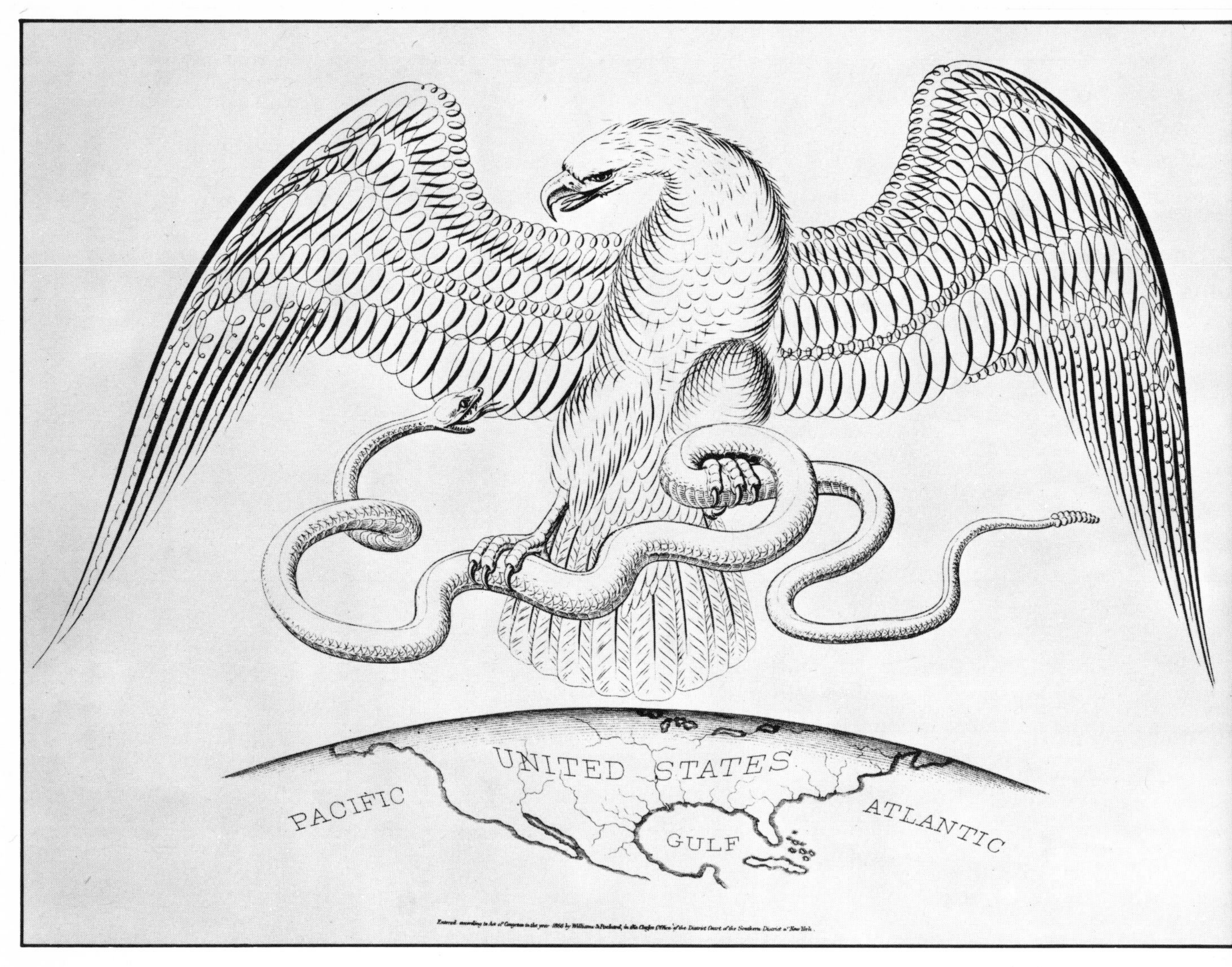

John D. Williams and S. S. Packard:
Williams & Packard's
original Gems of penmanship.
1867

Williams was a teacher of writing at Packard's in New York, and published several works jointly with him. As can be seen from this example, the ornamental aspect of the work tends to overshadow the writing, which is the standard business hand, but rather weak.

V&AM L 610-1916 25.5 × 30

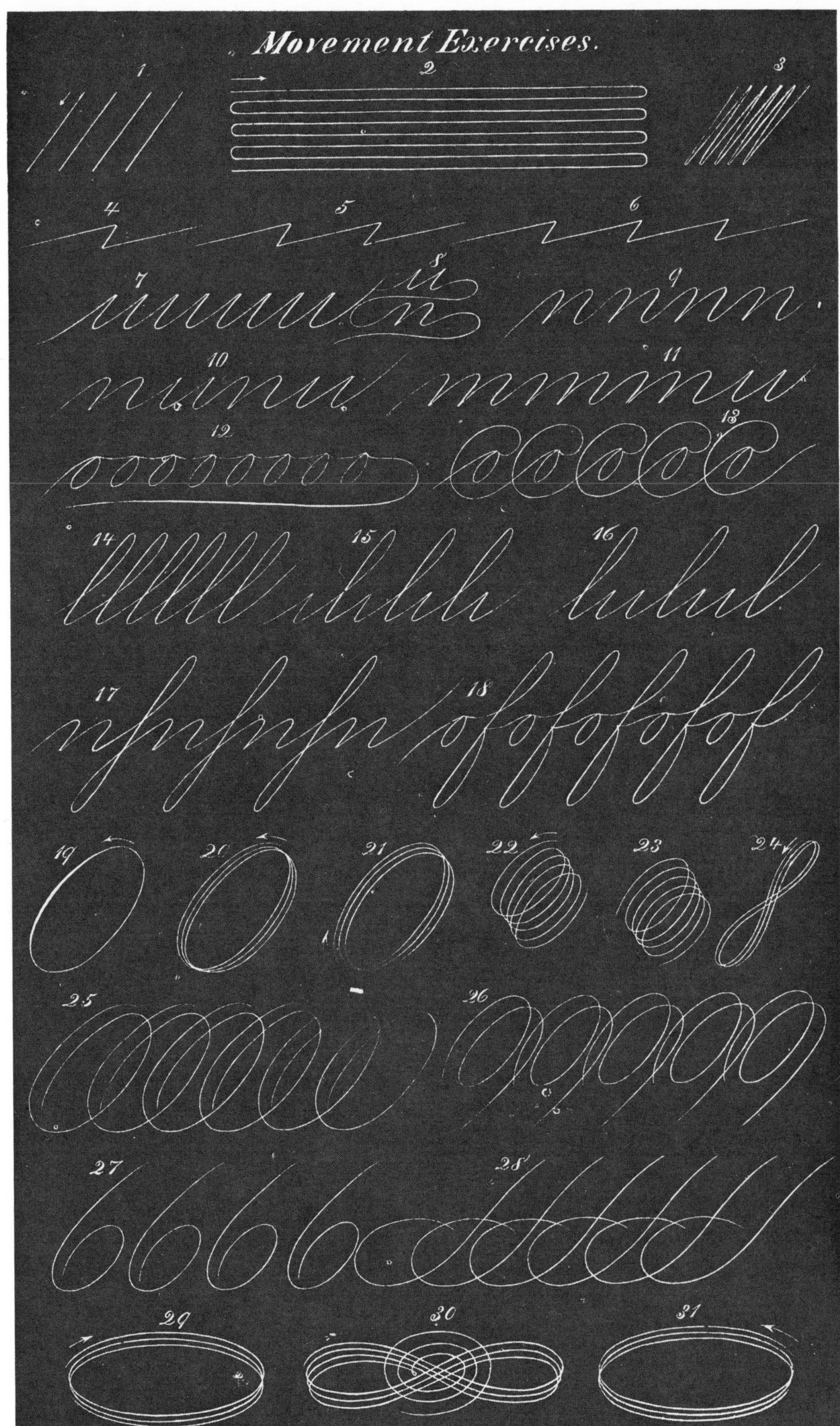

Platt Rogers Spencer: Spencerian key to practical penmanship. 1866

This book was published after the death of Spencer by one of his sons. Spencer himself published a number of copy books, in which he mostly concentrated on the business hand, and his work was widely used in the United States. Many of his examples however derive from the work of another American, Benjamin Franklin Foster.

V&AM L 612-1916 20.5 × 13.5

G. A. Gaskell: The penman's hand-book, for penmen and students [etc]. 1883

This work includes not only practical examples 'by the best American penmen', but also a history of writing, business letter writing, teaching penmanship, complete alphabets, and many other aspects of use and interest 'for penman and students'. The invitation cards shown here could have been produced in the 1980's as easily as in the 1880's, since this style of 'copperplate' writing in one form or another has continued to be considered as the traditional style for this type of work.

Author's collection. 27 × 21

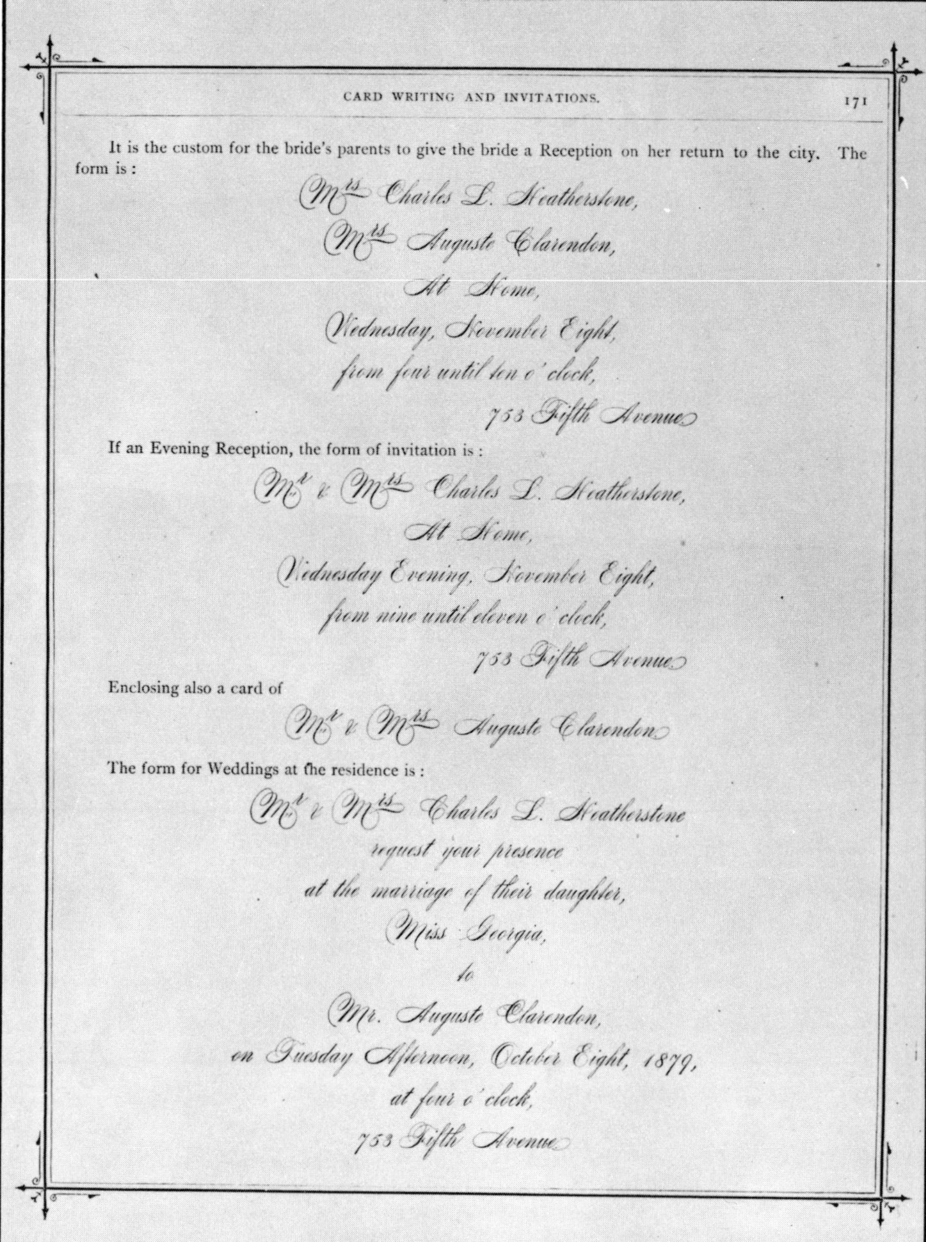

CARD WRITING AND INVITATIONS. 171

It is the custom for the bride's parents to give the bride a Reception on her return to the city. The form is:

Mrs Charles L. Heatherstone,
Mrs Auguste Clarendon,
At Home,
Wednesday, November Eight,
from four until ten o'clock,
753 Fifth Avenue

If an Evening Reception, the form of invitation is:

Mr & Mrs Charles L. Heatherstone,
At Home,
Wednesday Evening, November Eight,
from nine until eleven o'clock,
753 Fifth Avenue

Enclosing also a card of

Mr & Mrs Auguste Clarendon

The form for Weddings at the residence is:

Mr & Mrs Charles L. Heatherstone
request your presence
at the marriage of their daughter,
Miss Georgia,
to
Mr. Auguste Clarendon,
on Tuesday Afternoon, October Eight, 1879,
at four o'clock,
753 Fifth Avenue

10 The twentieth century and the calligraphic revival

THE FATHER of the 20th century revival of calligraphy was Edward Johnston (1872-1944). Johnston first studied medicine, but after 1897 he abandoned a medical career on account of ill-health, and devoted himself to the study and practice of calligraphy. He was encouraged in this study by Sydney Cockerell, who continued his support by giving him commissions as well as encouragement. Cockerell had been William Morris's secretary, and thus formed a link between the 19th and 20th century scribes. Johnston based his script on the writing found in manuscripts of the Winchester School of illumination of the 10th century, though later in life he experimented with a variety of other gothic and italic scripts. In 1906 he published his book *Writing & illuminating, & lettering*, a work which remains the classic text on these subjects to the present day. For many years he taught lettering and calligraphy at the Central School of Arts & Crafts in London. By his teaching and by his writings he influenced succeeding generations of scribes, both in England and elsewhere. Johnston's important discoveries about calligraphy arose from a very careful study of the medieval scribe and his work. He realised that the form of the letters was conditioned by the type of pen used to make them, and that an edged pen made thick and thin strokes by direction rather than by pressure. He also studied methods of cutting the reed or the quill, and likewise how to hold the pen in relation to the top of the writing surface. The type of ink and all the other materials required by the scribe were subject to his investigation.

One of Johnston's first pupils was William Graily Hewitt (1864-1946), who succeeded Johnston at the Central School of Arts & Crafts. He too influenced many later calligraphers, but his great contribution to the 20th century revival was in the field of illumination. Graily Hewitt carried out experiments in the art of gilding with gesso and gold leaf, to produce the burnished effect of the medieval illuminator, and his work in this field was outstanding. Many of the calligraphers whose works are illustrated in this section of the book were pupils of either Edward Johnston or Graily Hewitt, or pupils of their pupils. Calligraphers from other countries have also taken their teaching to the continents of Europe and America, and have there transmuted the work of the two masters into national styles of their own.

But the new calligraphy was not the only form of 20th century writing. For the most part the schools continued with the old style of 'copperplate' writing, with its 'pothooks and hangers', although some people were well aware that much was wrong with the handwriting currently taught in the schools. Mrs Bridges, wife of the poet Robert Bridges, published in 1911 *A new handwriting for teachers* and later Marion Richardson produced her influential work on the style which is still known by her name, and was especially aimed at teaching writing to young children. For the first half of the century most people remained unaware of the Johnston style of calligraphy, since this rarely penetrated educational establishments. 'Print-script' was one of the hands most frequently taught to the youngest children during the 1930's. It was easy to learn in the first instance, but difficult to transform into a cursive hand at a later stage. Of course most people are so used to the fact that the written and the printed forms of letters are different, that they tend to forget the young child's problem when being confronted with one or the other for the first time.

As a result of the influence of the Arts & Crafts Movement, especially strong in art schools in the first decades of this century, calligraphy was one of the subjects taught to art students, along with such other book crafts as binding. This gave many students a basic knowledge of letter forms and strengthened the calligraphic tradition in Britain. The professional craft body, the Society of Scribes and Illuminators, was founded in 1921, but the Society is also open to interested amateurs, who form a large group of lay members. After the last war, calligraphy was eventually dropped from the art college curriculum, while a change in the methods of teaching the 'three R's' to young children meant that there was little formal instruction in handwriting in the schools either. At the same time, interest in the humanist scripts, especially the italic, was stimulated by scholarly studies, and in 1952 a Society for Italic Handwriting was set up. This not only encourages and publishes scholarly articles on calligraphic subjects but it also stimulates the teaching of italic writing in schools by competitions and exhibitions. Many people are aware of the need to improve the standard of today's handwriting. But some consider that the discipline needed to obtain a good hand is unnecessary in the world of the telephone and the typewriter, when few people need ever do more than sign their name.

Nevertheless, as can be seen in the final section of this book, calligraphy has become much more a part of daily life in recent years, owing to the frequent use of pen-made letters in advertisement art, in place of printing types. At the same time developments have occurred in the last few decades which have been quite as revolutionary as those which swept away the quill pen in the early years of the 19th century. The almost ubiquitous use of the ball-point pen has had a disastrous effect on handwriting, which has hardly been compensated for by its convenience. The ball-point flows evenly over the surface, without the need of pressure to make strokes thick or thin, and the writing which is produced tends to lose all character. It is not impossible to write well with a ball-point pen, but it is certainly much more difficult.

Another important development, of more recent date, has been the felt-tip pen. This has quite a different effect on handwriting, because, unlike the ball-point, it does respond to the individual hand. It can also give a freedom of movement to produce more fluid letter forms and produce effects not unlike those made by the brush. Since many contemporary scribes have enjoyed working with the brush to form their letters, it will be obvious that the felt-tip can offer some advantages. The ease with which it flows over the surface can, however, lead to a lack of the discipline which the best of scripts has always required. Neverthless, the felt-tip can provide the amateur calligrapher with a chance to make exciting experiments, and certainly the brush-made script is popular in advertisement art.

Perhaps even more revolutionary in recent years has been the evolution of the computer alphabet. Although based on the traditional Roman alphabet, it shows a marked difference in many of the letter forms, and who knows what the future may hold in this field of machine-readable letters? Perhaps after nearly two thousand years of the Roman alphabet in calligraphy and in printing, we are about to witness an entirely new letter form.

So at the end of the 20th century, calligraphy has come to mean two different things. On the one hand there are professional bodies, such as the Society of Scribes & Illuminators in England, carrying out work to the highest specifications, supported by groups of amateurs who form the lay membership. On the other hand, there is mere writing, a subject taught, for the most part indifferently, in schools. Occasionally the two groups coalesce, when an enlightened teacher realises that writing is not just something that happens to a child, but needs practice and discipline. It is an interesting fact that most people admire good calligraphy when they see it; it is also true that many children (and indeed adults) have great pleasure in learning to write well. It is a skill that most people can acquire with a little practice, however inartistic or unskilled they may be, and the results are immediately visible – a fact that is especially rewarding for a child.

Many people are not even aware of calligraphy at all – or at least they think they are not. But its influence is all around today, since calligraphic forms have been so widely used in advertisements. Many of the forms so used have come, not from the direct Johnston tradition, which has become somewhat fossilised in Britain, but rather from its modifications in the United States and on the European continent. But the wide range of scripts included in this section of the book, indicate that calligraphic forms continue to offer a source of inspiration to those who wish to work within the older tradition as well as to those who prefer to use traditional forms as a point of departure for something entirely new.

Beispiele Kunstlerischer Schrift. Heraugegeben von Rudolf v. Larisch. 1900, 1906

These examples are taken from two of the portfolios issued in Vienna under the editorship of von Larisch, and containing the work of artists from most of the west European countries: Walter Crane and C. R. Ashbee represent England in these two volumes, and well-known people like Alphonse Mucha are also included. The scripts show how much contemporary art styles can affect calligraphy. The examples illustrated here are by Paul Burk of Darmstadt (right) and Felix Valloton of Paris (above).

V & AM L1052-1900, L1541-1910
23 × 28

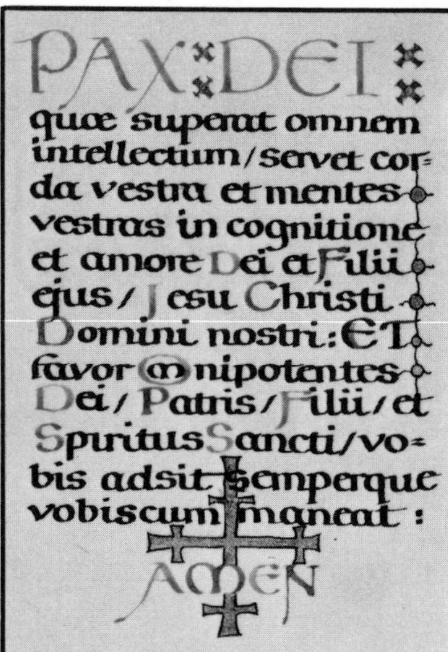

PAX DEI
quae superat omnem
intellectum/servet cor-
da vestra et mentes
vestras in cognitione
et amore Dei et Filii
ejus/Jesu Christi
Domini nostri: ET
favor omnipotentis
Dei/Patris/Filii/et
Spiritus Sancti/vo-
bis adsit semperque
vobiscum maneat:
AMEN

Edward Johnston: The order of the administration of the Lord's Supper or Holy Communion. 1900

This is a very early work by Edward Johnston, made as a personal present, for the colophon reads 'by mickle thought & little care this was wrought for cousin fair: by E.J.'. In this script he has gone back to the early Middle Ages and his writing has not yet gained the confidence it was to acquire later. The little manuscript is decorated with coloured inks and (not very good) gold.

V&AM MS L 131-1946 p 35
12 × 8.5

SURELY THERE
IS A MINE FOR
SILVER
And a place for gold
which they refine.
Iron is taken out
of the earth,
And brass is mol-
ten out of the stone
Man setteth an end
to darkness,
And searcheth out
to the furthest
bound
The stones of thick
darkness and of
the shadow of death.
HE BREAKETH
open a shaft away
from where men
sojourn;
They are forgotten
of the foot that
passeth by;
They hang afar from
men, they swing
to and fro.

AS FOR THE EARTH,
out of it cometh
bread:
And underneath it
is turned up as it
were by fire.
The stones thereof
are the place of
sapphires,
And it hath dust
of gold.
THAT PATH NO
BIRD OF PREY
KNOWETH,
Neither hath the
falcon's eye seen it:
The proud beasts
have not trodden it
Nor hath the fierce
lion passed thereby
HE PUTTETH FORTH
his hand upon
the flinty rock;
HE OVERTURNETH
the mountains
by the roots.
HE CUTTETH out

Black & Red

FIG. 93. 137

Edward Johnston: Writing & illuminating, & lettering. 1906

More than seventy years after it was first published, this work is still in print and still considered as one of the most important manuals of 20th century calligraphy. In it Johnston expressed his ideas on writing and provided instruction on all aspects of the craft, going back to the work of early scribes and studying their techniques. Various examples of his work at different periods of his life are illustrated in the present book; this page taken from the 1906 manual shows one of his earlier scripts.

V&AM L 4440-1959 18.5 × 12

enough, for diversity of Side Alleys: Unto which, the Two Covert Alleys of the Greene, may deliver you. But there must be, no Alleys with Hedges at either End, of this great Inclosure: Not at the Hither End, for letting your Prospect upon this Faire Hedge from the Greene: Nor at the Further End, for letting your Prospect from the Hedge, through the Arches, upon the Heath.

FOR the Ordering of the Ground, within the Great Hedge, I leave it to Variety of Device; Advising neverthelesse, that whatsoever forme you cast it into,

first it be not too Busie, or full of Worke. Wherein I, for my part, doe not like Images Cut out in Juniper, or other Garden stuffe: They be for Children. Little low Hedges, Round, like Welts, with some Pretty Pyramides, I like well: And in some Places, Faire Columnes upon Frames of Carpenters Worke. I would also have the Alleys, Spacious and Faire. You may have Closer Alleys upon the Side Grounds, but none in the Maine Garden. I wish also, in the very Middle, a Faire Mount, with three Ascents, and Alleys, enough for foure to walke

Edward Johnston: Of gardens, by Francis Bacon. 1911

Unlike Dorothy Pelton's version of this Bacon essay (p. 342), Johnston's manuscript is quite undecorated, except for a judicious use of red ink, which can just be perceived in this illustration. It is interesting to compare this thin, slightly angular script with that of the Holy Communion (p. 332) written only ten years earlier.

V & A M   MS L 26-1945   15 × 11.5

AVE Maria, gratia plena: Dominus tecum benedicta tu in mulieribus, et benedictus fructus ventris tui, Jesus. Sancta Maria, Mater Dei, ora pro nobis peccatoribus, nunc et in hora mortis nostræ. Amen.

CREDO in Deum Patrem omnipotentem, Creatorem cœli et terræ. Et in Jesum Christum,

Hail, Mary, full of grace; the Lord is with thee: blessed art thou among women, and blessed is the fruit of thy womb, Jesus. Holy Mary, Mother of God, pray for us sinners, now and at the hour of our death. Amen.

I believe in God, the Father Almighty, Creator of heaven and earth. And in Jesus Christ,

Edward Johnston: The Lord's Prayer, Hail Mary, and the Apostles' Creed. c1913

This little manuscript has an interesting history. It was written out by Johnston for Eric Gill, who in his leisure time had studied lettering and letter cutting under him. Gill later became better known for his carving, engraving and typography. This finely written work, with parallel texts in English and Latin, shows signs of wear, as if Gill made frequent use of it. Gill bequeathed it to his daughter, on whose death it became the property of Evan Gill; in 1959 the latter presented it to the calligrapher Heather Child as a token of her own devotion to the teaching of Edward Johnston. In 1977 Miss Child generously gave the manuscript to the Victoria and Albert Museum Library, which contains so many examples of Johnston's work.

V & A M   MS L 5316-1977
f.8v/9r   13 × 8

* most beautifully — with edges embroidered in white on the linen. She had dinner up in the bedroom with me (for I forgot to say, I am still kept in bed — but I am much better and am going to get up this afternoon for an hour or two. Poulticeing is finished & now I have got a belladonna plaster on my chest) and we had a long talk about everything — including the old subject — Latin services — how can children pray in Latin? I told her, among other things; that if you say "Glory be to the Father" etc. it means just as much as the english language can make the words mean (she agreed to that), but if you say "Gloria Patri et Filio & Spiritui Sancto" etc. it means as much as the Church means by the words.* That is their difficulty. They dont understand that there can be a church with divine authority to teach..... Well, then we had a tea-party in the bedroom. David J. was the only extra person (I didnt tell you, he gave me a splendid drawing of S. Peter — very good indeed) and Joan cut the birthday cake for me. At 5.30 grandma had to go to catch the 6.12 train & Petra walked to the top of Fullers Lane with her. (Mother has just brought me an extra cup of tea & some toast). In the evening after Complin Mr. P. & George M. came in & then David J. & then Uncle Charlie. So I am not exactly lonely — and I did have a most happy birthday xxxxxxxxxxxxx

This morning your letter of Sunday last has come & two most beautiful little drawings! Thank you again very much indeed my dear dear Elizabeth. We are all very much better, so you need not worry about us at all. Grippe is French for Influenza by the bye.

* You see English is a living language & it has the right to make words mean what it likes — but that meaning changes with the years — But Latin is a dead language — so it depends on something else to give meaning — either most scholars or the living Church

MARGARET of Cortona. She found her lover murdered and the sight of his corpse, the body she had embraced, showed her a figure of her own soul, disfigured by sin & dead to God. She immediately repented and gave herself to God & lived a life of heroic austerity and miraculous friendship with our Lord.
For Elizabeth 22 Feb 1922 E.G.

Eric Gill: Letter to his daughter Elizabeth, giving an account of his birthday celebrations. 22nd February 1922

Eric Gill was of course best known for his lettering rather than for his calligraphy, but this is a charming example of his informal hand in a family letter.

V&AM MS L 3382-1957 25.5 × 19

Edward Johnston: The House of David, his inheritance: a book of sample scripts. 1914

This manuscript was commissioned by Sir Sydney Cockerell, who presented it to the Library of the Victoria and Albert Museum in 1959. The work contains a great variety of scripts, from Johnston's early rounded form to the later more gothic style. It was his development of the chisel-edged quill nib of the medieval scribe that enabled him to produce his most characteristic hand. This illustration shows the title-page of the manuscript; the two following illustrations show the 'black italic' formed from his foundational hand, and his version of a modern uncial and half-uncial.

V & A M MS L 4391-1959 25 × 20

A Psalm of David. xxiij.

The LORD is my shepherd;
I shall not want.
He maketh me to lie down
in green pastures:
He leadeth me beside
the [1] still waters. 1. Heb. waters of rest.
He restoreth my soul:
He guideth me in the paths of
righteousness for his name's sake.
Yea, though I walk through the
valley of [2] the shadow of death,
I will fear no evil; 2. Or, deep darkness.

23

high dwelleth not in houses made
with hands; as saith the prophet,

The heaven is my
throne,
And the earth the foot-
stool of my feet:
What manner of house
will ye build me?
saith the Lord:
Or what is the place of
my rest?
Did not my hand make
all these things?

Acts. vij. 44–50.

25

William Graily Hewitt:
The Tempest, by William
Shakespeare c1938

Graily Hewitt originally trained as a barrister, but abandoned the legal profession in favour of calligraphy. He succeeded Edward Johnston at the Central School of Arts and Crafts and taught there for over thirty years; many of his pupils themselves became well-known calligraphers. His great contribution was to revive the art of gilding with gesso and gold leaf, and he gathered round him a group of artists. Ida Henstock worked longest with him, and it is her work which decorates the margin of this manuscript.

V & AM MS L 1801-1946 f.2r
30 × 20

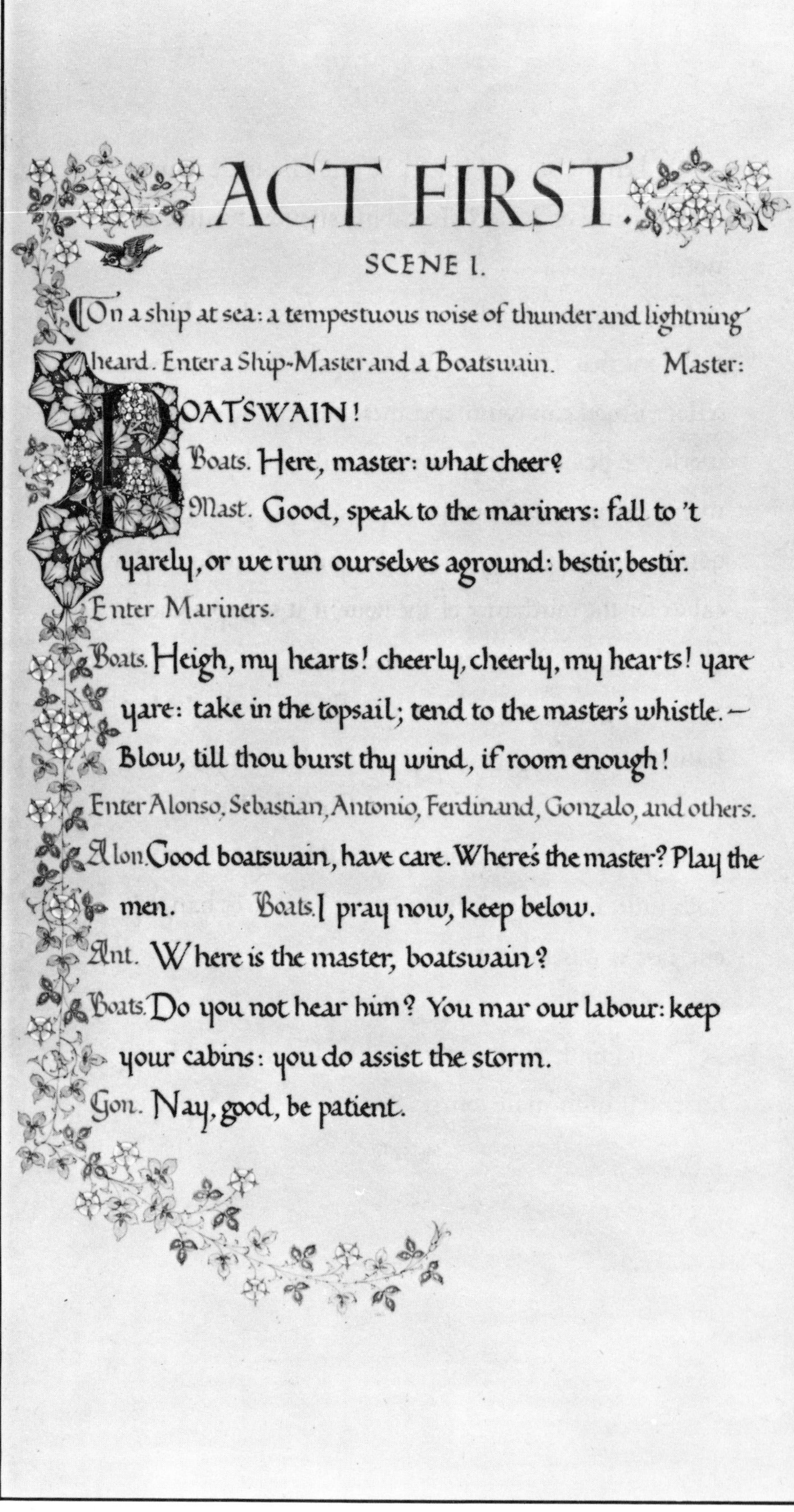

ACT FIRST.

SCENE I.

On a ship at sea: a tempestuous noise of thunder and lightning heard. Enter a Ship-Master and a Boatswain. Master:

BOATSWAIN!

Boats. Here, master: what cheer?

Mast. Good, speak to the mariners: fall to 't yarely, or we run ourselves aground: bestir, bestir.

Enter Mariners.

Boats. Heigh, my hearts! cheerly, cheerly, my hearts! yare yare: take in the topsail; tend to the master's whistle.— Blow, till thou burst thy wind, if room enough!

Enter Alonso, Sebastian, Antonio, Ferdinand, Gonzalo, and others.

Alon. Good boatswain, have care. Where's the master? Play the men. Boats. I pray now, keep below.

Ant. Where is the master, boatswain?

Boats. Do you not hear him? You mar our labour: keep your cabins: you do assist the storm.

Gon. Nay, good, be patient.

Opposite:
William Graily Hewitt: The order of the administration of the Lord's Supper or Holy Communion.
c1935

This is one of the finest of the Graily Hewitt manuscripts in the Library of the Victoria and Albert Museum. The illustration unfortunately cannot do justice to the fine gold lettering of the passages in capital letters. It is a large manuscript, and Hewitt's rounded script shows to much greater advantage on the more spacious page. With the completed work came the original roughs, so that it is possible to see how the calligrapher set about planning such a large work.

V & A M MS L 838-1953 38 × 26

before the people, & take the Cup into his hands, he shall say the Prayer of Consecration, as followeth.

ALMIGHTY GOD, OUR HEAVENLY FATHER, WHO OF THY tender mercy didst give thine only Son Jesus Christ to suffer death upon the cross for our redemption; who made there (by his one oblation of himself once offered) a full, perfect, and sufficient sacrifice, oblation, & satisfaction, for the sins of the whole world; & did institute, and in his holy Gospel command us to continue, a perpetual memory of that his precious death, until his coming again; Hear us, O merciful Father, we most humbly beseech thee; and grant that we receiving these thy creatures of bread and wine, according to thy Son our Saviour Jesus Christ's holy institution, in remembrance of his death and passion, may be partakers of his most blessed Body & Blood; who, in the same night that he was betrayed,[1] took Bread; and, when he had given thanks,[2] he brake it, and gave it to his disciples, saying, Take, eat,

[3] THIS IS MY BODY

which is given for you. Do this in remembrance of me.

Likewise after supper he[4] took the Cup; &, when he had given thanks, he gave it to them, saying, Drink ye all of this; for

[5] THIS IS MY BLOOD OF THE NEW TESTAMENT,

which is shed for you and for many for the remission of sins: Do this, as oft as ye shall drink it, in remembrance of me. AMEN.

1. Here the Priest is to take the Paten into his hands.
2. And here to break the Bread.
3. And here to lay his hand upon all the Bread
4. Here he is to take the Cup into his hand.
5. And here to lay his hand upon every vessel (be it Chalice or Flagon) in which there is any Wine to be consecrated.

William Graily Hewitt: The Hound of Heaven, by Francis Thompson. 1906

This hand is typical of Graily Hewitt's writing, and also shows the care with which the text is placed on the page. The work is written on vellum, and the initial is a fine example of the gilding Hewitt did so much to restore.

V&AM L 236-1953 20 × 14.5

I Sought no more that, after which I strayed,
In face of man or maid;
But still within the little children's eyes
Seems something, something that replies,
They at least are for me, surely for me!
I turned me to them very wistfully;
But just as their young eyes grew sudden fair
With dawning answers there,
Their angel plucked them from me by the hair.
Come then, ye other children, Nature's — share
With me (said I) your delicate fellowship;
Let me greet you lip to lip,
Let me twine with you caresses,
Wantoning
With our Lady-Mother's vagrant tresses,
Banqueting
With her in her wind-walled palace,
Underneath her azured daïs,

William Graily Hewitt: References made by Our Lord to nature and men's occupations. c1930?

Another manuscript, this time on a small scale, showing the co-operation between scribe and decorator — Graily Hewitt and Ida Henstock.

V&AM MS L 1588-1976 f.8v/9r 14 × 11

S:MARK

IV,26. SO IS THE KINGDOM
of God, as if a man should
cast seed into the ground;
And should sleep, & rise night
and day, & the seed should spring
and grow up, he knoweth not
how. For the earth bringeth forth
fruit of herself: first the blade,
then the ear, after that the full
corn in the ear.

S:LUKE

NO MAN HAVING DRUNK V.39.
old wine straightway desir-
eth new: for he saith, The old
is better.

A Good tree bringeth not forth cor- VI,43.
rupt fruit; neither doth a corrupt
tree bring forth good fruit. For every tree is known by his own fruit.
For of thorns men do not gather figs,

Louise Lessore (Mrs Louise Powell): Psalmi LXXXIC, CII, CIII. Canticum trium puerorum 1905

Louise Lessore was one of Edward Johnston's earliest pupils, and subsequently she became for a short time one of Graily Hewitt's assistants. During this period she and Hewitt worked on one of William Morris's incomplete manuscripts. Later she worked with Alfred Fairbank, and also produced decorations for publications of the Ashendene Press. In this manuscript, however, she was both scribe and illuminator, and it is interesting to note the medieval influence in both decoration and writing which is apparent in the work, so that although in the modern style the result is quite different from that of her contemporaries.

V & A M MS L 4393-1959 24 × 16.5

Percy J. Smith: Songs, by Robert Burns 1903

This little manuscript is typical of much of the work done at the beginning of the century, with the very rounded script which still at this period had an uncertain quality about it. The text here is written out in black, with the chorus to each of the poems in red.

V & A M MS L 4200-1967 f.1v/2r 19 × 14.5

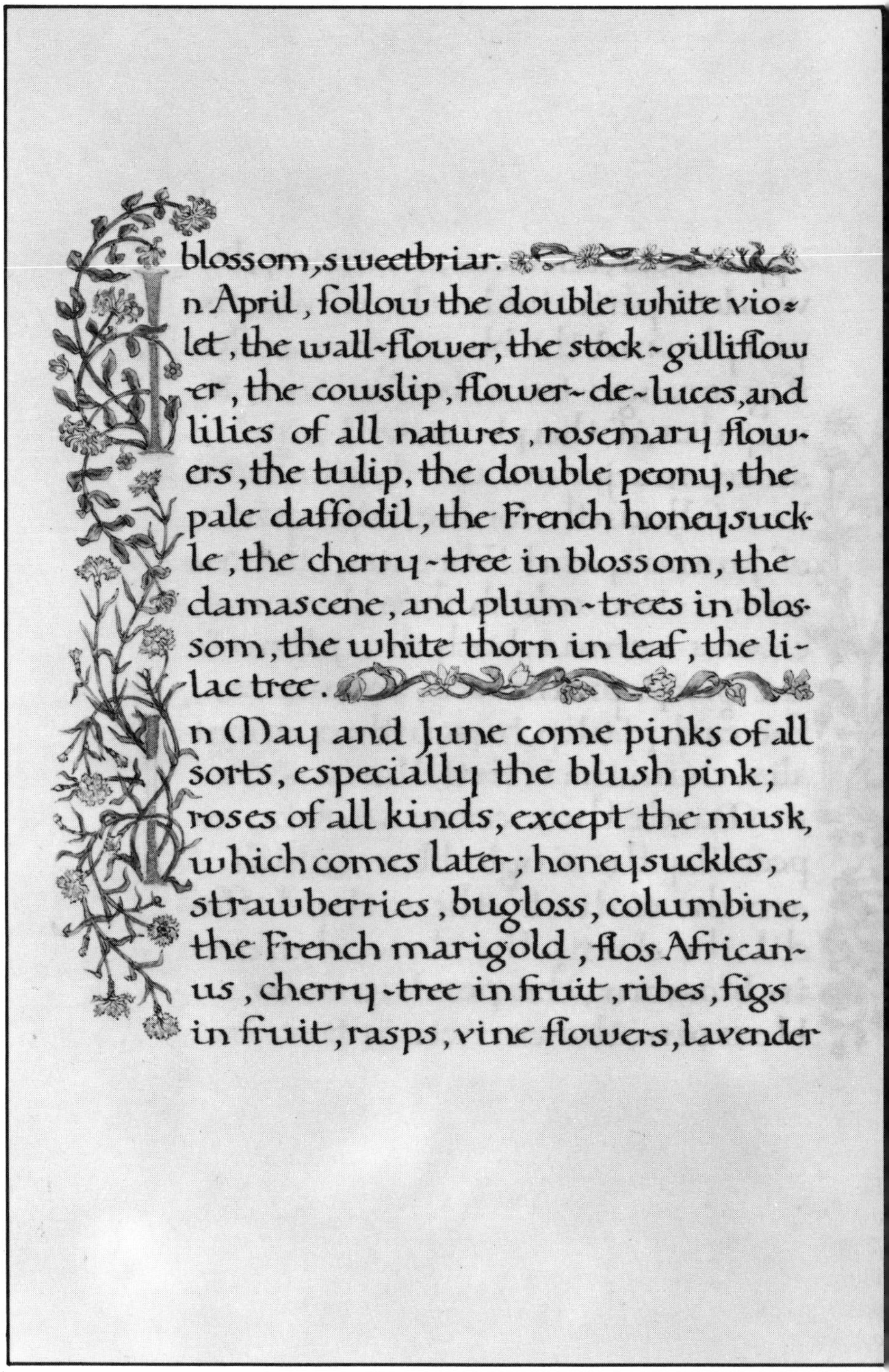

blossom, sweetbriar.

In April, follow the double white violet, the wall-flower, the stock-gilliflower, the cowslip, flower-de-luces, and lilies of all natures, rosemary flowers, the tulip, the double peony, the pale daffodil, the French honeysuckle, the cherry-tree in blossom, the damascene, and plum-trees in blossom, the white thorn in leaf, the lilac tree.

In May and June come pinks of all sorts, especially the blush pink; roses of all kinds, except the musk, which comes later; honeysuckles, strawberries, bugloss, columbine, the French marigold, flos Africanus, cherry-tree in fruit, ribes, figs in fruit, rasps, vine flowers, lavender

Dorothy Pelton: Of gardens, by Francis Bacon. c1905

Bacon's essay Of gardens *obviously attracted the 20th century scribe with the decorative possibilities it offered. This manuscript contains borders illustrating garden scenes, but the page shown here has been chosen for its concentration on the script. The writing is of the early Johnston style, but the book as a whole reflects the Arts & Crafts Movement. Floral borders were common in medieval manuscripts, but the 20th century illuminator handled them quite differently.*

V&AM MS L 2075-1972 22 × 17

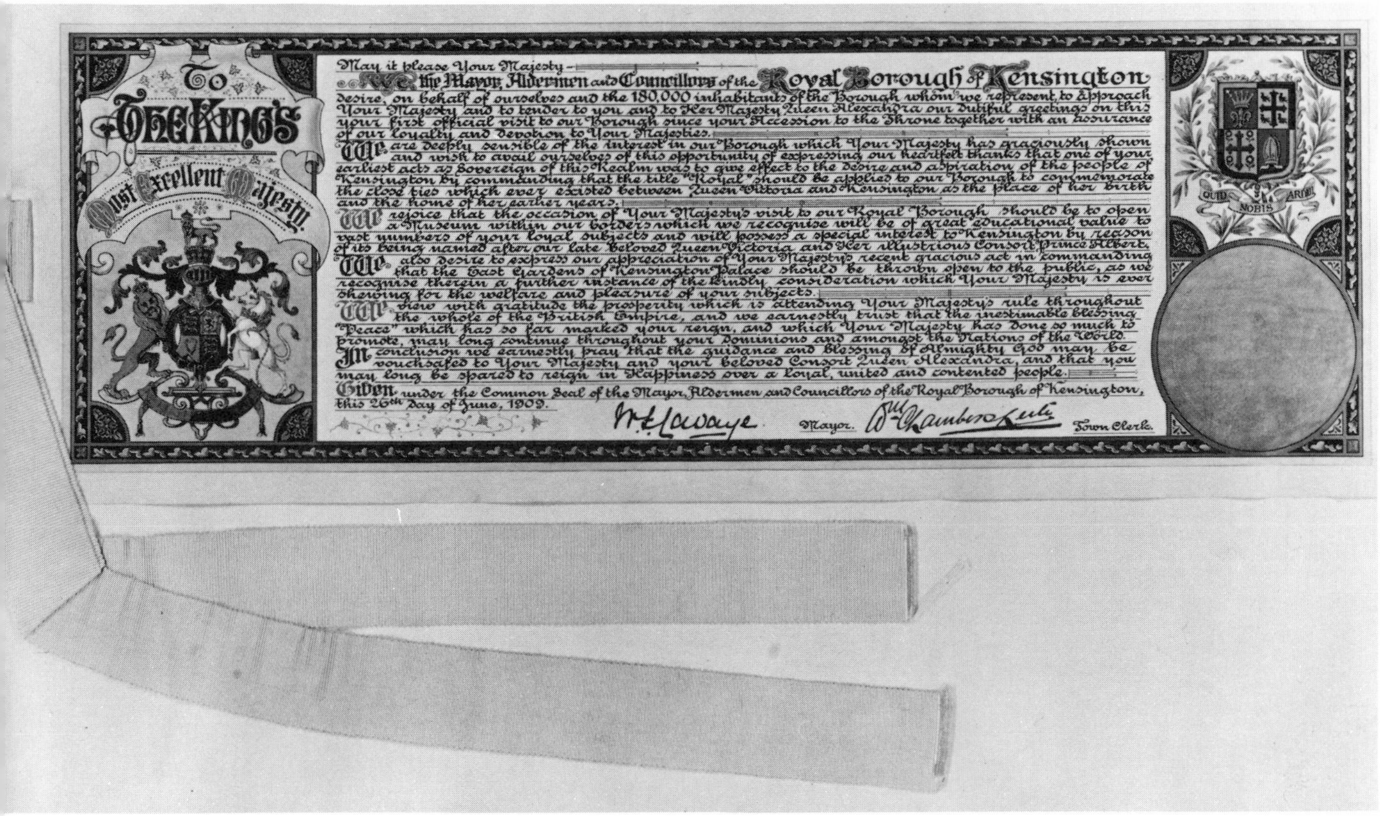

To The King's Most Excellent Majesty

May it please Your Majesty —

We the Mayor, Aldermen and Councillors of the Royal Borough of Kensington desire, on behalf of ourselves and the 180,000 inhabitants of the Borough whom we represent, to approach Your Majesty and to tender to you and to Her Majesty Queen Alexandra our dutiful greetings on this your first official visit to our Borough since your Accession to the Throne together with an assurance of our loyalty and devotion to Your Majesties.

We are deeply sensible of the interest in our Borough which Your Majesty has graciously shown and wish to avail ourselves of this opportunity of expressing our heartfelt thanks that one of your earliest acts as Sovereign of this Realm was to give effect to the desire and aspiration of the people of Kensington by commanding that the title "Royal" should be applied to our Borough to commemorate the close ties which ever existed between Queen Victoria and Kensington as the place of her birth and the home of her earlier years.

We rejoice that the occasion of Your Majesty's visit to our Royal Borough should be to open a Museum within our borders which we recognise will be of great educational value to vast numbers of your loyal subjects and will possess a special interest to Kensington by reason of its being named after our late beloved Queen Victoria and Her illustrious Consort Prince Albert.

We also desire to express our appreciation of Your Majesty's recent gracious act in commanding that the East Gardens of Kensington Palace should be thrown open to the public, as we recognise therein a further instance of the kindly consideration which Your Majesty is ever shewing for the welfare and pleasure of your subjects.

We view with gratitude the prosperity which is attending Your Majesty's rule throughout the whole of the British Empire, and we earnestly trust that the inestimable blessing "Peace" which has so far marked your reign, and which Your Majesty has done so much to promote, may long continue throughout your Dominions and amongst the Nations of the World.

In conclusion we earnestly pray that the guidance and blessing of Almighty God may be vouchsafed to Your Majesty and your beloved Consort Queen Alexandra, and that you may long be spared to reign in Happiness over a loyal, united and contented people.

Given under the Common Seal of the Mayor, Aldermen and Councillors of the Royal Borough of Kensington, this 26th day of June, 1909.

Mayor. Town Clerk.

Quid Nobis Ardui

Address presented to King Edward VII by the Royal Borough of Kensington on the occasion of his visit to open the new buildings of the Victoria and Albert Museum. 1909

By 1909 the revival of calligraphy was well under way in England and Edward Johnston's important manual Writing & illuminating, & lettering *had been published several years before. But this document is written very much in the traditional style which goes back over the centuries, and can be compared with other official manuscripts illustrated in this book. It was written and illuminated on paper (the modern scribe would usually prefer vellum) and was presented to the King in a gilt casket, on the front of which was a painting of the Museum (right).*

V&AM

Rudolf von Larisch: Unterricht in ornamentaler Schrift. 1911

Interest in calligraphy in the early years of the 20th century was not confined to the English-speaking countries. Larisch became interested in handwriting early in his career as an archivist, and a publication in 1899 on decorative writing led to his appointment as a lecturer on lettering at the Vienna School of Arts & Crafts. This work, first published in 1905, gave him the importance in Austria that Johnston achieved in England in the field of modern handwriting.

V&AM L 825-1912 25 × 16

Jupiter und Apollo ſtritten,
welcher von ihnen der bes:
te Bogenschütze ſei. Laſz
uns die Probe tun! ſagte
Apollo.-Er ſpannte ſeinen
Bogen und ſchoſz ſo mit:
ten in das bemerkte Ziel,
daſz Jupiter keine Mög:
lichkeit ſahe, ihn zu über;

24. 1/2 der Originalgröße. Vereinfachung einer bestimmten Buchstabenform. Stahlfeder.

Am andern Morgen fiel starker Schnee. Ein-
scharfer Ostwind fegte ihn über die Heide, über
die Marsch ins Meer. Wenn aber die Kleinen-,
vom Winde gejagten Flocken einen Halt fanden und
war es auch nur ein Heidestrauch oder ein Maul

25. 3/4 der Originalgröße. Gewöhnliche Schreibschrift eines Kursteilnehmers. „Grenzen" der gewöhnlichen Schreibschrift.

wöhnliche Schreibschriften sehr dekorativ wirken können. ■

■ Bei solchen Schriften kann am ehesten eine Anlehnung an Vorbilder Platz greifen. Je mehr sich der ornamentale Schriftcharakter der gewöhnlichen Schreibschrift nähert, umso geringer ist die Gefahr, daß durch Kopiatur das Handschriftliche verloren geht. Selbst in den

1

Leo Paul Fenz

2.

Ernſt G. Hart & Co

3.

4.

Dem Hochwohlgebor
Traugott Freit
wurde von der Gem

Lorenz Reinhard Spitzenpfeil: Die Behandlung der Schrift in Kunst und Gewerbe. 1911

At a time when Edward Johnston and his followers were reviving the art of calligraphy in England, there was considerable interest in the practical applications of handwritten letters in Germany. Here the gothic overtones of the 'Fraktur' script remained obvious, though, as in these examples, the influences of Art Nouveau and the Arts & Crafts Movement have also made their impact.

V&AM L 2253-1913 31 × 22.5

Bays yield no smell as they grow, rosemary
little, nor sweet marjoram ; that which, above
all others, yields the sweetest smell in the air, is
the violet ; especially the white double violet, wh.
comes twice a year - about the middle of April,
& about Bartholomew-tide. Next to that
is the musk rose ; then the strawberry leaves
dying, with a most excellent cordial smell ;
then the flower of the vines – it is a little
dust, like the dust of a bent, wh. grows
upon the cluster in the first coming forth ; then
sweetbriar, then wall-flowers

9

M. M. Bridges: A new handwriting for teachers. 1911

Johnston was by no means the only person to show an interest in improving the standard of handwriting in the early years of the 20th century. Mrs Bridges, the wife of the poet Robert Bridges, stated in her preface to this work that she had consciously altered her hand after 'making acquaintance with the Italianized Gothic of the sixteenth century'. The script shown here is the one she advocated to teachers.

V&AM L 1900-1929 23 × 19

Führen Sie bitte
den Quellstift
leicht und ohne
nennenswer-
ten Druck
Gottlieb
Landerer's
photographisches Atelier
Amselgasse 5

E. W. Baule: Scribtol. Anleitung zur Kunstschrift. 1912

This book combined an advertisement for writing ink ('Scribtol') with a copy book. This ornamental writing is suitably bold for use in advertisements, and is interesting in that it emanates from a country where an older style of writing and the 'fraktur' letters still prevailed.

V&AM L 2423-1912 30 × 22

FEDERTECHNISCHE ÜBUNGEN

ABCDEFGHIJKLM
NOPQRSTUVWXYZ

abcdefghijklmnot
pqrsuvwxyzз.,;!?(//)

EINFÜHRUNG IN DIE TECHNIK D. BREITFEDER

1234567890

DIE ALPHABETFORMEN DER MITTELSTUFE
TAFEL X

Paul Hulliger: Die neue Schrift. 1927

This illustration comes from the second edition of a report by a commission considering the reform of handwriting in schools in Basel, Switzerland. It indicates how pupils should be taught in each of their school years.

V&AM L 19-1928 25 × 19

thoughts shall be established.

The Lord hath made all things for himself: yea, even the wicked for the day of evil.

Every one that is proud in heart is an abomination to the Lord: though hand join in hand, he shall not be unpunished.

By mercy and truth iniquity is purged: and by the fear of the Lord men depart from evil.

When a man's ways please the Lord, he maketh even his enemies to be at peace with him.

Better is a little with righteousness than great revenues without right.

A man's heart deviseth his way: but the Lord directeth his steps.

A divine sentence is in the lips of the king: his mouth transgresseth not in judgment.

A just weight and balance are the Lord's: all the weights of the bag are his work.

It is an abomination to kings to commit wickedness: for the throne is established by righteousness.

Righteous lips are the delight of kings; and they love him that speaketh right.

The wrath of a king is as messengers of death: but a wise man will pacify it.

In the light of the king's countenance is life: and his favour is as a cloud of the latter rain.

How much better is it to get wisdom than gold! and to get understanding rather to be chosen than silver.

The highway of the upright is to depart from evil: he that keepeth his way preserveth his soul.

Pride goeth before destruction, and an haughty spirit before a fall.

Better it is to be of an humble spirit with the lowly, than to divide the spoil with the proud.

He that handleth a matter wisely shall find good: and whoso trusteth in the Lord, happy is he.

The wise in heart shall be called prudent: and the sweetness of the lips increaseth learning.

Understanding is a wellspring of life unto him that hath it: but the instruction of fools is folly.

The heart of the wise teacheth his mouth, and addeth learning to his lips.

Pleasant words are as an honeycomb, sweet to the soul, and health to the bones.

There is a way that seemeth right unto a man, but the end thereof are the ways of death.

He that laboureth laboureth for himself; for his mouth craveth it of him.

An ungodly man diggeth up evil: and in his lips there is as a burning fire.

A froward man soweth strife: and a whisperer separateth chief friends.

A violent man enticeth his neighbour, & leadeth him into the way that is not good.

He shutteth his eyes to devise froward things: moving his lips he bringeth evil to pass.

The hoary head is a crown of glory, if it be found in the way of righteousness.

He that is slow to anger is better than the mighty; and he that ruleth his spirit than he that taketh a city.

The lot is cast into the lap; but the whole disposing thereof is of the Lord.

CHAPTER XVII

BETTER is a dry morsel, and quietness therewith, than an house full of sacrifices with strife.

A wise servant shall have rule over a son that causeth shame, and shall have part of the inheritance among the brethren.

The fining pot is for silver, and the furnace for gold: but the Lord trieth the hearts.

A wicked doer giveth heed to false lips; and a liar giveth ear to a naughty tongue.

Whoso mocketh the poor reproacheth his Maker: and he that is glad at calamities shall not be unpunished.

Children's children are the crown of old men; and the glory of children are their fathers.

Excellent speech becometh not a fool: much less do lying lips a prince.

A gift is as a precious stone in the eyes of him that hath it: whithersoever it turneth, it prospereth.

He that covereth a transgression seeketh love; but he that repeateth a matter separateth very friends.

A reproof entereth more into a wise man than an hundred stripes into a fool.

An evil man seeketh only rebellion: therefore a cruel messenger shall be sent against him.

Let a bear robbed of her whelps meet a man, rather than a fool in his folly.

Whoso rewardeth evil for good, evil shall not depart from his house.

The beginning of strife is as when one letteth out water: therefore leave off contention, before it be meddled with.

He that justifieth the wicked, and he that condemneth the just, even they both are abomination to the Lord.

Wherefore is there a price in the hand of a fool to get wisdom, seeing he hath no heart to it?

A friend loveth at all times, and a brother is born for adversity.

A man void of understanding striketh hands, and becometh surety in the presence of his friend.

He loveth transgression that loveth strife: and he that exalteth his gate seeketh destruction.

He that hath a froward heart findeth no good: and he that hath a perverse tongue falleth into mischief.

He that begetteth a fool doeth it to his sorrow: the father of a fool hath no joy.

A merry heart doeth good like a medicine: but a broken spirit drieth the bones.

A wicked man taketh a gift out of the bosom to pervert the ways of judgment.

NO LONGER mourn for me when I am dead
Than you shall hear the surly sullen bell
Give warning to the world that I am fled
From this vile world, with vilest worms to dwell:
Nay, if you read this line, remember not
The hand that writ it, for I love you so,
That I in your sweet thoughts would be forgot,
If thinking on me then should make you woe.
O, if, I say, you look upon this verse
When I perhaps compounded am with clay,
Do not so much as my poor name rehearse,
But let your love even with my life decay;
Lest the wise world should look into your moan,
And mock you with me after I am gone.

THAT time of year thou mayst in me behold
When yellow leaves, or none, or few, do hang
Upon those boughs which shake against the cold,
Bare ruin'd choirs, where late the sweet birds sang.
In me thou see'st the twylight of such day
As after sunset fadeth in the west;
Which by and by black night doth take away,
Death's second self, that seals up all in rest.
In me thou see'st the glowing of such fire,
That on the ashes of his youth doth lie,
As the death-bed whereon it must expire,
Consumed with that which it was nourish'd by.
This thou perceivest, which makes thy love more strong,
To love that well which thou must leave ere long.

Opposite top:

Horace Higgins: From the Book of Proverbs c1927

There is a suggestion of the printed page about this piece of writing, which is emphasised by the regularity of the layout. The scribe has given himself a considerable problem with the need to blend so many initial capital letters with the rest of his text, but has succeeded remarkably well in assimilating them so that they do not call too much attention to themselves.

V & A M MS Circ.485-1927

Opposite bottom:

Alfred Fairbank: Two Sonnets, by William Shakespeare 1929?

Alfred Fairbank has played a most important part in the revival of calligraphy in the 20th century, and his influence has extended far and wide. Yet unlike most of the scribes whose work is featured in the 20th century section of this book, he was not a professional calligrapher, spending most of his working life in government employment. Through his writing and his teaching, as well as by his example, he has been a prime mover in the acceptance of italic writing in many schools and by many amateur calligraphers.

V & A M MS Circ.287-1929

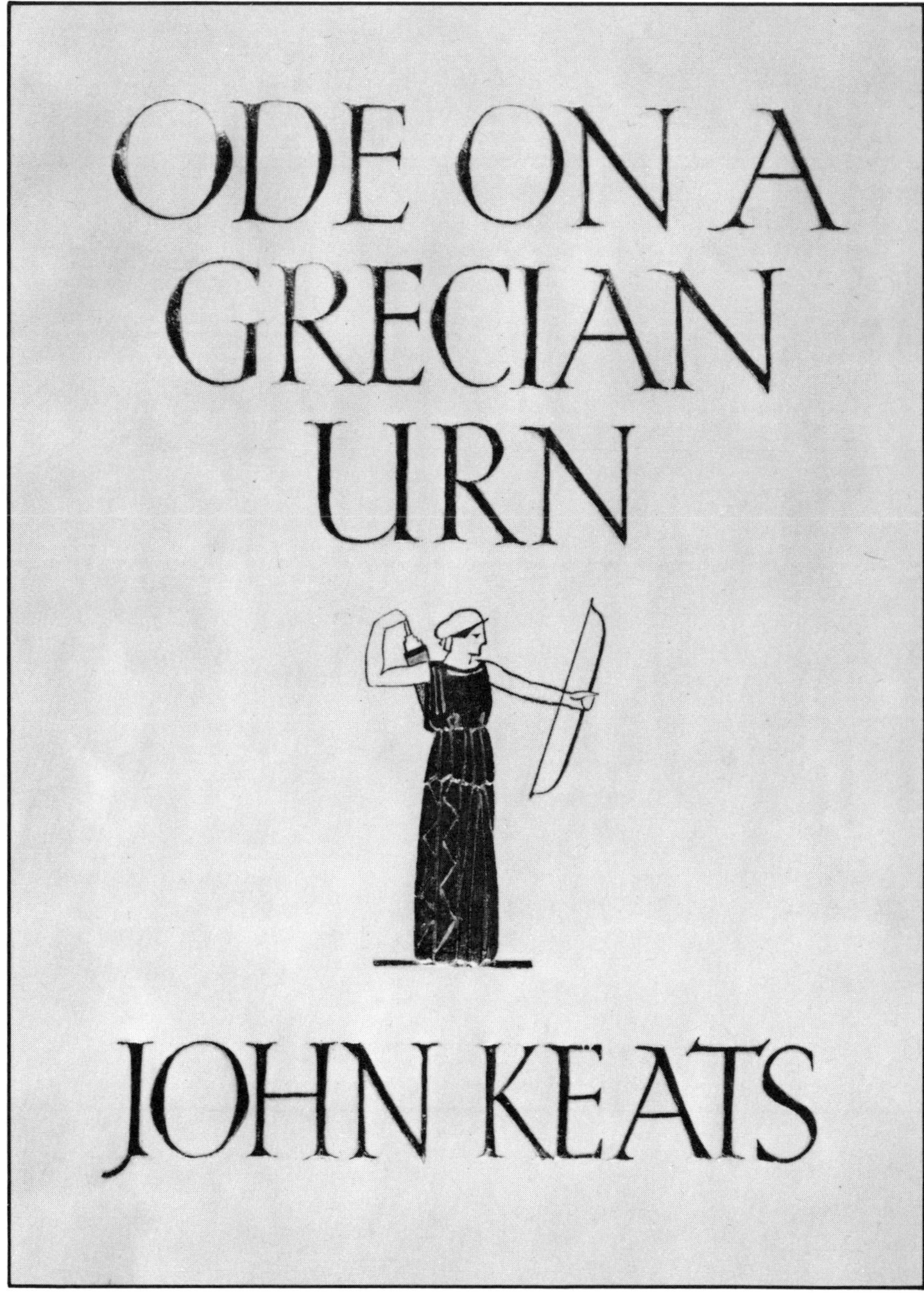

Irene Base: Ode on a Grecian urn, by John Keats c1930

This page is written out in burnished gold which, sadly, does not photograph well enough to do justice to Irene Base's skill as a calligrapher and illuminator; the importance of her work in this field caused her to be chosen to write the chapter on gilding in The calligrapher's handbook, *1956.*

V & A M MS Circ.41-1934

A CAROL

THE GLOOMY NIGHT EMBRACED THE PLACE
Wherein the noble Infant lay:
The Babe looked up and show'd His face;
In spite of darkness it was day
It was Thy day, Sweet, and did rise,
Not from the East but from Thine eyes.

WE SAW THEE IN THY BALMY NEST,
Young dawn of our eternal day,
We saw Thine eyes break from their east
And chase the trembling shades away.
We saw Thee and we blessed the sight;
We saw Thee by Thine own sweet light.

WELCOME, ALL WONDERS IN ONE SIGHT,
Eternity shut in a span,
Summer in winter, day in night,
Heaven in earth and God in man;
Great Little One, whose lowly birth
Lifts earth to heaven, stoops heaven to earth.

TO THEE MEEK MAJESTY, SOFT KING
Of simple graces and sweet loves,
Each one of us his lamb will bring,
And each his pair of silver doves;
Till burnt in fire of Thy fair eyes,
Ourselves become our sacrifice.

by
Richard Crashaw
1613
1649

Rosemary Ratcliffe: A carol, by Richard Crashaw c1930

Rosemary Ratcliffe succeeded Graily Hewitt as a teacher of calligraphy at the Central School of Arts & Crafts in London in 1930. The layout of this piece of work is interesting in that she has given such emphasis to the first line of each verse, but has balanced them with the title of the poem and the colophon (in the form of a cross), so that they act as a counterbalance to the horizontal lines. The curved ends to the descenders add weight to this effect.

V & A M MS Circ.50-134

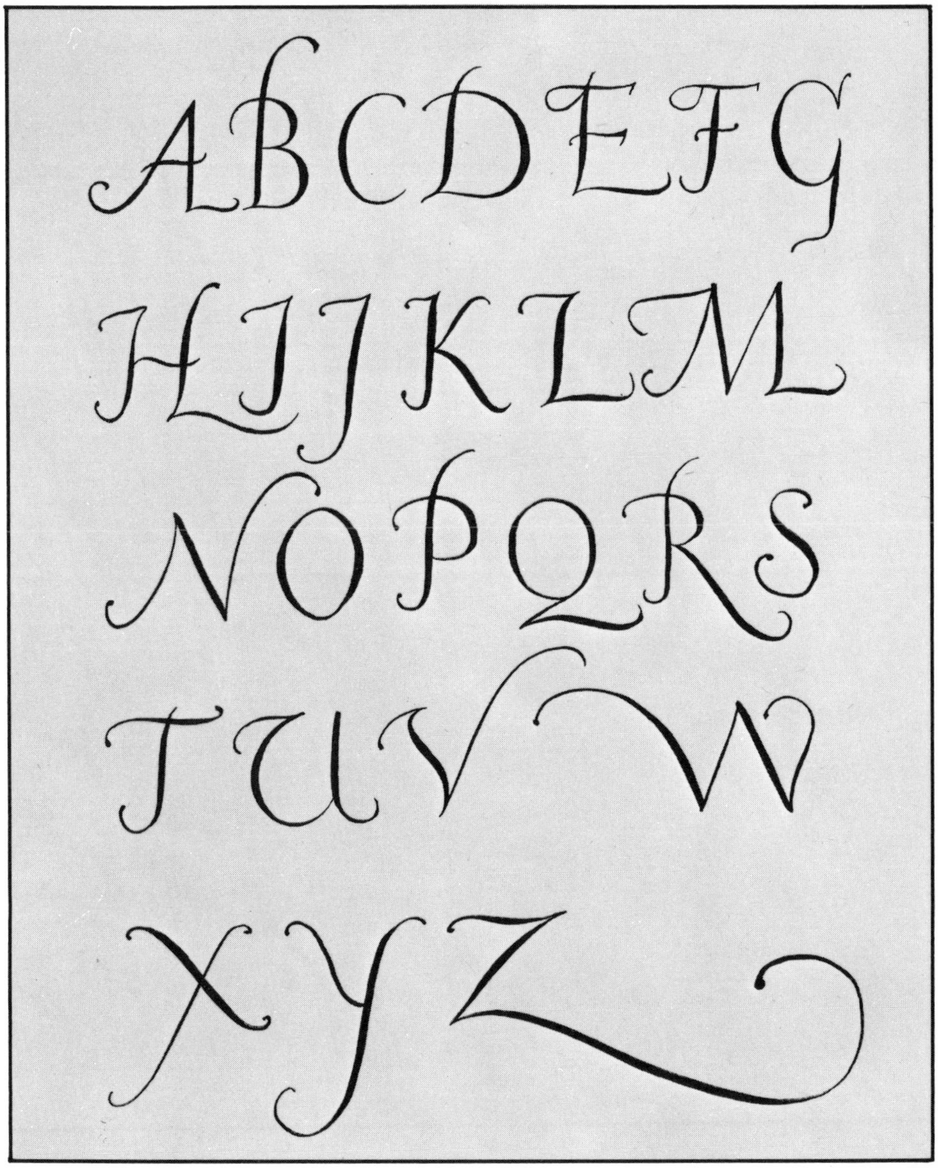

Reynolds Stone: A book of lettering. 1935

The name of Reynolds Stone has become associated with a particular style of writing which he made very much his own. It was based on the Italian Renaissance hands, and made use of restrained flourishes. Although a fine engraver of book illustration, it was his work in small personal items such as bookplates that showed his calligraphy at its best.

V & A M L 699-1935 23 × 17.5

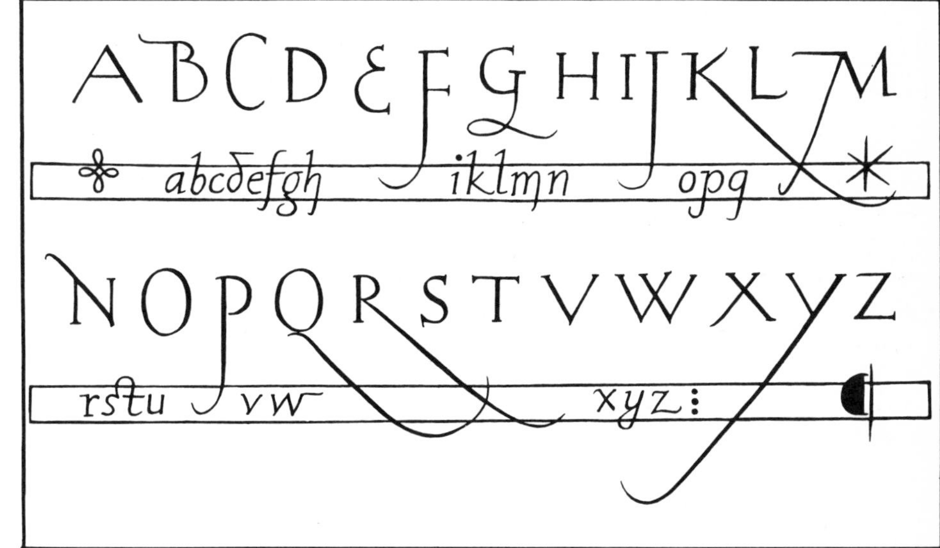

Rudolf Koch and Berthold Wolpe: Das ABC-Buchlein: Zeichnungen von Rudolf Koch und Berthold Wolpe. In Holz- und Metallschnitten von Fritz Kredel und Gustav Eichenauer. 1934

This little book was published in the year that Koch died. For much of his life he was interested in letter forms, both typographic and calligraphic, and the same is true of Berthold Wolpe, who has also published works on various aspects of both subjects.

V & AM L 678-1936 15 × 23

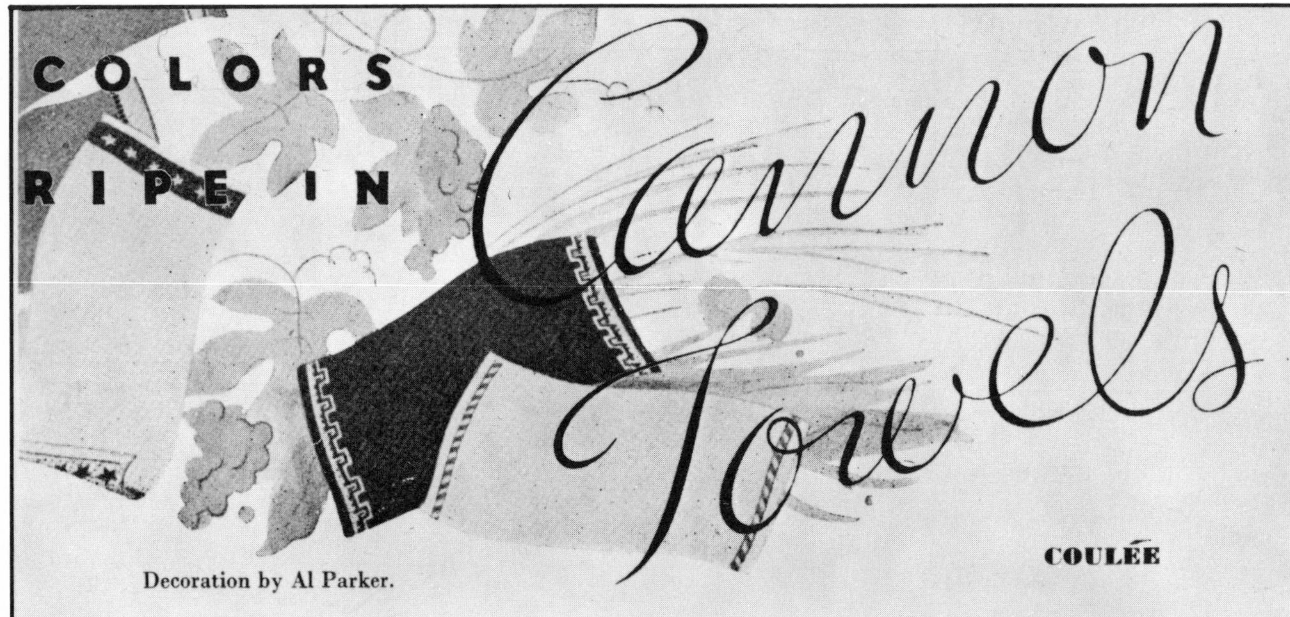

Decoration by Al Parker.

COULÉE

New 1931 Sterling
by Gorham

RONDE

Finesse

COULÉE

Ivory Soap

BÂTARDE

Opposite:

Tommy Thompson: The script letter, its form, construction and application. 1939 (One of the 'How to do it' series)

This illustration shows the use of scripts in commercial advertising art, and the author has given the styles the names which link them with traditional forms of writing.

V & A M L 662-1940 24.5 × 19

Right:

Irene Wellington: Il faut que France continue, by Charles Peguy 1950

Irene Wellington is one of the great names of modern calligraphy. She was a pupil of Edward Johnston and has herself taught many of the best-known later calligraphers. She has produced a great variety of work, both formal and informal, as well as the Irene Wellington Copy Books. *This is quite a late piece; it shows not only her script but also her feeling for its layout on the page. The work is written on vellum.*

V & A M MS L 4601-1978
Title-page 20.5 × 14

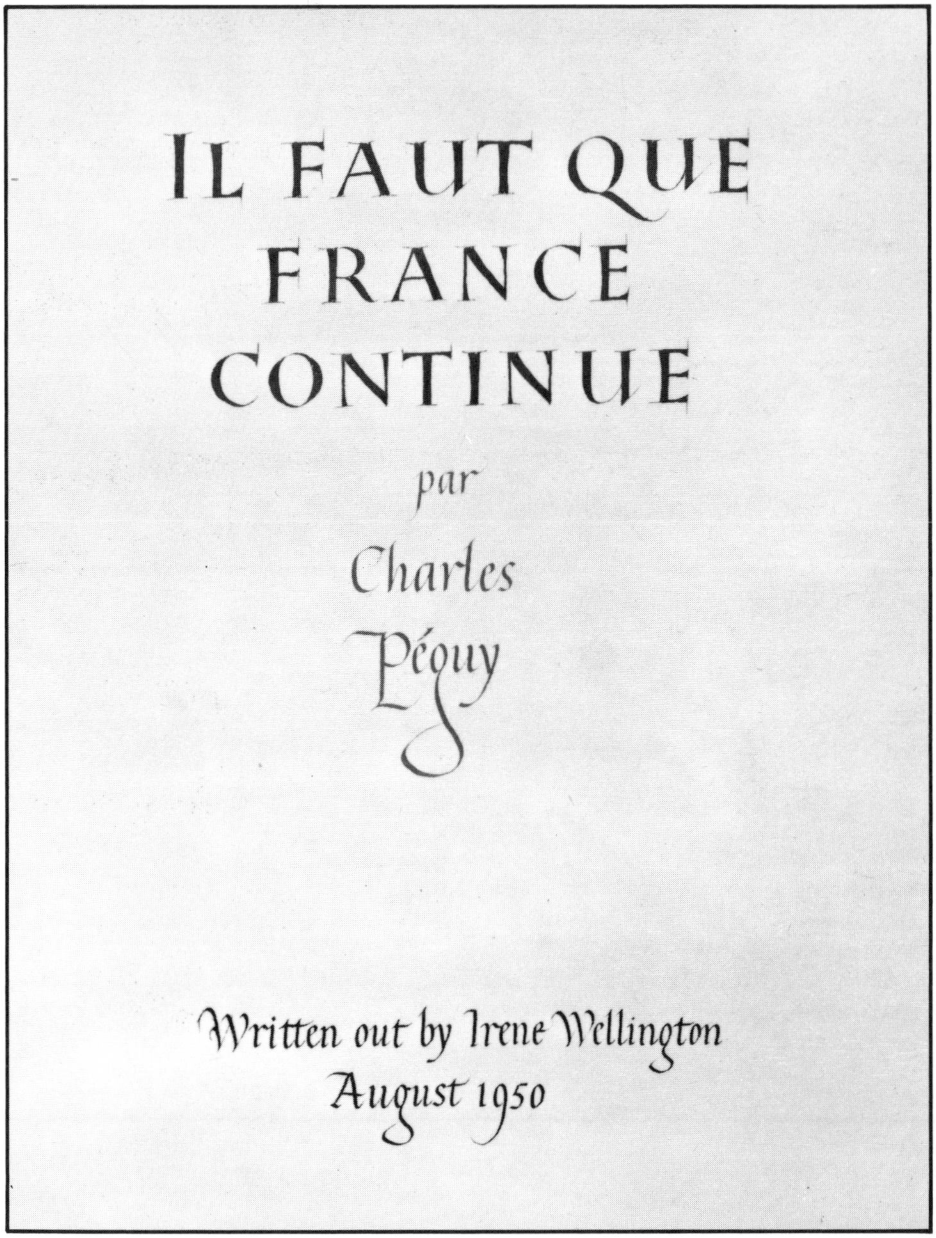

Hermann Zapf: Feder und Stichel: Alphabete und Schriftblätter in zeitgemässer Darstellung, Geschrieben von H. Zapf. 1950

This book indicates the interest in calligraphic forms among designers and typographers since the Second World War; the result has been the use of calligraphic forms in many ways, but especially in display and advertisement art. The essentially 20th century style of lettering here nevertheless looks back to uncial and half-uncial models of earlier centuries. Both Rudolf Koch and Hermann Zapf have played a significant rôle in the development of 20th century German calligraphy.

V & A M L 2422-1950 24 × 32

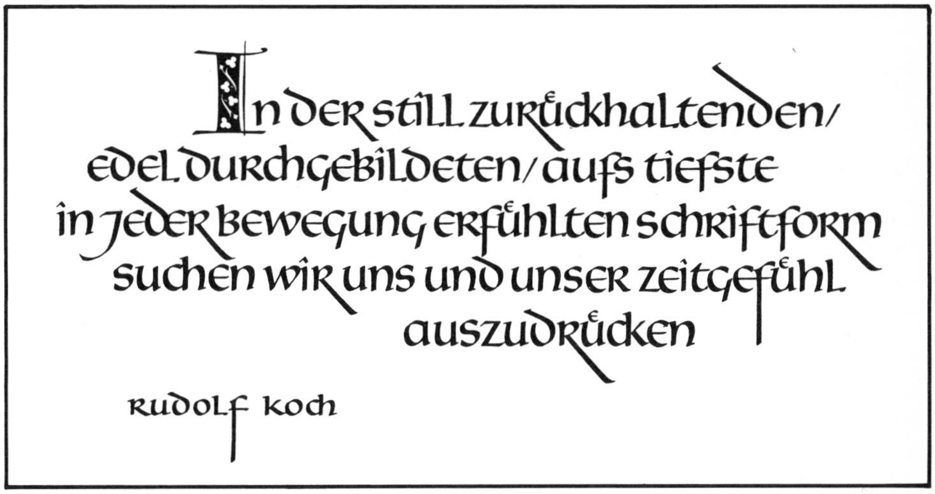

IL FAUT QUE
FRANCE
CONTINUE

par
Charles
Péguy

Written out by Irene Wellington
August 1950

In der still zurückhaltenden/
edel durchgebildeten/ aufs tiefste
in jeder bewegung erfühlten schriftform
suchen wir uns und unser zeitgefühl
auszudrücken

rudolf koch

Quelle est cette odeur agréable ?

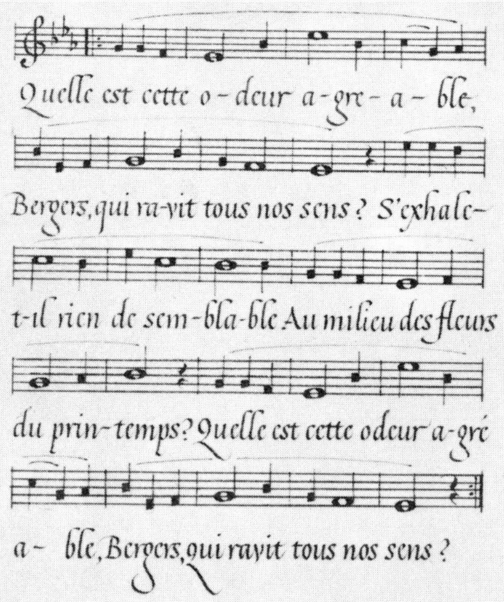

Quelle est cette o - deur a - gré - a - ble,
Bergers, qui ra-vit tous nos sens ? S'exhale-
t-il rien de sem - bla - ble Au milieu des fleurs
du prin - temps ? Quelle est cette odeur a - gré
a - ble, Bergers, qui ravit tous nos sens ?

Mais quelle éclatante lumière
Dans la nuit vient frapper nos yeux ?
L'astre du jour dans sa carrière,
Fut-il jamais si radieux ?
Mais quelle éclatante lumière
Dans la nuit vient frapper nos yeux ?

A Bethléem, dans une crèche,
Il vient de vous naitre un Sauveur.
Allons, que rien ne vous empêche
D'adorer votre rédempteur.
A Bethléem, dans une crèche,
Il vient de vous naître un Sauveur.

Dorothy Mahoney: Carol 1951

Dorothy Mahoney studied under Edward Johnston, and followed him in teaching lettering and calligraphy at the Royal College of Art in London and at the Central School of Arts & Crafts. She has thus been a means of transmitting Johnston's methods and ideas to a younger generation of scribes.

V & A M Circ.181-1953

Opposite:
Wendy Westover: A passage from 'The Land' by Victoria Sackville-West 1952

Wendy Westover studied calligraphy with Margaret Alexander, and she also studied lettering and letter cutting with David Kindersley. It is not surprising therefore that this manuscript has a bold, almost sculptural appearance. The form of lettering which she has chosen for the two lines of the heading should be noted, as well as her use of a typical medieval method of writing in smaller letters if it appeared that the text line would be too long for the page.

V & A M MS Circ.179-1953

IN FEBRUARY

IF THE DAYS BE CLEAR

The waking bee, still drowsy on the wing,
Will guess the opening of another year
And blunder out to seek another spring.
Crashing through winter sunlight's pallid gold,
His clumsiness sets catkins on the willow
Ashake like lambs' tails in the early fold.
But when the rimy afternoon turns cold
And undern squalls buffet the chilly fellow,
He'll seek the hive's warm waxen welcoming
And set about the chamber's classic mould.
And then pell-mell his harvest follows swift,
Blossom & borage, lime and balm & clover,
On Downs the thyme, on cliff the scantling thrift,
Everywhere bees go racing with the hours,
For every bee becomes a drunken lover
Standing upon his head to sup the flowers.

Taken from "The Land," by Victoria Sackville-West

Written out by Wendy Westover, December 1952

Margery Raisbeck: Part of a prayer by Dr Isaac Barrow 1953

Margery Raisbeck was a pupil of Edward Johnston, and her style of writing reflects her master, since it is based on the 12th century Winchester hand which he used later in his career. Although the extended hairlines with which she decorates her script have good medieval precedents, they do not add to its beauty, while the form of some of the letters appears to look back to the 18th century rather than to an earlier period.

V & A M *MS Circ.206-1953*

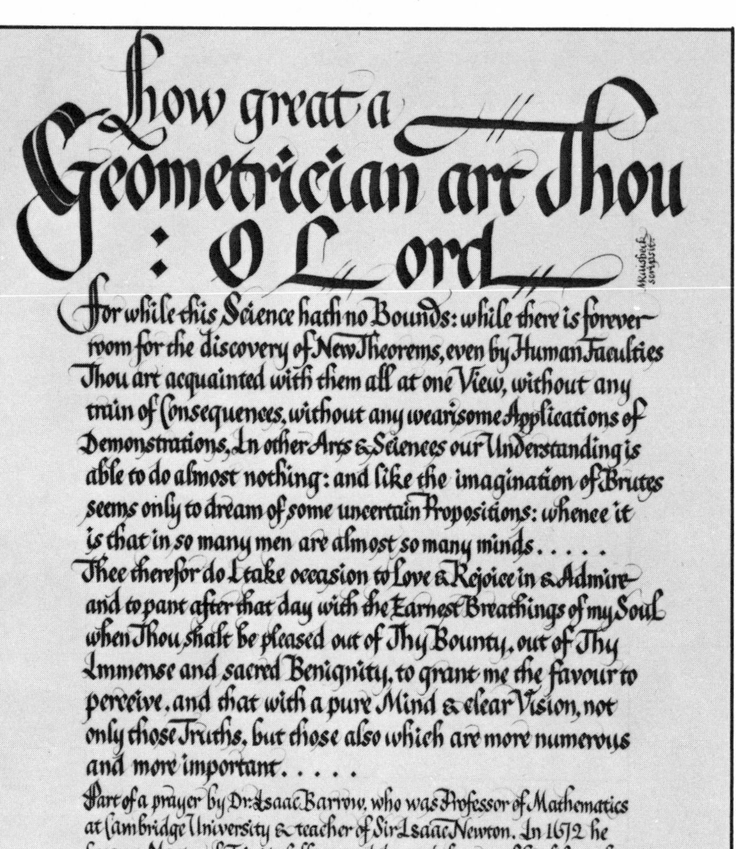
How great a Geometrician art Thou : O Lord

For while this Science hath no Bounds: while there is forever room for the discovery of New Theorems, even by Human Faculties Thou art acquainted with them all at one View, without any train of Consequences, without any wearisome Applications of Demonstrations, In other Arts & Sciences our Understanding is able to do almost nothing: and like the imagination of Brutes seems only to dream of some uncertain Propositions: whence it is that in so many men are almost so many minds.....
Thee therfor do I take occasion to Love & Rejoice in & Admire and to pant after that day with the Earnest Breathings of my Soul when Thou shalt be pleased out of Thy Bounty, out of Thy Immense and sacred Benignity, to grant me the favour to perceive, and that with a pure Mind & clear Vision, not only those Truths, but those also which are more numerous and more important.....

Part of a prayer by Dr. Isaac Barrow, who was Professor of Mathematics at Cambridge University & teacher of Sir Isaac Newton. In 1672 he became Master of Trinity College and devoted the rest of his life to the study of Divinity.

Sheila M. Salt: The singing-birds of Selbourne 1953

The charm of this piece arises to a certain extent from the contrasts which it offers. These are produced by the use of different coloured inks, by a variation in the scripts, and by the delicate use of colour in the depiction of the various birds.

V & A M *Circ.167-1953*

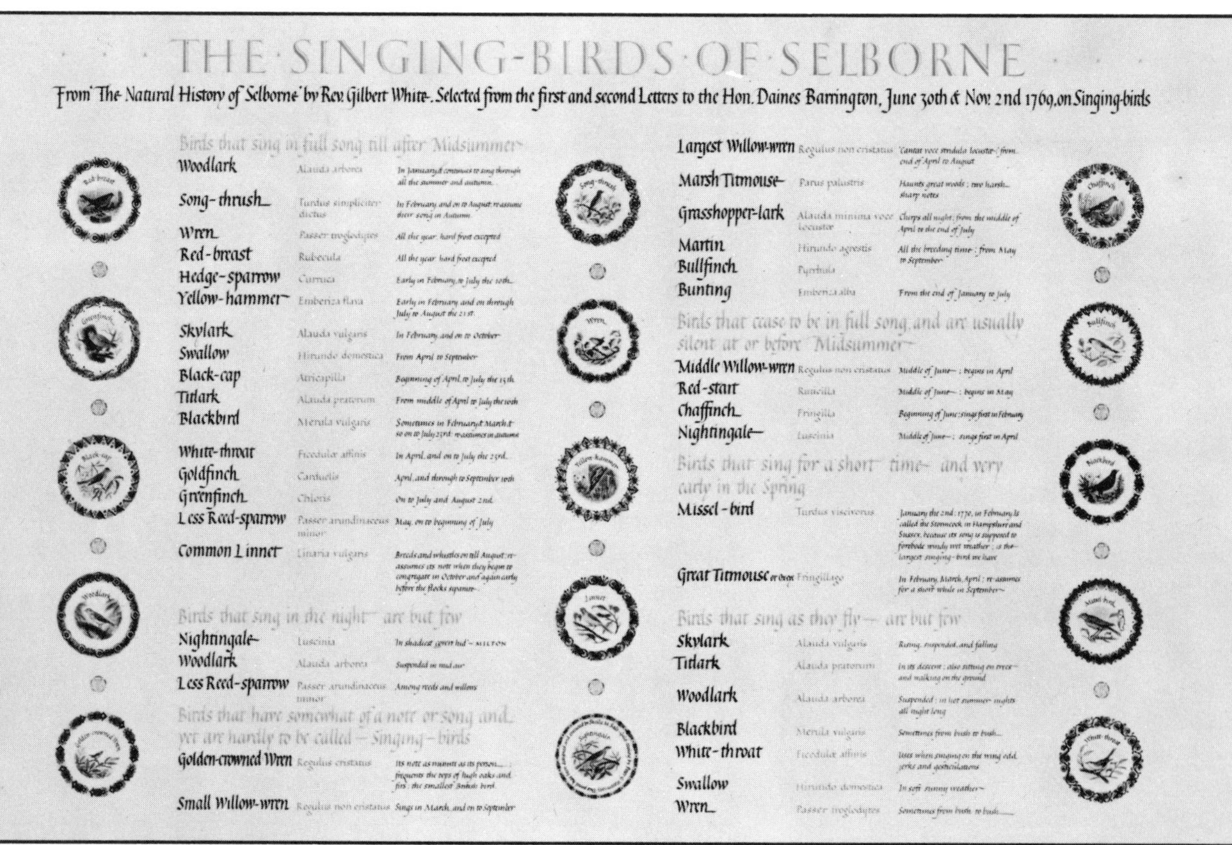
THE · SINGING-BIRDS · OF · SELBORNE

From 'The Natural History of Selborne' by Rev. Gilbert White. Selected from the first and second Letters to the Hon. Daines Barrington, June 30th & Nov. 2nd 1769, on Singing-birds

Birds that sing in full song till after Midsummer

Woodlark	Alauda arborea	In January & continues to sing through all the summer and autumn.
Song-thrush	Turdus simpliciter dictus	In February and on to August: re-assume their song in Autumn
Wren	Passer troglodytes	All the year: hard frost excepted
Red-breast	Rubecula	All the year: hard frost excepted
Hedge-sparrow	Curruca	Early in February, to July the 10th.
Yellow-hammer	Emberiza flava	Early in February and on through July to August the 21st.
Skylark	Alauda vulgaris	In February and on to October
Swallow	Hirundo domestica	From April to September
Black-cap	Atricapilla	Beginning of April, to July the 15th.
Titlark	Alauda pratorum	From middle of April to July the 10th
Blackbird	Merula vulgaris	Sometimes in February & March & so on to July 23rd: re-assumes in autumn
White-throat	Ficedulæ affinis	In April, and on to July the 23rd.
Goldfinch	Carduelis	April, and through to September 16th
Greenfinch	Chloris	On to July and August 2nd.
Less Reed-sparrow	Passer arundinaceus minor	May, on to beginning of July
Common Linnet	Linaria vulgaris	Breeds and whistles on till August: re-assumes its note when they begin to congregate in October and again early before the flocks separate.

Birds that sing in the night – are but few

Nightingale	Luscinia	'In shadiest cover hid' – MILTON
Woodlark	Alauda arborea	Suspended in mid air
Less Reed-sparrow	Passer arundinaceus minor	Among reeds and willows

Birds that have somewhat of a note or song and yet are hardly to be called – Singing-birds

Golden-crowned Wren	Regulus cristatus	Its note as minute as its person; frequents the tops of high oaks and firs: the smallest British bird.
Small Willow-wren	Regulus non cristatus	Sings in March, and on to September
Largest Willow-wren	Regulus non cristatus	'Cantat voce stridula locustæ'; from end of April to August
Marsh Titmouse	Parus palustris	Haunts great woods; two harsh sharp notes
Grasshopper-lark	Alauda minima voce locustæ	Chirps all night; from the middle of April to the end of July
Martin	Hirundo agrestis	All the breeding time; from May to September
Bullfinch	Pyrrhula	
Bunting	Emberiza alba	From the end of January to July

Birds that cease to be in full song, and are usually silent at or before Midsummer

Middle Willow-wren	Regulus non cristatus	Middle of June; begins in April
Red-start	Ruticilla	Middle of June; begins in May
Chaffinch	Fringilla	Beginning of June: sings first in February
Nightingale	Luscinia	Middle of June; sings first in April

Birds that sing for a short time and very early in the Spring

Missel-bird	Turdus viscivorus	January the 2nd: 1770, in February. Is called the Stormcock in Hampshire and Sussex, because its song is supposed to forebode windy wet weather; is the largest singing-bird we have
Great Titmouse or Ox-eye	Fringillago	In February, March, April; re-assumes for a short while in September

Birds that sing as they fly – are but few

Skylark	Alauda vulgaris	Rising, suspended, and falling
Titlark	Alauda pratorum	In its descent; also sitting on trees and walking on the ground
Woodlark	Alauda arborea	Suspended; in hot summer nights all night long
Blackbird	Merula vulgaris	Sometimes from bush to bush
White-throat	Ficedulæ affinis	Uses when singing on the wing odd jerks and gesticulations
Swallow	Hirundo domestica	In soft sunny weather
Wren	Passer troglodytes	Sometimes from bush to bush

V. Angelus domini nuntiavit Mariæ:
R. Et concepit de Spiritu Sancto:

Ave Maria, gratia plena, Dominus
tecum: benedicta tu in mulieribus, et
benedictus fructus ventris tui, Jesus.
Sancta Maria, mater Dei, ora
pro nobis peccatoribus, nunc et in
hora mortis nostræ: Amen.

V. Ecce ancilla Domini:
R. Fiat mihi secundum verbum tuum:

Ave Maria

V. Et verbum caro factum est:
R. Et habitavit in nobis:

Ave Maria

V. Ora pro nobis Sancta Dei Genitrix:
R. Ut digni efficiamur promissionibus Christi:

Oremus

Gratiam tuam, quæsumus Domine, menti-
bus nostris infunde, ut qui angelo nuntiante,
Christi Filii tui Incarnationem cognovim-
us per Passionem eius et crucem ad Res-
urrectionis gloriam perducamur. Per eundem Christum Dominum nostrum. Amen.

Ruth Mary Wood: The Angelus
1953

This manuscript is written out in red and black ink, and the text is placed interestingly on the page. Nevetheless, the script shows some of the faults of its medieval counterpart, in that the minims are so placed as to render some of the words illegible: nuntiavit *in the first line and* Dominus *in the third, are examples of this fault.*

V & A M Circ.201-1953

CHORUS

IN AN OLD HOUSE there is always listening, and more is heard than is spoken.
And what is spoken remains in the room, waiting for the future to hear it.
And whatever happens began in the past, and presses hard on the future.
The agony in the curtained bedroom, whether of birth or of dying,
Gathers in to itself all the voices of the past, and projects them into the future.

The treble voices on the lawn
The mowing of hay in summer
The dogs and the old pony
The stumble and the wail of little pain
The chopping of wood in autumn
And the singing in the kitchen
And the steps at night in the corridor
The moment of sudden loathing
And the season of stifled sorrow
The whisper, the transparent deception
The keeping up of appearances
The making the best of a bad job
All twined and tangled together, all are recorded.

There is no avoiding these things
And we know nothing of exorcism
And whether in Argos or England
There are certain inflexible laws
Unalterable, in the nature of music.

There is nothing at all to be done about it,
There is nothing to do about anything,
And now it is nearly time for the news
We must listen to the weather report
And the international catastrophes.

from "THE FAMILY REUNION" by T.S. Eliot O.M.

John Woodcock: Quotations from 'The Family Reunion' by T. S. Eliot 1953

John Woodcock studied with Dorothy Mahoney and Irene Wellington; he also wrote the chapter on the design of formal scripts in The Calligrapher's Handbook, *1956. His choice of layout and scripts for this piece is especially interesting, particularly the additional weight given to the initial* T *in three places, in order to indicate a break or pause in the development of the theme.*

V&AM MS Circ.169-1953

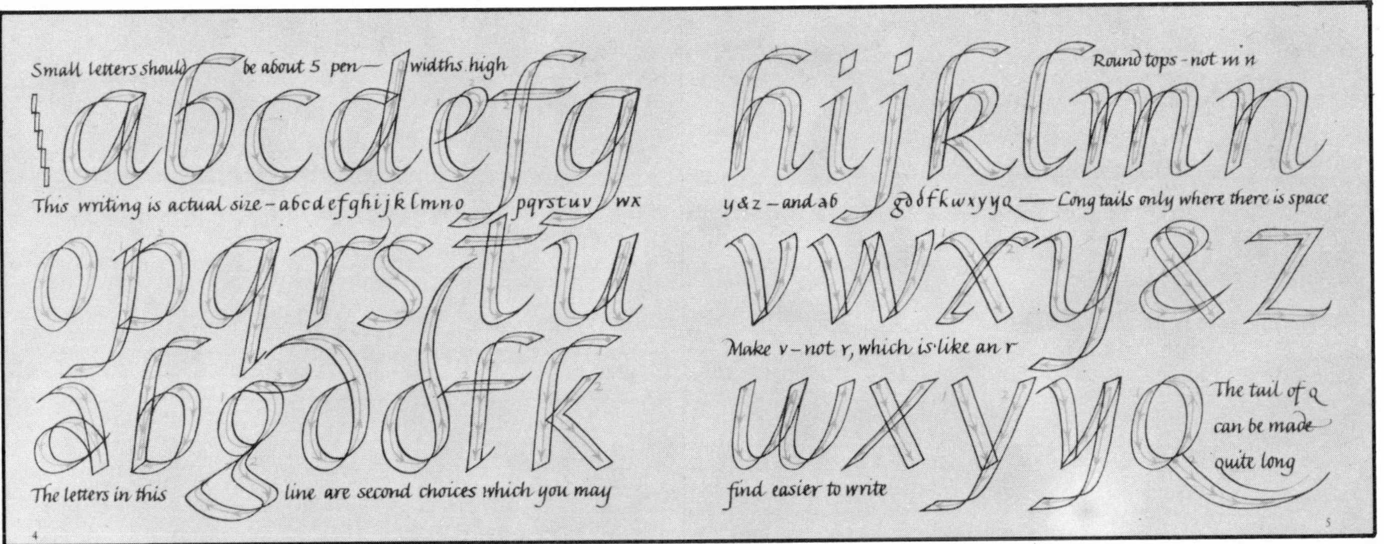

Small letters should be about 5 pen— widths high
Round tops - not m n
This writing is actual size - abcdefghijklmno pqrstuv wx
y&z - and ab
Long tails only where there is space
Make v - not r, which is like an r
The tail of q can be made quite long
The letters in this line are second choices which you may find easier to write

George L. Thomson: Better handwriting. (Puffin Picture Book 96) 1954

The title of this book, and the fact that it was issued in a popular paperback series, is indicative of the interest in handwriting among many people today. At a time when it is deteriorating, not least owing to the ubiquitous use of the ball-point pen, there is a desire for improvement, and a number of manuals have been published to meet this demand. In this work, Thomson advocates the italic hand as being not only more pleasing to the eye, but also less likely to disintegrate when written at speed.

V&AM L 2708-1954 18 × 22

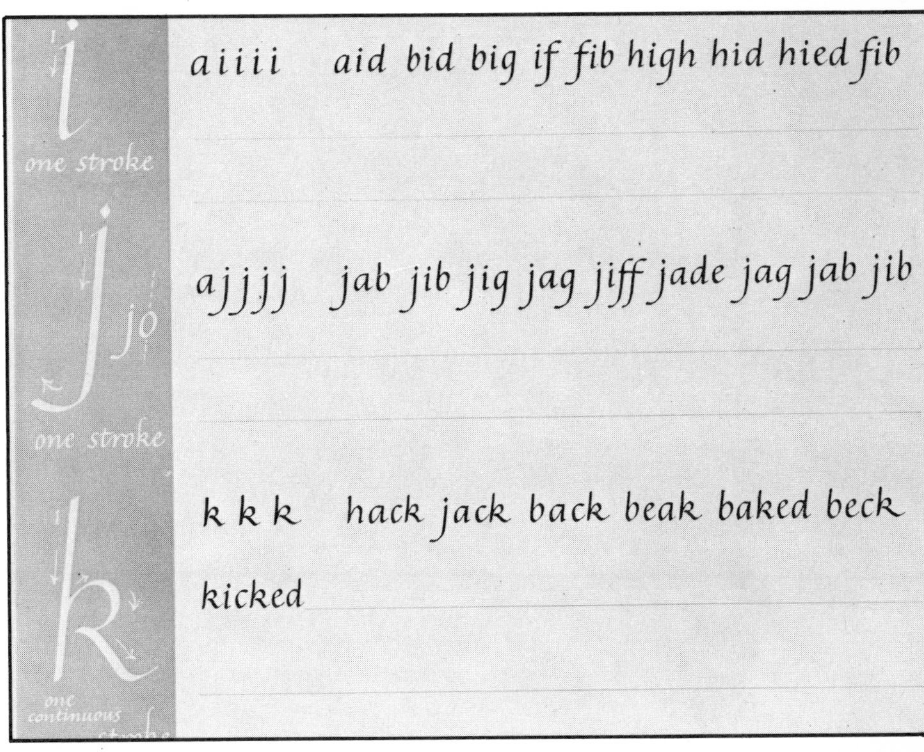

Irene Wellington: The Irene Wellington copy book 1957

Many of the modern scribes have also produced copy books as did the writing masters of past centuries. Irene Wellington has taught many of today's leading calligraphers, and an example of her manuscript work is also illustrated in the present book (p. 354).

V&AM L 3722-1957 18 × 23

Die Bücher sind einsame
Kapellen, die der Mensch in den
wildromantischen Gegenden des
Lebens auf den höchsten und
schönsten Standpunkten errich-
tet, und auf seinen Wanderungen
nicht bloß der Aussicht wegen,
sondern hauptsächlich deswegen
besucht, um sich in ihnen von
den Zerstreuungen des Lebens
zu sammeln und seine Gedanken
auf ein anderes Sein, als nur das
sinnliche, zu richten.

LUDWIG FEUERBACH

Opposite:
Friedrich Poppl: Quotation from Ludwig Feuerbach. 1960

Friedrich Poppl is a German calligrapher and this example of his script suggests a very swift and free movement of the pen, which can yet provide a disciplined result. The 'white-on-black' effect has good precedents and several examples are illustrated in this book. In this illustration the eye is held more by the decorative pattern of the piece as a whole than by the individual letter-forms.

V & A M MS Circ.164-1966

abcdefghij
klmnopqrs
ſtuvwxyz

Top:
Hans Burkardt: Pinselschriften 1958

Brushstroke scripts have had a considerable vogue since the 1940's and have been extensively employed in advertisement art. They convey a sense of directness and immediacy which is lacking in the more formal scripts, as well as offering greater freedom to the calligrapher.

V & A M L 2136-1961 25.5 × 20.

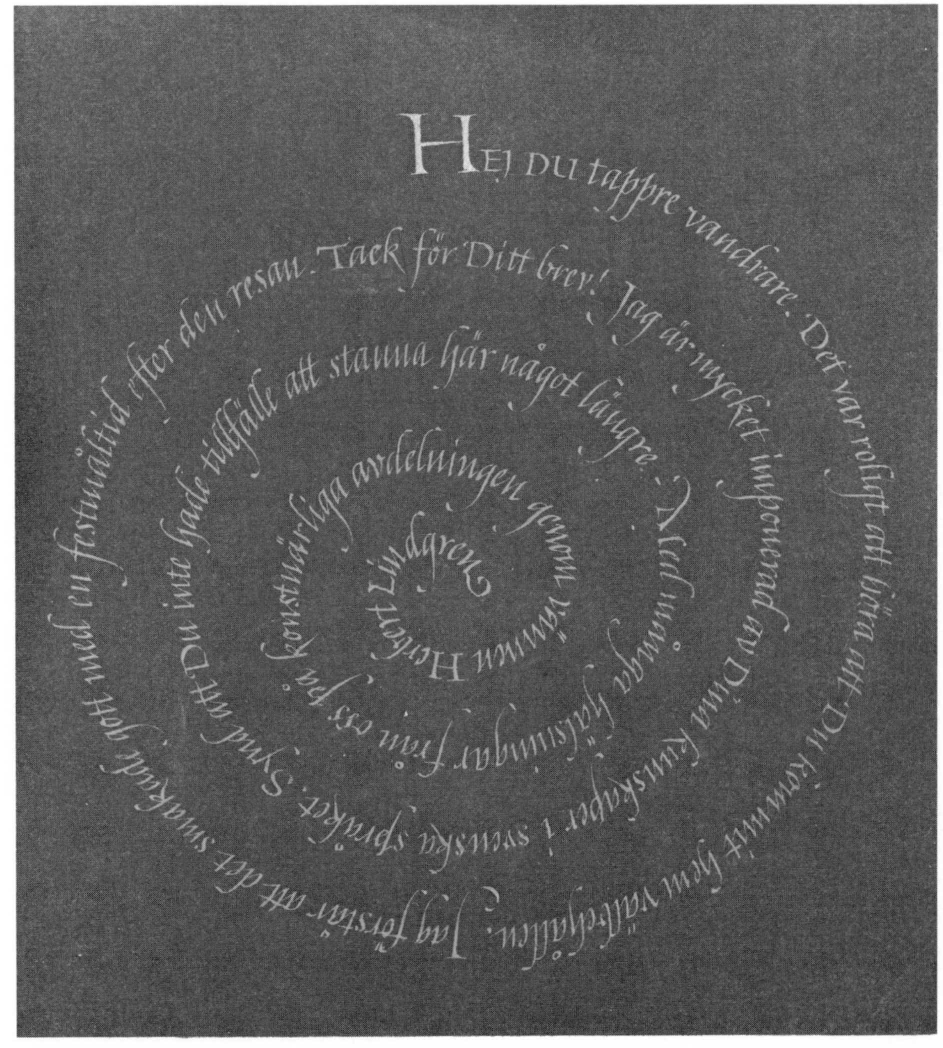

Bottom:
Herbert Lindgren: Circular greetings letter. 1960

The illustration does scant justice to this example of calligraphy from Sweden, which is written out in white ink on dark paper. The 'circular' form of writing has been quite popular among some later 20th century calligraphers — Anthony Gardner was another scribe who frequently used it.

V & A M Circ.723-1966

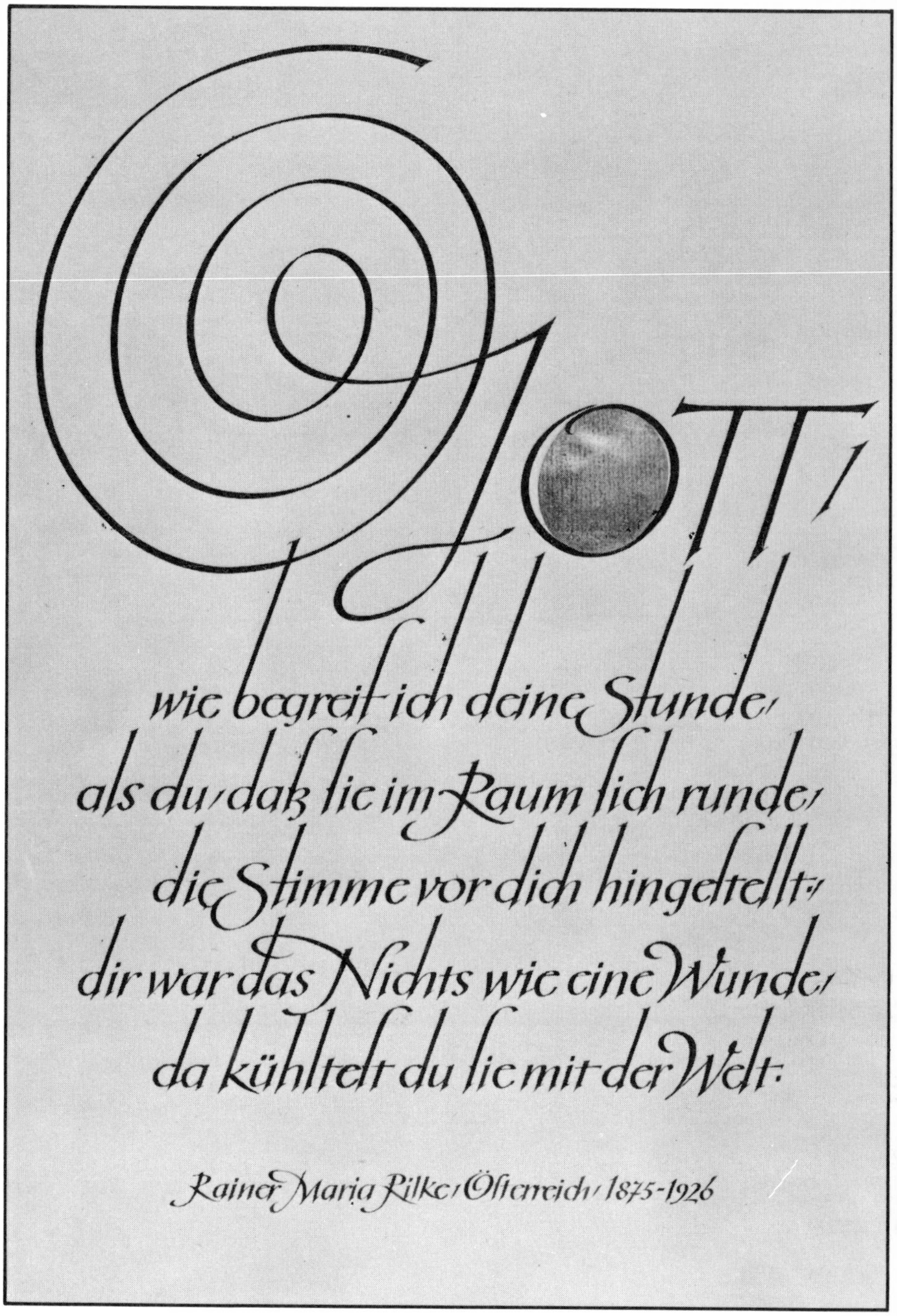

Friedrich Neugebauer: 'Gott, wie begreif ich'. . ., by Rainer Maria Rilke 1961

Neugebauer is Austrian, and the example of his work illustrated here is written out on blue paper, with the letter O of 'Gott' filled in with gold. In common with a number of European contemporary calligraphers, he experiments with the forms of the letters so that they make patterns on the page. This can sometimes lead to illegibility — the G here is hardly recognisable — but for some modern calligraphers the letters are only a starting point which lead, not to a readable text, but to an abstract design which happens to employ words.

V & A M MS Circ.294-1966

GOTT,
wie begreif ich deine Stunde,
als du, daß ſie im Raum ſich runde,
die Stimme vor dich hingeſtellt:
dir war das Nichts wie eine Wunde,
da kühlteſt du ſie mit der Welt.

Rainer Maria Rilke, Öſterreich, 1875-1926

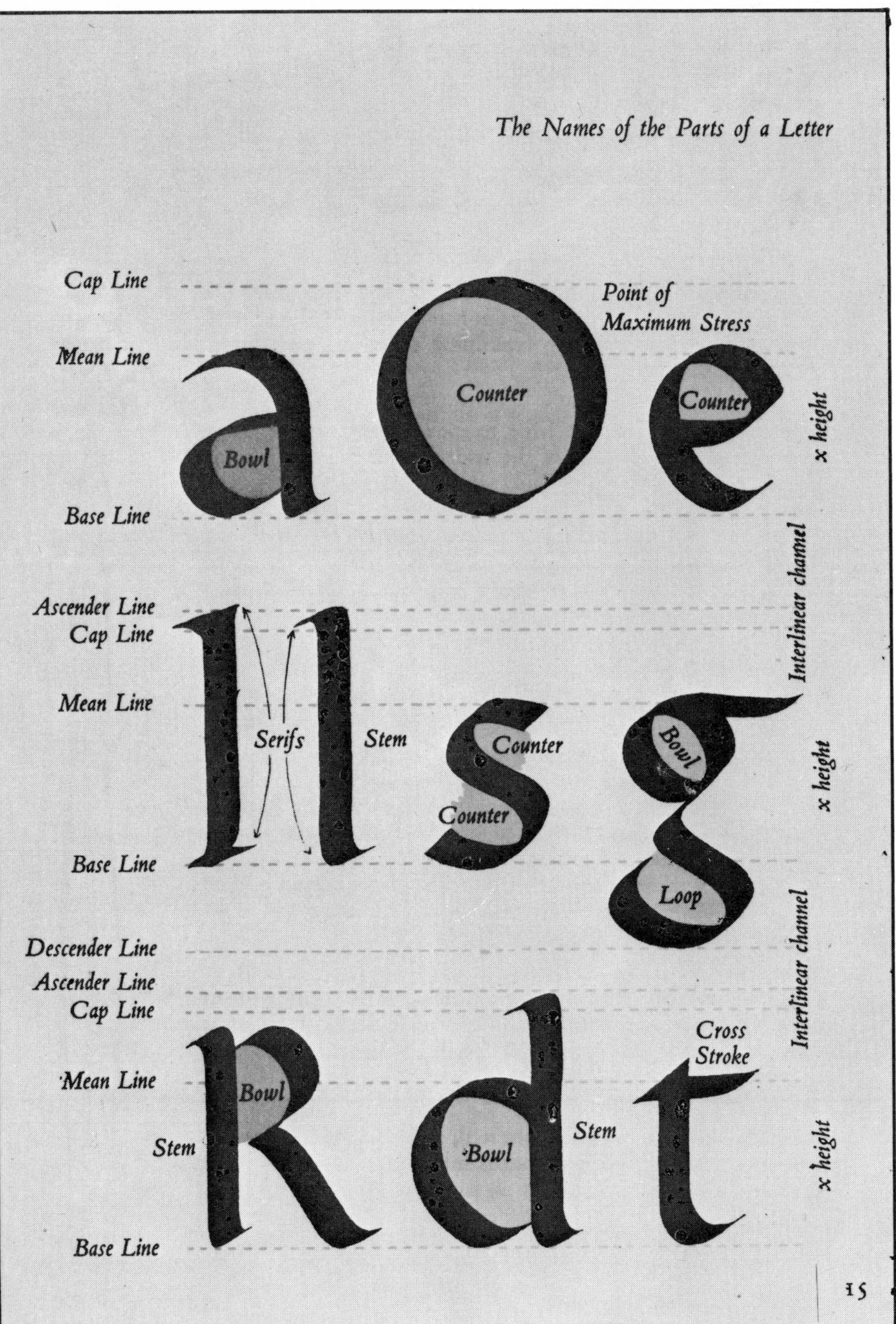

John R. Biggs: The craft of the pen 1961

John Biggs has written a number of books on calligraphy and typography. In this one he considers the pen as a suitable instrument for the production of small posters, bookjackets and other types of work where letters two or three inches high are required. This particular illustration is especially useful in that so many writers on calligraphy use technical terms for the parts of a letter, without ever defining them.

V&AM L3724-1961 22 × 15

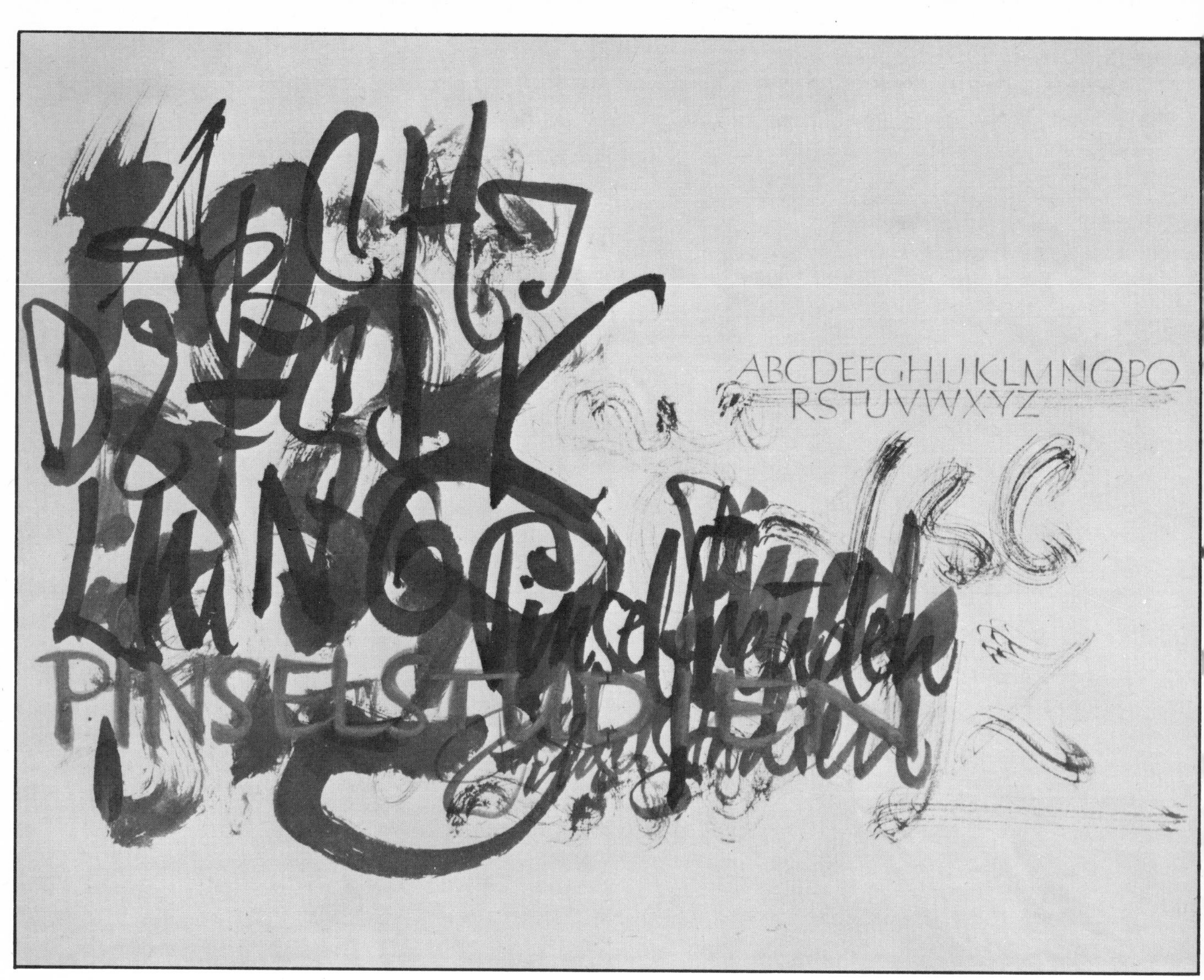

Forbilledet for trykskriften, kursiven såvel som antikva-skriften var de håndskrevne bog- & brevskrifter, som udvikledes af de tidlige italienske humanister under deres afskrivning af den klassiske litteratur. Den skrevne humanist-kursiv nåede med tiden en behersket og rendyrket form, som 1500-tallets kalligrafer benævnte CANCELLARESCA. Den blev forbilledet for to kursive trykskrifter, som byggede på hver sin version af cancellaresca-skriften og derfor blev væsensforskellige. Den tidligste af disse blev brugt fra 1501 af den venezianske forlægger og bogtrykker Aldus, som gennem sin skriftskærer Francesco Griffo, kopierede den dagligdags håndskrift, som blev anvendt i det pavelige kancelli til almindelig korrespondance og som benævnes Cancellaresca corsiva.

Opposite top:

Karl Georg Hoefer: Pinselstudien 1962

This work is in the form of a folder. It contains a variety of alphabets (some of them unrecognisable!). Colour and gold are also used. This illustration shows both a formal square capital as well as a flowing script of the kind that is sometimes used in advertisement art.

V & A M   MS L 136-1966   30 × 20

Opposite bottom:

Bent Rohde: An example of 'cancellaresca corsiva', as reproduced in 'ABC of lettering and printing types', by Erik Lindegren. 1964

This piece of writing was made for Lindegren's very informative work on calligraphy, lettering and printing. Rohde is a Danish calligrapher and it is interesting to note the widespread interest in the hands of the Renaissance among many contemporary scribes.

V & A M   MS Circ.298-1966

Die Weihnachtsgeſchichte

ES BEGAB SICH

ABER ZU DER ZEIT DASS

EIN GEBOT VON DEM

KAISER AVGVSTVS

ausging daß alle welt geſchätzt
würde ¢ Und dieſe ſchätzung
war die allererſte und geſchah
zu der zeit da cyrenius land-
pfleger in ſyrien war ¢ Und je-

Max Waibel: Die Erzählung von der Geburt Christi wie geschrieben steht bei Lukas 2, 1-52, Johannes 1, 1-14, Matthäus 1.23. 1964

The new school of calligraphy was taken from England to Germany by Anna Simons, one of Edward Johnston's pupils, who translated his manual Writing & illuminating, & lettering, *1906, and a lively interest in calligraphy has continued in Germany. Modern calligraphy there has taken many forms and has been much used in advertisement art; in this example we can see the continuing influence of the German traditional 'Fraktur' script. The opening lines of the text are written over colours of blue, pink and mauve.*

V & A M   MS L 604-1979   39.5 × 29.5

Just as one would wish to speak not only clearly but with some civilized and musical quality of grace, so one may write and the writing be worthy of the name of calligraphy – by which is meant handwriting considered as an art. Alfred Fairbank

The development of letters was a purely natural process in the course of which distinct and characteristik types were evolved and some knowledge of how these came into being will help us in understanding their anatomy and distinguishing good and bad forms. Edward Johnston

The letters should be designed by an artist, and not an engineer. William Morris

Geometry can produce legible letters, but art alone makes them beautiful. Art begins where geometry ends, and imparts to letters a character transcending mere measurement. Paul Standard

· All fine monumental inscriptions and types are but forms of writing modified according to the materials to which they are applied. W. R. Lethaby

Opposite:

Villu Toots: Passages from the writings of Alfred Fairbank, William Morris and W. R. Lethaby. 1965?

The layout and scripts selected for these passages are as interesting as the people whose work Toots has chosen to quote. The widespread appeal of modern calligraphy is emphasised by the fact that Villu Toots lives and works in Estonia.

V&AM MS Circ.176-1966

Top:

Tom Gourdie: The simple modern hand, Book 1. 1965

Tom Gourdie is a Scottish calligrapher and a pupil of Irene Wellington. He has done much to introduce italic writing in Scotland, by lecturing, organising exhibitions, and producing instructional books — of which this is one, with the illustration taken from the beginners' book.

V&AM L 1030-1966 18 × 22

Colours
The sky is blue today.
The grass is green.
Mummy has a yellow hat.
I have a purple dress.
I like a red pencil.
Which colour do you like?
31

Bottom:

Thomas Swindlehurst: From Edward Cocker's 'Multum in parvo; or, the pen's gallantrie 1660'. 1965

This text is taken from one of the most engaging of English writing masters, Edward Cocker, several of whose works are illustrated in the present book. But both in lay-out and style Thomas Swindlehurst has transformed it into a work very much in keeping with later 20th century calligraphy.

V&AM Circ.194-1966

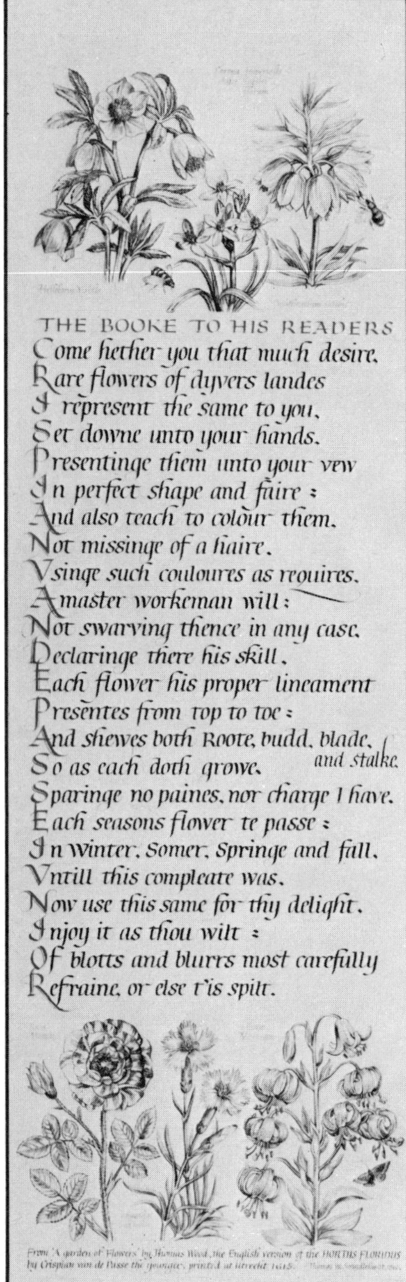
THE BOOKE TO HIS READERS
Come hether you that much desire.
Rare flowers of dyvers landes
I represent the same to you,
Set downe unto your hands.
Presentinge them unto your vew
In perfect shape and faire:
And also teach to colour them.
Not missinge of a haire.
Vsinge such coulours as requires.
A master workeman will:
Not swarving thence in any case.
Declaringe there his skill.
Each flower his proper lineament
Presentes from top to toe:
And shewes both Roote, budd, blade, and stalke.
So as each doth growe.
Sparinge no paines, nor charge I have.
Each seasons flower te passe:
In Winter, Somer, Springe and fall.
Vntill this compleate was.
Now use this same for thy delight.
Injoy it as thou wilt:
Of blotts and blurrs most carefully
Refraine, or else t'is spilt.

Thomas Swindlehurst: From 'A garden of flowers' by Thomas Wood. 1965

Many of the 20th century scribes have adorned their manuscripts with decorations as did their medieval predecessors. Birds and flowers have been especially favoured, even as they were in the margins of the illuminated manuscripts of the Middle Ages.

V & A M Circ.193-1966

OH THERE IS BLESSING
IN THIS GENTLE BREEZE,
A visitant that while it fans my cheek
Doth seem half-conscious of the joy it brings
From the green fields, and from yon azure sky.
Whate'er its mission, the soft breeze can come
To none more grateful than to me; escaped
From the vast city, where I long had pined
A discontented sojourner: now free
Free as a bird to settle where I will.
What dwelling shall receive me? in what vale
Shall be my harbour? underneath what grove
Shall I take up my home? and what clear stream
Shall with its murmur lull me into rest?
The earth is all before me. With a heart
Joyous, nor scared at its own liberty,
I look about; and should the chosen guide
Be nothing better than a wandering cloud,
I cannot miss my way. I breathe again!

Escape from the vast city

Joan Pilsbury: The Prelude, Book I, by William Wordsworth. 1967

Joan Pilsbury has worked with Irene Wellington, who considered her the best scribe of her generation. This manuscript contains a map of the Lakeland area, and Joan Pilsbury is especially known for her decorative maps. Her script here is fine and delicate, written in very black ink on a white page; additional coloured inks are used with great restraint.

V & A M MS L 5011-1970 f.7r
24 × 16

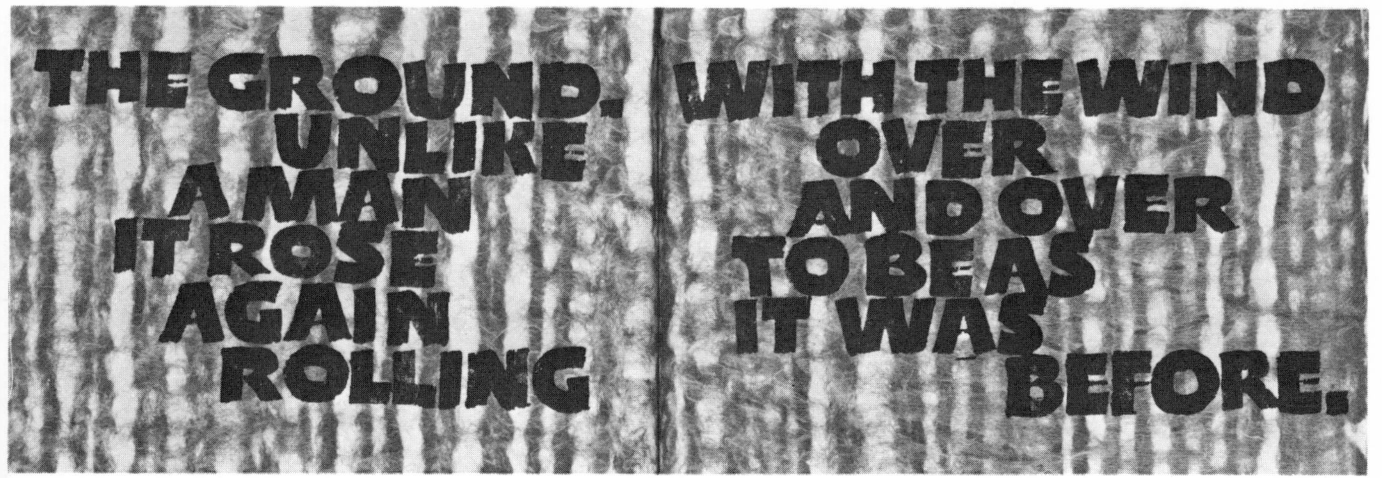

Above:

Pat Russell: The Term, by William Carlos Williams. 1968

This script is written on a rough textured paper of cream and brown stripes. A delicate letter form, of which Mrs Russell is quite capable, would have been out of place here. The scribe has therefore chosen to use a thick bold form which holds its own and forms a fitting complement to the texture and shape of the book as a whole.

V & A M *MS L 2889-1970* *10 × 16*

The Tale (contd.)

OUT of the corner of her eye, Yang could see Shan running towards her. He was chasing the same butterfly as Li, and as he was big--ger, there was just a chance he might catch it.

Above the bank by the lake two little rabbits were having a game, and Ying was chasing Pai, the little white rabbit, as fast as he could. They were both great pets of the children.

Soon, when the sun sinks behind the western hills, and the cool air brings the scent of flowers across the garden, the chil--dren will race each other to the big court, coming to say "good-night" to Ma-Tin with polite little bows, as was the custom with children in China long ago: while he, from a big mother-o'-pearl vase, gives to each child a large luscious sweetmeat to carry off to bed.

Dorothy Hutton: The Chinese cabinet, a tale, by Christobel Hardcastle. 1969

Dorothy Hutton studied under Graily Hewitt and is an accomplished scribe as well as an illuminator. She was also a founder member of the Society of Scribes and Illuminators. This is a late manuscript, and shows her use of a simple cursive italic set spaciously on the page.

V & A M *MS L 14154-1974* *30 × 25*

körper und stimme verleiht die Schrift
dem stummen Gedanken
durch der Jahrhunderte Strom trägt ihn
das redende Blatt

Bild 250

Bild 251

und die echte Sehnsucht muß stets produktiv sein, ein neues besseres erschaffen.

Bild 252

Bild 253

meine tinte ist gefroren und ausgeloschen der kamin

Hildegard Korger: Schrift und Schreiben: ein Fachbuch für alle, die mit dem Schreiben und Zeichnen von Schriften und ihre Anwendung zu tun haben. 1972

Hildegard Korger is herself a calligrapher, and this illustration includes examples of her work. The book not only assists the learner, but also deals with the history of calligraphy and its place at the present time. She therefore includes the practical application of calligraphy from its traditional use in the book arts to its employment in advertisements of all kinds.

V&AM L 4367-1972 27 × 24

Opposite:

Anthony Gardner: Draft of a work on italic handwriting, together with various examples. 1972?

This manuscript was written out by Anthony Gardner, also well-known as a binder of distinction, in the hand which he wished his students to copy. There has been a considerable interest in italic handwriting in the last few decades, and it is interesting to note the varieties of style that can emerge from the same basic models.

V&AM L 6905-1975 25 × 10.5

Formal and Cursive Italic Calligraphy.
A Sheet of points to bear in mind :–

Study Instruction Sheet No.1 each time you start writing.

Remember to keep the top of the nib wiped clean after dipping.

See that the pen is held at the correct angle: In plan, pointing over the right hand shoulder, & in elevation so that the nib makes an angle of abt. 45° to the paper.

Remember the essential Italic shape is this: a 8° and the slope of the letters is best at abt. 8°

Note that an excessive slope hinders legibility & slows up the writing, e.g: Calligraphy. Also an upright hand slows up the writing & is not true to the Italic form.

In branching letters observe these points :–
In n and m avoid this: n and m, and this: n and m.
See that u differs from n.
Mind your p's and q's & note g or g.

Ascenders start with a reverse action, wch. soon develops into a simple sleight of hand :– 1→ 2← l d b : Avoid: l d and l d.

Alison Urwick: From 'The spring' by Ezra Pound. 1975

This piece is written on hand-made paper with decorations in gouache and gold. The scribe has said that the ideas for the letter forms were taken from a tomb of 1451 in Florence and from inscriptions in the Catacombs.

V & A M MS L 5436-1979

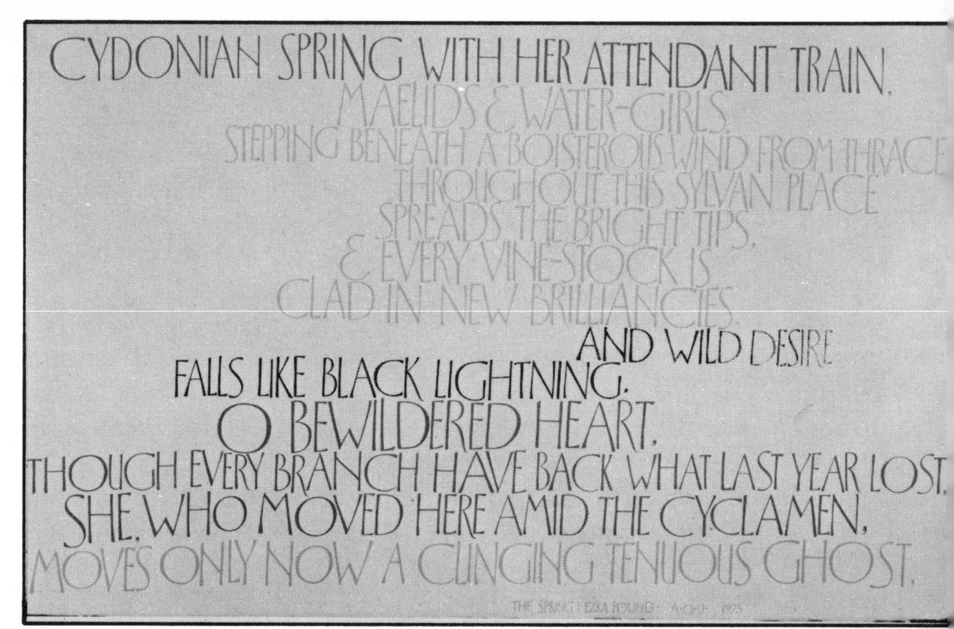

Alison Urwick: The song to Yasmin, from 'Hassan' by J. E. Flecker. 1977

This manuscript is written out on hand-made paper with decorations in gouache and shell gold. The scribe writes of it 'Hassan serenades Yasmin to the accompaniment of the lute, sitting by the fountain in the garden beneath her window'. Hassan's most precious possession is his old faded but very beautiful Persian carpet, and he eventually takes it with him on his journey to Samarkand, to be 'a little meadow in the waste of sand'. The illustrations and text are unusually disposed on the sheet, and the calligrapher is not afraid of blank spaces, which help to create the feeling of distance between the two lovers.

V & A M MS L 5435-1979

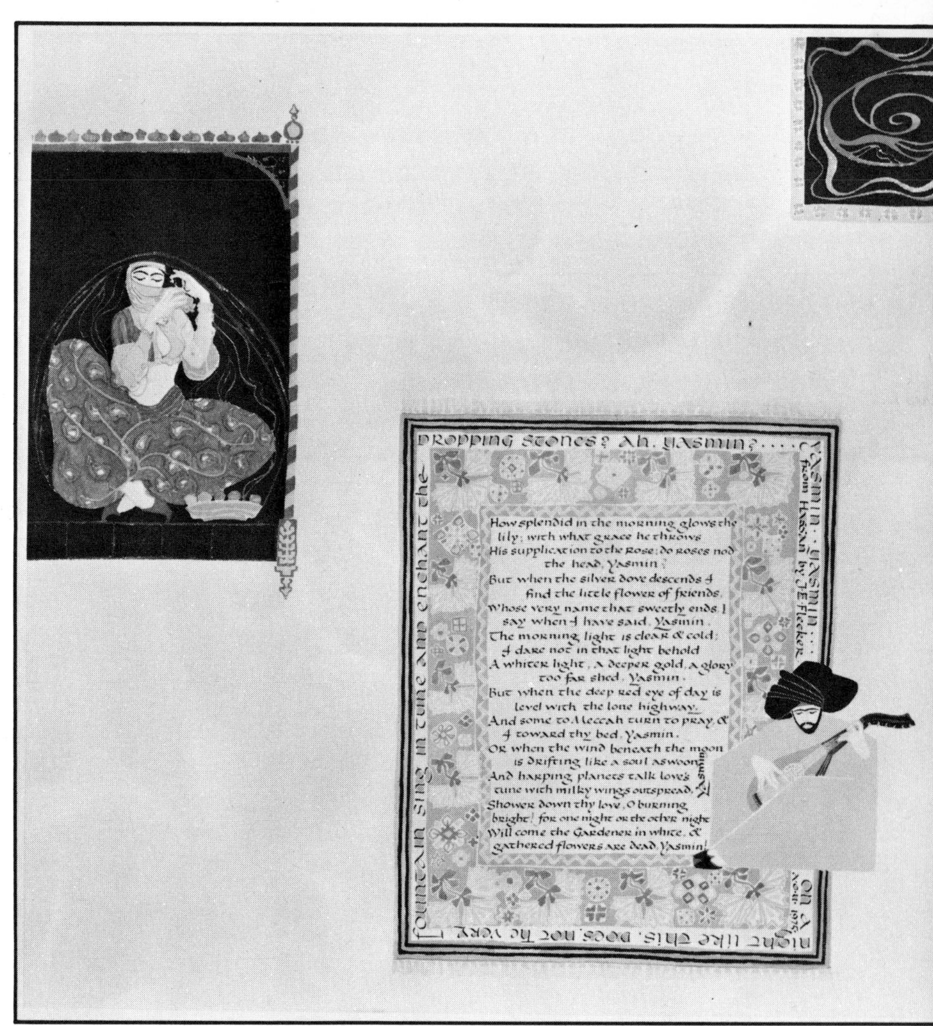

Ann Hechle: A calligraphic sampler. 1979

This piece of calligraphy was commissioned for the exhibition held at the Victoria and Albert Museum in 1980, but the choice of design was left entirely to the calligrapher. Ann Hechle was involved in various exhibition demonstrations at the Museum in recent years, and this Sampler arose directly out of her responses to the questions asked by members of the public during these demonstrations. In particular she has endeavoured to show how the different scripts can illuminate language and reflect the meaning of words. Most of the scripts included in this book will be found in this illustration.

V&AM

Now the bright morning Star, Day's harbinger,
Comes dancing from the East, and leads with her
The Flowry May, who from her green lap throws
The yellow Cowslip and the pale Primrose.
Hail bounteous May that dost inspire
Mirth and youth and warm desire,
Woods and Groves are of thy dressing,
Hill and Dale doth boast thy blessing.
Thus we salute thee with our early Song,
And welcome thee, and wish thee long.
John Milton

Buy my English posies!
Kent and Surrey may –
Violets of the Undercliff
Wet with Channel spray
Cowslips from a Devon combe
Midland furze afire –
Buy my English posies
And I'll sell your heart's desire!
Rudyard Kipling.

10.

Heather Child: The running winds of springtime, a selection of verses taken from various authors.

Heather Child has specialised in heraldry and maps, both of which suitably employ calligraphic inscriptions. She is also well known for her botanical illustrations. In this manuscript she combines her calligraphic text with drawings and paintings of flowers and natural scenes.

Reproduced by permission of the artist.

11 Calligraphic studies

THE ORIGIN of letters, like the origin of speech, has always fascinated some people. In both cases the desire is to get back to the very beginning of things. From the study of the origin of communicating by written or spoken forms, it is possible to pass to the study of special manifestations of those forms. The scholars and antiquarians who first studied written forms were primarily interested in classical or medieval scripts. The study of palaeography – of ancient writing – is therefore of much earlier date than the study of calligraphy. There are still today more published works on palaeographic subjects than calligraphic ones. It was probably not possible for people to take a dispassionate view of handwriting until printing was well established in the 16th century. Only with the rise of the writing masters, so many rivals all seeking pupils, was it possible to note differences and developments, and often the first to do this were the writing masters themselves. For several centuries the introductions to copy books were peppered with denigrations and carpings, as one master reviewed the work of another, in order to promote his own style or system. Thus a certain historicity is observable during the 16th and 17th centuries, as the various calligraphers cast a look back over their predecessors as well as a sideways glance at their contemporaries. The writings and counter-writings of this kind in Italy have been very well charted by Dr A. Osley in *Luminario: an introduction to the Italian writing books of the sixteenth and seventeenth centuries*, 1972.

But none of this really implies a serious *study* of the history of calligraphy. For this we must wait until the late 17th century and Samuel Pepys, who was sufficiently interested in the subject to collect as many examples of calligraphy, both English and foreign, as he could. In 1700 he had his collection mounted and annotated, and so it remains today, preserved in his three volumes in Magdalene College, Cambridge, where it was bequeathed on his death. Pepys was interested in the whole range of writing, from the earliest to the contemporary. Those who wished to please him, presented him with ancient examples taken from early manuscripts. These he passed to Humfrey Wanley, Bodley's Librarian, for his opinion and dating, which was duly recorded in volume I of the collection. For examples nearer his own time, Pepys was prepared to give his personal opinion. His interest in calligraphy can also be traced in his famous Diary, where, for example, Edward Cocker is mentioned with approbation. Pepys was undoubtedly primarily interested in the actual writing; all the engraved copy-book examples in his collection have been cut down to the plate-line, and any text which accompanied them has

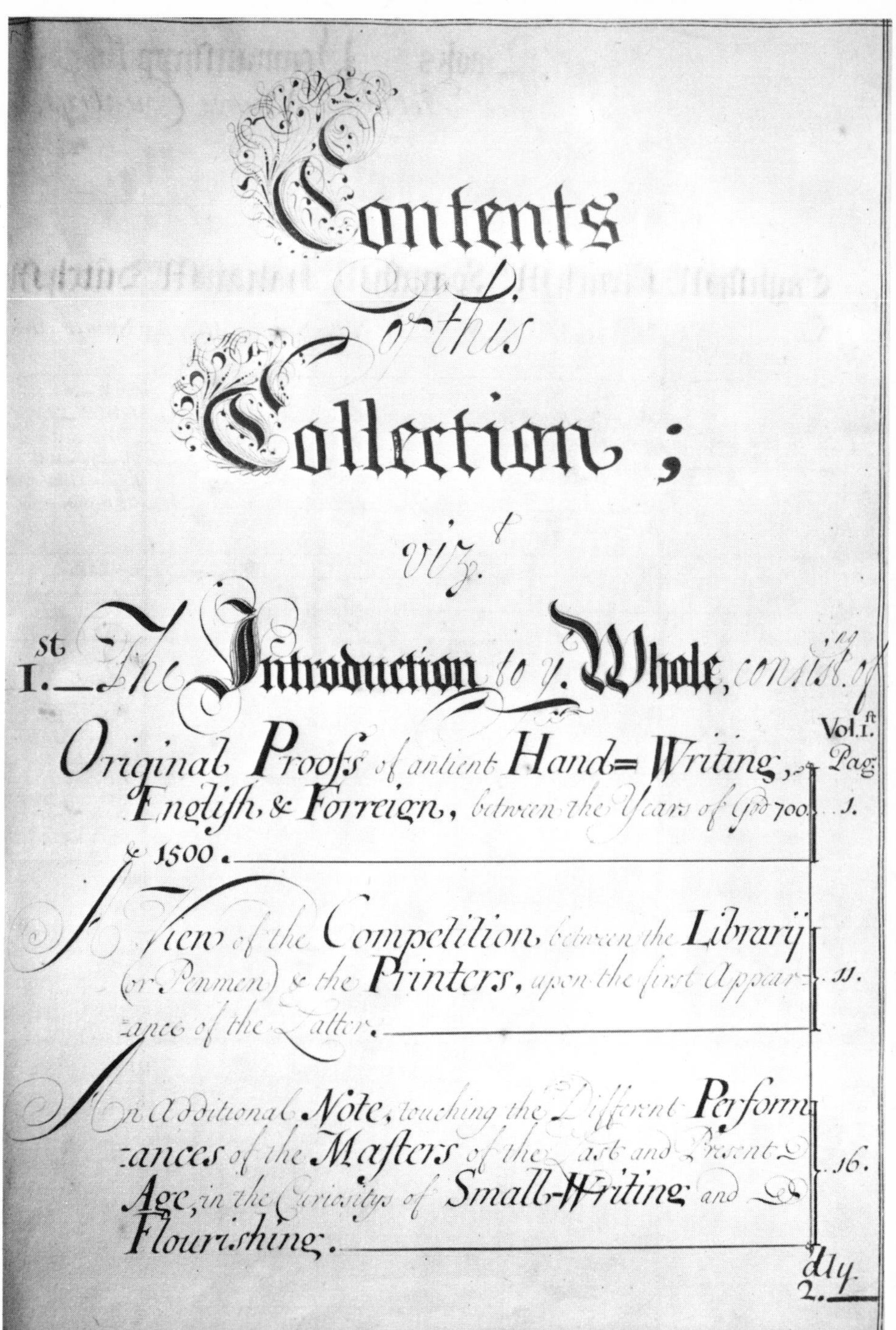
Contents of this Collection; viz.t

1.st — The Introduction to ye Whole, consist.g of

Original Proofs of antient Hand=Writing, English, & Forreign, between the Years of God 700 & 1500. — Vol. 1.st Pag. 1.

A View of the Competition between the Library (or Penmen) & the Printers, upon the first Apparance of the Latter. — 11.

An Additional Note, touching the Different Performances of the Masters of the Past and Present Age, in the Curiositys of Small-Writing and Flourishing. — 16.

2.dly

Samuel Pepys: My calligraphical collection. 1700

The contents page from Volume 1, showing the detailed way in which Pepys set about the arrangement of his large collection of examples. Of the copy books, only the engraved plates were preserved, all text pages being discarded.

Reproduced by permission of the Master and Fellows, Magdalene College, Cambridge.

been rejected. Since his copy may be the only known example of a particular writing book, its incompleteness means a loss to scholarship. Nevertheless, many of the copy books he preserved would have been altogether unknown if he had not retained the plates at least. The especially interesting aspect of the Pepys collection is that it was made by a non-professional – by an amateur in the true sense of the word. Certainly he was a man who had to use his pen a lot in the course of making his living, but he had no professional interest in the subject, whereas the earlier scraps of history were for the most part supplied by calligraphers themselves.

Pepys's interest in calligraphy seems to have been exceptional, and although the early 18th century produced other works on the study of alphabets and the origin of exotic scripts, it was not until 1763 that the next important work on calligraphy appeared in England. This was the book by William Massey *The origin and progress of letters*, which was divided into two parts, of which the first was the more traditional study of the origin of scripts. The second part however broke new ground. It was sub-titled 'A compendious account of the most celebrated English penmen, with the titles and characters of the books they have published both from the rolling and letter press. . . . A new species of biography never attempted before in English'.

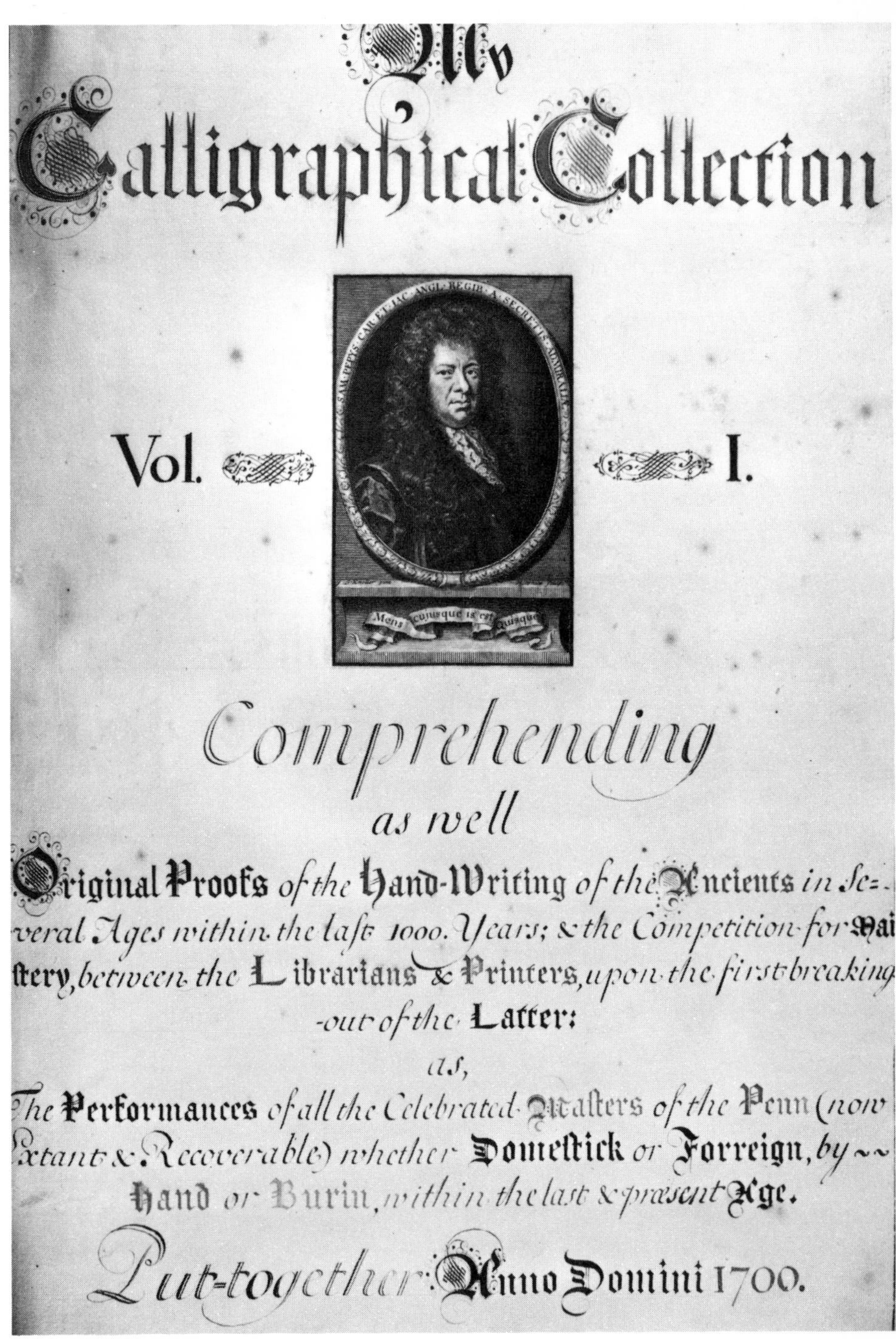
My Calligraphical Collection

Vol. I.

Mens cujusque is est quisque

Comprehending

as well

Original Proofs of the Hand-Writing of the Ancients in Several Ages within the last 1000. Years; & the Competition for Maistery, between the Librarians & Printers, upon the first breaking-out of the Latter:

as,

The Performances of all the Celebrated Masters of the Penn (now Extant & Recoverable) whether Domestick or Forreign, by Hand or Burin, within the last & præsent Age.

Put-together Anno Domini 1700.

Samuel Pepys: My calligraphical collection. 1700

This is the title-page from Volume 1 of the three volumes in which Samuel Pepys had his collection mounted, and it gives some idea of the wide range of his interest in writing, both 'domestick or forreign, by hand or burin, within the last & præsent age'. It will be noted that his title-page makes use of all the styles of script then current.

Reproduced by permission of the Master and Fellows, Magdalene College, Cambridge

22 *L'Idea dell'arte maggiore, e minore*

mo, da quali opere vengano le inuentioni di tante varie maniere di lettere cancellareſche, che hoggi da alcuni buoni dell'arte s'vſano, & inſieme tratteremo ampiamente, donde naſcano le imperfettioni de' Maeſtri moderni, e da quai loro effetti ſi comprendano.

Da quali opere venga quel poco, che ſanno al preſente i Maeſtri moderni dello ſcriuere cancellareſco corſiuo, et in che conſiſta per lo più l'imperfettione loro.

C A P. V.

VNA ſol coſa m'hà ſempre confortato, lodato ſia Dio, che a confuſione di alcuni mali ſpiriti inuidioſi, & ingrati a chi loro hà inſegnato, è paleſe a tutt'il Mondo, che quel poco, che hora ſanno di queſt'arte, viene dall'origine, & inuentione de' miei caratteri, che nelle quattro mie opere vn pezzo fà io diedi fuori in iſtampa, e ſpetialmente anche da quelle, che in diuerſi tempi con più perfettione hò ſcritte a penna, e che molti di loro tengono in mano per proprio ammaeſtramento: le quali paragonate con l'opere vecchie degli Scrittori di penna Gottica, e Longobarda, cioè di Lodouico Vicentino, di Giouan'Antonio Tagliente, e di Giouan Battiſta Palatino Cittadino Romano, innanzi, che al ſuo libro faceſſe la correttione, & anche con quelle di Frate Veſpaſiano Minoritano, e d'altri ſimili ſcrittori di que' tempi, ſi vedrà chiariſſimo, che non eſſendo dietro a quelle ſeguire

altre

A passage from Cresci's 'L'idea con le circonstanze naturali, che a quella si ricercano, per vole legittimamente posseder l'arte maggiore e minore dello scrivere', *published in 1622. Here he comments, often unfavourably, on his fellow writing masters, some of whose work is illustrated in the present book.*

V&AM L 956-1951 22 × 16

Massey surveyed the past as well as his contemporaries, and as a result was able to include much unwritten information in his account, since he was near enough in time to the great masters of the late 17th and early 18th centuries. Although much of his information has now been superseded by modern research, his work remains an important source book for anyone involved in the study of English handwriting.

Many writers who concerned themselves with scripts were of course practising scribes or writing masters, and it is in the introductions and prefaces of their printed works that we must search for any sign of serious interest in the history of calligraphy. Inevitably with such sources the information tends to support the writing master's own theories and practice. However a small amount of general consideration of the subject went on throughout the 18th century. Christoval Rodriguez for example in his *Bibliotheca universal de la polygraphia española*, 1738, which was a splendidly produced book, probably issued posthumously, took a wide survey of Spanish writing. Others used a study of the history of calligraphy to stir up a desire for improvement in their countrymen. Such a one was L. P. Vallain in his *Lettres à Mr de **** sur l'art d'écrire* published in 1760, in which he placed writing in its context: history, practice, and importance. Most calligraphers writing on the subject at all were mainly content to exalt the position of calligraphy among the arts and professions, and thereby enhance their own standing among their fellows.

The interest in medievalism which was so noticeable at the end of the 18th century certainly led to a greater interest in medieval books, and, to some extent, in the making of them. It led a number of people to attempt to copy such writings, but again little interest was shown in contemporary or near-contemporary scribes. One who did express an interest was Isaac D'Israeli, father of the famous statesman, who in 1791 produced a compilation which he called *Curiosities of literature*. Among the miscellaneous essays included in this book was one on 'The history of writing masters'. D'Israeli was very scathing in most of his comments, and denigrates Massey's pioneering work, but he reserved most of his scorn for his contemporary Thomas Tomkins,

This historical passage on French calligraphers is taken from L. P. Vallain's Lettres à Mr de **** sur l'art d'écrire, ou l'on voir les divers inconveniens d'une écriture trop negligée [etc], *published in 1760*.

V&AM L 3726-1977 13.5 × 8

148 *Lettres*

XIIIe LETTRE.

Utilité des Ouvrages que les habiles Maîtres d'Ecriture font graver.

La Province & les Pays Etrangers s'enrichiſſent, Monſieur, des travaux des Artiſtes de l'Ecriture, tandis que Paris reſte à cet égard dans la plus grande indifférence (*a*).

En 1680, Jean Alais de Beaulieu * mit au jour un Livre, qui par la ſimplicité de ſes principes ſur la formation des lettres, par les bons préceptes ſur la poſition du corps, des bras, & de

(*a*) Les Anglois ont enlevé une grande partie des piéces de Roſſignol.

* Il étoit neveu de celui que j'ai cité dans la précédente Lettre.

ſur l'Art d'écrire. 149

la main pour bien écrire; & par la beauté des piéces gravées ſur ſes modéles par Senault (*a*), auſſi habile Ecrivain que bon Graveur, eſt un des excellens Ouvrages qui ait paru.

Il n'eſt pas douteux que cet Ouvrage n'ait beaucoup ſervi à

(*a*) Il mit auſſi au jour en 1668 un Livre, qui eut des Amateurs; ſes caractères ſont beaux, fort délicats, & réguliers. J'ai fait l'éloge de ſon Burin dans la quatriéme Lettre. Il a écrit des Heures pour Louis XIV. qu'il a enſuite gravées. C'eſt lui qui a gravé le Livre de Laurent Fontaine qui parut en 1677. Cet Ouvrage de Laurent Fontaine eſt peu étendu; mais ingénieuſement diſtribué en trois Tables: le principe de chaque lettre y eſt bien développé pour le tems; les caractères en ſont bien liés, & d'une forme agréable. Le Livre de Nicolas Duval qui parut la même année eſt auſſi de ſon Burin, & cet Ouvrage décele beaucoup de goût & de main.

N iij

THE HISTORY OF WRITING-MASTERS. 189

let them meditate on the nothingness of their "Standard Rules," by the fate of Mr. Snell.

It was to be expected, when once these writing-masters imagined that they were artists, that they would be infected with those plague-spots of genius—envy, detraction, and all the *jalousie du métier*. And such to this hour we find them! An extraordinary scene of this nature has long been exhibited in my neighbourhood, where two doughty champions of the quill have been posting up libels in their windows respecting the inventor of *a new art of writing*, the Carstairian, or the Lewisian? When the great German philosopher asserted that he had discovered the method of fluxions before Sir Isaac, and when the dispute grew so violent that even the calm Newton sent a formal defiance in set terms, and got even George the Second to try to arbitrate (who would rather have undertaken a campaign), the method of fluxions was no more cleared up than the present affair between our two heroes of the quill.

A recent instance of one of these egregious caligraphers may be told of the late Tomkins. This vainest of writing-masters dreamed through life that penmanship was one of the fine arts, and that a writing-master should be seated with his peers in the Academy! He bequeathed to the British Museum his *opus magnum*—a copy of Macklin's Bible, profusely embellished with the most beautiful and varied decorations of his pen; and as he conceived that both the workman and the work would alike be darling objects with posterity, he left something immortal with the legacy, his fine bust, by Chantrey, unaccompanied by which they were not to receive the unparalleled gift! When Tomkins applied to have his bust, our great sculptor abated the usual price, and, courteously kind to the feelings of the man, said that he considered Tomkins as an artist! It was the proudest day of the life of our writing-master!

But an eminent artist and wit now living, once looking on this fine bust of Tomkins, declared, that "this man had died for want of a dinner!"—a fate, however, not so lamentable as it appeared! Our penman had long felt that he stood degraded in

A very scathing passage on writing masters taken from the chapter in Isaac D'Israeli's Curiosities of Literature, *first published in 1791, and here reproduced from Volume III of the edition issued in 1849. 'The late Tomkins' comes in for some especially hard words!*

V&AM Forster collection 2486
22 × 14

whom he referred to as 'the late Tomkins', in a very tetchy (and perhaps envious?) way.

The romantic approach to the Middle Ages so apparent in the 19th century continued to involve a study of manuscripts and the handwritten book. With the arrival of commercially viable colour printing in the middle of the century, far more people were able to see what manuscripts really looked like, and so to copy them. This led to an interest among some people as to what had happened to handwriting *after* the invention of printing. In particular, scholars began to study their own national hands, and to continue this study beyond the Middle Ages, which was where such studies had ended for so long. As a result many valuable studies on the calligraphy of individual countries began to appear, some of which are still the main sources of information for certain national hands. One such was Emilio Cotarelo y Mori's *Diccionario biográfico y bibliográfico de calígrafos españoles*, published in 1913-16, in two volumes. This contains an enormous amount of detailed information, sometimes almost too much, causing vital facts to become buried under a mass of verbiage, but it remains essential for anyone studying Spanish calligraphy. A slighter work on Portuguese calligraphy was published in 1923, and other countries such as Germany also produced important works on their own hands.

In England the study of the English writing masters was undertaken by Sir Ambrose Heal, who continued the tradition of Samuel Pepys in that he was an amateur or lover of the subject rather than a practitioner. His monumental work *The English writing-masters and their copy-books, 1570-1800: a biographical dictionary & a bibliography*, published in 1931 by the Cambridge University Press, also contained an important introduction by Stanley Morison on the development of handwriting. Heal's original notebooks, together with many items from his collection, were bequeathed to the Victoria and Albert Museum, thus greatly increasing the collection of calligraphy which had been built up by that Museum over a period of about one hundred years. American calligraphy had to wait until the post-war period for its main historian, in Ray Nash, whose studies have covered the period up to the mid-19th century. But in the United States, the study of calligraphy had already been acknowledged by museums and libraries, and a fine collection had been built up by the Newberry Library of Chicago for example. It was in the United States that the first major exhibition of calligraphy was held, in Baltimore in 1965, and the catalogue of that exhibition *Two thousand years of calligraphy* remains a vital work of reference for anyone interested in the development of scripts. Unlike so many scholarly studies, it brought the subject right up to date.

Meantime a completely different approach to the study of calligraphy had become observable, which moved away from the general study of national hands to a detailed study of certain periods, or individual hands and scribes. Among the pioneers of this kind of study was James Wardrop, for many years Deputy-Keeper of the Library of the Victoria and Albert Museum. A number of his early studies on individual scribes of the Italian Renaissance were published as articles in *Signature* in the 1950's, and it was this journal which also published a detailed catalogue by A. F. Johnson of Italian writing books of the 16th century. The post-war period has seen an increasing flow of works of scholarship on all aspects of calligraphy. In 1960 Alfred Fairbank (another pioneer of the study of humanist scripts) and Berthold Wolpe published *Renaissance handwriting: an anthology of italic scripts*. But it is undoubtedly the

Italian scripts and in particular the script of humanism (to use the title of Wardrop's own book) that has interested the contemporary scholar, and very often such studies have been produced in volumes which are themselves fine examples of modern book production. Examples are Emanuele Cassamassima's *Trattati di scrittura del Cinquecento italiano*, 1966, and Dr A. S. Osley's *Luminario: an introduction to the Italian writing books of the sixteenth and seventeenth centuries*, 1972. It is Dr Osley who, by his translations of the prefaces and texts to the writing books has made the calligraphers' own words available for general study. More recently the frontiers of our knowledge have been pushed even further back by Dr A. C. de la Mare's *The handwriting of the Italian humanists*, 1973, in which the author has identified even more and earlier calligraphers.

This survey of recent scholarship in the field of calligraphic studies selects only a few of the many works, books and articles, which have now made the study of the history of calligraphy a well-defined subject. There is still scope for more research, and obviously it is the detailed study of a person, a period, or a script which now most appeals. We have come a long way since Pepys could calmly accept scraps cut out of an early manuscript for him, or throw away all the textual matter of his copy books. However, the main study must always be of the scripts themselves and it is hoped that the illustrations in this book will assist in that study.

12 Applied calligraphy

CALLIGRAPHY is writing, and writing can be used in many ways. Most of the examples illustrated in this book are what might be called the obvious uses of calligraphy – the early manuscript books, letters, diplomas, and other ceremonial and similar 'one-off' documents. But with the invention of printing, and the development of typography along different lines from calligraphy, a choice arose. Hence when a handwritten type of letter was used in preference to a printed one, this meant that a conscious decision had been taken. What is interesting is to note how often pen-made letters continued to be used in a variety of different ways, even when printed letters might have been expected. This section therefore explores some of the ways in which calligraphy has continued to be used, either practically or decoratively, up to the present time.

One of the most obvious uses of calligraphy was in connection with the book. In any book the first point of impact is the title-page, and elaborately engraved title-pages continued to be provided for some centuries after printing was firmly established for most book work. Such title-pages usually followed the style of the contemporary copy book title-page, in that they displayed a great variety of different hands. No doubt in many cases the engraver of both kinds of title-pages would have been the same person, since few professional engravers could afford to specialise in one kind of work only, but would turn their hand to whatever commission was offered. Although an engraved title-page may have given a certain distinction to a book, it would seem that on occasions the publisher felt that something more was needed, and so provided his books with two title-pages – one engraved and one letter-press.

Books frequently have illustrations, and these need captions. Before the introduction of mechanical means of picture reproduction in the 19th century, illustrations were usually wood – or copper – engraved, with lithography and steel engraving being introduced in the late 18th and early 19th centuries respectively. If the illustration was engraved, it was often more convenient to engrave the caption also. In some cases this made use of the typographic forms to be found in the printed book, but much more frequently it was calligraphic letters which were used – in other words the caption was written. Sometimes, as can be seen from the illustrations here, such lettering was in the florid style of the contemporary copy books, but very often it was the italic script that was used. This script was neat and clear, and did not draw attention to itself and away from the picture it was intended to describe. It could also be written quite small and yet remain legible. This led to its frequent employment in maps and diagrams, where it was necessary to get information into as small a space as would be consistent with legibility. Even today, when printing is employed for these items, it is often an italic type which is chosen.

For a long time advertisements were engraved rather than printed, since they were rarely required in large numbers. Again calligraphic forms were frequently employed, although some advertisements show a mixture of letters taken from both printing and writing. Bill-heads can provide a fascinating display of calligraphy, often showing as many different forms of script as a contemporary copy book. The handwritten advertisement or document of any kind always suggests a personal touch, even today, when such 'handwritten' forms may in fact have been mechanically reproduced. As a result, wedding and other invitations, greetings cards and similar items, still continue the tradition of the personal 'handwritten' inscription, even though they may be mass-produced. In the same way, many contemporary advertisements prefer to use calligraphic forms of letters, so that handwritten styles of all kinds appear on many objects of daily use.

The modern use of calligraphy can take various forms, since it can be used in a variety of different media. Neon-light signs will give rise to quite different shapes of letters from those used on slate or glass. Inscriptions on glass or pottery are by no means something new since they can be found on similar artefacts of the 17th and 18th century or even earlier. But what perhaps is different in the use of calligraphic forms today, apart from the fact that we now find them daily on so many things from chocolate to cornflakes, is the ornamental use of the handwritten letters. Designers have taken up the various scripts and used them not only for what they say, but the way that they say it. From this it is a short step to using the letters as abstract designs. Some of the examples illustrated in the 20th century section of this book already show the calligrapher looking in that direction. In using calligraphic forms as abstract decoration the modern calligrapher and designer is close indeed to those writing masters whose work is illustrated in earlier sections of this book – scribes, whose intoxication with the magic of the calligraphic line led them to push their virtuosity to extremes – no wonder that today there is a revived interest in their work.

Opposite top:
A late 18th century engraved title-page, used here for quite a small children's book. It will be noted that the calligraphic styles are as varied as those to be found on the title-page of a contemporary copy book.

V & A M   L 722A-1961   12 × 8

Opposite bottom:
Urbis Romae aedificiorum illustrium, by G. B. de Cavalieri.
1569

Calligraphic captions were frequently used in illustrated books, especially when the plates were engraved. Usually such captions were placed below the illustration, but occasionally, as here, they were incorporated in it. The link with contemporary cursive hands is obvious in this example.

V & A M   21 × 27

Primrose ſurrounded by her little ſcholars.

The
RENOWNED HISTORY
of
Primrose Prettyface,
who
By her Sweetneſs of Temper, & Love of Learning, was raised from being the Daughter of a poor Cottager, to great Riches, and the Dignity
OF
Lady of the Manor.
set forth
For the Benefit & Imitation of those pretty little Boys & Girls,
Who by learning their Books & obliging Mankind,
Would to Beauty of Body, add Beauty of Mind.

LONDON.
Printed & ſold by J. Marſhall & Co. N°. 4,
Aldermary Church Yard in Bow Lane;
& N°. 17, Queen Street, Cheapside.

(Price 6^d. in Gilt Paper. — 9^d. bound in Red.)

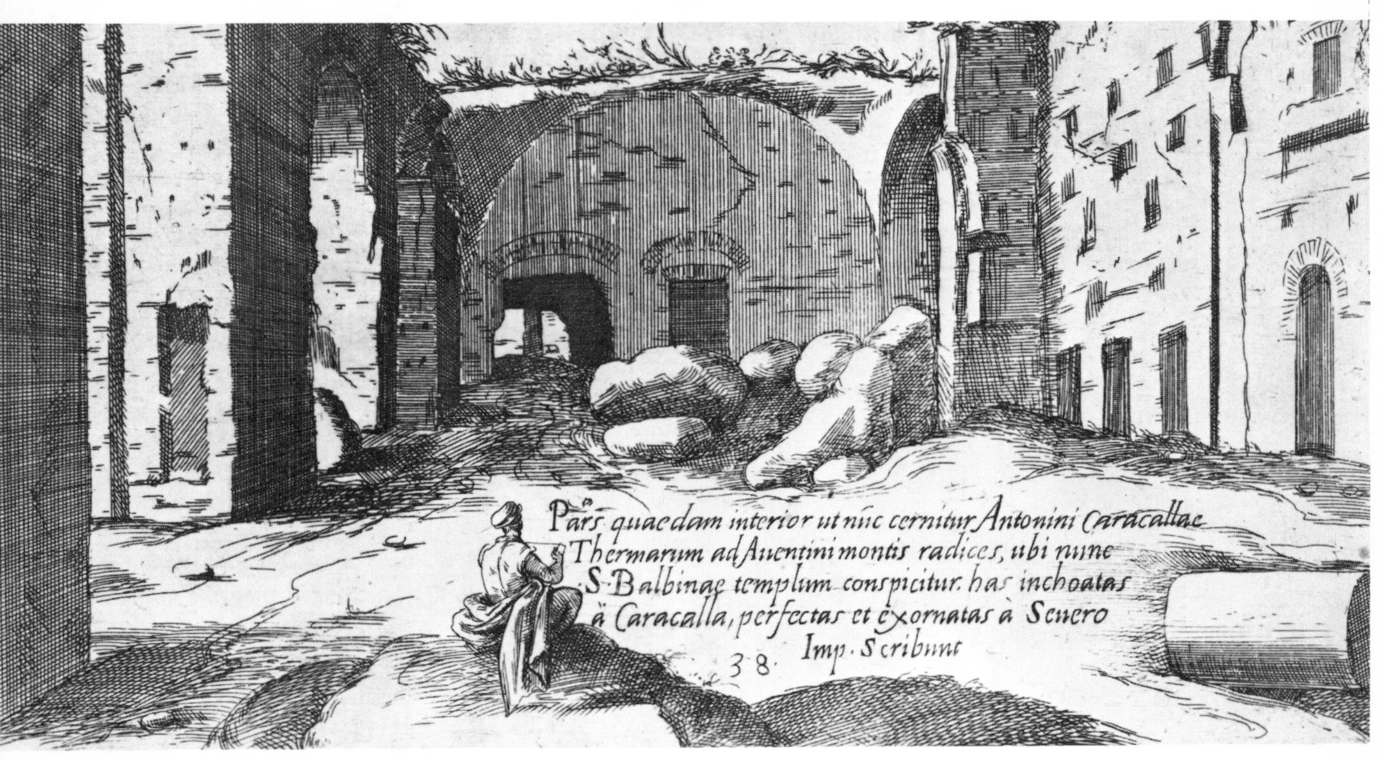

Pars quaedam interior ut nūc cernitur Antonini Caracallae
Thermarum ad Auentini montis radices, ubi nunc
S. Balbinae templum conspicitur. has inchoatas
à Caracalla, perfectas et exornatas à Seuero
Imp. Scribunt
38

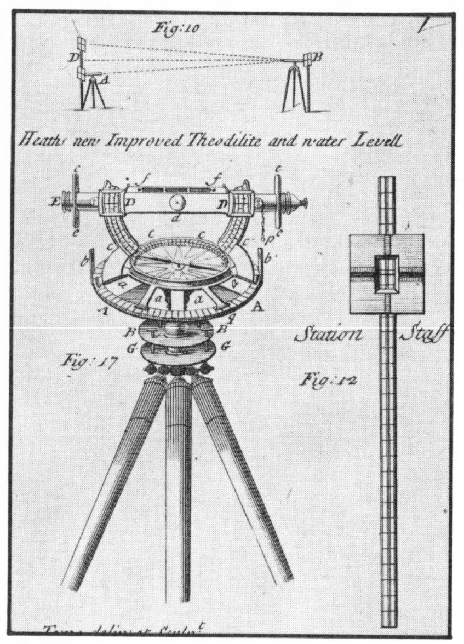

Above:
An engraved illustration in which the captions are based on handwritten forms. The italic script, small and neat, was frequently employed in this way. The diagrammatic illustration is taken from An introduction to a general system of hydrostaticks and hydraulicks, philosophical and practical, *by Stephen Switzer, published in 1729.*

V&AM L 2932-1948 25 × 18.5

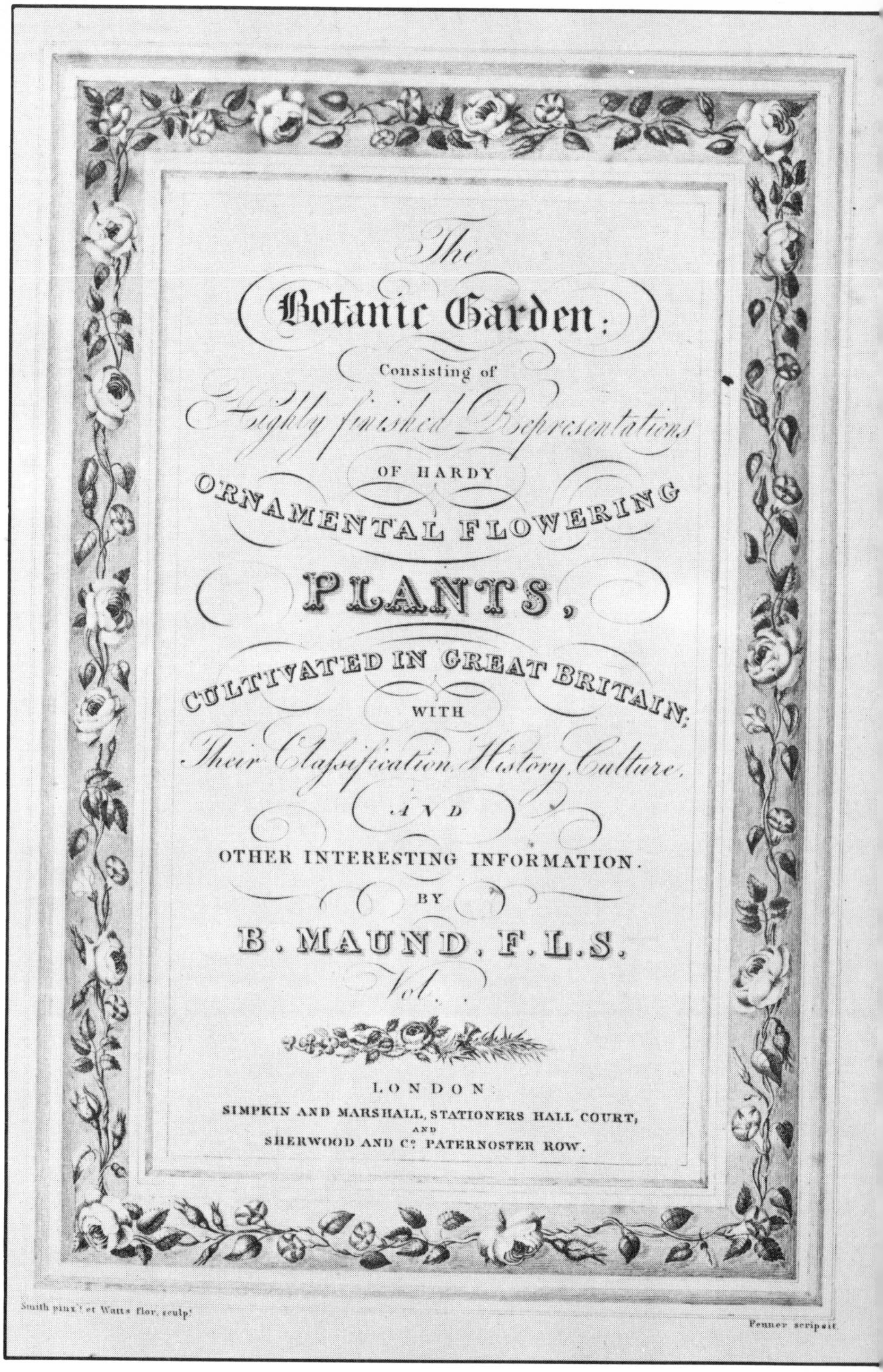

The
Botanic Garden:
Consisting of
Highly finished Representations
OF HARDY
ORNAMENTAL FLOWERING
PLANTS,
CULTIVATED IN GREAT BRITAIN;
WITH
Their Classification, History, Culture,
AND
OTHER INTERESTING INFORMATION.
BY
B. MAUND, F.L.S.
Vol.

LONDON:
SIMPKIN AND MARSHALL, STATIONERS HALL COURT;
AND
SHERWOOD AND Co. PATERNOSTER ROW.

Smith pinx.t et Watts flor. sculp. Fenner scripsit

This title-page from a work published in 1829-30 forms an interesting contrast with the earlier one from the children's book (p. 385). It still shows a great variety of calligraphic styles, but they bear an unmistakable 19th century stamp. The persistence of the traditional gothic letter, used in the main words of the title, should be noted.

V&AM 19.5 × 15.5

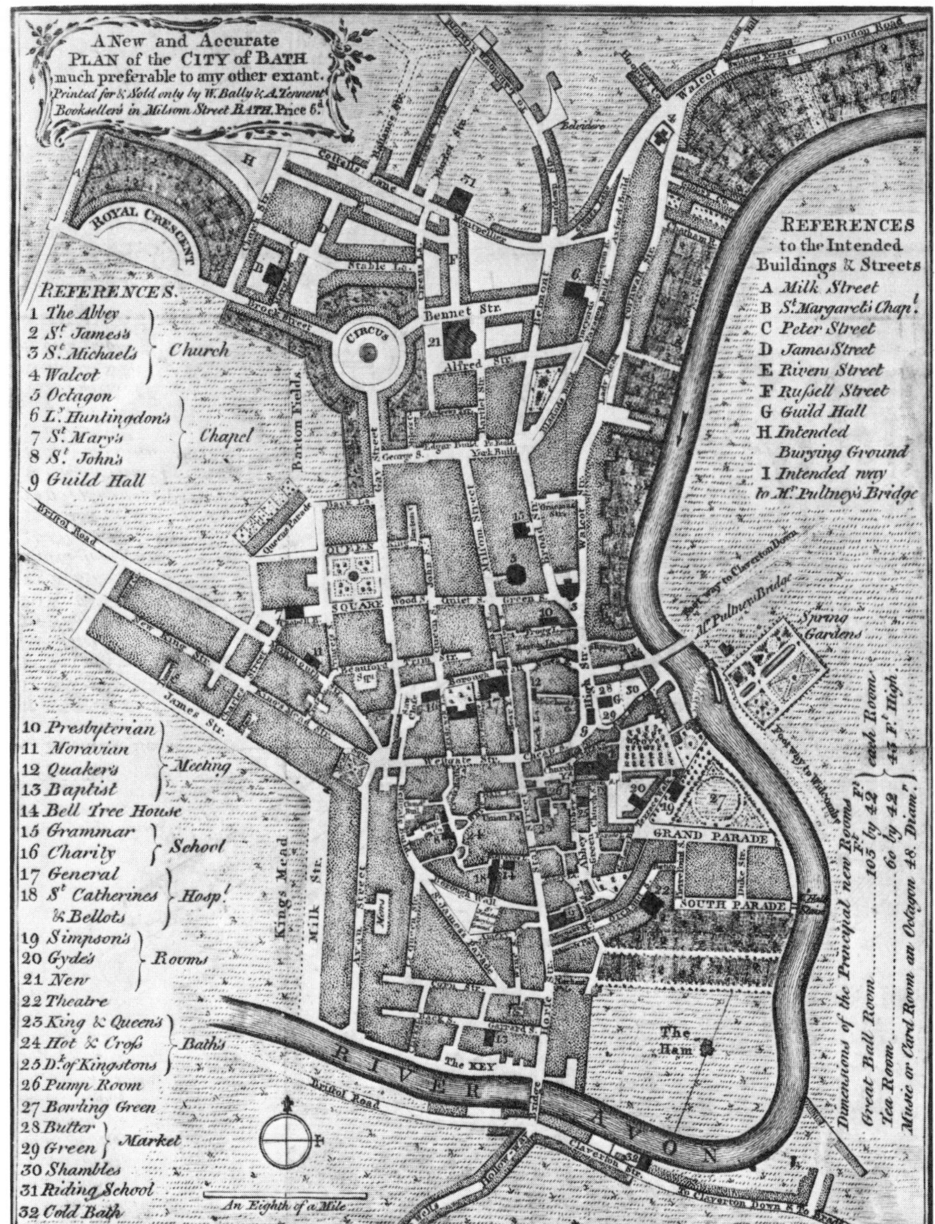

The strangers' assistant and guide to Bath. 1773

This is one of the small folding plans in the Bath guide and shows the use of written forms in the labelling of maps, although some of the lettering shows typographic rather than calligraphic influence.

V&AM L 6022-1976 23 × 17.5

SECOND-HAND PLATE
WATCHES & JEWELS.
Stafford Briscoe
JEWELLER and GOLDSMITH,
at his Old Shop
the three KINGS and GOLDEN BALL,
Opposite Foster Lane in Cheapside
LONDON.
Continues to Make it his particular Business,
to Deal in all Sorts of
New and Second-Hand Plate, Watches and Jewels,
of which he has constantly the greatest Variety and is
determind to Sell (as formerly) at Lower Prices than Common
and Likewise to Give the most Money for any Quantities of
Old Plate, Watches, Jewels, Pearls, & Colour'd-stones of all Kinds.
by Reason of the great Demand he has for the Same.
N.B The full Value Given for Pawnd Plate Watches, Jewels &c.

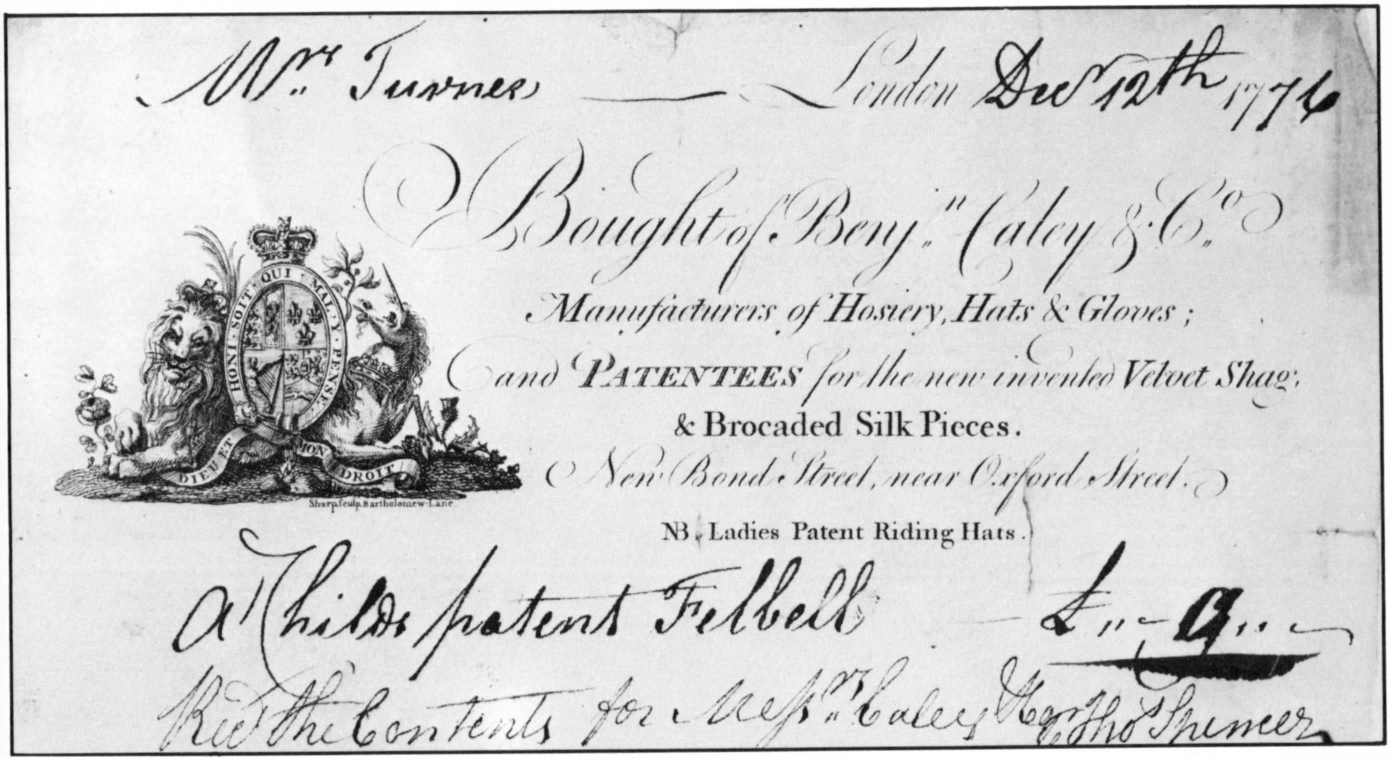

Mrs Turner — London Decr 12th 1776

Bought of Benjn Caley & Co

Manufacturers of Hosiery, Hats & Gloves;

and PATENTEES for the new invented Velvet Shag, & Brocaded Silk Pieces.

New Bond Street, near Oxford Street.

NB. Ladies Patent Riding Hats.

HONI SOIT QUI MAL Y PENSE

DIEU ET MON DROIT

Sharp sculp. Bartholomew Lane

a Childs patent Felbell £ " 9 ..

Recd the Contents for Messrs Caley & Co Thos Spencer

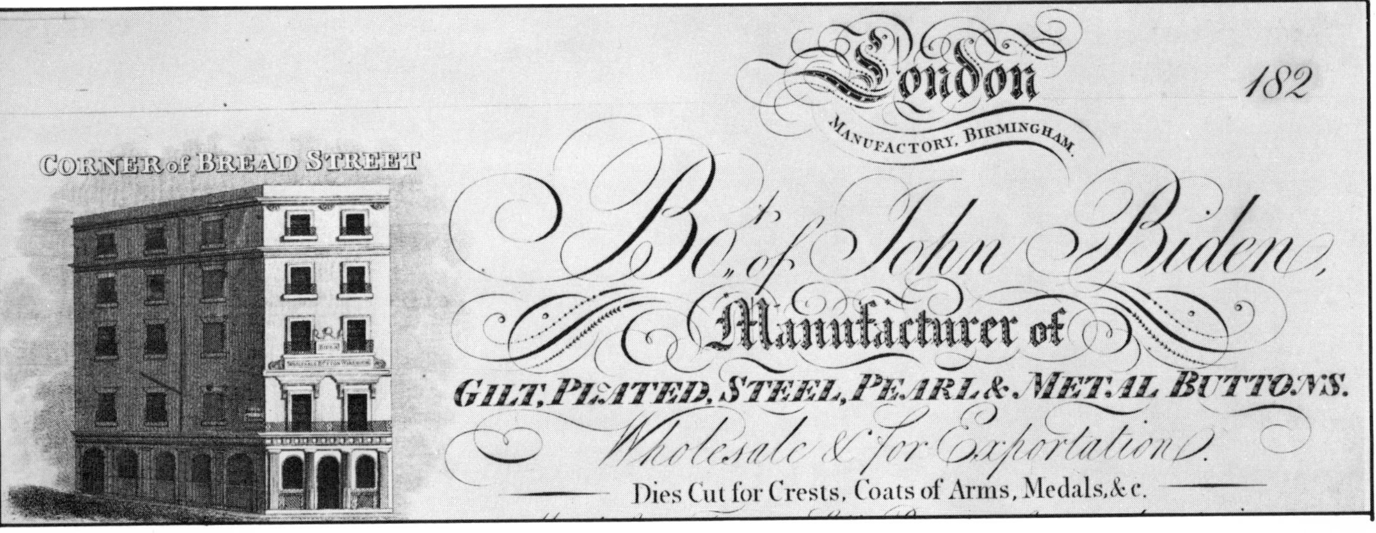

Opposite:
An elaborately written and engraved advertisement for an 18th century jeweller, which has been used as a bill, the debtor's name being written on the right-hand side 'Lady Colloney £19.6.9' — in fact the invoice should have been made out to Lady Conolly. The great variety of scripts used here is reminiscent of the title-page of a copy book.

V&AM

Two calligraphic bill-heads from the 18th and 19th centuries, showing the employment of diverse scripts. It will be noted that the handwriting on Mrs Turner's bill of 1776 falls far below that of the engraved examples!

V&AM

Next to St Mary's Gate is a picturesque half-timbered house dating from the 15 century. It is built on the stone base of the monastic Almonry, and evidence exists inside of a window used for the distribution of food and money to the poor. Today the Almoner's Lodging has a different use: that of preserving the County Records. This and the 18 century buildings of the west boundary of the Close comprise a visually harmonious group of houses, diverse yet unified. That part of No 12 having large windows was in 1750 described as "Mr Saunders' Great Room" and it served as a coffee-house as well as a dancing room

Gloucester Close, written out and illustrated by Aylwin Sampson. 1976

An example of a booklet whose text is entirely calligraphic; it is one of a series of such booklets on cathedral closes produced in this fashion.

God bless Queen Ann

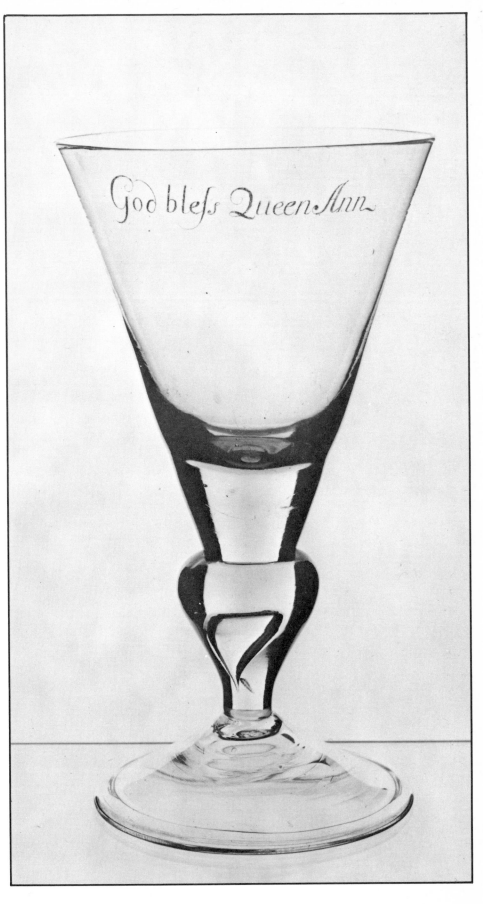

This shows a calligraphic inscription engraved on a drinking glass, and such decorations are quite frequently to be seen. The art of glass engraving, often employing calligraphic models, has been revived in the present century by Laurence Whistler and others. Today, designs based on pen-made forms (above) are to be found on many household objects while Steuben Glass in America has often commissioned important items.

V & A M C539-1936

These two pages show the varied uses of calligraphy in modern advertising. The familiarity of many of the names emphasises the ubiquity of pen-made letter forms in our daily life.

For Your Family
The Setting Room
Pentateuch
Clarks
Cosmetics
Lips 'n' nails
The London Book Fair
wooe
Dear Katie
pour toi
Delph
Walls
Eastham
Ladybird
Oneida
Readers Write
Coty
BREAKING OUT
Kellogg's
Halls
Colclough
Van-Dal
Gossard
Cabriole
Sherrys
Tropical
Rawlings
Octopus
Bygones
Cotswold
Grattan
JAEGER
Royal Albert

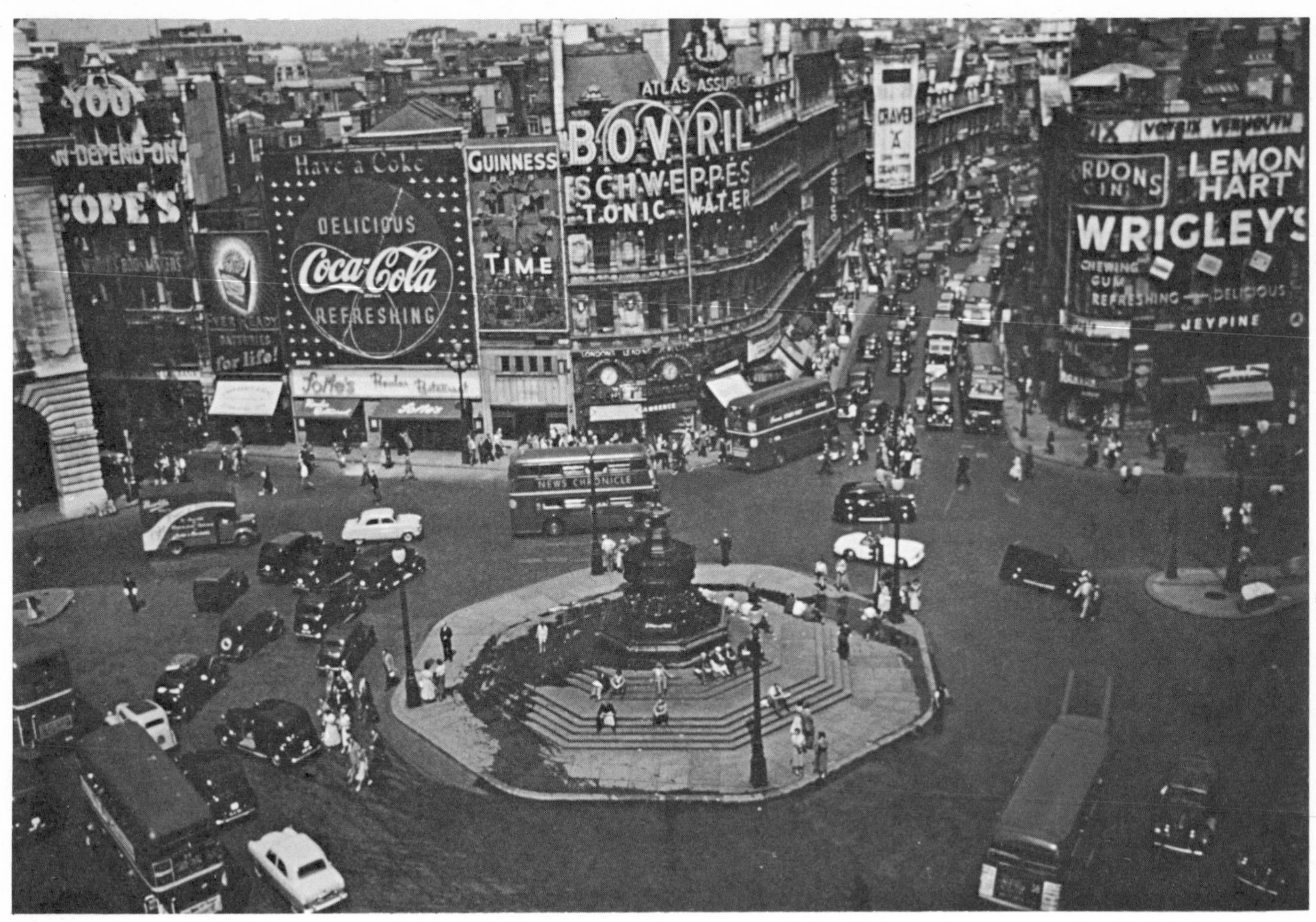

Calligraphy used as neon-sign advertising.

Bibliography

MOST OF the works listed in this bibliography also contain full bibliographies themselves; for this reason the books suggested for further reading have been limited to those most frequently consulted in the preparation of the present work, or which are especially relevant.

General works

Alexander, J. J. G. and de la Mare, A. C. *The Italian manuscripts in the Library of Major J. R. Abbey*. 1969
Anderson, D. M. *The art of written forms*. 1969
Astle, T. *The origin and progress of writing*. 1803
Blanco y Sanchez, R. *Catálogo de calígrafos y grabadores de letra*. 1920
Bonacini, C. *Bibliografia delle arti scrittorie e della calligrafia*. 1953
Brandi, K. *Unsere Schrift* [etc.], 1911
Campos Ferreira Lima, H. de. *Subsídios para um dicionário bio-bibliográfico dos calígrafos portugueses*. 1923
Cotarelo y Mori, *Diccionario biográfico y bibliográfico de calígrafos españoles*. 2 vols. 1913-16
Degering, H. *Die Schrift*. 1929
Fairbank, A. *A book of scripts*. 2ed. 1952
Federici, V. *La scrittura delle cancellerie italiane dal secolo XII al XVII*. 1964
Filby, P. W. (comp.) *Calligraphy and handwriting in America 1710-1962* (exhibition catalogue). 1963
Gray, N. *Lettering as drawing*. 1971
Johnston, E. *Writing & illuminating, & lettering*. 1906
Lamb, C. M. (ed.) *The calligrapher's handbook*. 1956
Lindegren, E. *The ABC of lettering and printing types*. 2 vols. 1964
Marinis, T. de. *Biblioteca napoletana dei re d'Aragona*. 4 vols. 1947-52
Marzoli, C. *Calligraphy 1535-1885: a collection of seventy-two writing books* [etc.]. 1962
Massey, W. *The origin and progress of letters*. 1763
Morison, S. *'Black letter' text*. 1942
Osley, A. S. (ed.) *Calligraphy and palaeography*. 1965
Prou, M. *Manuel de paléographie latine et française du VIe au XVIIe siècle*. 1890
Rodriguez, C. *Bibliotheca universal de la polygraphia española*. 1738
Tschichold, J. *Geschichte der Schrift in Bildern*. 1941
Schatzkammer der Schreibkunst. 1945

Medieval

Alexander, J. J. G. *The decorated letter*. 1978
Bishop, T. A. M. *English Caroline minuscule*. 1971
Corpus Inscriptionum Latinarum (T. Mommsen). 1863
Crous, E. and Kirchner, J. *Die gotischen Schriftarten*. 1928
Denholm-Young, N. *Handwriting in England and Wales*. 1954
Herbert, J. A. *Illuminated manuscripts*. Reprint, 1972

Hulshof, A. *Deutsche and lateinische Schrift in den Niederlander 1350-1650*. 1918
Jenkinson, H. *Later court hand in England from the fifteenth to the seventeenth century*. 2 vols. 1927
Johnson, C. and Jenkinson, H. *English court hand, AD 1066 to 1500*. 2 vols. 1915
Ker, N. *Mediaeval manuscripts in British libraries*. 1969-
Kirchner, J. *Scriptura Latina Libraria* [etc.]. 1955
Lindsay, W. M. *Early Irish minuscule script*. 1910
Lowe, E. A. *The Beneventan script*. 1914
'Handwriting' in *The legacy of the Middle Ages*. 1926
Scriptura Beneventana. 1929
Codices Latini antiquiores. 1935-
English uncial. 1960
Mallon, J., Marichal, R., and Perrat, C. *L'écriture latine de la capitale romaine à la minuscule*. 1939
Mallon, J. *Paléographie romaine*. 1952
Parkes, M. B. *English cursive book hands, 1250-1500*. 1969
Parkes, M. B., and Watson, A. G. (eds.) *Medieval scribes, manuscripts and libraries*. 1978
Rand, E. K. *A survey of the manuscripts of Tours*. 2 vols. 1929
Robinson, R. P. *Manuscripts 27 (S 29) and 107 (S 129) of the Municipal Library of Autun: a study of Spanish half-uncial and Visigothic minuscule and cursive scripts*. 1939
Schneider, A. *Deutsche und französische Cistercienser-Handschriften in englischen Bibliotheken*. 1962
Steffens, F. *Lateinische Paläographie*. 1929
Thompson, E. M. *Introduction to Greek and Latin palaeography*. 1912
Thomson, S. H. *Latin book hands of the later Middle Ages, 1100-1500*. 1969
Wright, C. E. *English vernacular hands from the twelfth to the fifteenth centuries*. 1960

Renaissance scripts

Casamassima, E. *Trattati di scrittura del Cinquecento italiano*. 1966
Dawson, G. E. and Kennedy-Skipton, L. *Elizabethan handwriting, 1500-1650*. 1968
De la Mare, A. C. *The handwriting of the Italian humanists*. 1973-
Fairbank, A. and Wolpe, B. *Renaissance handwriting*. 1960
Fairbank, A. and Dickens, B. *The italic hand in Tudor Cambridge*. 1962
Ullman, B. L. *The origin and development of the humanistic script*. 1960
Wardrop, J. *The script of humanism*. 1963

Post-Renaissance scripts and the writing masters

Borneman, H. S. *Pennsylvania German illuminated manuscripts: a classification of Fraktur-Schriften and an inquiry into their history and art*. 1973
Doede, W. *Bibliographie deutscher Schreibmeisterbücher von Neudörffer bis 1800*, 1958
Johnson, A. F. Catalogue of Italian writing-books of the sixteenth century, *Signature*, X, 1950
Lotz, A. Die deutschen Schreibmeisterbücher, *Philobiblon*, X, viii, 1939
Morison, S. *The calligraphic models of Ludovico degli Arrighi* [etc.]. 1926
Nash, R. *American writing masters and copy books: history and bibliography through colonial times*. 1939
Nash, R. *American penmanship, 1800-1850: a history of writing and a bibliography of copy books from Jenkins to Spencer*. 1969
Osley, A. S. *Luminario: an introduction to the Italian writing books of the sixteenth and seventeenth centuries*. 1972
Osley, A. S. and Wolpe, B. *Scribes and sources: handbook of the chancery hand in the sixteenth century*. 1980
Portalis, R., *Baron*. Nicolas Jarry et la calligraphie au XVIIe siècle, *Bulletin du Bibliophile* [etc.] 1896
Poulle, E. *Paléographie des écritures cursives en France du XVe au XVIIe siècle*. 1966
Ryder, J. *Lines of the alphabet in the sixteenth century*. 1965
Strange, E. F. Early English writing masters, *Bibliographica* III, 1897
Wardrop, J. 'Pierantonio Sallando and Girolamo Pagliarolo, scribes to Giovanni II Bentivoglio', *Signature* N.S.II, 1946

'Arrighi revived', *Signature* XII, 1939
'Civis Romanus sum': Giovanbattista Palatino and his circle, *Signature* N.S.XIV, 1952
A note on Giovantonio Tagliente, *Signature*, N.S.XVIII, 1959
The Vatican scriptors: documents for Ruano and Cresci, *Signature* N.S.V, 1948
Whalley, J. I. *English handwriting, 1540-1853*. 1969

19th and 20th centuries

Child, H. *Calligraphy today*. 2ed. 1976
Dunlap, J. William Morris, calligrapher. (*William Morris and the art of the book*, Pierpont Morgan Library exhibition) 1976
Hölscher, E. *Rudolf von Larisch und seine Schule*. 1938
Johnston, P. *Edward Johnston*. 1959

Periodicals

Journal (Bulletin) of the Society for Italic Handwriting, 1954-
Newsletter of the Society of Scribes and Illuminators, 1974-
Scriptorium: international review of manuscript studies, 1946/47-
Scriptura

Facsimiles

A number of facsimiles of copy books have been published in recent years, some containing useful information about the scribe and his period. Miland of Nieuwkoop (Neths.) has specialised in the production of many of the classic works. A short list of some of the more important facsimiles is included here, but it should be considered merely an indication of what is available in one public collection (the Victoria and Albert Museum Library) where many originals already exist, and should not be considered as a comprehensive record.

A newe book of copies, 1574 (ed. B. Wolpe) 1962
Cresci, G. F. *Essemplare* [etc.] (facsimile of 1578 ed. by A. S. Osley) 1968
Fugger, W. *Wolfgang Fugger's handwriting manual* (H. Carter & F. Plaat, transl.) 1955
Fugger, W. *Wolfgang Fuggers Schreibbuchlein von 1553* (A. Kapr and F. Funke eds.) 1958
Johnston, E. *House of David, his inheritance: a book of sample scripts* (J. P. Harthan ed.) 1966
Johnston, E. *Formal penmanship* (ed. H. Child) 1971
Neudörffer, J. *Neudörffer d. Ä., der grosse Schreibmeister der deutschen Renaissance* (ed. A. Kapr) 1956
Tagliente, G. *Opera di Giovanni Tagliente* (facsimile of 1525 ed. by J. M. Wells) 1952
Three classics of Italian calligraphy: Arrighi, Tagliente, Palatino (ed. O. Ogg) 1953
Wyss, U. *Das Schreibbuch der Urban Wyss* (H. Kienzle ed.) 1927
Yciar, J, de. *Juan de Yciar, a facsimile of Arte subtilissima, 1550* ed. (intro. by R. Stone, transl. by E. Shuckburgh) 1958

Index

Text references are indicated in roman
Illustrations in bold type
Coloured pages by plate numbers in italic

Photographic acknowledgements

The author and publisher wish to thank the following for permission to reproduce illustrations:

Arts & Metiers graphiques, Paris
Bodleian Library, Oxford
British Library, London
Courtauld Institute of Art, University of London
Institute of Archaeology, University of London
Magdalene College, Cambridge
Museum of London
Philadelphia Museum of Art
Victoria and Albert Museum, London